MANAGEMENT

ACCOUNTING

A STRATEGIC APPROACH

Wayne J. Morse,
Clarkson University

James R. Davis,
Clemson University

Al L. Hartgraves,
Emory University

SOUTH-WESTERN College Publishing

An International Thomson Publishing Company

Sponsoring Editor: Elizabeth A. Bowers
Developmental Editor: Leslie Kauffman
Production Editor: Peggy A. Williams
Production House: CompuText Productions, Inc.
Cover and Internal Designer: Michael H. Stratton
Cover and Internal Photos: Photonica
Marketing Manager: Steven W. Hazelwood

AQ68AA

ISBN: 0-538-84435-3

1 2 3 4 5 6 7 8 9 VH 3 2 1 0 9 8 7 6 5

Printed in the United States of America

I (T) P
International Thomson Publishing
South-Western College Publishing is an ITP Company. The ITP trademark is used under license.

Library of Congress Cataloging-in-Publication Data

Morse, Wayne J.
      Management accounting : a strategic approach / Wayne J. Morse,
James R. Davis, Al L. Hartgraves.
            p.   cm.
      Includes index.
      ISBN 0-538-84435-3
      1. Managerial accounting.   I. Davis, James Richard. 1947-
II. Hartgraves, Al L.   III. Title
HF5635.M865 1995
658. 15' 11--dc20   95-18158
                                                              CIP

PREFACE

Management accounting is a discipline concerned with the use of financial and related information by managers and other persons inside specific organizations to make strategic, organizational, and operational decisions. It provides a framework for identifying and analyzing decision alternatives and for evaluating success in accomplishing organizational goals. Although accountants have an important role to play in the management accounting process, management accounting is too important to be left exclusively to accountants. Furthermore, in an era of global competition, continuous improvement, process reengineering, and employee empowerment, management accounting is used by decision makers at all levels, rather than just by personnel traditionally classified as "managers." **The purpose of this book is to introduce students to management accounting as it is practiced today.**

Because this is an introductory text, we have elected to provide a survey of many topics, carefully relating them to each other. Whereas this book is written for a general audience, we have strived to place management accounting in a broad context, relating management accounting to other subject areas. We have left the in-depth coverage of many topics to other, more specialized, books on cost accounting, finance, production, statistics, marketing, policy, and so forth. We hope this book, like the trunk of a tree, will serve as a strong base for the future growth of knowledge and as a means of unifying the branches of management.

This book is intended for students who have had one course in accounting, a college-level economics course, and a college-level math course. While we use basic probability concepts, some statistical notation, and make reference to regression analysis, a background in statistics is not essential.

Although we are experienced authors, we elected to reengineer this textbook rather than to incrementally improve previous management accounting texts. The result is a book that is unique in several respects:

1. It is a 13-chapter text that can be covered in its entirety in a single semester.
2. It thoroughly integrates issues such as global competition, ethics, customer focus, the value chain, process management, activity-based costing, and target costing that have become important during the past ten years.
3. Its starting point is the use of management accounting as a tool for employee and manager empowerment.
4. It stresses the theme of global competition on the basis of price, quality, and service.
5. It focuses primarily on cost drivers within the value chain rather than on the distinction between product and nonproduct costs.
6. It is based on a belief that the accounting distinction between product and nonproduct costs (introduced early in virtually all management accounting texts):

- should not be the central theme of a management accounting text.
- is misleading.
- diverts attention from the analysis of the complete value chain.
- forces an unnecessary distinction between manufacturing and nonmanufacturing organizations.

We take a cost driver approach within the context of an organization's internal value chain. We believe the result is a book that is more relevant, interesting, and usable for students whose primary concerns are something other than financial reporting. Traditional financial reporting issues related to inventory costing are deferred to the end of the book, rather than introduced early in the book. Students use the knowledge gained in the early chapters to critically examine inventory cost system alternatives, rather than using basic "product costing" concepts (originally developed for financial reporting) as a foundation for learning. By taking this approach, the instructor also avoids the need to explain the shortcomings of traditional approaches to product costing to students who have just completed the first few weeks of studying management accounting.

In financial accounting, product costs are defined as the cost of direct materials and all costs incurred to convert direct materials into finished goods. We agree with the criticism that this definition starts too late and stops too early. Throughout the first three parts of this text, we place product costs in a strategic context, regarding them as the costs of physical products or services across the internal value chain. In the last part of the text, which considers product costing for financial reporting, we distinguish between strategic product costs and inventoriable product costs, stressing the importance of context in understanding the inclusiveness of product costs. The book ends on a philosophic note that relates topics examined throughout the text to each other and that suggests future directions for management accounting.

ORGANIZATION

The book is divided into four parts and 13 chapters:

I. Essentials of Management Accounting

1. World-Class Competition and Employee Empowerment
2. Cost Estimation and Cost-Volume-Profit Analysis
3. Relevant Costs and Differential Cost Analysis

II. Strategic Cost Management

4. Strategic Cost Management I: Value Chain Analysis and Activity-Based Costing
5. Strategic Cost Management II: Price, Cost, and Quality
6. Strategic Cost Management III: Capital Budgeting

III. Budgeting and Profitability Analysis

7. Operational Budgeting
8. Responsibility Accounting and Performance Assessment
9. Profitability Analysis of Strategic Business Segments

IV. Inventory and Service Costing
  10. Job Costing and the Manufacturing Environment
  11. Process Costing for Goods and Services
  12. Allocating Indirect Costs and Inventory Valuation Approaches
  13. Activity-Based Product Costing and Just-In-Time Inventory Management

Developing a book that can be used in a single semester, while integrating many new concepts, required careful attention to organization. Chapters build on each other and issues raised in early chapters are revisited in later chapters. Although some chapters (such as Chapters 6 and 11) or portions of some chapters (such as the second part of Chapter 12) and appendix materials may be omitted, we recommend assigning chapters in numerical order. Chapter 1 is important and worthy of study, rather than being a light overview that may be lectured on, but not assigned. In most management accounting texts, Chapter 2 is primarily concerned with terminology. To limit the number of chapters, we avoid the use of a terminology chapter and, instead, introduce terms where needed. **Key terms** are in bold type when they are first introduced and are defined at the end of each chapter, as well as in a comprehensive glossary at the end of the text.

All chapters contain **learning objectives** linked to major chapter headings and **management accounting practices** linked to chapter topics. The management accounting practices are adapted from real-life business scenarios and are intended to broaden students' perspectives and to motivate them by discussing interesting applications of chapter topics. **Additional examples** of the application of chapter materials are woven into the text. Many chapters contain **suggested readings**. The suggested readings may be used by students interested in learning more about chapter materials, as an initial reading list for papers, or as additional assignment material.

Global business activities, employee empowerment, the value chain, process management, activity-based costing, and competition on the basis of cost, quality, and service are so woven into the text that it is difficult to single out examples of these topics. **Ethics** also receives extensive coverage. Ethics is introduced within the context of measurement and management in Chapter 1 and discussed further in Chapters 5, 6, 7, and 8. Management accounting practices in Chapters 1, 6, 7, and 8 also highlight the importance of ethics in management accounting. Assignment material dealing with ethics is included in Chapters 1, 2, 3, 4, 5, 6, and 7.

ASSIGNMENT MATERIALS

A variety of assignment materials accompanies the chapters. Each chapter contains one or two review problems. Solutions to review problems are presented at the end of each chapter's assignment materials (rather than immediately following the review problem) to encourage students to solve the problems before reviewing the solutions. Chapters contain a range of assignment materials in the form of review questions, exercises, problems, discussion questions, and cases. Although many assignment materials deal with new concepts, there are ample materials dealing with important traditional topics.

- **Review questions**, sequenced to reflect the order of materials presented in the chapter, focus on the recall of basic chapter materials.
- **Exercises** are relatively short and straightforward applications of individual chapter topics. They focus on recall and application.
- **Problems** contain more rigorous and comprehensive applications of chapter materials, often requiring the ability to organize and present information. Many problems also contain straightforward requirements calling for decisions, interpretation, or "what if" analysis.
- **Discussion questions** typically require students to conceptualize chapter materials and, sometimes, relate them to materials in previous chapters. They focus on comprehension, synthesis, and evaluation. Discussion questions can be used as written assignments or, with relatively limited amounts of advanced student preparation, as a basis of classroom or group discussion.
- **Cases** involve rigorous analysis, synthesis, and evaluation. They often integrate materials contained in several chapters and require students to extend their thought processes to new situations. While the coverage of cases, especially at the undergraduate level, will likely require the guidance of the instructor, the selective use of case materials helps prepare students for the difficult transition from the classroom to the business world. The cases are also excellent for group assignments.

ANCILLARY MATERIALS

This textbook is part of a comprehensive and carefully prepared educational package that offers various forms of assistance to both instructors and students. A variety of ancillary materials is available.

- A **solutions manual**, prepared by the authors, contains detailed solutions to all assignment materials.
- **Transparency acetates** for the solutions to assignments requiring extensive computations are available to adopters.
- Computerized **PowerPoint™ teaching transparencies** of key exhibits and related text examples are available to adopters.
- A **test bank**, prepared by Professor Marvin Bouillon of Iowa State University, is available in printed and microcomputer (MicroExam III) versions. Comprised of a collection of problems, questions, and exercises, the test bank is designed to save time in preparing and grading periodic and final exams.
- A **study guide**, prepared by Professor Stephen V. Senge of Western Washington University, reemphasizes and reinforces basic concepts and techniques.
- Recognizing that some schools find it necessary to cover financial statement analysis and cash flows in management accounting, the authors have prepared a soft-cover supplement to cover these topics. The materials in

this supplement—Chapter 14, Financial Statement Analysis, and Chapter 15, Statement of Cash Flows—may be used before or after the other text materials. The solutions to supplement assignments are contained in the regular solutions manual.

OVERVIEW OF CHAPTER CONTENT

The following paragraphs provide an overview of the content of each chapter.

Part 1, Essentials of Management Accounting, consists of three chapters that place a number of essential management accounting topics within the framework of strategic cost management.

Chapter 1, World-Class Competition and Employee Empowerment, begins by contrasting financial accounting and management accounting and continues by examining organizations and their goals. Included is a discussion of strategic position analysis, a topic more often found in policy texts, and a discussion of how management accounting can assist in achieving goals. We stress how cost information can help individual employees do a better job. With reductions in the levels of management and the empowerment of employees to perform tasks previously reserved for upper and/or middle managers, employees at all levels need to use management accounting concepts. Along with empowerment comes an increased need to be aware of the ethical issues in developing and using information.

The chapter next discusses the changing business environment and the importance of competition on the basis of price, quality, and service. The theme of competing on these three interrelated dimensions is continued throughout the text. The chapter turns to a classification of cost drivers as (1) structural, (2) organizational, and (3) activity. This classification scheme was developed by the authors to relate the activity-based costing literature to the strategic cost management literature. Our task was to relate accepted ABC terminology to broader strategic cost management concepts. This framework is expanded in subsequent chapters.

Basic cost structures are introduced in Chapter 1 with a focus on how cost structures have changed during the past 50 years. We point out the difficulty of relating total costs to a single independent variable and the need to understand the multitude of factors that drive costs.

Chapter 2, Cost Estimation and Cost-Volume-Profit Analysis, contains many of the expected topics. Care is taken in the cost estimation materials to use illustrations where costs are logically driven by a single activity. Although the initial illustration of cost estimation uses the high-low method, the material continues through a discussion of multiple regression analysis. While reluctant to add the complexity of equations with summation signs and several independent variables, we felt exposure to multiple regression analysis was a good foundation for analyzing costs when there are multiple cost drivers. Optional appendices contain material on the computational details of least-squares analysis and the use of computer spreadsheets in least-squares analysis.

The CVP material stresses the usefulness of CVP analysis in the early stages of planning for a single product, event, or service where "it may be reasonable to assume the single independent variable is the cost driver." We discuss the limitations of CVP analysis when there are multiple cost drivers. We revisit the categories of cost drivers introduced in Chapter 1 and discuss how activity cost drivers (the third category) may be placed in a variety of hierarchies, depending on the interests of management. The chapter concludes by illustrating (1) cost prediction with a four-level activity cost hierarchy in a two-product firm and (2) the cost prediction errors that may occur when predictions are based on a single independent variable.

Chapter 3, Relevant Costs and Differential Cost Analysis, covers many traditional relevant cost topics such as to accept or reject special orders and to sell or process further. A unique aspect of Chapter 3 is the use of an activity cost hierarchy and a two-product example as the framework for identifying relevant costs. Other texts typically introduce this material within the framework of variable and fixed product and period costs for a single-product company. In this text, however, the make or buy decision is recast in a broader framework dealing with the internal or external acquisition of components or services. This allows us to consider the growing importance of outsourcing. The final topic in the chapter, how best to use limited resources, is related to the theory of constraints. An appendix considers the role of models in decision making, provides a classification scheme for models, and introduces linear programming as an illustrative optimizing model that uses accounting information.

Part 2, Strategic Cost Management, consists of three chapters.

Chapter 4, Strategic Cost Management I: Value Chain Analysis and Activity-Based Costing, begins with the introduction of the value chain, defined as the set of value producing activities stretching from basic raw materials to the final customer. We consider how an organization's internal value chain may be a link in a much longer value chain and the value enhancing opportunities of developing upstream linkages with vendors and downstream linkages with customers. The internal value chain is then broken into major processes, and the processes are further dissected into activities. We discuss the usefulness of process mapping and the development of storyboards in process analysis. The identification of processes and activities within the context of the value chain serves as the framework for examining continuous improvement, process reengineering, and the important distinction between value-added and nonvalue-added activities.

The chapter concludes with an introduction to the two-stage activity-based costing model. Significantly, ABC is first introduced within the context of an organization's entire internal value chain, rather than within the context of product costs. ABC is discussed, as appropriate, throughout the balance of the text, including Chapter 13, where the determination of product costs is studied as a specific application of ABC.

Chapter 5, Strategic Cost Management II: Price, Cost, and Quality, builds on Chapter 4 to discuss strategic management issues related to price competition, cost management, and quality. Most of the topics in Chapter 5 concern activity and organizational cost drivers. The chapter begins with an examination of traditional approaches to the pricing decision, including cost-based approaches to determining tax rates. Next, the shortcomings of cost-based pricing are examined and target costing is introduced as a proactive approach to cost management. Other topics, such as design for manufacture and life-cycle costs, are introduced within the context of target costing. We stress the interface between marketing, design, and manufacturing, and the need for people in these functions to understand the cost consequences of their actions.

This chapter extends the continuous improvement topic from Chapter 4 by introducing continuous improvement costing as the next logical step after target costing new products or services. Chapter 5 concludes with an examination of quality costs, ISO certification for quality management and environmental management, and benchmarking.

Chapter 6, Strategic Cost Management III: Capital Budgeting, relates capital budgeting to structural cost drivers, the most fundamental type of cost driver, introduced in Chapter 1. The chapter contains the expected material on capital budgeting models. There are also extensive discussions of the capital budgeting process and high-tech investments. An appendix provides an introduction to the time value of money.

While capital budgeting is often viewed as a finance topic, many capital expenditure decisions are strategic cost drivers and capital budgeting is frequently covered in management accounting. We elected to include this material but developed it so that Chapter 6 may be omitted without loss of continuity.

Part 3, Budgeting and Profitability Analysis, contains three chapters.

Planning elements were considered throughout Parts 1 and 2. **Chapter 7, Operational Budgeting,** integrates these plans in a budget. Institutional and behavioral factors dealing with the development of budgets and alternative approaches to budgeting are examined. In addition to the traditional example of an operating budget found in most texts, we consider activity-based budgeting for products and departments. Recognizing that some instructors prefer to defer the complexity of manufacturing budgets, our comprehensive budget example is for a merchandising organization. Manufacturing budgets are considered in an optional appendix. Review problems consider budgeting in both merchandising and manufacturing organizations.

Chapter 8, Responsibility Accounting and Performance Assessment, relates performance reporting to organizational structure and plans, considers nonfinancial as well as financial performance measures, and identifies several types of responsibility centers. The focal point is performance reports for cost and revenue centers. After introducing flexible budget variances and the computation of detailed variances for variable cost items, the interpretation of variances is examined in detail. Optional appendices take a closer look at fixed overhead variances and provide a simple reconciliation of budgeted and actual net income.

Chapter 9, Profitability Analysis of Strategic Business Segments, discusses the profitability analysis of investment and profit centers. After discussing the pros and cons of centralization and decentralization, the chapter examines reporting alternatives for strategic business segments, such as divisions, products, and territories. Special attention is given to direct and common segment costs and segment decisions. Chapter 9 also contains material on transfer pricing, return on investment, and residual income (sometimes referred to as economic value added).

Part 4, Inventory and Service Costing, consists of four chapters. The notions of product costs to this point have concerned costs across the internal value chain. To avoid confusion with previous product costing notions, we distinguish between strategic and inventoriable product costs and stress the importance of context in determining the scope of product costs.

Chapter 10, Job Costing and the Manufacturing Environment, begins with an examination of inventory costs in different organizations and the differences between inventory costing and service costing. The chapter continues with an analysis of inventory costing for financial reporting and the various types of product costs. After considering production planning and scheduling, and the impact of computers on manufacturing, job costing is examined in detail. The chapter concludes with a discussion of job costing for services.

Chapter 11, Process Costing for Goods and Services, provides an overview of process costing and the application of process costing concepts to services. Although mentioned, FIFO process costing is not illustrated because we believe this topic is better deferred to cost accounting. Chapter 11 concludes with a discussion of costing multiple products (where the problem of cross-subsidization is examined) and a consideration of issues involved in designing a costing system. These ending segments provide the basis for several innovative cost system design cases in the accompanying assignment materials.

Optional appendices provide a brief overview of costing joint products and by-products and illustrate the use of standard costs to simplify inventory costing. To boil down the presentation, only one account is used to accumulate all cost variances. Hence, students are able to understand this appendix even if they do not have a complete grasp of cost variance computations.

The first part of **Chapter 12, Allocating Indirect Costs and Inventory Valuation Approaches,** provides an introduction to traditional service department cost allocation topics, such as cost objectives, cost pools, allocation bases, and direct and indirect department costs. Service department cost allocation is related to the use of department overhead rates, and the direct and step methods of service department cost allocation are illustrated. While the linear algebra method is discussed, a detailed example of this method of service department cost allocation is deferred to cost accounting. The second part of the chapter considers absorption and variable costing for inventory valuation.

Chapter 13, Activity-Based Product Costing and Just-In-Time Inventory Management, concludes the book by tying inventory costing back to more current management accounting topics. ABC for inventory valuation is compared to traditional product costing systems. Included is a detailed example of the product costing continuum, anchored on one end by the use of a plant-wide overhead rate and at the other by ABC. The section on ABC concludes with a discussion of implementation issues.

Just-in-time inventory management is presented as a comprehensive inventory management philosophy that includes coordination through the value chain, reduced inventory, reduced production times, increased product quality, and increased employee involvement and empowerment. This theme allows us to examine accounting in a just-in-time environment and to revisit issues raised throughout the book. An optional appendix contains material on the economic order quantity for purchases and the economic lot size for manufacturing.

We were motivated in our approach to organizing this book by speakers at numerous meetings, conversations with business people, returning students with professional experience enrolled in graduate programs, participants in executive development programs, our colleagues in accounting and other disciplines, and researchers working on the cutting edge of management accounting. The writings of many of these people are included in the suggested readings at the end of most chapters. We were especially influenced by Peter Drucker's numerous writings on management, Robert Kaplan's and Robin Cooper's work in the areas of activity-based costing and activity-based management, John Shank's and Vijay Govindarajan's writings on the value chain and strategic cost management, and Michael Porter's writings on strategic position analysis and the value chain.

Five books that influenced our conceptual framework for thinking about management accounting are: *Megatrends* by John Naisbitt, published by Warner Books; *The Third Wave* by Alvin Toffler, published by William Morrow & Co.; *Relevance Lost* by H. Thomas Johnson and Robert S. Kaplan, published by the HBS Press; *Strategic Cost Management* by John K. Shank and Vijay Govindarajan, published by The Free Press; and *Reengineering the Corporation* by Michael Hammer and James Champy, published by Harper Business. These books helped us put management accounting within the context of the broad sweep of events affecting business and society at the end of the 20th century.

We are indebted to the following professors who served as reviewers and offered helpful comments on the manuscript:

- Susan Borkowski (LaSalle University)
- Margaret Gagne (University of Colorado at Colorado Springs)
- Judith Harris (Bryant College)
- Dolan Hinson (University of North Carolina at Charlotte)
- Ronald Huefner (State University of New York at Buffalo)
- Larry Paquette (Westfield State College)
- Jeffrey Schatzberg (University of Arizona)
- Stephen Senge (Western Washington University)
- Audrey Taylor (Wayne State University)
- Leslie Turner (Northern Kentucky University)

We thank our students at Clarkson University, Clemson University, and Emory University. We appreciate both their tolerance and their feedback as we tested many of the new ideas and assignment materials contained in this book. We also appreciate the assistance of our graduate students who reviewed the accuracy of assignment material. A special note of appreciation is extended to Dolan Hinson (University of North Carolina at Charlotte) and James Emig

(Villanova University) who provided a complete verification of the solutions to assignment materials; Margaret Gagne (University of Colorado at Colorado Springs) for verification of the test bank; and James Emig for verification of the study guide. Finally, we appreciate the encouragement, support, and detailed suggestions for improvement provided by Dave Shaut, Mary Draper, and Leslie Kauffman of South-Western College Publishing. Working with them has been a pleasure.

Appreciation is extended to the Institute of Certified Management Accountants for permission to use adaptations of problem materials from past Certified Management Accounting Examinations; these materials are identified as "CMA Adapted." We are also indebted to the American Institute of Certified Public Accountants for permission to use materials from the Uniform CPA Examination; these materials are identified as "CPA Adapted."

Despite the efforts of the many people who assisted in this project, there is always room for further improvement. To assist us in continuously improving this product so that it better fits your needs and the needs of your students, comments and suggestions are most welcome. Users wishing to contact us with comments, suggestions, or questions, may send electronic mail correspondence to us over the Internet through South-Western College Publishing at morse_mngt_acctg@itp.thomson.com.

Wayne J. Morse
Clarkson University

James R. Davis
Clemson University

Al L. Hartgraves
Emory University

BRIEF CONTENTS

CONTENTS

ESSENTIALS OF
MANAGEMENT ACCOUNTING

After completing this chapter, you should be able to:

LO 1

Contrast financial and management accounting and explain why financial accounting is not sufficient for management.

LO 2

Discuss how an organization's goals and strategies affect management accounting.

LO 3

Discuss how employee empowerment can affect the activities used to serve customers and how management accounting can be an important element of employee empowerment.

LO 4

Discuss the nature of the ethical dilemmas managers and accountants often confront.

LO 5

Discuss the fundamental changes affecting the nature of competition.

LO 6

Differentiate among structural, organizational, and activity cost drivers.

LO 7

Determine the behavior of activity costs.

LO 8

Describe how structural cost drivers have changed and how these changes have affected the behavior of an organization's total cost function.

WORLD-CLASS COMPETITION AND EMPLOYEE EMPOWERMENT

"Accounting," according to management philosopher Peter Drucker, "has become the most intellectually challenging area in the field of management, and the most turbulent one." Drucker believes this rebirth of accounting is taking place because accounting is the primary discipline attempting to answer questions "few executives yet know how to ask: What information do I need to do my job? When do I need it? and From whom should I be getting it?" Drucker believes accounting is being shaken to its roots by reform movements aimed at moving it away from being merely financial (dealing with assets, liabilities, and cash flows) and toward being operational.[1]

*Our aim, as authors, is to help you learn how to ask and answer the questions posed by Drucker, as well as other questions requiring the analysis of financial information. Our ultimate goal is to help you succeed in your chosen career—be it accounting, actuarial science, agriculture, business administration, financial management, engineering, hospital administration, marketing, retail management, or any other field. We hope to accomplish this by introducing you to **management accounting**, a discipline concerned with the use of financial and related information by managers and other persons inside specific organizations to make strategic, organizational, and operational decisions.*

The purpose of this chapter is to provide an overview of the factors making management accounting increasingly important. *We begin by distinguishing between financial and management accounting and by investigating how an organization's goals and strategies affect management accounting. Next, we consider how accounting can empower employees to do a better job managing the affairs of an organization and examine the interrelationships among measurement, management, and ethics. Finally, we explore how the emergence of global competition and changes in technology have increased the need to understand management accounting concepts such as cost driver and cost behavior analysis.*

1 Peter Drucker, "Be Data Literate—Know What to Know," *The Wall Street Journal,* December 1, 1992, p. A16.

FINANCIAL ACCOUNTING IS NOT SUFFICIENT FOR MANAGEMENT

L O 1

Most readers have had at least one course in **financial accounting** (a reporting system primarily concerned with providing financial information to persons outside the firm, including investors and creditors). The focal point of financial accounting is transactions processing and the development of general purpose financial statements, such as the balance sheet, income statement, and statement of cash flows, in accordance with generally accepted accounting principles.

The **balance sheet** is a picture of the economic health of an organization at a point in time, showing the organization's assets and the claims on those assets. The **income statement** is a summary of economic events during a period of time, showing the revenues generated by operating activities, the expenses matched to those revenues, and any gains and losses attributed to the period. The **statement of cash flows** is a summary of resource inflows and outflows stated in terms of cash. These financial statements, typically prepared quarterly and annually, report on the past affairs of the organization. Financial accounting is also concerned with keeping records of the organization's assets, obligations, and the collection and payment of debts. An organization cannot survive without keeping track of, and thereby helping safeguard, its assets, converting sales into cash, paying for purchases, and meeting payroll.

Managers often use income statements and balance sheets as a starting point in evaluating and planning the overall affairs of the firm. Because financial accounting data are widely available, managers learn a great deal by performing a comparative analysis of their firm and competing firms. Corporate goals are often stated using financial accounting numbers such as net income or ratios such as return on investment and earnings per share of common stock.

Despite financial accounting's importance, decision makers often find it of little value in managing day-to-day operating activities. They often complain that financial accounting information is too aggregated, too late, based on irrelevant past costs, and not action-oriented. The cost of all items produced and sold or all services rendered is summarized in a single line in most financial statements, making it impossible to determine the cost of individual products or services. When managers attempt to determine the cost of individual products, they may find that procedures acceptable for costing inventories as a whole produce misleading information when applied to individual products. Even when they can be accurately determined, the costs of individual products or services are rarely detailed enough to provide information needed for decisions concerning **cost drivers**, the factors that influence costs. Financial accounting reports, seldom prepared more than once a month, are not timely enough to direct attention to activities that cause excess costs. Finally, financial accounting reports are based on historical costs rather than on current or future costs. Because managers make decisions about the future, managers are more interested in future costs than in historical costs such as last year's depreciation.

In summary, while financial accounting information may be useful in making some management decisions, financial accounting does not have a primary emphasis on internal decision making.

Management Accounting Assists Internal Decision Makers

Management accounting, on the other hand, (1) provides a framework to evaluate information in light of an organization's goals and (2) provides information to managers and other persons inside the organization. Because the needs of internal users of accounting information can be known in advance, it is possible to design management accounting reports to meet their specific needs. Top management may only need summary information prepared once a month for each business unit. An engineer responsible for hourly production scheduling may need timely, detailed cost information on alternative ways of producing a product with available resources more frequently than once a month.

Many influential business executives now believe management accounting is too important to be left solely to accountants. Management accounting is a process for obtaining and analyzing relevant information to help achieve organizational goals. It should not be a function relegated only to accountants. Every manager must understand the financial implications of decisions. While accountants are available to assist in obtaining and evaluating relevant information, individual managers are responsible for requesting information, analyzing it, and making the final decisions.

Because management accounting information exists to serve the needs of management, it is subject to a cost-benefit analysis and should only be developed if the perceived benefits exceed the costs of development and use. Also, while financial measures are often used in management accounting, they are not used to the exclusion of other measures. Money is simply a convenient way of expressing events in a form suitable to summary analysis. When this is not possible or appropriate, nonfinancial measures are used. Time, for example, is often an important element of quality or service. Hence, many performance measures focus on time. For example:

- Federal Express keeps detailed information on the time required to make deliveries.
- Fire departments and police departments measure the response time to emergency calls.
- Delta Airlines monitors the number of on-time departures and arrivals.

No external standards (such as requirements of the Securities and Exchange Commission) are imposed on information provided to internal users. Consequently, management accounting information may be quite subjective. In developing a budget, management is more interested in a subjective prediction of next year's sales than in an objective report on last year's sales. The significant differences between financial and management accounting are summarized in Exhibit 1-1.

EXHIBIT 1-1: DIFFERENCES BETWEEN FINANCIAL AND MANAGEMENT ACCOUNTING

Financial Accounting	Management Accounting
• A reporting system	• A decision-making medium
• Information to external and internal users	• Information to internal users
• General purpose financial statements	• Special purpose information
• Statements highly aggregated	• Information may be aggregated or disaggregated, depending on need
• Relatively long reporting period	• Reporting period may be long or short, depending on need
• Report on past decisions	• Oriented toward future decisions
• Often required by law	• Not required by law
• Must conform to external standards	• No external standards
• Emphasizes objective data	• Allows subjective data if relevant

Strategic Cost Management Provides the Big Picture

During recent years, the rapid introduction of improved products has shortened the market lives of products. Some products such as personal computers may be obsolete within two or three years after introduction. At the same time, the use of complex automated equipment has made it difficult to change production procedures after production begins. As a consequence, more and more costs are determined by decisions, concerning product design and production procedures, made before production begins. Businesses are also working closer with suppliers to obtain the exact components they need at the highest quality and lowest possible cost. In response to these trends, a new approach to management accounting, referred to as strategic cost management, has emerged. According to John Shank, a major proponent of this new approach, strategic cost management has emerged from a blending of three themes:

1. **Cost driver analysis**, which concerns the study of factors that influence costs.
2. **Strategic position analysis**, which concerns an organization's basic way of competing to sell products or services.
3. **Value chain analysis**, which concerns the study of value-producing activities, stretching from basic raw materials to the final consumer of a product or service. [2]

We define **strategic cost management** as making decisions concerning specific cost drivers within the context of an organization's business strategy, internal value chain, and place in a larger value chain stretching from the development and use of resources to final consumers. Cost driver analysis and business strategy, including strategic position analysis, are introduced later in this chapter. Value chain analysis is introduced in Chapter 4.

---

2 John K. Shank, "Strategic Cost Management: New Wine, or Just New Bottles?" *Journal of Management Accounting Research* (Fall 1989), p. 50.

ORGANIZATIONS: THEIR GOALS AND STRATEGIES

An organization's **goal**[3] is the purpose toward which its activities are directed. Organizations vary widely in their goals. Whereas the goal of a college or university is to provide educational services (perhaps of a specific type and perhaps to a particular geographic area), the goal of a department store or steel company is to earn a profit by providing customers with goods, and the goal of the Red Cross is to provide humanitarian services. An organization is likely to have several goals. The goals of a paper mill located in a small town might include developing a reputation for quality and service in specialty markets, providing steady dividends, achieving a 7 percent return on assets, maintaining current profit levels, providing good jobs for area residents, and being regarded as a good community citizen. Other examples of organizational goals include market share, technological position, social performance, and cost leadership.

We frequently distinguish between organizations on the basis of profit motive. **For-profit organizations** have profit as a primary goal, whereas **not-for-profit organizations** do not have profit as a primary goal. Clearly, the General Electric Company is a for-profit organization, whereas the City of Chicago and the Red Cross are not-for-profit organizations.[4] Regardless of the presence or absence of a profit motive, an organization should use resources efficiently in accomplishing its goals. Every dollar the United Way spends for administrative salaries is a dollar that cannot be used to support charitable activities. Not-for-profit organizations can go bankrupt if they are unable to meet their financial obligations. Both for-profit and not-for-profit organizations should use management accounting concepts to ensure resources are used wisely.

Strategic Position Analysis

One of top management's most important jobs is the development and dissemination of realistic goals for an organization. A clear statement of goals provides an organization with an identity and unifying purpose, thereby ensuring that all employees are heading in the same direction, rather than working at cross-purposes. Having developed a set of goals, management is better prepared to make decisions concerning factors such as size, scope, and technology that influence costs. These elements should be properly integrated into the organization's strategic cost management system.

A fundamental goal that every organization should determine concerns its strategic position compared to that of its competition. Porter[5] has identified three potential strategic positions that lead to business success.

---

3 The term *mission* is frequently used to refer to what we have identified as *goal*.
4 The term *nonprofit* is frequently used to refer to what we have identified as *not-for-profit* organizations.
5 Michael E. Porter, *Competitive Strategy* (New York: The Free Press, 1980), p. 35.

These strategic positions relate to the goals of (1) cost leadership, (2) product or service differentiation, and (3) focus on a market niche.

> Cost leadership requires aggressive construction of efficient-scale facilities, vigorous pursuit of cost reductions from experience, tight cost and overhead control, avoidance of marginal customer accounts, and cost minimization in areas like R&D [research and development], service, sales force, advertising, and so on. A great deal of managerial attention to cost control is necessary to achieve these aims. Low cost relative to competitors becomes the theme running through the entire strategy, though quality, service, and other areas cannot be ignored. [Porter, p. 35]

Product or service differentiation involves creating something that is perceived as being unique and worth a premium price. Possible approaches to differentiation include a market image (the Energizer® bunny), technological leadership (Hewlett-Packard printers), customer service (L.L. Bean), and product features (Macintosh® computers). While differentiation may be a strategic theme, costs cannot be ignored. For a differentiation strategy to succeed, the resulting price premium must exceed the seller's cost of differentiation and be less than the differential value to the buyer.

Focusing on a specific market niche such as a buyer group, segment of the product line, or geographic market,

> . . . rests on the premise that the firm is thus able to serve its narrow strategic target more effectively or efficiently than competitors who are competing more broadly. As a result, the firm achieves either differentiation from better meeting the needs of the particular target, or lower costs in serving the target, or both. Even though the focus strategy does not achieve low costs or differentiation for the market as a whole, it does achieve one or both of these positions vis-à-vis its narrow market target. [Porter, pp. 38-39]

Following a focused strategy, regional breweries that cater to local taste preferences, such as Iron City® Beer in Pittsburgh, have prospered, while Miller®, Coors®, and Budweiser® dominate the U.S. market. Learjet follows a focused strategy in designing and building corporate aircraft, leaving the market for larger passenger aircraft to firms such as Boeing and the market for smaller private planes to firms such as Piper Aircraft. Management Accounting Practice 1-1 reports on the success of a Massachusetts textile mill that is becoming a world-class competitor through a product differentiation strategy with attention to competition on the basis of quality and service.

Determining competitive strategy is a fundamental goal with implications for the operation of an organization's management accounting system. Achieving cost leadership allows an organization to achieve higher

MANAGEMENT ACCOUNTING PRACTICE 1-1

Product Differentiation Helps Malden Mills Become a Massachusetts Textile Success

With scarce land, government regulation, taxes, and high labor costs, most textile makers long ago fled Massachusetts for greener, or at least less expensive, pastures. While family owned and managed Malden Mills was tempted to move, management elected instead to follow a strategy of producing high-tech specialty fabrics rather than one of producing final consumer products such as clothing or low-margin "commodity" products such as plain polyester sheets. Management believed this strategy would allow them to pay higher labor costs while taking advantage of the skills of loyal employees.

Malden's first breakthrough came working with outdoor garment-maker Patagonia to improve Polarfleece®, a double-faced fleece material originally developed by Patagonia. While the success of the new Polarfleece attracted imitations, Malden Mills stayed ahead of the competition by continuing to develop new products, including Polartec®, an active-wear fabric used in high-priced clothing.

To improve quality and control costs, profits have been reinvested in the business. The business has gone from labor-intensive to semiautomatic, capital-intensive. Automation allows Malden to produce weekly 1.4 million yards of fabric in 140 styles and 5,000 colors. Even with automation, financial success, reflected in an increase in sales from $119 million to $403 million during the past decade, has resulted in an increase in the labor force to 3,200 employees.

To continue sales growth, Malden Mills is paying increasing attention to international markets and striving to become a world-class competitor. Malden already exports almost 30 percent of its production, selling in 60 countries and developing marketing materials in six languages. Meanwhile, most U.S. textile mills export less than 10 percent, and few export more than 20 percent of their production. To better serve its growing European customer base quickly and economically, Malden intends to open a factory in Western Europe in 1996. This will eliminate the expense and delay of a 10-day boat trip while avoiding custom import duties.

Based on: Susan Diesenhouse, "A Textile Mill Thrives by Breaking All the Rules," *The New York Times* (July 24, 1994), p. F5.

profits selling at the same price as competitors or by allowing the firm to aggressively compete on the basis of price while remaining profitable. Johnson and Kaplan[6] have observed that this strategy was followed by the Carnegie Steel Company in the late nineteenth century.

> Carnegie's operating strategy was to push his own direct costs below his competitors so that he could charge prices that would always ensure enough demand to keep his plants

6 H. Thomas Johnson and Robert S. Kaplan, *Relevance Lost: The Rise and Fall of Management Accounting* (Boston: Harvard Business School Press, 1987).

running at full capacity. This strategy prompted him to require frequent information showing his direct costs in relation to those of his competitors. Possessing that information and secure in the knowledge that his costs were the lowest in the industry, Carnegie then mercilessly cut prices during economic recessions. While competing firms went under, he still made profits. In periods of prosperity, when customers' demands exceeded the industry's capacity to produce, Carnegie joined others in raising prices. [Johnson and Kaplan, pp. 33-34]

Achieving differentiation increases customer loyalty and reduces customer price sensitivity. Hence, organizations competing on the basis of differentiation are able to achieve higher profits by charging a premium price. While organizations may not achieve the market share of firms competing on the basis of cost leadership, differentiation may provide a high return on investment. Examples of differentiated products or services include Rolls Royce automobiles and Ben and Jerry's ice cream. In the late 1920s, General Motors employed a differentiation strategy, focusing on the rapid introduction of technological change in new automobile designs to overcome the market dominance of the Model T produced by Ford Motor Company. While Ford successfully followed a cost leadership strategy for years, Mr. Ford made the mistake of doing so to the exclusion of other considerations such as quality in the form of superior vehicle performance and meeting customer desires for different colors.[7]

According to Porter, firms that do not set one of these competitive strategies as a goal or try to be all things to all people are doomed to be "stuck in the middle." Unable to effectively compete on the basis of price or differentiation in the market as a whole or in a particular market niche, firms stuck in the middle are doomed to low profitability.

It should be noted that not all products, such as grain, can be substantively differentiated. One of the purposes of advertising, such as that for Chiquita bananas, is to attempt to differentiate products by creating an image of the product or service.

Management Accounting and Goal Attainment

Management accounting exists to support the achievement of an organization's goals. Hence, the information in management accounting reports should measure progress toward the organization's goals. Careful budgeting and cost control with frequent and detailed performance reports are critical with a goal of cost leadership. Here the product is difficult to distinguish from that of competitors, and price is the primary basis of competition. Under these circumstances, everyone in the organization should, like Andrew Carnegie, continuously apply management accounting concepts to achieve and maintain cost leadership.

---

7 William J. Abernathy and Kenneth Wayne, "Limits of the Learning Curve," *Harvard Business Review* (September-October 1974), pp. 109-119.

While frequent and detailed cost information is less important when a differentiation strategy is followed, managers must understand the financial consequences of their actions and realize there are limits to price premiums customers are willing to pay. On a more positive note, when a differentiation strategy is followed, it often pays to work closely with customers to find ways to enhance the value of a product or service to them. This leads to an analysis of costs from the customer's viewpoint. In designing its new 777 aircraft, Boeing invited potential customers to set up offices in Boeing plants and to work with the team of Boeing employees designing the aircraft. Many design changes were made to reduce customer costs. United Airlines, for example, convinced Boeing to move the location of the 777's fuel tanks to reduce the servicing costs.

Planning

In addition to developing overall goals, management needs to develop specific plans to achieve these goals. **Planning** is the formulation of a scheme or program for the accomplishment of a specific purpose or goal. A distinction is customarily made between long-range (strategic) planning and short-range planning. **Long-range planning** emphasizes the selection of programs to move the organization toward its goals over the next several years. Examples of long-range planning include decisions about the introduction of new products or the acquisition of plant and equipment.

Short-range planning is based on the organization's long-range plan as well as on its current situation and focuses on specific, near-term activities to move the organization from its current situation toward its long-range goals. **Short-range planning** involves the interpretation of goals and long-range plans into performance objectives for the coming year and the selection of specific actions to achieve these objectives. The following example illustrates the relationship between long-range and short-range planning.

Crown Department Stores currently operates three stores in the suburbs of a large metropolitan area. Professionals such as engineers, scientists, doctors, lawyers, and managers live in this market area. Crown's goals are to achieve the highest annual sales volume of all suburban department stores in the market area and to provide investors with an acceptable level of earnings by offering differentiated service in this market niche. To achieve these goals, Crown's long-range plans include opening one new store during each of the next five years, reorienting merchandise lines toward goods likely to be purchased by professional people, and increasing support for cultural activities. Crown's short-range plans for the coming year include hiring personnel and acquiring merchandise for one new store currently under construction. Discontinuing the sales of hardware, expanding the offerings of furniture and women's business apparel, adding an art department, and starting a Crown Summer Concert Series are also among management's plans. As reflected in Crown's budget, management believes these and other activities will produce a 40 percent increase in sales revenue and a 35 percent increase in after-tax profits during the coming year.

Crown's long-range plans are based on corporate goals, including Crown's competitive strategy for differentiated service. (How might products and services at Wal-Mart differ from Crown?) Care is taken to ensure that short-range plans support corporate goals and long-range plans. Because they are statements of actions to implement next year, short-range plans are more specific than long-range plans.

Organizing

Through **organizing**, the process of making the organization into a well-ordered whole, management structures tasks identified in the short-range plan and assigns them to specific individuals or groups. Authority to take action to accomplish plans and goals is delegated to other managers and employees.

An **organization chart** illustrates the formal relationships existing between the elements of an organization. An organization chart for Crown Department Stores is illustrated in Exhibit 1-2. The blocks represent organizational units, and the

EXHIBIT 1-2: CROWN DEPARTMENT STORES' ORGANIZATION CHART

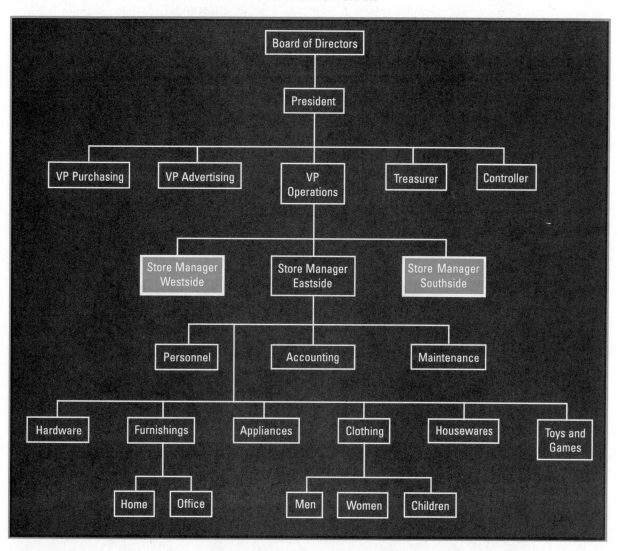

lines represent relationships between units. Authority flows down the organization. Top management delegates authority to use resources for limited purposes to subordinate managers who, in turn, delegate more limited authority to accomplish more structured tasks to their subordinates. Responsibility flows up the organization. People at the bottom are responsible for specific tasks, but the president is responsible for the operation of the entire organization.

A distinction is often made between line and staff departments. Line departments engage in activities that create and distribute goods and services to customers. Staff departments exist to facilitate the activities of line departments. In Exhibit 1-2, we see that Crown Department Stores has two levels of staff organizations—corporate and store. The corporate staff departments are Purchasing, Advertising, Treasurer, and Controller. Staff departments at the store level are Personnel, Accounting, and Maintenance. All other units are line departments. A change in plans can necessitate a change in the organization. For example, Crown's plan to discontinue the sale of hardware and add an art department during the coming year will necessitate an organizational change.

Controlling

Controlling is the process of ensuring that results agree with plans. In the process of controlling operations, actual performance is compared with plans. If actual results deviate significantly from plans, an attempt is made to bring operations into line with plans, or the plans are adjusted. The original plan is adjusted if it is deemed no longer appropriate because of changed circumstances. Hence, the process of controlling feeds back into the process of planning to form the continuous cycle illustrated in Exhibit 1-3. This is all coordinated through the organization's information system.

EXHIBIT 1-3: PLANNING, ORGANIZING, AND CONTROLLING ARE A CONTINUOUS CYCLE

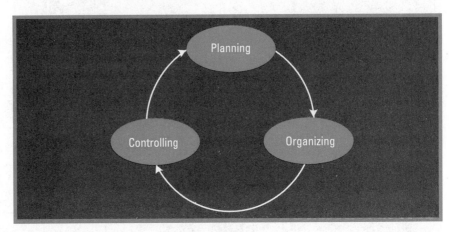

ACCOUNTING AS AN EMPOWERMENT TOOL

L O 3

For many years, organizations experienced a growth in staff size as tasks performed by line personnel were taken over by staff specialists. Unfortunately, many of the advantages of the staff's expertise were offset by increases in overall costs, a reduced feeling of decision ownership on the part of line personnel charged with implementing decisions, delays in decision making as coordination problems increased, and a tendency for employees in specific functional areas, such as sales, engineering, and accounting, to view problems from the narrow perspective of their discipline.

Since the early 1990s, there has been a movement toward empowering employees to make decisions at the lowest organizational level possible. This movement has flattened organization charts by reducing the number of management layers. It has also reduced the size of corporate staffs. Gone are the costs associated with the eliminated layers of management and staff positions. Activities previously performed by people in these positions have either been eliminated, assigned to other employees (often closer to the bottom of the organization chart), or combined with other activities. Perceived benefits of the empowerment movement include reduced costs, an increase in the speed with which decisions are made, and an increased feeling of ownership of (and interest in) decisions on the part of line employees.

Consider the following two examples. First, in some organizations, production employees now order raw materials directly from suppliers through prearranged purchase agreements. This contrasts with the traditional approach of having all purchase orders processed by a separate purchasing department. Second, to encourage employees to take more interest in product quality and to reduce the related costs of defects, some businesses have empowered workers to stop manufacturing operations when they identify a possible quality problem. This contrasts with the traditional approach of maintaining production and inspecting finished products for defects.

In both of these examples, employee empowerment results in a change in the activities performed and the costs incurred to fill customer needs. In the first example, the size of the purchasing department is reduced, the role of the purchasing department is changed, and the number of activities involved in placing a purchase order is reduced. Purchasing department employees now focus more on nonroutine tasks such as developing long-term relationships with a limited number of suppliers dedicated to helping both businesses prosper. Production employees perform the routine and streamlined activity of placing purchase orders. In the second example, the activities involving the inspection of finished goods may be eliminated. More significantly, the activities of continuing to work on defective products and the reworking of defective products are reduced or eliminated. Again, production employees are now responsible for the inspection activity. Hopefully, this can be done at lower cost, while employees are monitoring production or moving inventory. Management Accounting Practice 1-2 illustrates how one company improved performance after empowering its employees.

These changes have required organizations to open their books to employees and to provide them with information previously regarded as confidential. They have also forced the remaining staff to focus more on the needs of line personnel, who are the staff's customers. One specific result in the area of management accounting has been the emergence of **activity-based costing**, which involves the determination of costs for specific activities (such as the cost of packaging an order) performed to fill customer needs. The cost to fill the customer's needs is then determined as the sum of the cost of all related activities. When coupled with an analysis of alternative ways of filling customer needs or manufacturing a new product, activity-based cost information empowers line personnel to better manage activities under their control. Other examples of management accounting concepts developed to empower employee decision making include value chain analysis and quality cost measurements. These and related concepts will receive extensive treatment in subsequent chapters.

MANAGEMENT ACCOUNTING PRACTICE 1-2

Empowerment Brings Springfield Remanufacturing from the Brink to Profits

Although Springfield Remanufacturing Corporation is now profitable, in the late 1970s the company was bleeding red ink, and workers were so distrustful of management that they wore raincoats and galoshes to company meetings in preparation for another "snow job."

But, when Jack Stack became president, he opened the books, providing employees with information on all aspects of operations, ranging from revenue and purchasing costs to management and labor expenses. According to Mr. Stack, this open book policy is one of the actions responsible for bringing Springfield from the brink of bankruptcy to record earnings. "The more [employees] learned the more they could do....We matched up higher levels of thinking with higher levels of performance."

Candice Smalley, a nozzle rebuilder, says she didn't realize how much a factory floor worker could affect profits until she started seeing financials and hearing about usage and overhead. "... it made us start trying to improve our quality." Denise Bredfeldt, the training director, says that before Springfield adopted an open book policy, "people would just punch the clock and leave." Now, when things get bad, people start brainstorming about how to improve. Employees say they have a heightened sense of community and are willing to do whatever it takes to maintain competitiveness.

Based on: "Company Wins Workers' Loyalty by Opening Its Books," *The Wall Street Journal* (December 20, 1993), pp. B1-B2.

MEASUREMENT, MANAGEMENT, AND ETHICS

LO 4

Performance measurement, also referred to as **outcomes assessment**, is the determination of the extent to which actual outcomes correspond to planned outcomes. It is a management adage that "What you count is what you get." Because managers manage what is being measured, successful organizations are very careful about what they measure. Selecting inappropriate performance measures may lead employees to take actions that do not support attainment of organizational goals and plans. If performance is measured by return on assets (net income/total assets), managers may be reluctant to replace inefficient, fully depreciated equipment with new equipment because the resulting increase in the denominator will reduce return on investment. If the performance of a case worker is measured on the basis of the number of cases being worked on, the case worker will not be motivated to complete case assignments. If the performance of professional employees is measured on the basis of billable hours, the employees may be motivated to maximize billable hours, perhaps in an unethical manner. Management Accounting Practice 1-3 looks at the American Bar Association's efforts to control aggressive and ethically questionable billing practices.

Performance measurement draws attention *to* whatever is being measured and causes people to improve performance on the dimension that is being measured. It also draws attention *away* from other variables that, in fact, may be more critical for success. If on-time delivery is critical to success, but delivery costs rather than delivery times are reported in performance reports, employees will be more interested in minimizing delivery costs than maximizing on-time delivery.

Systematic Performance Measurement

Outcome assessment is a critical element of success. Management needs to determine the extent to which performance moves the organization toward achieving its goals and plans. Outcome assessment requires the determination of performance measures that support the achievement of goals and plans. It also requires the systematic measurement and reporting of outcomes in a timely manner and in a form most useful to management. Management will then use this performance information to improve processes, modify plans, or both. Managers should work with management accountants to identify appropriate measures and have them included in a systematic measurement and reporting system. See Exhibit 1-4 (page 17) for an overview of this process.

It is possible to develop such long lists of potential performance measures that it becomes difficult to know where to begin. If an attempt is made to report on everything, the costs of assessment will certainly exceed the benefits. Additionally, the number of items included in performance reports will make it difficult to address any of them. One possible solution is to agree on three or four measures most in need of immediate

MANAGEMENT ACCOUNTING PRACTICE 1-3

Performance Pressures Lead to Ethically Questionable Billing

On a six-hour trip, flying to consult a major client, a lawyer spends five hours preparing a brief for a second client. Upon arriving in the evening, the lawyer spends three hours preparing materials for a morning meeting with the major client. What is the total time billed for services rendered?

Lawyers, among the few professionals who typically bill by the hour, are experts at finding creative ways to increase billable hours and revenues. According to Amy Stevens, "Their reasons are a potent mix of elementary economics and raw survival instinct. A firm's earnings are a function of the firm's billable hours, and time sheets are usually a factor in determining individual associates' promotions and bonuses as well as partners' profit shares." Hence, the flying lawyer might bill for fourteen hours, even though the total time involved in the trip and evening work was only 9 hours.

The American Bar Association is considering a proposal to declare double billing, as well as a number of other billing practices, unethical. The ABA is concerned that questionable billing practices are contributing to a "discouraging" opinion of the profession.

Many clients are ahead of the ABA in trying to control aggressive billing practices. Zoe Baird, general council of Aetna Life & Casualty Co., requests that all significant outside legal work be done on a flat fee or similar basis. Sidney N. Herman, managing partner of Bartlit, Beck, Herman, Palenchar & Scott in Chicago, believes that more needs to be done about the practice of hourly billing, which he calls "a system that rewards inefficiency."

Based on: Amy Stevens, "ABA Tackles Firm's Tendencies for Creative Clockwork in Billing," *The Wall Street Journal* (December 17, 1993), p. B10.

attention and focus on them in performance reports. When performance of these items has improved, they are replaced by other performance measures now deemed more in need of improvement. While it may not be possible to concurrently improve performance on all dimensions, this approach supports the notion of continuous improvement.

Ethical Dilemmas

Ethics deals with the moral quality, fitness, or propriety of a course of action that may injure or benefit people. Ethics goes beyond legality, which refers to what is permitted under the law, to consider the moral quality of an action. Because situations involving ethics are not guided by well-defined rules, they are often subjective.

Although some actions are clearly ethical (working a full day in exchange for a full-day's pay) and others are clearly unethical (pumping contaminated waste into an underground aquifer used as a source of drinking water), managers and accountants are often faced with situations that do not obviously fall into either category:

- Accelerating shipments at the end of the quarter to improve current earnings.

EXHIBIT 1-4: DEVELOPING AND USING PERFORMANCE MEASURES BASED ON GOALS AND PLANS

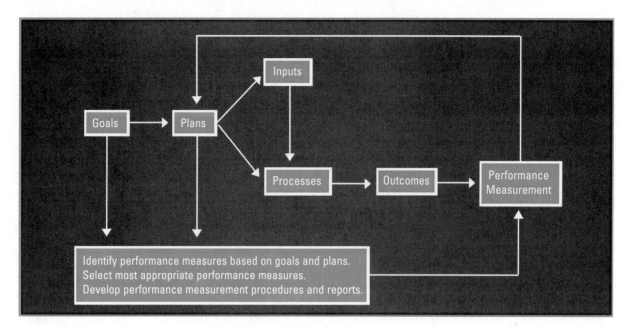

- Keeping inventory that is unlikely to be used on the books to avoid recording a loss.
- Purchasing supplies from a relative rather than seeking bids.
- Basing a budget on an overly optimistic sales forecast.
- Assigning some costs of contract A to contract B to avoid an unfavorable performance report on contract A.

Many ethical dilemmas involve actions that are perceived to have desirable short-run consequences and highly probable undesirable long-run consequences. The ethical action is to face an undesirable situation now to avoid a worse situation later. Yet, the decision maker may prefer to believe that things will work in the long run, be overly concerned with the consequences of not doing well in the short run, or simply not care about the future because the problem will then belong to someone else. In a situation that is clearly unethical, the future consequences are known to be avoidable and undesirable. In situations involving questionable ethics, there is some hope that things will work out:

- Next year's sales will more than make up for the accelerated shipments.
- The obsolete inventory can be used in a new nostalgia line of products.
- The relative may charge more but provides excellent service.
- You need to have more confidence in our sales staff.
- We can make up for the cost shift by working extra hard to be efficient with the remaining work on contract B.

When forced to think about the situation, most employees want to act in an ethical manner. The problem faced by personnel involved in measurement and reporting is that while they may question the propriety of a proposed action, the arguments may be plausible and their careers can be affected by "whistle-blowing." Of course, careers are also affected when individuals are found to be involved in unethical behavior. The careers of people who fail to point out unethical behavior may also be affected, especially if they have a responsibility for measurement and reporting.

Major ethical dilemmas often evolve out of a series of small compromises, none of which appears serious enough to warrant taking a stand on ethical grounds. Unfortunately, these small compromises establish a pattern of behavior that is increasingly difficult to reverse. The key to avoiding these situations is recognizing the early warning signs of situations that involve questionable ethical behavior and taking whatever action is appropriate.

Code of Ethics

To make members more aware of situations involving questionable ethical behavior and to provide a reference point for resisting pressures to engage in actions of questionable ethics, professional organizations such as the American Bar Association, the American Institute of Certified Public Accountants, the American Medical Association, and the Institute of Management Accountants (IMA) have developed codes of ethics. A representative code of professional ethics for the IMA is presented in Exhibit 1-5.

EXHIBIT 1-5: STANDARDS OF ETHICAL CONDUCT FOR MANAGEMENT ACCOUNTANTS

Competence

Management accountants have a responsibility to:

- Maintain an appropriate level of professional competence by ongoing development of their knowledge and skills.
- Perform their professional duties in accordance with relevant laws, regulations, and technical standards.
- Prepare complete and clear reports and recommendations after appropriate analysis of relevant and reliable information.

Confidentiality

Management accountants have a responsibility to:

- Refrain from disclosing confidential information acquired in the course of their work except when authorized, unless legally obliged to do so.
- Inform subordinates as appropriate regarding the confidentiality of information acquired in the course of their work and monitor their actions to assure the maintenance of that confidentiality.
- Refrain from using or appearing to use confidential information acquired in the course of their work for unethical or illegal advantage either personally or through third parties.

(continued)

Integrity

Management accountants have a responsibility to:

- Avoid actual or apparent conflicts of interest and advise all appropriate parties of any potential conflict.
- Refrain from engaging in any activity that would prejudice their ability to carry out their duties ethically.
- Refuse any gift or hospitality that would influence or appear to influence their actions.
- Refrain from actively or passively subverting the attainment of the organization's legitimate and ethical objectives.
- Recognize and communicate professional limitations or other constraints that would preclude responsible judgment of successful performance of an activity.
- Communicate unfavorable as well as favorable information and professional judgments or opinions.
- Refrain from engaging in or supporting any activity that would discredit the profession.

Objectivity

Management accountants have a responsibility to:

- Communicate information fairly and objectively.
- Disclose fully all relevant information that could reasonably be expected to influence an intended user's understanding of the reports, comments, and recommendations presented.

Resolution of Ethical Conflict

In applying the standards of ethical conflict, management accountants may encounter problems in identifying unethical behavior or in resolving an ethical conflict. When faced with significant ethical issues, management accountants should follow the established policies of the organization bearing on the resolution of such conflict. If these policies do not resolve the ethical conflict, management accountants should consider the following courses of action.

- Discuss such problems with the immediate supervisor except when it appears that the supervisor is involved, in which case the problem should be presented initially to the next higher managerial levels. If satisfactory resolution cannot be achieved when the problem is initially presented, submit the issue to the next higher management level.

  If the immediate supervisor is the chief executive officer, or equivalent, the acceptable reviewing authority may be a group such as the audit committee, executive committee, board of directors, board of trustees, or owners. Contact with levels above the immediate supervisor should be initiated only with the supervisor's knowledge, assuming the superior is not involved.

- Clarify relevant concepts by confidential discussion with an objective advisor to obtain an understanding of possible courses of action.
- If the ethical conflict still exists after exhausting all levels of internal review, the management accountant may have no other recourse on significant matters than to resign from the organization and to submit an informative memorandum to an appropriate representative of the organization.

  Except when legally prescribed, communication of such problems to authorities or individuals not employed or engaged by the organization is not considered appropriate.

Source: Institute of Management Accountants, *Statements on Management Accounting: Standards of Ethical Conduct for Management Accountants*, Statement No. 1C, New York, NY, June 1983.

Many organizations have also established codes of ethics. One of the important goals of corporate codes of ethics is to provide employees with a common foundation for addressing ethical issues. A survey conducted by two members of the IMA's Ethics Committee found that 56 percent of the responding companies have corporate codes of conduct. Unfortunately, the same survey also reported that while senior management and middle management usually received copies of the code, only 57 percent of the responding companies with corporate codes of conduct provided copies of the code to all employees.[8] Perhaps more important than a published code of ethics is the ethical tone set by top management. If top management is perceived to take unethical actions or be less than 100 percent committed to high ethical standards, employees will be less inclined to make the difficult decisions often required to maintain ethics.

A basic rule used by General Motors Corporation is that employees should never do anything they would be ashamed to explain to their families or to see in the front page of the local newspaper. Former GM chairman and CEO Roger Smith added that:

> Ethical conduct in business goes beyond this, however. For example, one of the basic needs of top management is to receive reliable data and honest opinions from people throughout the organization. Too often, subordinates are reluctant to tell all the details of a project or assignment that has failed or is in trouble. This very human trait occurs in all walks of life, whether personal, business, or governmental, and contributes to the making of bad decisions. In short, ethics is an essential element of success in business.[9]

WORLD-CLASS COMPETITION ON COST, QUALITY, AND SERVICE

L O 5

For the past 50 years, the move away from isolated, national economic systems toward an interdependent global economic system has become increasingly pronounced. International treaties, such as the 1993 North American Free Trade Agreement and the 1994 General Agreement on Tariffs and Trade, merely recognize an already existing and inevitable condition made possible by advances in telecommunications to move data, in computers to process data into information, and in transportation to move products and people. The labels of origins on goods (Japan, Germany, Canada, Taiwan, United States, and so forth) only scratch the surface of existing global relationships. Behind labels designating a product's final assembly point are components from all over the world.

---

8 Robert B. Sweeney and Howard L. Siers, "Survey: Ethics and Corporate America," *Management Accounting* (June 1990), pp. 34-40.
9 Roger B. Smith, "Ethics in Business: An Essential Element of Success," *Management Accounting* (June 1990), p. 50.

The move toward a global economy has heightened competition and reduced selling prices to such an extent that there is little or no room for error in managing costs or pricing products. Well-informed buyers routinely search the world for the product or service that best fits their needs. Moreover, customers are not just looking for the best price. Today's competition takes place on the three interrelated dimensions of cost, quality, and service. Cost includes not only the initial purchase price, but also subsequent operating and maintenance costs. Quality refers to the degree to which products or services meet the customer's needs. Service includes such things as the helpfulness of sales personnel, special product modifications to meet the buyer's needs, timely delivery, and subsequent support. Management Accounting Practice 1-4 takes a look at how Federal Express and United Parcel Service compete on the basis of quality, service, and price.

Managers of successful companies know they compete in a global market with instant communications. Because the competition is hungry and always striving to gain a competitive advantage, world-class companies must continuously struggle to improve performance in these three interrelated dimensions: cost, quality, and service. Throughout this text, we

MANAGEMENT ACCOUNTING PRACTICE 1-4

FedEx and UPS Stage Battle Customer Is Sure to Win

To increase customer service in the $18 billion express delivery business, Federal Express introduced FedEx Ship®, a personal computer-based system that lets even its smallest customers use a modem to order pickups, print shipping labels, and track deliveries. "We have to stay ahead of the competition" was the theme of remarks describing this new service by Dennis Jones, FedEx's chief information officer.

Almost immediately, United Parcel Service revealed it is developing a new alliance with Prodigy on-line computer service to provide a similar service. Responding to a reporter's question, Joe Pyne, vice-president of marketing at UPS, commented, "There's no question we track FedEx, just like they track us."

Both companies are also investing heavily in new equipment and infrastructure to continue to meet increasingly tight delivery deadlines they set. UPS is investing $120 million in sorting hubs for air shipments. FedEx is investing $1.8 billion in new aircraft.

While both companies battle to improve quality and service, and thereby differentiate their product, they are increasingly reaching technological limits that make further differentiation difficult. The result is customers who benefit from high quality and service at lower and lower costs. FedEx and UPS have cut prices in recent years for large-volume customers, reducing their profit margins on each sales dollar by one-third during the past five years.

Based on: David Greising, "Watch Out for Flying Packages," *Business Week* (November 14, 1994), p. 40, and advertisements such as that in *Business Week* (January 30, 1995), p. 12.

will examine how firms can successfully compete on these three dimensions. As a starting point in our journey, we introduce cost driver concepts and basic cost behavior patterns in the remaining sections of this chapter.

COST DRIVERS INFLUENCE COSTS

L O 6

An **activity** is a unit of work. To serve a customer at a restaurant, a waiter or waitress might perform the following units of work:

- Seat customer and offer menu.
- Take customer order.
- Bring order to kitchen.
- Bring food to customer.
- Determine and bring bill to customer.
- Collect money and give change.
- Clear table.

Each of these is an activity, and the performance of each activity costs money. To manage activities and their costs, it is necessary to understand how costs respond to **cost drivers**, the factors that influence costs. While cost drivers may be classified in a variety of ways, we believe that dividing them into the three categories of structural, organizational, and activity cost drivers provides a useful foundation for the study of management accounting.

Structural cost drivers are fundamental choices about the size and scope of operations and technologies employed in delivering products or services to customers.[10] The types of activities and the costs of activities performed to satisfy customer needs are influenced by an organization's size, the scope of its operations, and the technologies used. Decisions affecting structural cost drivers are made infrequently; and, once made, the organization is committed to a course of action that will be difficult to change. For a chain of discount stores, possible structural cost drivers include:

- Determining the size of the stores. This will affect the variety of merchandise that can be carried and operating costs.
- Determining the type of construction. While a lean warehouse type of construction may be less expensive, it may not be an appropriate setting for selling high-fashion clothing.

---

10 John Shank [1989] and John Shank and Vijay Govindarajan [1993], building on the work of Riley, identify five structural and six executional cost drivers. We identify their executional drivers as operational drivers and add the third category of activity cost drivers. See Daniel Riley, "Competitive Cost Based Investment Strategies for Industrial Companies," *Manufacturing Issues* (New York: Booz, Allen, Hamilton, 1987).

- Determining the location of the stores. Locating in a shopping mall may cost more and subject the store to mall regulations but provide for more customer traffic and shared advertising.
- Determining kind of technology employed in the stores. A computerized system for maintaining all inventory and sales data requires a large initial investment and fixed annual operating costs while providing more current information. However, the computerized inventory and sales systems may be less expensive at high sales volumes than a less expensive system relying more on clerks taking physical inventory.

Organizational cost drivers are choices concerning the organization of activities and choices concerning the involvement of persons inside and outside the organization in decision making. Like structural cost drivers, organizational cost drivers influence costs by affecting types of activities and the costs of activities performed to satisfy customer needs. Decisions affecting organizational cost drivers are made within the context of previous decisions affecting structural cost drivers. In a manufacturing organization, previous decisions about plant, equipment, and location are taken as a given when decisions affecting organizational cost drivers are made. Examples of organizational cost drivers at a manufacturing organization include:

- Deciding to work closely with a limited number of suppliers. This may assist in ensuring that the proper materials are available in the proper quantities and the optimal time. Developing linkages with suppliers may also result in suppliers' initiatives that improve the profitability of both organizations.
- Providing employees with cost information and empowering them to make decisions. This may improve decision speed, reduce costs, and make employees more oriented toward customers. Production employees may, for example, offer product design suggestions that reduce manufacturing costs or reduce defects.
- Deciding to reorganize the existing equipment in the plant so that sequential operations are closer. This may reduce the cost of moving inventory between workstations.

Activity cost drivers are specific units of work (activities) performed to serve customer needs that consume costly resources. Several examples of activities in a restaurant were mentioned previously. The customer may be outside the organization, such as a client of an advertising firm, or inside the organization, such as an accounting office that receives maintenance services. Because the performance of activities consumes resources and resources cost money, the performance of activities drives costs.

The basic decisions concerning which available activities will be used to respond to customer requests have already been made. At this level, execution of previous plans and following prescribed activities is important. Hence, in the following list of activity cost drivers for a manufacturing organization, note the absence of the decision-oriented words.

- Placing a purchase order for raw materials.
- Inspecting incoming raw materials.
- Moving items being manufactured between workstations.
- Setting up a machine to work on a product.
- Machine time spent working on a product.
- Labor time spent working on a product.
- Time spent determining how a specific product will be produced.
- Hiring and training a new employee.
- Packing an order for shipment.
- Processing a sales order.
- Shipping a product.

In managing costs, management makes choices concerning structural and organizational cost drivers. These decisions affect the types of activities required to satisfy customer needs. Because different types of activities have different costs, management's decisions ultimately affect activity costs and profitability. Hence, good decision making at the level of structural and organizational cost drivers requires an understanding of the linkages among the three types of cost drivers and knowledge of the costs of different activities. We will examine these linkages throughout our study of management accounting.

THE BEHAVIOR OF ACTIVITY COST DRIVERS

L O 7

Cost behavior concerns how costs respond to changes in the number of units of an activity cost driver. Structural and organizational cost drivers affect the selection of activities to serve customer needs as well as the cost per unit of activity.

Four Basic Cost Behavior Patterns

While there are an unlimited number of ways that costs can respond to changes in activity cost drivers, as a starting point it is useful to classify cost behavior into four categories: variable, fixed, mixed, and step. Graphs of each are presented in Exhibit 1-6. Observe that total cost is measured on the vertical axis, and total activity for some time period of interest is measured on the horizontal axis.

1. **Variable costs** are uniform for each incremental unit of activity. Total variable costs change in direct proportion to changes in activity, equaling zero dollars when activity is zero and increasing at a constant amount per unit of activity. The higher the variable cost per

EXHIBIT 1-6: IMPORTANT TOTAL COST BEHAVIOR PATTERNS

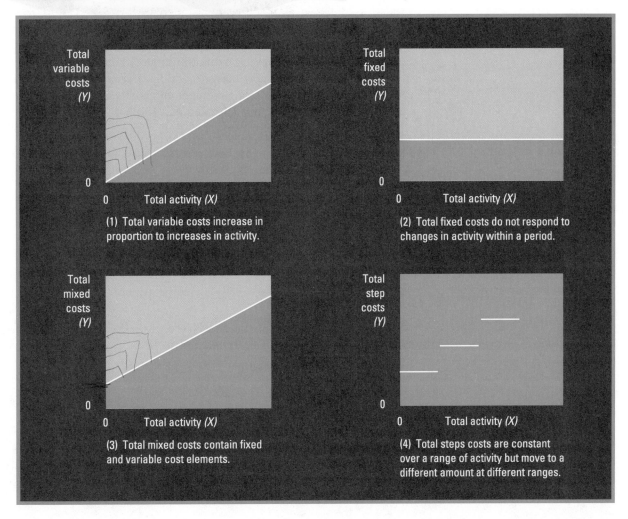

(1) Total variable costs increase in proportion to increases in activity.

(2) Total fixed costs do not respond to changes in activity within a period.

(3) Total mixed costs contain fixed and variable cost elements.

(4) Total steps costs are constant over a range of activity but move to a different amount at different ranges.

unit of activity, the steeper the cost curve. With sales revenue as the activity cost driver in a department store, sales commissions and the cost of goods sold are examples of variable costs.

2. **Fixed costs** are a constant amount per period of time. Hence, the fixed cost curve is flat with a slope (incline) of zero. Examples of fixed costs include salaries of professional employees, annual depreciation, property taxes, and rent. While fixed costs may respond, over time, to structural and organizational cost drivers, they do not respond to short-run changes in activity cost drivers.

3. **Mixed costs** (sometimes called **semivariable costs**) contain a fixed and a variable cost element. Total mixed costs are positive (like fixed costs) when activity is zero, and they increase in a linear fashion (like total variable costs) as activity increases. Assuming annual machine hours is the cost driver in a manufacturing plant, maintenance cost is an example of a mixed cost. Some maintenance

is required to keep equipment from deteriorating, and additional maintenance is required as machine hours increase.

4. **Step costs** are constant within a given range of activity but different between ranges of activity. Total step costs increase in a step-like fashion as activity increases. With the annual number of patient-days in a hospital as the cost driver, nursing salaries are an example of a step cost. Up to a certain number of patients only one nurse needs to be on duty at a time. Beyond that limit an additional nurse is required, and so forth.

Mathematically, the relationship between total cost (Y axis) and total activity (X axis) is expressed as follows for the four cost behavior patterns:

$$(1)\ \text{Variable cost:}\quad Y = bX$$

where:
b = the variable cost per unit, sometimes referred to as the slope of the cost function.

$$(2)\ \text{Fixed cost:}\quad Y = a$$

where:
a = total fixed costs. Note that, because fixed costs do not change with activity, the slope of the fixed cost function is zero.

$$(3)\ \text{Mixed cost:}\quad Y = a + bX$$

where:
a = total fixed cost element
b = variable cost element per unit of activity.

$$(4)\ \text{Step costs:}\quad Y = a_i$$

where:
a_i = the step cost within a specific range of activity, identified by the subscript i.

Other Factors Affecting Cost Behavior Patterns

The cost behavior patterns presented above are based on the assumptions that the time period is too short to incorporate changes in strategic cost drivers such as the scale of operations. While this assumption is useful for short-range planning, for the purpose of developing plans for extended time periods, it is more appropriate to take into consideration possible variations in one or more strategic cost drivers. When this is done, many costs previously classified as fixed are better classified as variable.

Even the cost of depreciable assets can be viewed as variable if the time period is long enough. Assuming sales revenue is the cost driver, for a single month the depreciation on all the Pizza Hut Restaurants in the world is a fixed cost. Over several years, if sales are strong, additional restaurants will be opened; and, if sales are weak, some restaurants will likely be closed and sold or torn down. Hence, for planning over a multiple-year period, the number of restaurants varies with sales volume, and depreciation becomes a variable cost with sales revenue as a cost driver. In general, the longer the time period, the greater the number of variable costs.

Identifying the appropriate cost driver for a particular cost requires judgment and professional experience. Analytic tools such as regression analysis can assist in selecting the most appropriate cost driver. In general, the cost driver should have a logical, causal relationship with costs. Failure to identify the most appropriate cost driver can hinder cost management.

Total Cost Function for an Organization or Business Segment

It is often useful to consider how the sum of all costs associated with an organization or a business segment respond to a single independent variable of interest to management. This may be done to obtain a general understanding of cost behavior, to compare the cost structures of different organizations, or to perform preliminary planning activities. Presenting all costs as a function of a single independent variable is not accurate enough to make specific decisions concerning products, services, or activities. Because of the multitude of the underlying factors that drive costs, it is seldom appropriate to identify the independent variable of a total cost function as a cost driver. Doing so would imply that total costs can be manipulated by changing the level of a single item that is responsible for all costs. This is seldom true.

In developing a total cost function, the independent variable usually represents some measure of the goods or services provided customers such as total student credit hours in a university, total sales revenue in a store, total guest-days in a hotel, or total units manufactured in a factory. The resulting cost function is illustrated in Exhibit 1-7.

EXHIBIT 1-7: TOTAL COST BEHAVIOR

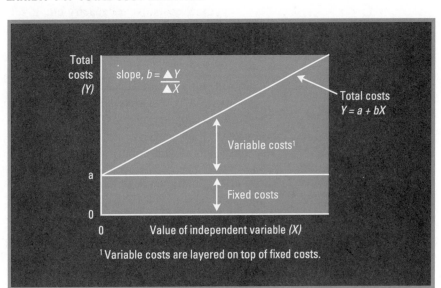

The resulting equation for total costs is:

$$Y = a + bX$$

where:

Y = total costs
a = vertical axis intercept (an approximation of fixed costs)
b = slope (an approximation of variable costs per unit of X)
X = value of independent variable

Relevant Range for Cost Functions

The use of straight lines in accounting models of cost behavior assumes a linear relationship between cost and activity with each additional unit of activity being accompanied by a uniform increment in total cost. Accountants identify this uniform increment as the variable cost of one unit.

Economic models show a curvilinear relationship between cost and activity with each incremental unit of activity being accompanied by a varying increment in total cost. Economists identify the varying increment in total cost as the **marginal cost** of one unit.

It is useful to relate marginal costs to three levels of activity:

1. Below the activity range for which the facility was designed, the existence of excess capacity results in relatively high marginal costs. Having extra time, employees complete their assignments at a leisurely pace, increasing the time and the cost to produce each unit above what it would be if employees were more pressed to complete work. Frequent starting and stopping of equipment may also add to costs.
2. Within the normal activity range for which the facility was designed, activities take place under optimal circumstances, and marginal costs are relatively low.
3. Above the activity range for which the facility was designed, the existence of capacity constraints again results in relatively high marginal costs. Near capacity employees may be paid overtime wages, less experienced employees may be used, regular equipment may operate less efficiently, and old equipment with high energy requirements may be placed in service.

Based on marginal cost concepts, the economists' short-run total cost function is illustrated in Exhibit 1-8(a). The vertical axis intercept represents capacity costs. Corresponding to the high marginal costs at low levels of activity, the initial slope is quite steep. In the normal activity range, where marginal costs are relatively low, the slope becomes less steep. Then, corresponding to high marginal costs above the normal activity range, the slope of the economists' total cost function increases again.

If the economists' total cost curve is valid, how can we reasonably approximate it with a straight line? The answer to this question is in the notion of a relevant range. A linear pattern may be a poor approximation of the economists' curvilinear pattern over the entire range of possible

activity, but a linear pattern, illustrated in Exhibit 1-8(b), is often sufficiently accurate within the range of probable operations. The range of
operations within which a linear cost function is valid is called the **relevant range**. Linear estimates of cost behavior are only valid within the
relevant range. Extreme care must be exercised when making comments
about cost behavior outside the relevant range.

**Other Cost
Behavior
Patterns**

While we have considered the most frequently used cost behavior patterns, remember that there are an almost unlimited number of ways that
costs can respond to changes in activity. You should avoid the temptation
to automatically assume that the cost in question conforms to one of the
patterns discussed in this chapter. Think through each situation and then
select a behavior pattern that seems logical and fits the known facts.
Additional cost behavior patterns are considered in the assignment material and subsequent chapters.

EXHIBIT 1-8: ECONOMIC AND ACCOUNTING COST STRUCTURES

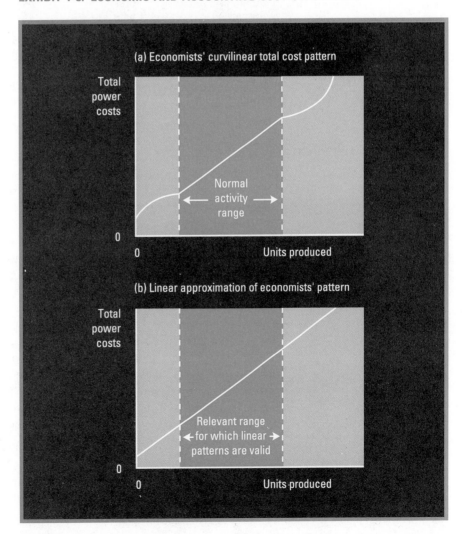

Particular care needs to be taken with the vertical axis. So far, all Chapter 1 graphs have placed *total* costs on the vertical axis. Miscommunication is likely if one party is thinking in terms of total costs, while the other is thinking in terms of variable or average costs. Consider the following cost function:

$$\text{Total costs} = \$3,000 + \$5X$$

where:

$$X = \text{customers served}$$

The total, variable, and average costs for various levels of activity are shown below and graphed in Exhibit 1-9, parts (a), (b), and (c). Note that as the number of customers served increases, total costs increase by the amount of the variable costs per unit, and the average cost decreases because fixed costs are spread over a larger number of units. Because division by zero is not possible, the average cost line is not extended to zero customers.

Customers Served	Total Costs	Average Cost*	Variable Costs per Customer
100	$3,500	$35.00	$5
200	4,000	20.00	$5
300	4,500	15.00	$5
400	5,000	12.50	$5
500	5,500	11.00	$5

*Total costs/Customers served

To predict total costs for the coming period, management is interested in the graph in Exhibit 1-9(a). To determine the minimum price required to avoid a loss on each additional customer served, management is interested in the variable costs per customer. Yet, if a manager inquired as to the cost of serving a customer, a financial accountant would probably provide average cost information, as illustrated in Exhibit 1-9(b). The specific average cost would likely be a function of the number of customers served during the most recent accounting period.

Errors can occur if last period's average costs, perhaps based on a volume of 500 customers, were used to predict total costs for a future period when the anticipated volume was some other amount, say 300 units. Using average costs, the predicted total costs of 300 units are $3,300 ($11 × 300). In fact, using the proper total cost function, a more accurate prediction of total costs is $4,500 ($3,000 + [$5 × 300]). The prediction error could cause a number of problems. If management planned to pay bills of $3,300 when the bills actually totaled $4,500, the company might have to curtail activities or borrow cash under unfavorable terms to avoid running out of cash.

Committed and Discretionary Fixed Costs

Fixed costs are often classified as "committed" or "discretionary," depending on their immediate impact on the organization if they are changed. **Committed fixed costs**, sometimes identified as **capacity costs**,

EXHIBIT 1-9: TOTAL, VARIABLE, AND AVERAGE COSTS

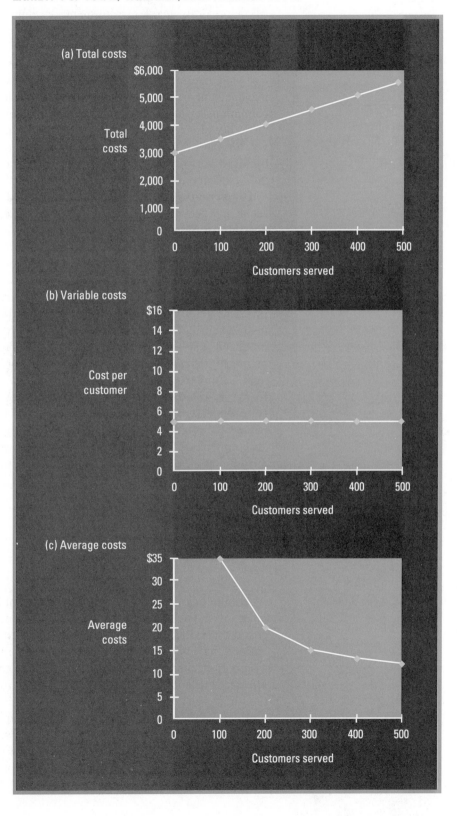

are required to maintain the current service or production capacity or to fill a previous legal commitment. Examples of committed fixed costs include depreciation, property taxes, rent, and interest on previously issued bonds.

Committed fixed costs are the result of structural decisions about the size and nature of an organization. For example, many years ago the management of the Santa Fe Railroad made decisions concerning what communities the railroad would serve. Track was laid on the basis of those decisions, and the Santa Fe Railroad now pays property taxes each year on the railroad's miles of track. These property taxes can be reduced by disposing of track. However, reducing track will also reduce the Santa Fe's capacity to serve.

Discretionary fixed costs, sometimes called **managed fixed costs**, are set at a fixed amount each year at the discretion of management. It is possible to reduce discretionary fixed costs without reducing production or service capacity *in the near-term*. Typical discretionary fixed costs include advertising, charitable contributions, employee training, and research and development.

Expenditures for discretionary fixed costs are frequently regarded as investments in the future. Research and development, for example, is undertaken to develop new or improved products that can be profitably produced and sold in future periods. During periods of financial well-being, organizations may make large expenditures on discretionary cost items. Conversely, during periods of financial stress, organizations will likely reduce discretionary expenditures before reducing capacity costs. Unfortunately, fluctuations in the funding of discretionary fixed costs may reduce the effectiveness of long-range programs. A high-quality research staff may be difficult to reassemble if key personnel are laid off; even the contemplation of such layoffs may reduce the staff's effectiveness. In all periods, discretionary costs are subject to debate and are likely to be changed in the budgeting process.

CHANGING STRUCTURAL COST DRIVERS AND COST FUNCTIONS

L O 8

As technology has advanced and competition has intensified, the management of most organizations has made decisions affecting structural cost drivers. Perhaps the most fundamental shift in manufacturing organizations has been the movement from labor-intensive to automated assembly techniques. These changes in structural cost drivers have affected the specific activities performed to meet customer needs and total cost behavior.

Many years ago, the rate of technological change was slower, production procedures were relatively straightforward, production was labor-paced, and only a limited number of related products were produced in a single plant. It was said of the Model T Ford that "You could have any color you wanted, as long as it was black." The largest cost elements of most manufactured goods were the cost of raw materials and the wages paid to production employees. Both of these costs were highly variable with sales volume as the independent variable.

In Exhibit 1-10, line A illustrates the traditional relationship between total costs and annual unit sales. Line B illustrates the relationship often found in the 1990s. There has been a significant shift away from traditional labor-paced activities that have variable cost functions toward production procedures requiring significant investments in automated equipment. The result has been a decrease in variable costs, represented by the flatter slope of line B, and an increase in fixed costs, represented by the higher vertical axis intercept of line B.

In the past, production employees used equipment to assist them in performing their job. Now employees spend considerable time scheduling, setting up, maintaining, and moving materials to and from equipment. They spend relatively little time on actual production. The equipment does the work, and the employees keep it running efficiently. Increased complexity of production procedures and an increase in the variety of products produced in a single facility have also caused a shift towards more support personnel and fewer production employees. When compared to the traditional behavior of total costs, fixed costs have increased and variable costs have decreased, resulting in relatively higher costs at low sales volumes and relatively lower costs at high sales volumes.

Given the variety and number of factors that drive costs, it is apparent that cost functions are multidimensional. Today, it is seldom possible to accurately describe the cost behavior of an entire organization or facility with an equation that has a single independent variable. What's more, the specific set of cost drivers differs from organization to organization. To manage costs, it is necessary to manage an organization's activities and

EXHIBIT 1-10: CHANGING TOTAL COST STRUCTURES

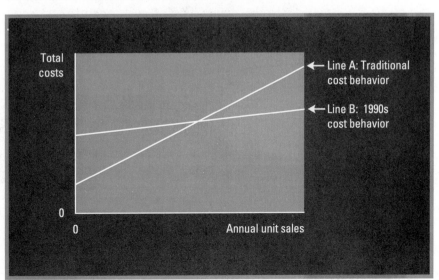

the factors that drive activity costs. This need to understand and manage the multitude of structural, organizational, and activity cost drivers underlies Peter Drucker's observation that "accounting has become the most intellectually challenging area in the field of management."

SUMMARY

Management accounting is concerned with the use of financial and related information by persons inside specific organizations to make strategic, organizational, and operational decisions. In general, management accounting helps organizations achieve their goals. A fundamental goal of every organization concerns its strategic position compared to the competition in its industry. Careful budgeting and cost management with frequent and detailed performance reports are critical with a goal of cost leadership. If the goal is product differentiation, management needs to view products or services from the customer's perspective and work to enhance the value of the organization's products or services to the customer.

The establishment of goals is followed by long-range and short-range planning (to achieve goals), organizing (to structure tasks and assign them to specific people), and controlling (to revise plans or bring operations into line with plans). Performance measurement is an important part of this ongoing process. Critical elements of performance measurement include determining which performance outcomes to measure and establishing systematic procedures for reporting outcomes. Care must be taken to ensure that performance measures and other accounting information are reliable and based on honest opinions. To help foster such ethical behavior as honest financial measurement, many professional associations and businesses have developed codes of ethics.

World-class companies must constantly improve their performance on the dimensions of cost, quality, and service (including time). Success requires managing the multitude of factors that drive costs. These cost drivers may be placed into three categories:

1. Structural cost drivers are fundamental choices about the size and scope of operations.
2. Organizational cost drivers are choices concerning the organization of activities and the involvement of persons inside and outside the organization in decision making.
3. Activity cost drivers are specific units of work performed to serve customer needs.

While costs can respond to activity cost drivers in an unlimited number of ways, as a starting point in analyzing cost behavior, it is useful to consider four basic cost behavior patterns—those for variable, fixed, mixed, and step costs.

SUGGESTED READINGS

Bridges, William. "The End of The Job," *Fortune* (September 19, 1994), pp. 62-74.

Collins, John W. "Is Business Ethics an Oxymoron?" *Business Horizons* (September-October, 1994), pp. 1-8.

Johnson, H. Thomas, and Robert S. Kaplan. *Relevance Lost: The Rise and Fall of Management Accounting* (Boston: Harvard Business School Press, 1987).

Porter, Michael E. *Competitive Strategy* (New York: The Free Press, 1980), Chapters 1 and 2.

Shank, John K. "Strategic Cost Management: New Wine, or Just New Bottles?" *Journal of Management Accounting Research* (Fall 1989), pp. 47-65.

Shank, John K., and Vijay Govindarajan. *Strategic Cost Management* (New York: The Free Press, 1993), Chapters 1 and 9.

REVIEW PROBLEM

Classifying Cost Drivers and Costs Behavior

(a) Classify each of the following as a structural, organizational, or activity cost driver.

1. Meals served to airplane passengers.
2. General Motor's decision to start manufacturing the Saturn, a completely new automobile in completely new facilities.
3. Zenith's decision to sell Zenith's computer operations and focus on the core television business.
4. Number of tax returns filed electronically by H & R Block.
5. Number of passenger cars in a Via train.
6. Coor's decision to expand its market area east from the Rocky Mountains.
7. Boeing's decision to invite airlines to assist in designing the new model 777 airplane.
8. Chrysler Motor's decision to use cross-disciplinary teams to design the Neon automobile.
9. A hospital's decision to establish review committees to evaluate the appropriateness and effectiveness of medical procedures with the goal of improving patient care.
10. Harley-Davidson's efforts to restructure production procedures to reduce inventories and machine set-up times.

(b) Identify each of the following cost behavior patterns as variable, fixed-committed, fixed-discretionary, mixed, or step.

1. Total cost of bakery products used at a McDonald's Restaurant when meals served is the activity driver.

2. Total cost of operating a health clinic where patients served is the cost driver.
3. Total property taxes for a Monroe Muffler Shop when vehicles serviced is the cost driver.
4. Total cost of motherboards used by Apple Computer when computers manufactured and shipped is the cost driver.
5. Total cost of secretarial services at a university where each secretary can handle the needs of ten faculty and part-time secretarial help is not possible. Number of faculty is the cost driver.
6. Total advertising costs for International Business Machines where sales revenue is the cost driver.
7. Automobile rental costs at Alamo in Orlando, Florida, where there is no mileage charge. The cost driver is miles driven.
8. Automobile rental cost at Hertz in Dallas, Texas, where there is a base charge plus a mileage charge. The cost driver is miles driven.
9. Salaries paid personnel while conducting on-campus employment interviews at Champion International. Number of on-campus interviews is the cost driver.
10. The cost of contributions to educational institutions by Xerox Corporation. Number of employees hired is the cost driver.

The solution to the review problem is found at the end of the Chapter 1 assignment material. To maximize your learning, you should make a serious attempt to develop a written solution to the review problem before looking at the solution. If there are errors in your solution, you should then attempt to determine the causes of the errors.

KEY TERMS

Activity—a unit of work.

Activity-based costing—a type of costing that is based on the cost for specific activities performed to fill customer needs.

Activity cost drivers—specific units of work (activities) performed to serve customer needs that consume costly resources.

Balance sheet—a picture of the economic health of an organization at a point in time, showing the organization's assets and the claims on those assets.

Committed fixed costs (sometimes called **capacity costs**)—costs required to maintain the current service or production capacity or to fill a previous legal commitment.

Controlling—the process of ensuring that results agree with plans.

Cost behavior—how costs respond to changes in the number of units of an activity cost driver.

Cost driver—a factor that influences costs.

Cost driver analysis—the study of factors that influence costs.

Discretionary fixed costs (sometimes called **managed fixed costs**)—costs set at a fixed amount each period at the discretion of management.

Ethics—the moral quality, fitness, or propriety of a course of action that may injure or benefit people.

Financial accounting—a reporting system primarily concerned with providing financial information to persons outside the firm.

Fixed costs—costs that are a constant amount for a time period. Their total amount does not respond to short-run changes in activity.

For-profit organization—an organization that has profit as a primary goal.

Goal—the purpose toward which an organization directs its activities.

Income statement—a summary of economic events during a period of time, showing the revenues generated by operating activities, the expenses incurred in generating those revenues, and any gains or losses attributed to the period.

Long-range planning—a type of planning that emphasizes the selection of programs to move the organization toward its goals over the next several years.

Management accounting—a discipline concerned with the use of financial and related information by managers and other persons inside specific organizations to make strategic, organizational, and operational decisions.

Marginal cost—in economics, the varying increment in total costs with an additional unit of activity.

Mixed costs (sometimes called **semivariable costs**)—costs that contain a fixed and a variable cost element.

Not-for-profit organization—an organization that does not have profit as a primary goal.

Organizational cost drivers—cost consequences resulting from choices concerning the organization of activities and the involvement of persons inside and outside the organization in decision making.

Organization chart—a diagram illustrating the formal relationships existing between the elements of an organization.

Organizing—the process of making the organization into a well-ordered whole.

Performance measurement (sometimes called **outcomes assessment**)—the determination of the extent to which actual outcomes correspond to planned outcomes.

Planning—the formulation of a scheme or program for the accomplishment of a specific purpose or goal.

Relevant range—the range of activity within which a linear cost function is valid.

Short-range planning—the interpretation of goals and long-range plans into performance objectives for the coming year and the selection of specific actions to achieve these objectives.

Statement of cash flows—a summary of resource inflows and outflows stated in terms of cash.

Step costs—costs that are constant within a given range of activity but different between ranges of activity. Total step costs increase in a step-like fashion as activity increases.

Strategic cost management—making decisions concerning specific cost drivers within the context of an organization's business strategy, internal value chain, and place in a larger value chain stretching from the development and use of resources to final consumers.

Strategic position analysis—an organization's basic way of competing to sell products or services.

Structural cost drivers—the result of fundamental choices about the size and scope of operations and technologies employed in delivering products or services to customers. These choices affect the types of activities and the costs of activities performed to satisfy customer needs.

Value chain analysis—the study of value-producing activities, stretching from basic raw materials to the final consumer of a product or service.

Variable costs—costs that are uniform for each incremental unit of activity. Their total amount increases proportionately as activity increases.

REVIEW QUESTIONS

1-1
Contrast financial and management accounting on the basis of: user orientation, purpose of information, level of aggregation, length of time period, orientation toward past or future, conformance to external standards, and emphasis on objective data.

1-2
Describe the three strategic positions that lead to business success.

1-3
Distinguish between how management accounting would support the strategy of cost leadership and the strategy of product differentiation.

1-4
Briefly describe employee empowerment and the role of activity-based costing in employee empowerment.

1-5

Describe how pressures to have desirable short-run outcomes can lead to ethical dilemmas.

1-6

lean production;

Identify three advances that have fostered the move away from isolated, national economic systems toward an interdependent global economy.

1-7

What are the three interrelated dimensions that today's competition takes place on and their meanings? *cost, quality & serv.*

1-8

Differentiate among structural, organizational, and activity cost drivers.

1-9

Act. cost drivers

Briefly describe variable, fixed, mixed, and step costs and indicate how the total cost function of each changes as activity increases within a time period.

1-10

cost drivers are varied.

Why is presenting all costs of an organization as a function of a single independent variable, while useful in obtaining a general understanding of cost behavior, not accurate enough to make specific decisions concerning products, services, or activities?

1-11

Describe the economists' short-run total cost function and identify the range within which a linear pattern is a reasonable approximation of total costs.

1-12

How have changes in structural cost drivers changed the short-run total cost functions of many organizations?

EXERCISES

1-1 Matching

Required:

Match the following terms with the best descriptions. Each description is used only once.

1. Ethics
2. Fixed costs
3. Controlling
4. Goal
5. Not-for-profit organization
6. Total variable costs
7. Balance sheet
8. Income statement
9. Cost driver

a. Increase with each additional unit
b. The Starlight Foundation raises money to grant wishes for terminally ill children.
c. Prepared as of a point in time
d. Accounting for external users
e. The Computer Company wishes to develop the best computer in the industry.

10. Financial accounting
11. Capacity cost
12. Discretionary cost
13. Management accounting
14. Step costs
15. Marginal cost

f. Shows the results of operations for a period of time
g. Annual rent paid under a lease agreement
h. Do not vary with the level of activity in the short run
i. Constant within a range of activity but vary between ranges
j. Used internally to make decisions
k. The amount of advertising expenditures to make this year
l. The propriety of taking some action.
m. The number of machine hours used to produce a certain product
n. To produce 1 more unit requires $10
o. Comparing the budget with the actual results

1-2 Line and Staff Organization
Presented are the names of some departments often found in a merchandising organization.

(a) Maintenance
(b) Home Furnishings
(c) Store Manager
(d) Payroll
(e) Human Resources
(f) Advertising

Required:
Identify each as a line or a staff department.

1-3 Line and Staff Organization
Presented are the names of some departments often found in a manufacturing organization.

(a) Manager, Plant 2
(b) Design Engineering
(c) President
(d) Controller
(e) Property Accounting
(f) Sales Manager, District 1

Required:
Identify each as a line or a staff department.

1-4 Classifying Cost Drivers
Required:
Classify each of the following as structural, organizational, or activity cost drivers.

(a) Onita Silversmiths reorganizes production facilities from a layout in which all similar types of machines are grouped together to one in which a set of machines is designated for the production of a particular product and that set of machines is grouped together.

(b) A cable television company decides to start offering telephone service.

(c) Xerox Corporation's decision to stop making personal computers

(d) Canon decides to start making high-volume photocopy equipment to compete head-to-head with Xerox.

(e) The number of meals served in a cafeteria

(f) The number of miles driven by a taxi cab

(g) Eliminating the position of supervisor and having each work group elect a team leader

(h) Toyota empowers employees to halt production if a quality problem is identified.

(i) The number of tons of grain loaded on a ship

(j) Crossgate Mall's decision to build space for 80 additional stores

1-5 Classifying Cost Behavior

Required:

Classify the total costs of each of the following as variable, fixed, mixed, or step. Sales volume is the cost driver.

(a) Pulpwood in a papermill

(b) Salaries of two supervisors

(c) Real estate taxes

(d) Salaries of quality inspectors when each inspector can evaluate a maximum of 1,000 units per day

(e) Wages paid production employees for the time spent working on products

(f) Electric power in a factory

(g) Raw materials used in production

(h) Automobiles rented on the basis of a fixed charge per day plus an additional charge per mile driven

(i) Sales commissions

(j) Depreciation on office equipment

1-6 Classifying Cost Behavior

Required:

Classify the total costs of each of the following as variable, fixed, mixed, or step.

(a) Maintenance costs at a college

(b) Property taxes on a building

(c) Rent on a photocopy machine charged as a fixed amount per month plus an additional charge per copy

(d) Cost of goods sold in a bookstore

(e) Salaries paid temporary instructors in a college as the number of sections offered of a course varies

(f) Lumber used by a house construction company

(g) The costs of operating a research department

(h) The cost of hiring a dance band for three hours

(i) Typing paper used in a steno pool

(j) Electric power in a restaurant

1-7 Classifying Cost Behavior

Required:

For each situation, select the most appropriate cost behavior pattern (shown below). Lines represent the cost behavior pattern. The vertical axis represents costs. The horizontal axis represents total volume. Dots represent actual costs. Each pattern may be used more than once.

Situation:

(a) Variable costs per unit
(b) Total mixed costs
(c) Total fixed costs
(d) Average fixed costs per unit
(e) Total current manufacturing costs
(f) Average variable costs
(g) Employees are paid $10 per hour for the first 40 hours worked each week and $15 per each additional hour.
(h) Employees are paid $10 per hour and guaranteed a minimum weekly wage of $200.

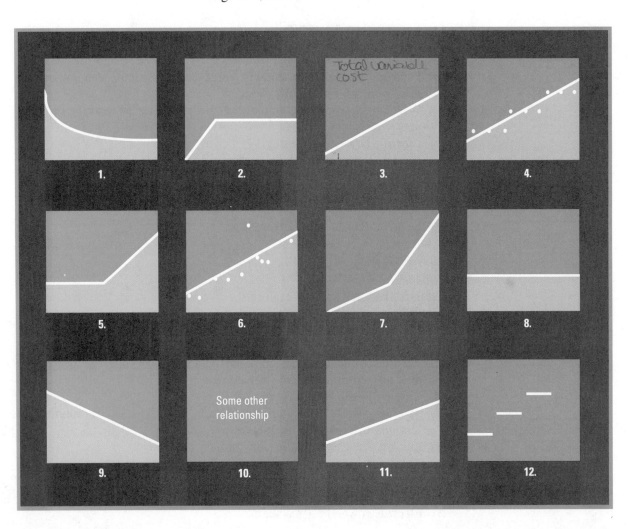

2 (i) A consultant is paid $50 per hour with a maximum fee of $1,000.

3 (j) Total variable costs

12 (k) Salaries of social workers where each social worker can handle a maximum of 20 cases

5 (l) A water bill where a flat fee of $800 is charged for the first 100,000 gallons and additional water costs $0.005 per gallon

4 (m) Variable costs properly used to estimate step costs

3 (n) Total materials costs in a factory

8 (o) Rent on exhibit space at a convention

1-8 Classifying Cost Behavior

Required:

For each situation, select the most appropriate cost behavior pattern (shown below). Lines represent the cost behavior pattern. The vertical axis represents total costs. The horizontal axis represents total volume. Dots represent actual costs. Each pattern may be used more than once.

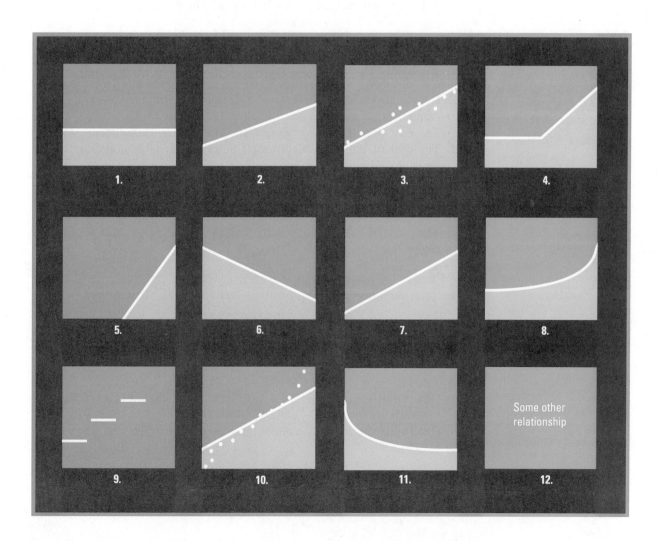

Situation:

4 (a) A telephone bill where a flat fee is charged for the first 20 calls per month and additional calls cost $0.25 each

2 (b) Total selling and administrative costs

7 (c) Total labor costs when employees are paid per unit produced

5 (d) Total overtime premium paid production employees

11 (e) Average total cost per unit

9 (f) Salaries of supervisors when each can supervise a maximum of 10 employees

6 (g) Total idle time costs when employees are paid for a minumum 40-hour week

1 (h) Materials costs per unit

3 (i) A good linear approximation of actual costs

2 (j) Electric power consumption in a restaurant

8 (k) Total costs when high volumes of production require the use of over-time and obsolete equipment

7 (l) Total sales commissions

10 (m) A linear cost estimation valid only within the relevant range

1-9 Classifying Discretionary and Committed Fixed Costs

Required:

Identify each of the following costs as discretionary or committed.

C (a) Depreciation on equipment used to produce widgets

C (b) Annual property taxes for Barb's Bridal Shop

D (c) The cost of television commercials for Allhere Department Store

D (d) The cost of the local Methodist Church's charitable donation to The Starlight Foundation

D (e) After a new computer system is installed, the costs of training the employees

C (f) The annual rent Betty must pay to operate her bakery

D (g) The cost of research done by federal agencies to find a cure for cancer

1-10 Computing Average Unit Costs

The total monthly operating costs of Del Rio Chili To Go are:

$$\$10,000 + \$0.30X$$

where:

$$X = \text{servings of chili}$$

Required:

(a) Determine the average cost per serving at each of the following monthly volumes: 10, 100, 200, 400, 800.

(b) Determine the monthly volume at which the average cost per serving is $0.50.

1-11 Automatic Versus Manual Processing

The Fast Photo Company operates a 60-minute film development and print service. The current service, which relies extensively on manual

$10,000 + .30x$

$\dfrac{10,000 + (.30)(10)}{10} = 1000.30$

$\dfrac{10,000 + (.30)(100)}{100} = 100.30$

$\dfrac{10,000 + (.30)(200)}{200} = 50.30$

$\dfrac{10,000 + (.30)(400)}{400} = 25.30$

$\dfrac{10,000 + (.30)(800)}{800} = 12.80$

$\dfrac{10,000 + .30x}{x} = .50 \qquad 10,000 + 30x = .50x$

$50,000 = x$

(handwritten notes in left margin)

$5000 + 2x = 45000$

$23,000 + 1.40x = 51000$

$105,000$

$93,000$

1) $500,000$
   $5000 \times 25 = 500$
   $1,500,000$
   $1,500$
2) $1,140 + (.05)(500)$
   $1,140 + (.05)(1500)$
   $1,140 + 25 = 1165$
   $1,140 + 75 = 1215$
   $1,140 + .05x$
   $\frac{1,000}{5,000}$
   $\frac{x}{5000}$
   $\$ 1,200,000.00$

operations, has monthly operating costs of $5,000 plus $2 per roll of film developed and printed. Management is evaluating the desirability of acquiring a machine that will automatically develop film and make prints. If the machine is acquired, the monthly fixed costs will increase to $23,000, and the variable costs of developing and printing a roll of film will decline to $1.40.

Required:

(a) Determine the total costs of developing and printing 20,000 and 50,000 rolls per month:
  (1) With the current process.
  (2) With the automatic process.
(b) Determine the monthly volume at which the automatic process becomes preferable to the manual process.

20,000

1-12 Automatic Versus Manual Processing

The Kopy Tat Photocopy Service processes 1,000,000 photocopies per month at its mid-town service center. Approximately 60 percent of the photocopies require collating. Collating is currently performed by high school and college students who are paid $5.00 per hour. Each student collates an average of 5,000 copies per hour.

Management is contemplating the lease of an automatic collating machine that has a monthly capacity of 5,000,000 photocopies with lease and operating costs totaling $1,140, plus $0.05 per 1,000 units collated.

Required:

(a) Determine the total costs of collating 500,000 and 1,500,000 per month:
  (1) With student help.
  (2) With the collating machine.
(b) Determine the monthly volume at which the automatic process becomes preferable to the manual process.
(c) Should Kopy Tat lease the automatic collating machine at this time?

No. Cheaper to do labor.

DISCUSSION QUESTIONS

1-13 Financial and Management Accounting

Michelle Jones has just been promoted to product manager for Crunch and Spice cereal at a large food company. Although she is an accomplished sales representative and well versed in market research, her accounting background is limited to reviewing her paycheck, balancing her checkbook, filing income tax returns, and reviewing the company's annual income statement and balance sheet. She commented that while the financial statements are no doubt useful to investors, she just doesn't see how accounting can help her be a good product manager.

Based on her remarks, it is apparent that Michelle's view of accounting is limited to financial accounting.

Required:

Explain to Michelle some of the important differences between financial and management accounting and suggest some ways management accounting can help her be a better product manager.

1-14 Product Differentiation

You are the owner of Louie Lobster's Limited. You have no trouble catching lobsters, but you have difficulty in selling all that you catch. The problem is that all lobsters from all vendors look the same. You do catch high-quality lobsters, but you need to be able to tell your customers that your lobsters are better.

Required:

(a) What are some possible ways of distinguishing your lobsters from those of other vendors?
(b) Explain the possible results of this differentiation.

1-15 Identifying Performance Measures

Required:

Identify possible monetary and nonmonetary performance measures for each of the following situations. One nonmonetary measure should relate to quality and one should relate to time.

(a) Central University wishes to evaluate the success of last year's graduating class.
(b) Cook County Hospital wishes to evaluate the performance of its emergency room.
(c) L.L. Bean wishes to evaluate the performance of its telephone order filling operations.
(d) Hilton Hotels wishes to evaluate the performance of registration activities at one of its hotels.
(e) United Parcel Service wishes to evaluate the success of its operations in Knoxville.

1-16 Applying Ethical Standards for Management Accountants

Required:

Assume you are a recently hired management accountant and that you intend to follow the Institute of Management Accountants' Standards of Ethical Conduct. Indicate the ethical standard applicable to each of the following situations and determine the appropriate *initial* course of action.

(a) Late Thursday afternoon you learn that your company has received a large government contract that will have a significant impact on future earnings. The award is to be publicly announced by the government agency on Friday afternoon. That evening at a family dinner, your brother-in-law, a stock broker, asks if this would be a good time to buy stock in the company you work for.
(b) You are aware that your company has obsolete inventory recorded at cost in its accounting records. Disposing of this inventory or writing

it down to its fair market value would significantly reduce reported earnings for the current period. While speaking with your firm's independent external auditor, you learn that your immediate supervisor recently told the auditor that the company has no obsolete or slow-moving inventory.

(c) Prior to accepting your current position at a manufacturing organization, you spent four years in public accounting where your primary duties involved tax planning. While you believe your firm's accounting system does a good job of providing the information for compliance with external reporting and income tax requirements, you have become increasingly concerned about negative comments from internal decision makers concerning the usefulness of the accounting information. To date, you have not spent much time reading relevant professional journals or attending any professional continuing education programs. You believe you have too many other more important things to do and are concerned that your supervisor will recognize your lack of expertise in cost accounting.

(d) One of your first jobs with your new employer was assisting with the preparation of the budget for the coming year. Based on a predicted 20 percent increase in sales volume during the Christmas season, the budget for the early part of the year calls for large expenditures financed by borrowing that is to be repaid after the Christmas sales. The final meeting of the budget preparation committee was this morning. After having lunch with several other new employees in marketing, you come away with a concern that the sales forecast is unrealistic. The budget is to be forwarded to corporate headquarters for final approval tomorrow.

1-17 Ethics and Revenue Recognition

John is in charge of recording sales for a department of a retail firm. His supervisor, Mark, is evaluated based on year-end profits. This has been an especially bad year for the firm, and sales are lower than expected. However, Mark wants to show the highest possible profits for the year. Mark has discreetly asked John to record sales that occur on the first few days of next year as if they had happened in the current year. Doing this would increase revenues and thus make profits higher. John knows that he should record sales in their proper periods, but his evaluation from Mark will determine whether he gets a raise. In addition, if John does not do what Mark asks, he may be fired. However, if John does do what Mark asks, he could be fired if his actions are detected.

Required:
What should John do?

1-18 Ethics and "Short-Term Borrowing"

Ethel, a secretary, is in charge of petty cash for a local law firm. Normally, about $200 is kept in the petty cash box. When Ethel needs a little cash for lunch or to pay her babysitter and she is short on cash, she sometimes takes a few dollars from the box. Since she is in charge of the box, nobody knows that she takes the money, and she always replaces it within a few days.

Required:

(a) Is Ethel's behavior ethical?
(b) Assume that Ethel has recently had major problems meeting her bills. She also is in charge of purchasing supplies for the office from petty cash. Last week when she needed $5 for the babysitter, she falsified a voucher for the amount of $5. Is this behavior ethical?

1-19 Ethics and Travel Reimbursement

Scott takes many business trips throughout the year. All of his expenses are paid by his company. Last week he travelled to Rio De Janeiro, Brazil, and stayed there on business for 5 days. He is allowed a maximum of $28 per day for food and $100 per day for lodging. To his surprise, the food and accommodations in Brazil were much less than he expected. Not too happy about having to travel last week because he couldn't use tickets to a Red Sox baseball game that he had purchased, he decided to inflate his expenses a bit. He increased his lodging expense from $50 per day to $75 per day and his food purchased from $10 per day to $20 per day. Therefore, for the 5-day trip, he overstated his expenses by $175 total. After all, the allowance was higher than the amount he spent.

Required:

Assume that the company would never find out that he had actually spent less. Are Scott's actions ethical? Are they acceptable?

1-20 Applying Ethical Standards in Various Professional Positions

Many professional organizations have developed ethical standards such as those presented in Exhibit 1-5 for management accountants.

Required:

Using the code of professional ethics presented in Exhibit 1-5 as a model for your profession, indicate the ethical standard(s) applicable to each of the following situations and determine the appropriate *initial* course of action.

(a) You are the manager of product development for a rapidly growing telecommunications company. You and your spouse have just been invited to join a former college roommate, who is now a stock analyst, for an all-expense-paid ski vacation. Your friend explains that you will be staying at a condominium owned by her firm and that she won the rights to a fully paid vacation for four in a firm contest based on her performance as a stock analyst. "Besides," she added at the end of her invitation, "you might give me the insight needed to win another vacation next year."

(b) You are the chief environmental engineer at a facility located in a small town. After a careful evaluation of plant facilities and a recently enacted law, you inform the plant manager that the plant will not be able to meet new emissions standards without an expenditure of $5 million. The plant manager is concerned that because of the low profitability of plant operations, this new information might lead to a decision to close the plant, causing significant disruption of the local economy. Consequently, he reports to corporate headquarters that the changes needed to meet the new emissions requirements would be minimal.

1-21 Ethics and False Claims Act

In 1986, the U.S. Government passed the Federal False Claims Act to encourage persons to bring forward evidence of fraudulent charges on government contracts. Under the provisions of the Act, whistle-blowers receive up to 25 percent of any money recovered as a result of evidence they bring forth. To date, the largest settlement under the terms of the Act was a $7.5 million dollar reward to a former employee of a defense contractor who filed a suit after leaving his former employer to accept a position as a price analyst for the Department of Defense.

Required:

Evaluate the likely impact of the Federal False Claims Act on corporations doing business with the U.S. Government. Do you believe the Act is a good idea?

1-22 Management Decisions Affecting Cost Drivers

An avid bicycle rider, you have decided to use an inheritance to start a new business to sell and repair bicycles. Two college friends have already accepted offers to work for you.

Required:

For your new business:

(a) Suggest one strategic position you might strive for to compete with area hardware and discount stores that sell bicycles.
(b) Formulate two items that might be part of your long-range plan.
(c) Formulate two items that might be part of your short-range plan for the coming year.
(d) Mention two decisions that will be structural cost drivers.
(e) Mention two decisions that will be organizational cost drivers.
(f) Identify two activity cost drivers.

SOLUTION TO REVIEW PROBLEM

(a)
1. Activity cost driver
2. Structural cost driver
3. Structural cost driver
4. Activity cost driver
5. Activity cost driver
6. Structural cost driver
7. Organizational cost driver

8. Organizational cost driver
9. Organizational cost driver
10. Organizational cost driver

(b)

1. Variable cost
2. Mixed cost
3. Committed fixed cost
4. Variable cost
5. Step cost
6. Discretionary fixed cost
7. Fixed cost. Without knowing the purpose of renting the car, we cannot classify the cost as committed or discretionary
8. Mixed cost
9. Step cost
10. Discretionary fixed cost

After completing this chapter, you should be able to:

L O 1

Develop a linear cost estimating equation and discuss problems encountered in cost estimation.

L O 2

Prepare and explain a cost-volume-profit analysis.

L O 3

Discuss why the use of a single activity measure limits the usefulness of cost-volume-profit analysis.

L O 4

Discuss the hierarchy of activity cost drivers and use the hierarchy to classify specific activity costs.

L O 5

Identify the limitations of cost-volume-profit analysis for fundamental decisions concerning products, services, or activities.

COST ESTIMATION AND COST-VOLUME-PROFIT ANALYSIS

Activities undertaken to achieve an organization's short-range and long-range goals cause costs to be incurred. Because economic resources are limited, managers must carefully control costs and the activities that cause them. This requires knowledge of how costs respond to changes in activities. In Chapter 1, we considered four basic cost behavior patterns and the types of activities that produce each. We identified:

- *Cost of goods sold as a variable cost with sales revenue being the cost driver.*
- *Property taxes as a fixed cost.*
- *Maintenance costs as a mixed cost with machine hours being the cost driver.*
- *Nursing salaries as a step cost with patient-days being the cost driver.*

The first purpose of this chapter is to continue our study of cost behavior by examining and evaluating methods used to estimate the slope and the vertical axis intercept in models of cost behavior. Having done this, we will be able to develop equations to assist in planning and controlling activities and their resulting costs.

In Chapter 1, we also noted that as a preliminary planning device, the sum of all costs associated with an organization or business segment is often expressed as a function of a single independent variable of interest to management. This total cost equation is frequently combined with a total revenue equation so that management can analyze the relationships among the organization's volume, costs, and profits.

Cost-volume-profit analysis is a technique used to examine the relationships among the total volume of some independent variable, total costs, total revenues, and profits during a time period. Cost-volume-profit analysis is particularly useful in the early stages of planning because it provides a framework for discussing planning issues and organizing relevant data. Cost-volume-profit (CVP) analysis is widely used in for-profit and in not-for-profit organizations. It is equally applicable to service, merchan-

dising, and manufacturing organizations. In for-profit organizations, CVP analysis is used to answer such questions as: How many photocopies must the College Avenue Copy Service produce to earn a profit of $20,000? At what dollar sales volume will Burger King's total revenues and total costs be equal? What profit will General Electric earn at an annual sales volume of $30 billion? What will happen to the profit of Duff's Smorgasbord if there is a 20 percent increase in the cost of food and a 10 percent increase in the selling price of meals?

In not-for-profit organizations, CVP analysis is used to plan service levels, plan fund-raising activities, and determine funding requirements. How many meals can the Downtown Salvation Army serve with an annual budget of $200,000? How many tickets must be sold for the benefit concert to raise $10,000? Given the current cost structure, current tuition rates, and projected enrollments, how much money must City University raise from other sources? ***The second purpose of this chapter is to introduce cost-volume-profit analysis.***

The chapter begins by considering methods used to estimate how costs respond to changes in the number of units of an activity cost driver. Once this is done, the resulting cost estimating equation is used for cost prediction. We then examine cost-volume-profit relationships and consider their use in short-range planning. We also examine the limitations of cost-volume-profit analysis when costs are driven by a multitude of activity drivers. Finally, we consider the usefulness of classification schemes in understanding cost behavior when there are numerous activity drivers. The chapter culminates with a sophisticated cost management model that uses multiple activity cost drivers.

COST ESTIMATION

L O 1

Cost estimation, the determination of previous or current relationships between activity and cost, is an important part of cost management. To properly estimate the relationship between activity and cost, it is necessary to be familiar with basic cost behavior patterns and to be knowledgeable of cost estimating techniques.

Costs known to have a variable or a fixed pattern are readily estimated by interviews or analyzing available records. Sales commissions per sales dollar, a variable cost, might be determined to be 15 percent of sales on the basis of interviews or a review of company records. In a similar manner, annual property taxes might be determined by consulting tax documents.

Mixed (or semivariable) costs, that contain fixed and variable cost elements, are more difficult to estimate. According to a basic rule of algebra, two equations are needed to determine two unknowns. Following this rule, at least two observations are needed to determine the variable and fixed elements of a mixed cost.

High-Low Cost Estimation

The most straightforward approach to determining the variable and fixed elements of mixed costs is to use the **high-low method of cost estimation**. This method utilizes data from two time periods, a representative high activity period and a representative low activity period, to estimate fixed and variable costs. Assuming identical fixed costs in both periods, the difference in total costs between these two periods is due entirely to the difference in variable costs; and the variable costs per unit are found by dividing the difference in total costs by the difference in total activity:

$$\text{Variable costs per unit} = \frac{\text{Difference in total costs}}{\text{Difference in activity}}$$

Once variable costs are determined, fixed costs, which are identical in both periods, are computed by estimating total variable costs of either the high or the low activity period and subtracting them from the corresponding total costs.

$$\text{Fixed costs} = \text{Total costs} - \text{Variable costs}$$

Assume a mail-order company wants to develop a monthly cost function for its packaging department. Further assume that the number of shipments is believed to be the primary cost driver and that the following observations are available for the first four months of 19X7.

		Number of Shipments	Packaging Costs
Low activity period ⟶	January	6,000	$17,000
	February	9,000	26,000
High activity period ⟶	March	12,000	32,000
	April	10,000	20,000

Equations for total packaging department costs in January and March, the periods of lowest and highest activity, are:

$$\text{January: } \$17{,}000 = a + b(6{,}000 \text{ shipments})$$
$$\text{March: } \$32{,}000 = a + b(12{,}000 \text{ shipments})$$

where:

$$a = \text{fixed costs per month}$$
$$b = \text{variable costs per shipment}$$

Solving for the estimated variable costs:

$$b = \frac{\text{Difference in total costs}}{\text{Difference in activity}}$$

$$b = \frac{\$32{,}000 - \$17{,}000}{12{,}000 - 6{,}000}$$

$$= \$2.50$$

Next, the estimated monthly fixed costs are determined by substituting the $2.50 variable costs per unit in *either* the January or March total cost equation:

$$a = \text{Total costs - Variable costs}$$

January: $17,000 = a + ($2.50 per shipment x 6,000 shipments)
$$a = \$17,000 - (\$2.50 \text{ per shipment x } 6,000 \text{ shipments})$$
$$= \$2,000$$

or

March: $32,000 = a + ($2.50 per shipment x 12,000 shipments)
$$a = \$32,000 - (\$2.50 \text{ per shipment x } 12,000)$$
$$= \$2,000$$

The cost estimating equation for total packing department costs is:

$$Y = \$2,000 + \$2.50X$$

where:

$$X = \text{number of shipments}$$
$$Y = \text{total packing department costs}$$

The concepts underlying the high-low method of cost estimation are illustrated in Exhibit 2-1.

Cost prediction, the forecasting of future costs, is a common purpose of cost estimation. If 5,000 shipments are budgeted for June 19X7, the predicted June 19X7 shipping   department costs are $14,500 ($2,000 + [$2.50 per shipment x 5,000 shipments]).

EXHIBIT 2-1: HIGH-LOW COST ESTIMATION

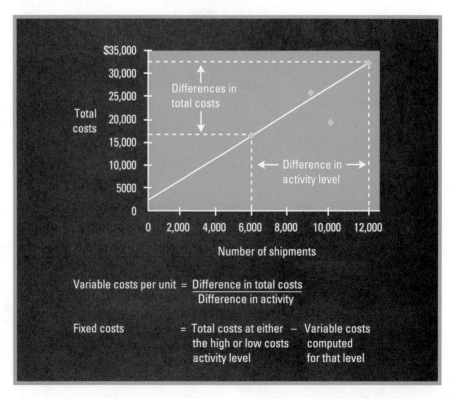

Scatter Diagrams

A **scatter diagram** is a graph of past activity and cost data, with individual observations represented by dots. Plotting historical cost data on a scatter diagram is a useful approach to cost estimation, especially when used in conjunction with other cost estimating techniques. As illustrated in Exhibit 2-2, a scatter diagram helps in selecting high and low activity levels representative of normal operating conditions. The periods of highest or lowest activity may not be representative because of the cost of overtime, the use of less efficient equipment, strikes, and so forth. If the goal is to develop an equation to predict costs under normal operating conditions, then the equation should be based on observations of normal operating conditions. A scatter diagram is also useful in determining if costs can be reasonably approximated by a straight line.

Scatter diagrams are sometimes used alone as a basis of cost estimation. This requires the use of professional judgment to draw a representative straight line through the plot of historical data. Typically, the analyst tries to ensure that an equal number of observations are on either side of the line, while minimizing the vertical differences between the line and actual cost observations at each value of the independent variable. Once a line is drawn, cost estimates at any representative volume are made by studying the line. Alternatively, an equation for the line may be developed by applying the high-low method to any two points on the line.

Least-Squares Regression Analysis

Least-squares regression analysis uses a mathematical technique to fit a cost estimating equation to the observed data. The technique mathematically accomplishes what the analyst does visually with a scatter diagram. The least-squares technique creates an equation that minimizes the sum of the vertical squared differences between the estimated and the actual costs at each obser-

EXHIBIT 2-2: SELECTING REPRESENTATIVE HIGH AND LOW ACTIVITY LEVELS

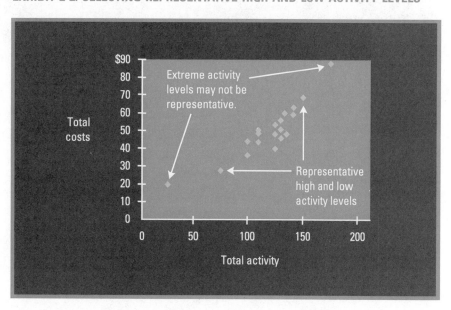

vation. Each of these differences is an estimating error. Using the packaging department example, the least-squares technique is illustrated in Exhibit 2-3. Estimated values of total monthly packaging costs are represented by the straight line, and the actual values of total monthly packaging costs are represented by the dots. For each dot, such as the one at a volume of 10,000 shipments, the line is fit to minimize the vertical squared differences.

Values of a and b can be calculated manually using a set of equations developed by mathematicians, as in Chapter 2, Appendix A, or by using spreadsheet software packages such as Microsoft Excel® or Lotus 1-2-3®. Many calculators also have built-in functions to compute these coefficients. In any case, the least-squares equation for monthly packaging costs is:

$$Y = \$3,400 + \$2.20X$$

Using the least-squares equation, the predicted June 19X7 shipping department costs, when there are 5,000 budgeted shipments, are $14,400 ($3,400 + [$2.20 per shipment x 5,000 shipments]). Recall that the high-low method predicted June 19X7 costs of $14,500. Given this difference, it is reasonable to ask which prediction is more reliable.

Goodness of Fit

Mathematicians regard least-squares regression analysis as superior to the high-low and the scatter diagram methods. It uses all available data, rather than just two observations, and does not rely on subjective judgment in drawing a line. Statistical measures are also available to determine how well a least-squares equation fits the historical data. These measures are

EXHIBIT 2-3: LEAST-SQUARES TECHNIQUE

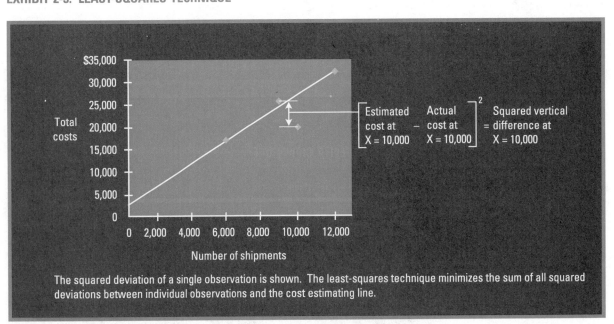

The squared deviation of a single observation is shown. The least-squares technique minimizes the sum of all squared deviations between individual observations and the cost estimating line.

often contained in the output of spreadsheet software packages. A typical output, obtained using Lotus 1-2-3®, is presented in Chapter 2, Appendix B. The appendix also contains brief descriptions of each item of output.

In addition to the vertical axis intercept and the slope, we will focus our attention on the coefficient of determination. The **coefficient of determination** is a measure of the percent of variation in the dependent variable (such as total packaging department cost) that is explained by variations in the independent variable (such as total shipments). Statisticians often refer to the coefficient of determination as R-squared and represent it as R^2. The coefficient of determination can take on values between zero and 1, with values close to zero suggesting that the equation is not very useful and values close to 1 indicating that the equation explains a large percent of the variation in the dependent variable. When choosing between two cost estimating equations, the one with the higher coefficient of determination is generally preferred. The coefficient of determination for the packaging department cost estimation equation, determined using least-squares regression analysis, is 0.68. This means that 68 percent of the variation in packaging department costs is explained, using the least-squares estimating equation, by the number of shipments.

Although computers make least-squares regression easy to use, analysts should not merely enter data into a computer and accept the output as correct. Always exercise judgment when considering the validity of the least-squares approach, the solution, and the data. If the objective is to predict future costs under normal operating conditions, observations reflecting abnormal operating conditions should be deleted. Verify that the cost behavior pattern is linear. Scatter diagrams assist in both of these judgments. Finally, stop and think about the results and ask, "Does this make sense?" Even if the relationship has a high R-squared, if it "doesn't make sense," there is probably something wrong. When a large number of possible relationships between cost and activity are examined, it is possible to have a high R-squared purely by chance.

Simple and Multiple Regression

Least-squares regression analysis is identified as "simple regression analysis" when there is only one independent variable and as "multiple regression analysis" when there are two or more independent variables. The general form for simple regression analysis is:

$$Y = a + bX$$

The general form for multiple regression analysis is:

$$Y = a + \Sigma b_i X_i$$

In this case, the subscript i is a general representation of each independent variable. When there are several independent variables, i is set equal to 1 for the first, 2 for the second, and so forth. The total variable costs of each independent variable is computed as $b_i X_i$, with b_i representing the variable cost per unit of independent variable X_i. The Greek symbol sigma, Σ, indicates the costs of all independent variables are summed in determining total variable costs.

As an illustration, assume shipping costs at a mail-order company are a function of two activity cost drivers, the number of packages shipped and kilograms shipped. Also assume it costs $4,000 per month to operate the shipping department with each package costing an additional $5, plus $1.50 per kilogram. The mathematical representation of monthly shipping costs in general terms is:

$$Y = a + b_1X_1 + b_2X_2$$

where:

a = $4,000
b_1 = $5
b_2 = $1.50
X_1 = number of packages shipped
X_2 = total kilograms shipped

During a month when 1,200 packages with a total weight of 24,000 kilograms are shipped, the total shipping costs are:

$$Y = \$ 4,000 + \$5(1,200) + \$1.50(24,000)$$
$$= \underline{\underline{\$46,000}}$$

Additional Issues in Cost Estimation

We have mentioned several items to be wary of when developing cost estimating equations:

- Data that are not based on normal operating conditions.
- Nonlinear relationships between total costs and activity.
- Obtaining a high R-squared purely by chance.

Additional items of concern include:

- Changes in technology or prices.
- Matching activity and cost within each observation.
- Identifying activity cost drivers.

Changes in Technology or Prices

Changes in technology and prices make cost estimation and prediction difficult. When telephone companies changed from using human opera-tors to using automated switching equipment to place long-distance tele-phone calls, cost estimates based on the use of human operators were of little or no value in predicting future costs. Care must be taken to make sure data used in developing cost estimates are based on the same tech-nology. When this is not possible, professional judgment is required to make appropriate adjustments.

Only data reflecting a single price level should be used in cost estima-tion and prediction. If prices have remained stable in the past but then uniformly increase by 20 percent, cost estimating equations based on data from previous periods will under predict future costs. In this case, all that is required is a 20 percent increase in the prediction. Unfortunately, adjustments for price changes are seldom this simple. The prices of vari-ous cost elements are likely to change at different rates and at different times. Furthermore, there are apt to be several different price levels included in the past data used to develop cost estimating equations. Always be suspicious of old data. If data from different price levels are used, an attempt should be made to restate them to a single price level.

Matching Activity and Costs

Costs and activity must be matched within each observation. Accuracy is reduced if activity is recorded in one time period and costs are recorded in another. The shorter the time period, the higher the probability of error in matching costs and activity. The cost of electricity consumed this month might, for example, not be recorded until next month when the electric bill is received. There may also be a lag between an activity and the resulting costs. Consider automobile oil and lubrication costs. Because an auto may be driven several months between servicing, weekly observations of miles driven and maintenance costs are unlikely to match the costs of oil and lubrication with the activity, miles driven, that drives these costs. The cost analyst must carefully review the data base to verify that activity and cost are matched within each observation. If matching problems are found, it may be possible to adjust the data (perhaps by moving the cost of electricity from one observation to another). Under other circumstances, it may be necessary to use longer time periods to match costs and activity.

Identifying Activity Cost Drivers

In many cases, the identity of the most appropriate activity cost driver, such as miles driven for the cost of automobile gasoline, is apparent. In other situations, where different activity cost drivers might be used, scatter diagrams and statistical measures, such as the coefficient of determination, are helpful in selecting the activity cost driver that best explains past variations in cost. When scatter diagrams are used, the analyst can study the dispersion of observations around the cost estimating line. In general, a small dispersion is preferred. If regression analysis is used, the analyst considers the coefficient of determination. In general, a higher coefficient of determination is preferred. Of course, the relationship between the activity cost driver and the cost must seem logical, and the activity data must be available. Management Accounting Practice 2-1 indicates activity cost drivers for several department cost centers in a hospital.

COST-VOLUME-PROFIT ANALYSIS

L O 2

Cost-volume-profit (CVP) analysis is a technique used to examine the relationships among the total volume of some independent variable, total costs, total revenues, and profits during a time period (typically a month or year). In CVP analysis, volume refers to a single activity cost driver, such as unit sales, that is assumed to correlate with changes in revenues, costs, and profits.

MANAGEMENT ACCOUNTING PRACTICE 2-1

MedCenter Uses Different Measures of Activity to Analyze Costs in Different Departments

MedCenter Hospital is organized into a number of different department cost centers. To analyze costs, different measures of activity are used for each cost center. Representative information on department cost centers and each center's activity cost driver for Year 2 are as follows:

Cost Center	Activity	Units of Activity Year 2	Total Cost Year 2
Routine services:			
Adult	Patient-days	30,137	$4,417,693
Intensive care	Patient-days	858	439,808
Newborn	Patient-days	2,722	322,041
Operating room	Surgeries	3,291	788,591
Anesthesiology	Surgeries	3,291	29,014
Radiology	Exams	19,719	986,580
Laboratory	Tests	297,934	1,096,615
Ultra Sound	Treatments	1,059	86,722
Blood Bank	Transfusions	888	101,501

The high-low method was used to study cost behavior for each cost center. Because two observations are required, data for Year 1 were obtained and adjusted for changes in such things as wage rates. High-low analysis was then performed on the adjusted data for Year 1 and the data for Year 2. Take adult routine services as an example.

	Year 2		Year 1 (adjusted)	
	Patient-Days	Total Cost	Patient-Days	Total Cost
Adult routine services	30,137	$4,417,783	33,485	$4,493,017

Finally, the following cost estimating equation was developed for adult routine services:

$$Y = \$3,740,609 + \$22.47 \text{ per patient-day}$$

The variable component represents the cost of linens and laundry, services of aids and orderlies, housekeeping, supplies, and some utilities. The fixed component represents nursing services, furniture, fixtures, medical equipment, and some utilities.

....

Based on: Maryanne M. Mowen, *Accounting for Costs as Fixed & Variable* (Montvale, NY: Institute of Management Accountants [Formerly National Association of Accountants] 1986), pp. 53-55.

Assumptions   CVP analysis is subject to a number of limiting assumptions. Although these assumptions do not negate the usefulness of CVP models in the early stages of planning, they do suggest the need for further analysis before plans are completed. Among the more important assumptions are:

1. *All costs are classified as fixed or variable.* It is assumed that all other costs, such as mixed costs, can be broken into fixed and variable cost elements.
2. *The total cost function is linear within the relevant range.* This assumption may be valid within a relevant range of normal operations, but over the entire range of possible activity, changes in efficiency are likely to result in a curvilinear cost function.
3. *The total revenue function is linear within the relevant range.* Unit selling prices are assumed to be constant over the range of possible volumes. This implies a purely competitive market for final products or services. In some economic models (monopolistic and oligopolistic) where demand responds to price changes, the revenue function is curvilinear. In these situations, the linear approximation is accurate only within a limited range of activity.
4. *The analysis is for a single product, or the sales mix of multiple products is constant.* The **sales mix** refers to the relative portion of unit or dollar sales derived from each product or service. If products have different selling prices and costs, changes in the mix will affect CVP model results.
5. *There is only one cost driver: unit or dollar sales volume.* Reviewing the many cost drivers in Management Accounting Practice 2-1, it becomes apparent that in a complex organization, it is seldom possible to represent the multitude of factors that drive costs for an entire organization with a single cost driver.

When applied to a single product (such as kilograms of potato chips), service (such as the number of pages printed), or event (such as the number of tickets sold to a concert), it may be reasonable to assume the single independent variable is the cost driver. The total costs associated with the single product, service, or event during a specific time period are often determined by this single activity cost driver.

Although cost-volume-profit analysis is often used to understand the overall operations of an organization or business segment, accuracy decreases as the scope of operations being analyzed increases. After introducing CVP analysis, we further consider the single cost driver assumption.

The Profit Formula

The profit associated with a product, service, or event is equal to the difference between total revenues and total costs:

$$\text{Profit} = \text{Total revenues} - \text{Total costs}$$

The revenues are a function of the unit sales volume and the unit selling price:

$$\text{Total revenues} = \text{Selling price} \times \text{Unit sales volume}$$

Total costs for a time period are a function of the fixed costs per period and the variable costs of unit sales:

$$\begin{array}{c} \text{Total} \\ \text{costs} \end{array} = \begin{array}{c} \text{Fixed} \\ \text{costs} \end{array} + \left(\begin{array}{c} \text{Variable costs} \\ \text{per unit} \end{array} \times \begin{array}{c} \text{Unit sales} \\ \text{volume} \end{array} \right)$$

The equation for profit can be expanded to include the details of the total revenue and total cost equations:

$$\text{Profit} = \left(\begin{array}{c} \text{Selling} \\ \text{price} \end{array} \times \begin{array}{c} \text{Unit sales} \\ \text{volume} \end{array} \right) - \left(\begin{array}{c} \text{Fixed} \\ \text{costs} \end{array} + \left[\begin{array}{c} \text{Variable costs} \\ \text{per unit} \end{array} \times \begin{array}{c} \text{Unit sales} \\ \text{volume} \end{array} \right] \right)$$

Given information on the selling price, fixed costs per period, and variable costs per unit, this formula is used to predict profit at any specified activity level. Consider the following example.

The Benchmark Paper Company's only product is high-quality photocopy paper that it manufactures and sells to wholesale distributors at $8 per carton. Following modern inventory minimization techniques, Benchmark does not maintain inventories of raw materials or finished goods. Instead, newly purchased raw materials are delivered directly to the factory, and finished goods are loaded directly onto trucks for shipment. Benchmark's variable and fixed costs are detailed below:

1. **Direct materials** is the cost of the primary raw materials converted into finished goods. Because the consumption of raw materials increases as the quantity of goods produced increases, direct materials is a variable cost. Benchmark's raw materials consist primarily of paper purchased in large rolls and packing supplies such as boxes. Benchmark also treats the costs of purchasing, receiving, and inspecting raw materials as part of the cost of direct materials. All together, these costs total $1 per carton of finished product.

2. **Direct labor** is wages earned by production employees for the time they spend working on the conversion of raw materials into finished goods. Based on Benchmark's manufacturing procedures, direct labor is a variable cost. These costs are $0.25 per carton.

3. **Variable manufacturing overhead** includes all other variable costs associated with converting raw materials into finished goods. Benchmark's variable manufacturing overhead costs include the cost of lubricants for cutting and packaging machines, the cost of electricity to operate these machines, and the cost to move materials between receiving and shipping docks and the cutting and packaging machines. These costs equal $1.25 per carton.

4. **Variable selling and administrative costs** include all variable costs other than those directly associated with converting raw materials into finished goods. At Benchmark, these costs include sales commissions, transportation of finished goods to wholesale distributors, and the cost of processing the receipt and disbursement of cash. These costs amount to $0.50 per carton.

5. **Fixed manufacturing overhead** includes all fixed costs associated with converting raw materials into finished goods. Benchmark's fixed manufacturing costs include depreciation, property taxes, and insurance on buildings and machines used for manufacturing, salaries of

manufacturing supervisors, and the fixed portion of electricity used to light the factory. These costs total $5,000 per month.

6. **Fixed selling and administrative costs** include all fixed costs other than those directly associated with converting raw materials into finished goods. Included are the salaries of Benchmark's president and many other staff personnel such as accounting and marketing. Also included are depreciation, property taxes, insurance on facilities used for administrative purposes, and any related utilities costs. These costs equal $10,000 per month.

Benchmark's variable and fixed costs are summarized below:

Variable Costs per Carton			**Fixed Costs per Month**	
Manufacturing:			Manufacturing overhead	$ 5,000
Direct materials	$1.00		Selling and administrative	10,000
Direct labor	0.25		Total	$15,000
Manufacturing				
overhead	1.25	$2.50		
Selling and administrative		0.50		
Total		$3.00		

The cost estimation techniques discussed earlier in this chapter would probably be used to determine many detailed costs. Least-squares regression, for example, might be used to determine the variable and monthly fixed amount of electricity used in manufacturing. Because Benchmark manufactures and sells a single product on a continuous basis with all sales to distributors under standing contracts, it is reasonable to assume that in the short-run Benchmark's total monthly cost function responds to a single cost driver, cartons sold. Combining all of this information, Benchmark's profit equation is:

$$\text{Profit} = \$8X - (\$15,000 + \$3X)$$

where:

$$X = \text{cartons sold}$$

Using this equation, Benchmark's profit at a volume of 5,400 units is $12,000 ($8(5,400) - [$15,000 + $3(5,400)]).

Contribution Income Statement

To provide more detailed information on anticipated or actual financial results at a particular sales volume, a contribution income statement can be prepared. Benchmark's contribution income statement for a volume of 5,400 units is presented in Exhibit 2-4. Note that in a **contribution income statement**, costs are classified according to behavior as variable or fixed, and the **contribution margin** (the difference between total revenues and total variable costs) that goes toward covering fixed costs and providing a profit is emphasized.

While Exhibit 2-4 presents detailed revenues and cost information, it is sometimes useful to present abbreviated information, perhaps with information per unit or as a portion of sales as follows:

EXHIBIT 2-4: CONTRIBUTION INCOME STATEMENT

Benchmark Paper Company
Contribution Income Statement
For a Monthly Volume of 5,400 Cartons

Sales (5,400 x $8)		$43,200
Less variable costs:		
Direct materials (5,400 x $1.00)	$ 5,400	
Direct labor (5,400 x $0.25)	1,350	
Manufacturing overhead (5,400 x $1.25)	6,750	
Selling and administrative (5,400 x $0.50)	2,700	- 16,200
Contribution margin		$27,000
Less fixed costs:		
Manufacturing overhead	$ 5,000	
Selling and administrative	10,000	- 15,000
Profit		$12,000

	Total	Per Unit	Ratio to Sales
Sales (5,400 units)	$43,200	$8	1.000
Variable costs	- 16,200	- 3	-0.375
Contribution margin	$27,000	$5	0.625
Fixed costs	- 15,000		
Profit	$12,000		

The per unit information is very useful in short-range planning. The **unit contribution margin** is the difference between the unit selling price and the unit variable costs. It is the amount, $5 in this case, that each unit contributes toward covering fixed costs and earning a profit.

The contribution margin is widely used in **sensitivity analysis**, the study of the responsiveness of a model to changes in one or more of its independent variables. Benchmark's income statement is an economic model of the firm, and the unit contribution margin indicates how sensitive Benchmark's income model is to changes in unit sales. If, for example, sales increase by 100 cartons per month, the increase in profit is readily determined, multiplying the 100 carton increase in sales by the $5 unit contribution margin:

100 Carton sales increase × $5 Unit contribution margin = $500 Profit increase

There is no increase in fixed costs, so the new profit level becomes $12,500, ($12,000 + $500) per month.

When expressed as a ratio to sales, the contribution margin is identified as the contribution margin ratio. The **contribution margin ratio** is the portion of each dollar of sales revenue contributed toward covering fixed costs and earning a profit. In the abbreviated income statement presented above, the portion of each dollar of sales revenue contributed toward covering fixed costs and earning a profit was computed to be 0.625, ($27,000/$43,200). This is Benchmark's contribution margin ratio. If sales revenue increase by $800 per month, the increase in profits is computed as follows:

$800 Sales increase × 0.625 Contribution margin ratio = $500 Profit increase

The contribution margin ratio is especially useful in situations involving several products or when unit sales information is not available.

Break-Even Point

The **break-even point** occurs at the unit or dollar sales volume where total revenues equal total costs. The break-even point is of great interest to management. Until break-even sales are reached, the product, service, event, or business segment of interest operates at a loss. Beyond this point, increasing levels of profits are achieved. Consequently, management is always interested in the break-even point of a current or planned activity. Management often wants to know the **margin of safety**, the amount by which actual or planned sales exceed the break-even point. Other questions of interest include the probability of exceeding the break-even sales volume and the effect of some proposed change on the break-even point.

To determine the break-even point, set the equation for total revenues equal to the equation for total costs and solve for the break-even unit sales volume. Using the general equations for total revenues and total costs, the following results are obtained.

Setting total revenues equal to total costs:

$$\underbrace{\begin{pmatrix} \text{Selling} & & \text{Break-even} \\ \text{price} & \times & \text{unit sales} \\ \text{per unit} & & \text{volume} \end{pmatrix}}_{\textbf{Total revenues}} = \underbrace{\begin{pmatrix} \text{Fixed} \\ \text{costs} \end{pmatrix} + \begin{bmatrix} & \text{Break-even} \\ \text{Variable costs} \times & \text{unit sales} \\ \text{per unit} & \text{volume} \end{bmatrix}}_{\textbf{Total costs}}$$

Solving for the break-even sales volume:

$$\begin{matrix} \text{Break-even} \\ \text{unit sales} \\ \text{volume} \end{matrix} = \frac{\text{Fixed costs}}{\begin{matrix}\text{Selling price} & - & \text{Variable costs} \\ \text{per unit} & & \text{per unit}\end{matrix}}$$

The denominator in the above equation is the unit contribution margin. Hence, the break-even point is also computed as the fixed costs divided by the unit contribution margin.

$$\begin{matrix} \text{Break-even} \\ \text{unit sales} \\ \text{volume} \end{matrix} = \frac{\text{Fixed costs}}{\text{Unit contribution margin}}$$

Letting X equal the break-even unit volume, Benchmark's break-even point is 3,000 units per month:

$$\$8X = \$15,000 + \$3X$$

Solving for X:

$$\$8X - \$3X = \$15,000$$
$$\$5X = \$15,000$$
$$X = \$15,000/\$5$$
$$X = 3,000 \text{ units}$$

At a $5 per unit contribution margin, 3,000 units of contribution are required to cover $15,000 of fixed costs. If the anticipated sales for some month total 5,400 units, the margin of safety would be 2,400 units, (5,400 anticipated sales - 3,000 break-even sales), and profit would be $12,000, (2,400 unit margin of safety × $5 per unit contribution margin).

Profit Planning

Establishing profit objectives is an important part of planning in for-profit organizations. Profit objectives are determined in many ways. They can be set as a percent of last year's profits, as a percent of total assets at the start of the current year, or as a percent of owner's equity. They might be based on a profit trend, or they might be expressed as a percent of sales. The economic outlook for the firm's products and anticipated changes in products, costs, and technology are also considered in establishing profit objectives.

Before incorporating profit plans into a detailed budget, it is useful to obtain some preliminary information on the feasibility of profit plans. Cost-volume-profit analysis is one way of doing this. By manipulating cost-volume-profit relationships, management can determine the sales volume corresponding to a desired profit. Management might then evaluate the feasibility of this sales volume. If the profit plans are feasible, a complete budget might be developed for this activity level. The required sales volume might be infeasible because of market conditions or because the required volume exceeds production or service capacity, in which case management must lower its profit objective or consider other ways of achieving it. Alternatively, the required sales volume might be less than management believes the firm is capable of selling, in which case management might raise its profit objective.

Assume Benchmark's management desires to know the unit sales volume required to achieve a monthly profit of $18,000. Using the profit formula, the required unit sales volume is determined by setting profits equal to $18,000 and solving for X, the unit sales volume:

$$\text{Profit} = \text{Total revenues} - \text{Total costs}$$
$$\$18,000 = \$8X - (\$15,000 + \$3X)$$

Solving for X:

$$\$8X - \$3X = \$15,000 + \$18,000$$
$$X = (\$15,000 + \$18,000)/\$5$$
$$= 6,600 \text{ units}$$

The total contribution must now cover the desired profit as well as the fixed costs. Hence, the sales volume required to achieve a desired profit is computed as the fixed costs plus the desired profit, all divided by the unit contribution margin.

$$\text{Desired profit unit sales volume} = \frac{\text{Fixed costs} + \text{Desired profit}}{\text{Unit contribution margin}}$$

Cost-Volume-Profit Graph

A **cost-volume-profit graph** illustrates the relationships among volume, total revenues, total costs, and profits. Its usefulness comes from highlighting the break-even point and depicting revenues and cost relationships over a range of activity. This representation allows management to view the relative amount of important variables at any graphed volume. Benchmark's monthly CVP graph is presented in Exhibit 2-5. Total revenues and total costs are measured on the vertical axis, and unit sales is measured on the horizontal axis. Separate lines are drawn for total variable costs, total costs, and total revenues. The amount of profit or loss at a given volume is depicted by the vertical distance between the total revenue and the total cost lines. Losses occur when total revenues are less than total costs, and profits occur when total revenues exceed total costs.

The total contribution margin is shown by the difference between the total revenue and the total variable cost lines. Observe that as unit sales increase, the contribution margin first goes to cover the fixed costs; and, beyond the break-even point, any additional contribution margin provides a profit.

EXHIBIT 2-5: TYPICAL COST-VOLUME-PROFIT GRAPH

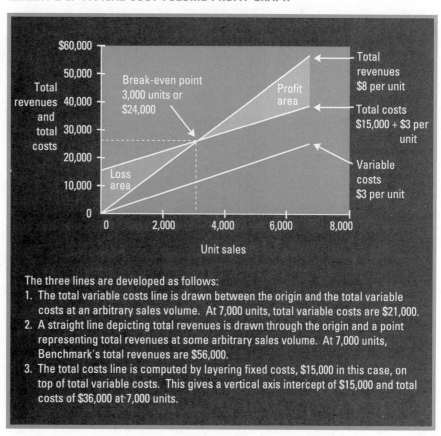

The three lines are developed as follows:
1. The total variable costs line is drawn between the origin and the total variable costs at an arbitrary sales volume. At 7,000 units, total variable costs are $21,000.
2. A straight line depicting total revenues is drawn through the origin and a point representing total revenues at some arbitrary sales volume. At 7,000 units, Benchmark's total revenues are $56,000.
3. The total costs line is computed by layering fixed costs, $15,000 in this case, on top of total variable costs. This gives a vertical axis intercept of $15,000 and total costs of $36,000 at 7,000 units.

Profit-Volume Graph

In cost-volume-profit graphs, profits are represented by the difference between total revenues and total costs. When management is primarily interested in the impact on profits of changes in sales volume, and less interested in the related revenues and costs, a profit-volume graph is sometimes used instead of a cost-volume-profit graph. A **profit-volume graph** illustrates the relationship between volume and profits; it does not show revenues and costs. Profits are read directly from a profit-volume graph rather than being computed as the difference between total revenues and total costs. Profit-volume graphs may be developed plotting either unit sales or total revenues on the horizontal axis.

Benchmark's monthly profit-volume graph, with total revenues plotted on the horizontal axis, is presented in Exhibit 2-6. Profit or loss is measured on the vertical axis, and volume is measured on the horizontal axis, which intersects the vertical axis at zero profit. A single line, representing total profit, is drawn intersecting the vertical axis at a zero unit sales volume loss equal to the fixed costs. The profit line crosses the horizontal axis at the break-even unit or dollar sales volume. The profit or loss at any volume is depicted by the vertical difference between the profit line and the horizontal axis.

Note that the slope of the profit line is determined by the contribution margin. The greater the contribution margin ratio or the unit contribution margin, the steeper the slope of the profit line.

EXHIBIT 2-6: PROFIT-VOLUME GRAPH

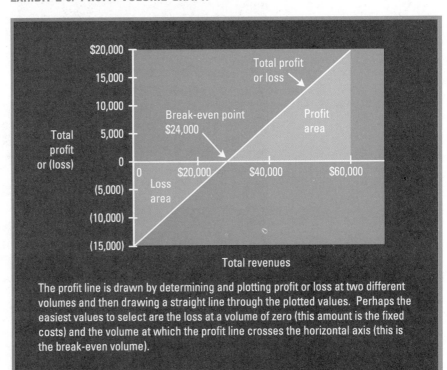

The profit line is drawn by determining and plotting profit or loss at two different volumes and then drawing a straight line through the plotted values. Perhaps the easiest values to select are the loss at a volume of zero (this amount is the fixed costs) and the volume at which the profit line crosses the horizontal axis (this is the break-even volume).

Multiple-Product Cost-Volume-Profit Analysis

Unit cost information may not be available or appropriate when analyzing cost-volume-profit relationships of multiple-product firms. In this case, assuming the sales mix is constant, the contribution margin ratio (the portion of each sales dollar contributed toward covering fixed costs and earning a profit) may be used to determine the break-even dollar sales volume or the dollar sales volume required to achieve a desired profit. Treating a dollar of sales revenue as a unit, the break-even point in dollars is computed as fixed costs divided by the number of cents from each dollar of revenue contributed to covering fixed costs and providing a profit.

$$\text{Dollar break-even point} = \frac{\text{Fixed costs}}{\text{Contribution margin ratio}}$$

If unit selling price and cost information were not available, Benchmark's dollar break-even point could be computed as $24,000, ($15,000/0.625).

Analogous computations can be made to find the dollar sales volume required to achieve a desired profit.

$$\text{Desired profit dollar sales volume} = \frac{\text{Fixed costs} + \text{Desired profit}}{\text{Contribution margin ratio}}$$

To achieve a desired profit of $12,000, Benchmark needs sales of $43,200, ([$15,000 + $12,000]/0.625).

These relationships can be graphed by placing sales dollars, rather than unit sales, on the horizontal axis. Management Accounting Practice 2-2 demonstrates how CVP information can be developed from the published financial statements of multiple-product firms such as American Brands, Inc.

MANAGEMENT ACCOUNTING PRACTICE 2-2

Determining CVP Relationships by Analyzing Published Financial Statements

Presented is condensed information from the 1991 and 1992 income statements of American Brands, Inc. (in millions).

	1992	1991
Revenues	$14,623.6	$14,063.8
Operating expenses	- 12,868.6	- 12,433.0
Operating income	$ 1,755.0	$ 1,630.8

By applying the high-low method of cost estimation to this information, it is possible to determine American Brands' cost-volume-profit relationships. Start by determining the variable costs as a portion of each sales dollar.

$$\text{Variable cost ratio} = \frac{\text{Difference in total costs}}{\text{Difference in total sales revenue}} = \frac{\$12,868.6 - \$12,433.2}{\$14,623.6 - \$14,063.8} = 0.7778$$

(continued)

Annual fixed costs are determined by subtracting the variable costs for either period, computed as a portion of total sales revenue, from the corresponding total costs.

$$\text{Annual fixed costs} = \$12{,}868.6 - (0.7778 \times \$14{,}623.6) = \$1{,}494.4 \text{ million}$$

The contribution margin ratio is 1 minus the variable cost ratio.

$$\text{Contribution margin ratio} = 1 - 0.778 = 0.222$$

American Brands break-even point is $6,731.5 million ($1,494.4/0.222).

Applying these concepts to 1993 sales of $13,701.4 million, we obtain an expected profit of $1,550.1 million. American Brands' actual 1993 profit was $1,397.9 million, an error of $152.2 million, or 9.8%. Interestingly, management reported that 1993 income was adversely affected by foreign currency translation losses of $100.3 million and by inventory adjustments of $29.9 million. This analysis worked for American Brands because of its stable sales mix and cost structure.

Based on: 1993 *American Brands, Inc. Annual Report*, pp. 21 and 29.

The Impact of Income Taxes

Income taxes are imposed on individuals and for-profit organizations by units of government. The amount of an individual's or an organization's income tax is determined by laws that specify the calculation of taxable income (the income subject to tax) and the calculation of the amount of tax on taxable income. Income taxes are computed as a percentage of taxable income, with increases in taxable income usually subject to progressively higher tax rates. The laws governing the computation of taxable income differ in many ways from the accounting principles and standards that guide the computation of accounting income. This is especially true concerning the timing of the recognition of revenues and expenses.[1] Consequently, taxable income and accounting income are seldom the same in the short run.

In the *early stages* of profit planning, income taxes are sometimes incorporated in CVP models by assuming that taxable income and accounting income are equal and that the tax rate is constant. Although these assumptions are seldom true, they are useful because they assist management in developing an early prediction of the sales volume required to earn a desired after-tax profit. Once management has developed a general plan, this early prediction should be refined with the advice of tax experts.

Assuming taxes are imposed at a constant rate per dollar of before-tax profit, income taxes are computed as before-tax profit multiplied by the tax rate. After-tax profit is equal to before-tax profit minus income taxes:

---

1 The timing of depreciation for tax purposes is considered in Chapter 6.

$$\begin{array}{c} \text{After-tax} \\ \text{profit} \end{array} = \begin{array}{c} \text{Before-tax} \\ \text{profit} \end{array} - \left(\begin{array}{c} \text{Before-tax} \\ \text{profit} \end{array} \times \begin{array}{c} \text{Tax} \\ \text{rate} \end{array} \right)$$

After-tax profit can also be expressed as before-tax profit times 1 minus the tax rate:

$$\begin{array}{c} \text{After-tax} \\ \text{profit} \end{array} = \begin{array}{c} \text{Before-tax} \\ \text{profit} \end{array} \times \left(1 - \begin{array}{c} \text{Tax} \\ \text{rate} \end{array} \right)$$

This formula can be rearranged to isolate before-tax profit as follows:

$$\begin{array}{c} \text{Before-tax} \\ \text{profit} \end{array} = \frac{\text{After-tax profit}}{(1 - \text{Tax rate})}$$

Since all costs and revenues in the profit formula are expressed on a before-tax basis, the most straightforward way of determining the unit sales volume required to earn a desired after-tax profit is to:

1. Determine the required before-tax profit.
2. Substitute the required before-tax profit into the profit formula.
3. Solve for the required unit sales volume.

Assume Benchmark is subject to a 40 percent tax rate and that management desires to earn a November 19X9 after-tax profit of $18,000. The required before-tax profit is $30,000, ($18,000/[1 - 0.40]), and the unit sales volume required to earn this profit is 9,000 units, ([$15,000 + $30,000]/$5).

It is apparent that income taxes increase the sales volume required to earn a desired after-tax profit. A 40 percent tax rate increased the sales volume required for Benchmark to earn a profit of $18,000 from 6,600 to 9,000 units. These amounts are verified in Exhibit 2-7.

EXHIBIT 2-7: CONTRIBUTION INCOME STATEMENT

Benchmark Paper Company
Contribution Income Statement
Planned for the Month of November 19X9

Sales (9,000 x $8)		$72,000
Less variable costs:		
Direct materials (9,000 x $1.00)	$ 9,000	
Direct labor (9,000 x $0.25)	2,250	
Manufacturing overhead (9,000 x $1.25)	11,250	
Selling and administrative (9,000 x $0.50)	4,500	- 27,000
Contribution margin		$45,000
Less fixed costs:		
Manufacturing overhead	$ 5,000	
Selling and administrative	10,000	- 15,000
Before-tax profit		$30,000
Income taxes ($30,000 x 0.40)		- 12,000
After-tax profit		$18,000

Operating Leverage

Operating leverage refers to the extent that an organization's costs are fixed. The **degree of operating leverage** is computed as the contribution margin divided by income before taxes.

$$\frac{\text{Degree of}}{\text{operating leverage}} = \frac{\text{Contribution margin}}{\text{Income before taxes}}$$

The rationale underlying this computation is that as fixed costs are substituted for variable costs, the contribution margin as a percent of income before taxes increases. Hence, the higher the degree of operating leverage, the greater the portion of fixed costs.

The higher the degree of operating leverage, the greater the opportunity for profit with increases in sales. Conversely, a higher degree of operating leverage magnifies the risk of large losses with a decrease in sales.

Assume Benchmark Card Company competes with High Fixed Card Company. Information for both companies at a monthly volume of 4,000 units is as follows:

	Benchmark	High Fixed
Unit selling price	$ 8.00	$ 8.00
Unit variable costs	- 3.00	- 1.50
Unit contribution margin	$ 5.00	$ 6.50
Unit sales	× 4,000	× 4,000
Contribution margin	$20,000	$26,000
Fixed costs	- 15,000	- 21,000
Profit before taxes	$ 5,000	$ 5,000
Contribution margin	$20,000	$26,000
Profit before taxes	÷ 5,000	÷ 5,000
Degree of operating leverage	4.0	5.2

Although both companies have identical net incomes at a sales volume of 4,000 units, High Fixed has a higher degree of operating leverage, and its profits vary more with changes in sales volume.

If sales increase by 12.5 percent, from 4,000 to 4,500 units, the percent increase in each firm's profits can be computed as the percent change in sales multiplied by the degree of operating leverage.

	Benchmark	High Fixed
Change in sales	12.5%	12.5%
Degree of operating leverage	× 4.0	× 5.2
Change in profits	50.0%	65.0%

This can be verified by multiplying each firm's unit contribution margin by the increase in unit sales:

	Benchmark	High Fixed
Unit contribution margin	$ 5.00	$ 6.50
Unit change in sales	× 500	× 500
Change in profit	$2,500	$3,250
Percent increase from $5,000 profit	50%	65%

Management is interested in measures of operating leverage to determine how sensitive profits are to changes in sales. Risk averse managers will strive to maintain a lower operating leverage, even if this results in some loss of profits. One way to reduce operating leverage is to use more direct labor and less automated equipment. Another way is to contract to have outside organizations perform tasks that might be done internally. This approach to reducing operating leverage is considered in Chapter 3, where we examine the external acquisition of goods and services. Of course, while operating leverage is a useful analytic tool, long-run success comes from keeping the overall level of costs down, while providing customers with the products or services they want at competitive prices. Management Accounting Practice 2-3 looks at how Naxos Records does just that.

COST DRIVER AND CVP ANALYSIS

L O 3

In Chapter 1, three types of cost drivers were discussed:

1. *Structural cost drivers* are fundamental choices about the size and scope of operations and technologies employed in delivering products or services to customers.

MANAGEMENT ACCOUNTING PRACTICE 2-3

Classical Music at Aggressive Prices Bring High Notes and Profits to Listeners and Investors

When Klaus Heymann founded Hong Kong-based Naxos in 1987, his goal was to bring quality classical music to the masses on compact disks at affordable prices. Up to then, major recording companies followed a two market strategy of (1) hiring well-known performers to record new digital masters sold on compact disks for premium prices and (2) placing old analogue recordings on compact disks sold for budget prices.

Heymann's strategy was to seek unknown talent to record new digital masters sold on compact disks at budget prices. Naxos keeps costs low by operating with a small administrative staff out of modest facilities, finding talent willing to work for what Naxos will pay them, and watching recording costs carefully. According to Heymann, "Our artists don't fly first class, stay in five-star hotels or drink champagne."

By keeping the fixed costs of each newly issued compact disk down, Naxos can get by with a much lower unit contribution margin than can major competitors. This allows Naxos to sell digitally recorded compact disks for $6, whereas major competitors sell digitally recorded compact disks for $18 and analogue recorded compact disks for $6. With lower prices comes higher volume (an average Naxos release sells 50,000 copies, five times the industry average), further reducing the fixed product costs averaged over each disk.

Based on: Andrew Tanzer, "All the Music Without the Trimming," *Forbes* (February 14, 1994), pp. 43-44.

2. *Organizational cost drivers* are choices concerning the organization of activities and choices concerning the involvement of persons inside and outside the organization in decision making.

3. *Activity cost drivers* are specific activities performed to serve customer needs that consume costly resources.

Cost-volume-profit analysis, with its focus on costs during a relatively short period of time such as a year or month, considers only activity cost drivers. While the activities selected to respond to customer needs are affected by strategic and organizational decisions, such decisions are not explicitly considered in CVP analysis. The management of structural and organizational cost drivers is considered in Chapters 4, 5, and 6.

CVP analysis uses a single cost driver or independent variable. Moreover, because that single variable must relate to revenues as well as to costs, it is of necessity a measure of final output such as unit sales or sales revenue. The Benchmark Paper Company example involved the continuous production of a single product. Additionally, sales and shipping activities were streamlined by using a single wholesale distributor. These assumptions made the use of a single activity driver, cartons sold, reasonable.

If Benchmark produced additional products such as writing paper, envelopes, and note pads with sales and shipments in various size lots, the multitude of independent activities that caused the incurrence of costs could not be reasonably approximated by a single cost driver. In this case, Benchmark's activity cost drivers would include the number of purchase orders for raw materials, the quantity of raw materials used, the number of sales orders processed, the number of production runs for each product, the number of units in each production run, the number of machine setups, and the number of units shipped. Additional cost drivers could be determined by identifying the major categories of activities required to satisfy customer needs, especially activities that differed among customers or products. Procedures useful in determining activities are considered in Chapter 4.

HIERARCHY OF ACTIVITY COSTS

L O 4

Because CVP analysis is intended to be a simplified, preliminary planning model, incorporating all activities that drive costs into the model would so complicate the model that its primary usefulness would be destroyed. Instead, in complex situations, CVP analysis uses a single independent variable, such as unit sales or sales revenue, that correlates with revenues and costs. When this is done, it is important to understand the inadequacies of the resulting model for anything other than providing the "big picture." To make specific decisions, additional information is required concerning activities and activity costs.

As noted in Chapter 1, providing customers with products or services requires the performance of numerous activities, and the performance of activities consume costly resources:

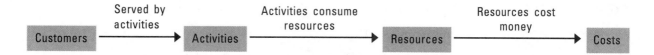

Efforts to manage costs require an understanding of the multitude of activities performed to serve customer needs. Because classification schemes help in understanding underlying phenomenon, several researchers have developed frameworks for categorizing activity costs. The most well-known framework, developed by Cooper[2] and Cooper and Kaplan[3] for manufacturing situations, classifies activities into four categories:

1. **Unit level activities**, performed *for each unit* of product produced.
2. **Batch level activities**, performed *for each batch* of product produced.
3. **Product level activities**, performed *to support* the production of each different type of product.
4. **Facility level activities**, performed *to maintain* general manufacturing capabilities.

According to Cooper and Kaplan:

> Some activities, like drilling a hole or machining a surface, are performed on individual units. Others—setups, materials movements, and first part inspections allow batches of units to be processed. Still others—engineering product specifications, process engineering, product enhancements, and engineering change notices—provide the overall capability that enables the company to produce the product. And plant management, building and grounds maintenance, and heating and lighting sustain the manufacturing facility. [Cooper and Kaplan, p. 131]

Several additional examples of the costs driven by activities at each level are presented in Exhibit 2-8.

We have broadened the scope of activities at each level to include general administrative, selling, and distribution. Consider the Benchmark Paper Company example. Some activities, such as placing packages of copy paper in a carton, are performed for individual cartons of product (unit). Others, such as processing a sales order or recording the collection of cash for a sales invoice, are performed for each sale (batch). Still others, such as specialized advertising for copy paper, are performed for each product. Finally, general advertising might be acquired to enhance Benchmark's overall reputation.

The hierarchy developed by Cooper is but one of many possible ways of classifying activities and their costs. Classification schemes can be

---

2 Robin Cooper, "Cost Classification in Unit-Based and Activity-Based Manufacturing Cost Systems," *The Journal of Cost Management* (Fall 1990), pp. 4-14.
3 Robin Cooper and Robert S. Kaplan, "Profit Priorities From Activity-Based Costing," *Harvard Business Review* (May-June 1991), pp. 130-135.

EXHIBIT 2-8: HIERARCHY OF ACTIVITY COSTS

Activity Level	Why Activity Is Performed	Examples of Activity Cost
1. Unit level	Performed for each unit of product produced and sold	• Cost of raw materials • Cost of inserting a component • Utilities cost of operating equipment • Some costs of packaging • Sales commissions
2. Batch level	Performed for each batch of product produced or sold	• Cost of processing sales order • Cost of issuing and tracking work order • Cost of equipment setup • Cost of moving batch between workstations • Cost of inspection (assuming same number of units inspected in each batch)
3. Product level	Performed to support each different product that can be produced	• Cost of product development • Cost of product marketing such as advertising • Cost of specialized equipment • Cost of maintaining specialized equipment
4. Facility level	Performed to maintain general manufacturing capabilities	• Cost of maintaining general facilities such as buildings and grounds • Cost of nonspecialized equipment • Cost of maintaining nonspecialized equipment • Cost of real property taxes • Cost of general advertising • Cost of general administration such as the plant manager's salary

easily developed to meet user needs. In the preceding paragraph, we modified the definition of a batch to include either a production batch or a sales order. If management were interested in analyzing the profitability of sales to particular types of customers, an activity level might be inserted for market segment. If Benchmark only sold copy paper, and this product was sold to three customer groups (for-profit private, not-for-profit private, and government), the cost hierarchy might be modified to consider the activities performed to support sales to each market segment:

Unit level
Batch level
Market segment
Facility level

If Benchmark sold multiple products (copy paper, writing paper, and note paper) to distinct customer groups, costs might be classified using a five-level activity hierarchy:

Unit level
Batch level
Product level
Market segment
Facility level

Foster and Gupta[4] recommend the cost hierarchy *and* the costs included in the hierarchy be tailored to meet the specific circumstances of an organization and the interests of management. They offer the following hierarchy for marketing costs with a focus on customers:

1. Customer-transaction specific costs such as a sales discount for a customer's early payment of a sale on account.
2. Customer specific costs such as the cost of a customer credit report.
3. Customer group costs such as the cost of television advertising.
4. Marketing support costs such as the salary of the general marketing manager. [Foster and Gupta, p. 56]

FROM CVP ANALYSIS TO COST MANAGEMENT

L O 5

To accurately analyze costs in situations where there are multiple cost drivers, the cost estimating equation should include an independent variable for each cost driver. Based on Cooper's activity hierarchy, a revised total cost equation might appear as follows:

$$Y = \Sigma\, b_{1i} X_{1i} + \Sigma\, b_{2i} X_{2i} + \Sigma\, b_{3i} X_{3i} + \Sigma\, b_{4i} X_{4i}$$

where:

Y = total costs for a period

X_{1i} = unit level cost drivers, where the subscript *1* refers to the unit level and the subscript *i* refers to a specific driver

X_{2i} = batch level cost drivers, where the subscript *2* refers to the batch level and the subscript *i* refers to a specific driver

X_{3i} = product level cost drivers, where the subscript *3* refers to the product level and the subscript *i* refers to a specific driver

X_{4i} = facility level cost drivers, where the subscript *4* refers to the facility level and the subscript *i* refers to a specific driver

b_{1i}, b_{2i}, b_{3i}, b_{4i} = the cost per unit of cost driver

Σ = summation symbol indicating need to add the total costs at each level together

There are no residual fixed costs per period. Costs are completely specified as a function of distinct cost drivers. When a less complete cost function is used, such as one that focuses only on the unit level, costs driven by higher levels of activity will show up either as fixed costs or as an increase in the estimation error. The use of a single independent variable for cost

---

4 George Foster and Mahendra Gupta, "Marketing, Cost Management and Management Accounting," *Journal of Management Accounting Research*, 6 (Fall 1994), pp. 43-77.

estimation, as is the case in CVP analysis, can lead to significant errors when costs are driven by a multitude of activities and there is a change in the mix of activities. Consider the following example. While it may appear complex at first reading, studying it with paper and pencil will help you understand both the limitations of simple approaches to cost estimation and the potential contribution of activity-based costing.

The Pace Company manufactures and sells two products, A and B. Pace's activities have been analyzed and placed into a hierarchy of activity costs. Presented below is information on activity cost drivers and costs per unit of cost driver at each activity level.

Activity Level	Activity Cost	Activity
Unit	$b_{11} = \$8$	$X_{11} =$ A acquire direct materials
	$b_{12} = \$12$	$X_{12} =$ B acquire direct materials
	$b_{13} = \$2$	$X_{13} =$ A conversion
	$b_{14} = \$5$	$X_{14} =$ B conversion
Batch level	$b_{21} = \$300$	$X_{21} =$ A setup
	$b_{22} = \$300$	$X_{22} =$ B setup
	$b_{23} = \$50$	$X_{23} =$ A movement
	$b_{24} = \$50$	$X_{24} =$ B movement
Product level	$b_{31} = \$20,000$	$X_{31} =$ A advertising
	$b_{32} = \$15,000$	$X_{32} =$ B advertising
Facility level	$b_{41} = \$10,000$	$X_{41} =$ Maintenance
	$b_{42} = \$2,000$	$X_{42} =$ Rent
	$b_{43} = \$5,000$	$X_{43} =$ Administrative salaries

To simplify the example as much as possible, the number of activities has been limited. Selected information on costs at each activity level is described as follows. At the unit level, each unit of product A requires raw materials costing $8 and conversion activities (which would be detailed in a more complete example) costing $2. At the batch level, each batch of A (consisting of one or more units) requires setting up producing equipment at a cost of $300 per setup and moving the items in the batch at a cost of $50. At the product level, management spends $20,000 per month to promote the sale of product A. Finally, at the facilities level, monthly maintenance costs total $10,000.

During June 19X9, Pace produced 2,000 units of product A in 5 batches containing 400 units each and produced 10,000 units of product B in 10 batches of 1,000 units each. Total costs at each activity level and total predicted costs for the month are as follows:

Unit: $\sum b_{1i}X_{1i} = 2,000(\$8) + 2,000(\$2) + 10,000(\$12) + 10,000(\$5)$
$= \$190,000$

Batch: $\sum b_{2i}X_{2i} = 5(\$300) + 5(\$50) + 10(\$300) + 10(\$50)$
$= \$5,250$

Product: $\sum b_{3i}X_{3i} = 1(\$20,000) + 1(\$15,000)$
$= \$35,000$

Facility: $\sum b_{4i}X_{4i} = 1(\$10,000) + 1(\$2,000) + 1(\$5,000)$
$= \$17,000$

Total: $Y = \$190,000 + \$5,250 + \$35,000 + \$17,000$
$= \underline{\$247,250}$

During July 19X9, Pace produced 3,200 units of product A in 4 batches of 800 and produced 10,000 units of product B in 10 batches of 1,000. With no changes in activity costs, the total costs for the month were $258,900. As an exercise, you should verify this amount to ensure your understanding of the total cost equation with a hierarchy of activity cost.

Let us use detailed information, developed using a complete analysis of cost drivers, to illustrate the errors likely to be incurred when using a simple model that contains only one independent variable. As a baseline, we will use our previous computations of June and July 19X9 costs.

Following the single variable approach to developing a cost estimating equation, we can analyze these costs using the high-low method as follows:

Production	Total Cost
12,000, (2,000 + 10,000) units	$247,250
13,200, (3,200 + 10,000) units	$258,900

The variable and fixed costs are determined using the high-low method to be:

$$b = (\$258,900 - \$247,250)/(13,200 - 12,000)$$
$$= \$9.708$$
$$a = \$247,250 - \$9.708(12,000)$$
$$= \$130,754$$

The resulting equation for total monthly costs with units produced and sold as the independent variable is:

$$Y = \$130,754 + \$9.708X$$

where:

$$X = \text{total production}$$

If this equation were used to predict costs for August, when management anticipated producing 1,500 units of A in 5 batches and 13,000 units of B in 13 batches, predicted costs would amount to $271,520.

$$Y = \$130,754 + \$9.708(1,500 + 13,000)$$
$$= \$271,520$$

But, if we perform a complete analysis of activities and activity costs, the predicted costs for August are $294,300:

Unit: $\sum b_{1i}X_{1i}$ = 1,500($8) + 1,500($2) + 13,000($12) + 13,000($5)
$$= \$236,000$$

Batch: $\sum b_{2i}X_{2i}$ = 5($300) + 5($50) + 13($300) + 13($50)
$$= \$6,300$$

Product: $\sum b_{3i}X_{3i}$ = 1($20,000) + 1($15,000)
$$= \$35,000$$

Facility: $\sum b_{4i}X_{4i}$ = 1($10,000) + 1($2,000) + 1($5,000)
$$= \$17,000$$

Total: Y = $236,000 + $6,300 + $35,000 + $17,000
$$= \underline{\$294,300}$$

In this example, the use of a single independent variable for cost prediction produced an error of $(22,780), ($271,520 prediction - $294,300 correct). Changes in the mix of cost drivers at the unit and batch level led to significant errors when cost estimates were based on a single independent variable.

It is apparent that cost estimating errors can have severe economic consequences to individuals and organizations of all sizes. Management Accounting Practice 2-4 reports on a study demonstrating that by using a single cost driver for determining reimbursable hospital inpatient costs, Medicare *subsidizes* private health insurers.

MANAGEMENT ACCOUNTING PRACTICE 2-4

Use of a Single Cost Driver Produces Medicare Subsidy to Private Health Insurers

At the beginning of a report on a research project that had surprising results, Hwang and Kirby observed that "hospitals must annually complete a Medicare Cost Report to be eligible for government reimbursement for services rendered to Medicare patients. This cost information is used in determining values of Medicare reimbursement parameters. This same cost information is also often used as the basis for determining the charges for privately insured patients. For inpatient care costs, Medicare reporting requires that all operating costs pertaining to patient care are allocated to patients based only on the number of patient-days. Thus Medicare cost reporting does not take account explicitly of the possibility of multiple cost drivers."

Hwang and Kirby noted that patient care costs can be attributed to at least two cost drivers: (1) the number of days a patient spends in the hospital and (2) the number of inpatients admitted. Patient-day costs include such "hotel" costs as meals, laundry, and basic nursing care, while admission costs include costs related to taking patients' history upon admission, preparing patients for surgery, intensively tending them immediately following surgery, housekeeping costs related to preparing rooms for new patients, and administrative costs related to medical coding and billing. Patient-days are a unit cost driver, and admissions are a batch cost driver.

Using publicly available information, Hwang and Kirby compared the results of current Medicare reimbursement procedures, which are based on a single unit level cost driver (patient-days) with the results that would be obtained if Medicare reimbursements were based on two cost drivers: a unit level driver (patient-days) and a batch level driver (number of admissions). Contrary to the general wisdom, which often suggests that Medicare payments do not cover hospital costs, Hwang's and Kirby's results suggest that Medicare is potentially overcharged for hospital patient care by between $66 million and $1.98 billion per year! The explanation is simple when the underlying data is analyzed. Medicare patients tend to be older and have a much longer average length of hospitalization than private insurance patients. Because Medicare reimbursements only consider patient-days, Medicare is charged for a disproportionately large share of the costs of admitting patients.

....

Based on: Yuhchang Hwang and Alison J. Kirby, "Distorted Medicare Reimbursements: The Effect of Cost Accounting Choices," *Journal of Management Accounting Research*, 6 (Fall 1994), pp. 128 - 143.

The above comparison of the total cost function based on the hierarchy of activity costs with the simple cost function used in CVP analysis provides some awareness of the limitations of CVP analysis. It is apparent that information far beyond that provided by CVP models is required to make specific decisions pertaining to products or services and the activities required to provide them to customers. Obtaining and analyzing this underlying information is the subject of the next several chapters.

SUMMARY

Cost estimation, the determination of previous or current relationships between activity and cost, is an important part of cost management. While costs known to display a variable or fixed pattern are readily estimated by interviews or analyzing available data, mixed costs are more difficult to estimate. Although we focused on the high-low method of cost estimation, the use of scatter diagrams and least-squares regression analysis was also considered. The use of scatter diagrams is especially useful in selecting representative high and low activity levels and in determining if costs can reasonably be approximated by a straight line. Least-squares regression analysis applies a mathematical technique to all available data and provides useful information on how well the cost estimating equation fits the historical data. In developing a cost estimation equation, particular care must be taken to ensure that the equation reflects normal operating conditions, that technology and prices are consistent, and that activity and costs are matched within each observation.

Equations for total costs, developed using the techniques discussed early in this chapter, are widely used in cost-volume-profit analysis. Because cost-volume-profit analysis provides a framework for discussing planning issues and organizing relevant data, it is widely used in the early stages of planning. In CVP analysis, volume refers to a single independent variable that is assumed to correlate with changes in revenues, costs, and profits. When applied to a single product, service, or event, where costs can logically be assumed to be driven by a single cost driver, the use of a single independent variable appears reasonable. Although CVP analysis is often used to develop an understanding of the overall operations of an organization or business segment, accuracy decreases as the scope of operations being analyzed increases.

With a broader scope of operations, it is seldom possible to represent the multitude of factors that drive costs for an organization or business segment by a single cost driver. To help understand and analyze the multitude of factors that drive costs, it is useful to organize activities into a hierarchy. A hierarchy for a manufacturing organization might consist of unit level, batch level, product level, and organization level activities. When important factors that drive costs are omitted from the cost estimating equation, the omitted costs will increase errors in cost estimation and cost prediction.

Appendix A: Determining Cost Coefficients Using Least-Squares Regression Analysis

Mathematicians have proven that the values of a and b can be found by this simultaneous solution of the following equations:

$$\Sigma XY = a\Sigma X + b\Sigma X^2 \qquad\qquad (2\text{-}1)$$
$$\Sigma Y = an + b\Sigma X \qquad\qquad (2\text{-}2)$$

where:

Σ = capital sigma, meaning the sum of (i.e.; ΣXY means the sum of the products of X and Y)

n = the number of observations

The above equations, called normal equations, are used to compute the constant term and slope that best meet the least-squares technique. This is done below.

Observation	Number of Shipments X	Packaging Costs Y	XY	X^2
1	6,000	$17,000	102,000,000	36,000,000
2	9,000	26,000	234,000,000	81,000,000
3	12,000	32,000	384,000,000	144,000,000
4	10,000	20,000	200,000,000	100,000,000
	$\Sigma X = 37,000$	$\Sigma Y = \$95,000$	$\Sigma XY = 920,000,000$	$\Sigma X^2 = 361,000,000$

Substituting these values into the normal equations, we obtain:

$$920,000,000 = a37,000 + b361,000,000 \qquad\qquad (2\text{-}3)$$
$$95,000 = a4 + b37,000 \qquad\qquad (2\text{-}4)$$

We can solve for b by eliminating a from an equation for the difference between equations 2-3 and 2-4. To do this, we must have the same coefficient for a in each equation. We can accomplish this in a number of ways, including multiplying equation 2-3 by 4 and multiplying equation 2-4 by 37,000:

$$3,680,000,000 = 148,000a + 1,444,000,000b \qquad\qquad (2\text{-}5)$$
$$3,515,000,000 = 148,000a + 1,369,000,000b \qquad\qquad (2\text{-}6)$$
$$\overline{165,000,000 = \qquad\qquad\qquad 75,000,000b} \qquad\qquad (2\text{-}7)$$

Equation 2-7 is computed as equation 2-5 minus equation 2-6. Solving for b in equation 2-7 and then solving for a by substituting the value of b in equation 2-5 or 2-6, we obtain:

$$b = \$2.20$$

$$a = \$3,400$$

APPENDIX B: LEAST-SQUARES REGRESSION ANALYSIS USING A COMPUTER SPREADSHEET

X	Y	
6000	17000	This data was entered into the computer and identified as the X range and the Y range.
9000	26000	
12000	32000	
10000	20000	

Regression Output:

Constant	3400	This informa-tion was calculated by the spreadsheet program. Each item is briefly described below.
Std Err of Y Est	4582.576	
R-Squared	0.683616	
No. of Observations	4	
Degrees of Freedom	2	
X Coefficient	2.2	
Std Err of Coef.	1.058301	

Constant—the value of a. Within the range of normal operations, the monthly fixed costs of operating the packaging department are $3,400.

Standard error of Y estimate (Std Err of Y Est.)—a measure of the dispersion of actual values around the trend. If a value of Y is computed using the estimating equation, mathematicians have determined that under certain circumstances, there is a 68 percent probability that the true value of Y will be equal to the computed value ± the standard error of the Y estimate. If we were interested in costs for a month when there were 10,000 shipments, the estimated value is $25,400 ($3,400 + $2.20[10,000]), and there is a 68 percent probability that the actual value of Y is between $25,400 ± $4,583.576.

Coefficient of determination (R-Squared)—a measure of the percent of variation in the dependent variable (such as total cost) that is explained by variations in the independent variable (such as total shipments) when the least-squares estimation equation is used. Statisticians often refer to the coefficient of determination as R-squared and represent it as R^2. The coefficient of determination can take on values between zero and plus 1, with values close to zero suggesting that the equation is not very useful and values close to 1 indicating that the equation explains a large percent of the variation in the dependent variable. In this case, 68.3616 percent of the variation in monthly packing department costs is explained by the variation in the number of shipments.

No. of observations—simply the number of paired values used in computations.

Degrees of freedom—as demonstrated using the high-low method, two observations are required to compute two coefficients: a and b. The degrees of freedom refers to the number of extra observations.

X coefficient—the value of b. Within the range of normal observations, this is $2.20 per package.

Standard error of X coefficient (Std Err of Coef.)—A measure of the dispersion of actual values of the X coefficient around the computed value. Mathematicians have determined that under certain circumstances, there is a 68 percent probability that the true value of X will be equal to the computed value ± the standard error of the X coefficient. This is useful if we are particularly interested in estimating the variable cost per shipment. There is a 68 percent probability that the actual value of b, the variable cost, is between $2.20 ± $1.058301.

SUGGESTED READINGS

Cooper, Robin. "Cost Classification in Unit-Based and Activity-Based Manufacturing Cost Systems," *The Journal of Cost Management* (Fall 1990), pp. 4-14.

Cooper, Robin, and Robert S. Kaplan. "Profit Priorities from Activity-Based Costing," *Harvard Business Review* (May-June 1991), pp. 130-135.

Foster, George, and Mahendra Gupta. "Marketing, Cost Management and Management Accounting," *Journal of Management Accounting Research* (Fall 1994), pp. 43-77.

REVIEW PROBLEMS

2-1 Estimating Cost Behavior and Predicting Future Costs

Dan's Submarine Sandwich Shop reported the following results for April and May 19X2:

	April	May
Unit sales	2,100	2,700
Cost of food sold	$1,575	$2,025
Wages and salaries	1,525	1,675
Rent on building	1,500	1,500
Depreciation on equipment	200	200
Utilities	710	770
Supplies	225	255
Miscellaneous	113	131
Total	$5,848	$6,556

Required:
(a) Identify each cost as being fixed, variable, or mixed.
(b) Using the high-low method, develop an equation for the cost of food, wages and salaries, rent on building, and total monthly costs.
(c) Predict total costs for monthly volumes of 1,000 and 2,000 units.

(d) Predict the average cost per unit at monthly volumes of 1,000 and 2,000 units and explain why the average costs differ at these two volumes.

The solution to the review problem is found at the end of Chapter 2 assignment material. To maximize your learning, you should make a serious attempt to develop a written solution to the review problem before looking at the solution. If there are errors in your solution, you should then attempt to determine the causes of the errors.

2-2 Cost-Volume-Profit Analysis

The Memorabilia Cup Company produces keepsake 16-ounce beverage containers for educational institutions. Memorabilia sells the cups for $40 per box of 50 containers. Variable and fixed costs are as follows:

Variable Costs per Box			Fixed Costs per Month	
Manufacturing:			Manufacturing overhead	$15,000
Direct materials	$15		Selling and administrative	10,000
Direct labor	3		Total	$25,000
Manufacturing overhead	10	$28		
Selling and administrative		2		
Total		$30		

In September 20X3, Memorabilia produced and sold 3,000 boxes of beverage containers.

Required:

(a) Prepare a contribution income statement for September 20X3.
(b) Prepare a cost-volume-profit graph with unit sales as the independent variable. Label the revenue line, total costs line, fixed costs line, loss area, profit area, and break-even point. The recommended scale for the horizontal axis is 0 to 5,000 units, and the recommended scale for the vertical axis is $0 to $200,000.
(c) Determine Memorabilia's unit contribution margin and contribution margin ratio.
(d) Determine Memorabilia's monthly break-even point in units.
(e) Determine the monthly dollar sales required to produce a monthly profit of $5,000. Ignore taxes.
(f) Assuming Memorabilia is subject to a 40 percent income tax, determine the monthly unit sales required to produce a monthly after-tax profit of $4,500.

The solution to the review problem is found at the end of Chapter 2 assignment material. To maximize your learning, you should make a serious attempt to develop a written solution to the review problem before looking at the solution. If there are errors in your solution, you should then attempt to determine the causes of the errors.

KEY TERMS

Batch level activity—an activity performed for each batch of product produced.

Break-even point—the unit or dollar sales volume where total revenues equal total costs.

Coefficient of determination (R_2)—a measure of the percent of variation in the dependent variable that is explained by variations in the independent variable when the least-squares estimation equation is used.

Contribution income statement—an income statement where costs are classified according to behavior as variable or fixed and the contribution margin that goes toward covering fixed costs and providing a profit is emphasized.

Contribution margin—the difference between total revenues and total variable costs that goes toward covering fixed costs and providing a profit.

Contribution margin ratio—the portion of each dollar of sales revenue contributed toward covering fixed costs and earning a profit.

Cost estimation—the determination of previous or current relationships between activity and cost.

Cost prediction—the forecasting of future costs.

Cost-volume-profit analysis—a technique used to examine the relationships among total volume of some independent variable, total costs, total revenues, and profits during a time period.

Cost-volume-profit graph—an illustration of the relationships among activity volume, total revenues, total costs, and profits.

Degree of operating leverage—a measure of operating leverage, computed as the contribution margin divided by income before taxes.

Direct labor—wages earned by production employees for the time they spend working on the conversion of raw materials into finished goods.

Direct materials—the cost of the primary raw materials converted into finished goods.

Facility level activity—an activity performed to maintain general manufacturing capabilities.

Fixed manufacturing overhead—all fixed costs associated with converting raw materials into finished goods.

Fixed selling and administrative costs—all fixed costs other than those directly associated with converting raw materials into finished goods.

High-low method of cost estimation—utilizes data from two time periods, a representative high activity period and a representative low activity period, to estimate fixed and variable costs.

Least-squares regression analysis—uses a mathematical technique to fit a cost estimating equation to the observed data in a manner that minimizes the sum of the vertical squared estimating errors between the estimated and actual costs at each observation.

Margin of safety—the amount by which actual or planned sales exceed the break-even point.

Operating leverage—refers to the extent that an organization's costs are fixed.

Product level activity—an activity performed to support the production of each different type of product.

Profit-volume graph—illustrates the relationship between volume and profits; it does not show revenues and costs.

Sales mix—the relative portion of unit or dollar sales derived from each product or service.

Scatter diagram—a graph of past activity and cost data, with individual observations represented by dots.

Sensitivity analysis—the study of the responsiveness of a model to changes in one or more of its independent variables.

Unit contribution margin—the difference between the selling price and the unit variable costs.

Unit level activity—an activity performed for each unit of product produced.

Variable cost ratio—variable costs as a portion of sales revenue.

Variable manufacturing overhead—all variable costs, except direct labor and direct materials, associated with converting raw materials into finished goods.

Variable selling and administrative costs—all variable costs other than those directly associated with converting raw materials into finished goods.

REVIEW QUESTIONS

2-1

How are variable and fixed costs determined using the high-low method of cost estimation?

2-2

Distinguish between cost estimation and cost prediction.

2-3

Why is a scatter diagram helpful when used in conjunction with other methods of cost estimation?

2-4

Identify two advantages of least-squares regression analysis as a cost estimation technique.

2-5

What is cost-volume-profit analysis and when is it particularly useful?

2-6

When is the use of a single independent variable in cost-volume-profit analysis most appropriate?

2-7

What is the unit contribution margin? How is it used in computing the unit break-even point?

2-8

How does a profit-volume graph differ from a cost-volume-profit graph? When is a profit-volume graph most likely to be used?

2-9

What is the impact of income taxes on the sales volume required to earn a desired after-tax profit?

2-10

What categories of cost drivers are and are not considered in cost-volume-profit analysis? How do the excluded categories affect cost-volume-profit analysis?

2-11

For a single product, distinguish among the unit level, batch level, and product level activities found in a manufacturing facility.

2-12

What is the effect of changes in the mix of cost drivers on the accuracy of cost-volume-profit models that contain only one independent variable?

EXERCISES

2-1 High-Low Cost Estimation

Jack's Taxi Company has the following information available about fleet miles and operating costs:

Year	Miles	Operating Costs
19X3	556,000	$115,060
19X4	684,000	132,340

Required:

Use the high-low method to develop a cost estimating equation for total annual operating costs.

2-2 Scatter Diagrams and High-Low Cost Estimation

Presented are information on the number of sales orders received and order processing costs:

Month	Sales Orders	Order Processing Costs
1	3,000	$40,000
2	1,500	28,000
3	4,000	65,000
4	2,800	39,000
5	2,300	32,000
6	1,000	20,000
7	2,000	30,000

Required:
(a) Use information from the high- and low-volume months to develop a cost estimating equation for monthly order processing costs.
(b) Plot the data on a scatter diagram. Using the information from *representative* high- and low-volume months, develop a cost estimating equation for monthly production costs.
(c) What factors might have caused the difference in the equations developed for requirements (a) and (b)?

2-3 Scatter Diagrams and High-Low Cost Estimation

From April 1 through October 31, the Central County Highway Department hires temporary employees to mow and clean the right of way along county roads. The County Road Commissioner has asked you to help her in determining the variable labor cost of mowing and cleaning a mile of road. The following information is available regarding 19X5 operations:

Month	Miles Mowed and Cleaned	Labor Costs
April	350	$7,500
May	300	7,000
June	400	8,500
July	250	5,000
August	375	8,000
September	200	4,500
October	100	4,300

Required:
(a) Use the information from the high- and low-volume months to develop a cost estimating equation for monthly labor costs.
(b) Plot the data on a scatter diagram. Using the information from *representative* high- and low-volume months, develop a cost estimating equation for monthly labor costs.
(c) What factors might have caused the difference in the equations developed for requirements (a) and (b)?
(d) Adjust the equation developed in requirement (b) to incorporate the effect of an anticipated 7 percent increase in wages.

2-4 Cost Behavior Analysis in a Restaurant: High-Low Cost Estimation

The Pizza House Restaurant has the following information available regarding costs at representative levels of monthly sales:

	Monthly Sales in Units		
	5,000	8,000	10,000
Cost of food sold	$ 5,250	$ 8,400	$10,500
Wages and fringe benefits	4,250	4,400	4,500
Fees paid delivery help	1,250	2,000	2,500
Rent on building	1,200	1,200	1,200
Depreciation on equipment	300	300	300
Utilities	500	560	600
Supplies (soap, floor wax, etc.)	150	180	200
Administrative costs	1,300	1,300	1,300
Total	$14,200	$18,340	$21,100

Required:
(a) Identify each cost as being variable, fixed, or mixed.
(b) Use the high-low method to develop a schedule identifying the amount of each cost that is fixed per month or variable per unit. Total the amounts under each category to develop an equation for total monthly costs.
(c) Predict total costs for a monthly sales volume of 9,500 units.

2-5 Developing an Equation from Average Costs
The Dog House is a pet hotel located on the outskirts of town. In March, when dog- (occupancy) days were at an annual low of 500, the average cost per dog-day was $18.50. In July, when dog-days were at a capacity level of 3,100, the average cost per dog-day was $5.50.

Required:
(a) Develop an equation for *monthly* operating costs.
(b) Determine the average cost per dog-day at an annual volume of 24,000 dog-days.

2-6 Selecting an Independent Variable: Scatter Diagrams
Valley Production Company produces backpacks that are sold to sporting goods stores throughout the Rocky Mountains. Presented is information on production costs and inventory changes for five recent months:

	January	February	March	April	May
Finished goods inventory in units:					
Beginning	30,000	40,000	50,000	30,000	60,000
Manufactured	60,000	90,000	80,000	90,000	100,000
Available	90,000	130,000	130,000	120,000	160,000
Sold	- 50,000	- 80,000	- 100,000	- 60,000	- 120,000
Ending	40,000	50,000	30,000	60,000	40,000
Manufacturing costs	$300,000	$500,000	$450,000	$450,000	$550,000

Required:
(a) With the aid of scatter diagrams, determine whether units sold or units manufactured is a better predictor of manufacturing costs.

(b) Prepare an explanation for your answer to requirement (a).
(c) Which independent variable, units sold or units manufactured, should be a better predictor of selling costs? Why?

2-7 Selecting a Basis for Predicting Shipping Expenses: Requires Spread sheet Program

The Tyson Company assembles and sells computer boards in western Pennsylvania. In an effort to improve the planning and control of shipping expenses, management is trying to determine which of three variables—units shipped, weight shipped, or sales value of units shipped—has the closest relationship with shipping expenses. The following information is available:

Month	Units Shipped	Weight Shipped (lbs.)	Sales Value of Units Shipped	Shipping Expenses
May	3,000	6,200	$50,000	$2,500
June	5,000	8,000	55,000	3,500
July	4,000	8,100	40,000	3,000
August	7,000	10,000	57,000	5,000
September	6,000	7,000	70,000	4,000
October	4,500	8,000	80,000	3,800

Required:

(a) With the aid of a spreadsheet program, determine whether units shipped, weight shipped, or sales value of units shipped has the closest relationship with shipping expenses.
(b) Using the independent variable that appears to have the closest relationship to shipping expense, develop a cost estimating equation for total monthly shipping expenses.
(c) Use the equation developed in requirement (b) to predict total shipping expenses in a month when 5,000 units, weighing 7,000 lbs., with a total sales value of $57,000 are shipped.

2-8 Contribution Income Statement and Cost-Volume-Profit Graph

The Alberta Company produces a product that is sold for $50 per unit. Variable and fixed costs are shown below:

Variable Costs per Unit			Fixed Costs per Month	
Manufacturing:			Factory overhead	$40,000
Direct materials	$ 8		Selling and administrative	20,000
Direct labor	12		Total	$60,000
Factory overhead	10	$30		
Selling and administrative		5		
Total		$35		

The company produced and sold 6,000 units during May 19X3. There were no beginning or ending inventories.

Required:

(a) Prepare a contribution income statement for May.

(b) Prepare a cost-volume-profit graph. Label the horizontal axis in units with a maximum value of 8,000. Label the vertical axis in dollars with a maximum value of $350,000. Draw a vertical line on the graph for the current, 6,000 unit sales level and provide labels for total variable costs, total fixed costs, and total profits at 6,000 units.

2-9 Contribution Margin Concepts

The following information is taken from the 19X5 records of the Duke Art Shop:

	Fixed	Variable	
Sales			$800,000
Costs:			
Goods sold		$300,000	
Labor	$160,000	60,000	
Supplies	2,000	5,000	
Utilities	12,000	3,000	
Rent	24,000	—	
Advertising	6,000	2,000	
Miscellaneous	6,000	10,000	
Total costs	$210,000	$380,000	- 590,000
Net income			$210,000

Required:

(a) Determine the annual break-even dollar sales volume.
(b) Determine the current margin of safety in dollars.
(c) Prepare a cost-volume-profit graph for the Duke Art Shop. Label both axes in dollars with maximum values of $1,000,000. Draw a vertical line on the graph for the current, $800,000 sales level and provide labels for total variable costs, total fixed costs, and total profits at $800,000 sales.
(d) What is the annual break-even dollar sales volume if management makes a decision that increases fixed costs by $52,500?

2-10 Cost-Volume-Profit Graph: Identification and Sensitivity Analysis

Presented is a typical cost-volume-profit graph.

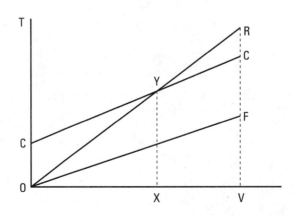

Required:
(a) Identify each of the following:
    (1) Line *OF*
    (2) Line *OR*
    (3) Line *CC*
    (4) The difference between lines *OF* and *OV*
    (5) The difference between lines *CC* and *OF*
    (6) The difference between lines *CC* and *OV*
    (7) The difference between lines *OR* and *OF*
    (8) Point *X*
    (9) Area *CYO*
    (10) Area *RCY*
(b) Indicate the effect of each of the following independent events on lines *CC*, *OR*, and the break-even point:
    (1) A decrease in fixed costs
    (2) An increase in unit selling price
    (3) An increase in the variable costs per unit
    (4) An increase in fixed costs and a decrease in the unit selling price
    (5) A decrease in fixed costs and a decrease in the unit variable costs

2-11 Profit-Volume Graph: Identification and Sensitivity Analysis

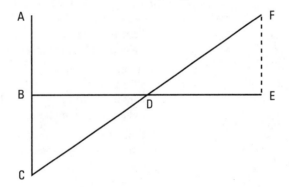

Required:
(a) Identify each of the following:

(1) Area *BDC*   (4) Line *AC*
(2) Area *DEF*   (5) Line *BC*
(3) Point *D*   (6) Line *EF*

(b) Indicate the effect of each of the following on line *CF* and the break-even point:
    (1) An increase in the unit selling price
    (2) An increase in the variable costs per unit
    (3) A decrease in fixed costs
    (4) An increase in fixed costs and a decrease in the unit selling price
    (5) A decrease in fixed costs and an increase in the variable costs per unit

2-12 Preparing Cost-Volume-Profit and Profit-Volume Graphs

Little Nero's Pizza Shop has the following monthly revenue and cost functions:

$$\text{Total revenues} = \$6.00X$$
$$\text{Total costs} = \$9,000 + \$1.50X$$

Required:

(a) Prepare a graph, similar to that in Exhibit 2-5, illustrating Little Nero's cost-volume-profit relationships. The vertical axis should vary between $0 and $18,000, with increments of $3,000. The horizontal axis should vary between 0 units and 3,000 units, with increments of 1,000 units.

(b) Prepare a graph, similar to that in Exhibit 2-6, illustrating Little Nero's profit-volume relationships. The horizontal axis should vary between 0 units and 3,000 units, with increments of 1,000 units.

(c) When is it most appropriate to use a profit-volume graph?

2-13 Profit Planning with Taxes

In 19X5, the Fenwick Processing Company had the following income statement:

Sales		$950,000
Variable costs:		
Cost of goods sold	$420,000	
Selling and administrative	150,000	- 570,000
Contribution margin		$380,000
Fixed costs:		
Factory overhead	$110,000	
Selling and administrative	80,000	- 190,000
Net income before taxes		$190,000
Income taxes (36 percent)		- 68,400
Net income		$121,600

Required:

(a) Determine the 19X5 break-even point in sales dollars.

(b) Determine the 19X5 margin of safety in sales dollars.

(c) What is the break-even point in sales dollars if management makes a decision that increases fixed costs by $50,000?

(d) What dollar sales volume is required to provide an after-tax net income of $200,000? Assume fixed costs are $190,000.

(e) Prepare an abbreviated contribution income statement to verify that the solution to requirement (d) will provide the desired after-tax income.

2-14 Not-for-Profit Applications

Determine the solution to each of the following independent cases:

(a) Lakeside College has annual fixed operating costs of $5,000,000 and variable operating costs of $1,000 per student. Tuition is $4,000 per student for the academic year. The projected enrollment for the coming year is 1,500 students. Expected revenues from endowments and federal and state grants are $250,000. Determine the amount Lakeside must obtain from other sources.

(b) The Lakeside College Student Association is planning a fall concert. Expected costs of renting a hall, hiring a band, and so forth, are $30,000. Assuming 5,000 people attend the concert, determine the break-even price per ticket. How much will the association lose if this price is charged and only 4,250 tickets are sold?

(c) City Hospital has a contract with the city to provide indigent health care on an out-patient basis for $25 per visit. The patient will pay $5 of this amount, and the city will pay the balance of $20. Determine the amount the city will have to pay if the hospital has 10,000 patient visits.

(d) A civic organization is engaged in a fund-raising program. On Civic Sunday, it will sell newspapers at $1.25 each. The organization will pay $0.75 for each newspaper. Costs of the necessary permits, signs, and so forth, are $500. Determine the amount the organization will raise if 5,000 newspapers are sold.

(e) Christmas for the Needy is a civic organization that provides Christmas presents to disadvantaged children. The annual costs of this activity are $5,000, plus $10 per present. Determine the number of presents the organization can provide with $20,000.

2-15 Alternative Production Procedures and Operating Leverage

Candice Corporation has decided to introduce a new product. The new product can be manufactured by either a capital-intensive method or a labor-intensive method. The predicted manufacturing costs for each method are as follows:

	Capital-Intensive	Labor-Intensive
Direct materials per unit	$ 5.00	$ 5.60
Direct labor per unit	6.00	7.20
Variable manufacturing overhead per unit	3.00	4.80
Fixed manufacturing overhead per year	2,440,000	1,320,000

Candice's market research department has recommended an introductory unit sales price of $30. The incremental selling costs are predicted to be $500,000 per year, plus $2 per unit sold.

Required:
(a) Calculate the annual break-even point in units of the new product if Candice used the:
  (1) Capital-intensive manufacturing method.
  (2) Labor-intensive manufacturing method.
(b) Determine the annual unit volume at which Candice would be indifferent between the two manufacturing methods.

(c) In deciding which manufacturing method to use, you recommend that management consider operating leverage. Write a report to management that:
    (1) Explains operating leverage and the relationship between operating leverage and the volatility of earnings.
    (2) Illustrates the computation of operating leverage at a volume of 250,000 units.
    (3) Explains the difference in operating leverage.

(CMA Adapted)

2-16 Contribution Income Statement and Operating Leverage

The Alabama Berry Basket harvests early season strawberries for shipment throughout the eastern United States in late March. The strawberry farm is maintained by a permanent staff of 10 employees and a large number of seasonal workers who pick and pack the strawberries. The strawberries are sold in crates containing 100 individually packaged one-quart containers. Affixed to each one-quart container is the distinctive Alabama Berry Basket logo inviting buyers to "Enjoy the berry best strawberries in the world!" The selling price is $90 per crate, variable costs are $80 per crate, and fixed costs are $275,000 per year. In 19X8, Alabama Berry Basket sold 40,000 crates.

Required:
(a) Prepare a contribution income statement for the year ended December 31, 19X8.
(b) Determine Alabama Berry Basket's 19X8 operating leverage.
(c) Calculate the percentage change in profits if sales decrease by 10 percent.
(d) Management is considering the purchase of several berry-picking machines. This will increase annual fixed costs to $375,000, while reducing variable costs to $77.50 per crate. Calculate the effect this acquisition will have on operating leverage. Explain the change in operating leverage.

PROBLEMS

2-17 Cost-Volume-Profit Relationships: Missing Data

Supply the missing data in each independent case.

	Case 1	Case 2	Case 3	Case 4
Unit sales	1,000	800	?	?
Sales revenue	$20,000	?	?	$60,000
Variable cost per unit	$ 10	$ 1	$ 12	?
Contribution margin	?	$800	?	?
Fixed costs	$ 8,000	?	$80,000	?
Net income	?	$400	?	?
Unit contribution margin	?	?	?	$ 15
Break-even point (units)	?	?	4,000	2,000
Margin of safety (units)	?	?	300	1,000

2-18 Cost-Volume-Profit Relationships: Missing Data
Supply the missing data in each independent case.

	Case 1	Case 2	Case 3	Case 4
Sales revenue	$100,000	$80,000	?	?
Contribution margin	$ 60,000	?	$20,000	?
Fixed costs	$ 30,000	?	?	?
Net income	?	$15,000	$10,000	?
Variable cost ratio	?	0.25	?	0.20
Contribution margin ratio	?	?	0.40	?
Break-even point (dollars)	?	?	?	$ 25,000
Margin of safety (dollars)	?	?	?	$ 15,000

2-19 Profit Planning with Taxes
The Brown Manufacturing Company produces a product that is sold for $35 per unit. Variable and fixed costs are shown below:

Variable Costs per Unit		Fixed Costs per Year	
Manufacturing	$ 18	Manufacturing	$ 80,000
Selling and administrative	7	Selling and administrative	30,000
Total	$ 25	Total	$110,000

Last year, Brown manufactured and sold 20,000 units to obtain a net income after taxes of $49,500.

Required:
(a) Determine the tax rate Brown paid last year.
(b) What unit sales volume is required to provide an after-tax net income of $88,000?
(c) If Brown reduces the unit variable cost by $2.50 and increases fixed manufacturing costs by $20,000, what unit sales volume is required to provide an after-tax income of $88,000?
(d) What assumptions are made about taxable income and tax rates in requirements (a) through (c)?

2-20 High-Low Cost Estimation and Profit Planning
Presented are comparative 19X8 and 19X9 income statements for Montana Products, Inc.:

Montana Products, Inc.
Comparative Income Statements
For the Years Ending December 31, 19X8 and 19X9

	19X8	19X9
Unit sales	5,000	8,000
Sales revenue	$ 65,000	$ 104,000
Expenses	- 75,000	- 90,000
Net income (loss)	$(10,000)	$ 14,000

Required:

(a) Determine the break-even point in units.

(b) Determine the unit sales volume required to earn a profit of $10,000.

2-21 Break-Even Analysis in a Not-for-Profit Organization

Melford Hospital operates a general hospital but rents space to separately owned entities rendering specialized services such as pediatrics and psychiatric. Melford charges each separate entity for patients' services such as meals and laundry and for administrative services such as billings and collections. Space and bed rentals are fixed charges for the year, based on bed capacity rented to each entity.

Melford charged the following costs to Pediatrics for the year ended June 30, 19X2:

	Patient-Days (Variable)	Bed Capacity (Fixed)
Dietary	$ 600,000	
Janitorial		$ 70,000
Laundry	300,000	
Laboratory	450,000	
Pharmacy	350,000	
Repairs and maintenance		30,000
General and administrative		1,300,000
Rent		1,500,000
Billings and collections	300,000	
Total	$2,000,000	$2,900,000

In addition to the above charges from Melford Hospital, Pediatrics incurred the following personnel costs:

	Annual Salaries
Supervising nurses	$100,000
Nurses	200,000
Assistants	180,000
Total	$480,000

These salaries are fixed within the ranges of annual patient-days considered in this problem.

During the year ended June 30, 19X2, Pediatrics charged each patient $300 per day, had a capacity of 60 beds, and had revenues of $6,000,000 for 365 days. Pediatrics operated at 100 percent of capacity on 90 days during the year ended June 30, 19X2. It is estimated that during these 90 days, the demand exceeded 80 beds (Pediatrics' capacity is 60 beds). Melford has an additional 20 beds available for rent during the year ending June 30, 19X3. Such additional rental would proportionately increase Pediatrics' annual fixed charges based on bed capacity.

Required:

(a) Calculate the minimum number of patient-days required for Pediatrics to break even for the year ending June 30, 19X3, if additional beds are not rented. Patient demand is unknown, but assume that revenue per patient-day, cost per patient-day, cost per bed, and salary rates for the year ending June 30, 19X3, remain the same as for the year ended June 30, 19X2.

(b) Assume that patient demand, revenue per patient-day, cost per patient-day, cost per bed, and salary rates for the year ending June 30, 19X3, remain the same as for the year ended June 30, 19X2. Prepare a schedule of increases in revenue and increases in costs for the year ending June 30, 19X3, in order to determine the net increase or decrease in earnings from an additional 20 beds if Pediatrics rents this extra capacity from Melford.

(CPA Adapted)

2-22 Cost-Volume-Profit Analysis of Alternative Products

Siberian Ski Company recently expanded its manufacturing capacity to allow production of up to 15,000 pairs of cross-country skis of the Mountaineering model or the Touring model. The sales department assures management that it can sell between 9,000 and 13,000 of either product this year. Because the models are very similar, Siberian Ski will produce only one of the two models.

The following information was compiled by the accounting department:

| | Model | |
	Mountaineering	Touring
Selling price per unit	$88.00	$80.00
Variable costs per unit	$52.80	$52.80

Fixed costs will total $369,600 if the Mountaineering model is produced, but only $316,800 if the Touring model is produced. Siberian Ski Company is subject to a 40 percent income tax rate.

Required:

(a) Determine the contribution margin ratio of the Touring model.

(b) If Siberian Ski Company desires an after-tax net income of $24,000, how many pairs of Touring model skis will the company have to sell? Round answer to nearest unit.

(c) Determine the *unit* sales volume at which Siberian Ski Company would make the same before-tax profit or loss regardless of the ski model it decides to produce. Also determine the resulting before-tax profit or loss.

(d) Determine the *dollar* sales volume at which Siberian Ski Company would make the same before-tax profit or loss regardless of the ski model it decides to produce. Also determine the resulting before-tax profit or loss. *Hint:* Work with contribution margin ratios.

(e) What action should Siberian Ski Company take if the annual sales of either model were guaranteed to be at least 12,000 pairs? Why?

(f) Determine how much the unit variable costs of the Touring model would have to change before both models have the same break-even point in units. Round calculations to the nearest cent.

(g) Determine the new unit break-even point of the Touring skis if their variable costs per unit decrease by 10 percent and their fixed costs increase by 10 percent. Round answer to nearest unit.

(CMA Adapted)

2-23 Unit and Batch Cost Drivers

Fried Mania, a fast-food restaurant, serves fried chicken, fried fish, and french fries. The managers have estimated the costs of a batch of fried chicken for Fried Mania's all-you-can-eat Friday Fried Fiesta. Each batch must be 100 pieces. The chicken is precut by the chain headquarters and sent to the chain store in 10-piece bags. Each bag costs $3. Preparing a batch of 100 pieces of chicken with Fried Mania's special coating takes one employee two hours. The current wage rate is $4.50 an hour. Another cost driver is the cost of putting fresh oil into the fryers. New oil, costing $5, is used for each batch.

Required:
(a) Determine the cost of preparing one batch of 100 pieces.
(b) If management projects that it will sell 300 pieces of fried chicken, determine the total unit and batch costs.
(c) If management estimates the sales to be 350 pieces, determine the total costs.
(d) How much will the batch costs increase if the government raises the minimum wage to $5 an hour?
(e) If management decided to reduce the number of pieces in a batch to 50, determine the cost of preparing 350 pieces. Assume that the batch would take half as long to prepare and management wants to replace the oil after 50 pieces are cooked.
(f) Refer to your solutions to requirements (c) and (e). Would management be wise to reduce the batch size to 50?

2-24 Hierarchy of Activity Costs

Dolls Incorporated manufactures and sells two products: the Amanda Doll (A) and the Betsy Star Doll (B). The firm's activities have been analyzed and placed into a hierarchy of activity costs. Presented is information on activity cost drivers and costs per unit of cost driver at each activity level.

Activity Level	Activity Cost	Activity
Unit	$b_{11} = \$3$	X_{11} = A acquire direct materials
	$b_{12} = \$5$	X_{12} = B acquire direct materials
	$b_{13} = \$1$	X_{13} = A conversion
	$b_{14} = \$2$	X_{14} = B conversion
Batch level	$b_{21} = \$100$	X_{21} = A setup
	$b_{22} = \$150$	X_{22} = B setup
	$b_{23} = \$25$	X_{23} = A movement
	$b_{24} = \$25$	X_{24} = B movement
Product level	$b_{31} = \$10,000$	X_{31} = A advertising
	$b_{32} = \$15,000$	X_{32} = B advertising
Facility level	$b_{41} = \$5,000$	X_{41} = Maintenance
	$b_{42} = \$3,000$	X_{42} = Rent
	$b_{43} = \$7,000$	X_{43} = Administrative salaries

During August 19X8, Dolls Incorporated produced 10,000 units of product A and 5,000 units of product B.

During September of 19X8, Dolls Incorporated produced 15,000 units of product A and 10,000 units of product B. Production increased because the marketing staff had underestimated sales for the holiday season.

Each batch of product A and each batch of product B contain 1,000 units.

Required:

(a) Determine the total costs for each activity level and the total predicted costs for August.
(b) Determine the total costs for each activity level and the total predicted costs for September.

DISCUSSION QUESTIONS AND CASES

2-25 Negative Fixed Costs

"This is crazy!" exclaimed the production supervisor as he reviewed the work of his new assistant. "You and that dumb computer are telling me that my fixed costs are negative! Tell me, 'genius,' how did you get these negative fixed costs, and what am I supposed to do with them?"

Required:

Try to salvage the situation by explaining the meaning of the negative "fixed costs" and what can be done with them.

2-26 Significance of High R-Squared

Oliver Morris had always been suspicious of newfangled mathematical stuff, and the most recent suggestion of his new assistant merely confirmed his belief that schools are putting a lot of useless junk in students' heads. It seems that after an extensive analysis of historical data, the assistant suggested that pounds of scrap was the best basis of predicting manufacturing overhead.

In response to Mr. Morris's rage, the slightly intimidated assistant indicated that pounds of scrap had the highest coefficient of determination with manufacturing overhead of the 35 equations he tried.

Required:

Comment on Morris's reaction. Is it justified? Is it likely that pounds of scrap is a good basis for predicting manufacturing overhead? Is it a feasible basis for predicting manufacturing overhead?

2-27 Estimating Machine Repair Costs

In an attempt to determine the best basis for predicting machine repair costs, the production supervisor accumulated daily information on these costs and production over a one-month period. Applying simple regression analysis to the data, she obtained the following estimating equation:

$$Y = \$800 - \$2.601X$$

where:

$$Y = \text{total daily machine repair costs}$$
$$X = \text{daily production in units}$$

Because of the negative relationship between repair costs and production, she was somewhat skeptical of the results, even though the R-squared was a respectable 0.765.

Required:
(a) What is the most likely explanation of the negative variable costs?
(b) Suggest an alternative procedure for estimating machine repair costs that might prove more useful.

2-28 Ethics and Pressure to Improve Profit Plans

Art Conroy is the assistant controller of New City Muffler, Inc., a subsidiary of New City Automotive, which manufactures tail pipes, mufflers, and catalytic converters at several plants throughout North America. Because of downward pressure on selling prices, New City Muffler has had disappointing financial performance in recent years. Indeed, Art Conroy is aware of rumblings from corporate headquarters threatening to close the plant.

One of Art Conroy's responsibilities is to present the plant's financial plans for the coming year to the corporate officers and board of directors. In preparing for the presentation, Art was intrigued to note the focal point of the budget presentation was a profit-volume graph projecting an increase in profits and a reduction in the break-even point.

Curious as to how the improvement would be accomplished, Art ultimately ended up speaking with Paula Mitchell, the plant manager. Paula indicated that a planned increase in productivity would reduce variable costs and increase the contribution margin ratio.

When asked how the productivity increase would be accomplished, Paula became thoughtful. Finally, she made a vague reference to increasing the speed of the assembly line. Art commented that speeding up the assembly line could lead to labor problems because the speed of the line was set by union contract. Paula responded that she was afraid that if the speedup were opened to negotiation, the union would make a big "stink" that could result in the plant being closed. She indicated that the speedup was the "only way to save the plant, our jobs, and the jobs of all plant employees." Besides, she did not believe employees would notice a 2 or 3 percent increase in speed. Paula concluded the meeting observing that, "You need to emphasize the results we will accomplish next year, not the details of how we will accomplish those results. Top management does not want to be bored with details. If we accomplish what we set out in the budget, we will be in for a big bonus."

Required:
What advice do you have for Art Conroy?

2-29 Ethical Problem Uncovered by Cost Estimation

Mighty Mall Management Company owns and provides management services for several shopping centers. After 5 years with the company, Mike Moyer was recently promoted to the position of manager of X-Town, an 18-store mall on the fringe of a downtown area. When he accepted the assignment, Mike was told that he would only hold it for a couple of years because X-Town would likely be torn down and paved over to make way for a new sports stadium. Mike was also told that if he did well in this assignment, he would be in line for heading one of Mighty Mall's new 200-store operations currently in the planning stage.

While reviewing X-Town's financial records for the past few years, Mike observed that last year's oil consumption was up by 8 percent even though the number of heating degree days were down by 4 percent. Somewhat curious, Mike uncovered the following information:

- X-Town is heated by forced-air oil heat. The furnace is 5 years old and has been well maintained.
- Fuel oil is kept in four, 5,000-gallon underground oil tanks. The oil tanks were installed in 1968.
- Replacing the tanks would cost $80,000, assuming no pollution was found. If pollution was found, cleanup costs could go as high as $2,000,000, depending on how much oil leaked into the ground and how far it traveled.
- Replacing the tanks would also add further congestion to parking at X-Town.

Required:

What should Mike do?

2-30 Simple and Multiple Regression: Requires Spreadsheet Program

Wanda Sable is employed by a mail-order distributor and reconditions used tuner/amplifiers, tape decks, and compact disk players. Wanda is paid $8 per hour, plus an extra $4 per hour for work in excess of 40 hours per week.

The distributor just announced plans to outsource all reconditioning work. Because the distributor is pleased with the quality of Wanda's work, she has been asked to enter into a long-term contract to recondition used CD players at a rate of $25 per player, plus all parts. The distributor also offered to rent her all necessary equipment at a rate of $200 per month. She has been informed that she should plan on reconditioning as many CD players as she can handle, up to a maximum of 20 CD players per week.

Wanda has room in her basement to set up a work area, but she is unsure of the economics of accepting the contract, as opposed to working for a local Radio Stuff store at $6 per hour.

Data related to the time spent and the number of units of each type of electronic equipment Wanda has reconditioned in recent weeks is as follows:

Week	Tuner Amplifiers	Tape Decks	Compact Disk (CD) Players	Total Units	Total Hours
1	4	5	5	14	40
2	0	7	6	13	42
3	4	3	7	14	40
4	0	2	12	14	46
5	11	6	4	21	48
6	5	8	3	16	44
7	5	8	3	16	44
8	5	6	5	16	43
9	2	6	10	18	53
10	8	4	6	18	46
Total				160	446

Required:

What should Wanda do? Assume she wants to work an average of 40 hours per week.

2-31 Cost Estimation, CVP Analysis, and Hierarchy of Activity Costs
Presented are the 19X6 and 19X7 income statements of Regional Distribution, Inc.:

Regional Distribution, Inc.
Income Statements
For the Years Ending December 31, 19X6 and 19X7

	19X7	19X6
Sales	$5,520,000	$5,000,000
Expenses:		
Cost of goods sold	$4,140,000	$3,750,000
Shipping	215,400	200,000
Sales order processing	52,500	50,000
Customer relations	120,000	100,000
Depreciation	80,000	80,000
Administration	250,000	250,000
Total	- 4,857,900	- 4,430,000
Before-tax profit	$ 662,100	$ 570,000
Income taxes at 40 percent	- 264,840	- 228,000
After-tax profit	$ 397,260	$ 342,000

Required:
(a) Determine the following:
   (1) Regional Distribution's break-even point in sales dollars.
   (2) Anticipated after-tax profit at 19X8's budgeted sales of $6,000,000
   (3) The sales volume required to earn an after-tax profit of $480,000.
(b) In an effort to increase sales volume, Regional Distribution has been increasing its customer base. Management is concerned about the profitability of small orders and customers who only place one or two orders each year. Should Regional Distribution specify a minimum order size? If so, what should it be? What annual volume

is necessary to continue customers who only place one or two orders each year?

Before beginning, you acquire the following additional information:

Operating statistics:

	19X7	19X6
• Total customers	240	220
• Number of orders	2,100	2,000

Activity cost driver information:

- The cost of goods sold is driven by sales dollars, at the rate of 75 percent of sales.
- Shipping expenses are driven by sales dollars, at the rate of 2 percent of sales, and by the number of orders, at the rate of $50 per order.
- Sales order processing is driven by the number of sales orders.
- Customer relations is driven by the number of customers.
- Depreciation and administration are facility level costs.

(c) Reevaluate your answers to requirement (a). Under what circumstances will your previous answers be correct?

(d) Assume management's $6,000,000 sales forecast for 19X8 is based on the following assumptions:

- 340 total customers
- 2,750 total orders

Using activity cost hierarchy concepts, predict 19X8 after-tax profits.

SOLUTIONS TO REVIEW PROBLEMS

Review Problem 2-1

(a)

Fixed costs are easily identified. They are the same at each activity level. Variable and mixed costs are determined by dividing the total costs for an item at two activity levels by the corresponding units of activity. The quotients of variable cost items will be identical at both activity levels. The quotients of mixed costs will differ, being lower at the higher activity level because the fixed costs are being spread over a larger number of units.

Cost	Behavior
Cost of food sold	Variable
Wages and salaries	Mixed
Rent on building	Fixed
Depreciation on equipment	Fixed
Utilities	Mixed
Supplies	Mixed
Miscellaneous	Mixed

(b)

The cost of food sold was classified as a variable cost. Hence, the cost of food may be determined by dividing the total costs at either observation by the corresponding number of units.

$$b = \frac{\$1,575 \text{ total variable costs}}{2,100 \text{ units}}$$

$$= \underline{\underline{0.75X}}$$

Wages and salaries were previously classified as a mixed cost. Hence, the cost of wages and salaries is determined using the high-low method.

$$b = \frac{\$1,675 - \$1,525}{2,700 - 2,100}$$

$$= \underline{\underline{0.25X}}$$

$$a = \$1,525 \text{ total costs} - \$0.25(2,100) \text{ variable costs}$$

$$= \underline{\underline{\$1,000}}$$

Rent on building was classified as a fixed cost.

$$a = \underline{\underline{\$1,500}}$$

Total monthly costs most likely follow a mixed cost behavior pattern. Hence, they can be determined using the high-low method.

$$b = \frac{\$6,556 - \$5,848}{2,700 - 2,100}$$

$$b = \underline{\underline{\$1.18X}}$$

$$a = \$5,848 - \$1.18(2,100)$$

$$= \underline{\underline{\$3,370}}$$

Total costs = \$3,370 + \$1.18X

where:

$$X = \text{unit sales}$$

(c) and (d)

Volume	Total Costs	Average Cost per Unit
1,000	\$3,370 + \$1.18(1,000) = \$4,550	\$4,550/1,000 = \$4.55
2,000	\$3,370 + \$1.18(2,000) = \$5,730	\$5,730/2,000 = \$2.865

The average costs differ at 1,000 and 2,000 units because the fixed costs are being spread over a different number of units. The larger the number of units, the smaller the average fixed cost per unit.

Review Problem 2-2

(a)

Memorabilia Cup Company
Contribution Income Statement
For the Month of September 20X3

Sales (3,000 x $40)		$120,000
Less variable costs:		
Direct materials (3,000 x $15)	$45,000	
Direct labor (3,000 x $3)	9,000	
Manufacturing overhead (3,000 x $10)	30,000	
Selling and administrative (3,000 x $2)	6,000	- 90,000
Contribution margin		$ 30,000
Less fixed costs:		
Manufacturing overhead	$15,000	
Selling and administrative	10,000	- 25,000
Profit		$ 5,000

(b)

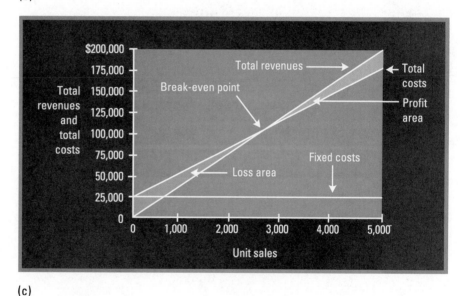

(c)

Selling price	$40 per unit
Variable costs	- 30 per unit
Contribution margin	$10 per unit

Contribution margin ratio = Unit contribution margin/Unit selling price
= $10/$40
= 0.25

(d)

Break-even point = Fixed costs/Unit contribution margin
= $25,000/$10
= 2,500 units

(e)

$$\text{Required dollar sales} = \frac{\text{(Fixed costs + Desired Profit)}}{\text{Contribution margin ratio}}$$

$$= (\$25{,}000 + \$5{,}000)/0.25$$

$$= \underline{\underline{\$120{,}000}}$$

(f)

$$\text{Desired before-tax profit} = \frac{\text{Desired after-tax profit}}{\text{(1.0 - tax rate)}}$$

$$= \$4{,}500/(1 - 0.40)$$

$$= \underline{\underline{\$7{,}500}}$$

$$\text{Required unit sales} = \frac{\text{(Fixed costs + Desired before-tax profit)}}{\text{Unit contribution margin}}$$

$$= (\$25{,}000 + 7{,}500)/\$10$$

$$= \underline{\underline{3{,}250 \text{ units}}}$$

After completing this chapter, you should be able to:

L O 1

Differentiate between relevant and irrelevant revenues and costs.

L O 2

Organize relevant costs in a manner that clearly indicates how they differ under decision alternatives.

L O 3

Discuss issues involved in predicting relevant costs.

L O 4

Apply differential analysis to a variety of decisions, including multiple changes in profit plans, whether to accept or reject a special order, whether to make or buy a product or service, and whether to sell a product or process it further.

L O 5

Determine how to allocate limited resources for the purpose of maximizing short-run profit.

RELEVANT COSTS AND DIFFERENTIAL COST ANALYSIS

Cost-volume-profit analysis was presented in Chapter 2 as a useful framework for discussing planning issues and organizing relevant data. Cost-volume-profit analysis is especially useful in the early stages of planning. The overview it provides of the relationships among revenues, costs, and volume helps managers avoid becoming lost in the details of individual decisions. Yet, despite the immense value of cost-volume-profit analysis, our previous discussion of the hierarchy of activity costs makes it clear that a sharper focus is needed to make specific decisions. This is particularly evident in multiple-product or multiple-service organizations for which it is difficult to develop a single CVP model. When evaluating alternate actions, managers should focus their attention on those costs and revenues that differ under alternative actions.

***The purpose of this chapter is to examine approaches to identifying and analyzing revenue and cost information for specific decisions.** Our emphasis will be on identifying **relevant costs**—that is, future costs that differ among competing decision alternatives—and distinguishing relevant costs from other costs that do not differ among competing decision alternatives. We will consider a number of frequently encountered decisions: multiple changes in profit plans, to accept or reject a special order, to acquire a component or service internally or externally, to sell a product or process it further, and how best to use limited capacity. These decision situations are not exhaustive; they only illustrate relevant cost concepts. Once you understand these concepts, you may apply them to a variety of decisions.*

To better focus on relevant cost concepts, the emphasis in this chapter is on decisions that only involve an analysis of activity cost drivers. In Chapters 4 through 6, we emphasize decisions affecting structural and organizational cost drivers. Although our focus in this chapter is on profit maximization, keep in mind that decisions should not be based solely on the criterion of profit maximization, especially short-run profit maximization. Decision makers must consider the long-run profit implications of decisions as well as legal, ethical, social, and other nonquantitative factors. These factors may lead management to select a course of action other than that selected by financial information alone.

IDENTIFYING RELEVANT COSTS

L 0 1

The key to differential cost analysis is to (1) identify the relevant costs (and revenues) that differ among competing decision alternatives and (2) organize them in a manner that clearly indicates how they differ under each alternative. Consider the following equipment replacement decision:

The Ace Welding Company manufactures frames for Mountain bicycles and Touring bicycles. Mountain bicycle frames have a unit selling price of $20, and Touring bicycle frames have a unit selling price of $15. Annual production and sales total 10,000 Mountain bicycle frames and 11,000 Touring bicycle frames. Each product is manufactured with separate equipment in a shared building. Activity cost information is as follows:

Activity Level	Mountain	Touring	Common
Unit level:			
Direct materials	$3.00 per unit	$2.50 per unit	
Conversion	5.00 per unit	3.50 per unit	
Selling and distribution	1.00 per unit	0.75 per unit	
Batch level:			
Inspection and adjustment	$500 per batch of 1,000 units	$400 per batch of 1,000 units	
Product level:			
Depreciation on welding machines	$15,000 per year	$12,000 per year	
Machine maintenance	$200 per month	$500 per six months	
Advertising	$5,000 per year	$4,500 per year	
Facility level:			
Administrative salaries			$65,000 per year
Building operations			23,000 per year
Building rent			24,000 per year

In the unit level costs listed above, **conversion costs** include all costs (direct labor and variable manufacturing overhead) required to convert raw materials into finished goods. Note that total unit activity costs follow a variable cost function (they increase in direct proportion to increases in activity), total batch activity costs follow a step cost function (they are fixed over a range of activity but differ between ranges of activity), and total product and total facility activity costs follow fixed cost functions (once plans are set for a time period, they do not vary with activity).

The Model I welding machine used in the manufacture of Mountain bicycle frames is 2 years old and has a remaining useful life of 4 years. It cost $90,000 when new and has an estimated salvage value of zero dollars at the end of its useful life. Its current book value (original cost less accumulated depreciation) is $60,000, but its current disposal value is only $35,000.

Management is evaluating the desirability of replacing the Model I welding machine with a new Model II welding machine. The new machine costs $80,000, has a useful life of 4 years, and a predicted salvage value of zero dollars at the end of its useful life. Though the new machine has the same productive capacity as the old machine, its operating costs would be lower because it would consume less electricity. Furthermore, because of a computer control system, the Model II machine will allow production of twice as many units between inspections and adjustments, and the cost of inspections and adjustments will be lower. Finally, the Model II machine requires only annual, rather than monthly, overhauls. Hence, machine maintenance costs will be significantly reduced. The new conversion, inspection and adjustment, and machine maintenance costs are predicted to be as follows:

Conversion costs	$4.00 per unit
Inspection and adjustment	$300 per batch of 2,000 units
Machine maintenance	$200 per year

All other costs and all revenues remain unchanged.

The decision at hand is either to keep the old Model I welding machine or to replace it with a new Model II welding machine. To assist management in making this decision, an analysis of differential costs and revenues should be prepared. Although the clearest presentation is one that contains only those costs and revenues that differ, the first objective of this chapter is to study the distinction between relevant and irrelevant items. To help accomplish this objective, a complete analysis of all costs and revenues under each alternative is presented in Exhibit 3-1. After evaluating the relevance of each item, a more focused analysis of relevant costs is prepared.

The first thing to notice about Exhibit 3-1 is that many costs and revenues are the same under each alternative. These items are not relevant to the replacement decision. The only relevant items are those that have an entry in the Difference column. For emphasis, the relevant costs are shaded.

Future Revenues May Be Relevant

Revenues, which are inflows of resources from the sale of goods and services,[1] are relevant if they differ between alternatives. In this example, revenues are not relevant because they are identical under each alternative. They would be relevant if the new machine had greater capacity that would be used or if management intended to change the unit selling price should it acquire the new machine.

1 The $35,000 disposal value of the Model I machine is an inflow of resources. However, revenues refer to resources from the sales of goods and services the organization is established to provide to customers in the normal course of business. We include the sale of the Model I machine under a separate category, "disposal and salvage values."

EXHIBIT 3-1: COMPLETE ANALYSIS OF ALL COSTS AND REVENUES

	Complete Analysis of Four-Year Totals		
	(1) Replace With New Model II Machine	(2) Keep Old Model I Machine	(1) - (2) Difference (Effect of Replacement on Income)
Sales:			
Mountain (10,000 units x $20 x 4 years)	$ 800,000	$ 800,000	
Touring (11,000 units x $15 x 4 years)	660,000	660,000	
Total	$1,460,000	$1,460,000	
Direct materials:			
Mountain (10,000 units x $3 x 4 years)	$ 120,000	$ 120,000	
Touring (11,000 units x $2.50 x 4 years)	110,000	110,000	
Conversion:			
Mountain, Model I (10,000 units x $5 x 4 years)		200,000	
Mountain, Model II (10,000 units x $4 x 4 years)	160,000		$40,000
Touring (11,000 units x $3.50 x 4 years)	154,000	154,000	
Selling and distribution:			
Mountain (10,000 units x $1 x 4 years)	40,000	40,000	
Touring (11,000 units x $0.75 x 4 years)	33,000	33,000	
Inspection and adjustment:			
Mountain, Model I (10* setups x $500 x 4 years)		20,000	
Mountain, Model II (5* setups x $300 x 4 years)	6,000		14,000
Touring (11** setups x $400 x 4 years)	17,600	17,600	
Depreciation, write-off, or disposal:			
Mountain, Model I, depreciation ($15,000 x 4 years) or write-off ($60,000 book value)	60,000	60,000	
Touring depreciation on welding machine ($12,000 x 4 years)	48,000	48,000	
Mountain, Model I, disposal value	(35,000)		35,000
Cost of Model II	80,000		(80,000)
Machine maintenance:			
Mountain, Model I ($200 x 12 months x 4 years)		9,600	
Mountain, Model II ($200 x 4 years)	800		8,800
Touring ($500 x 2 per year x 4 years)	4,000	4,000	
Advertising:			
Mountain ($5,000 x 4 years)	20,000	20,000	
Touring ($4,500 x 4 years)	18,000	18,000	
Administrative salaries ($65,000 x 4 years)	260,000	260,000	
Building operations ($23,000 x 4 years)	92,000	92,000	
Building rent ($24,000 x 4 years)	96,000	96,000	
Total costs	- 1,284,400	- 1,302,200	
Profit	$ 175,600	$ 157,800	$17,800

*Model I: 10,000 units / 1,000 units per batch
Model II: 10,000 units / 2,000 units per batch
**11,000 units / 1,000 units per batch

The keep-or-replace decision facing Ace's management might be called a **cost reduction proposal** because it is based on the assumption that the organization is committed to an activity and that management desires to minimize the cost of activities. Here, the alternatives are: (1) continue operating with the old machine or (2) replace with a new machine.

Although this approach is appropriate for many activities, managers of for-profit organizations should remember that they have another alternative; namely, discontinue operations. To simplify the analysis, managers normally do not consider the alternative to discontinue when operations appear to be profitable. However, if there is any doubt about an operation's profitability, this alternative should be considered. Because revenues will change if an operation is discontinued, revenues are relevant whenever this alternative is considered.

Outlay Costs May Be Relevant

Outlay costs are costs that require future expenditures of cash or other resources. Outlay costs that differ under the decision alternatives at hand are relevant; those that do not differ are irrelevant. It is a mistake to assume that variable costs are always relevant and fixed costs are always irrelevant or to assume that costs affected by unit activity drivers are relevant, while costs affected by other activity drivers are irrelevant. The relevant and the irrelevant outlay costs for Ace Welding Company's equipment replacement decision follows:

Relevant Outlay Costs	Irrelevant Outlay Costs
Mountain frame conversion costs	Mountain frame direct materials
Mountain frame inspection and adjustment costs	Mountain frame selling and distribution
Cost of new Model II machine	Mountain frame advertising
Mountain frame machine maintenance	Touring frame outlay costs
	Facility level outlay costs

Because unit level costs are variable and respond to changes in the level of activity, they are relevant when decision alternatives have different activity levels or different costs per unit of activity. Unit level costs are not relevant when decision alternatives have the same activity level and the same cost per unit of activity. In this example, while the level of activity was unchanged, there were changes in unit level activity costs. In this case, Mountain frame conversion costs are relevant because they are $5 per unit for Model I and $4 per unit for Model II.

Batch level activity costs are also relevant when decision alternatives have a different number of batches or different costs per batch. In this example, for Mountain bicycle frames, there was a change in both the number of batches and the inspection and adjustment cost per batch.

For the organization as a whole, product level activity costs are relevant if decision alternatives involve a different number of products or different costs per product. In this example, while there was no change in the number of products, there were changes in Mountain frame product level costs for machine maintenance. There was also a product level cash outlay to acquire the new Model II machine.

In the short run, facility level activity costs do not change in direct response to the number of units, batches, or products. Facility level costs are relevant, however, if management is contemplating an action that affects the availability of, or method of, performing facility level activities. In this example, there are no changes being considered for facility level activities. If, however, both Mountain and Touring bicycle frames were produced using the same machines and management was contemplating replacing these common machines, then there would be facility level costs involved in the replacement decision.

When a change involves several products, outlay costs associated with all involved products may be relevant. In this example, the machinery replacement decision only affects the production of Mountain bicycle frames. Hence, all unit, batch, and product outlay costs for Touring bicycle frames are irrelevant. While including them in the analysis does not change the bottom line in Exhibit 3-1, including them may distract attention from relevant costs and revenues.

Sunk Costs Are Never Relevant

Sunk costs result from past decisions that cannot be changed. Though the relevance of outlay costs is determined by the decision at hand, sunk costs (aside from possible tax consequences) are never relevant. The cost of the Model I machine is a historical cost, not a future cost. This historical cost, and the related depreciation, results from the past decision to acquire the old machine. Even though all the outlay costs discussed above would be relevant to a decision to continue or discontinue operations, the sunk cost of the Model I machine is not relevant even to this decision.

If management elects to keep the old machine, its book value will be depreciated over its remaining useful life of 4 years, whereas if management elects to replace the old machine, its book value will be written off when it is replaced. You can see the irrelevance of the Model I machine's historical cost in Exhibit 3-1, where the $60,000 does not differ between decision alternatives. Even if management elects to discontinue operations, the book value of the old machine must be written off in the accounting records.

Sunk Costs May Cause Ethical Dilemmas

Although the book value of the old machine has no economic significance, the accounting treatment of past costs can make it psychologically difficult for managers to regard them as irrelevant. If management replaces the old machine, an accounting loss from disposal of $25,000 will be recorded in the year of replacement:

Book value	$60,000
Disposal value	- 35,000
Loss on disposal	$25,000

The possibility of recording an accounting loss may place managers in an ethical dilemma. While, over a period of years, an action may be desirable from the viewpoint of the organization, in the short run choosing the action may result in an accounting loss. Fearing the loss will lead superiors to question his or her judgment, a manager might prefer using the old machine, with lower total profits over the four-year period, to replacing it and being forced to record a loss on disposal. Although this action may avoid raising troublesome questions in the near-term, the cumulative effect of many decisions of this nature will be harmful to the long-run economic health of the organization.

From an economic viewpoint, the analysis should focus on future costs and revenues that differ. The decision should not be influenced by sunk costs. Though there is no easy solution to this behavioral and ethical problem, managers and management accountants should be aware of its potential impact.

Disposal and Salvage Values

Revenues are inflows of resources from operations. The Ace Welding Company's revenues from the sale of Mountain and Touring bicycle frames were discussed above. The sale of fixed assets is also a source of resources. Because the sale of fixed assets is a nonoperating item, cash inflows obtained from these sales are discussed separately.

The disposal value of the Model I welding machine is a relevant cash inflow. It is obtained only if the replacement alternative is selected. Any salvage value available at the end of the useful life of either machine would also be relevant. A loss on disposal may have a favorable tax impact if the loss can be offset against taxable gains or taxable income. In this case, although the book value of the old asset remains irrelevant, the expected tax reduction would be relevant.

DIFFERENTIAL ANALYSIS OF RELEVANT COSTS

L O 2

Differential cost analysis is an approach to the analysis of relevant costs that focuses on the costs that differ under alternative actions. A differential analysis of relevant costs for the Ace Welding Company's equipment replacement decision is presented in Exhibit 3-2. Replacement provides a net advantage of $17,800 over the life of both machines.[2]

Assuming the organization is committed to providing a particular product or service, a differential analysis of relevant costs (such as the one in Exhibit 3-2) is preferred to a complete analysis of all costs and revenues (such as the one in Exhibit 3-1) for a number of reasons:

- Focusing only on those items that differ provides a clearer picture of the impact of the decision at hand. Management is less apt to be confused by a differential analysis than by an analysis that commingles relevant and irrelevant items.

_____

2 Our current objectives are to (1) distinguish between relevant and irrelevant costs and (2) demonstrate the advantages of analyzing only relevant costs. An analysis of long-term projects should also consider the time value of money. The time value of money is discussed in Chapter 6.

EXHIBIT 3-2: DIFFERENTIAL ANALYSIS OF RELEVANT COSTS

| | Differential Analysis of Four-Year Totals | | |
	(1) Replace with New Model II Machine	(2) Keep Old Model I Machine	(1) - (2) Difference (Effect of Replacement on Income)
Conversion:			
Mountain, Model I (10,000 units x $5 x 4 years)		$200,000	
Mountain, Model II (10,000 units x $4 x 4 years)	$160,000		$40,000
Inspection and adjustment:			
Mountain, Model I (10* setups x $500 x 4 years)		20,000	
Mountain, Model II (5* setups x $300 x 4 years)	6,000		14,000
Machine maintenance:			
Mountain, Model I ($200 x 12 months x 4 years)		9,600	
Mountain, Model II ($200 x 4 years)	800		8,800
Disposal of Model I	(35,000)		35,000
Cost of Model II	80,000		(80,000)
Total costs	$211,800	$229,600	$17,800
Advantage of replacement		$17,800	

*Model I: 10,000 units / 1,000 units per batch
 Model II: 10,000 units / 2,000 units per batch

- Because a differential analysis contains fewer items, it is easier and quicker to prepare.
- In complex situations, such as those encountered by multiple-product or multiple-plant firms, it is difficult to develop complete firm-wide statements to analyze all decision alternatives.

Before preparing a differential analysis, it is always desirable to reassess the organization's commitment to a product or service. This helps avoid "throwing good money after bad." If Ace Welding Company currently had large annual losses, acquiring the Model II machine would merely reduce total losses over the next four years by $17,800. In this case, a third alternative, discontinuing operations should be considered.

An advantage of a complete analysis of costs and revenues, such as that in Exhibit 3-1, is that it does disclose overall profitability, thereby helping management assess the desirability of continuing operations. Unfortunately, the analysis in Exhibit 3-1 does not distinguish between the profitability of Mountain and Touring bicycle frames. Perhaps, if there were ongoing losses, they are attributable to Touring rather than to Mountain frames. Then Ace's management might decide to acquire the new Model II machine but discontinue the sale of Touring frames. Segment analysis, which concerns the analysis of the profitability of a business segment such as a product or service, could be used to separately determine the profitability of Mountain and Touring frames. Segment analysis is considered in Chapter 9. For now, the key point to remember is that a differential analysis assumes a commitment to a product or service. When this commitment is justified, differential analysis is an efficient analytical tool. When this commitment is not justified, a more thorough approach, such as a complete analysis of all costs and revenues or a segment analysis, is required.

PREDICTING RELEVANT COSTS

L O 3

Information on relevant costs is almost always given in textbook examples and problems. Here the task is to (1) distinguish between relevant and irrelevant costs and (2) properly classify the relevant costs. In practice, the analyst would have the difficult job of obtaining the relevant cost information, which is a very time-consuming process that requires questioning, observing, and analyzing. Obviously, an understanding of relevant cost concepts is a prerequisite to obtaining relevant cost information. Simply stated, the analyst must know what to look for. This knowledge helps guide the search for the few pieces of relevant information contained in voluminous sets of data. Management Accounting Practice 3-1 discusses how credit card companies can help businesses measure travel costs, a prerequisite to controlling these costs.

MANAGEMENT ACCOUNTING PRACTICE 3-1

Before Controlling Travel Costs, It Is Necessary to Measure Them

Price Waterhouse (PW) is one of the largest accounting firms in the world. With over 100 offices and 10,000 employees in the United States making travel arrangements through 300 travel agencies, PW estimated that annual travel expenditures were approximately $30 million. A travel consultant predicted PW could reduce these costs by up to 20 percent, or $6 million, by developing uniform travel policies, working through a single travel agency, and negotiating contracts with hotel chains and rental car companies.

To successfully negotiate these contracts, management found that specific data were needed on dollars spent on particular types of services in particular locations. To obtain this information, PW turned to a national credit card company. By having all employee travel charged to a specific credit card, PW was able to obtain a detailed analysis of how and where travel dollars were spent.

The surprising outcome of the analysis of travel costs was that annual travel expenditures were between $40 and $50 million, rather than the $30 million previously estimated. Hence, the potential savings were $10 million, rather than $6 million. Realizing such savings could make PW more profitable and more competitive.

Based on a presentation by representatives of American Express and Carl E. Schwab, "Price Waterhouse's Experience," *Management Accounting* (August 1990), p. 37.

Predicting relevant costs may involve an examination of past cost trends. If one of the alternatives under consideration is to continue operations as in the past, the techniques discussed in Chapter 2 can be used to estimate past costs and to develop predictions of future costs. The predicted operating costs of the Model I welding machine would be developed in this manner.

It is more difficult to predict costs when technology changes. The substitution of the Model II for the Model I welding machine is an example of a technological change. Because the Model II machine is new, the Ace Welding Company's historical information is of limited value in predicting its operating costs. Cost predictions for the Model II machine must be deduced from information obtained from the manufacturer, other users, trade associations, publications, and engineers employed by Ace. Management should carefully evaluate the credibility of this information.

A **cost prediction error** is the difference between a predicted future cost and the actual amount of the cost when, or if, it is incurred. Because cost predictions may be inaccurate, management should determine how sensitive a decision is to prediction errors. This would include, for example, determining how much a prediction could change before affecting the decision.

The Ace Welding Company's new machine has a net advantage of $17,800 over its 4-year life; hence, cost predictions could increase by $17,800 before affecting the decision. Given the size of the relevant operating costs, a $17,800 prediction error seems unlikely. If the net advantage of the new machine were smaller, say $5,000, management might want to consider the likelihood of a $5,000 prediction error.

APPLICATIONS OF DIFFERENTIAL ANALYSIS

LO 4

Differential analysis is used to provide information for a variety of planning and decision situations. Illustrated in this section are some of the more frequently encountered applications of differential analysis. To focus on differential analysis concepts and to avoid the complexities introduced by multiple cost drivers, we will use a relatively simple example of a company that produces one product on a continuous basis with all output sold to a single customer. Because of continuous production, there are no batch level costs; and because there is only one product, there is no need to distinguish among product, customer, or facility costs. From the viewpoint of our single-product, single-customer firm, all costs can be classified as either (1) unit level costs that vary with units produced and sold or (2) facility level costs that are fixed in the short run.

Multiple Changes in Profit Plans

Mind Trek, Limited, located in Lancaster, England, manufactures an electronic game sold to distributors for £22 per unit (a pound, represented by the symbol £, is the basic unit of currency of the United Kingdom). Variable costs per unit and fixed costs per month are as follows:

Variable Costs per Unit		Fixed Costs per Month	
Direct materials	£ 5	Manufacturing overhead	£30,000
Direct labor	3	Selling and administrative	15,000
Manufacturing overhead	2	Total	£45,000
Selling	2		
Total	£12		

The unit contribution margin (UCM) is £10 (£22 selling price - £12 variable costs). Mind Trek's April 19X6 contribution income statement is presented in Exhibit 3-3. The April 19X6 operations are typical. Monthly production and sales average 5,000 units, and monthly profits average $5,000.

Management wants to know the effect on monthly profits of the following three mutually exclusive alternative actions:

1. Increasing the monthly advertising budget by £4,000, which should result in a 1,000 unit increase in monthly sales.
2. Increasing the unit selling price by £3, which should result in a 2,000 unit decrease in monthly sales.
3. Decreasing the unit selling price by £2, which should result in a 2,000 unit increase in monthly sales. However, because of capacity constraints, the last 1,000 units would be produced during overtime, when the direct labor costs increase by £1 per unit.

It is possible to develop contribution income statements for each alternative and then determine the profit impact of the proposed change by comparing the new income with the current income. A more direct approach is to use differential analysis and focus only on those items that differ under each alternative:

EXHIBIT 3-3: CONTRIBUTION INCOME STATEMENT

Mind Trek, Limited
Contribution Income Statement
For the Month of April 19X6

Sales (5,000 units x £22)		£110,000
Less variable costs:		
Direct materials (5,000 units x £5)	£25,000	
Direct labor (5,000 units x £3)	15,000	
Manufacturing overhead (5,000 units x £2)	10,000	
Selling and administrative (5,000 units x £2)	10,000	- 60,000
Contribution margin		£ 50,000
Less fixed costs:		
Manufacturing overhead	£30,000	
Selling and administrative	15,000	- 45,000
Profit		£ 5,000

Alternative 1:

Profit increase from increased sales	
(1,000 additional unit sales x £10 UCM)	£ 10,000
Profit decrease from increased advertising	(4,000)
Increase in monthly profit	£ 6,000

Alternative 2:

Profit decrease from reduced sales if there were no changes in prices or costs	
(2,000 lost unit sales x £10 UCM)	£(20,000)
Profit increase from increased selling price ([5,000 old unit sales - 2,000 lost unit sales] x £3 increase in unit selling price)	9,000
Decrease in monthly profit	£(11,000)

Alternative 3:

Profit increase from increased sales if there were no changes in prices or costs	
(2,000 increased unit sales x £10 UCM)	£ 20,000
Profit decrease from reduced selling price of all units ([5,000 old unit sales + 2,000 additional unit sales] x £2 decrease in unit selling price)	(14,000)
Profit decrease from increased direct labor costs of the last 1,000 units (1,000 units x £1 increase in unit direct labor costs)	(1,000)
Increase in monthly profit	£ 5,000

Alternative 2 is undesirable because it would result in a decrease in monthly profit. Because Alternative 1 results in a larger increase in monthly profit, it is preferred to Alternative 3.

Special Orders

Assume a Brazilian distributor offered to place a special, one-time order for 1,000 units next month at a reduced price of £12 per unit. The distributor will pay all packing and transportation costs, and there will be no unit or batch level selling or administrative expenses associated with the order. Mind Trek has sufficient production capacity to produce the additional units without reducing sales to other customers. Management desires to know the profit impact of accepting the order. The following analysis focuses on those costs and revenues that will differ if the order is accepted:

Increase in revenues (1,000 units x £12)		£12,000
Increase in costs:		
Direct materials (1,000 units x £5)	£5,000	
Direct labor (1,000 units x £3)	3,000	
Variable manufacturing overhead (1,000 units x £2)	2,000	- 10,000
Increase in profits		£ 2,000

Accepting the order will result in a profit increase of £2,000.

If management were unaware of relevant cost concepts, they might be tempted to compare the special order price to some average unit cost information developed from accounting reports. Based on Mind Trek's 19X6 contribution income statement in Exhibit 3-3, the average cost of all manufacturing, selling, and administrative expenses was £21 per unit:

Variable costs:	
Direct materials (5,000 units x £5)	£ 25,000
Direct labor (5,000 units x £3)	15,000
Manufacturing overhead (5,000 units x £2)	10,000
Selling and administrative (5,000 units x £2)	10,000
Fixed costs:	
Manufacturing overhead	30,000
Selling and administrative	15,000
Total costs	£105,000
Unit production and sales	÷ 5,000
Average unit cost of manufacturing, selling, and administration	£ 21

Comparing the special order price of £12 per unit to the average unit cost of £21, management might conclude the order would result in a loss of £9 per unit.

It is apparent that the £21 figure encompasses variable costs of £12 per unit (including irrelevant costs for selling and administration of £2 per unit) and irrelevant fixed costs of £45,000 spread over 5,000 units. But remember that management may not have detailed cost information. To obtain appropriate information for decision-making purposes, management must ask their accounting staff for the specific information needed. Different configurations of cost information are provided for different purposes. In the absence of special instructions, the accounting staff might supply some average cost information.

Importance of Time Span

The special order is a one-time order for 1,000 units that will use current excess capacity. Because no special setups or equipment are required to produce the order, it is appropriate to consider only variable costs in computing the order's profitability.

But what if the Brazilian distributor wanted Mind Trek to sign a multiyear contract to provide 1,000 units per month at £12 each? Under these circumstances, management would be well advised to reject the order because there is a high probability that cost increases would make the order unprofitable in later years. At the very least, management should insist that a cost escalation clause be added to the purchase agreement, specifying that the selling price be increased to cover any cost increases and detailing how cost is computed.

Of more concern is the variable nature of all long-run costs. Given adequate time, management must replace fixed assets and may adjust both the number of machines as well as the size of machines used to manufacture. Accordingly, *in the long run all costs, including costs classified as fixed in a given period, are relevant.* To remain in business in the long run, Mind Trek must replace equipment, pay property taxes, pay administrative salaries, and so forth. Consequently, management should consider all costs (fixed and variable, manufacturing and nonmanufacturing) in evaluating a long-term contract.

Full costs include all costs, regardless of their behavior pattern or activity level. The average full cost per unit is sometimes used to approximate long-run variable costs. If accepting a long-term contract increases the monthly production and sales volume to 6,000 units, the average full cost per unit will be £19.5 (nineteen and a half pounds):

Direct materials	£ 5.0
Direct labor	3.0
Variable manufacturing overhead	2.0
Variable selling and administration	2.0
Fixed manufacturing overhead (£30,000 / 6,000 units)	5.0
Fixed selling and administrative (£15,000 / 6,000 units)	2.5
Average full cost per unit	£19.5

If the Brazilian distributor agrees to pay separately all variable selling and administrative expenses associated with the contract, the estimated long-run variable costs are £17.5 per unit (£19.5 - £2). Many managers would say this is the minimum acceptable unit selling price for the order, especially if the order extends over a long period of time.

Opportunity Costs May Also Be Relevant

An **opportunity cost** is the net cash inflow that could be obtained if the resources committed to one action were used in the most desirable other alternative. Because Mind Trek has excess productive capacity, no opportunity cost is associated with accepting the Brazilian distributor's one-time order. There is no alternative use of the productive capacity in the short run, so there is no opportunity cost.

But what if Mind Trek were operating with no excess capacity? In this case, accepting the special order would require either reducing regular sales or using overtime. To simplify the illustration, assume overtime production is not possible. Because Mind Trek is operating at capacity, there is an alternative use of the productive capacity and, hence, an opportunity cost associated with its use to fill the special order. Each unit sold to the Brazilian distributor could generate a £10 contribution from regular customers. Accepting the special order would cause Mind Trek to incur an opportunity cost of £10,000, the net benefit of the most desirable other action, selling to regular customers:

Lost sales to regular customers	1,000	units
Regular unit contribution margin	x £10	unit
Opportunity cost of accepting special order	£10,000	

Because this opportunity cost exceeds the £2,000 contribution derived from the special order, management should reject the special order. Accepting the order will reduce profits by £8,000 (£2,000 contribution - £10,000 opportunity cost).

Nonquantitative Considerations

Although an analysis of cost and revenue information may indicate that a special order would be profitable in the near-term, management might still reject the order because of nonquantitative, short-run or long-run considerations. Because of a concern for the order's impact on regular customers, management might reject an order even if they had excess capacity. If the order involves a special low price, regular customers might demand a similar price reduction and threaten to take their business elsewhere. Alternatively, management might accept the special order even though they were operating at capacity if they believed there were long-term benefits associated with penetrating a new market. Legal factors must also be considered if the special order is from a buyer who competes with regular customers. These legal factors are discussed later in conjunction with the pricing decision in Chapter 5.

Internal or External Acquisition of Components or Services

Organizations often have the opportunity to acquire services or components of products they manufacture externally, rather than providing the service or manufacturing the component internally. The external acquisition of services or components is called **outsourcing**. In recent years, many companies have been focusing more on what they do best and developing long-term relationships with outside suppliers that specialize in producing a particular component or service. Colleges and universities buy services they used to perform themselves. Marriott and ARA food services now run many college dining halls and Barnes & Noble manages many university bookstores. Organizations such as Detroit's Attention to Detail have even replaced the internal custodian. Because of their high volume and focus, these outside specialists often provide better services at a lower cost. Management Accounting Practice 3-2 examines a company that is performing inventory and equipment management decisions for hospitals.

Suppose a Canadian manufacturer has offered a *one-year* contract to supply Mind Trek with an electronic component at a cost of £2 per unit. Mind Trek is now faced with the decision to continue to make the electronic component internally or to buy the component from the external Canadian company. This is often called a "make or buy" decision. An analysis of the materials and operations required to manufacture the component internally reveals that if Mind Trek accepts the offer, it will be able to reduce:

- Materials costs by 10 percent per unit.
- Direct labor and variable factory overhead costs by 20 percent per unit.
- Fixed manufacturing overhead by £20,000 per year.

A differential analysis of Mind Trek's make or buy decision is presented in Exhibit 3-4. Continuing to make the component has a net advantage of £10,000.

But what if the space currently used to manufacture the electronic component can be rented to a third party for £40,000 per year? In this case, the productive capacity has an alternative use, and the net cash flow from this alternative use is an opportunity cost of making the component. Treating the rent Mind Trek will not receive if it continues to make the component as an opportunity cost of making the component, the analysis in Exhibit 3-5 indicates that buying now has a net advantage of £30,000.

Even if outsourcing appears financially advantageous in the short run, management should not decide to outsource before considering a variety of

EXHIBIT 3-4: DIFFERENTIAL ANALYSIS OF MAKE OR BUY DECISION

	(1) Cost to Make	(2) Cost to Buy	(1) - (2) Difference (Effect of Buying on Income)
Cost to buy (£2 x 60,000* units)		£ 120,000	£ (120,000)
Cost to make:			
Direct materials (£5 x 0.10 x 60,000 units)	£ 30,000		30,000
Direct labor (£3 x 0.20 x 60,000 units)	36,000		36,000
Variable manufacturing overhead (£2 x 0.20 x 60,000 units)	24,000		24,000
Fixed manufacturing overhead	20,000		20,000
Total	£ 110,000	£ 120,000	£ (10,000)
Advantage of making		£10,000	

*5,000 units per month x 12 months

MANAGEMENT ACCOUNTING PRACTICE 3-2

Baxter International Helps Hospitals Heal Finances Through Outsourcing

Proving that specialists often know best, Baxter International, a $9 billion health-care products and services company, has long provided consulting services to hospitals to streamline distribution and standardize equipment and supplies. Baxter's newest service, known as Value Link, goes much further.

Hospitals participating in Value Link transfer ownership and management of inventories to Baxter. Baxter will go so far as to deliver supplies to hospital floors several times a day. In 1994, Baxter further expanded its hospital services to cleaning and sterilizing equipment. Baxter's presence at hospitals participating in Value Link has expanded to the point where Baxter employees are on-site up to 24 hours a day.

While Baxter has been pleased with the success of Value Link, customers are just as happy. At Seton Medical Center in Daly City, California, George Ryan, the director of materials management, estimated that the cost of supplies decreased approximately $300,000.

Based on: "Why Some Customers Are More Equal than Others," *Fortune* (September 19, 1994), pp. 215-224.

EXHIBIT 3-5: DIFFERENTIAL ANALYSIS OF MAKE OR BUY DECISION WITH OPPORTUNITY TO RENT FACILITIES

	(1) Cost to Make	(2) Cost to Buy	(1) - (2) Difference (Effect of Buying on Income)
Cost to buy (£2 x 60,000* units)		£120,000	£ (120,000)
Cost to make:			
Direct materials (£5 x 0.10 x 60,000 units)	£ 30,000		30,000
Direct labor (£3 x 0.20 x 60,000 units)	36,000		36,000
Variable manufacturing overhead (£2 x 0.20 x 60,000 units)	24,000		24,000
Fixed manufacturing overhead	20,000		20,000
Opportunity cost of lost rent income	40,000		40,000
Total	£150,000	£120,000	£ 30,000
Advantage of buying		£30,000	

*5,000 units per month x 12 months

nonquantitative factors. Is the outside supplier interested in developing a long-run relationship or merely attempting to use some temporarily idle capacity? If so, what will happen at the end of the contract period? Will the supplier extend the contract at all, or at a higher price? What impact would a decision to outsource have on the morale of Mind Trek's employees? Will Mind Trek have to rehire laid-off employees after the contract expires? Will the outside supplier meet delivery schedules? Does the supplied part meet Mind Trek's quality standards, and will it continue to meet them? Organizations often manufacture products or provide services they can obtain elsewhere in order to control quality and to have an assured source of supply with on-time delivery.

The movement toward outsourcing has grown to include many units of government, where elected officials have concluded that a profit motive in a competitive environment often leads to higher quality services at lower costs. Consider the following examples:

- The California Private Transportation Co. is building toll roads.
- BFI collects and disposes of trash in many communities.
- Rural/Metro is contracting to run fire departments and provide medical services.
- Corrections Corporation of America even runs prisons.

According to Mark Liebner, chief financial officer of Rural/Metro, by focusing on the bottom line, his company provides better service at a fraction of the cost of traditional government-run services. He cites Scottsdale, Arizona, where fire losses have declined 84 percent since 1985, as an example. Some politicians have even proposed that package carriers, such as Federal Express and United Parcel Service, should be allowed to compete with the U.S. Postal Service in delivering first-class mail. Experts have estimated that the increased competition would reduce costs of first-class mail by 25 percent.[3]

Sell or Process Further

We will consider two types of sell or process further decisions (1) for a single product and (2) for joint products.

Single Product Decisions

When a product is salable at various stages of completion, management must determine the product's most advantageous selling point. As each stage is completed, management must determine whether to sell the product then or to process it further. Assume the Boston Rocking Company manufactures rocking chairs from precut and shaped wood. The chairs are salable once they are assembled; however, Boston Rocking sands and paints all chairs before they are sold. Management wishes to know if this is the optimal selling point.

A complete listing of unit costs and revenues for the alternative selling points is as follows:

	Per Chair		
	Sell After Assembly	Sell After Painting	Difference (Effect of Painting on Income)
Selling price	$ 40	$ 75	$ 35
Assembly costs	(25)	(25)	
Sanding and painting costs		(12)	(12)
Contribution margin	$ 15	$ 38	$ 23
Advantage of painting		$23	

The chairs should be sold after they are painted. The sanding and painting operation has an additional contribution of $23 per unit.

Note that the assembly costs are the same under both alternatives. This illustrates that *all costs incurred prior to the decision point are irrelevant.* Given the existence of an assembled chair, the decision alternatives are to sell it now or to process it further. A differential analysis for the decision to sell or process further should include only revenues and the incremental costs of further processing.

Increase in revenues:		
Sell after painting	$ 75	
Sell after assembly	- 40	$ 35
Additional costs of sanding and painting		- 12
Advantage of sanding and painting		$ 23

---

3 Eric Schine, Richard S. Dunham, and Christopher Farrell, "America's New Watchword: If It Moves, Privatize It," *Business Week* (December 12, 1994).

The identical solution is obtained if the selling price without further processing is treated as an opportunity cost:

Revenues after painting		$ 75
Additional costs of sanding and painting	$ 12	
Opportunity cost of not selling after assembly	40	- 52
Advantage of sanding and painting		$ 23

By processing the chairs further, Boston Rocking has foregone the opportunity to receive $40 from its sale. Since the chair is already made, this $40 is the net cash inflow from the most desirable alternative; hence, it is the opportunity cost of painting.

Joint Product Decisions

Two or more products simultaneously produced from a common set of inputs by a single process are called **joint products**. Joint products are often found in basic industries that process natural raw materials such as dairy products, chemicals, meat products, petroleum, and wood products. In the petroleum industry, crude oil is refined into fuel oil, gasoline, kerosene, lubricating oil, and other products.

The point in the process where the joint products become separately identifiable is called the **split-off point**, and materials and conversion costs incurred prior to the split-off point are called **joint costs**. For external reporting purposes, a number of techniques are used to allocate joint costs among joint products. (Some of these techniques are considered in the appendix to Chapter 11.) We will not discuss these techniques here, except to note that none of them provide information that is useful in determining what to do with a joint product once it is produced. Because joint costs are incurred prior to the decision point, they are sunk costs. Consequently, *joint costs are irrelevant to a decision to sell a joint product or to process it further.*

HOW BEST TO USE LIMITED RESOURCES

L O 5

No doubt, you have experienced time as a limiting or constraining resource. With two exams the day after tomorrow and a paper due next week, your problem is how to allocate limited study time. The solution depends on your objectives, your current status (grades, knowledge, skill levels, and so forth), and the available time. Given this information, you devise a work plan to best meet your objectives.

Managers must also decide how best to use limited resources to accomplish organizational goals. A supermarket may lose sales because limited shelf space prevents stocking all available brands of soft drinks. A manufacturer may lose sales because limited machine or labor hours prevent filling all orders. Managers of for-profit organizations will likely find the problems of capacity constraints less troublesome than the problems of excess capacity; nonetheless, these problems are real. Management Accounting Practice 3-3 gives an illustration of the efforts organizations will make to overcome production delays or provide additional capacity as quickly as possible.

If the limited resource is not a core business activity, such as manufacturing computer chips at Intel, it may be appropriate to acquire additional units of the limited resource externally. For example, many organizations have a small legal staff to handle routine activities; but if the internal staff becomes fully committed, the organization seeks outside legal council. The external acquisition of such resources was discussed previously.

The long-run solution to the problem of limited resources to perform core activities may be to expand capacity. However, this is usually not feasible in the short run. Economic models suggest that another solution is to reduce demand by increasing the price. Again, this may not be desirable. The supermarket, for example, may want to maintain competitive prices; and the manufacturer might want to maintain a long-run price to retain customer goodwill and to avoid attracting competitors or accusations of "price gouging."

Single Constraint

The allocation of limited resources should be made only after a careful consideration of many nonquantitative factors. The following rule provides

MANAGEMENT ACCOUNTING PRACTICE 3-3

From Guns to Diesels and Pepsi: Russian-Built Military Aircraft Becomes Capitalist Tool

It burns 3.3 tons of fuel to taxi on a runway, some of its engines need replacement after 1,000 hours (as opposed to 8,000 to 10,000 hours before maintenance is required on a jet engine manufactured in the West), it has a crew of 19 so emergency repairs can be made promptly, and you can rent it for approximately $11,000 per flying hour. Compared to a Boeing 747-400 cargo jet, the Russian Antonov 124, built to move military cargo, is a gas-guzzling clunker. Yet, this relic of the Cold War is an important tool of capitalists trying to compete on the basis of time.

The secret to the Antonov's success is not high technology. It is massive capacity and raw power. At 330,639 lbs., its maximum payload is almost 70,000 pounds more than a Lockheed C-5B; and with a cargo tunnel 14 feet high, 20 feet wide, and 134 feet long, the Antonov can handle cargo that won't fit into a Boeing 747-400.

When production delays jeopardized General Motors Corporation's sale of locomotives to an Irish railroad, an Antonov carried a 240,000-lb. locomotive across the Atlantic. And, when Pepsi wanted to get a bottling line manufactured in Italy to Mexico as soon as possible, Pepsi's management called upon an Antonov. This allowed the new 1,200 cans-a-minute line to begin operations one month sooner than would have been possible if the next feasible method of transportation, a cargo ship, were used.

Based on: Douglas Lavin, "The Mighty Antonov Is Only Way to Fly Your Locomotive," *The Wall Street Journal* (December 29, 1994), pp. 1, 4.

a useful starting point in making short-run decisions of how best to use limited resources: *To achieve short-run profit maximization, a for-profit organization should allocate limited resources in a manner that maximizes the contribution per unit of the limited resource.* The application of this rule is illustrated in the following example.

The Delta Manufacturing Company produces three products: A, B, and C. A limitation of 120 machine hours for machine Z1 per week prevents Delta from meeting the sales demand for these products. Product information is as follows:

	A	B	C
Unit selling price	$100	$80	$50
Unit variable costs	- 90	-50	-25
Unit contribution margin	$ 10	$30	$25
Machine hours per unit	2	2	1

Product A has the highest selling price, product B has the highest unit contribution margin, and product C is shown below to have the highest contribution per Z1 machine hour.

	A	B	C
Unit contribution margin	$10	$ 30	$ 25
Machine hours per unit	÷ 2	÷ 2	÷ 1
Contribution per machine hour	$ 5	$ 15	$ 25

Following the rule of maximizing the contribution per unit of constraining factor, Delta should use its limited machine hours to produce product C. As shown in the following analysis, any other plan would result in lower profits:

	A Highest Selling Price	B Highest Contribution per Unit	C Highest Contribution per Unit of Constraining Factor
Machine hours available	120	120	120
Machine hours per unit	÷ 2	÷ 2	÷ 1
Weekly production	60	60	120
Unit contribution margin	x $10	x $30	x $25
Total weekly contribution margin	$ 600	$1,800	$ 3,000

Despite this analysis, management may decide to produce some units of A, or B, or both to satisfy the requests of some "good" customers or to offer a full product line. However, such decisions sacrifice short-run profits. Each machine hour used to produce A or B has an opportunity cost of $25, the net cash flow from using that hour to produce a unit of C, the most desirable other alternative. Producing all A, for example, results in an opportunity cost of $3,000 (120 units of C x $25). The net disadvantage of producing all A is $2,400:

Contribution from A	$ 600
Opportunity cost of not producing C	- 3,000
Net disadvantage of producing A	$(2,400)

The opportunity cost of producing all C is $1,800. This is the net cash flow from the most desirable other alternative, producing B. However, when compared to producing B, producing C has a net advantage of $1,200:

Contribution from C	$3,000
Opportunity cost of not producing B	-1,800
Net advantage of producing C	$1,200

When there is a single constraint, it is very often related to time.

Multiple Constraints

If the weekly demand for product C was less than 120 units, say 80 units, the limited production capacity of machine Z1 should be used to satisfying the demand for this product with any remaining capacity going to produce the product with the next highest contribution per unit of constraining factor, or product B. This will provide a total weekly contribution of $2,600:

Available hours	120
Required for C (80 units × 1 machine hour)	80
Available for B	40
Machine hours per unit	÷ 2
Production of B in units	20
Unit contribution margin of B	× $30
Contribution from B	$ 600
Contribution from A ($25 per unit × 80 units)	2,000
Total weekly contribution margin	$2,600

When an organization has alternative uses for several limiting resources, the optimal use of those resources cannot be determined using the rule for short-run profit maximization. In these situations, techniques such as linear programming (discussed in the appendix to this chapter) may be used to assist in determining the optimal mix of products or services.

Theory of Constraints

The theory of constraints is similar to our general rule for how best to use limited resources. It focuses, however, on the scheduling of work. The goal of the theory of constraints is to maximize the flow of work through a constraining resource while minimizing the backlog of work waiting for the constraining resource. The **theory of constraints** states that every process has a bottleneck (constraining resource) and that production cannot take place faster than it can be processed through the bottleneck.[4] The theory has several implications for management.

---

4 The concepts underlying the theory of constraints are presented in the form of a novel in *The Goal*, by Eliyahu M. Goldratt and Jeff Cox. See the suggested readings. Goldratt has developed a scheduling system, called Optimum Production Technology, to schedule production in a manner that maximizes throughput in organizations that have internal bottlenecks.

- Management should identify the bottleneck. This may be difficult when several different products are produced in a facility containing many different production activities. One approach might be to walk around and observe where inventory is building up and awaiting further processing. The bottleneck will likely have the largest piles of work that have been waiting for the longest time.
- Management should schedule production to maximize the efficient use of the bottleneck resource. Efficiently using the bottleneck resource might necessitate inspecting all units before they reach the bottleneck rather than after the units are completed. The bottleneck resource is too valuable to waste on units that may already be defective.
- Production should be scheduled to avoid a buildup of inventory. Reducing inventory reduces the cost of inventory investments and the cost of carrying inventory. It also assists in improving quality by making it easier to identify quality problems that might otherwise be hidden in large piles of inventory. Reducing inventory will require a change in the attitude of managers who like to see machines and people working all the time. Keeping machines and people working full-time will guarantee a buildup of inventory in front of the bottleneck. To avoid this buildup, it may be necessary for people and equipment to remain idle until the bottleneck resource calls for additional input.
- Management should work to eliminate the bottleneck, perhaps by increasing the capacity of the bottleneck resource, redesigning products so they can be produced with less use of the bottleneck resource, rescheduling production procedures to substitute nonbottleneck resources, or outsourcing work performed by bottleneck resources.

The theory of constraints has implications for management accounting performance reports. Keeping people and equipment working on production full-time is often a goal of management. To support this goal, management accounting performance reports have traditionally highlighted underutilization as an unfavorable variance. This has encouraged managers to have people and equipment producing inventory, even if the inventory is not needed or cannot be processed further because of bottlenecks. The theory of constraints suggests that it is better to have nonbottleneck resources idle than it is to have them fully utilized. To support the theory of constraints, performance reports should:

- Measure the utilization of bottleneck resources.
- Measure factory throughput.
- Not encourage the full utilization of nonbottleneck resources.
- Discourage the buildup of excess inventory.

It is important to understand that there will always be a bottleneck resource. If all internal bottlenecks are eliminated, the ultimate bottleneck, customer demand, remains. This external bottleneck is becoming increasingly important. As worldwide production capacity and competition expands, the bottleneck is changing from production capacity to customer requirements for quality and service at the lowest possible cost. How management accounting can assist in meeting these customer expectations is the focal point of the next two chapters.

SUMMARY

A number of special decisions were presented in this chapter, including whether to accept or reject a special order, whether to make or buy a product or service, whether to sell a product or to process it further, and how best to use limited resources. When evaluating alternative actions such as these, managers should focus on the decision at hand. They should evaluate only those costs and revenues that differ under each alternative.

Relevant costs include all future costs that differ under each alternative, and sometimes they include an opportunity cost. An outlay cost is a future cost that requires a future expenditure. When resources are limited, the initiation of one action requires management to forego competing alternative actions. The net cash inflow from the most desirable other alternative is the opportunity cost of the action selected.

Irrelevant costs, which include sunk costs and certain other outlay costs, do not differ among competing alternatives. Sunk costs are historical costs resulting from past decisions. There is absolutely nothing management can do to change the total amount of these costs. All outlay costs are relevant to some decisions, such as the decision to continue or discontinue operations, but not all outlay costs are relevant to all decisions. Outlay costs that do not differ under decision alternatives are not relevant to that decision. A summary classification of relevant and irrelevant costs is presented in Exhibit 3-6.

Although this chapter has focused on profit maximization, decisions should not be based solely on profit maximization, especially short-run profit maximization. The long-run profit, legal, ethical, and social implications of decisions must always be recognized.

EXHIBIT 3-6: SUMMARY CLASSIFICATION OF RELEVANT AND IRRELEVANT COSTS

Relevant Costs			Irrelevant Costs
Future costs that differ among competing alternatives			Costs that do not differ among competing alternatives
Opportunity Costs	Outlay Costs		Sunk Costs
Net cash flow from the best alternatives	Future costs requiring future expenditures that differ	Future costs requiring future expenditures that do not differ	A historical cost resulting from a past decision

APPENDIX: RELEVANT COST INFORMATION FOR QUANTITATIVE MODELS SUCH AS LINEAR PROGRAMMING

A **model** is a simplified representation of some real-world phenomenon. Models are used to learn about the related phenomenon and to quickly and inexpensively determine the effect of some proposed action. Museums contain educational models of buildings, spaceships, prehistoric animals, and ecosystems. Airframe manufacturers study the aerodynamics of model planes in wind tunnels. Airplane pilots learn how to pilot their craft using flight simulators. These are all examples of **physical models**, scaled down versions or replicas of physical reality.

Managers and other decision makers also use quantitative models that are simply a set of mathematical relationships. **Quantitative models** can be further classified into **descriptive models** that merely specify the relationships between a series of independent and dependent variables and **optimizing models** that suggest a specific choice between decision alternatives. Cost-volume-profit relationships, contribution income statements, and operating budgets are all descriptive models. While CVP models do not suggest an optimal action, they help managers understand how profits respond to changes in volume, selling price, or costs.

The purpose of this appendix is to discuss the proper use of accounting data in linear programming, a widely used optimizing model. While linear programming is not an accounting model per se, accounting data are frequently used in linear programming. Consequently, the accuracy and relevance of accounting data are critical to the proper use of linear programming models.

QUANTITATIVE MODELS ARE DECISION AIDS

Quantitative models, especially optimizing models, are often criticized as being overly simplistic, unrealistic, and prone to "make" incorrect decisions. It is true that models are a simplified representation of reality, but this is also one of their strengths. The use of a model helps decision makers focus on the few variables that are most critical to a decision. Furthermore, the assumptions that underlie a model can be specified and evaluated.

All quantitative models, descriptive and optimizing, are intended to *assist* in decision making. People cannot relinquish their decision-making responsibility to models that are merely intended to be decision support systems. In the final analysis, *people, not models, make decisions*. Managers must carefully evaluate the data used in the model, the assumptions underlying the model, and the output of the model. If everything appears satisfactory, a manager may decide to implement the action suggested by an optimizing model. If the responsible person suspects faulty data, an oversimplistic assumption, or changed circumstances that invalidate the model, the suggested action should not be implemented. Instead, the manager should undertake further analysis or make a decision based on professional judgment.

LINEAR PROGRAMMING

Linear programming is an optimizing model used to assist managers in making decisions under constrained conditions when linear relationships exist among all variables. The constraints can represent limited resources (such as labor hours, machine hours, raw materials, or financial resources), limited consumer demand, or required physical characteristics of the final product (such as a minimum percentage of protein or a maximum percentage of fat).

Linear programming may be applied to a variety of business decisions, including product mix, raw materials mix, production scheduling, transportation scheduling, and cash management. The objective in linear programming is to determine the action that will maximize profits or minimize costs.

Although the concepts underlying linear programming are straightforward, the actual solution to linear programming problems can be extremely complex. Fortunately, the availability of computers and modeling software has resulted in situations where the manager need not be concerned about the detailed operation of the solution technique. The manager should, of course, have a general understanding of how the solution is determined (the model's assumptions) and be able to evaluate both the data used and the suggested solution.

Assumptions and Uses of Accounting Data

As its name implies, the most critical linear programming assumption is that linear relationships exist among all variables. The total contribution from the sale of products X and Y, for example, must be of the form aX $+ b$Y, where a is the unit contribution of product X and b is the unit contribution of product Y. Curvilinear relationships are not allowed.

Another assumption of linear programming is that fractional solutions are permitted.[5] The suggested solution to a linear programming problem might, for example, specify the production and sale of 25.2 units of X and 32.7 units of Y. When these assumptions are not valid, the manager might elect to use other models. Alternatively, if it seems appropriate, the manager might use professional judgment to adjust the suggested linear programming solution. The production of X and Y might be rounded *down* to 25 and 32 units. In linear programming, the existence of resource constraints prevent upward rounding. Hence, while 32.7 would normally be rounded up to 33, in linear programming, we can only round down to 32.

Every linear programming model includes an **objective function**, or goal to be maximized or minimized. Accounting data are often used in the objective function. *If the objective is to maximize profits, the coefficients of the variables in the objective function should be unit contribution margins.* If the objective is to minimize costs, the coefficients should be unit

---

5 A special type of linear programming, known as integer programming, can also be used when the solution must be in whole numbers. A discussion of integer programming is beyond the scope of this book.

variable costs. The total contribution margin or variable costs of each product will vary in proportion to changes in volume. Profit and cost measures that include an allocation of fixed costs should not be used in the objective function. They do not vary in direct proportion to changes in production. A limitation of linear programming is the difficulty of incorporating batch and product level costs. In this appendix, we assume that all costs are either variable at the unit level or fixed at the facility level.

Graphic Analysis of Product Mix Decisions

We use graphic analysis to illustrate the solution of linear programming problems. Though graphic analysis can be used to solve problems containing only two variables, it provides the general understanding necessary to evaluate more complex problems containing three or more variables. The following steps are involved in graphic analysis:

1. *Develop an equation for the objective function,* indicating how each variable affects the profit maximization or cost minimization goal.
2. *Develop an equation for each constraint,* indicating how each variable affects the total use of the constraint.
3. *Graph the constraints.*
4. *Identify the feasible solutions* that are bounded by the constraints.
5. *Determine the optimal solution* that maximizes or minimizes the value of the objective function.

Assume the Martin Company produces two products, A and B, in two departments, Assembly and Finishing. Product A has a unit contribution margin of $50, and product B has a unit contribution margin of $40. There are no batch level costs. The demand for each product exceeds Martin's capacity to produce. Production information is as follows:

	Labor Hours per Unit		Total Labor Hours Available per Week
	A	B	
Assembly Department	20	20	600
Finishing Department	20	10	400

Martin can only obtain raw materials sufficient to produce 25 units of B each week. Management desires the product mix that will maximize the weekly contribution of products A and B toward fixed costs and profits. Using the five steps in graphic analysis, the problem is solved as follows:

1. *Objective function.* The objective is to maximize the total weekly contribution of products A and B. Given information on the unit contribution margin, Martin's objective function is:

$$\text{Maximize } \$50A + \$40B$$

2. *Constraints.* There are constraints for maximum assembly hours, maximum finishing hours, and maximum production of product B.

Because each constraint indicates an upper limit on the use of some resource, the less than or equal to symbol is used in each:

$$20A + 20B \leq 600 \text{ Assembly Department hours}$$
$$20A + 10B \leq 400 \text{ Finishing Department hours}$$
$$B \leq 25 \text{ units}$$

The assembly hours constraint indicates that any combination of A and B can be produced, providing it does not require more than 600 assembly hours. The finishing hours constraint indicates that any combination of A and B can be produced, providing it does not require more than 400 finishing hours. Finally, because of raw materials limitations, no more than 25 units of B can be produced.

To be technically precise, two more constraints are added to indicate that negative production is prohibited:

$$A \geq 0$$
$$B \geq 0$$

Hence the production of A and the production of B must be greater than or equal to zero.

3. *Graph.* One axis must be designated to represent each variable. In Exhibit 3-7, the horizontal axis represents production and sales of product A, and the vertical axis represents production and sales of product B. The opposite could also have been done.

The set of all feasible A and B production values is determined by solving each constraint for its maximum A and B values, assuming all production was devoted to that product, and drawing lines on graph paper connecting, for each constraint, the maximum value of each product. We compute the maximum values of A and B as the maxi-

EXHIBIT 3-7: GRAPHIC APPROACH TO LINEAR PROGRAMMING

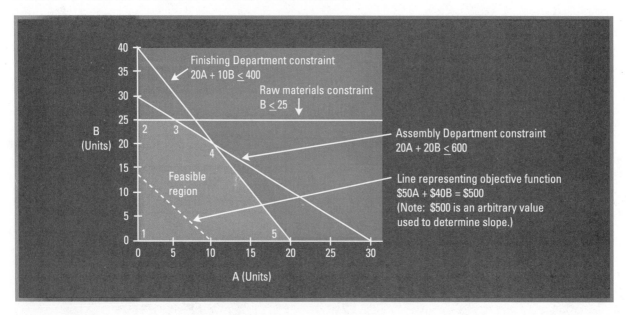

mum amount of each constraint divided by the units of the constraint required to produce a unit of A or a unit of B:

| | Maximum Values | |
	Product A	Product B
Assembly hours	600/20 = 30	600/20 = 30
Finishing hours	400/20 = 20	400/10 = 40
Raw materials		25

The lines connecting these maximum values are illustrated in Exhibit 3-7. Because the raw materials constraint affects only product B, it does not intersect the horizontal axis for product A. Instead, it is drawn parallel to the horizontal axis. The nonnegativity constraints are represented by the horizontal and vertical axes.

4. *Feasible solutions.* After the lines representing each constraint are drawn, the **feasible region**, representing all possible production volumes and mixes, is depicted by the area between the vertical and horizontal axes and the first set of enclosing lines that represent constraints (this is the area enclosed by the solid lines from points 1-2-3-4-5 in Exhibit 3-7). The firm can produce anywhere within the feasible region; however, it is likely that one product mix will provide a higher total contribution than any other mix.

5. *Optimal solution.* In linear programming, the **optimal solution** is the feasible solution that maximizes or minimizes the value of the objective function, depending on management's goal. An important characteristic of linear programming is that *if there is a single optimal solution, it is found at a corner point where the lines representing two or more constraints intersect.* Knowing this, it is only necessary to evaluate the solutions represented by corner points. In Exhibit 3-7, there are five corner points, which, for convenience, are numbered 1 through 5. The value of the objective function at each corner point is computed in Exhibit 3-8. The maximum optimal solution, represented by corner 4, calls for a weekly production of 10 units of product A and 20 units of product B. This solution will provide a weekly contribution of $1,300. Fixed costs, of course, would be deducted from this amount to determine the weekly profit.

EXHIBIT 3-8: EVALUATION OF ALTERNATIVE CORNER SOLUTIONS

| Corner | Value of | | Value of Objective Function |
	A	B	$50A + $40B =
1	0	0	$ 0
2	0	25	1,000
3	5	25	1,250
4	10*	20*	1,300*
5	20	0	1,000

*Optimal solution

The Corner Solution

The reason that the unique solution is always found at a corner point can be illustrated by drawing a line representing some arbitrary value for the objective function. In the Martin Company case, the end points for an objective function with an arbitrarily selected value of $500 are 10 units of product A and 12.5 units of product B. In general,

Desired contribution / Unit contribution = End point

For A,

$500 / $50 = 10 units

For B;

$500 / $40 = 12.5 units

Drawing this line in Exhibit 3-7, observe that 10 units of A or 12.5 units of B or any combination along this line will provide a weekly contribution of $500. An objective function having a higher value would be drawn farther from the origin, parallel to the first line. To maximize the value of the objective function, additional lines are drawn parallel to the first line, but farther from the origin, until only one point on a line touches the feasible solution. This one unique point will be a corner point; corner 4 in this case. You may draw these additional lines as an exercise.

Simplex Method

Though it is possible to solve two variable problems with the aid of graphic analysis, linear programming problems containing three or more variables must be solved by a mathematical solution technique known as the **simplex method**. The mechanics of the simplex method are far from simple, even though the method arrives at a solution by comparing objective function values at multidimensional corner points, just as was done earlier with the graphic approach. To solve the Martin Company's product mix problem, the same set of equations would be used as in the previous illustration. Software packages are available to solve linear programming problems on most computers.

SUGGESTED READINGS

Goldratt, Eliyahu M., and Jeff Cox. *The Goal* (Croton-on-Hudson, New York: North River Press, Inc., 1984).

Goldratt, Eliyahu M. *Theory of Constraints* (Croton-on-Hudson, New York: North River Press, Inc., 1990).

REVIEW PROBLEM

Applications of Differential Analysis

Final Copy Company produces color cartridge ribbons for dot matrix printers. The ribbons are sold to mail-order distributors for $4.80. Manufacturing and other costs are as follows:

Variable Costs per Unit		Fixed Costs per Month	
Direct materials	$2.00	Factory overhead	$15,000
Direct labor	0.20	Selling and administration	5,000
Factory overhead	0.25	Total	$20,000
Distribution	0.05		
Total	$2.50		

The variable distribution costs are for transportation to mail-order distributors. The current monthly production and sales volume is 15,000. Monthly capacity is 20,000 units.

Required:

Determine the effect of the following situations on monthly profits. Each situation is to be evaluated independent of all others.

(a) A $1.50 increase in the unit selling price should result in a 1,800 unit decrease in monthly sales.

(b) A $1.80 decrease in the unit selling price should result in a 6,000 unit increase in monthly sales. However, because of capacity constraints, the last 1,000 units would be produced during overtime, when the direct labor costs increase by 50 percent.

(c) A New Zealand distributor has proposed to place a special, one-time order for 4,000 units next month at a reduced price of $4 per unit. The distributor would pay all transportation costs. There would be additional fixed selling and administrative costs of $500.

(d) An Australian distributor has proposed to place a special, one-time order for 8,000 units at a special price of $4 per unit. The distributor would pay all transportation costs. There would be additional fixed selling and administrative costs of $500. Assume overtime production is not possible.

(e) A Mexican manufacturer has offered a one-year contract to supply cartridges for the ribbons at a cost of $1.00 per unit. If Final Copy accepts the offer, it will be able to reduce variable manufacturing costs by 40 percent and rent some space currently used to manufacture cartridges for $1,000 per month.

(f) The cartridge ribbons are currently unpackaged; that is, they are sold in bulk. Packaging them individually would increase costs by $0.10 per unit. However, the units could now be sold for $5.05.

The solution to the review problem is found at the end of the Chapter 3 assignment material. To maximize your learning, you should make a serious attempt to develop a written solution to the review problem before looking at the solution. If there are errors in your solution, you should then attempt to determine the causes of the errors.

KEY TERMS

Conversion costs—costs (direct labor and variable manufacturing overhead) required to convert raw materials into finished goods.

Cost prediction error—the difference between a predicted future cost and the actual amount of the cost when, or if, it is incurred.

Cost reduction proposal—a proposed action or investment intended to reduce the cost of an activity that the organization is committed to keeping.

Differential cost analysis—an approach to the analysis of relevant costs that focuses on the costs that differ under alternative actions.

Full costs—include all variable and fixed costs and costs at all activity levels.

Joint costs—all materials and conversion costs of joint products incurred prior to the split-off point.

Joint products—two or more products simultaneously produced from a common set of inputs by a single process.

Opportunity cost—the net cash inflow that could be obtained if the resources committed to one action were used in the most desirable other alternative.

Outlay costs—costs that require future expenditures of cash or other resources.

Outsourcing—the external acquisition of services or components.

Relevant costs—future costs that differ between competing decision alternatives.

Revenues—inflows of resources from the sale of goods and services.

Split-off point—the point in the process where joint products become separately identifiable.

Sunk costs—costs resulting from past decisions that cannot be changed.

Theory of constraints—every process has a bottleneck (constraining resource) and production cannot take place faster than it can be processed through the bottleneck.

Appendix Key Terms

Descriptive model—a model that merely specifies the relationships between a series of independent and dependent variables.

Feasible region—in linear programming models, includes all possible production volumes and mixes.

Linear programming—an optimizing model used to assist managers in making decisions under constrained conditions when linear relationships exist among all variables.

Model—a simplified representation of some real-world phenomenon.

Objective function—in linear programming models, the goal to be minimized or maximized.

Optimal solution—in linear programming models, the feasible solution than maximizes or minimizes the value of the objective function, depending on the decision maker's goal.

Optimizing model—a model that suggests a specific choice between decision alternatives.

Physical model—a scaled-down version or replica of physical reality.

Quantitative model—a set of mathematical relationships.

Simplex method—a mathematical approach to solving linear programming models containing any number of variables.

REVIEW QUESTIONS

3-1
Distinguish between relevant and irrelevant costs.

3-2
In evaluating a cost reduction proposal, what three alternatives are available to management?

3-3
When are outlay costs relevant and when are they irrelevant?

3-4
When are product level activity costs relevant and when are they irrelevant?

3-5
Why is a differential analysis of relevant items preferred to a detailed listing of all costs and revenues associated with each alternative?

3-6
How can cost predictions be made when the acquisition of new equipment results in a technological change?

3-7
When are opportunity costs relevant to the evaluation of a special order?

3-8
Mention some nonquantitative considerations important in evaluating a decision to make or buy a part.

3-9
In a decision to sell or to process further, of what relevance are costs incurred prior to the decision point? Explain your answer.

3-10
How should limited resources be used to achieve short-run profit maximization?

3-11

What should performance reports do in support of the theory of constraints?

EXERCISES

3-1 Relevant Cost Terms: Matching

A company that produces three products, M, N, and O, is evaluating a proposal that will result in doubling the production of N and discontinuing the production of O. The facilities that are currently used to produce O will be devoted to the production of N. Furthermore, additional machinery will be acquired to produce N. The production of M will not be affected. All products have a positive contribution margin.

Presented are a number of phrases or statements related to the proposal. For each phrase or statement, select the most appropriate cost term. Each term is used only once.

1. Increased revenues from the sale of N
2. Increased variable costs of N
3. Property taxes on the new machinery
4. Revenues from the sale of M
5. Cost of the equipment used to produce O
6. Contribution margin of O
7. Variable costs of M
8. The salary of the company president

a. Opportunity cost
b. Sunk cost
c. Irrelevant variable outlay cost
d. Irrelevant fixed outlay cost
e. Relevant variable outlay cost
f. Relevant fixed outlay cost
g. Relevant revenues
h. Irrelevant revenues

3-2 Relevant Cost Terms: Matching

A company that produces and sells 4,000 units per month, but has the capacity to produce 5,000 units per month, is evaluating a one-time, special order for 2,000 units from a large chain store. Accepting the order will result in an increase in variable manufacturing costs and certain fixed selling and administrative costs. It will also require the company to forego the sale of 1,000 units to regular customers.

Presented are a number of statements related to the proposal. For each statement, select the most appropriate cost term. Each term is used only once.

1. Cost of existing equipment used to produce special order
2. Lost contribution margin from foregone sales to regular customers
3. Increased revenues from special order
4. Variable cost of 4,000 units sold to regular customers

a. Irrelevant variable outlay cost
b. Irrelevant fixed outlay cost
c. Sunk cost
d. Relevant variable outlay cost
e. Relevant fixed outlay cost
f. Opportunity cost
g. Relevant revenues
h. Irrelevant revenues

e 5. Increase in fixed selling and administrative expenses

h 6. Revenues from 4,000 units sold to regular customers

b 7. Salary paid to current supervisor who oversees manufacture of special order

a 8. Increased variable costs of special order

3-3 Identifying Relevant Costs and Revenues

The village of Twin Falls operates a hydro plant on the west side of a river that flows through town. The village uses some of the electricity generated by the plant to operate a water treatment plant and sells the excess electricity to a local utility. The village council is evaluating two alternative proposals:

Proposal 1 calls for replacing the generators used in the plant with more efficient generators that will produce more electricity and have lower operation costs. The salvage value of the old generators is greater than their removal cost.

Proposal 2 calls for raising the level of the dam to retain more water for power generation and increasing the force of water flowing through the dam. This will significantly increase the amount of electricity generated by the plant. Operating costs will not be affected.

Presented are a number of cost and revenue items. Under the columns for proposals 1 and 2, indicate whether each item is relevant or irrelevant to that proposal.

	Proposal 1	Proposal 2
1. Cost of new fire engine	Irr.	Irr.
2. Cost of old generators	Irr.	
3. Cost of new generators	Rel.	
4. Operating cost of old generators	Rel.	
5. Operating cost of new generators	Irr.	Irr.
6. Mayor's salary	Irr.	
7. Depreciation on old generators	Rel.	Rel.
8. Salvage value of old generators	Rel.	
9. Removal cost of old generators	Irr.	Rel.
10. Cost of raising dam	Rel.	Irr.
11. Maintenance costs of water plant	Rel.	Rel.
12. Revenues from sale of electricity		

3-4 Classifying Relevant and Irrelevant Items

Taylor, Taylor, and Tower, attorneys at law, have been asked to represent a local client in proceedings to be held in Washington, D.C. Classify each of the following items on the basis of their relationship to this engagement. Items may have multiple classifications.

	Relevant Costs		Irrelevant Costs	
	Opportunity	Outlay	Outlay	Sunk
1. The case will require three attorneys to stay four nights in a Washington hotel. The predicted hotel bill is $1,200.		1200		
2. Taylor, Taylor, and Tower's professional staff is paid $800 per day for out-of-town assignments.		(3 x 800) 2400		
3. Last year, depreciation on Taylor Taylor, and Tower's office was $12,000.				12,000
4. Round-trip transportation to Washington is expected to cost $250 per person for the engagement.		(250 x 3) 750		
5. The firm has recently accepted an engagement that will require partners to spend two weeks in Atlanta. The predicted out-of-pocket costs of this engagement are $8,500.			8,500	
6. The firm has a maintenance contract on its word processing equipment that will cost $2,200 next year.			2,200	
7. If the firm accepts the engagement in Washington, it will have to decline a conflicting engagement in Hilton Head that would have provided a net cash inflow of $7,200.	7,200			
8. The firm's variable overhead is $8 per client-hour.		$8	$8/client	
9. The firm pays $50 per year for Mr. Tower's subscription to a law journal.			$50	
10. Last year the firm paid $3,500 to increase the insulation in its building.				$3500

3-5 Special Order

The Produce Patch is a new health-food restaurant situated on a busy highway in Pomona, California. The Produce Patch specializes in a chef's salad dinner selling for $6. Daily fixed costs are $1,500, and variable costs are $3 per meal. An average of 750 meals are served each day even though the capacity is 800 meals per day.

Handwritten annotations (top):
current var. cost (300x .750) 2,250
Fixed costs 1,500
Total Cost 3,750
Meals 750
Avg. cost/meal 5.00

Handwritten annotations (left):
a) 300 + (1,500/150) ÷ 2 = $5.00

150/40 = 3.75

5.00
-3.75
1.25

P/u cont. is .75
3.25
-3.00
.75

only cover fixed costs.

Required:

(a) Determine the current average cost per meal.

(b) A bus load of 40 Girl Scouts, on their way home from the San Bernardino National Forest, stops by, and the scoutmaster offers to bring them in if the scouts can all be served a meal for a total of $150. The owner refuses, saying he would lose $1.25 per meal if he accepted this offer. Comment.

(c) A local businessman on a tomato juice break overhears the conversation with the scoutmaster and offers the owner a one-year contract to feed 300 of his employees at the special price of $3.75 per meal. Should the restaurant owner accept? Why or why not?

3-6 Special Order: High-Low Cost Estimation

The Quality Belt Company produces seat belts that are sold to North American automobile manufacturers. Although the company has a capacity of 300,000 belts per year, it is currently producing at an annual rate of 180,000 belts.

Quality Belt has received an order from a German manufacturer to purchase 60,000 belts at $9.50 each. Budgeted costs for 180,000 and 240,000 units are as follows:

Units	180,000	240,000
Manufacturing costs:		
Direct materials	$ 450,000	$ 600,000
Direct labor	315,000	420,000
Factory overhead	1,215,000	1,260,000
Total	$ 1,980,000	$ 2,280,000
Selling and administrative	765,000	780,000
Total	$ 2,745,000	$ 3,060,000
Costs per unit:		
Manufacturing	$ 11.00	$ 9.50
Selling and administrative	4.25	3.25
Total	$ 15.25	$ 12.75

Sales to North American manufacturers are priced at $20 per unit, but the sales manager believes Quality Belt should aggressively seek the German business even if it results in a loss of $3.25 per unit. She believes obtaining this order would open up several new markets for the company's product. The general manager commented that Quality Belt cannot tighten its belt enough to absorb the $195,000 loss ($3.25 x 60,000) it would incur if the order is accepted.

Required:

(a) Determine the financial implications of accepting the order.

(b) How would your analysis differ if Quality Belt were operating at capacity? Determine the new advantage or disadvantage of accepting the order under these circumstances.

3-7 Make or Buy

Fresh Air Limited manufactures a line of room air fresheners. Management is currently evaluating the possible production of an air freshener for the passenger compartment of automobiles. Based on an annual volume of 10,000 units, the predicted cost of an auto air freshener is as shown below:

Direct materials	$ 8.00 per unit
Direct labor	1.50 per unit
Factory overhead	7.00 per unit
Total	$16.50 per unit

These cost predictions include $50,000 in facility level fixed factory overhead averaged over 10,000 units. *Fixed $5.00*

One of the component parts of the auto air freshener is a battery-operated electric motor. Fresh Air does not currently manufacture battery-operated electric motors. However, the above cost predictions are based on the assumption that Fresh Air will assemble such a motor.

The Mini Motor Company has offered to supply an assembled battery-operated motor at a cost of $4.00 per unit, with a minimum annual order of 5,000 units. If Fresh Air accepts this offer, it will be able to reduce the variable labor and variable overhead costs of the auto air freshener by 50 percent. The electric motor's components will cost $2.00 if Fresh Air assembles the motors.

Required:
(a) Determine whether Fresh Air should make or buy the electric motor.
(b) If Fresh Air could rent the space the motors would be assembled in for $8,000 per year, should it make or buy this component?
(c) What additional factors should Fresh Air consider in deciding whether it should make or buy the electric motors?

3-8 Make or Buy

John Rahavy, III, MD, is a general practitioner whose offices are located in the South Falls Professional Building. In the past, Dr. Rahavy has operated his practice with a nurse, a receptionist/secretary, and a part-time bookkeeper. Dr. Rahavy, like many small-town physicians, has billed his patients and their insurance companies from his own office. The part-time bookkeeper, who works 10 hours per week, is employed exclusively for this purpose.

The North Falls Physician's Service Center has offered to take over all of Dr. Rahavy's billings and collections for an annual fee of $7,500. If Dr. Rahavy accepts this offer, he will no longer need the bookkeeper. The bookkeeper's wages and fringe benefits amount to $8 per hour, and the bookkeeper works 50 weeks per year. With all the billings and collections done elsewhere, Dr. Rahavy will have 2 additional hours available per week to see patients. Dr. Rahavy sees an average of 3 patients per hour at an average fee of $30 per visit. His practice is expanding, and new patients often have to wait several weeks for an appointment. Dr. Rahavy has resisted expanding his office hours or working more than 50 weeks per year.

Finally, if Dr. Rahavy subscribes to the computer service, he will no longer need to rent a records storage locker in the basement of the Professional Building. The locker rents for $100 per month.

Required:
Determine whether or not Dr. Rahavy should subscribe to the service.

3-9 Sell or Process Further

The Finger Lakes Boat Company manufactures sailboat hulls at a cost of $4,200 per unit. The hulls are sold to boat yards for $5,000. Finger Lakes Boat Company is evaluating the desirability of adding masts, sails, and rigging to the hulls prior to sale. The additional parts would cost $1,500. However, the completed sailboats could then be sold for $5,800 each.

Required:
Determine whether Finger Lakes should sell sailboat hulls or process them further into complete sailboats. Assume sales volume will not be affected.

3-10 Sell or Process Further

The Morristown Chemical Company processes raw material D into joint products E and F. Each 100 liters of D yield 60 liters of E and 40 liters of F. Raw material D costs $5 per liter, and it costs $100 to convert 100 liters of D into E and F. Product F can be sold immediately for $5 per liter or processed further into product G at an additional cost of $4 per liter. Product G can then be sold for $15 per liter.

Required:
Determine whether product F should be sold or processed further into product G.

3-11 Limited Resources

The Cape Town Manufacturing Company, Ltd. produces three products: X, Y, and Z. A limitation of 200 labor hours per week prevents Cape Town Manufacturing from meeting the sales demand for these products. Product information is as follows:

	X	Y	Z
Unit selling price	$ 160	$ 100	$ 200
Unit variable costs	- 100	- 50	- 180
Unit contribution margin	$ 60	$ 50	$ 20
Labor hours per unit	SO 4	100 2	SO 4
	15	25	5

Required:
(a) Determine the weekly contribution from each product when total labor hours re allocated to the product with the highest:
(1) Unit selling price.
(2) Unit contribution margin.
(3) Contribution per labor hour.
Hint: Each situation is independent of the others.

(b) What generalization can be made regarding the allocation of limited resources to achieve short-run profit maximization?

(c) Determine the opportunity cost Cape Town Manufacturing will incur if management requires the weekly production of 10 units of X.

3-12 Limited Resources

John Drive, a regional sales representative for the Byte Computer Supply Company, has been working more than 80 hours per week calling on a total of 140 regular customers each month. Because of family and health considerations, he has decided to spend no more than 40 hours per week, or 160 per month, with customers. Unfortunately, this cutback will require John to turn away some of his regular customers or, at least, serve them less frequently than once a month. John has developed the following information to assist him in determining how to best allocate his time:

	Customer Classification		
	Large Business	Small Business	Individual
Number of customers	10	50	80
Average monthly sales per customer	$2,000	$1,000	$500
Commission percentage	5%	7%	10%
Hours per customer per monthly visit	4.0	2.0	2.5

Required:

(a) Develop a monthly plan, indicating the number of customers John should call on in each classification to maximize his monthly sales commissions.

(b) Determine the monthly commissions John will earn if he implements this plan.

3-13 Linear Programming with Graphic Analysis (Appendix)

The Menz Company produces two products, X and Y, in one department. Product X has a unit contribution margin of $40, and product Y has a unit contribution margin of $70. The demand for product X exceeds Menz's production capacity, which is limited by available labor- and machine hours. The maximum demand for product Y is 8 units per week. Product information follows:

	Hours per Unit		Total Hours Available per Week
	X	Y	
Labor	12	18	180
Machine	6	4	60

Management desires the product mix that will maximize the weekly contribution toward fixed costs and profits.

Required:

(a) Formulate the objective function and constraints necessary to determine the optimal product mix.

(b) Determine the optimal solution and the corresponding value of the objective function with the aid of graphic analysis.

3-14 Linear Programming with Graphic Analysis (Appendix)

The Old Salt Desk Company produces two styles of desks, Captain's and Mate's, in two departments, Assembly and Finishing. The Captain's desks have a unit contribution margin of $200, and Mate's desks have a unit contribution margin of $150. The demand for Captain's desks exceeds Old Salt's production capacity, which is limited by the available hours in each department. The demand for Mate's desks is 80 units per month. Production information follows:

| | Hours per Unit | | Total Hours |
	Captain's	Mate's	Available per Month
Assembly Department	10	10	1,500
Finishing Department	40	20	4,000

Management desires the product mix that will maximize the monthly contribution toward fixed costs and profits.

Required:

(a) Formulate the objective function and constraints necessary to determine the optimal product mix.
(b) Determine the optimal solution and the corresponding value of the objective function with the aid of graphic analysis.

PROBLEMS

3-15 Multiple Changes in Profit Plans

Presented is the Mountainside Company's April 19X6 contribution income statement.

Mountainside Company
Contribution Income Statement
For the Month of April 19X6

Sales (10,000 units x $40)		$ 400,000
Less variable costs:		
Direct materials (10,000 units x $5)	$ 50,000	
Direct labor (10,000 units x $14)	140,000	
Variable factory overhead (10,000 units x $6)	60,000	
Selling and administrative (10,000 units x $5)	50,000	- 300,000
Contribution margin (10,000 units x $10)		$ 100,000
Less fixed costs:		
Factory overhead	$ 50,000	
Selling and administrative	60,000	- 110,000
Net income (loss)		$ (10,000)

In an attempt to improve the company's profit performance, management is considering a number of alternative actions. They have asked your help in evaluating the consequences of each.

Required:

Determine the effect of each of the following situations on monthly profit. Each situation is to be evaluated independent of all others.

(a) Purchasing automated assembly equipment. This action should reduce direct labor costs by $6 per unit. It will also increase variable overhead costs by $2 per unit and fixed factory overhead by $20,000 per month.

(b) Reducing the unit selling price by $5 per unit. This should increase the monthly sales by 5,000 units. At this higher volume, additional equipment and salaried personnel would be required. This will increase fixed factory overhead by $3,000 per month and fixed selling and administrative costs by $2,500 per month.

(c) Buying rather than manufacturing a component of Mountainside's final product. This will increase direct materials costs by $15 per unit. However, direct labor will decline $4 per unit, variable factory overhead will decline $1 per unit, and fixed factory overhead will decline $10,000 per month.

(d) Increasing the unit selling price by $3 per unit. This action should result in a 1,000-unit decrease in monthly sales.

(e) Combining requirements (a) and (d).

3-16 Multiple Changes in Profit Plans: Multiple Products

Information on Flamingo Bay's three products follow:

	A	B	C
Unit sales per month	800	1,400	900
Selling price per unit	$ 5.00	$ 7.50	$ 4.00
Variable costs per unit	- 5.20	- 6.00	- 2.00
Unit contribution margin	$(0.20)	$ 1.50	$ 2.00

Required:

Determine the effect of each of the following situations on monthly profits. Each situation is to be evaluated independent of all others.

(a) Product A is discontinued.

(b) Product A is discontinued, and the subsequent loss of customers causes sales of B to decline by 100 units.

(c) The selling price of A is increased to $5.50 with a sales decrease of 200 units.

(d) The price of B is increased to $8.00 with a sales decrease of 200 units. However, some of these customers shift to product A, and sales of product A increase by 100 units.

(e) Product A is discontinued, and the plant in which A was produced is used to produce D, a new product. Product D has a unit contribution margin of $0.30. Monthly sales of product D are predicted to be 700 units.

(f) The selling price of product C is increased to $5, and the selling price of product B is decreased to $7. Sales of C decline by 200 units, and sales of B increase by 300 units.

3-17 Relevant Costs and Differential Analysis

The Third National Bank of Outback paid $50,000 for a check-sorting machine in January 19X1. The machine had an estimated life of 10 years and annual operating costs of $40,000, excluding depreciation. Although management is pleased with the machine, recent technological advances have made it obsolete. Consequently, as of January 19X5, the machine has a book value of $30,000, a remaining operating life of 6 years, and a salvage value of $0.

The manager of operations is evaluating a proposal to acquire a new Perfect Reader II—Optical Scanning and Sorting Machine. The new machine would cost $60,000 and reduce annual operating costs to $25,000, excluding depreciation. Because of expected technological improvements, the manager believes the new machine will have an economic life of only 6 years and no salvage value at the end of that life.

Prior to signing the papers authorizing the acquisition of the new machine, the president of the Third National Bank prepared the following analysis:

Six-year savings ([$40,000 - $25,000] x 6 years)	$ 90,000
Cost of new machine	(60,000)
Loss on disposal of old machine	(30,000)
Advantage (disadvantage) of replacement	$ -0-

After looking at these numbers, he rejected the proposal and commented that he was "... tired of looking at marginal projects. This bank is in business to make a profit, not to break even. If you want to break even, go work for the government."

Required:

(a) Evaluate the president's analysis.
(b) Prepare a differential analysis of six-year totals for the old and the new machines.

3-18 Special Order

Thousand Islands Propulsion Company produces a variety of electric trolling motors. Management follows a pricing policy of manufacturing cost, plus 60 percent. In response to a request from Northern Sporting Goods, the following price has been developed for an order of 300 Minnow Motors (this is the smallest motor Thousand Island produces):

Manufacturing costs:	
Direct materials	$ 10,000
Direct labor	12,000
Factory overhead	18,000
Total	$ 40,000
Markup (60 percent)	24,000
Selling price	$ 64,000

Mr. Bass, the president of Northern Sporting Goods, rejected this price as too high and offered to purchase the 300 Minnow Motors at a price of $44,000.

Additional information:
- Thousand Islands has sufficient excess capacity to produce the motors.
- Factory overhead is applied on the basis of direct labor-dollars.
- Budgeted factory overhead is $400,000 for the current year. Of this amount, $100,000 is fixed. Hence, of the $18,000 of factory overhead assigned to the Minnow Motors, only $13,500 is driven by the order. $3,500 is a facility level cost.
- Selling and administrative expenses are budgeted as follows:

| Fixed | $ 90,000 per year (facility level) |
| Variable | $ 20 per unit manufactured and sold |

Required:
(a) The president of Thousand Islands Propulsion wants to know if he should allow Mr. Bass to have the Minnows for $44,000. Determine the effect on profits of accepting Mr. Bass's offer.
(b) Briefly explain why you omitted certain costs from your analysis in requirement (a).
(c) Assume Thousand Islands is operating at capacity and it could sell the 300 Minnows at its regular markup.
    (1) Determine the opportunity cost of accepting Mr. Bass's offer.
    (2) Determine the effect on profits of accepting Mr. Bass's offer.

3-19 Special Order
Every Halloween, the Glacier Ice Cream Shop offers a Trick-or-Treat package of 20 coupons for $3. The coupons are redeemable, by children of 12 or under, for a single-scoop cone of Glacier ice cream, with a limit of one coupon per child per visit. Coupon sales average 500 books per year. The printing costs are $60.

A single-scoop cone of Glacier ice cream normally sells for $0.60. The variable costs of a single-scoop cone are $0.40.

Required:
(a) Determine the loss if all coupons are redeemed without any other effect on sales.
(b) Not all coupons will be redeemed. Assuming regular sales are not affected, determine the coupon redemption rate at which Glacier will break even on the offer.
(c) Assuming regular sales are not affected and that each time a coupon is redeemed one additional single-scoop cone is sold at the regular price, determine the coupon redemption rate at which Glacier will break even on the offer.
(d) Determine the profit or loss incurred on the offer if the coupon redemption rate is 60 percent and:
    (1) One-fourth of the redeemed coupons have no effect on sales.
    (2) One-fourth of the redeemed coupons result in additional sales of 2 single-scoop cones.
    (3) One-fourth of the redeemed coupons result in additional sales of 3 single-scoop cones.

(4) One-fourth of the redeemed coupons come out of regular sales of single-scoop cones.

3-20 Applications of Differential Analysis

The Bird Box produces squirrel-proof bird feeders. The bird feeders are sold to mail-order distributors for $25.00. Manufacturing and other costs are as follows:

Variable Costs per Unit		Fixed Costs per Month	
Direct materials	$ 8.00	Factory overhead	$10,000
Direct labor	7.00	Selling and administrative	5,000
Factory overhead	2.00	Total	$15,000
Distribution	3.00		
Total	$20.00		

The variable distribution costs are for transportation to mail-order distributors. The current monthly production and sales volume is 5,000 units. Monthly capacity is 6,000 units.

Required:

Determine the effect of each of the following situations on monthly profits. Each situation is to be evaluated independent of all others.

(a) A $2.50 increase in the unit selling price should result in a 1,000-unit decrease in monthly sales.
(b) A $2.00 decrease in the unit selling price should result in a 2,000-unit increase in monthly sales. However, because of capacity constraints, the last 1,000 units would be produced during overtime, when the direct labor costs increase by 60 percent.
(c) A British distributor has proposed to place a special, one-time order for 1,000 units next month at a reduced price of $20 per unit. The distributor would pay all transportation costs. There would be additional fixed selling and administrative costs of $100.
(d) A Dutch distributor has proposed to place a special, one-time order for 2,500 units at a special price of $20 per unit. The distributor would pay all transportation costs. There would be additional fixed selling and administrative costs of $200. Assume overtime production is not possible.
(e) A Canadian manufacturer has offered a one-year contract to supply a squirrel guard that attaches to the bottom of the feeder at a cost of $4 per unit. If Bird Box accepts the offer, it will be able to reduce variable manufacturing costs by 10 percent, reduce fixed costs by $500 per month, and rent some space currently used to manufacture bird feeders for $900 per month.
(f) The bird feeders are currently sold assembled and ready for mounting. Selling the feeders unassembled would reduce costs by $5.00 per unit. However, the units could now be sold for only $21.00.
(g) The Bird Box produces a variety of bird feeders. The given information is for an average unit. Determine the variable cost markup required to earn a monthly profit of $20,000.

3-21 Applications of Differential Analysis

Bush-Wack Expeditions offers guided back-country hiking/camping trips in British Columbia. Bush-Wack provides a guide and all necessary food and equipment at a fee of $50 per person per day. Bush-Wack currently provides an average of 600 guide-days per month in June, July, August, and September. Based on available equipment and staff, maximum capacity is 800 guide-days per month. Monthly variable and fixed operating costs are as follows:

Variable Costs per Guide-Day		Fixed Costs per Month	
Food	$ 5.00C *	Equipment rental	$ 5,000C
Guide salary	25.00C	Administration	5,000C
Supplies	2.00C	Advertising	2,000C
Insurance	8.00C	Total	$12,000C
Total	$40.00C		

*C = Canadian dollars.

Required:

Determine the effect of each of the following situations on monthly profits. Each situation is to be evaluated independent of all others.

(a) A $12C increase in the daily fee should result in a 200-unit decrease in monthly sales.

(b) A $5C decrease in the daily fee should result in a 300-unit increase in monthly sales. However, because of capacity constraints, the last 100 guide-days would be provided by subcontracting to another firm at a cost of $46C per guide-day.

(c) A French tour agency has proposed to place a special, one-time order for 80 guide-days next month at a reduced fee of $45C per guide-day. The agency would pay all insurance costs. There would be additional fixed administrative costs of $200C.

(d) An Italian tour agency has proposed to place a special, one-time order for 300 guide-days next month at a special fee of $45C per guide-day. The agency would pay all insurance costs. There would be additional fixed administrative costs of $200C. Assume additional capacity beyond 800 guide-days is not available.

(e) An Alberta outdoor supply company has offered to supply all necessary food and camping equipment at $7.50C per guide-day. This eliminates the current food costs and reduces the monthly equipment rental costs to $1,500C.

(f) Clients must currently carry a backpack and assist in camp activities such as cooking. Bush-Wack is considering the addition of mules to carry all food and equipment and the hiring of college students to perform camp activities such as cooking. This will increase variable costs of $10C per guide-day and fixed costs by $1,200C per month. However, 600 full-service guide-days per month could now be sold at $75C each.

(g) Bush-Wack provides a number of different types of wilderness experiences. The given information is for an average tour. Determine the variable cost markup required to earn a monthly profit of $6,000C.

3-22 Differential Analysis of Alternative Facilities

Williams Company owns and operates a nationwide chain of movie theaters. The 500 properties in the Williams chain vary from low-volume, small-town, single-screen theaters to high-volume, big-city, multiscreen theaters.

Management is considering installing machines that will make popcorn on the premises. These machines would allow the theaters to sell freshly popped popcorn daily rather than the prepopped popcorn that is currently purchased in large bags. This proposed feature would be properly advertised and is intended to increase patronage at the company's theaters.

The machines are available from a leasing company in several different sizes. The annual rental and operating costs vary with the size of the machine. The machine capacities and costs are shown below:

	Popper Model		
	Economy	**Regular**	**Super**
Annual capacity (boxes)	50,000	120,000	300,000
Costs:			
Annual machine rental	$ 8,000	$ 11,000	$ 20,000
Popcorn cost per box	0.13	0.13	0.13
Other costs per box	0.22	0.14	0.05
Cost of each box	0.08	0.08	0.08

Required:

(a) Calculate the sales volume in boxes at which the Economy Popper and the Regular Popper would earn the same profit.
(b) Management can estimate the number of boxes to be sold at each theater. Present a decision rule, based on sales volume in boxes, that would enable Williams's management to select the most profitable machine without having to make a separate cost calculation for each theater.
(c) Could management use the average number of boxes sold per seat for the entire chain and the capacity of each theater to develop the decision rule? Explain your answer.

(CMA Adapted)

3-23 Relevant Costs for Various Decisions

The income statement for Davann Co. presented on page 156 represents the operating results for the fiscal year just ended. Davann had sales of 1,800 tons of product during the current year. The manufacturing capacity of Davann's facilities is 3,000 tons of product.

Davann Co.
Income Statement
For the Year Ended December 31, 19X0

Sales	$ 900,000
Variable costs:	
Manufacturing	$ 315,000
Selling	180,000
Total variable costs	- 495,000
Contribution margin	$ 405,000
Fixed costs:	
Manufacturing	$ 90,000
Selling	112,500
Administrative	45,000
Total fixed costs	- 247,500
Net income before taxes	$ 157,500
Income taxes (40%)	- 63,000
Net income	$ 94,500

Required:

(a) Determine the 19X0 break-even volume in tons of product.

(b) Determine the expected 19X1 after-tax net income, assuming sales volume of 2,100 tons and no changes in selling prices or cost behavior.

(c) Assume demand from regular customers equals 1,800 tons in 19X1 and there are no changes in regular selling prices or cost behavior. Davann has a potential foreign customer that has offered to buy 1,500 tons at $450 per ton. What net income after taxes would Davann make in 19X1 if it took this order and rejected some business from regular customers so as not to exceed capacity?

(d) Assume Davann will have additional capacity in 19X1 and there are no changes in sales to regular customers, selling prices, or cost behavior. Davann plans to market its product at the regular price in a new territory. This will require an additional promotion program costing $61,500 annually. Additionally, an extra $25 per ton sales commission over and above the current sales commission would be required in the new territory. How many tons would have to be sold in the new territory to maintain Davann's current after-tax income of $94,500?

(e) Davann is considering replacing a highly labor-intensive process with an automatic machine. This would result in an increase of $58,500 in annual fixed manufacturing costs. The variable manufacturing costs would decrease by $25 per ton. Determine the new break-even volume in tons.

(f) Davann estimates the per ton selling price will decline by 10 percent next year. If variable costs increase $40 per ton and fixed costs remain unchanged, what sales volume *in dollars* would be required to earn an after-tax net income of $94,500?

(CMA Adapted)

3-24 Accounting Inputs to Linear Programming: Graphic Analysis

The Smile Camera Company manufactures two popular cameras, Little Smile and Big Smile. Recent increases in demand have pushed Smile Camera to the limits of its production capacity. The president is a former engineer who knows that linear programming can be used to determine the optimal product mix. However, he needs your assistance in formulating the objective function coefficients and in determining the profit implications of the optimal solution.

The following information is available from the accounting records:

	Little Smile	Big Smile
Unit selling price	$150	$220
Unit manufacturing costs:		
Direct materials	$ 38	$ 54
Direct labor	30	30
Factory overhead	48	80
Total	$116	$164

Production employees are paid $10 per direct labor-hour. A total of 450 direct labor hours is available each month. Factory overhead is assigned to units manufactured at the rate of $16 per machine-hour. Seventy-five percent of the overhead rate is for variable costs, and 25 percent is for fixed costs. Although averaged over units produced for financial accounting purposes, the fixed factory overhead is driven by facility level activities rather than by unit level activities. A total of 750 machine hours is available each month. The factory overhead rate is based on the full utilization of 750 machine hours each month.

Additional information:

- Because of insufficient raw materials, only 100 Big Smile cameras can be produced each month.
- Variable selling and administrative expenses are $6 per unit of either product.
- Fixed selling and administrative expenses are $2,300 per month.

Required:

(a) Formulate the objective function and constraints necessary to determine the optimal monthly production mix.
(b) Determine the optimal solution and the corresponding value of the objective function with the aid of graphic analysis.
(c) Determine the Smile Camera Company's expected monthly profit. (*Hint*: Determine the fixed factory overhead assigned to each unit at 750 machine hours and then determine monthly fixed factory overhead.)

3-25 Accounting Inputs to Linear Programming: Graphic Analysis

Kyoto Electric produces two video cassette recorders, a manual model that does not contain an automatic timer and an automatic model that does.

Though demand for the automatic model is only 75 units per month, Kyoto has been unable to satisfy the demand for the lower priced manual model. The following information is available from the accounting records:

	Manual	Automatic
Unit selling price	$ 200	$ 329
Unit manufacturing costs:		
Direct materials	$ 105	$ 190
Conversion:		
Department 1	24	24
Department 2	45	90
Total	$ 174	$ 304

The per unit conversion costs include direct labor, variable overhead, and fixed overhead. The fixed factory overhead is driven by facility rather than by unit level activity. In Department 1, conversion costs are assigned at the rate of $20 per hour. Fifty percent is for variable costs, and 50 percent is for fixed costs. A total of 180 hours is available each month in Department 1. In Department 2, conversion costs are assigned at the rate of $30 per hour. Eighty percent is for variable costs, and 20 percent is for fixed costs. A total of 300 hours is available each month in Department 2. The fixed overhead rates, as a portion of total conversion costs, are based on the full utilization of production capacity.

Additional information:

- Variable selling and administrative expenses are $10 per unit of either product.
- Fixed selling and administrative expenses are $1,200 per month.

Required:

(a) Formulate the objective function and the constraints necessary to determine the optimal monthly production mix.
(b) Determine the optimal solution and the corresponding value of the objective function with the aid of graphic analysis.
(c) Determine Kyoto Electric's expected monthly profit.

3-26 Formulating Objective Function

A processing department of the East Orange Chemical Company can vary the production mix of two products, compound B1 and compound B2. Because of the high demand for these products, a chemical engineer has been requested to determine the optimal monthly volumes of each product. The engineer has formulated all the constraints needed to determine the optimal mix with the aid of linear programming and has asked you to assist in developing the objective function coefficients. The engineer has provided you with the following production information:

	Per Two-Liter Bottle*	
	Compound B1	Compound B2
Raw materials:		
C25	1 liter	2 liters
D80	3 liters	1 liter
MA5	—	1 liter
Bottle	1	1
Direct labor	0.4 hours	0.6 hours

*The difference between total inputs and outputs is due to shrinkage, waste, and evaporation.

You obtain the following information from an analysis of the accounting records:

Selling prices:
    Compound B1 $ 12.20/bottle
    Compound B2   18.00/bottle
Raw materials costs:
    C25 $ 0.80/liter
    D80   0.40/liter
    MA5   0.65/liter
    Bottles   0.50 each
Direct labor rate $ 9.00/hour

Monthly factory overhead = $20,000 + 0.40 direct labor dollars
Monthly selling and administrative costs = $15,000 + 0.25 sales revenue

Required:
Formulate the objective function necessary to determine the optimal monthly production in bottles.

DISCUSSION QUESTIONS AND CASES

3-27 Ethics of Frequent Flyer Mile Incentives

In an attempt to attract and retain loyal customers, many organizations offer frequent flyer miles. Consider the following examples:

- Airlines offer frequent flyer miles, sometimes with a minimum of 500 or 750 miles per flight segment.
- Major automobile rental agencies award frequent flyer mile credits on cooperating airlines.
- Many hotel chains award frequent flyer mile credits on cooperating airlines, sometimes at the rate of 1,000 miles per night.
- A few credit cards have even joined in, offering frequent flyer miles on cooperating selected airlines at the rate of one mile per dollar charged.

In exchange for accumulated frequent flyer miles, airlines offer free tickets, free upgrades, and membership in airport clubs. Cooperating hotels offer free lodging in exchange for frequent flyer miles.

Frequent flyer programs are structured so that frequent flyer miles can only accrue to the traveler. Hence, organizations paying for employee travel cannot accumulate frequent flyer miles as an asset. Some frequent flyer programs are structured so that travelers can reassign their unused frequent flyer miles to a charitable purpose sponsored by the airline. The charity then pools these miles to accomplish its goals.

Required:

(a) Discuss the potential impact of frequent flyer incentive programs on the travel costs of organizations.

(b) Discuss why the programs are structured so that organizations paying for employee travel cannot accumulate frequent flyer miles.

(c) Discuss the ethics of frequent flyer programs. Are there any circumstances when taking advantage of frequent flyer incentives is clearly ethical or clearly unethical? Are the administrators of frequent flyer programs encouraging unethical behavior by not allowing organizations that pay for employee travel to accumulate frequent flyer miles?

3-28 Ethics of Markups on Services Charges

Resellers of a variety of products, such as computers, often perform marketing services for manufacturers. In billing manufacturers, there is some question about the ethics and legality of adding a markup to the out-of-pocket cost of marketing services. Consider the following statements by executives in manufacturing and reselling organizations:[6]

- Paul Thomas, a marketing executive for Apple (a major computer manufacturer), said that Apple allows "no scope for profit-making on any Apple [marketing] program."

- Robert Sutis, in-house counsel for Hewlett-Packard (a major manufacturer of computer printers), noted that H-P bases marketing reimbursements on "claim forms that have documentation attached," such as "invoices or tear sheets or other paperwork."

- Curtis J. Scheel, a vice president of MicroAge, Inc. (a computer reseller), commented that to the extent that a company charges more than it spends, it does so to offset costs of running its marketing operations. He added that if vendors discovered that marketing money was going to the bottom line, "they might stop funding."

Susan Thompson just accepted a position with Digital Distributors (DD), a regional computer wholesale company, as DD's new marketing director. In reviewing company records, she determined that DD was charging manufacturers much more than was spent on marketing activities. Big Pear Computing, for example, was charged $2.9 million in 19X8 for advertising, while only $1.5 million was recorded as advertising expenses on Big Pear's account.

---

6 Raju Narisetti, "Intelligent Electronics Made Much of Its Profit At Suppliers Expense," *The Wall Street Journal* (December 6, 1994), pp. A1, A17.

The cumulative effect of these markups was very significant to DD's overall profitability. After asking a few questions and analyzing some data with a spreadsheet program, Susan determined that in 19X8 marketing took in $15 million more from charges to manufacturers than it spent for all marketing operations. Meanwhile, DD's profit after taxes was $24 million.

Concerned about the situation, Susan spoke with Mike Murdstone, DD's controller. He immediately commented that DD has done nothing wrong. Mike observed that DD sends invoices to vendors with a simple statement, such as, "For marketing services $235,000." Mike continued with the following advice: "We do not claim to only bill for actual outlay costs. If manufacturers feel we are overcharging, they could do business with someone else. In the meantime, I recommend you not kill the goose that lays the golden egg."

Required:

Discuss the ethics and legality of DD's billing practices for marketing services. What advice do you have for Susan?

3-29 Special Order and Ethics

Award Plus Co. manufactures medals for winners of athletic events and other contests. Its manufacturing plant, which has the capacity to produce 10,000 medals each month, currently produces 7,500 per month. The company normally charges $175 per medal. Monthly variable and fixed costs for the current activity level are as follows:

Variable costs:		
Manufacturing:		
Labor	$ 375,000	
Material	262,500	
Marketing	187,500	$ 825,000
Fixed costs:		
Manufacturing	$ 275,000	
Marketing	175,000	450,000
Total costs		$ 1,275,000
Variable costs per unit		$110
Average fixed costs per unit		60
Average unit cost		$170

Award Plus has just received a special, one-time order for 2,500 medals at $100 per medal. For this particular order, no variable marketing costs will be incurred. Cathy Senna, a management accountant with Award Plus, has been assigned the task of analyzing this order and recommending whether or not the company should accept or reject it. After examining the costs, Cathy suggests to her supervisor, Gerard LePenn, the controller, that they request competitive bids for the raw materials as the current quote seems high. LePenn insisted that the prices are in line with other vendors and told her that she was not to discuss her observations with anyone else.

Required:
(a) Identify and explain the costs that will be relevant to Cathy's analysis of the special order.
(b) Determine if Award Plus Co. should accept the order. For this requirement, assume that the materials costs of the order are the same as materials costs for regular medals.
(c) Discuss any additional considerations that Cathy should include in her analysis of the special order.
(d) How should Cathy try to resolve the ethical conflict arising out of the controller's insistence that the company avoid competitive bidding?

(CMA Adapted)

SOLUTION TO REVIEW PROBLEM

Unit selling price	$ 4.80
Unit variable costs	- 2.50
Unit contribution margin	$ 2.30

(a)

Profit decrease from reduced sales if there were no changes in prices or costs (1,800 units x $2.30)	$ (4,140)
Profit increase from increase in selling price ([15,000 units - 1,800 units] x $1.50)	19,800
Increase in monthly profit	$ 15,660

(b)

Profit increase from increased sales if there were no changes in prices or costs (6,000 units x $2.30)	$ 13,800
Profit decrease from reduced selling price of all units ([15,000 units x 6,000 units] x $1.80)	(37,800)
Profit decrease from increased direct labor costs of the last 1,000 units (1,000 units x [$0.20 x 0.50])	(100)
Decrease in monthly profit	$ (24,100)

(c)

Increase in revenues (4,000 units x $4)		$ 16,000
Increase in costs:		
Direct materials (4,000 units x $2.00)	$8,000	
Direct labor (4,000 units x $0.20)	800	
Factory overhead (4,000 units x $0.25)	1,000	
Selling and administrative	500	- 10,300
Increase in profits		$ 5,700

(d)

Increase in revenues (8,000 units x $4)		$ 32,000
Increase in costs:		
Direct materials (8,000 units x $2.00)	$16,000	
Direct labor (8,000 units x $0.20)	1,600	
Factory overhead (8,000 units x $0.25)	2,000	
Selling and administrative	500	
Opportunity cost of lost regular sales ([15,000 units + 8,000 units - 20,000 unit capacity] x $2.30)	6,900	- 27,000
Increase in profits		$ 5,000

(e)

	Cost to Make	Cost to Buy	Difference (Effect of Buying on Income)
Cost to buy (15,000 units x $1)		$15,000	$(15,000)
Cost to make:			
Direct materials (15,000 units x $2.00 x 0.40)	$12,000		12,000
Direct labor (15,000 units x $0.20 x 0.40)	1,200		1,200
Factory overhead (15,000 units x $0.25 x 0.40)	1,500		1,500
Opportunity cost	1,000		1,000
Totals	$15,700	$15,000	$ 700
Advantage of buying		$700	

(f)

Increase in revenues:		
Package individually (15,000 units x $5.05)	$75,750	
Sell in bulk (15,000 units x $4.80)	- 72,000	$ 3,750
Additional packaging costs (15,000 units x $0.10)		- 1,500
Advantage of individual packaging		$ 2,250

PART ▸ 2

STRATEGIC COST
MANAGEMENT

After completing this chapter, you should be able to:

LO 1

Describe strategic cost management.

LO 2

Discuss the importance of the value chain approach to analyzing decision alternatives.

LO 3

Analyze an organization's internal value chain, dividing it into processes and activities.

LO 4

Explain how process and activity-based management can help improve organizational performance.

LO 5

Determine the costs of individual activities and the activity costs associated with various cost objectives.

STRATEGIC COST MANAGEMENT I: VALUE CHAIN ANALYSIS AND ACTIVITY-BASED COSTING

In Chapter 2, cost-volume-profit analysis was introduced as useful in the early stages of planning because it provides a framework for discussing planning issues and organizing relevant data. Building on the contribution margin, relevant costs were defined in Chapter 3 as future costs that differ between competing decision alternatives. To focus on relevant costs concepts, the emphasis in Chapters 2 and 3 was on decisions that only involve an analysis of activity cost drivers; that is, units of work performed to serve customers needs that influence costs.

The analytic approach in Chapters 2 and 3 is limited in that structural and organizational cost drivers are given. Recall that structural cost drivers are fundamental choices about the size and scope of operations and the technologies employed in delivering products or services to customers. Also, recall that organizational cost drivers are choices affecting the organization of activities and the involvement of persons inside and outside the organization in decision making. The omission of possible structural and organizational cost driver decisions produced a simplistic environment where the possible ways of serving customers was not subject to change. While this static analysis of unchanging cost structures is often appropriate for analyzing short-run decision alternatives, a more inclusive approach is required for strategic planning.

*In Chapters 4 through 7, we examine how management accounting assists in strategic planning and strategic cost management. **The purpose of this chapter is to broaden our analytic viewpoint from that of the contribution margin for a narrowly defined decision alternative to encompass the place of an organization in a much larger value chain stretching from basic resources to final consumers.** First, the elements of strategic planning and strategic cost management are considered. We continue by examining the value chain and considering some of the advantages of taking a value chain perspective to decision making. We then illustrate how major links in an organization's internal value chain may be broken into processes and activities. Including cost information in our analysis, we determine the costs of individual activities. Finally, we illustrate the accumulation of activity costs to determine the cost of products, projects, and services across an organization's internal value chain.*

STRATEGIC PLANNING AND STRATEGIC COST MANAGEMENT

L O 1

An organization's goal is the purpose toward which its activities are directed. Its long-range goals identify what planners hope an organization will be like in several years. Its **strategic plan** indicates the basic way people in the organization are to go about achieving these long-range goals. The strategic plan serves as a guideline or framework for making medium-range and specific short-run decisions. In a similar manner, strategic cost management provides a framework for making specific short-run or tactical decisions concerning costs.

Many researchers believe strategic cost management has three key elements:

1. The organization's strategic plan, which strategic cost management is designed to support.
2. The **value chain**, which is the set of value-producing activities stretching from basic raw materials to the final customer.
3. **Activity-based management (ABM),** which concerns the identification and selection of activities that maximize the value of activities while minimizing the cost of activities from the viewpoint of the final customer.

Strategic cost management is defined as making decisions concerning specific cost drivers within the context of an organization's business strategy, its internal value chain, and its place in a larger value chain stretching from the development and use of resources to final consumers. Strategic cost management decisions most often affect structural and organizational cost drivers. The focus is on selecting the best way to serve customer needs in the long run.

THE VALUE CHAIN

L O 2

The word *value* has several different definitions. In ethics and religion, *value* refers to moral quality. In mathematics, *value* refers to a numerical quantity. For our purposes, **value** is the worth in usefulness or importance of a product or service to the customer. Unfortunately, while we all make decisions based on what we value, it is a concept that is difficult to quantify. We might decide to purchase a paperback book by John Grisham rather than go to a movie, even though both cost the same, because we derive more personal satisfaction (value) from reading the book. But we cannot easily specify how much more we value reading the book. Nor can we quantify the value of an automobile air bag that prevents serious injury in an accident.

The value chain for a product or service is the set of value-producing activities that stretches from basic raw materials to the final consumer. When we go to a movie, purchase a hamburger, have our car serviced, or buy a newspaper, we are the final consumer at the end of a value chain. Each product or service has a distinct value chain, and that value chain may be analyzed at varying levels of detail.

Illustration of a Value Chain

Developing a value chain from the perspective of the final consumer requires working backwards from the product or service we buy all the way to the basic raw materials entering into the product or service. Developing a value chain from the viewpoint of an organization that is part of a value chain requires working forward (downstream) to the final consumer and backward (upstream) to the source of raw materials.

Depending on the needs of management, value chains are developed at varying levels of detail. If management wants to understand the overall economics associated with a product or service, the value chain might identify only economic entities. Exhibit 4-1 contains a possible value chain for whole chickens purchased at a grocery store. The value chain is presented at three levels, with each level containing additional detail. The first level represents business entities: the hatchery, the poultry farmer, the chicken processor, the wholesale distributor, the grocery store, and the final consumer. Hatcheries breed and hatch chickens. Poultry farms grow the chickens until they are ready for market. Chicken processors slaughter, clean, and pack the chickens. Wholesale distributors purchase chickens in large lots from chicken processors and distribute them in varying lot sizes to grocery stores. Finally, grocery store customers purchase and consume the chickens.

EXHIBIT 4-1: ELEMENTS OF A VALUE CHAIN

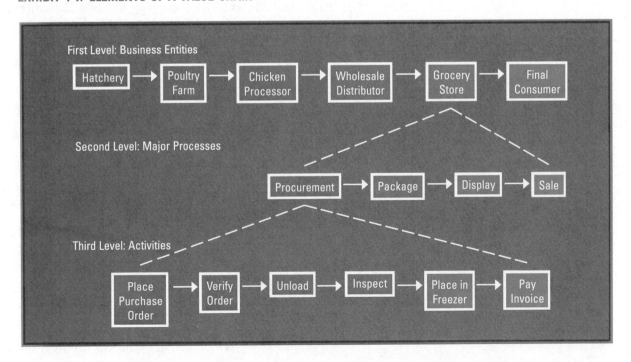

To better understand how a business entity within the chain adds value and incurs costs, management might further refine the value chain into **processes**; that is, collections of related activities intended to achieve a common purpose. The second level in Exhibit 4-1 represents major processes concerning the procurement and sale of chickens by a grocery store. To simplify our illustration, we only show the processes for the grocery store related to chickens. They include procuring chickens from wholesale distributors, packaging the chickens, displaying the packaged product, and selling the packaged chickens.

Because processes often cut across the boundaries of departments within an organization, studying processes helps managers understand how activities in one department are linked to—and can drive—activities and costs in other departments. While the focus in cost management is often on department budgets and costs, the value chain suggests that cost management might more effectively be done from the viewpoint of a process. It is this broader perspective that leads us to place the word *strategic* before the phrase *cost management*. The way processes cut across department boundaries becomes clear as we proceed to the third level in Exhibit 4-1, where the grocery store process of procurement is further disaggregated into major activities.

An **activity** is a unit of work. For clarity, we only show grocery store activities for a single process, procuring chickens. These activities include placing a purchase order for chickens, verifying that the chickens were delivered pursuant to an actual order, unloading the chickens from the delivery truck, inspecting the chickens to verify they meet quality standards, placing the chickens in the freezer until needed, and paying for the chickens after the invoice arrives from the distributor.

Usefulness of Value Chain Concept

All entities along the value chain are dependent on the final customer's perception of the value and cost of a product or service. It is the final customer who ultimately pays all costs and provides all profits to organizations along the entire value chain. Consequently, *the goal of every organization should be to maximize the value while minimizing the cost of a product or service to final customers.* Because it recognizes the importance of final customers, the value chain provides a vantage point that encompasses all activities performed to deliver products and services to final customers.

The goal of maximizing final customer value while minimizing final customer cost leads organizations to examine *internal links* and *external links* in the value chain rather than to examine departments, processes, or activities independently. From a value chain perspective, it is total value chain cost, not the cost of individual businesses, departments, processes, or activities, that is most important.

Focus on Processes, Not Departments
It is difficult to control costs by focusing on departments when processes require activities in several departments. Looking at departments, upper-level managers are tempted to implement across-the-board cuts in department budgets. Unfortunately, across-the-board cuts are often

counterproductive in the long run. They may lead to frustration on the part of employees who still have the same amount of work to perform with fewer resources. Unless there is excess capacity, pressure to perform the same amount of work with fewer resources may lead to reduced quality and service that will harm the organization's competitive position and put further pressure on costs.

Using departments, rather than processes and activities, as the focal point of cost reduction may also result in individual departments taking actions that increase rather than reduce overall costs. A production department might reduce its total batch level costs (such as machine setup) by significantly increasing batch size (the number of units produced each time machines are setup to produce a particular product). While this might reduce the department's costs, the increase in batch size will likely increase handling and storage costs elsewhere in the organization.

In the long run, simply mandating cost cuts will not produce profits or help an organization fulfill its mission. If managers really want to reduce costs, they should keep in mind that the only sure way to eliminate costs is to cease operations.

Looking at the activities that are part of a process, management might determine that certain activities can be combined or eliminated. *As a long-run approach to profit-enhancing cost reductions, it is better to eliminate or reduce activities that drive costs than to merely cut budgets.*

By examining activities within a process, management might determine that the best way to reduce total costs is to increase the budgets of departments that perform activities found early in the internal value chain while reducing the budgets of departments that perform activities late in the internal value chain. Spending more to design a product so that it is easy to manufacture may reduce subsequent manufacturing costs, and spending more on employee training might reduce the cost of rework or response to customer complaints. Saving money may even require an upfront expenditure. For example, a textile manufacturer in North Carolina was able to reduce the cost of spoiled goods by providing employees with free eye exams and glasses.

Treat Suppliers and Buyers as Partners

In the past, relationships between suppliers and buyers were often adversarial. Contact between suppliers and buyers was done solely through purchasing and selling departments. Buyers encouraged competition among possible suppliers with the primary—and often single—goal of obtaining the lowest purchase price. Suppliers strived merely to meet purchasing contract specifications at the lowest possible cost.

Exploiting cost reduction and value-enhancing opportunities in the value chain has led many buyers and suppliers to view each other as partners rather than as adversaries. Buyers have reduced the number of suppliers they deal with, often developing long-term partnerships with a single supplier. Once they establish mutual trust, both proceed to share detailed information on internal operations and help each other solve problems.

Partners work closely to examine mutual opportunities by studying their common value chain. Supplier engineers might determine that a minor relaxation in buyer specifications can produce significant reductions in seller manufacturing costs with only minor increases in subsequent processing costs on the part of the buyer. Working together, they determine how best to modify processes to reduce overall costs and share increased profits.

Companies such as Xerox and Ford now involve their suppliers in design, development, and manufacturing decisions. Motorola has even developed a survey asking suppliers to assess Motorola as a buyer. Among other questions, the survey asks sellers to evaluate Motorola's performance in helping suppliers identify major cost drivers and in helping them to increase their profitability. These questions clearly represent the concerns of a partner rather than those of an adversary. Management Accounting Practice 4-1 describes how relationships with buyers have changed at Chrysler and PPG Industries as these organizations moved toward regarding suppliers as partners.

On a smaller scale, the grocery store in Exhibit 4-1 (page 168) should examine its external links. It may be willing to pay more for chickens if the meat packers and distributors:

MANAGEMENT ACCOUNTING PRACTICE 4-1

Value Chain Perspective Leads to Partnering and a Change in Attitude at Chrysler and PPG Industries

". . . after becoming a quality partner with Chrysler, Valient Machine and Tool, Inc., a manufacturer of automotive and aerospace frame assembly lines, noticed a marked change in Chrysler's handling of its pricing on the 'L-H' midsized car project. Normally, Chrysler would put a large multimillion dollar contract for the building of its major assembly lines out for bid. Instead, Valient was asked to present its cost figures and explain how its costs were derived. Chrysler executives thought some parts of the complex assembly line were too expensive, while others were priced too low. Eventually, Chrysler and Valient settled on prices. This was a big shift in attitude—and behavior—on Chrysler's part. Chrysler didn't award the tender to the lowest bidder, but instead treated its supplier as a close collaborator . . .

"Another attitude change apparent in buyer-seller partnering arrangements is more open access to the buying partner's premises by the seller. For example, at PPG Industries' Lake Charles (Louisiana) chemical manufacturing plant, several of the distributor partners' personnel are preauthorized by plant security to gain access day or night to provide any necessary technical or distribution support. These key staff members have often saved PPG time and money by offering quick, on-the-spot technical support. For instance, when an electrical switch button in the factory would fail, a very expensive replacement unit would routinely be ordered by the plant maintenance staff. The distributor's on-site technical support people advised PPG to order a new switch button costing only six dollars."

Based on: Exposure draft of *Building World Class Buyer/Seller Partnerships,* The Society of Management Accountants of Canada (September 1994), p. 26.

- Make more frequent delivery in small lots so the store can reduce its need for storage.
- Enhance quality to guarantee that chickens meet the store's requirements, enabling the store to reduce inspection costs.
- Streamline ordering and payment procedures so the store can reduce bookkeeping costs.

If the store is able to reduce its total costs by any of these partnering arrangements with upstream suppliers, it can maintain or enhance its competitive position and profitability while reducing the selling price of products to final consumers. Remember that competitors are also striving to reduce costs and enhance their competitive position. Hence, failing to strive for improvement will likely result in reduced sales and profits.

The development of partnerships between entities in the value chain has had a significant impact on marketing. Customers now expect sales representatives to be technical experts who understand the customers' businesses and can offer advice on how best to perform specialized activities or processes. Hence, sales representatives are often technical experts in some engineering or scientific discipline who receive additional education in business and marketing. National Starch and Chemical Company, for example, hires chemical engineers for technical sales positions.

Value-Added and Value Chain Perspectives

The value chain perspective is often contrasted with a value-added perspective. Under a value-added perspective, decision makers only consider the cost of resources to their organization and the selling price of products or services to their immediate customers. Using a value-added perspective, the goal is to maximize value-added (the difference between the selling price and costs) by the organization. To do this, the value-added perspective focuses primarily on internal activities and costs. Under a value chain perspective, the goal is to maximize value and minimize cost to final customers, often by developing linkages or partnerships with suppliers and customers. Even though there is nothing inherently wrong with a value-added perspective, it is inadequate in a highly competitive environment and certainly not a basis for world-class competition. Contrasted with the value chain perspective, the value-added perspective starts too late and stops too soon.

Although initial efforts to enhance competitiveness might start with a value-added perspective, it is important to expand to a value chain perspective. World-class competitors need to utilize both a value-added and a value chain perspective. These firms always keep the final customer in mind and recognize that the profitability of each entity in the value chain is dependent on the overall value and cost of the product or service delivered to final customers.

Note that the value-added perspective is the foundation of the make or buy decision considered in Chapter 3. The key differences between the partnering decisions considered here and the make or buy decision discussed in Chapter 3 concern time frame, perspective, and attitude. The make or buy decision is a stand-alone, often short-run decision that does not view vendors and customers as partners. The value chain perspective is:

- Comprehensive.
- Focused on the final customers.
- Strategic.
- A basis for partnerships between vendors and customers.

For organizations along the value chain, enhancing or maintaining a competitive position requires an understanding of the entire system used to develop and deliver value to final customers. All organizations along the value chain are in business together and should work together as partners rather than as adversaries.

Determining the Entities in the Value Chain of a Product or Service

The task of identifying the links in the value chain for an organization or one of its products or services can be approached in a systematic manner. As a starting point, the analyst should identify the major business entities in the value chain. He or she might start with library research to gain an overall understanding of an industry and then continue by interviewing personnel that interface with customers and suppliers. The analyst will also need to speak with personnel from downstream and upstream entities. These people are most knowledgeable in issues concerning their customers and suppliers.

Marketing personnel might inform an analyst developing a value chain for a paperboard manufacturer that most of the firm's paperboard is sold to companies that coat the paperboard with a plastic and convert the coated paperboard into beverage containers. Speaking with customers, the analyst might further determine that the beverage containers are purchased by beverage companies to hold fruit juices and that the fruit juices are sold to final consumers in grocery stores. Further research might reveal that most of the juice containers are used in packed lunches. The resultant value chain is shown in Exhibit 4-2.

Equipped with this information, the paperboard manufacturer might consider changes to make the final product more competitive. Perhaps a minor

EXHIBIT 4-2: VALUE CHAIN FOR PAPERBOARD MANUFACTURER WITH UPSTREAM AND DOWNSTREAM LINKS

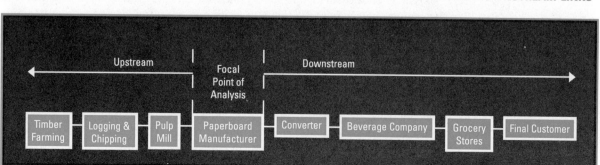

change in the paperboard can enhance the capability of the containers to keep beverages cold, or a lighter stock of paperboard might be used, reducing weight and cost. Another possibility is that the manufacturer can change the width of the paperboard to reduce scrap or eliminate costly cutting operations currently performed by paperboard buyers.

Turning attention upstream, the analyst might talk with purchasing personnel to identify the sources of pulp used in manufacturing paperboard and even continue further upstream to pinpoint the organizations that provide logs and chips to the pulp mill and even to locate the timber farms where the trees are grown. It is possible that changes in the composition of pulp might enhance the capability of the beverage containers to keep fruit juices cold. This enhanced value to final customers would help ensure the long-run viability of all organizations along the value chain.

A **vertically integrated organization** is one that operates two or more units that might be regarded as independent links in a value chain. Tyson Foods, for example, operates across most of the value chain represented in Exhibit 4-1 (page 168). Its poultry business includes hatcheries, poultry farms, and chicken processors. A **horizontally integrated organization** is one that operates many entities in the same industry. P&C Supermarkets, for example, runs numerous grocery stores in the northeastern United States. P&C has also integrated vertically by developing its own wholesale operations. Exhibit 4-3 illustrates the value chain for whole chickens with additional information about the scope of Tyson Foods' and P&C's operations.

Although Tyson Foods and P&C Supermarkets operate across two or more possible independent entities in the value chain, an analyst developing a value chain for either organization should include the more fundamental entities in the value chain. This encourages management to consider all possible decision alternatives. Tyson Foods competes against organizations that specialize in hatching, growing, and processing. To maximize its profit potential, Tyson must manage each value chain link as efficiently as independent competitors.

If Tyson's poultry farms are not competitive, Tyson might consider ways to improve their performance, using the performance of their independent competitors as a benchmark or standard of comparison. Alternatively, Tyson might consider selling chicks produced in hatcheries to outside poultry farms and then buying mature chickens from poultry farms. Considering all possible entities also allows Tyson to uncouple units. Tyson might, for example, hatch more chickens than its poultry farms can accommodate and sell the excess to independent poultry farms.

An organization may participate in several value chains. General Electric is involved in value chains for products ranging from electric turbines to home appliances and electric light bulbs. P&C Supermarkets is involved in the sale of thousands of food and household products. Obviously P&C is not able to develop separate value chains for each product it carries. Instead, an analyst at P&C would be more apt to focus on families of products and internal processes and activities common to many products.

EXHIBIT 4-3: VERTICAL INTEGRATION AND THE VALUE CHAIN

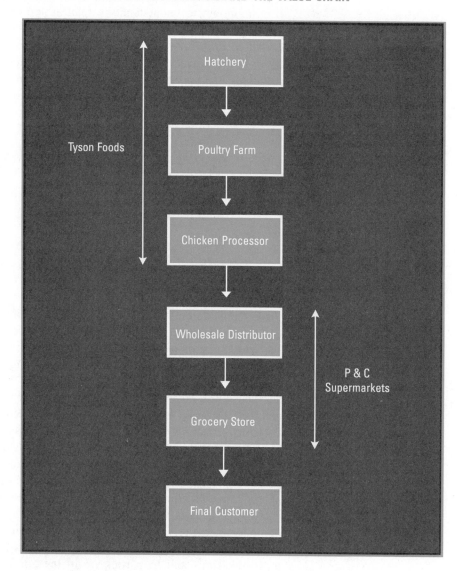

**DISAGGREGATING AN
ENTITY LEVEL LINK
INTO INTERNAL
PROCESSES AND
ACTIVITIES**

The development of a schematic representation of a value chain is a subjective art rather than an objective science. The specific elements included in a value chain vary, depending on the perceptions of the analyst. There is no single correct answer. Likewise, when it comes to developing a schematic representation of an internal value chain, analysts will develop different renditions.

Before considering procedures used to develop an internal value chain, it is important to understand the relationship between cost drivers and the value chain. Cost drivers, factors that influence costs, were previously classified into three major categories: structural, organizational, and activity. While the most obvious cost drivers are activities that consume costly resources, the specific activities that an organization utilizes to serve customer needs are predetermined by previous structural and organizational decisions (or the failure to make such decisions).

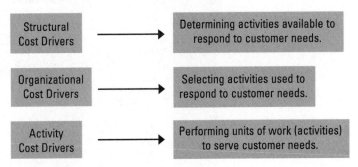

Consider the grocery store in Exhibit 4-1 (page 168). *Structural cost drivers* include determination of the organization's goals (to enter the grocery store business), as well as decisions concerning location (freestanding buildings or part of strip mall), scale (horizontal integration and size of each store), scope (vertical integration through ownership of wholesale distributors), technology (bar code scanning at cash registers linked to computers for inventory control and reordering), and complexity (number and type of products offered for sale). *Organizational cost drivers* include decisions affecting the organization of processes (Will purchase orders be placed by the manager of the meat department, or will all orders be placed by the assistant store manager?), layout efficiency (relative locations of unloading dock and freezer), product configuration (Through genetic engineering and breeding, how much of the total weight of the chicken is comprised of parts final customers regard as most desirable?), exploitation of linkages in the value chain (the development of partnerships with suppliers and customers), work force involvement (empowering employees to make decisions and to participate in the continuous improvement of the organization), and attitudes toward total quality management (continuously striving to deliver a product that maximizes value for and minimizes the costs to final customers).

Previous examples cited in this chapter of ways to reduce costs or to improve value to final customers concerned organizational decisions about the organization of activities. These included allocating more resources to product design for the purpose of reducing subsequent manufacturing costs and developing partnerships with suppliers and vendors up and down the value chain. Exhibit 4-4 contains a brief overview of structural, organizational, and activity cost drivers.

The activity cost drivers in the lower portion of Exhibit 4-4 have been matched with possible ways of measuring the volume of the activity. The performance of each activity, such as verifying that a shipment received at

EXHIBIT 4-4: COST DRIVERS AND ACTIVITIES

Structural Cost Drivers—determining activities available to respond to customer needs.

Mission and goals (decision to enter the grocery store business)
Location (freestanding stores or mall location)
Scale (horizontal integration for the number of stores and the size of each store)
Scope (vertical integration through ownership of wholesale distributors)
Technology (bar code scanning at cash registers linked to computers for inventory control and reordering)
Complexity (number and type of products offered for sale)

Organizational Cost Drivers—selecting activities used to respond to customer needs.

Work force involvement (participation, empowerment, commitment)
Total quality management (attitudes and achievements concerning quality)
Plant layout efficiency (efficiency of plant layout)
Product configuration (effectiveness and efficiency of design)
Exploitation of linkages in value chain (partnerships with suppliers and customers)

Activity Cost Drivers—performing units of work (activities) to serve customer needs.

Activities (Within Procurement Process for Whole Chickens at a Grocery Store)

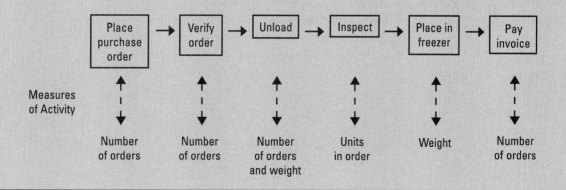

the unloading dock is the result of a legitimate order, consumes resources. In this case, the resources consumed include the time spent by the receiving clerk to verify that the order is legitimate, in addition to any time and materials consumed to provide the receiving clerk with the necessary information.

Exhibit 4-5 (page 178) contains a "generic" internal value chain. It is generic in the sense that it represents the major internal processes of virtually any organization. Note that in addition to processes directly related to serving customer needs, such as inbound logistics and operations, Exhibit 4-5 recognizes the existence of supporting activities such as accounting, design, finance, human resources, and maintenance.

EXHIBIT 4-5: GENERIC INTERNAL PROCESSES

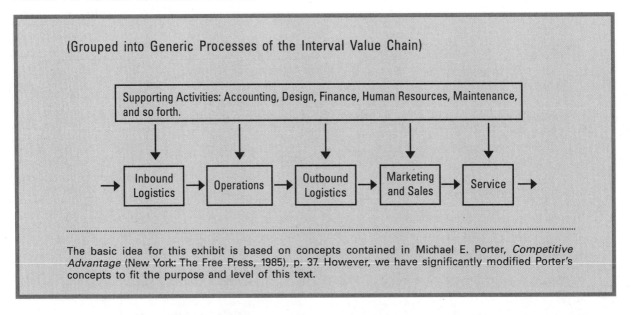

(Grouped into Generic Processes of the Interval Value Chain)

Supporting Activities: Accounting, Design, Finance, Human Resources, Maintenance, and so forth.

Inbound Logistics → Operations → Outbound Logistics → Marketing and Sales → Service

The basic idea for this exhibit is based on concepts contained in Michael E. Porter, *Competitive Advantage* (New York: The Free Press, 1985), p. 37. However, we have significantly modified Porter's concepts to fit the purpose and level of this text.

Representative services provided by these supporting activity areas include:

Accounting:
- Processing employee paychecks
- Developing budgets
- Determining activity costs
- Verifying the existence of recorded assets

Design:
- Developing specifications for products or services delivered to customers
- Developing specifications for procedures to produce products or services

Finance:
- Signing checks
- Obtaining financial resources

Human resources:
- Hiring employees
- Training employees

Maintenance:
- Repairing equipment
- Cleaning buildings

The generic internal value chain is a useful starting point in identifying major processes. It is equally applicable to service and manufacturing, profit, not-for-profit, and government organizations. Consider the following examples of inbound logistics and operations processes in various organizations:

Organization	Type of Organization	Inbound Logistics	Operations
• McDonalds'	Service, for-profit	Order food from suppliers	Food preparation
• Internal Revenue Service	Service, government	Receive tax returns electronically	Transfer data to IRS data base
• Zenith Television	Manufacturing, for-profit	Receive TV components	Assemble TV components
• University of Southern California	Service, not-for-profit	Unload office supplies	Teach courses

Process Map

Once the major processes performed to serve customer needs are identified, the next step is to determine the activities involved in each process. The best way to do this is to develop a process map. A **process map,** or process flow-chart, is a schematic overview of all the activities required to complete a process. Each major activity is represented by a rectangle on the map. Like a road map, a process map indicates how to get from point A (input) to point B (output) and all the communities (activities) along the way. The activities level of Exhibit 4-1 (page 168) contains a simple process map for procurement.

It is important to make sure the process map represents the process as it actually exists, rather than as the analyst imagines that it should exist. Developing an accurate process map requires the assistance of personnel involved in the process. When developing a process map, it often becomes apparent that while each person involved in a process is an expert in his or her own specialty, no one understands the whole process. This is particularly likely to occur when a process crosses department boundaries. People typically focus on activities within their department, rather than on processes across the entire organization.

Recognizing the point at which to stop is a problem in developing a process map. While the map needs to be comprehensive enough to include every step in performing a process, it is counterproductive to identify every single action as a separate activity. In the case of completing a purchase order, the detailed actions might start as follows:

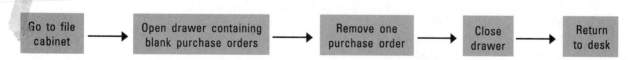

This level of detail is analogous to writing lines of code for a computer program. We don't need every single step. We do need to understand the process and its major activities. Consequently, in developing a process map of the procurement process, completing the purchase order would likely be a single step. If management wanted to specifically evaluate the subprocess of completing the purchase order, we might go to a further level of detail.

Like developing a value chain, developing a process map is more of an art than an exact science. Different analysts will likely develop somewhat different maps when studying the same process. As noted in Chapter 1, management accounting allows subjective data when subjective information is relevant. It also varies the level of aggregation or disaggregation, depending on the needs of management.

Storyboards and Employee Empowerment

The most knowledgeable people are most frequently the people who perform activities. Very often they operate in isolation, knowing their part of the process, but unable to communicate with others. They may have ideas for improving their activities; but because they do not have a forum for expressing their thoughts and do not know how the pieces fit together, their valuable knowledge is unused. Having employees develop storyboards is a useful approach to process mapping. It is also an excellent way of empowering employees to make process improvements.

A **storyboard** is a process map developed by employees who perform the component activities required to complete a process. In the storyboard, employees tell the story of how they complete their part of a process. One approach to developing a storyboard is to have employees write a brief summary of activities they perform on index cards. Then all the cards are organized in a sequential manner and pinned to a corkboard (the storyboard). It may take some time to get activities in the proper sequence, and it may be desirable to stack cards that appear to be detailed parts of a single activity together under a single header card. When employees are satisfied with the storyboard, the board will show an overview of the current process. This overview may be transcribed to paper for communication to others.

To study work flows, the storyboard might be organized around an outline of the organization's physical facilities. The cards, representing activities performed by employees, would be pinned to the board at the location of the appropriate employee workstation. String is then attached to the pins holding the index cards to visualize the flow of work. A college might do this to see how students move from office to office during registration.

Process and Activity-Based Management

L O 4

It is not unusual to have people make comments such as, "I can't believe we do this!" "That doesn't make sense," and "That can't be correct," as the map takes shape. One use of process maps is to improve processes. Things that "I can't believe," "doesn't make sense," or "can't be correct" are obviously in need of improvement. Once employees understand the overall process of which their activities are a part of, they can make recommendations for improvement. And these recommendations can pay off handsomely.

At General Electric's Evendale, Ohio, plant, the focus used to be on the efficiency of individual workers and machines. In pursuit of high machine utilization, parts used to go to a central steam-cleaning facility between operations. Developing a process map revealed that establishing several cleaning booths closer to workstations would save enough time to more than pay for the additional equipment. Working with the map, employees were also able to rearrange equipment to achieve a more continuous flow of work through the factory. The result was a 50 percent savings in processing time and a $4 million reduction in work-in-process inventories.[1] Management Accounting Practice 4-2 (page 182) contains another example of how developing a process map facilitated process improvements.

Continuous Improvement and Reengineering

In today's highly competitive market, world-class companies must constantly strive to improve the value and reduce the costs of their products or services. In **continuous improvement**, an organization's employees constantly evaluate products, services, and processes, seeking ways to do better. As demonstrated in Management Accounting Practice 4-2, having an up-to-date process map is a useful starting point in continuous improvement.

Process reengineering is the fundamental redesign of a process to serve internal or external customers. While continuous improvement focuses on improving existing processes, reengineering reinvents a process. The goal in process reengineering is to radically reduce costs or to radically improve quality or service. In process reengineering, employees start with a blank sheet of paper and determine how the process should be performed under ideal circumstances. They should not be constrained by current facilities or work relationships. Although it may not be possible to immediately implement the reengineered process, it is a useful goal to work toward.

Phoenix Designs, Inc. sold custom-designed furniture through independent dealers. Sales representatives would gather information about customer needs and forward the information to Phoenix Designs. Employees at Phoenix Designs would then design furniture to meet the customer needs. The furniture designs were returned to the appropriate sales representative who met with the customer to review the design. After receiving requested changes from the customer, the process of finalizing the design and obtaining a sales contract took up to six weeks. Rather than attempting to improve this process, Phoenix Designs reengineered it by providing sales representatives with a personal computer and special software. The sales representative was now able to design the furniture at the customer's office. The result was a radical reduction in the time to develop a final design and obtain a sales contract, a 1,000 percent increase in dealer sales and a 27 percent increase in income.[2]

Value-Added and Nonvalue-Added Activities

The total time required to complete a process is referred to as **cycle time**. Minimizing cycle time is becoming increasingly important as companies strive to compete on the basis of time. Management Accounting Practice 4-3 (page 183) examines the increasing importance of cycle time as manufacturing companies such as Levi, Ross Operating Valve, and Caterpiller move to mass customization and agile manufacturing.

After developing a map of the current process, a good way to start improving the process is to classify each activity as value-added or nonvalue-added and then determine how to minimize or eliminate nonvalue-added activities. A **value-added activity** is an activity that adds value to a

---

1 Thomas Stewart, "GE Keeps Those Ideas Coming," *Fortune* (August 1991), p. 48.
2 Marshall Romney, "Business Process Reengineering," *The CPA Journal* (October 1994), pp. 30-31.

MANAGEMENT ACCOUNTING PRACTICE 4-2

Process Maps Facilitate Process Improvements at Brooktree

Brooktree manufactures computer chips from wafers. The wafers are manufactured to Brooktree's specifications by a foundry. Scheduling manufacturing activities at Brooktree depends on the foundry committing to delivery dates for wafer orders. Brooktree wanted to reduce the time to obtain delivery date commitments in order to better schedule its own facilities and to reduce the time required to fill customer orders for computer chips. A team of Brooktree and foundry personnel developed a map for the process of obtaining a commitment date for wafer delivery. As shown below, the map revealed that 15 days were required for delivery date commitment. Working together, representatives of both firms developed a new process, also shown below, that requires only six days to obtain a delivery date commitment.

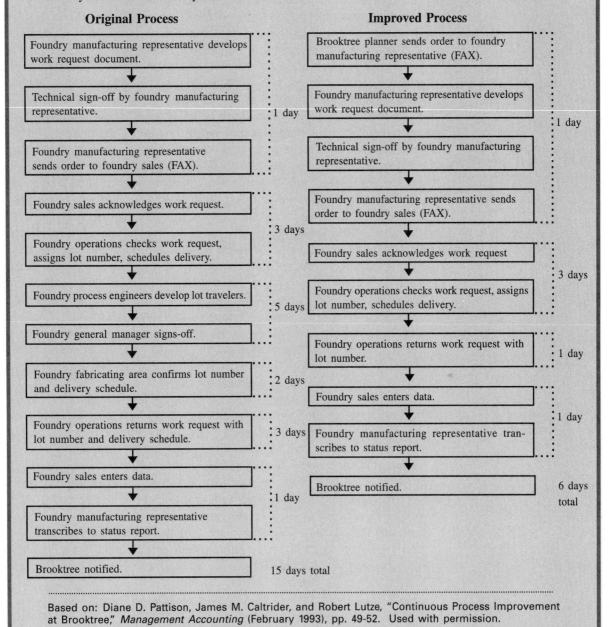

Based on: Diane D. Pattison, James M. Caltrider, and Robert Lutze, "Continuous Process Improvement at Brooktree," *Management Accounting* (February 1993), pp. 49-52. Used with permission.

MANAGEMENT ACCOUNTING PRACTICE 4-3

Agile Manufacturing Satisfies Customers and Increases Profits by Reducing Cycle Time

The ability to manufacture custom products as quickly and inexpensively as mass produced products is the ultimate goal of the movement toward mass customization. While a recent article in *Business Week* suggested that mass customization would be the factory focus of the 21st century, for many companies it is already here, and it is changing how and where they do business.

For an extra $10, made-to-fit blue jeans are available at some Original Levi's Stores. Clerks note and forward customer's vital statistics to a Levi's factory in Tennessee where a computer instructs a robotic tailor to cut fabric precisely to the customer's measurements. It takes about three weeks for the customer to receive the custom jeans.

A factory that is capable of producing custom products on a mass scale is referred to as an agile factory. Although the situation may change in a few years, today agile factories still provide a service or function advantage that allows them to charge a premium price. Ross Operating Valve Co. uses computers and automated machine tools to design and manufacture one-of-a kind valves in as little as 72 hours. According to David Ross, marketing director at Ross Operating Valve Co., once customers realize that agile suppliers can provide exactly what is needed on a tight schedule, "price is no longer a factor."

The need to reduce cycle times as companies strive to compete in an increasingly agile marketplace is also affecting where some products are manufactured. Caterpillar moved the manufacture of earthmoving equipment back to the U.S. from Korea after determining that the time moving products through international pipelines more than offset any labor savings.

Based on: "Custom-Made, Direct From the Plant," *Business Week/21st Century Capitalism*, 1994, pp. 158-159, and "Computer Lets Levi's Offer Custom Jeans," *Watertown Daily Times* (November 25, 1994), pp. 11-12.

---

product or service from the viewpoint of the customer. A **nonvalue-added activity** is an activity that does not add value to a product or service from the viewpoint of the final customer. Because the performance of nonvalue-added activities takes time and requires the use of costly resources, continuous improvement and process reengineering both seek to minimize or eliminate nonvalue-added activities. As noted in Exhibit 4-6 (page 184), the four classic examples of nonvalue-added activities within a manufacturing process are movement, waiting, setup, and inspection.

The string in a storyboard represents movement between workstations. After visualizing the movement involved in a process using a storyboard, employees might offer suggestions for rearranging workstations for the purpose of minimizing movement. The introduction of the electronic filing of tax returns has allowed the Internal Revenue Service to eliminate some physical movement without rearranging workstations. Likewise, many colleges are now using electronic registration to minimize student movement.

Waiting customers or materials cost money. Facilities have to be provided to store materials or for customers who are waiting. These facilities could be eliminated or devoted to value-added activities if waiting time is reduced. The faster customers can be served at a fast-food restaurant, such as Wendy's, the less space that needs to be devoted to waiting lines and the more space

EXHIBIT 4-6: NONVALUE-ADDED ACTIVITIES WITHIN A MANUFACTURING PROCESS

- **Movement**—time spent being shifted between workstations where value-added activities are performed.
- **Waiting**—time spent in suspense between value-added activities.
- **Setup**—time spent getting ready to perform a value-added activity.
- **Inspection**—time spent verifying that a value-added activity was done correctly.

that can be devoted to tables. In a manufacturing organization, excessive work-in-process ties up money in inventory, clutters the shop flow, increasing the difficulty of locating things, and increases the danger of obsolete and damaged inventory.

Setup involves getting ready to do work. Gathering your book, calculator, paper, and pencil prior to starting homework is an example of setup. Fifteen minutes spent trying to locate your calculator is a nonvalue-added activity. Keeping your calculator in the top drawer of your desk will reduce nonproductive setup time prior to doing homework.

Inspection involves verifying that goods or services meet quality standards. If processes can be established to ensure a job is done right the first time, every time, inspection can be eliminated.

While continuous improvement and process reengineering should strive to minimize or eliminate nonvalue-added activities, it may not be feasible to drive the time devoted to nonvalue-added activities to zero. Examining nonvalue-added activities for possible time and cost savings is, however, a useful starting point that may yield significant results. After examining nonvalue-added activities, attention should be shifted to value-added activities for possible improvements. Indeed, the way value-added activities are performed may impact nonvalue-added activities such as the need for inspection.

Activity Cost Data

Information on the cost of activities is helpful in process improvement and reengineering. In the early stages of implementing an improvement process, it is important to justify the project with cost savings. Hence, the most costly nonvalue-added activities are often selected for initial improvement efforts. Projected cost savings from reducing nonvalue-added movement time may be used to justify the cost of rearranging equipment in a factory. Information on the cost of alternative activities may assist in determining the best way to perform a process.

Many Japanese companies have developed detailed cost tables to assist in product and process design, continuous improvement, and process reengineering.[3] These **cost tables** are data bases that indicate the effect on costs of using different materials, production methods, and product designs. A hypothetical example of a simple cost table is presented in Exhibit 4-7.

The development of cost tables requires a significant investment of resources, and their availability provides a competitive advantage. According

---

3 Takeo Yoshikawa, John Innes, and Falconer Mitchell, "Japanese Cost Management Practices," in *Handbook of Cost Management*, Barry J. Brinkler, ed. (Boston: Warren Gorhan Lamont, 1992) Sec. F3. Cost tables are examined on pp. F3-23 - F3-29.

to a study jointly sponsored by the Society of Management Accountants of Canada, the Institute of Management Accountants, and the Consortium for Advanced Manufacturing—International:

> A primary role of the management accountant in Japanese companies employing cost tables is to maintain such tables. To do that requires that the management accountant understand design alternatives, procurement practices, process engineering, and production. During the product development process, the management accountant brings the content of the cost tables to the inevitable trade-off discussions. If the existing tables are not adequate, the management accountant may have to extend the existing tables to satisfy new issues.[4]

Developing cost information for current activities is illustrated in the next section of this chapter. To maximize the usefulness of activity cost information for product design, process improvement, and process reengineering, management accountants must go beyond tracing current activity costs and examine the effects of technological developments, inside and outside the company, on costs.

Through this chapter, we have focused attention on processes and activities rather than on traditional organizational units such as departments. Because processes cut across departments and because processes are composed of individual activities, managers should focus their attention on processes rather than on activities. **Activity-based management (ABM)** stresses the identification and selection of activities that maximize the value while minimizing the cost of activities from the viewpoint of the final customer. **Process-based management** goes further than ABM by emphasizing that in evaluating activities, managers must consider the entire process of which activities are a part. Activity- and process-based management are complementary concepts. Furthermore, the improvement or optimization of processes requires information on the cost of activities included in the process.

EXHIBIT 4-7: ILLUSTRATION OF A COST TABLE

Activity: Welding
Equipment: Welding Machine I
Cost per Inch

Type of Metal	Thickness of Metal			
	1/8 inch	1/4 inch	1/2 inch	1 inch
Type A	$1.20	$2.50	$5.20	$11.00
Type B	1.50	3.20	7.00	16.00
Type C	1.60	3.50	7.50	18.00

---

4 *Implementing Target Costing*, Management Accounting Guideline 28 (Hamilton, Ontario: The Society of Management Accountants of Canada, 1994), p. 34.

ACTIVITY-BASED COSTING

L O 5

A **cost objective** is an object to which costs are assigned. In management accounting, the selection of cost objectives and subsequent cost assignments is made to assist in internal decision making. Consequently, the selection of a cost objective depends on the decision for which the cost information will be used. Possible cost objectives include processes, products, projects, services, and customers. Management might be interested in the cost of processing a purchase order to assist in continuous improvement. They might be interested in the cost of a product or service to determine the profitability of the product or service. They might be interested in the cost of alternative long-distance telephone carriers (MCI versus Sprint versus AT&T) to identify the carrier with the best combination of quality, service, and cost. Activity-based costing is used to develop cost information for these and other purposes.

Activity-based costing (ABC) involves determining the cost of activities and tracing the cost of activities to cost objectives on the basis of the cost objective's utilization of units of activity. ABC concepts were introduced in Chapter 2 when we considered the hierarchy of activity costs and in Chapter 3 when activity cost information was used in an equipment replacement decision. However, the material in Chapters 2 and 3 was highly aggregated, and the starting point was revenue, cost, and contribution margin information per unit of activity. Having introduced the value chain, processes within the value chain, and activities within processes, we are now ready to consider the assignment of costs to activities and the determination of the cost per unit of activity.

The concepts underlying ABC can be summarized in two statements and illustrations:

1. Activities performed to fill customer needs consume resources that cost money.

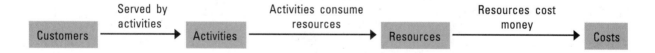

2. The cost of resources consumed by activities should be assigned to cost objectives on the basis of the units of activity consumed by the cost objective.

*Based on units of activity utilized by the cost objective

The cost objective is typically a product or service provided to a customer. Depending on the information needs of decision makers, the cost objective might be the customer.

Two-Stage Model

The most widely used approach to activity-based costing involves the use of a two-stage model. In the first stage, costs are assigned to activities. In the second stage, costs are reassigned from activities to cost objectives on the basis on the cost objective's use of activities. Operationalizing the two-stage model requires:

1. Identifying activities.
2. Assigning costs to activities.
3. Determining the basis for assigning the cost of activities to cost objectives.
4. Determining the cost per unit of activity.
5. Reassigning costs from the activity to the cost objective on the basis of the cost objective's consumption of activities.

Identifying Activities

Most of the material in this chapter has concerned the development of value chains, the identification of processes within a value chain, and the determination of activities within a process. To simplify the illustration of ABC concepts, we restrict ourselves to an example involving two processes: (1) inbound logistics and (2) operations in a manufacturing organization. These are the first two generic internal processes in Exhibit 4-5 (page 178). We will also assume that our purpose is to determine the total cost and profitability of jobs. The Chapter 4 review problem continues the example with the addition of activity costs for outbound logistics, marketing and sales, and service. When combined with the following example, the review problem illustrates the use of activity-based costing across an organization's entire internal value chain.

Assume the Ace Metal Shop produces custom metal parts in response to customer job orders. All inbound logistics are handled by the Purchasing Department whose activities include placing purchase orders for raw materials used in specific jobs and receiving raw materials. All operations are handled in the Machining and Finishing departments. Machining Department activities include setup, performed once for each job, and conversion, which is a function of the time (work) required to complete machine operations on the job. Conversion activities are performed automatically by machines once the machines are set up. In the Finishing Department, the metal parts are hand polished and packed. Ace's inbound logistics and operations activities are summarized as follows:

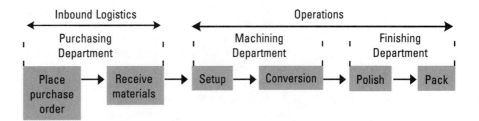

Assigning Costs to Activities

Because accounting systems are typically designed to assign costs to departments, additional analysis is required to determine the cost of activities performed in each department. The assignment of costs to activities may be based on objective data, perhaps from job descriptions or engineering time studies. Cost assignments are just as likely to be based on subjective estimates obtained from interviews and questionnaires. The costs and benefits of increasingly accurate cost assignments must be considered. While it may be possible to have employees keep detailed logs of how they spend their time, keeping such a log is very time-consuming and costly. Consequently, in assigning costs to activities, the analyst will often settle for approximately correct information.

Analysis of available records and interviews with Purchasing Department personnel reveals the following:

- The total costs of operating the Purchasing Department during a month, when the department is operating at its practical capacity of 200 purchase orders for $800,000 of direct materials, amount to $45,000. Included in the $45,000 are salaries and wages of $33,000 and other costs of $12,000.
- Three purchasing agents are involved in contacting suppliers and processing purchase orders. Each purchase order receives identical attention, regardless of its dollar value. Purchasing agents earn an average of $4,000 per month.
- Five receiving employees are involved in unloading, unpacking, and inspecting incoming goods. During interviews, the receiving employees indicated that they spend approximately 20 percent of their time verifying the specific requirements for each order and 80 percent of their time on factors related to the dollar amount of each order. Receiving employees are paid $3,000 per month.
- The department supervisor indicated that his time is divided equally among each of the eight purchasing agents and receiving room employees. The supervisor is paid $6,000 per month.
- Other Purchasing Department costs are related to space. Ignoring the space of the supervisor's office, the purchase order processing activity uses approximately 15 percent of the department's space, and the receiving area uses the remaining 85 percent.

Monthly costs of Purchasing Department activities are as follows:

	Placing Purchase Orders	Receiving Materials
Purchasing agent salaries ($4,000 x 3 agents)	$12,000	
Receiving room employees ($3,000 x 5 employees)		$15,000
Supervisor:		
($6,000 x 3/8 of time with purchasing agents)	2,250	
($6,000 x 5/8 of time with receiving employees)		3,750
Other costs:		
($12,000 x 0.15 purchasing space)	1,800	
($12,000 x 0.85 receiving space)		10,200
Total	$16,050	$28,950

Determining the Basis for Assigning the Cost of Activities to Cost Objectives

The basis for assigning activity costs to cost objectives can be identified from direct observation, from interviews, from questionnaires, from statistical analysis, and from logical analysis. Interviews with Ace Metal Shop's purchasing agents reveal that the number of purchase orders is the single best basis for assigning the costs of the activity "placing purchase orders."

Interviews with receiving employees reveal that the activity "receiving materials" has two important subactivities: (1) verifying the purchase order and (2) unloading/unpacking/inspecting. It is then determined that the number of purchase orders is the best basis for assigning the costs of the activity "verifying purchase orders" and that the dollar amount of purchase orders is the best basis for assigning the costs of the activity "unloading/unpacking/inspecting."[5]

This refinement of data is an inherent part of a subjective procedure intended to provide relevant information for management decisions. Note how this differs from financial accounting where the procedures to be followed are well known in advance. Reanalyzing the Purchasing Department costs, we now have three major activities and the following activity costs:

	Placing Purchase Orders	Verifying Purchase Orders	Unloading/ Unpacking/ Inspecting
Purchasing agent salaries			
($4,000 x 3 agents)	$12,000		
Receiving room employees			
($3,000 x 5 employees x 0.20 verifying time)		$3,000	
($3,000 x 5 employees x 0.80 unloading/unpacking/inspecting time)			$12,000
Supervisor:			
($6,000 x 3/8 of time with purchasing agents)	2,250		
($6,000 x 5/8 of time with receiving employees x 0.20 employees' verifying time)		750	
($6,000 x 5/8 of time with receiving employees x 0.80 employees' unloading/unpacking/inspecting time)			3,000
Other costs*:			
($12,000 x 0.15 purchasing space)	1,800		
($12,000 x 0.85 receiving space)			10,200
Total	$16,050	$3,750	$25,200

*Because the purchase order is verified before delivery trucks are unloaded, the space devoted to this activity is assumed to be insignificant.

---

5 If data from several periods were available, multiple regression might be used to determine the cost per order and the cost per dollar.

Note that the number of purchase orders is to be used for assigning the cost of two activities; namely, "placing purchase orders" and "verifying purchase orders." To minimize computations, when the costing purpose is to determine the cost of a product or service, some analysts recommend combining activities that have the same basis of cost assignment.

Determining the Cost per Unit of Activity

After the cost of activities and the activity cost drivers have been identified, the determination of the cost per unit of cost driver is straightforward:

$$\frac{\text{Cost per unit of}}{\text{activity cost driver}} = \frac{\text{Cost of activity}}{\text{Units of cost driver}}$$

For the Ace Metal Shop:

	Placing Purchase Orders	Verifying Purchase Orders	Unloading/ Unpacking/ Inspecting
Total cost of activity	$16,050	$3,750	$ 25,200
Units of activity cost	÷ 200 orders	÷ 200 orders	÷$800,000
Cost per unit of activity	$ 80.25 per order	$18.75 per order	$ 0.0315 per dollar

Assigning Activity Costs to Cost Objectives

Once the cost per unit of activity is known, the assignment of activity costs to cost objectives is done on the basis of the number of units of activity performed to serve the cost objective. Ace Metal Shop's management wishes to know the total costs of jobs. The cost of direct materials is an important element of the final cost of each job. Assume that Job 102 requires two purchase orders for direct materials, in the amounts of $5,000 and $3,500, respectively.

An activity-based cost system treats these two purchases as cost objectives, assigning costs as follows:

	Purchase Order 1	Purchase Order 2	Total
Direct materials costs	$5,000.00	$3,500.00	$8,500.00
Reassigned activity costs:			
Placing purchase orders	$ 80.25	$ 80.25	$ 160.50
Verifying purchase orders	18.75	18.75	37.50
Unloading/unpacking/inspecting			
($5,000 x 0.0315)	157.50		
($3,500 x 0.0315)		110.25	267.75
Total	256.50	209.25	465.75
Total costs assigned to cost objective	$5,256.50	$3,709.25	$8,965.75

The relationships between the Purchasing Department, the three activities performed in the department, and purchase orders are illustrated by the following diagram:

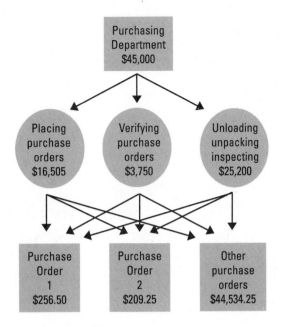

Observe that in the hierarchy of activity costs, the costs of placing the purchase order and verifying the purchase order are batch level costs, while the costs of unloading, unpacking, and inspecting are unit level costs.

Continuing the Ace Metal Shop example, assume that procedures similar to those discussed for Purchasing Department activities were used to determine the following activity costs in the Machining and Finishing departments:

> Machining Department:
>   Setup $ 250 per job
>   Conversion   100 per machine hour
> Finishing Department:
>   Polish $ 50 per labor hour
>   Pack   5 per kilogram

If Job 102 requires 35 machine hours in the Machining Department and 20 labor hours in the Finishing Department, with a final weight of 450 kilograms, the total costs assigned to this cost objective for operations processes are $7,000.

	Job 102
Reassigned activity costs:	
Machining Department:	
Setup	$ 250.00
Conversion ($100 × 35 machine hours)	3,500.00
Finishing Department:	
Polish ($50 × 20 labor hours)	1,000.00
Pack ($5 × 450 kilograms)	2,250.00
Total costs assigned to cost objective	$7,000.00

The relationships among the Machining and Finishing Departments, the four activities performed in them, and Job 102 are illustrated by the following diagram:

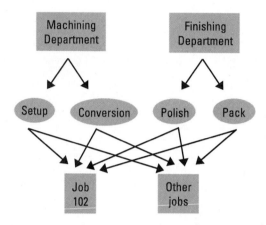

The total costs assigned to Job 102 through the end of inbound logistics and operations are $15,965.75.

Direct materials		
Order 1	$5,000.00	
Order 2	3,500.00	$ 8,500.00
Reassigned inbound logistics:		
Placing purchase orders	$ 160.50	
Verifying purchase orders	37.50	
Unloading/unpacking/inspecting	267.75	465.75
Reassigned operations:		
Setup	$ 250.00	
Conversion	3,500.00	
Polish	1,000.00	
Pack	2,250.00	7,000.00
Total costs assigned to Job 102		$15,965.75

Management Accounting Practice 4-4 describes the information provided by a prototype ABC system at Farrall, Inc.

A generalized version of the two-stage activity-based costing model is presented in Exhibit 4-8 (page 194). Note that:

- Some departments (Department 1) perform multiple activities that are contained wholly within the department.
- Some departments (Department 5) perform only one activity.
- Some departments (Departments 2, 3, and 4) participate with other departments in the performance of an activity such as activity 5. Perhaps Department 4 is the purchasing department and activity 5 is

MANAGEMENT ACCOUNTING PRACTICE 4-4

ABC Reveals Ten Percent of Customers Provide Two-Hundred and Thirty Percent of the Profits at Farrall, Inc.

When Farrall, Inc., a manufacturer of specialized filter materials, started an ABC pilot project, management was seeking more accurate information on product costs and customer profitability. Management also wanted to identify cost reduction opportunities and more accurately evaluate proposals to acquire technologically advanced equipment. Analyzing data obtained from the pilot study provided some surprises.

Farrall found that when costs were properly assigned to products and customers, less than 10 percent of the customers provided 230 percent of the firm's profits. ABC revealed that specialized products were being sold to many customers for less than the cost to manufacture the product and to serve the customer. This suggests that Farrall should work to strengthen its relationships with highly profitable customers and take actions to eliminate or improve the profitability of dealings with unprofitable customers.

Farrall had assumed that 52 percent of its costs varied with unit volume, while the rest were fixed. Developing a hierarchy of activity costs revealed that only 23 percent of the costs varied with unit level activities. Because of the customized nature of Farrall's products, the ABC analysis revealed that 21 percent of the costs varied with batch volume, 15 percent were related to products, and an additional 41 percent were facility sustaining.

Based on: Robin Cooper, Robert S. Kaplan, Lawrence S. Maisel, Eileen Morrissey, and Ronald M. Oehm, *Implementing Activity-Based Cost Management: Moving From Analysis to Action* (Montvale, NJ: Institute of Management Accountants, 1992). See Chapter 5, Farrall, Inc., pp. 63-98. We have highlighted results. The emphasis in the original is on implementing ABC.

processing a purchase requisition. If purchase requisitions are initiated in Departments 2 and 3, it follows that all three departments are involved in activity 5.

Additional Considerations

Activity-based costing is a relatively new approach to cost assignment. However, because of its ability to provide a more detailed and relevant analysis of costs for internal decision making, ABC is rapidly gaining acceptance as superior to traditional cost assignment systems used for financial reporting. The use of activity-based costing for inventory valuation is considered in Chapter 13.

A 1993 survey by The Society of Management Accountants of Canada revealed that 14 percent of the respondent firms had implemented ABC and another 15 percent were assessing the desirability of implementing ABC.[6] A 1994 survey by the Institute of Management Accountants of leading U.S. industrial companies found that 29 percent of surveyed companies were using ABC as the primary means of cost assignment, up from 25 percent in

---

6 "Actvity-Based Costing," Management Accounting Issue Paper 3 (Hamilton, Ontario: The Society of Management Accountants of Canada, 1993), p. 22.

EXHIBIT 4-8: TWO STAGE ACTIVITY BASED COSTING MODEL

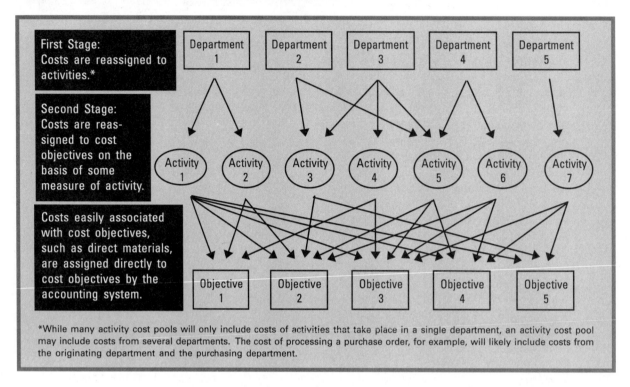

First Stage: Costs are reassigned to activities.*

Second Stage: Costs are reassigned to cost objectives on the basis of some measure of activity.

Costs easily associated with cost objectives, such as direct materials, are assigned directly to cost objectives by the accounting system.

*While many activity cost pools will only include costs of activities that take place in a single department, an activity cost pool may include costs from several departments. The cost of processing a purchase order, for example, will likely include costs from the originating department and the purchasing department.

1993. Significantly, another 56 percent were using ABC to supplement traditional cost assignment systems developed for external reporting.[7] Although both surveys indicate a growing use of ABC, the Canadian and U.S. surveys are not directly comparable. While the U.S. survey focused on large industrial firms, the group most likely to lead in implementing performance enhancing techniques such as ABC, the Canadian survey included a much wider range of organizations in terms of size and type of business. An interesting aspect of the Canadian survey is its revelation that organizations as diverse as manufacturing and financial services are using ABC.

Because activity-based costing is not guided by financial accounting requirements, there is wide variation in the components of ABC systems. One size does not fit all. Each ABC system is designed to fit the needs and circumstances of a particular organization. These characteristics make the implementation of ABC systems time-consuming and expensive. Consequently, many organizations develop ABC cost information on an irregular basis to assist with strategic decisions such as analyzing the profitability of products or services. Some organizations only develop ABC data for processes management deems critical for success such as manufacturing or marketing and sales.

---

7 "ABC Beats Old-Style Costing, Survey Finds," *Accounting Today* (June 6, 1994), p. 14 , and "More Companies Turn to ABC," *Journal of Accountancy* (July 1994), p. 14.

Activity-Based Costs Are Strategic

Some analysts argue that activity-based costs would be more useful for short-range decision making if separate rates were developed for variable costs that changed with the volume of activity and fixed costs that do not change with the volume of activity. Others respond that activity-based costing is intended to assist in making long-term structural and organizational decisions rather than day-to-day short-range decisions and, in the long run, all costs are variable. One danger of separating fixed and variable costs in a model for strategic planning is to leave decision makers with a feeling that variable costs are more important than fixed costs because fixed costs cannot be controlled in the near-term. Such an attitude leads to continual growth of fixed costs and a feeling of helplessness on the part of managers. ABC was intended to help decision makers reassert control over costs during a period in which there has been significant increases in short-term fixed costs and significant reductions in short-term variable costs.

Activity-Based Costs Should Be Based on Practical Capacity

With most costs other than direct materials being fixed in the short run, activity costs assigned to cost objectives are heavily influenced by the number of units of cost driver used to compute the cost per unit of cost driver.

$$\text{Cost per unit of activity} = \frac{\text{Cost of activity}}{\text{Units of activity cost driver}}$$

To avoid variations in cost assignments that result solely from capacity utilization, activity costs should be developed assuming facilities are used at their practical capacity. **Practical capacity** is the maximum possible activity, allowing for normal repairs and maintenance.

Practical capacity will produce lower cost assignments to cost objectives than will actual activity or average activity over some period of time. The resulting cost assignments are a better indication of what costs would be if capacity and utilization were in balance. For an organization to be a world-class competitor, management must strive to balance capacity and utilization. Other competitors are doing this, and few customers are willing to pay for excess capacity. In the accounting records, unassigned costs resulting from the underutilization of capacity can be identified as an idle capacity variance. The existence and magnitude of the variance are clear signals to management that excess capacity exists.

Measuring the Performance of Activities and Processes

The use of management accounting information to develop performance reports for departments and functional areas, such as marketing, manufacturing, and administration, is considered in Chapter 8. Those performance reports are developed in a relatively straightforward manner from the accounting records.

Using ABC, it is possible to develop financial performance reports for processes or activities. Returning to our example of the Ace Metal Shop, assume that the total budget for the activity "placing purchase orders" is

$16,050 for the month and that at a practical capacity of 200 orders, the activity cost per order is $80.25. Now assume that during the month of July 19X3, the actual cost of this activity was $15,500 and that 180 orders were placed.

Actual activity costs were less than budgeted activity costs, producing a $550 ($16,050 - $15,500) favorable (F) activity cost variance. Because there were only 180 orders, the costs assigned to cost objectives amounted to $14,445 ($80.25 × 180), and the idle capacity variance was $1,605 ($16,050 - $14,445) unfavorable (U). These two variances are summarized as follows:

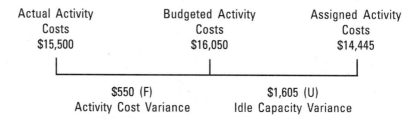

The activity cost variance indicates that actual activity costs were less than the budgeted activity costs. Management might try to find out why this took place. Perhaps it is possible and appropriate to plan on similar cost reductions in future budgets. The idle capacity variance is a reminder of the existence of excess capacity.

Number and Hierarchy of Activities

A major issue in developing ABC models is knowing when to stop. While accuracy can always be increased by including more activities, there comes a point where the marginal improvements from expanding the model are more than offset by the additional costs. A recent survey revealed that 30 percent of the organizations using ABC had between 20 and 30 activities in their model.[8] In the final analysis, the determination of the number of activities to use is a subjective decision based on the professional judgment of the people developing the ABC model.

Establishing and using an appropriate cost hierarchy are important parts of designing an ABC system. The hierarchy helps clarify thinking and guides the proper assignment of activity costs to cost objectives. In most situations, the highest volume of activity will be at the unit and batch levels. Depending on the situation, product, facility, and customer costs may also be significant.

Multiple-Stage ABC Models

We have presented the widely discussed and utilized two-stage ABC model. The literature contains discussions of even more sophisticated multiple-stage models in which some costs are reassigned from one activity to another before being assigned to final cost objectives. While multiple-stage models might

---

8 "Activity-Based Costing," Management Accounting Issue Paper 3 (Hamilton, Ontario: The Society of Management Accountants of Canada, 1993), p. 18.

more accurately trace the cost of activities in supporting departments to final cost objectives, few multistage ABC models are encountered in practice, and a discussion of such models is beyond the scope of this text.

SUMMARY

Strategic cost management involves making decisions concerning specific cost drivers within the context of an organization's business strategy, internal value chain, and position in a larger value chain stretching from basic resources to final consumers. The goal of every organization should be to maximize the value and minimize the cost of a product or service to final customers. This goal leads to an examination of internal and external links in the value chain rather than a focus on independent departments, processes, or activities. From a value chain perspective, it is total value chain cost, not the cost of individual economic units, departments, processes, or activities, that is most important.

To better understand how an economic entity adds value and incurs costs, management might further refine the value chain into processes. Because processes often cut across the boundaries of departments within an organization, studying processes helps managers understand how activities in one department are linked to—and can drive—activities and costs in another department. Once the major processes performed to serve customer needs are identified, the next step is to determine the activities and activity costs involved in each process.

Activity-based costing involves determining the cost of activities and tracing the cost of activities to cost objectives on the basis of the cost objectives' utilization of units of activity. ABC is based on the premise that customer needs are the immediate cause of the performance of activities that consume resources that cost money. Consequently, the cost of resources consumed by activities should be assigned to cost objectives on the basis of their consumption of activities. Operationalizing the two-stage ABC model requires five steps: (1) identifying activities, (2) assigning costs to activities, (3) determining the basis for assigning the cost of activities to cost objectives, (4) determining the cost per unit of activity, and (5) reassigning costs from the activity to the cost objective on the basis of the cost objective's consumption of activities. This chapter and the accompanying review problem considered activity-based costing across an organization's entire internal value chain. The use for activity-based costing for the narrower purpose of inventory valuation is examined further in Chapter 13.

SUGGESTED READINGS

Brimson, James A., and John Antos. *Activity-Based Management for Service Industries, Government Entities, and Nonprofit Organizations* (New York: John Wiley & Sons, Inc., 1994).

Cokins, Gary, Alan Stratton, and Jack Helbling. *An ABC Manager's Primer* (Montvale, NJ: Institute of Management Accountants and Arlington, TX: Consortium for Advanced Manufacturing-International/Cost Management Systems, 1993).

Cooper, Robin, Robert S. Kaplan, Lawrence S. Maisel, Eileen Morrissey, and Ronald M. Oehm. *Implementing Activity-Based Cost Management: Moving From Analysis to Action* (Montvale, NJ: Institute of Management Accountants, 1992).

DeBruine, Marinus, and Parvez R. Sopariwala, "The Use of Practical Capacity for Better Management Decisions," *Journal of Cost Management* (Spring 1994), pp. 25-31.

Exposure Draft *Building World Class Buyer/Seller Partnerships* (Hamilton, Ontario: The Society of Management Accountants of Canada, September 1994).

Implementing Activity-Based Costing, Statement on Management Accounting Number 4T. (Montvale, NJ: Institute of Management Accountants, September 30, 1993).

Lawson, Raef. "Beyond ABC: Process-Based Costing," *Journal of Cost Management* (Fall 1994), pp. 33-43.

Mecimore, Charles D., and Alice T. Bell. "Are We Ready for Fourth-Generation ABC?" *Management Accounting* (January 1995), pp. 22-26.

Pattison, Diane D., James M. Caltrider, and Robert Lutze. "Continuous Process Improvement at Brooktree," *Management Accounting* (February 1993), pp. 49-52.

Porter, Michael E., *Competitive Advantage* (New York: The Free Press, 1985), Chapters 1 through 3.

Romano, Patrick L., ed. *Activity-Based Management in Action* (Montvale, NJ: Institute of Management Accountants, 1994).

Romney, Marshall. "Business Process Reengineering," *The CPA Journal* (October 1994), pp. 30-32, 60.

Shank, John K., and Vijay Govindarajan. "Strategic Cost Management and the Value Chain," *Journal of Cost Management* (Winter 1992), pp. 5-21.

Shank, John K., and Vijay Govindarajan. "Strategic Cost Management: The Value Chain Perspective," *Journal of Management Accounting Research* 4, (Fall 1992), pp. 179-197.

Turney, Peter. "Beyond TQM with Work Force Activity-Based Management," *Management Accounting* (September 1993), pp. 28-31.

Yoshikawa, Takeo, John Innes, and Falconer Mitchell. "Cost Tables: A Foundation of Japanese Cost Management," *Journal of Cost Management* (Fall 1990), pp. 30-36.

REVIEW PROBLEM

Activity-Based Costing

The Ace Metal Shop example in the body of Chapter 4 concerned the processes for inbound logistics and operations. Direct materials and activity costs for inbound logistics and operations were assigned to Job 102 as follows:

Direct materials		
Order 1	$5,000.00	
Order 2	3,500.00	$ 8,500.00
Inbound logistics:		
Placing purchase orders ($80.25 × 2 orders)	$ 160.50	
Verifying purchase orders ($18.75 × 2 orders)	37.50	
Unloading/unpacking/inspecting ($8,500 × 0.0315)	267.75	465.75
Operations:		
Setup ($250 × 1 setup)	$ 250.00	
Conversion ($100 × 35 machine hours)	3,500.00	
Polish ($50 × 20 labor hours)	1,000.00	
Pack ($5 × 450 kilograms)	2,250.00	7,000.00
Total costs assigned to Job 102 through operations		$ 15,965.75

This review problem concerns outbound logistics, marketing and sales, and service. When combined with the example in the body of Chapter 4, you will have completed an illustration of activity-based costing across an organization's entire internal value chain.

After studying the activities, costs, and measures of activity cost drivers for each of these processes, you have obtained the following information:

- Outbound logistics is handled by an independent trucking service that charges $10 per pickup, $10 per delivery, and $0.50 per kilogram of weight.
- Marketing and sales are handled by highly skilled professional employees who are paid an annual salary and no commission. Their primary activities relate to maintaining customer relationships, assisting customers in developing specifications and taking orders, and providing subsequent service. The annual costs of maintaining a customer are $1,000 per customer. Each visit to develop specifications, take an order, or provide subsequent service costs an average of $175.
- Ace Metal Shop does not have a separate service staff. The service activities, as described above, are handled by the professional marketing and sales staff.

Job 102 was produced in response to an order from the Orleans Company. Developing the order specifications and taking the order for Job 102 required three site visits to Orleans's headquarters. The order contains parts for delivery to two separate facilities operated by Orleans. Subsequent to delivery, Ace representatives made one visit to one Orleans facility to offer technical advice. The final selling price of Job 102 was $20,000.

Required:

(a) Using appropriate measures of activity, assign all remaining activity costs that can be specifically identified with Job 102.

(b) Identify any costs that are not specifically related to Job 102.

(c) Determine the profitability of Job 102 by developing a statement that shows sales revenue and summarizes costs in each of five generic processes.

(d) Assuming Job 102 is the only order received this year from the Orleans Company, determine the current year profitability of relationships with the Orleans Company.

(e) Classify each activity cost driver included in the textbook example of the Ace Metal Shop and the related review problem as unit, batch, or customer.

The solution to the review problem is found at the end of the Chapter 4 assignment material. To maximize your learning, you should make a serious attempt to develop a written solution to the review problem before looking at the solution. If there are errors in your solution, you should then attempt to determine the causes of the errors.

KEY TERMS

Activity—a unit of work.

Activity-based costing (ABC)—determining the cost of activities and tracing the cost of activities to cost objectives on the basis of the cost objective's utilization of units of activity.

Activity-based management (ABM)—the identification and selection of activities that maximize the value of activities while minimizing the cost of activities from the viewpoint of the final customer.

Continuous improvement—the constant evaluation of products, services, and processes, seeking ways to do better.

Cost objective—an object to which costs are assigned.

Cost tables—data bases that indicate the effect on costs of using different materials, production methods, and product designs.

Cycle time—the total time required to complete a process.

Horizontally integrated organization—an organization that operates many entities in the same industry.

Nonvalue-added activity—an activity that does not add value to a product or service from the viewpoint of the final customer.

Practical capacity—the maximum possible activity, allowing for normal repairs and maintenance.

Process—a collection of related activities.

Process-based management—an approach to the evaluation of activities emphasizing the importance of considering the entire process of which activities are a part.

Process map (or **process flowchart**)—a schematic overview of all the activities required to complete a process. Each major activity is represented by a rectangle on the map.

Process reengineering—the fundamental redesign of a process to serve internal or external customers.

Storyboard—a process map developed by employees who perform the component activities required to complete a process.

Strategic cost management—making decisions concerning specific cost drivers within the context of an organization's business strategy, its internal value chain, and its place in a larger value chain stretching from the development and use of resources to final consumers.

Strategic plan—a plan indicating the basic way people in the organization are to go about achieving the organization's long-range goals.

Value—the worth in usefulness or importance of a product or service to the customer.

Value-added activity—an activity that adds value to a product or service from the viewpoint of the customer.

Value chain—the set of value-producing activities stretching from basic raw materials to the final customer.

Vertically integrated organization—an organization that operates two or more units that might be regarded as independent links in a value chain.

REVIEW QUESTIONS

4-1
In what way is strategic cost management similar to a strategic plan?

4-2
What is the relationship among a value chain, processes, and activities?

4-3
What should be the goal of every organization along a value chain?

4-4
What is wrong with across-the-board cuts in budgets as an approach to cost reduction?

4-5
Distinguish between the value-added and the value chain perspective.

4-6

Why should the people who perform activities be involved in developing process maps?

Pg. 18 + **4-7**

Distinguish between continuous improvement and process reengineering.

+ **4-8**

Pg. 183

Why do both continuous improvement and process reengineering seek to eliminate nonvalue-added activities?

Pg. 186 4-9 *Focus on eliminating the non-value added act.*

Summarize the concepts underlying activity-based costing in two sentences.

+ **4-10**

Pg. 195

Why do some analysts prefer not to develop separate fixed and variable rates in activity-based costing?

+ **4-11**

Pg. 195

Why should activity-based costs be based on practical capacity?

4-12 *what a company can efficiently produce*

Why is the development of an activity cost hierarchy an important part of designing an ABC system?

EXERCISES

4-1 Matching Terms and Descriptions

Required:

Match the following terms with the best description of each term. Each description is used only once.

1. Horizontal integration
2. Process
3. Process reengineering
4. Nonvalue-added activity
5. Value chain
6. Activity-based managementment
7. Upstream
8. Direct materials
9. Value
10. Structural cost driver
11. Process map
12. Activity-based costing
13. Organizational cost driver
14. Storyboard
15. Activity

a. Worth or usefulness
b. A unit of work
c. Selecting activities to maximize value while minimizing cost
d. Has a goal of radical improvement
e. A decision to pursue vertical integration
f. Element of a value chain
g. Assigned directly to cost objectives
h. Is frequently accomplished using a two-stage model
i. Used to develop a process map
j. Entities between the one being analyzed and sources of raw materials

k. Operating several ice cream stores
l. A decision to have all quality inspection performed by independent quality specialists
m. Something to be minimized
n. Set of value-producing processes and activities
o. Useful starting point in continuous improvement

4-2 Activities and Cost Drivers

Required:

For each of the following activities, select the most appropriate cost driver. Each cost driver may be used only once.

1. Pay vendors
2. Evaluate vendors
3. Inspect raw materials
4. Plan for purchases of raw materials
5. Packaging
6. Supervision
7. Employee training
8. Clean tables
9. Machine maintenance
10. Move patients to and from surgery

a. Number of different kinds of raw materials
b. Number of classes offered
c. Number of tables
d. Number of employees
e. Operating hours
f. Units of raw materials received
g. Number of moves
h. Number of vendors
i. Number of checks issued
j. Number of customer orders

4-3 Developing a Value Chain from the Perspective of the Final Customer

Assume that you purchase bottled orange juice for personal consumption at an on-campus cafeteria.

Required:

Prepare a value chain for bottled orange juice.

4-4 Developing a Value Chain: Upstream and Downstream Entities

Assume that your firm produces cotton T-shirts.

Required:

Prepare a value chain for your firm's product. Clearly identify upstream and downstream entities in the value chain.

4-5 Classifying Activities Using the Generic Internal Value Chain: Aluminum Wire Manufacturer

Required:

Classify each of the following activities of an aluminum cable manufacturer, using the generic internal value chain shown in Exhibit 4-5 (page 178), as inbound logistics, operations, outbound logistics, marketing and sales, service, or support.

(a) Advertising in a construction magazine
(b) Inspecting incoming aluminum ingots
(c) Placing bar codes on coils of finished products
(d) Borrowing money to finance a build up of inventory
(e) Hiring new employees
(f) Heating aluminum ingots
(g) Drawing wire from aluminum ingots
(h) Coiling wire
(i) Visiting a customer to determine the cause of cable breakage
(j) Filing tax returns

4-6 Classifying Activities Using the Generic Internal Value Chain: Cable TV Company

Required:

Classify each of the following activities of a cable television company, using the generic internal value chain shown in Exhibit 4-5 (page 178), as inbound logistics, operations, outbound logistics, marketing and sales, service, or support.

(a) Installing cable in the apartment of a new customer
(b) Repairing cable after a windstorm
(c) Mailing brochures to prospective customers
(d) Meeting with a local government body to discuss a rate increase
(e) Selling shares of stock in the company
(f) Monitoring the quality of reception at the company's satellite downlink
(g) Preparing financial statements
(h) Visiting a customer to determine the cause of poor-quality television pictures
(i) Traveling to a conference to learn about how technological changes are affecting the industry
(j) Inspecting television cables for wear

4-7 Classifying Activities as Value-Added or Nonvalue-Added in a Manufacturing Firm

Required:

Classify each of the following activities in a manufacturing organization as value-added or nonvalue-added.

(a) Receive order to manufacture a product for Big Value Hardware Stores.
(b) Schedule production of order for Big Value Hardware Stores.
(c) Place order for necessary raw materials.
(d) Unload raw materials.
(e) Pay for raw materials.
(f) Move raw materials to Grinding Department.
(g) Set up grinding machinery to work on raw materials.
(h) Grind raw materials.
(i) Place partially finished product in storage area to await further work.
(j) Maintain storage area for partially finished product.

(k) Remove partially finished product from storage area.
(l) Move partially finished product to Assembly Department.
(m) Complete production in Assembly Department.
(n) Move finished product to Shipping Department.
(o) Pack finished product for shipment in display cases used by Big Value Hardware Stores.
(p) Load packed display cases on truck.
(q) Send invoice to Big Value Hardware Stores.
(r) Receive payment of invoice from Big Value Hardware Stores.
(s) Deposit payment in checking account.

4-8 Classifying Activities as Value-Added or Nonvalue-Added at a Physician's Office

Required:

Classify each of the following activities in a physician's office as value-added or nonvalue-added.

(a) Patient phones and appointment is scheduled.
(b) Patient checks in with receptionist and is placed on waiting list.
(c) Patient goes to waiting room.
(d) Large waiting room is furnished, stocked with magazines, cleaned, and heated.
(e) Patient is placed in one of several examining rooms.
(f) Patient's file is obtained and placed outside door.
(g) Physician reviews file.
(h) Physician interviews patient.
(i) Physician examines patient.
(j) Physician advises patient.
(k) Physician dictates notes to be transcribed by receptionist to patient's file.
(l) Patient returns to receptionist to complete billing information and schedule any further appointments.

4-9 Developing a List of Activities for Baggage Handling at an Airport

As part of a continuous improvement program, you have been asked to determine the activities involved in the baggage handling process of a major airline at one of the airline's hubs. Prior to conducting observations and interviews, you decide to develop a sequential list of possible activities. You believe this list will help you observe key activities and ask meaningful questions.

Required:

For incoming aircraft only, develop a sequential list of baggage handling activities. Your list should contain between 8 and 10 activities.

4-10 Developing a Process Map

One part of the complex procedures of manufacturing cars concerns the attachment of tires to the car. Presented below is a brief description of this process:

Tires and rims are delivered directly to the assembly area by subcontractors according to a predetermined schedule. At the assembly area, the tires are attached to the rim, inflated, and balanced. Next, four sets of tires and rims are bolted to each car, and one set is secured in the trunk of the car. Finally, the five sets of tires and rims are inspected.

Required:

Develop a process map from the information given.

4-11 Stage One ABC: Assigning Costs to Activities

An economics professor at Western College devotes 60 percent of his time to teaching, 20 percent of his time to research and writing, and 20 percent of his time to service activities such as committee work and student advising. The professor teaches two semesters per year, and each semester he teaches two sections of an introductory economics course (with a maximum enrollment of 80 students each) and one section of a graduate economics course (with a maximum enrollment of 30 students). Including course preparation, classroom instruction, and meeting with students, each course (not each section) requires equal amounts of time. The economics professor is paid $58,000 per year.

Required:

Determine the activity cost of instruction per student in the introductory and in the graduate economics course.

4-12 Stage One ABC: Assigning Costs to Activities

As the chief engineer of a small machine shop, Barry Tanner refers to himself as a "jack of all trades." When an order for a new product comes in, Barry has to:

1. Design the product to meet customer requirements.
2. Prepare a bill of materials, which is a list of materials required to produce the product.
3. Prepare an operations list, which is a sequential list of the steps involved in manufacturing the product.

Each time the foundry manufactures a batch of the product, Barry must:

1. Schedule the job.
2. Supervise the setup of machines that will work on the job.
3. Inspect the first unit produced to verify that it meets specifications.

The actual work on individual units of product is left to production employees whom Barry supervises. Barry is also responsible for employee training, ensuring that production facilities are in proper operating condition, and attending professional meetings.

Barry's estimates of time spent on each of these activities last year are as follows:

1.	Product design	15%
2.	Preparing bills of materials	5%
3.	Preparing operations lists	10%

4.	Job scheduling	18%
5.	Supervising setup	5%
6.	First unit inspection	2%
7.	Supervising production	20%
8.	Employee training	15%
9.	Facility maintenance	7%
10.	Attending professional meetings	3%

(handwritten annotations: "both" bracketing items 4–6, "unit" next to 7, "facility" bracketing items 8–10)

Required:

Assuming Barry Tanner's salary is $80,000 per year, determine the dollar amount of his salary assigned to unit, batch, product, and facility level activities.

4-13 Stage Two ABC: Reassign Costs to Cost Objectives

Presented is information on the activity costs of the New England Wholesale Company:

Activity	Activity Cost
Customer relations	$200.00 per customer per month
Selling	0.06 per sales dollar
Accounting	5.00 per order
Warehousing	0.50 per unit shipped
Packing	0.25 per unit shipped
Shipping	0.10 per pound shipped

The following information is available about the March 19X2 New England Wholesale Company's activities in Vermont:

Sales orders	235
Sales revenue	$122,200
Cost of goods sold	73,320
Customers	25
Units shipped	4,700
Pounds shipped	70,500

Required:

Determine the profitability of March 19X2 sales in Vermont.

4-14 Stage Two ABC: Reassign Costs to Cost Objectives

Davenport Fabricating has developed the following activity cost information for its manufacturing activities:

Machine setup	$ 50 per batch
Movement	10 per batch per move, plus $0.10 per pound
Drilling	3 per hole
Welding	4 per inch
Shaping	25 per hour
Assembly	15 per hour
Inspection	2 per unit

Filling an order for 60 fireplace inserts that weighed 150 pounds per unit required:

1. Three batch moves
2. Two sets of inspections
3. Drilling five holes in each unit
4. Completing 80 inches of welds on each unit
5. Thirty minutes of shaping for each unit
6. One hour of assembly per unit

Required:
Determine the activity cost of converting raw materials into 60 fireplace inserts.

4-15 Activity Cost Variance Analysis

The instructional budget for Central City Evening University indicates that the budget for teaching an evening class in general psychology is $5,000. The Psychology Department has determined that the maximum class size for an evening class in general psychology is 40 students. Last semester, when 35 students enrolled in the evening general psychology class, the related instructional costs amounted to $5,200.

Required:
(a) Determine the activity cost variance and the idle capacity variance.
(b) Discuss the implications of each variance.

PROBLEMS

4-16 Two-Stage Activity-Based Costing

Hendricks Manufacturing has developed the following activity cost pool information for its 19X1 manufacturing activities:

Activity	Budgeted Activity Cost	Activity Cost Driver at Practical Capacity
Purchasing and materials handling	$ 675,000	900,000 kilograms
Setup	700,000	1,400 setups
Machine operations	960,000	12,000 hours
First unit inspection	50,000	800 batches
Packaging	250,000	312,500 units

Actual 19X1 production information is as follows:

	Standard Product A	Standard Product B	Specialty Products
Units	150,000	100,000	50,000
Batches	100	80	600
Setups*	300	160	900
Machine operations	6,000	3,000	2,000
Kilograms of raw materials	400,000	300,000	200,000
Direct materials costs	$900,000	$600,000	$800,000

*Some products require setups on two or more machines.

Required:

(a) Determine the unit cost of each product.

(b) Explain why the unit cost of the specialty products is so much higher than the unit cost of Standard Product A or Standard Product B.

(c) Determine the total idle capacity variance for 19X1.

(d) What arguments can be made in favor of basing activity costs on practical capacity rather than on actual activity?

4-17 Value-Added Analysis and Organizational Changes in Manufacturing Procedures

Perfect Support Chair Company manufactures three styles of office chairs in batches of 100 units. The direct materials and manufacturing activity costs per batch of each product are as follows:

	Task Chair	Desk Chair	Executive Chair
Direct materials	$1,500	$1,700	$2,500
Molding Department:			
Setup	400	500	600
Operations	500	600	800
Movement to Fabric Department*	100	100	100
Fabric Department:			
Setup	150	175	190
Operations	600	800	1,000
Movement to Assembly Department*	100	100	100
Assembly Department operations	500	750	1,000
Movement to Packing Department*	100	100	100
Packing Department operations	300	400	500
Total	$4,250	$5,225	$6,890

*$1 per unit

Last year, Perfect Support manufactured and sold 10,000 task chairs, 5,000 desk chairs, and 4,000 executive chairs.

Required:

(a) For each batch of each product, determine the total cost of the value-added and the total cost of the nonvalue-added activities.

(b) For each product, determine the materials, value-added activity costs, and nonvalue-added activity costs per chair. Determine the total cost per chair.

(c) On an annual basis, how much money might be saved by increasing the batch size to 500 units? Mention some factors that should be considered before increasing the batch size.

(d) Management is contemplating the rearrangement of the manufacturing facilities to allow each product to be manufactured on a separate assembly line. This would virtually eliminate setup and movement activities. It would, however, require renting some specialized high-volume equipment. Determine the annual cost savings that should be considered in evaluating the desirability of the change in manufacturing procedures.

4-18 Determining Activity Costs and the Activity Cost Hierarchy

Extra Oomph, a new startup company, is owned and operated by Percilla Snyder and Jane Cummings, two young bicycle enthusiasts. To form their company, Percilla gave up a job paying $28,000 per year and Jane gave up a job paying $32,000 year.

Extra Oomph's only product is a small electric motor, called the Extra Oomph, that provides supplementary power for bicycling up hills. The direct materials cost for this product are as follows:

Electric motor	$ 75
Battery holder	10
Switch and wire	15
Total	$100

Other materials costs include:

Instructional brochure (included with motor)	$0.25
Display package (one motor per package)	3.00
Shipping box (10 display packages per box)	5.00

International Express picks up the shipping boxes and delivers them to customers for an average cost of $8.50 per box.

Percilla devotes her time to four activities with the following time breakdowns:

1. Ordering raw materials (in lots of 100 units)	15%
2. Unpacking and 100% inspection of raw materials	5%
3. Assembling Extra Oomphs	65%
4. Product development	15%

Jane devotes her time to three activities with the following time breakdowns:

1. Packaging Extra Oomphs	
Into individual display packages	15%
Into shipping boxes	10%
2. Marketing and sales	60%
3. Recordkeeping	15%

Other 19X3 operating costs were:

Telephone used for marketing Extra Oomphs	$ 900
Rent and utilities space used for unpacking/inspecting,	
assembling, and packing	6,000
Sundry costs	5,000

Approximately 25 percent of the space is used for unpacking/inspecting, 50 percent is used for assembly, and 25 percent is used for packaging (15 percent into display packages and 10 percent into shipping boxes). The joint nature of the sundry costs makes it impractical to assign them to specific activities.

In 19X3, Extra Oomph produced and sold 600 units at a selling price of $300 each.

Required:
(a) Identify all major activities performed by Extra Oomph and classify them into the six generic processes contained in Exhibit 4-5 (page 178).
(b) Assuming Percilla and Jane want a personal income equal to the opportunity cost they incurred in giving up their former jobs, prepare a detailed analysis of 19X3 costs. Determine the total unit, batch, product, and facility level costs for 19X3.
(c) Determine Extra Oomph's 19X3 income.
(d) What factors would make it difficult to perform a traditional cost-volume-profit analysis of Extra Oomph?

4-19 Using Activity Cost Data: Value-Added and Nonvalue-Added Activities

Morvis, Inc. has developed the following activity cost data for its purchasing and manufacturing activities:

Purchase order and receiving report	$20.00/order
Unpack and inspect incoming goods	$0.50/unit purchased
Raw materials inventory carrying cost	1% of invoice cost
Issue raw materials	$4.00/type of item/batch
Move to a work or inspection station in-process or to finished goods	$1.50/unit in batch
In-process inventory carrying cost*	$0.50/unit in batch/day
Labor activities	$25.00/hour
Quality inspection	$0.50/inspection
Machine activities:	

	A	B	C
Setup	$50.00/batch	$60.00/batch	$55.00/batch
Operation	40.00/hour	42.00/hour	30.00/hour

*Applicable to all units, regardless of whether they are being worked on or are awaiting work

Management is contemplating the production of a new product, number G57, and desires to know the average annual unit cost at an annual production volume of 10,000 units in 10 batches of 1,000 units.

Purchasing, engineering, and production scheduling have developed the following information for an annual volume of 10,000 units:

Raw Material	Annual Requirements	Order Quantity	Orders per Year	Unit Price
D34	20,000	5,000	4	$ 5.00
G77	30,000	10,000	3	0.50
H65	10,000	1,000	10	20.00

Production requirements per batch of 1,000 units is as follows:

• Raw materials:
    D34   2,000   units
    G77   3,000   units
    H65   1,000   units

- Machine activities:
    - A   100   hours
    - B   50   hours
    - C   50   hours
- Labor: 60 hours
- Two quality inspections per unit

All raw materials required for the batch will be issued at the start of production. All machines will be set up before production on the batch begins, and units will be moved directly from one operation to the next as each is ready. This will reduce work-in-process inventories to the extent possible. The average cycle time for a unit from start to finish is estimated to be three days.

Required:

(a) Use activity cost data to determine the total annual and average unit cost of product G57. Round computations to the nearest cent.
(b) At a recent seminar, a discussion leader told management that all materials movement, inspection, and carrying activities are nonvalue-added. What's more, conversion costs related to materials movement, inspection, and carrying inventory are wasted, and management should strive to eliminate the activities that cause them. Management has asked you to break total conversion costs into the categories of value-added and nonvalue-added.

4-20 Activity-Based Costing at a Service Organization

The Gothom National Bank has 10 automatic teller machines spread throughout the city. The machines are maintained by the Automatic Teller Department. You have been assigned the task of determining the cost of operating each machine. Management will use the information you develop, along with other information pertaining to the volume and type of transactions at each machine, to evaluate the desirability of continuing to operate each machine and/or changing security arrangements for a particular machine.

The Automatic Teller Department consists of a total of 6 employees: a supervisor, a head cashier, 2 cashiers, and 2 maintenance personnel. The cashiers make between 2 and 4 routine trips each day to each machine for the purpose of replenishing and collecting cash, supplies, deposit tickets, and so forth. Each machine contains a small computer that automatically summarizes and reports transactions to the head cashier. The activities of the 2 cashiers are reconciled to the computerized reports by the head cashier and reviewed by the supervisor, who does not handle cash.

When a problem is reported at an automatic teller, the 2 maintenance employees and a cashier are dispatched immediately. The cashier removes all cash and transaction records, while the maintenance employees repair the machine. Maintenance employees spend all of their time on maintenance-related activities, and the cashiers spend approximately 50 percent of their time on maintenance-related activities. The cashiers spend the other 50 percent of their time on routine trips.

Seventy-five percent of the time of the head cashier is directly related to routine trips to each machine, while 25 percent is related to supervising cashiers on maintenance calls. Twenty percent of the supervisor's time is related to routine trips to each machine, while 80 percent is related to the equal supervision of each employee.

Cost information for a recent month is as follows:

Supervisor's salary	$ 3,000
Head cashier's salary	2,000
Other salaries ($1,800 each)	7,200
Lease and operating costs:	
Cashiers' service vehicle	1,200
Maintenance service vehicle	1,400
Office rent and utilities	2,300
Machine lease, space rent, and utilities ($1,500 each)	15,000
Total	$32,100

Related monthly activity information is as follows:

Machine	Routine Trips	Maintenance Hours
1	30	5
2	90	17
3	60	15
4	60	30
5	120	15
6	30	10
7	90	25
8	120	5
9	60	20
10	60	18
Total	720	160

Additional information:

- The office is centrally located with approximately equal travel time to each machine.
- Maintenance-hours include travel time.
- The cashiers' service vehicle is used exclusively for routine visits.
- The office space is divided equally between that assigned to the supervisor and that assigned to the head cashier.

Required:
(a) Determine the monthly operating costs of machines 7 and 8 when cost assignments are based on the number of machines.
(b) Determine the activity cost of a routine trip and a maintenance-hour for the month given. Round answers to the nearest cent.
(c) Determine the operating costs assigned and reassigned to machines 7 and 8 when activity-based costing is used.

4-21 Cycle Efficiency

Cycle time is the total time required to complete a manufacturing process. It is computed as the sum of five elements:

$$\frac{\text{Cycle}}{\text{time}} = \frac{\text{Setup}}{\text{time}} + \frac{\text{Process}}{\text{time}} + \frac{\text{Move}}{\text{time}} + \frac{\text{Wait}}{\text{time}} + \frac{\text{Inspection}}{\text{time}}$$

Of the five elements of cycle time, only process time adds value from the perspective of final customers. This leads to the following measure of cycle efficiency:

$$\text{Cycle efficiency} = \frac{\text{Processing time}}{\text{Cycle time}}$$

Required:
(a) What would the computed amount of cycle efficiency equal if nonvalue-added activities were completely eliminated?
(b) Should the failure to eliminate all nonvalue-added activities be considered in evaluating the performance of management? Why or why not?
(c) If cycle time only consisted of processing time, does this mean that no further reduction in cycle time is possible?
(d) Why might management select a low-speed, rather than a high-speed, machine to perform a manufacturing activity?
(e) Assume management can manufacture a product using one of three processes. Cycle time and cost information on each process are as follows:

	Alternative A		Alternative B		Alternative C	
	Time	Cost	Time	Cost	Time	Cost
Setup	30 min.	$ 90	35 min.	$ 100	5 min.	$ 200
Process	300	600	500	650	100	800
Move	50	75	50	75	20	60
Wait	180	90	180	90	30	60
Inspect	30	120	30	120	10	40
Total	590 min.	$975	795 min.	$1,035	165 min.	$1,160

Which alternative would management prefer if management's performance was based on:

1. Minimizing cycle time?
2. Minimizing manufacturing costs?
3. Maximizing cycle efficiency?

4-22 Is Marketing a Value-Added Activity?

Custom Office Furniture designs and manufactures office furniture to meet customer specifications. Bill Martinez, senior marketing manager for Custom Office Furniture, was pleased to attend a manufacturing seminar focusing on process reengineering. He believed that attending the seminar, along with Carl Janaro, Custom Office Furniture's chief production engineer, and Susan Brafman, the firm's production cost accountant, would provide him with useful insights into emerging topics and make him a better member of the corporate team.

As he listened to the seminar leader's opening comments, Bill began to wonder if attending the program was a good idea. According to the seminar leader: "The only value-added activity in a manufacturing organization is the physical transformation of raw materials into a final product that meets customer wants." Throughout the seminar, the focus continued to be on eliminating paperwork, movement, waiting, and checking, and seeking the least-cost method of transforming raw materials into finished goods.

Riding home, Carl and Susan engaged in a detailed conversation about the ideal way to manufacture office furniture at the lowest possible costs. Finally, the moment Bill feared arrived, and Carl commented that one sure-fire way of reducing costs at Custom Office Furniture would be to eliminate all marketing activities and put in an 800 number directly to production scheduling.

Required:
Respond to Carl's comment and explain how marketing adds value to the customers of Custom Office Furniture.

4-23 Across-the-Board Budget Cuts
Midstate Pipe manufactures plumbing supplies used primarily in the construction of new houses. Recent increases in interest rates have led to a decline in the purchase and construction of new houses, placing financial pressure on Midstate Pipe. To maintain profits, management has announced a hiring freeze and an across-the-board cut of 15 percent in all department budgets.

Required:
Discuss the potential consequences of Midstate Pipe's approach to solving its financial problems. Recommend an alternative approach to reducing costs that might avoid many of these undesirable consequences and explain why this alternative approach is better.

4-24 The Cost and Ethics of Unlimited Returns[9]
Is it possible to have too much emphasis on pleasing final customers? Many manufacturers of consumer electronics argue that the answer is "Yes."

"There is an escalation of problems with returns, and it is frightening," says Jerry Kalov, president of Cobra Electronic Corp. "I think of this as a problem of consumer ethics and retailer ethics." Mr. Kalov and others are unhappy with the product return policies of discount retail stores such as that of Kmart Corp. Its policy guarantees a full refund, no questions asked, any time a product is returned, no matter how long since the date of purchase.

Return policies, such as Kmart's, have resulted in televisions being returned the Monday after a Superbowl, camcorders being returned shortly after a wedding, and radar detectors being returned after a long trip. Mr. Kalov says

---

9 Based on Timothy L. O'Brien, "Unjustified Returns Plague Electronics Makers," *The Wall Street Journal* (September 26, 1994), pp. B1, B2.

Cobra even received a two-year-old cordless telephone, that was obviously chewed by a dog, from a retailer who gave the customer a complete refund.

Robert Shaw, president of International Jensen, estimates that "bogus returns" lower his company's profits by 25 percent. Mr. Shaw believes that only 15 percent of the products returned to International Jensen are defective.

In an attempt to reduce returns, many small companies are opening customer assistance phone numbers to supply the kind of technical expertise that is not available from sales personnel at discount stores. But, according to Mr. Johnson, the cost of customer assistance services will ultimately be passed along to customers in the form of higher prices.

Required:

(a) Does an unlimited return policy such as Kmart's pose an ethical problem? Is it unethical to buy a product with the intention of returning it? Is it unethical to return a product that has been subject to abuse?

(b) Over an extended period of time, what are the likely consequences of unlimited returns on small manufacturers, small specialized retail stores, large manufactures, discount superstores, and customers?

4-25 Ethical Issues with Supplier/Buyer Partnerships

John Snyder was excited to learn of his appointment as Central Switching Corporation's new vendor sales representative to March Label Appliance, Inc. For the past 4 years, Central Switching has supplied all the electric switches used in March Label washers and dryers. As Central Switching's vendor sales representative, John Snyder's threefold assignment involves: (1) working with March Label engineers in designing electric switches that can be manufactured to meet cost and quality requirements, (2) assisting March Label in resolving any problems related to electric switches, and (3) monitoring the inventory levels of electric switches at March Label, placing orders for additional switches as appropriate.

This appointment will require John to move to Bonn, Germany, for 2 years. While John has mixed feelings about the move, he is familiar with the success of the program in improving Central Switching's financial performance and very much aware of the fact that the two previous vendor sales representatives received promotions at the end of their appointments.

As John toured the March Label factory in Bonn with his predecessor, Janet Smith, his excitement turned into concern. It became apparent that Central Switching had not been supplying March Label with the best available switches at the lowest possible costs. Although the switches were adequate, they were more likely to wear out after five or six years of use than would switches now on the market (and being used by March Label's competitors). Furthermore, when the switches currently in transit by ship from North America to Europe were counted, it also appeared that the inventory level of electric switches would soon be more than enough to satisfy March Label's needs for the next four months.

Required:

If you were John, what would you do?

SOLUTION TO REVIEW PROBLEM

(a)

Additional costs of Job 102:

Outbound logistics:			
Pickup ($10 x 1 pickup)		$ 10.00	
Deliveries ($10 x 2 deliveries)		20.00	
Weight ($0.50 x 450 kilograms)		225.00	$ 255.00
Marketing and sales:			
Site visits ($175 x 3 visits)			525.00
Service:			
Site visit ($175 x 1 visit)			175.00
Total remaining costs assigned to Job 102			$ 955.00

(b)

The annual costs of maintaining customer relations are not specifically driven by Job 102.

(c)

Profitability of Job 102:

Selling price		$20,000.00
Costs:		
Direct materials	$8,500.00	
Inbound logistics	465.75	
Operations	7,000.00	
Outbound logistics	255.00	
Marketing and sales	525.00	
Service	175.00	-16,920.75
Profit		$ 3,079.25

(d)

Profitability of relationships with Orleans Company:

Profit on Job 102	$3,079.25
Annual costs to maintain customer	- 1,000.00
Profitability of customer	$2,079.25

(e)

Classification of costs:

Placing purchase orders	Batch
Verifying purchase orders	Batch
Unloading/unpacking/inspecting	Unit
Setup	Batch
Conversion	Unit
Polish	Unit
Pack	Unit
Pickup	Batch
Delivery	Batch
Weight	Unit
Maintain customer	Customer
Marketing site visit	Batch or unit (Arguments can be made either way.)
Service site visit	Batch or unit (Arguments can be made either way.)

After completing this chapter, you should be able to:

L O 1

Distinguish between economic and cost-based approaches to pricing.

L O 2

Describe target costing and explain why it is gaining widespread acceptance in highly competitive industries.

L O 3

Explain the relationship between target costing and continuous improvement costing.

L O 4

Distinguish among the four basic types of quality costs and discuss how quality cost information can assist in a program of quality management.

L O 5

Explain how benchmarking can assist in quality management, continuous improvement, and process reengineering.

STRATEGIC COST MANAGEMENT II: PRICE, COST, AND QUALITY

In Chapter 1, we noted that well-informed customers evaluate products or services on the three interrelated dimensions of cost, quality, and service. Cost includes both the initial purchase price and subsequent operating and maintenance costs. Quality refers to the degree to which the product or service meets customers' needs. And service includes such things as helpfulness of sales personnel, special product modifications to meet the buyer's needs, timely delivery, and subsequent support.

The purpose of this chapter is to examine approaches to pricing, the interrelationship between price and cost, and the role of quality costs and benchmarking in meeting customer needs at the lowest possible price. *We begin by investigating the theoretical pricing model presented by economists to explain price equilibrium. After mentioning the limitations of this long-run equilibrium model for actually determining the price of a product or service, we consider the widely used cost-plus approach to identifying initial prices. Next, we examine how intense competition has inverted the cost-plus pricing model into one that starts with an acceptable market price and subtracts a desired profit to determine a target cost.*

We consider life-cycle costs and quality costs from the perspectives of both (1) the seller who increasingly plans for all costs before production begins and (2) the buyer who regards subsequent operating, maintenance, repair, and disposal costs as important as the purchase price. This leads to efforts undertaken to improve quality and minimize quality costs and considerations of quality certification requirements often imposed on vendors. Finally, we consider how benchmarking can assist in improving competitiveness and profitability.

THE PRICING DECISION

L O 1

Product pricing is one of the most important and complex decisions facing management. The salability of individual products or services is directly affected by pricing decisions, as is the profitability—and even the survival—of the organization. This section examines the determination of long-run equilibrium prices in economic models and considers the traditional role of costs in pricing.

Economic Approaches to Pricing

In economic models, the firm has a profit maximizing goal and known cost and revenue functions. Typically, increases in sales quantity require reductions in selling prices, causing **marginal revenue**, the varying increment in total revenue derived from the sale of an additional unit, to decline as sales increase. Increases in production can only be achieved with increases in **marginal cost**, the varying increment in total cost required to produce and sell an additional unit of product. In economic models, profits are maximized at the sales volume where marginal revenues equal marginal costs. Firms continue to produce as long as the marginal revenue derived from the sale of each additional unit exceeds the marginal cost of producing that unit.

Economic models provide a useful framework for thinking about pricing decisions. The ideal price is the one that will lead customers to purchase all the units a firm can provide up to the point where the last unit has a marginal cost exactly equal to its marginal revenue.

Despite their conceptual merit, economic models are seldom used for day-to-day pricing decisions. Perfect information and an indefinite time period are required to achieve equilibrium prices where marginal revenues equal marginal costs.[1] In the short run, most for-profit organizations attempt to achieve a target profit rather than a maximum profit. One reason for this is an inability to determine the single set of actions out of all possible actions that will lead to profit maximization. Furthermore, managers are more apt to strive to satisfy a number of goals (such as profits for investors, job security for themselves and their employees, and being a "good" corporate citizen) than to strive for the maximization of a single profit goal. In any case, to maximize profits, a company's management would have to know the cost and revenue functions of every product the firm sells. For most firms, this information cannot be developed at a reasonable cost.

Cost-Based Approaches to Pricing

Though cost is not the only consideration in pricing, it has traditionally been important. There are several reasons for this:

---

1 Amanda Bennett, "Sugarscape Model Shows Flaws in Textbook Economics," *The Wall Street Journal* (November 21, 1994), p. B1.

- *Cost data are available*. When hundreds of different prices must be set in a short time, cost may be the only feasible basis for product pricing.
- *Cost-based prices are defensible*. Managers threatened by legal action or public scrutiny feel secure using cost-based prices. They can argue that prices are set in a manner that provides a "fair" profit.
- *Revenues must exceed costs if the firm is to remain in business*. In the long run, the unit selling price must exceed the full cost of each unit.

The general approach to cost-based pricing is illustrated in Exhibit 5-1. The process begins with market research to determine customer wants. If the product requires components to be designed and produced by vendors, the process of obtaining prices may be time-consuming. When some costs, such as those at the facility level, are not assigned to specific products, a

EXHIBIT 5-1: TRADITIONAL COST-BASED PRICING FOR A NEW PRODUCT

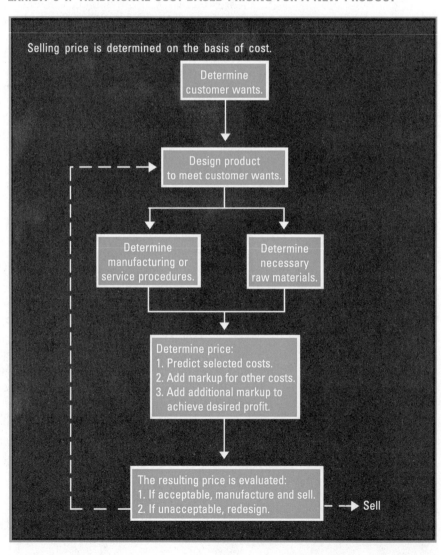

markup is added to cover these costs. An additional markup is added to achieve a desired profit. The selling price is then set as the sum of the assigned costs, the markup to cover unassigned costs, and the markup to achieve the desired profit.

The proposed selling price is evaluated in the light of competitive information and what customers are willing to pay. If the price is acceptable, the product or service is produced. If the price is too high, the product may be redesigned, manufacturing procedures may be changed, and different kinds of materials may be considered until either an acceptable price is achieved, or it is determined that the product cannot be produced at an acceptable price.

Cost-Based Pricing in Regulated Industries

The use of cost-based pricing is most apparent in regulated industries such as electric utilities and cable television. In these industries, prices are set by regulatory commissions. Utility companies apply to the regulatory commission for a price per kilowatt hour of electricity or per customer for monthly cable service. The company's application details the expected demand for its service, its operating costs, and the profit required to obtain a reasonable return on investment. Based on this information, the utility proposes a rate per unit of service. While the regulatory commission may not approve the proposed rate, the starting point for negotiation is a cost-based price.

In the 1980s, there was a movement toward deregulation of the U.S. transportation and communications industries. This movement is now spreading to electric utilities. The deregulation of the U.S. airline industry presented significant opportunities for super-efficient airlines, such as Southwest, to profitably compete with low fares. Deregulation also presented problems for less efficient carriers, such as Eastern Airlines, which went out of business. As noted in Management Accounting Practice 5-1, deregulation is spreading to Europe, with similar consequences for European airlines.

Cost-Based Pricing for Government Contracts

Cost-based pricing is widely used by defense contractors. In this case, unique and expensive products are designed and manufactured to government specifications. Because the final cost cannot be known in advance, the government typically enters into a contract that calls for the vendor to be reimbursed for costs incurred in connection with the contract and to receive a profit as specified in the terms of the contract. Obvious problems are how to determine what costs should be assigned to the contract and how to ensure that only allowed costs are assigned to the contract. To solve the first problem, the U.S. government established the Cost Accounting Standards Board and gave it the task of specifying what costs are allowable and how allowable costs should be assigned to government contracts. To solve the second problem, organizations such as the Defense Contract Audit Agency were established to ensure that the costing guidelines are followed on government contracts.

MANAGEMENT ACCOUNTING PRACTICE 5-1

Airline Deregulation Spreads Price Competition to Europe

Although all European domestic airline markets will be completely open to competition by 1997, some newly formed carriers are getting a jump on deregulation to the delight of travelers. Newly formed EuroBelgian Airways (EBA) recently introduced no-frills service between Brussels and Rome for $175 per round trip. Competitors, used to price regulation, are charging $1,146.

EBA Managing Director Victor Hasson has vowed that, "We will shake up the European airline industry." His strategy for success is modeled after U.S.-based Southwest Airlines, which has made money under deregulation with low fares and super-efficient use of equipment and personnel, while giants such as American and USAir have been awash in red ink.

Industry analysts see clouds on the horizon for Europe's old-style carriers. Nick Cunningham of a London brokerage firm asks: "If they didn't make money under regulation, how are they going to make money in a deregulated environment?" Perhaps by starting over with a clean sheet of paper. German-based Lufthansa has started Lufthansa Express, and Italy's Altalia plans to start a no-frills subsidiary, to compete with low-fare carriers.

Based on: "Now Lifting Off in Europe: No-Frills Flying," *Business Week* (November 28, 1994), p. 72.

Cost-Based Approaches to Determining Tax Rates

Property taxes in most cities, counties, and school districts are also set by elected officials on the basis of cost. The starting point is typically a proposed budget for the coming year and information on the total assessed valuation on all taxable property in the jurisdiction. The price, a rate per unit of assessed valuation, is determined by dividing the amount of the proposed budget that must be obtained from property taxes by the total taxable assessed valuation. The amount a particular property owner must pay is computed as the assessed valuation of his or her property multiplied by the rate per unit of assessed valuation. Again, while the elected officials (or voters) may decide that the proposed tax rate is so high that the budget needs to be revised, the starting point is based on costs.

Cost-Based Pricing in Single-Product Companies

Implementing cost-based pricing in a single-product company is straight-forward if everything is known but the selling price. In this case, all known information is entered into the profit formula, which is then solved for the variable price.

Assume the Bright Rug Company has annual facility level costs of $200,000 and unit costs of $10 per rug cleaned. Management desires to achieve an annual profit of $30,000 at an annual volume of 10,000 rugs. To simplify the example, assume management charges the same price re-gardless of the type, size, or shape of the rug. Using the profit formula, the cost-based price is determined to be $33:

$$\text{Profit} = \text{Total revenues} - \text{Total costs}$$
$$\$30,000 = (\text{Price} \times 10,000 \text{ rugs}) - (\$200,000 + [\$10 \times 10,000 \text{ rugs}])$$

Solving for the price:

$$(\text{Price} \times 10,000) = \$300,000 + \$30,000$$
$$\text{Price} = \$330,000/10,000$$
$$= \$33$$

A price of $33 to clean a rug will allow Bright to achieve its desired profit. Before setting the price at $33, management should evaluate the competitive situation and consider what customers are willing to pay for this service.

Cost-Based Pricing in Multiple-Product Companies

In multiple-product companies, desired profits are determined for the company as a whole, and standard procedures are established for determining the initial selling price of each product. These procedures typically specify the initial selling price as the costs assigned to products or services, plus a markup to cover unassigned costs and provide for the desired profit.

Depending on the sophistication of the organization's accounting system, possible cost bases in a manufacturing organization include markups based on (1) a combination of cost behavior and function and (2) activity hierarchy.

For markups based on behavior and function, the possible cost bases are:

- Direct materials costs
- Variable manufacturing costs
- Variable costs (manufacturing, selling, and administrative)
- Full manufacturing costs

For markups based on activity hierarchy, the possible cost bases are:

- Unit level costs
- Unit and batch level costs
- Unit and batch and product level costs

Markup on Variable Costs

We will illustrate two possible cost bases: variable costs and full manufacturing costs. When the markup is based on variable costs, it must be large enough to cover all fixed costs and the desired profit:

$$\frac{\text{Markup on}}{\text{variable costs}} = \frac{\text{Predicted fixed costs} + \text{Desired profit}}{\text{Predicted variable costs}}$$

Once the markup is determined, it is then used to determine the initial selling price of each product:

$$\frac{\text{Initial}}{\text{selling price}} = \frac{\text{Variable costs}}{\text{per unit}} + \left(\frac{\text{Variable costs}}{\text{per unit}} \times \frac{\text{Markup on}}{\text{variable costs}} \right)$$

Assume the predicted 19X9 variable and fixed costs for Magnum Enterprises are as follows:

Variable Costs		Fixed Costs	
Manufacturing	$600,000	Manufacturing	$300,000
Selling and		Selling and	
administrative	200,000	administrative	100,000
Total	$800,000	Total	$400,000

Also assume that Magnum Enterprises has total assets of $1,250,000 and management has determined that an annual return of 16 percent on total assets is appropriate in their industry. A 16 percent return translates into a desired annual profit of $200,000 ($1,250,000 x 0.16). To achieve a desired profit of $200,000, Magnum Enterprises needs a 75 percent markup on variable costs:

$$\text{Markup on variable costs} = \frac{\$400,000 + \$200,000}{\$800,000}$$

$$= 0.75$$

If the predicted variable costs for product A1 are $12 per unit, the initial selling price for product A1 is $21:

$$\text{Initial selling price} = \$12 + (\$12 \times 0.75)$$

$$= \$21$$

To make competitive pricing decisions that at least ensure breaking even, management might wish to separate the markup required to cover unassigned costs from the markup to achieve a desired profit. For Magnum Enterprises, these two markups are determined as follows:

$$\text{Markup to cover unassigned costs} = \frac{\$400,000 \text{ unassigned costs}}{\$800,000 \text{ variable costs}}$$

$$= 0.50 \text{ of variable costs}$$

$$\text{Markup to achieve desired profit} = \frac{\$200,000 \text{ desired profit}}{\$800,000 \text{ variable costs}}$$

$$= 0.25 \text{ of variable costs}$$

To break even at the predicted level of activity, products must carry a markup of 50 percent on variable costs. To achieve Magnum's desired profit, products must carry an additional markup of 25 percent on variable costs.

Markup on Manufacturing Costs

When the markup is based on manufacturing costs, it must be large enough to cover selling and administrative expenses and to provide for the desired profit:

$$\text{Markup on manufacturing costs} = \frac{\text{Predicted selling and administrative costs} + \text{Desired profit}}{\text{Predicted manufacturing costs}}$$

For Magnum, the markup on manufacturing costs would be 55.6 percent:

$$\text{Markup on manufacturing costs} = \frac{\$300,000 + \$200,000}{\$900,000}$$

$$= 0.556$$

To compute the markup on manufacturing costs, it is necessary to determine the desired profit and predict all costs for the pricing period. The initial prices of individual products are then determined as their unit manufacturing costs, plus the markup:

$$\text{Initial selling price} = \text{Manufacturing costs per unit} + \left(\text{Manufacturing costs per unit} \times \text{Markup on manufacturing costs} \right)$$

If the predicted manufacturing costs for product B1 were $10, the initial selling price for product B1 is $15.56:

$$\text{Initial selling price} = \$10 + (\$10 \times 0.556)$$

$$= \$15.56$$

Again, management may desire separate information on the markup required to cover unassigned costs and the markup required to achieve a desired profit.

A Critique of Cost-Based Pricing

Cost-based pricing has four major drawbacks:

1. Cost-based pricing requires accurate cost assignments. If costs are not accurately assigned, some products may be priced too high, losing market share to competitors, and other products may be priced too low, gaining market share but being less profitable than anticipated.
2. The greater the portion of unassigned costs, the greater the likelihood of overpricing and underpricing individual products.
3. Cost-based pricing assumes goods or services are relatively scarce and customers who want a product or service are, generally, willing to pay the price.
4. In a competitive environment, cost-based approaches increase the time and cost of bringing new products to market.

Cost-based pricing became the dominant approach to pricing during an era when products were relatively long-lived and there was relatively little competition. While they are easy to implement, reflect the need to recover costs and earn a return on investment, and easily justified, cost-based prices may not be competitive. Today's worldwide competition puts intense downward pressure on prices and removes slack from pricing formulas. There is little margin for error in pricing. In a highly competitive market, small variations in pricing make significant differences in success.

Furthermore, competitive pressures have reduced the life cycle of products and the time companies have to bring new products to market. One problem with the cost-plus model illustrated in Exhibit 5-1 is the failure to involve suppliers in the early stages of product design. When component parts must be developed and manufactured by vendors, the failure to involve vendors until after the final product is designed causes significant delays and misses helpful suggestions from the vendor's technical experts. The model also reflects a split between design and manufacturing that may cause further delays and quality problems. Perhaps a simple design change could simplify and speed up manufacturing operations. When people in design and manufacturing do not work together, cost saving and quality-enhancing opportunities may go unnoticed. Finally, when the cost-plus price is determined to be unacceptably high, the redesign, reworking of manufacturing procedures, and soliciting additional bids from vendors may require so much time that competitors have an insurmountable lead in developing and introducing new products. These problems have led to the development of target costing, discussed later in this chapter.

Ethical and Legal Considerations in Pricing

In response to intense pressure to achieve an adequate return on investment, managers of competing businesses may be tempted to work together for their mutual benefit. Highway contractors may be tempted to share available business and earn more profits by rigging bids. In an attempt to lessen competition and maintain prices, large automobile manufacturers appeal to the government, protesting that foreign competitors are selling below cost. Large retail organizations pressure manufacturers to give them price concessions not available to other merchants. A major manufacturer that buys more than half of a vendor's product refuses to accept a price increase. A valued customer, experiencing financial problems, requests price reductions and payment terms not available to others. In these circumstances, managers are frequently faced with the problem of trying to determine what is ethical. They also need to be aware of laws prohibiting price discrimination and price fixing.

Price discrimination involves illegally charging different purchasers different prices. The **Robinson-Patman Act** prohibits price discrimination when purchasers compete with one another in the sale of their products or services to third parties unless:

1. The discriminatory lower price is in response to changing conditions in the market for, or marketability of, the commodities involved (such as the sale of discontinued products).
2. The discriminatory lower price is made to meet an equally low price of a competitor.
3. The discriminatory lower price makes only due allowance for specific cost differences such as those resulting from long production runs and bulk shipments.

Efficient, large-volume retailers, such as Wal-Mart, evoke the resentment of smaller merchants because they often sell products for less than the smaller retailer's cost of the same products. While some of the lower prices may be "loss leaders" intended to attract customers, most of the lower prices at large-volume retailers reflect lower operating costs per dollar of sales revenue and lower costs for merchandise. Wholesalers and manufacturers charge Wal-Mart less than they charge smaller independent stores.

These lower prices are justified under the Robinson-Patman Act as resulting from bulk shipments and reduced order processing costs.

Price fixing, the organized setting of prices by competitors, is prohibited by the **Sherman Antitrust Act**. The goal of price fixing is to reduce competition on the basis of price. The argument in favor of price fixing is that it forces companies to compete on the basis of factors other than price, while it ensures that companies remain financially viable. In recent years, the U.S. Justice Department has vigorously enforced regulations against price fixing. The goal of the Justice Department is to enhance competition and lower prices.

For many years, an agency of the U.S. government set air fares. This was done in a belief that a financially viable airline industry was in the national best interest and that, without the protection of set prices, financial concerns would reduce airline safety. The airline industry has since been deregulated, and the dramatic reduction in air fares has led to a significant increase in air travel. While the Federal Aviation Administration maintains that increased competition has not affected airline safety, it has led several airlines into financial difficulty. Following the deregulation of the airline industry, the Department charged American, Delta, Continental, Northwest, TWA, and Alaska Airlines with communicating proposed airfares to each other and informally agreeing to set airfares by way of computer systems maintained by the Airline Tariff Publishing Company.

TARGET COSTING

L O 2

Peter Drucker has identified cost-based (he calls it "cost-driven") pricing as a "deadly business sin." According to Drucker:

> Most American and practically all European companies arrive at their prices by adding up costs and then putting a profit margin on top. And then, as soon as they have introduced the product, they have to start cutting the price, have to redesign the product at enormous expense, have to take losses—and, often have to drop a perfectly good product because it is priced incorrectly.[2]

Drucker believes that cost-based pricing is the reason why, despite technological success, there is no longer an American consumer-electronics industry. He believes that the only sound way to price is to start with what the market is willing to pay and to design a product or service to meet that price. This approach to the pricing and design of new products was formalized at Toyota[3] and quickly utilized by other successful Japanese companies such as Nissan, Canon, and Ricoh. It is referred to as *target costing*.

---

2 Peter F. Drucker, "The Five Deadly Business Sins," *The Wall Street Journal* (October 21, 1993), p. A18.
3 Takao Tanaka, "Target Costing at Toyota," *Journal of Cost Management* (Spring 1993), p. 4.

Target costing starts with determining what customers are willing to pay for a product or service and then subtracts a desired profit on sales to determine the allowable, or target, cost of the product or service. This target cost is then communicated to a cross-functional team of employees representing such diverse areas as marketing, product design, manufacturing, and management accounting. Reflecting value chain concepts and the notion of partnerships up and down the value chain, suppliers of raw materials and components are often included in the teams. The target costing team is assigned the task of designing a product that meets customer price, function, and quality requirements, while providing a desired profit. Its job is not completed until the target cost is met, or a determination is made that the product or service cannot be profitably introduced under the current circumstances. Exhibit 5-2 contains an overview of target costing.

While a formula may be used to determine a markup on cost, it is not possible to develop a formula indicating how to achieve a target cost. Hence, target costing is not a technique. It is more of a philosophy or an approach to pricing and cost management. It takes a proactive approach to cost management, reflecting a belief that *costs are best managed by decisions made during product development.* This contrasts with the more passive cost-plus belief that costs result from design, procurement, and manufacture. Like the value chain, target costing helps orient employees toward the final customer and reinforces the notion that all departments within the organization and all organizations along the value chain must work together. Target costing also empowers employees, who will be assigned responsibility for carrying out activities necessary to deliver a product or service, with the authority to determine what activities will be selected. Like process mapping, it helps employees better understand their role in serving the customer.

In the absence of a target costing orientation, design engineers are apt to focus on incorporating leading-edge technology and the maximum number of features in a product. Target costing keeps the customer's function, quality, and price requirements in the forefront at all times. If customers do not want leading-edge technology (which may be expensive and untested) and several product features, they will resist paying for them. Focusing on achieving a target cost keeps design engineers tuned in to the final customer.

Left on their own, design engineers may believe that their job ends when they design a product that meets the customer's functional requirements. There is a tendency to simply pass on the design to manufacturing and let manufacturing determine how best to produce the product. Further down the line, if the product needs servicing, it then becomes the service department's responsibility to determine how best to service the product. A target costing orientation forces design engineers to explicitly consider the costs of manufacturing and servicing a product while designing it. This is known as **design for manufacture**.

EXHIBIT 5-2: TARGET COSTING IN A HIGHLY COMPETITIVE ENVIRONMENT

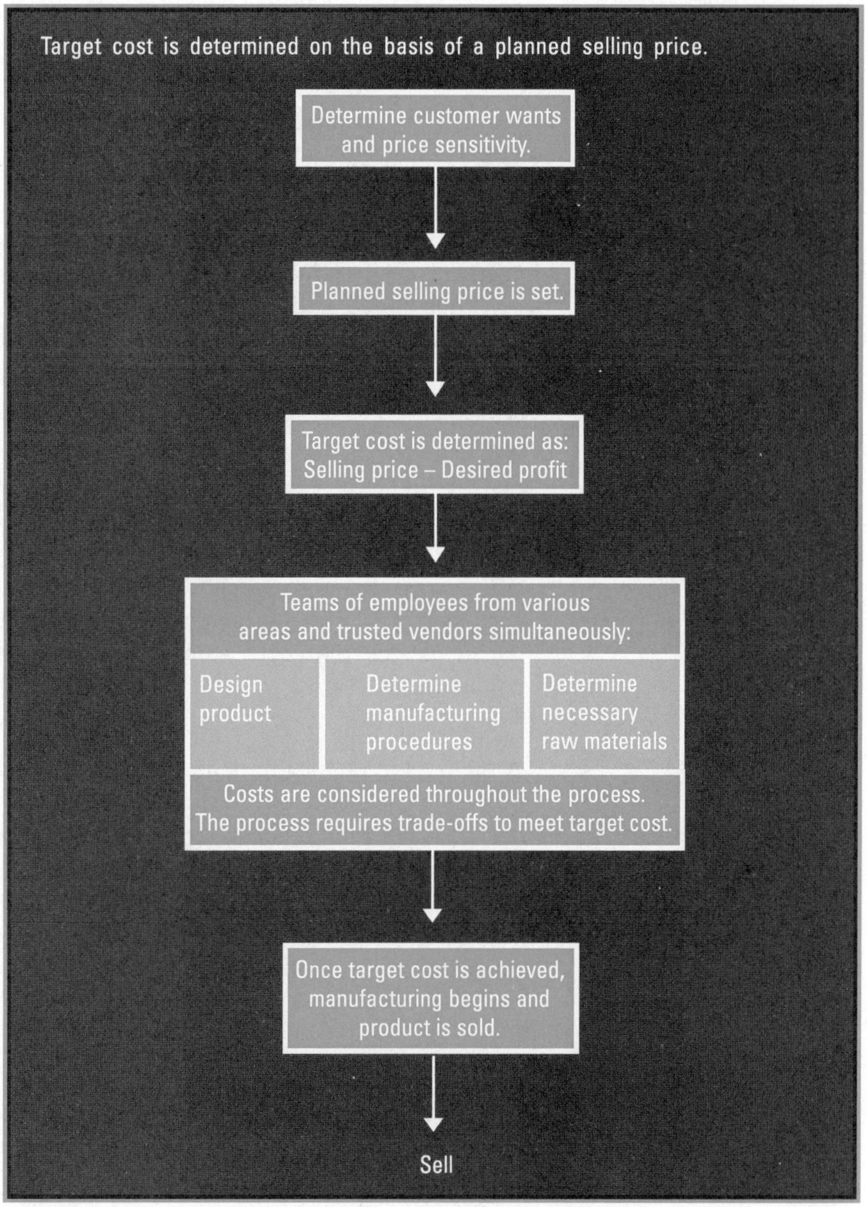

Target cost is determined on the basis of a planned selling price.

> Determine customer wants
> and price sensitivity.

> Planned selling price is set.

> Target cost is determined as:
> Selling price – Desired profit

> Teams of employees from various
> areas and trusted vendors simultaneously:

| Design product | Determine manufacturing procedures | Determine necessary raw materials |

> Costs are considered throughout the process.
> The process requires trade-offs to meet target cost.

> Once target cost is achieved,
> manufacturing begins and
> product is sold.

Sell

Minor changes in design that do not affect functionality can often produce dramatic savings in manufacturing and service costs. Examples of design for manufacture include:

- Using molded plastic parts to avoid assembling several small parts.
- Designing two parts that must be fit together so that joining them in the correct manner is obvious to assembly workers.
- Placing an access panel in the side wall of an appliance so service personnel can make repairs quickly.

- Using standard-size parts to reduce inventory requirements, to reduce the possibility of assembly personnel inserting the incorrect part, and to simplify the job of service personnel.
- Ensuring that tolerance requirements for parts that must fit together can be met with available equipment.
- Using manufacturing procedures that are common to other products.

The successful implementation of target costing requires employees from all involved disciplines to be familiar with activity-based costing concepts and the notions of value-added and nonvalue-added activities. When considering the manufacturing process, team members should minimize nonvalue-added activities such as movement, storage, inspection, and setup. They should also select the lowest cost value-added activities that will do the job properly.

Target Costing Reduces Time to Introduce New Products

By designing a product to meet a target cost rather than evaluating the marketability of a product at a cost-plus price and having to recycle the design through several departments, target costing reduces the time required to introduce new products. Involving vendors in target costing design teams also makes vendors aware of the necessity of meeting a target cost and facilitates the concurrent engineering of components to be produced outside the organization. This reduces the time required to obtain components.

Target Costing Components

Although target costing is most frequently associated with the development of new products, target costing concepts can be applied to components. A cost management expert at Isuzu Motors once illustrated target costing for components by taking apart a pen. "This is what we do with our competitors' products . . . . We would analyze the material it is made of, the way it is molded, the process used to assemble it. From this we would determine the product's probable cost." Isuzu would then use the component's probable cost to a competitor as a target cost to meet or beat.[4]

Target Costing Requires Detailed Cost Information

Implementing target costing requires detailed information on the cost of alternative activities. This information allows decision makers to select design and manufacturing alternatives that best meet function and price requirements. Tables containing detailed data bases of cost information for various manufacturing variables are occasionally used in designing products and selecting processes to meet target costs. The development and use of cost tables were considered in Chapter 4.

Target Costing Requires Coordination

The primary limitations of target costing concern employee and supplier attitudes and the many meetings required to coordinate product design and to select manufacturing processes. Everyone needs to have a basic under-

---

4 Ford S. Worthy, "Japan's Smart Secret Weapon," *Fortune* (August 12, 1992), p. 74.

standing of the overall processes required to bring a product to market and an appreciation of the cost consequences of alternative actions. They must also respect, cooperate, and communicate with other team members and be willing to engage in a negotiation process involving trade-offs. Finally, they must understand that while the total time required to bring a new product to market may be reduced, the countless coordinating meetings may be quite intrusive on their otherwise orderly schedule. Exhibit 5-3 contains an evaluation of target costing.

Short Product Life Cycles Increase the Importance of Target Costing

From a traditional marketing perspective, products with a relatively long life go through four distinct stages during their life cycle:

1. Startup. Sales are low when a product is first introduced. Traditionally, initial selling prices are set high and customers tend to be relatively affluent trendsetters.
2. Growth. Sales increase as the product gains acceptance. Traditionally, prices have remained high during this stage because of customer loyalty and the absence of competitive products.
3. Maturity. Sales level off as the product matures. Because of increased competition, there is increasing pressure on selling prices; and some reductions may be necessary.
4. Decline. Sales decline as the product becomes obsolete. Significant price cuts may be required to sell remaining inventories.

The sales revenue over a product's marketing life cycle is represented by the vertical axis, and time is represented by the horizontal axis in Exhibit 5-4. Part (a) of Exhibit 5-4 represents a product with a relatively long market life cycle, such as a Model T Ford, Coca Cola, Levi's blue jeans, or Bounty paper towels. Some of these products, such as the Model T Ford, have completed their life cycle. Others, such as Coke, seem to remain mature products indefinitely.

EXHIBIT 5-3: PROS AND CONS OF TARGET COSTING

Pros
- Proactive approach to cost management
- Orients organization toward customer
- Breaks down barriers between departments
- Enhances employee awareness and empowerment
- Fosters partnerships with suppliers
- Minimizes nonvalue-added activities
- Encourages selection of low cost value-added activities
- Reduces time to market

Cons
- Effective use requires the development of detailed cost data
- Requires willingness to cooperate
- Requires many meetings for coordination

EXHIBIT 5-4: PRODUCT MARKETING LIFE CYCLES

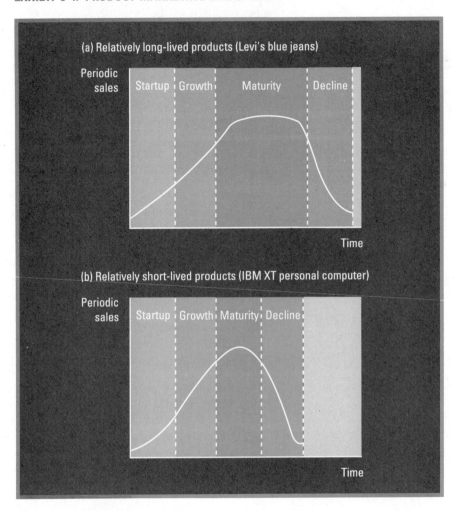

Part (b) represents a product with a relatively short market life cycle, such as IBM XT personal computers or Intel 386 computer chips. In general, as the rate of technological change increases, product life cycles decrease, especially for products that utilize advanced technology.

Target costing is more important for products with a relatively short market life cycle. When products have a long life cycle, there are many opportunities to continuously improve design and manufacturing procedures. These opportunities are not available when a product has a short life cycle. Hence, extra care must go into the initial planning for short-lived products. This is especially true when short product life cycles are combined with increased worldwide competition. It is important to introduce a product first and to introduce it at a price that ensures rapid market penetration. Management Accounting Practice 5-2 illustrates how being first and using highly competitive pricing made Hewlett-Packard's inkjet printers a market success.

MANAGEMENT ACCOUNTING PRACTICE 5-2

Better Print Quality and Competitive Pricing Makes Inkjet Printers a Success

More than a decade ago Hewlett-Packard was the world leader in the manufacture and sale of hand-held calculators, a business it pioneered. H-P lost the market to Japanese companies, such as Sharp, that introduced mass market products at lower prices, while H-P went after the limited market for scientific calculators.

Learning from its mistakes, H-P invested heavily in product research and vowed to move quickly, go for the mass market with low prices and low costs, and target "the enemy." This new competitive strategy is a major reason for the success of Hewlett-Packard's inkjet printers.

The first inkjet printers were envisioned to be a low cost variation on H-P's well-known laser printers. H-P concluded, however, that with a low enough price (and cost), the inkjet could profitably dominate the lower end of the printer market, perhaps driving out dot matrix printers. H-P decided to go after the dot matrix market dominated by Epson. Wearing "Beat Epson" football jerseys, teams of H-P employees began studying Epson to learn what made it a success and what its weaknesses were. They identified high reliability and a design that simplified manufacturing as Epson's strengths and a commitment to dot matrix printers as a major weakness.

To hold down costs and introduce inkjet printers as soon as possible, H-P engineers were convinced to use existing platforms and processes wherever possible and to avoid expensive product features. H-P was the first company to introduce inkjet printers in 1988. By continuously introducing improved variations of the inkjet and aggressively meeting or beating competitors' prices, H-P has become one of the fastest growing U.S.-based multinational companies.

Based on: "How H-P Used Tactics of the Japanese to Beat Them at Their Games," *The Wall Street Journal* (September 8, 1994), pp. A1, A9.

Target Costing Helps Manage Life-Cycle Costs

Life-cycle costs include all costs associated with a product or service ranging from those associated with initial conception through design, preproduction, production, and after-production support. The lower line in Exhibit 5-5 (page 234) illustrates the cumulative expenditure of funds over the life of a product. For low-technology products with relatively long product lives, decisions committing the organization to spend money are made at approximately the same time the money is spent. However, for high-technology products with relatively short product lives, most of the critical decisions affecting cost, such as product design and the selection of manufacturing procedures, are made before production begins. The top line in Exhibit 5-5 represents decisions committing the organization to expenditures for a product. It has been estimated that up to 95 percent of the total costs associated with high-technology products are committed before the first unit is produced.[5]

5 Benjamin S. Blanchard, *Design and Manage to Life Cycle Cost* (Portland, Oregon: M/A Press, 1978), p. 15.

EXHIBIT 5-5: THE COMMITMENT AND EXPENDITURE OF MONEY FOR HIGH-TECHNOLOGY PRODUCTS WITH RELATIVELY SHORT PRODUCT LIFE

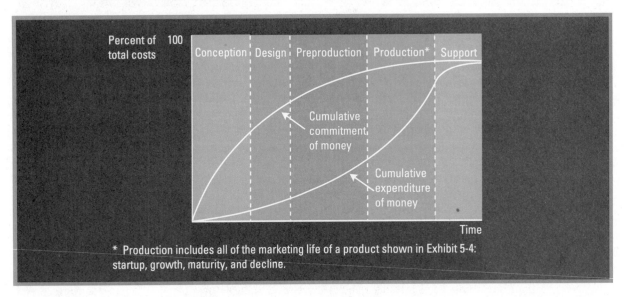

* Production includes all of the marketing life of a product shown in Exhibit 5-4: startup, growth, maturity, and decline.

CONTINUOUS IMPROVEMENT (KAIZEN) COSTING

L O 3

Continuous improvement costing calls for establishing cost reduction targets for products or services an organization is currently providing to customers. Because this approach to cost management was developed in Japan, it is often referred to as *Kaizen costing. Kaizen* means "continuous improvement" in Japanese. Continuous improvement costing begins where target costing ends. While target costing takes a proactive approach to cost management during the conception, design, and preproduction stages of a product's life, continuous improvement costing takes a proactive approach to cost management during the production stage of a product's life:

		Time		→
Conception	Design	Preproduction		Production
	Target Costing			Continuous Improvement Costing

Continuous improvement costing is accomplished through continuous improvement techniques, such as process mapping, discussed in Chapter 4. What continuous improvement costing adds to the continuous improvement concept discussed previously is a specific target to be achieved during a time period.

Successful world-class companies use continuous improvement costing to avoid complacency. Competitors are constantly striving to win market share through better quality or lower prices. Hewlett-Packard studied Epson to determine Epson's strengths and weaknesses. Isuzu Motors takes competitors' products apart to determine a target cost it must beat. To fend off competition, prices and costs must be continuously reduced. A failure to reduce prices and costs will result in a loss of market share. To maintain its competitive position, Hewlett-Packard reduced the list price of the inkjet printer from $995 in 1988 to $365 in 1993. In 1995, a basic H-P inkjet printer could be purchased for less than $250. This could not have been done without continuous reductions in costs.

At the Daihatsu Motor Company of Osaka, Japan, Kaizen cost reduction targets are set for each cost element, including purchased parts per car, direct materials per car, labor hours per car, and office utilities.[6] Performance reports are developed at the end of each month, comparing targeted and actual cost reductions. If actual cost reductions are more than the targeted cost reductions, the results are favorable; and if the actual cost reductions are less than the targeted cost reductions, the results are unfavorable.

Because cost reduction targets are set before it is known how they will be achieved, continuous improvement costing can be stressful to employees. To help reduce this stress at Daihatsu, a period of about three months following the introduction of a new product is allowed before organizational units are expected to meet target costs and Kaizen costing targets. A critical element in motivating employee cooperation and teamwork in aggressive cost management techniques, such as target and continuous improvement costing, is to avoid using performance reports to place blame for failure. The response to an unfavorable performance report must be an offer of assistance rather than a demand that failure be explained.

QUALITY COSTS

L O 4

Life-cycle costs were previously considered from the seller's perspective within the context of developing target costs. From the buyer's perspective, life-cycle costs include the total costs associated with a cost objective such as a refrigerator, furnace, X-ray machine, or tractor over its entire life. Sophisticated buyers look beyond acquisition cost to life-cycle costs in making decisions. Major home appliances now come with attached stickers estimating their annual operating costs, and new automobiles have attached stickers with information on fuel efficiency. The life-cycle costs of a furnace include the purchase price, operating costs such as fuel, maintenance costs such as cleaning the burner, and repair costs such as replacing an exhaust fan. The preferred furnace is the one that provides the desired heat at the lowest life-cycle cost.

---

6 Yasuhiro Monden and John Lee, "How a Japanese Auto Maker Reduces Costs," *Management Accounting* (August 1993), pp. 22-26.

Applying life-cycle cost concepts, the total cost of materials to a manufacturing company include much more than the purchase price. They also include costs caused by potential and actual materials' quality problems. A concern that some materials are defective may require purchasing extra materials or the inspection of materials. The use of defective materials may cause a manufacturer to incur costs for production downtime and rework. When life-cycle costs are considered, purchasing decisions are less likely to be made solely on the basis of price. When the effect of quality on subsequent costs is considered, raw materials quality becomes just as important as price.

Quality, defined as conformance to customer expectations, is an important competitive factor.[7] Successful companies know they must meet customers' quality and price expectations. In addition to being ethically questionable, reducing quality to achieve a target cost will not lead to long-run profits in today's highly competitive worldwide markets. Consistent product quality is a component in the success of companies such as Federal Express, Ford, McDonald's, Toyota, and Xerox.

In manufacturing photocopy equipment, Xerox has found that an emphasis on quality does more than satisfy customers. Focusing on quality also leads to lower manufacturing costs, lower inventory levels, higher productivity, and increased profits. Purchasing high-quality materials reduces the need to inspect incoming materials, reduces the need for extra inventory, and facilitates delivery of materials directly to the shop floor. In manufacturing and repetitive services activities, such as processing checks at a bank, an emphasis on "doing it right the first time" reduces the need for inspection, the production of extra units, and the need for rework. By eliminating the effort devoted to detecting and reworking defective units, many organizations have been able to increase their productivity and profitability.

Productivity is the relationship between outputs and inputs:

$$\text{Productivity} = \text{Outputs/Inputs}$$

Measurement of productivity requires a measure of output and a measure of input. Partial measures of productivity are based on the relationship of units produced to a single input such as the number of employees, direct labor hours, or machine hours. Total measures of productivity convert all inputs into dollars (a common denominator) and restate outputs in terms of sales dollars.

Improvements in quality increase productivity by reducing the inputs required to obtain a given level of output. These improvements in productivity increase profits by lowering costs for a given level of output. If some of the cost savings are passed on to customers in the form of lower selling prices, an increase in sales volume may generate increased profits. Additionally, if an organization achieves a reputation for quality, it may be able to charge premium prices. The known quality of international brands, such

---

7 Much of the material in this section is based on *Measuring, Planning, and Controlling Quality Costs*, by Wayne J. Morse, Harold P. Roth, and Kay M. Poston (Montvale, NJ: National Association of Accountants, 1987).

as Coke and Pepsi, allow vendors of these products to charge higher prices than those of local brands of soft drinks.

An emphasis on quality is a critical element of modern approaches to inventory management that strive to minimize inventories throughout the organization. As inventories are reduced, the presence of defective units becomes increasingly disruptive. Indeed, without buffer stocks, manufacturers may have to stop operations as soon as a defective unit is detected. While costly in the short run, these disruptions call attention to quality problems and encourage changes that prevent their reoccurrence.

Quality of Design and Quality of Conformance

A key to improving quality is recognizing that quality is everyone's responsibility. The responsibility for quality starts with determining customer expectations and concludes with the delivery of products and services that conform to these expectations. The process of delivering a quality product or service can be broken into five steps:

Step 1 → Step 2 → Step 3 → Step 4 → Step 5
Customer Expectations / Functional Specifications / Design Specifications / Manufacturing Specifications / Actual Results

1. Quality starts with determining customer expectations. There needs to be an agreement as to what customers expect and what the vendor will deliver. If customers at a McDonald's restaurant expect table service, lobster, and candlelight, they will be disappointed. If they expect fast, courteous service and low prices, they are unlikely to be disappointed.

2. The next step in delivering a quality product is to develop functional specifications for the product or service. These are explicit statements regarding the service or product capabilities, expressed in quantitative terms whenever possible. Functional specifications for a new automobile engine might include specifications for horsepower, fuel consumption, and emissions. Functional specifications at a hotel might refer to the types of services provided guests, such as prompt room service.

3. The functional specifications then need to be turned into design specifications. These are detailed statements regarding the physical characteristics of the product and engineering drawings illustrating those physical characteristics. At a Holiday Inn hotel, the number of towels to be left in each room is a design specification.

4. Detailed specifications of how a product will be manufactured to meet design specifications or how a service will be performed must also be developed. At a McDonald's restaurant, manufacturing specifications include the specified sequence of activities required to prepare a hamburger.

5. Finally, a product or service is delivered in conformance with its design specifications.

For clarity, we have identified five distinct steps in delivering a quality product or service. In reality, these steps are often intermingled. As indicated in the discussion of target costing, teams of employees from various functional areas should work on steps 1 through 4 concurrently. Many efforts to deliver quality products succeed or fail during the design stage. Quality problems and manufacturing costs increase when a complex design makes manufacture difficult. Warranty costs and buyers' life-cycle costs increase when a design does not consider ease of service.

To develop standards for evaluating product quality, it is necessary to distinguish between quality of design and quality of conformance. **Quality of design** refers to the degree of conformance between customer expectations for a product or service and the design specifications of the product or service. **Quality of conformance** refers to the degree of conformance between a product and its design specifications. The relationship between quality of design and quality of conformance is illustrated in Exhibit 5-6.

A failure to develop design specifications that conform to customer expectations results in poor quality of design. Because design specifications serve as the benchmark for evaluating the quality of finished products, poor quality of design reduces the usefulness of internal measures of quality. Internally, the quality of finished products is evaluated using design specifications. Products that fail to conform to design specifications have poor quality of conformance and are classified as defective or spoiled.

When First Alert started manufacturing household carbon monoxide detectors, the units delivered to customers conformed to design specifications. Hence, First Alert believed it had a quality product. Unfortunately, the carbon monoxide detectors were so sensitive that atmospheric air stagnation caused thousands of false alarms in the Chicago area during December of 1994. The design specifications did not conform to customer expectations because they led to an excessive number of false alarms. Hence, the carbon monoxide detectors had poor quality of design.[8]

Types of Quality Costs

Many managers find financial information related to quality useful for determining the financial significance of quality problems, developing an overall strategy for improving quality, evaluating proposals to invest in quality improvement activities, and evaluating the performance of quality improvement activities. Quality costs concepts serve as the basis for these special purpose management accounting reports.

Quality costs are costs incurred because poor quality of conformance exists or may exist. There are two basic types of quality costs, and each basic type is further divided into two subcategories:

Quality costs incurred *because of the possibility of poor conformance*:

1. **Prevention costs** are incurred to prevent nonconforming products from being produced or nonconforming services from being performed.
2. **Appraisal costs** are incurred to identify nonconforming products or services before they are delivered to customers.

---

8 "Officials Sound Off About Carbon Monoxide Detectors," *Watertown Daily Times* (February 18, 1995), pp. 9-10. An interesting aspect of this incident is that the First Alert detectors were designed to detect extended exposure to low levels of carbon monoxide, which some medical experts say is dangerous to fetuses and people with heart disease.

EXHIBIT 5-6: QUALITY OF DESIGN AND QUALITY OF CONFORMANCE*

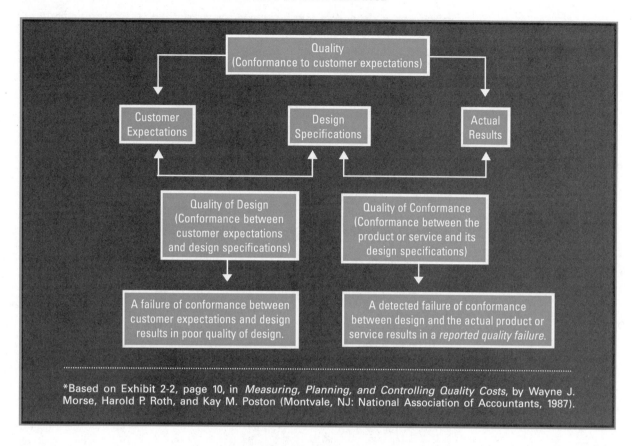

*Based on Exhibit 2-2, page 10, in *Measuring, Planning, and Controlling Quality Costs*, by Wayne J. Morse, Harold P. Roth, and Kay M. Poston (Montvale, NJ: National Association of Accountants, 1987).

Quality costs incurred *because of poor conformance between actual products or services and their design standards*:

1. **Internal failure costs** occur when materials, components, products, or services are identified as defective before delivery to customers.
2. **External failure costs** occur when nonconforming products or services are delivered to customers.

Examples of costs in each category are presented in Exhibit 5-7. Note how quality cost information cuts across organizational boundaries.

Quality cost information is periodically summarized in a quality cost report such as the one in Exhibit 5-7 for a hypothetical Swiss company. To provide a benchmark for comparison between periods with different levels of activity, quality cost information is often restated as a percent of sales or total manufacturing costs.

Notice in Exhibit 5-7 that external failure costs are very high in comparison with other quality costs. This indicates quality problems are not being identified and corrected before goods are delivered to customers, a situation frequently encountered before the initiation of a quality improvement program. In this case, expenditures on appraisal and prevention might pay off handsomely in reductions of failure costs.

EXHIBIT 5-7: QUALITY COST REPORT

Geneva Clock Company
Quality Cost Report
For the Period Ending March 31, 19X1

	Amount (In Swiss Francs Fr)	Percent of Sales*
Prevention:		
Design for manufacture	0 Fr	
Quality planning	2,000	
Quality training	3,000	
Supplier verification	0	
Total prevention	5,000 Fr	0.25%
Appraisal:		
Accuracy review of sales orders	0 Fr	
Depreciation of testing equipment	1,000	
Field inspection and testing	8,000	
In-process inspection and testing	0	
Total appraisal	9,000 Fr	0.46
Internal failure:		
Downtime due to quality problems	0 Fr	
Reinspection	400	
Retest	0	
Rework labor and overhead	10,000	
Scrap	1,600	
Total internal failure	12,000 Fr	0.61
External failure:		
Complaint adjustment	30,000 Fr	
Product recalls	60,000	
Returns and allowances	10,000	
Warranty repairs	50,000	
Warranty replacement	80,000	
Insurance for product liability	20,000	
Legal fees for product liability	0	
Total external failure	250,000 Fr	12.68
Total quality costs	276,000 Fr	13.99%

*Sales for the period total $1,972,208, or 100%.

Quality cost information may be prepared for any time period or cost objective such as a machine, a department, a plant, a division, a company, a product, or a product line. Depending on management's information needs, quality cost reports may include fewer than four cost categories. They may even include subjective information such as an estimate of lost sales resulting from quality problems (an external failure cost). Management Accounting Practice 5-3 examines how two hotel chains are trying to internalize the cost of lost sales.

MANAGEMENT ACCOUNTING PRACTICE 5-3

Internalizing the Cost of Lost Sales Due to Quality Problems

If you can't measure it, goes the cliché, you can't manage it. One of the biggest problems in getting a handle on total quality costs is measuring the opportunity cost of lost customer sales. One possible approach is to internalize it with an out-of-pocket expenditure management believes is equal to or greater than the unmeasurable opportunity cost of lost sales.

Hampton Inns internalizes the possible cost of lost customer sales by offering guaranteed refunds to any customer dissatisfied with his or her stay for any reason. In the process of internalizing and measuring this quality cost, Hampton Inns improved employee morale and helped identify and respond to customers' major complaints. Employee morale improved because of their empowerment to satisfy customers. Learning that one of the major complaints at Hampton's Embassy Suites chain was the delay in getting irons and ironing boards to guests, the chain put an iron and board in every room. Management estimates that the refund program cost $1.1 million dollars in 1993 and that the irons and boards cost an average of $475,000 per year, but that the program brought in an additional $11 million in revenue in 1993.

To build customer loyalty and to avoid the cost of lost sales due to quality problems, the Ritz-Carlton Hotel Co. authorizes employees to spend up to $2,000 to redress a guest's grievance. Furthermore, employees are permitted to break from their routine work as long as needed to make a guest happy. The underlying philosophy is that guests, remembering the level of service and the effort taken to resolve problems, will tell their friends and colleagues, and they will return. More than 90 percent of Ritz-Carlton's customers return.

....

Based on: "Why Some Customers Are More Loyal than Others," *Fortune* (September 19, 1994), pp. 215-224 and "Quality: How to Make It Pay," *Business Week* (August 8, 1994), pp. 54-80.

Quality Cost Trend Analysis

A trend analysis illustrating the effect on quality costs of successfully implementing a quality improvement program is presented in Exhibit 5-8. The most immediate action management can take to prevent the delivery of poor-quality products is to implement a rigorous inspection program and identify defective goods before they are delivered. If the inspection program is successful, there should be a shift in quality costs as a percent of sales, with external failure costs declining and appraisal and internal failure costs increasing. At this stage in a quality improvement program, total known quality costs are likely to increase. The ultimate solution to quality problems is to increase efforts to prevent the occurrence of defects. In addition to reducing external and internal failure costs, a successful quality improvement program will make it possible to reduce appraisal costs when management is confident the job is done right the first time.

While the implementation of a quality improvement program may have a significant effect on the total amount and distribution of quality costs, it is unlikely that quality costs can be reduced to zero. Management must continue to invest in prevention as new products are introduced and production procedures are changed. Even if the goal of zero defects is reached,

EXHIBIT 5-8: QUALITY COST TREND ANALYSIS OF A SUCCESSFUL QUALITY
IMPROVEMENT PROGRAM

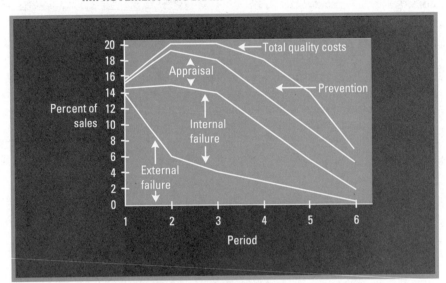

some prevention will be required to maintain this ideal state. Appraisal and internal failure costs are better than external failure costs, and prevention costs are preferred to appraisal or failure costs. While quality is not free, it is less expensive than the alternative.

Exhibit 5-9 shows a hypothesized short-run relationship between the quality of conformance and quality costs. Assuming static conditions with a given technology and level of knowledge, the graph shows that total quality costs are high when quality is low. Total quality costs decline as expenditures for appraisal and prevention improve quality. As quality nears perfection the incremental returns to additional efforts to improve quality decline to such an extent that total quality costs begin to rise.

While this hypothesized relationship is a useful way of thinking about quality costs in the short run, keep in mind that these are static relationships applicable for a given technology and level of knowledge. Advances in technology or knowledge should have the effect of shifting the prevention and appraisal cost curve down and to the right, increasing the optimal level of quality. The search for quality improvements is never-ending. Once a temporary optimal level of quality is achieved, management should strive for advances in technology and knowledge that will permit further improvements. Competitors who continue to work toward quality improvements may achieve breakthroughs that improve quality, productivity, sales volume, and profitability.

International Organization for Standardization (ISO)

The ability to demonstrate a commitment to quality is becoming increasingly important for companies doing business in globalized markets. As noted in Management Accounting Practice 5-4, the opening up of former communist countries in Eastern Europe to external competition has had a dramatic impact on how managers and employees in Hungarian companies view customers and the need for quality.

EXHIBIT 5-9: SHORT-RUN ANALYSIS OF THE ECONOMICS OF QUALITY

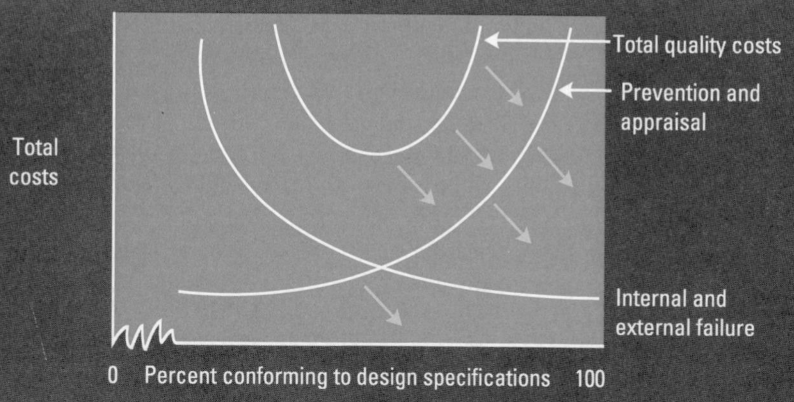

Arrows represent the effect of technological breakthrough in prevention. They cause the prevention and appraisal cost curve to shift down and to the right. This, in turn, causes the total quality costs curve to shift down and to the right. The net result is an increase in the percent conforming that minimizes total quality costs.

ISO 9000 Certification for Quality Management

In 1987, the 92-member International Organization for Standardization (ISO) issued a series of five quality assurance and management standards. These standards, known as ISO 9000 standards, provide organizations with internationally recognized models for the operation of a quality management system. However, they do not specify quality requirements for products or services. Meeting ISO 9000 standards beyond the first level requires an independent examination by an outside organization. Certification that ISO 9000 standards are being met is assessed for individual plants rather than for organizations as a whole. Plants passing the exam receive ISO 9000 certification, indicating that they have the specified quality assurance and management procedures in place.

Obtaining ISO 9000 certification is often a requirement for supplying products. The European Economic Community requires suppliers of certain products to have ISO 9000 certification. The North Atlantic Treaty Organization, the U.S. Department of Defense, and many American companies, such as Motorola, IBM, and General Electric, also require suppliers to be ISO 9000 certified. Even where it is not a requirement, achieving ISO 9000 certification enables companies to differentiate themselves from noncertified competitors. It can also serve as a catalyst for improving quality. At DuPont's Emigsville, Pennsylvania, plant, which makes plastic connectors for computers, the defect rate fell from 30 percent to 8 percent as a result of participating in the ISO 9000 program.[9]

---

9 Peter C. Brewer and Tina Y. Mills, "ISO 9000 Standards: An Emerging CPA Service Area," *Journal of Accountancy* (February 1994), p. 64.

MANAGEMENT ACCOUNTING PRACTICE 5-4

Quality Improvements Help Hungarian Paperboard Manufacturer in Quest to Compete with Western Counterparts

Before the decline of Communism in Eastern Europe, the sales staff of Petofi Printing and Packaging of Kecskemet, Hungary, did not make calls on customers. Instead, the sales staff set visiting hours when customers could plead their case. Meanwhile, on the factory floor, employees drank beer and flies got stuck in the paint and pressed into the paperboard. Containers were delivered in wrong colors and sizes. But, having no alternative sources of supply, customers didn't complain. Instead, they bribed the sales staff with chocolates and liquor to take their orders.

Things changed rapidly after privatization in 1990. Petofi invested $35 million in new equipment. Petofi also set up a quality assurance lab to inspect materials and provided incentives for employees to produce quality products. Workers were offered 40 percent pay raises, year-end bonuses, and better working conditions. Customers were brought onto the shop floor, and workers were taken to trade shows to learn firsthand the importance of quality. Opening a beer on the job now results in a loss of a third of a month's wages.

With new equipment, more motivated and empowered employees, and relatively low but rising wages, Petofi is competitive in price and is becoming competitive in quality. In a dramatic change from just a few years ago, most of its products are now exported to companies such as Unilever NV of the Netherlands and General Electric of the U.S. Petofi's quality "compares very favorably," says Gerry Flanagan, a purchaser for PepsiCo, Inc., "They have filled the gap between competitive quality and best cost."

Based on: "New Competitor: East Europe's Industry Is Raising Its Quality and Taking on West," *The Wall Street Journal* (September 21, 1994), pp. A1 and A7.

ISO Certification for Environmental Management

ISO is currently working on a series of environmental management standards, similar to ISO 9000 quality standards. The first draft of these standards was released in 1995. The standards are intended to help management communicate environmental information within and outside the company and to provide management with information to help assess the impact of business decisions on the environment. It is likely that the ISO environmental standards will call for certification that suppliers have environmental management programs in place and that achieving environmental ISO certification will become a prerequisite for supplying some customers.[10]

ISO certification will accelerate the trend in making environmental accounting an important management accounting issue, rather than simply a financial accounting issue of tracking costs and noting any contingent liability. Environmental costs, such as those associated with waste treatment, landfill disposal, the disposal of hazardous waste, and environmental inspections, are an important part of the life-cycle costs of many products.

---

10 Michael Murray, "ISO Moves to Draft Environmental Standards," *Manufacturing Issues* (Winter 1994), p. 12.

Previously, future costs, such as those associated with removing oil storage tanks and cleaning up any possible pollution, were seldom considered. Including environmental expenditures as part of a product's life-cycle costs may reveal that a product with low acquisition costs but high environmental costs is less desirable than a product with a higher initial cost.

A 1994 agreement between Arizona Public Service and Niagra Mohawk Power further illustrates the growing importance of environmental accounting to internal decision making. Under the Clean Air Act, limits are set for emissions, and utilities are allowed to exchange credits when their emissions are below maximums. According to the agreement, Arizona Public Service gave Niagara Mohawk sulfur dioxide credits valued at $3 million in exchange for carbon dioxide credits.[11]

BENCHMARKING

L O 5

When Isuzu Motors takes a competitor's product apart to determine the competitor's manufacturing costs and when Hewlett-Packard studies Epson to determine Epson's strengths and weaknesses, both are engaging in benchmarking, a practice that has been around for centuries. But, in recent years, as globalization and increased competitiveness have forced businesses to more aggressively compete on the bases of cost, quality, and service, benchmarking has become more formalized and open. Benchmarking is no longer regarded as spying. **Benchmarking** is now a systematic approach to identifying the best practices to help an organization take action to improve performance.

The formalization of benchmarking is largely attributed to the 1989 publication of a book by Robert Camp of Xerox. Since then, many managers have come to believe that benchmarking is a requirement for success. Although benchmarking can focus on anything of interest, it typically deals with target costs for a product, service or operation, customer satisfaction, quality, inventory levels, inventory turnover, cycle time, and productivity. While benchmarking initially focused on studying competitors, benchmarking efforts have changed dramatically in recent years. According to Camp:

> Although you must focus strongly on the competition, if that is the sole objective, playing catch-up is the best you can do. Watching the competition does not tell you how to outdistance them. The mix of our benchmark activities have changed 180 degrees. In the early days, we spent 80 percent of our benchmark time looking at the competition. Today we spend 80 percent of that time outside our industry, because we have found innovative ideas from businesses in other industries.[12]

---

11 "Making a Market in Pollution Credits," *Business Week* (November 28, 1994), p. 59.
12 Robert Camp, "A Bible for Benchmarking, by Xerox," *Financial Executive* (July/August 1993), p. 24.

Benchmarking provides measurements useful in setting goals. It can lead to dramatic innovations, and it helps overcome resistance to change. When presented with a major cost reduction target, employees often believe they are being asked to do the impossible. Benchmarking can be a psychological tool that helps overcome resistance to change by showing how others have already met the target. As part of an effort to reduce the cost of manufacturing aircraft 25 percent by 1998, Boeing set a target of reducing the time to build a 767 model aircraft from 18 months in 1992 to eight months in 1996. To help overcome arguments that such a target was unrealistic, Boeing benchmarked against General Electric's heavy manufacturing operations and the world's best producers of other products ranging from computers to ships. After overcoming resistance to change, process reengineering efforts have already reduced the time required to build 767 model aircraft from 18 months to 12 months.[13]

Although each organization has its own approach to benchmarking, the following six steps used by Alcoa are typical:

1. Deciding what to benchmark
2. Planning the benchmark project
3. Understanding your own performance
4. Studying others
5. Learning from the data
6. Taking action[14]

In recent years, professional organizations, such as the Institute of Management Accountants, have set up clearinghouses for benchmark information or performed benchmarking studies of interest to members. Management Accounting Practice 5-5 describes a benchmarking project undertaken by the National Association of College and University Business Officers.

SUMMARY

Product pricing is one of the most important and complex decisions facing management today. The salability of individual products or services is directly affected by pricing decisions, as is the profitability—and even the survival—of the organization. Cost-based pricing starts with determining the cost of a product or service and then adding a markup to cover unassigned costs and to provide for a profit. While cost-based pricing remains a frequently used approach to pricing, it is based on the assumptions that goods or services are relatively scarce and that customers who want a product or service are willing to pay the price. When those assumptions are incorrect, firms using cost-based pricing may find that both their cost structure and the time required to develop and deliver new products or services are uncompetitive.

---

13 Shawn Tully, "Why to Go for Stretch Targets," *Fortune* (November 14, 1994), p. 154.
14 Karen Bemowski, "The Benchmark Bandwagon," *Quality Progress* (January 1991), pp. 22-23.

MANAGEMENT ACCOUNTING PRACTICE 5-5

Benchmarking to Improve the Quality and Reduce the Cost of Higher Education

One advantage of large-scale benchmark surveys performed by professional associations is to help members identify areas most in need of improvement. To create a data base for benchmarking by member schools, the National Association of College and University Business Officers (NACUBO) started gathering data on college and university operations and administrative costs in 1992. Institutions participating in the study provided information on more than forty functional areas, including:

Accounts payable	Library
Admissions	Mail
Collections	Processing a purchase requisition
Development office	Producing a report card
Food services	

A typical result of the study is given for the operation of the development (fund-raising) office below:

Development Office Cost per Donor

		Type of School		
	Public	Private	Liberal Arts	All
High	$130	$187	$1,071	$1,071
Low	15	53	85	15
Median	66	115	145	100
Average	71	119	152	112

An institution with costs at the high end of the scale might decide to reevaluate its operations to determine if they are cost-effective. It might then want to learn more about the processes at benchmark institutions, perhaps by site visits.

Based on: "Benchmarking in Higher Education," *Higher Education Management Newsletter* (November 1992), pp. 6-9.

Target costing starts with determining what customers are willing to pay for a product or service and then subtracting a desired profit on sales to determine the allowable, or target, cost of the product or service. The organization then assigns cross-functional teams of employees to design a product that meets the customer's price, function, and quality requirements. In addition to achieving a more competitive price, target costing, by encouraging the concurrent consideration of design, manufacturing, and service issues, is more focused on life-cycle costs and may bring products to market in a shorter time.

While target costing is most appropriate for new products, continuous improvement calls for establishing cost reduction targets for products or services an organization is currently providing customers. Continuous improvement costing is accomplished through continuous improvement techniques, such as process mapping, discussed in Chapter 4. Continuous improvement costing adds a specific cost target to be achieved during a time period to the continuous improvement concept.

Meeting customer needs and desires and doing the job right the first time are the essence of quality management. Organizations that continuously strive to improve quality are more apt to attract and retain customers and to meet cost reduction and continuous improvement targets. Quality costs concepts are often used to understand the cost reduction potential of improvements in quality, to justify investments in quality enhancing technology, and to serve as cost targets.

Organizations have always attempted to obtain information concerning their competitors, often in informal ways. In today's highly competitive environment, benchmarking has become a systematic approach to identifying best practices and taking action to improve performance. It is used to support continuous improvement, process reengineering, target costing, continuous improvement costing, and quality management activities. Significantly, benchmarking is often done with benchmark partners in noncompeting industries. Focusing on competitors only tells companies what they need to do to catch up. Benchmarking against best practices across all industries tells a company how to outdistance competitors.

SUGGESTED READINGS

Becoming ISO 9000 Registered, Management Accounting Guideline 25 (Hamilton, Ontario: The Society of Management Accountants of Canada, 1994).

Berliner, Callie, and James A. Brimson. *Cost Management for Today's Advanced Manufacturing* (Boston: Harvard Business School Press, 1988).

Brewer, Peter C., and Tina Y. Mills. "ISO 9000 Standards: An Emerging CPA Service Area," *Journal of Accountancy* (February 1994), pp. 63-67.

Camp, Robert C. *Benchmarking* (Milwaukee, Wisconsin: ASQC Press, 1989).

Committee, Bruce E., and D. Jacque Grinnell. "Predatory Pricing, the Price-Cost Test, and Activity-Based Costing," *Journal of Cost Management* (Fall 1992), pp. 52-58.

Implementing Target Costing, Management Accounting Guideline 28 (Hamilton, Ontario: The Society of Management Accountants of Canada, 1994).

Kreuze, Jerry G., and Gale Newell. "ABC and Life-Cycle Costing for Environmental Expenditures," *Management Accounting* (February 1994), pp. 38-42.

Managing Quality Improvements, Statement 4-R (Montvale, NJ: Institute of Management Accountants, 1993).

Morse, Wayne J., Harold P. Roth, and Kay P. Poston, *Measuring, Planning, and Controlling Quality Costs* (Montvale, NJ: Institute of Management Accountants (formerly National Association of Accountants), 1987).

Product Life Cycle Management, Management Accounting Guideline 29 (Hamilton, Ontario: The Society of Management Accountants of Canada, 1994).

Sakurai, Michiharu. "Target Costing and How to Use It," *Journal of Cost Management* (Summer 1989), pp. 39-50.

Simon, Hermann. "Pricing Opportunities—And How to Exploit Them," *Sloan Management Review* (Winter 1992), pp. 55-65.

Spendolini, Michael J. *The Benchmarking Book* (New York, AMACO, 1992).

Tanaka, Takao. "Target Costing at Toyota," *Journal of Cost Management* (Spring 1993), pp. 4-11.

Thornton, Daniel B. "Green Accounting and Green Eyeshades," *CA Magazine* (October 1993), pp. 34-40.

Worthy, Ford S. "Japan's Smart Secret Weapon," *Fortune* (August 12, 1991), pp. 72-75.

REVIEW PROBLEM

Cost-Based Pricing and Target Costing

Presented is the 19X8 contribution income statement of the Knox Company.

Knox Company
Contribution Income Statement
For the Year Ending December 31, 19X8

Sales (100,000 units at $12 per unit)		$1,200,000
Less variable costs:		
Manufacturing	$300,000	
Selling and administrative	150,000	- 450,000
Contribution margin		$ 750,000
Less fixed costs:		
Manufacturing	$400,000	
Selling and administrative	200,000	- 600,000
Net income		$ 150,000

Knox has total assets of $2,000,000, and management desires an annual return of 10 percent on total assets.

Required:

(a) Determine the amount in dollars by which Knox Company exceeded or fell short of the desired annual rate of return in 19X8.

(b) Given the current sales volume and cost structure, determine the unit selling price required to achieve an annual profit of $250,000.

(c) Assume management wants to state the selling price as a percent of variable manufacturing costs. Given your answer to requirement (b) and the current sales volume and cost structure, determine the selling price as a percent of variable manufacturing costs.

(d) Restate your answer to requirement (c) into two separate markup percentages: (1) the markup on variable manufacturing costs required to cover unassigned costs and (2) the additional markup on variable manufacturing costs required to achieve an annual profit of $250,000.

(e) Market analysis has revealed that the sales volume can be increased to 180,000 units per year if the selling price is set at $9 per unit. At this price and sales volume, determine the target cost that will provide an annual profit of $250,000.

The solution to the review problem is found at the end of the Chapter 5 assignment material. To maximize your learning, you should make a serious attempt to develop a written solution to the review problem before looking at the solution. If there are errors in your solution, you should then attempt to determine the causes of the errors.

KEY TERMS

Appraisal costs—quality costs incurred to identify nonconforming products or services before they are delivered to customers.

Benchmarking—a systematic approach to identifying the best practices to help an organization take action to improve performance.

Continuous improvement (Kaizen) costing—establishing cost reduction targets for products or services an organization is currently providing to customers.

Design for manufacture—the explicit consideration of the costs of manufacturing and servicing a product while designing it.

External failure costs—quality costs incurred when nonconforming products or services are delivered to customers.

Internal failure costs—quality costs incurred when materials, components, products, or services are identified as defective before delivery to customers.

Life-cycle costs—from the seller's perspective, all costs associated with a product or service ranging from those associated with initial conception through design, preproduction, production, and after-production support. From the buyer's perspective, they include all costs associated with a purchased product or service, including initial acquisition costs and subsequent costs of operation, maintenance, repair, and disposal.

Marginal cost—the varying increment in total cost required to produce and sell an additional unit of product.

Marginal revenue—the varying increment in total revenue derived from the sale of an additional unit.

Prevention costs—quality costs incurred to prevent nonconforming products from being produced or nonconforming services from being performed.

Price discrimination—illegally charging different purchasers different prices.

Price fixing—the organized setting of prices by competitors.

Productivity—the relationship between outputs and inputs.

Quality—conformance to customer expectations.

Quality costs—costs incurred because poor quality of conformance does or may exist.

Quality of conformance—the degree of conformance between a product and its design specifications.

Quality of design—the degree of conformance between customer expectations for a product or service and the design specifications of the product or service.

Robinson-Patman Act—prohibits price discrimination when purchasers compete with one another in the sale of their products or services to third parties.

Sherman Antitrust Act—prohibits price fixing.

Target costing—establishes allowable costs of a product or service by starting with determining what customers are willing to pay for a product or service and then subtracting a desired profit on sales.

REVIEW QUESTIONS

5-1
Why are economic models seldom used for day-to-day pricing decisions?

5-2
Identify three reasons why cost-based approaches to pricing have traditionally been important.

5-3
Identify four drawbacks with cost-based pricing.

5-4
Distinguish between price discrimination and price fixing.

5-5
How does target costing differ from cost-based pricing?

5-6

Why is cost-based pricing more of a technique and target costing more of a philosophy? Which approach takes a more proactive approach to cost management?

5-7

Distinguish between the marketing life cycles of products incorporating advanced technology, such as household electronic equipment, and those using more traditional technology, such as household paper products. Why would life-cycle costing be more important to a manufacturer of household electronic equipment than to a manufacturer of household paper products?

5-8

What is the relationship between target costing and continuous improvement costing?

5-9

Distinguish between the seller's and the buyer's conceptions of life-cycle costs.

5-10

Distinguish between quality of design and quality of conformance. Which is used for internal appraisals? What is the ultimate determination of the quality of a product or service?

5-11

Considering the four types of quality costs, which is most preferred and which is least desirable?

5-12

What is the purpose of ISO 9000 certification?

5-13

What advantage is derived from benchmarking against firms other than competitors?

EXERCISES

5-1 Matching

Required:

Match the numbered term or phrase in the left column with the letter corresponding to the best answer in the right column. Each answer is used only once.

1. Sherman Antitrust Act	a. Prohibits price discrimination when purchasers compete with each other
2. Appraisal cost	
3. Worst kind of quality cost	
4. Benchmark	
5. Argument in favor of cost-based prices	b. Increase the importance of target costing
6. Quality of design	c. Assumes relatively scarce goods or services and customers willing to pay the price

7. Argument against cost-based prices
8. Target costing
9. Robinson-Patman Act
10. Short product life cycles and increased competition

d. Comparison of design specifications with customer expectations
e. Used to manage costs during product development
f. Prohibits price fixing
g. The best way of performing a task, determined by a study of other organizations
h. They are legally defensible
i. External failure
j. Inspecting a product before it is delivered to customers

5-2 Cost-Based Pricing with Variable Costs

Johnson Services provides computerized inventory consulting. The office and computer expenses are $600,000 annually. The consulting hours available for 19X5 total 20,000, and the average consulting hour has $20 of variable costs.

Required:
(a) If the company desires a profit of $100,000, what should it charge per hour?
(b) What is the markup on variable costs if the desired profit is $120,000?
(c) If the desired profit is $80,000, what is the markup on variable costs to cover:
    (1) Unassigned costs?
    (2) Desired profit?

5-3 Markups

The predicted 19X6 costs for Tabor Motors are as follows:

Manufacturing Costs		Selling and Administrative Costs	
Variable	$100,000	Variable	$300,000
Fixed	200,000	Fixed	200,000

Average total assets for 19X6 are predicted to be $5,000,000.

Required:
(a) If management desires a rate of return of 12 percent on total assets, what are the markup percentages on total variable costs and on total manufacturing costs?
(b) If the company desires a rate of return of 10 percent on total assets, what is the markup percentage on total manufacturing costs:
    (1) For unassigned costs?
    (2) For desired profits?

5-4 Product Pricing: Single Product

Mary Morgan is planning to open a soft ice cream franchise. The franchise will operate in a resort community during the summer months. Fixed operating costs for the three-month period are projected to be $5,250. Variable costs per serving include the cost of the ice cream and cone, $0.25, and a franchise fee payable to Snowdrift Cooler, $0.05. A market analysis prepared by Snowdrift Cooler indicates that summer sales in the resort community should total 22,500 units.

Required:
Determine the price Mary should charge for each ice cream cone to achieve a profit of $6,000 for the three-month period.

5-5 Product Pricing: Single Product
Presented is the 19X2 contribution income statement of Simplex Products.

Simplex Products
Contribution Income Statement
For the Year Ending December 31, 19X2

Sales (12,000 units)		$1,440,000
Less variable costs:		
Cost of goods sold	$480,000	
Selling and administrative	132,000	- 612,000
Contribution margin		$ 828,000
Less fixed costs:		
Manufacturing overhead	$520,000	
Selling and administrative	210,000	- 730,000
Net income		$ 98,000

During the coming year, it is expected that variable manufacturing costs will increase by $6 per unit and fixed manufacturing costs will increase by $48,000.

Required:
(a) If sales remain at 12,000 units, what price should Simplex charge to produce the same profit as last year?
(b) Management believes that sales can be increased to 16,000 units if the selling price is lowered to $107. Is this action desirable?
(c) After taking into consideration the expected increases in costs, what sales volume is needed to earn a profit of $98,000 with a unit selling price of $107?

5-6 Product Pricing: Two Products
Magic Data manufactures two products: 5 1/4-inch and 3 1/2-inch disks. Both products are produced on the same assembly lines. The predicted sales are 400,000 packs (10 disks each) of 5 1/4-inch disks and 500,000 packs (10 disks each) of 3 1/2-inch disks. The predicted costs for 19X9 are as follows:

	Variable Costs	Fixed Costs
Materials	$ 200,000	$ 400,000
Other	300,000	800,000

Each product uses half of the materials costs. Based on manufacturing time, 40 percent of the other costs are assigned to the 5 1/4-inch disks, and 60 percent of the other costs are assigned to the 3 1/2-inch disks.

The management of Magic Data desires an annual profit of $100,000.

Required:

(a) What price should be charged for each disk pack if management believes the 3 1/2-inch disks sell for 20 percent more than the 5 1/4-inch disks?
(b) What is the total profit per product?
(c) Based on your results in requirement (b), how should the company evaluate the status of the two products?

5-7 Target Costing

North Woods Equipment Company wants to develop a new log-splitting machine for rural homeowners. Market research has determined that North Woods could sell 5,000 log-splitting machines per year at a retail price of $500 each. Sales would be handled through an independent catalog company for an annual fee of $2,000, plus $50 per unit sold. The cost of the raw materials required to produce the log-splitting machines amount to $95 per unit.

Required:

If North Woods's management desires a return equal to 10 percent of the final selling price, what is the target unit cost for conversion and administration?

5-8 Kaizen Costing

Koto Photo manufactures cameras. At its Pacific Plant, cost control has become a concern of management. The actual costs per unit for 19X6 and 19X7 were as follows:

	19X6	19X7
Direct materials:		
Plastic case	$ 4.00	$ 3.80
Lens set	17.00	17.20
Electrical component set	6.00	5.40
Film track	12.00	10.00
Direct labor	32.00 (1.6 hours)	30.00 (1.5 hours)
Indirect manufacturing costs:		
Variable	8.00	7.10
Fixed	2.00 (100,000 unit base)	1.90 (120,000 unit base)

The company manufactures all camera components except the lens sets, which are furnished by several vendors.

The company has used target costing in the past but has not been able to meet very competitive global pricing. Beginning in 19X7, the company is implementing a continuous improvement program that requires cost reduction targets.

Required:

If Kaizen costing sets a first-year target of a 10-percent reduction of the 19X6 base, how successful was the company in meeting 19X7 per unit cost reduction targets? Support your answer with appropriate computations.

5-9 Productivity Measures

Ingram Iron, Inc., has not had strong earnings during the last several quarters of operation. Production management has decided that it needs more information than the current cost accounting system is supplying. The following nonfinancial information is available for the current quarter:

Production in units	20,000
Direct labor hours	14,000
Tons of materials used	5,200
Machine hours	6,000

The standards for the production of each unit are as follows:

41 minutes of direct labor
1/4 ton of direct materials
20 minutes of machine time

Required:

Compute several productivity measures the production managers may use. Was the current quarter acceptable in meeting the measures you selected? Explain.

5-10 Quality Costs: Service Emphasis

Required:

Categorize each of the following quality costs as either prevention, appraisal, internal failure, or external failure.
(a) Inspection of incoming supplies
(b) Service department for follow-up complaints
(c) Training of new employees
(d) Reconciliation of agency contracts with billing statements
(e) Retraining staff members who are not current in their area of expertise
(f) Toll-free telephone costs for client questions
(g) Redesigning reception area so clients have privacy during consultations
(h) Dismissing staff member found guilty of unethical acts regarding company matters
(i) Inspection of final report by senior staff before given to client

5-11 Quality Costs: Manufacturing Emphasis

Required:

Categorize each of the following quality costs as prevention, appraisal, internal failure, or external failure.
(a) Disposal of spoiled work-in-process inventory
(b) Downtime due to quality problems
(c) Expediting work to meet delivery schedule
(d) Field testing

(e) Internal audits of inventory
(f) Maintaining complaint department
(g) Opportunity cost of lost sales because of bad quality reputation
(h) Product liability
(i) Quality circles
(j) Quality training
(k) Reinspection
(l) Revision of computer programs due to software errors
(m) Rework labor and overhead
(n) Scrap
(o) Supplier verification
(p) Technical support provided to vendors
(q) Test and inspection of equipment
(r) Test and inspection of purchased raw materials
(s) Utilities in inspection area
(t) Warranty repairs

5-12 Quality Costs for a Manufacturing Firm

Expandable Computer incurred the following quality-related costs during November:

Spoiled work-in-process inventory disposal	$23,000
Downtime due to quality problems	43,000
Field testing of new computer	84,000
Maintaining a customer complaint department	22,000
Product liability insurance	6,000
Quality training	12,000
Reinspection	2,000
Rework labor and overhead	18,000
New vendor verification and facility inspections	28,000
Technical support provided to vendors	3,000
Equipment inspection	33,000
Test and inspection of purchased parts	42,000
Warranty repairs	15,000

November sales totaled $4,200,000.

Required:

Prepare a quality cost report with appropriate classifications.

5-13 Quality Cost Report for a Food Processor

Dakota City Packers incurred the following costs during July:

Livestock inspection at auction yard	$ 4,800
Livestock inspection upon delivery	6,000
Inspection training—finished products	2,000
Redesign of processing procedures and sequence	10,000
Packing procedure inspection and testing	8,200
Product liability insurance	4,000
Product returns	7,400

Scrap disposal	$ 6,600
Downtime due to spoiled products	12,000
Contract negotiations with large vendor	1,500
Rework labor due to processing errors	4,900

Sales for July totaled $2,000,000, and the company's return on investment is expected to be 15 percent for the year.

Required:

Prepare a quality cost report with appropriate classifications.

PROBLEMS

5-14 Multiple-Product Price Setting

The Sussex Company's predicted 19X0 variable and fixed costs are as follows:

	Variable Costs	Fixed Costs
Manufacturing	$ 400,000	$ 200,000
Selling and administrative	100,000	50,000
Total	$ 500,000	$ 250,000

Sussex produces a wide variety of small tools. Per unit manufacturing cost information about one of these products, the Type-A Clamp, is as follows:

Direct materials	$ 5
Direct labor	7
Manufacturing overhead:	
Variable	6
Fixed	6
Total manufacturing costs	$24

Variable selling and administrative costs for the Type-A Clamp is $3 per unit. Management has set a target profit for 19X1 of $150,000.

Required:

(a) Determine the markup percentage on variable costs required to earn the desired profit.
(b) Use variable cost markup to determine a suggested selling price for the Type-A Clamp.
(c) For the Type-A Clamp, break the markup on variable costs into separate parts for fixed costs and profit. Explain the significance of each part.
(d) Determine the markup percentage on manufacturing costs required to earn the desired profit.
(e) Use the manufacturing costs markup to determine a suggested selling price for the Type-A Clamp.
(f) Evaluate the variable and the manufacturing cost approaches to determine the markup percentage.

5-15 Multiple-Product Price Setting

The Chesapeake Tackle Company produces a wide variety of commercial fishing equipment. In the past, the prices of individual products have been set by product managers on the basis of professional judgment. John Marlin, the new controller, believes this practice has led to the significant underpricing of some products (and lost profits) and the significant overpricing of other products (and lost sales volume). You have been asked to assist Mr. Marlin in developing a corporate approach to pricing. The output of your work should be a cost-based formula that can be used to develop initial selling prices for each product. Though product managers are allowed to adjust these prices to meet competition and to take advantage of market opportunities, they must explain such deviations in writing.

You have obtained the following 19X4 cost information from the accounting records:

	Manufacturing Costs	Selling and Administrative Costs
Variable	$ 350,000	$ 50,000
Fixed	150,000	200,000

In 19X4, Chesapeake reported earnings of $80,000. However, the controller believes that proper pricing should produce earnings of at least $120,000 on the same sales mix and unit volume. Accordingly, you are to use the above cost information and a target profit of $120,000 in developing a cost-based pricing formula.

Selling and administrative expenses are not currently associated with individual products. However, you have obtained the following unit production cost information for the Tigershark Reel:

Variable manufacturing costs	$120
Fixed manufacturing costs	60
Total	$180

Required:

(a) Determine the standard markup percentage for each of the following cost bases. Round answers to three decimal places.
  (1) Full costs, including fixed and variable manufacturing costs, and fixed and variable selling and administrative costs
  (2) Manufacturing costs, plus variable selling and administrative costs
  (3) Manufacturing costs
  (4) Variable costs
  (5) Variable manufacturing costs
(b) Explain why the markup percentages become progressively larger between parts (1) and (5) of requirement (a).
(c) Determine the initial price of a Tigershark Reel using the manufacturing cost markup and the variable manufacturing cost markup.
(d) Do you believe the controller's approach to product pricing is reasonable? Why or why not?

5-16 Predicting External Failure Costs[15]

In December 1994, in response to pressure from computer manufacturers, the communications media, and the general public, Intel offered to replace any Pentium processor that had a "floating-point divide flaw" with an updated version of the Pentium processor. Intel's management remained convinced, however, that the floating-point divide flaw was a minor issue that should not cause a problem for most users.

It was estimated that it will cost Intel about $200, including service fees, to replace each chip. A total of 5.3 million flawed Pentium chips were sold before the recall was announced.

The following information is available about the response rate to product calls:

- The response rate in automobile recalls, where safety is an issue, averages 68 percent.
- Sears, Roebuck & Co. reports that the response rate to a recall of a toaster with a safety defect might be as high as 40 percent, but it would be much lower without a safety issue.
- An independent analyst predicted that 30 to 40 percent of the Pentium processors were sold to companies and that half of these companies will not ask for replacements. The analyst also estimated that 90 percent of the individual consumers will not ask for a replacement because the applications they run are not affected by the flaw.

Required:

Based on the above information, develop several alternative predictions of the external failure cost of replacing flawed Pentium processors. If you were to select one estimate, what would it be? Are there any other external failure costs that should be considered?

5-17 Preparing and Analyzing Quality Cost Reports

Concerned about competitive pressures, the Hitec Company implemented a program in 19X4 to reduce inventory levels, improve productivity, improve on-time delivery of goods to customers, and reduce customer complaints about quality. To help evaluate the success of these efforts, management requested you to prepare a quality cost report for the year ended December 31, 19X4.

After a detailed review of the accounting records and several interviews with key personnel, you have developed the following data for 19X4:

Sales	$ 5,100,000
Inspection of purchased raw materials	50,000
Inspection of finished goods	110,000
Rework	80,000
Disposal cost of spoiled goods	30,000
Reinspection of finished goods	10,000

---

15 Based on Jim Carlton, "Humble Pie: Intel to Replace Its Pentium Chips," *The Wall Street Journal* (December 21, 1994), pp. B1, B6.

Planning a design for manufacture program	$ 5,000
Customer out-of-warranty adjustments	50,000
Warranty adjustments	60,000
Returns and allowances	8,000
Indirect costs of inspection department	25,000
Developing quality control training programs	8,000
Downtime due to quality problems	210,000

Required:

(a) Prepare a quality control cost report with appropriate classifications.

(b) Management is concerned about the success of the recently implemented program. The vice president of finance observed, "Although sales were essentially unchanged from 19X3, profits declined. Furthermore, the decline in profits appears entirely due to increases in inspection, downtime, rework, and similar costs. Increases in these costs far exceeded the cost savings from lower customer complaints." Prepare a response to the concerns expressed by the vice president of finance.

5-18 Quality Cost Trend Analysis

Presented below is information pertaining to quality costs and total sales for Ray Company for the years 19X1 through 19X5.

	19X1	19X2	19X3	19X4	19X5
Prevention	$ 20,000	$ 40,000	$ 25,000	$ 10,000	$ 5,000
Appraisal	10,000	10,000	10,000	5,000	5,000
Internal failure	50,000	55,000	40,000	20,000	10,000
External failure	50,000	25,000	15,000	55,000	65,000
Sales	1,000,000	1,500,000	1,600,000	1,200,000	1,000,000

Required:

(a) Prepare a quality cost trend analysis based on total dollars of quality costs in each category.

(b) Prepare a quality cost trend analysis based on quality costs as a percent of total sales.

(c) Compare the graphs prepared for requirements (a) and (b). Which is more meaningful? Why?

(d) Based on the graphs, can any conclusions be made about the Ray Company's quality control program?

5-19 Activity-Cost Analysis: Quality Costs and Nonvalue-Added Costs

Borroth Manufacturing has developed the following activity cost data for its purchasing and manufacturing activities:

Purchase order and receipt of order	$ 36.00/order
Unpack and inspect incoming goods	0.50/unit purchased
Move in-process goods	2.50/unit in job
In-process holding costs (no work being performed)	0.50/unit in job/day
Machine setup	60.00/machine/job

Machine operation A	$ 80.00/hour
Machine operation B	60.00/hour
Rework	150.00/hour
Inspect work-in-process or finished goods	1.50/unit
Pack and ship finished goods	5% previous costs
	+ $25.00/job

Borroth only produces to fill customer orders. Because suppliers deliver on 24-hours' notice, Borroth does not maintain raw materials inventories. Materials are purchased as needed in the quantities needed and, after being unpacked and inspected, are sent immediately to the shop floor. Finished goods are inspected, packed, and immediately shipped to customers.

The following information is available for job 91-Z24, which consisted of 20 units of a special machine part:

Activity

Purchase order 91-B34:		
Material M1	100 units	$1,200 purchase price
Material J2	300 units	300 purchase price
Purchase order 91-B35:		
Material N6	50 units	800 purchase price
Move materials for job to machine A		
Store at machine A	1 day	
Setup machine A		
Run time on machine A	4 hours	
Setup machine B		
Move job to machine B		
Run time on machine B	12 hours	
Move job to inspection		
Inspect goods	20 units	
Move job to rework station		
Store at rework station	2 days	
Rework	2.5 hours	
Move job to inspection		
Inspect reworked goods	6 units	
Move to packing and shipping		
Pack and ship finished goods		

Required:
(a) Use activity cost data to determine the total cost of job 91-Z24. Round computations to the nearest cent.
(b) Determine the quality costs associated with job 91-Z24. Assume 40 percent of the costs of unpacking and inspecting incoming goods are attributable to inspection.
(c) Determine the cost of nonvalue-added activities associated with job 91-Z24.

DISCUSSION QUESTIONS

5-20 Telephone Pole Rental Rates

Most utility poles carry electric and telephone lines. In areas served by cable television, they also carry television cables. However, cable television companies rarely own any utility poles. Instead, they pay utility companies a rental fee for the use of each pole on a yearly basis. The determination of the rental fee is a source of frequent disagreement between the pole owners and the cable television companies. In one situation, pole owners were arguing for a $7 annual rental fee per pole because this was the standard rate the electric and telephone companies charged each other for the use of poles.

"We object to that," stated the representative of the cable TV company. "With two users, the $7 fee represents a rental fee for one-half the pole. This fee is too high because we only use about six inches of each 40-foot pole."

"You are forgetting federal safety regulations," responded a representative of the electric company. "They specify certain distances between different types of lines on a utility pole. Television cables must be a minimum of 40 inches below power lines and 12 inches above telephone lines. If your cable is added to the pole, the total capacity is reduced because this space cannot be used for anything else. Besides, we have an investment in the poles; you don't. We should be entitled to a fair return on this investment. Furthermore, speaking of fair, your company should pay the same rental fee that the telephone company pays us and we pay them. We do not intend to change this fee."

In response, the cable TV company representative made two points. First, any fee represents incremental income to the pole owners because the cable company would pay all costs of moving existing lines. Second, because the electric and telephone companies both strive to own the same number of poles in a service area, their pole rental fees cancel themselves. Hence, the fee they charge each other is moot.

Required:

Evaluate the arguments presented by the cable TV and electric company representatives. What factors should be considered in determining a pole rental fee?

5-21 Target Costing

The president of Household Electronics was pleased with the company's newest product, the HE Versatile CD. The HE Versatile CD is portable and can be attached to a computer to play or record computer programs or sound. It can be attached to an amplifier to play or record music. It can be attached to a television to play or record TV programs, or it can be used with a headset to play or record sound. It can even be attached to a camcorder to record videos directly on compact disks rather than on tape.

The proud president announced that this unique and innovative product would be an important factor in reestablishing the North American consumer electronics industry.

Based on development costs and predictions of sales volume, manufacturing costs, and distribution costs, the cost-based price of the HE Versatile CD was determined to be $375. Following a market skimming strategy, management set the initial selling price at $450. The marketing plan was to reduce the selling price by $50 during each of the first two years of the product's life in order to obtain the highest contribution possible from each market segment.

The initial sales of the HE Versatile CD were strong, and Household Electronics found itself adding a second and even a third production shift. Although the second and third shifts were expensive, at a selling price of $450, the product had ample contribution margin to remain highly profitable.

The president was talking with the company's major investors about the desirability of obtaining financing for a major plant expansion when the bad news arrived. A foreign company announced that it would shortly introduce a similar product that would incorporate new design features and sell for only $250. The president was shocked. "Why," she remarked, "it costs us $260 to put a complete unit in the hands of customers."

Required:

How could the foreign competitor profitably sell a similar product for less than it costs Household Electronics to manufacture it? What advice do you have for the president concerning the HE Versatile CD? What advice would you have to help Household Electronics avoid similar problems in the future?

5-22 Electronic Scanning Errors

Law enforcement officials and the general public are becoming increasingly concerned about errors in electronic checkout scanning systems. Consider the following:

- A survey by Vermont's attorney general found that local outlets of Ames Department Stores, Inc., and Rich's Department Stores had serious errors in their scanning systems.
- Michigan's attorney general announced the detection of errors in scanning systems at Sears, Roebuck & Company and Wal-Mart stores.
- An official of the Morris County New Jersey Office of Weights and Measures found many mistakes at the checkout counter of a Bradlees, Inc., store.[16]

While authorities and retailers say the mistakes are the result of human error, not fraud, experts believe electronic scanning errors, typically caused by the failure to update price data in computers, are a serious problem. The

---

16 Based on Catherine Yang and Willy Stern, "Maybe They Should Call Them Scammers," *Business Week* (January 16, 1995), pp. 32-33.

problem is most likely to occur when merchandise is placed on sale. Exacerbating the problem is the fact that electronic scanning allows stores to save money by not placing a price sticker on each item of merchandise. Some communities have responded to concerns about scanning errors by requiring local merchants to continue attaching stickers to each item so that customers can review their bill when they unpack their purchases.

Required:

(a) Identify some costs that merchants are likely to incur because of scanning errors.
(b) Are these costs related to prevention, appraisal, internal failure, or external failure?
(c) Mention several actions a merchant can take to reduce the costs identified in requirement (a). Classify the costs of each action as prevention, appraisal, internal failure, and external failure.

5-23 Developing Quality Cost Categories for a Service Company

The management of Good Morning Inn, a national hotel chain, is interested in implementing a total quality control program. Although management is not interested in developing a quality cost reporting system at this time, the controller believes that identification of activities and types of costs the hotel may incur in each of the four quality cost categories would be useful as a starting point in initiating the program. However, she is somewhat limited in her knowledge of the four quality cost categories.

Required:

Based on your knowledge of quality costs and the hotel industry, identify activities and costs in each of the four basic quality cost categories.

5-24 Costs of Nonquality Work

The production manager and the plant controller of Quartz Limited are having trouble agreeing on the importance and extent of using quality cost reports as part of the normal monthly reporting operations of the Boise Plant. The Boise operations are very material-intensive with most per unit costs being the actual cost of the materials used. Also, defective units require substantial replacement of most of the original materials used.

The production manager argues that the cost of preparing the report (including major efforts to collect the data) is more than the benefits to be received. He argues that other than the cost of rework of nonquality (defective) units, the costs are negligible and the quality costs reports would not add anything to the decision model that he doesn't already know.

The controller disagrees with this assessment of quality cost reports and presents the production manager with a list of possible cost categories that could be used to classify the cost of quality. However, knowing that the production manager is not receptive to more information on quality cost, the controller is planning on a tactic to provide the manager with a list of costs labeled as the cost of nonquality work.

Required:

Using the production manager's example of rework as a nonquality cost, assist the controller in developing a list of nonquality costs in addition to rework.

5-25 Ethics and Quality of Design

In the short run, high concentrations of carbon monoxide can cause death. In the long run, low concentrations can cause a variety of health problems. In 1991, the U.S. Consumer Product Safety Commission, concerned about health problems resulting from carbon monoxide, started a campaign to encourage all homeowners to buy carbon monoxide detectors. The City of Chicago even passed an ordinance mandating the installation of carbon monoxide detectors.

In accordance with Commission guidelines, First Alert, a well-known manufacturer of smoke detectors, designed a carbon monoxide detector to warn when relatively low levels of carbon monoxide were present. By December 1994, First Alert had sold more than 3 million detectors at about $45 each. Most other manufacturers set their detectors so that only life-threatening amounts of carbon monoxide would trigger an alarm.

After nearly 10,000 false carbon monoxide alarms were sounded within a 48-hour period in December 1994, Chicago officials were so angry that they threatened to sue First Alert. While the false alarms were blamed on an unusual temperature inversion that trapped auto exhausts and other pollutants near the ground, officials charged that the First Alert detectors were too sensitive. A fire department representative in another city noted that five out of six false carbon monoxide alarms were caused by First Alert detectors.

Yet, Underwriters Laboratories, Inc., although it recommended an increase in the alarm threshold standard set by the Consumer Products Safety Commission, indicated that First Alert detectors warranted its endorsement. While First Alert endorsed Underwriters Laboratories' proposed standards, the Carbon Monoxide Safety and Health Association, a manufacturers' trade group, proposed a standard with an even higher alarm threshold.

Required:

Discuss the issues the management of First Alert faced in setting the design standards for their carbon monoxide detector. What arguments can be made in favor of setting relatively low alarm thresholds and in favor of setting relatively high alarm thresholds? Are there any ethical issues involved in setting alarm standards? How should First Alert respond to the public relations problem caused by the "false" alarms?

5-26 Benchmarking

Your company is developing a new product for the computer printer industry. You have talked to several material vendors about being able to supply quality components for the new product. The product designers are satisfied with the company's ability to make the product in the current facilities. Also, numerous potential customers have been surveyed, and most have indicated a willingness to buy the product if the price is competitive.

Required:

What are some means of benchmarking the development and production of your new product?

5-27 Benchmarking

"Rampant downsizing has been sweeping across most parts of Corporate America since the early 1990s, producing huge layoffs and shutdowns of operations. Commercial banks, though, have been virtually immune. Despite numerous mergers and consolidations, bank employment has remained remarkably steady. And, even though electronic banking is expanding, bank branches, often regarded as relics of the past, have actually increased."[17]

Presented is benchmark information on the number of bank employees per 1,000 people in various countries:

Germany	3.2
France	3.5
Japan	3.7
Canada	4.9
United States	5.8

Required:

Based on this information, what conclusions can you draw concerning the relative efficiency and operating costs of U.S. commercial banks? Are you aware of any unique circumstances that might lead to the above results? What do you predict will happen to employment at U.S. commercial banks during the next several years?

SOLUTION TO REVIEW PROBLEM

(a)

Desired annual profit ($2,000,000 × 0.10)		$ 200,000
Actual profit		- 150,000
Amount actual profit fell short of achieving the desired return		$ 50,000

(b)

Predicted costs:		
Variable	$450,000	
Fixed	600,000	$1,050,000
Desired profit		250,000
Required revenue		$1,300,000
Unit sales		÷ 100,000
Required unit selling price		$ 13

---

17 Kelly Holland, "Blood on the Marble Floors," *Business Week* (February 27, 1995), p. 98.

(c)

Markup on variable manufacturing costs to achieve an annual profit of $250,000:

Unassigned costs:		
Variable selling and administrative	$150,000	
Fixed costs	600,000	$ 750,000
Desired profit		250,000
Total markup		$ 1,000,000
Variable manufacturing costs		÷ 300,000
Markup percent		333 1/3%

(d)

Detail of markup on variable manufacturing costs:

Unassigned costs:		
Variable selling and administrative	$150,000	
Fixed costs	600,000	$ 750,000
Variable manufacturing costs		÷ 300,000
Markup on variable manufacturing costs to cover unassigned costs		250%
Desired profit		$ 250,000
Variable manufacturing costs		÷ 300,000
Additional markup on variable manufacturing costs to achieve desired profit		83 1/3%

(e)

Projected revenue (180,000 units × $9)	$ 1,620,000
Less desired profit	- 250,000
Target cost	$ 1,370,000

CHAPTER ►

After completing this chapter, you should be able to:

L O 1

Discuss the role of capital budgeting in long-range planning.

L O 2

Apply capital budgeting models, such as net present value and internal rate of return, that consider the time value of money.

L O 3

Apply capital budgeting models, such as payback period and the accounting rate of return, that do not consider the time value of money.

L O 4

Evaluate the strengths and weaknesses of alternative capital budgeting models.

L O 5

Discuss the importance of judgment, attitudes toward risk, and obtaining relevant cash flow information in making capital budgeting decisions.

L O 6

Determine the net present value of investment proposals taking tax effects into consideration.

◄ O B J E C T I V E S

STRATEGIC COST MANAGEMENT III: CAPITAL BUDGETING

In the preceding chapters, much of our attention centered on decisions affecting activity and organizational cost drivers where we assume the organization's basic facilities and products or services do not change. In this chapter, we turn our attention to a portion of long-range planning that deals with the identification and evaluation of major investment proposals to expand or change the organization's activities or facilities.

***Capital expenditures** involve investments of significant financial resources in projects to develop or introduce new products or services, to expand current production or service capacity, or to change current production or service facilities. Capital expenditure decisions affect structural cost drivers. They are made infrequently but once made are difficult to change. They commit the organization to the use of certain facilities and activities to satisfy customer needs. General Motor's construction of a completely new "green field" facility to manufacture Saturn automobiles and the city of Denver's replacement of Stapleton airport with a completely new airport are examples of major capital expenditures. Both had a significant impact on structural cost drivers and will continue to have an impact for many years to come. Interestingly, because United Airlines uses Denver as a hub, the increased landing fees charged by the city, in an attempt to recover its investment, have increased United's activity costs.*

***Capital budgeting** is a process that involves the identification of potentially desirable projects for capital expenditures, the subsequent evaluation of capital expenditure proposals, and the selection of proposals that meet certain criteria. A number of quantitative models have been developed to assist managers in evaluating capital expenditure proposals. **The purpose of this chapter is to introduce important capital budgeting concepts and models and to discuss the proper use of accounting data in these models**.*

The best capital budgeting models are similar in many respects to the short-range planning models used in Chapters 2 and 3. They all emphasize cash flows and focus on future costs (and revenues) that differ between decision alternatives. The major difference is that capital budgeting models involve cash flows over several years, whereas short-range planning models involve cash flows for a year or less. When the cash flows associated with a proposed activity extend over several years, an adjustment is necessary to make the cash flows expected to occur at different points in time comparable.

The time value of money concept explains why monies received or paid at different points in time must be adjusted to make them comparable. The time value of money is introduced in the appendix to this chapter. If you have not previously studied the time value of money, or if you believe you would benefit from a review of time value concepts, read the appendix before continuing this chapter.

LONG-RANGE PLANNING AND CAPITAL BUDGETING PROCEDURES

L O 1

Most organizations plan not only for operations in the current period, but also for the longer term, perhaps five to ten, or even twenty years in the future. Most planning beyond the next budget year is called *long-range planning*.

Increased uncertainty and an increased number of alternatives makes planning more difficult as the planning horizon increases. Nevertheless, the fact that long-range planning is difficult and involves uncertainties does not relieve management of long-range planning and capital expenditure decisions. Capital expenditure decisions will be made; the question is: How will they be made? Will they be made on the basis of the best information available? Will care be taken to ensure that capital expenditure decisions are in line with the organization's long-range goals? Will the potential consequences, both good and bad, of capital expenditures be considered? Will important alternative uses of the organization's limited financial resources be considered in a systematic manner? Will managers be held accountable for the results of major capital expenditure programs they initiate? The alternative to a systematic approach to capital budgeting is the haphazard expenditure of significant resources on the basis of hunch, immediate need, and persuasion—without accountability by the person(s) making the capital expenditure decisions.

A basic requirement for a systematic approach to capital budgeting is a well-formulated set of long-range goals the organization desires to achieve over a multiyear period. These goals serve as a guideline, thereby reducing the types of capital expenditure decisions considered by management. If, for example, KFC's primary goal is to become the largest fast-food restaurant chain in North America, its management should not consider a proposal to purchase and operate a bus line.

Accompanying its goals, an organization should also have a well-defined business strategy. The strategy will likewise guide capital expenditure decisions. If Hewlett-Packard is following a strategy of technological leadership, it might seriously consider a proposal to meet customer needs by investing in innovative production facilities while rejecting out-of-hand a proposal to purchase and refurbish used, but seemingly cost-efficient, equipment.

Procedures should also be developed for the review, evaluation, approval, and post-audit of capital expenditure proposals. Central to these procedures in a large organization is a capital budgeting committee that provides guidance to managers in the formulation of capital expenditure proposals.

Additionally, this committee reviews, analyzes, and approves or rejects major capital expenditure proposals. Very significant projects may require the approval of top management and even the board of directors. The capital budgeting committee should include persons knowledgeable of capital budgeting models, financing alternatives and costs, operating procedures, cost estimation and prediction methods, research and development efforts, the organization's goals and basic strategy, and the expectations of the organization's stockholders or owners. A management accountant—who is generally expert in data collection, retrieval, and analysis—is normally part of the capital budgeting committee.

Not all capital expenditure proposals will require committee approval or be subject to formal evaluation. With the approval of top management, the committee may provide guidelines to line managers at each level of the organization, indicating the type and dollar amount of capital expenditures they can make without formal evaluation, or committee approval, or both. The guidelines might state that expenditures of less than $5,000 do not require committee approval and that only expenditures of more than $10,000 need to be evaluated using capital budgeting models.

Typically, managers at higher levels have greater discretion in making capital expenditures. In a college or university, for example, a department chairperson may have authority to purchase office and instructional equipment with a maximum limit of $3,000 per year; a dean may have authority to renovate offices or classrooms with a maximum limit of $20,000 per year; but the formal review of a capital budgeting committee and final approval of the board of trustees may be required to convert the power plant from fuel oil to wood chips at a cost of $225,000.

The post-audit of approved capital expenditure proposals is an important part of a well-formulated approach to capital budgeting. A post-audit involves the development of project performance reports comparing planned and actual results. Project performance reports should be provided to the manager who initiated the capital expenditure proposal, to the manager assigned responsibility for the project (if a different person), to the project manager's supervisor, and to the capital budgeting committee. These reports help keep the project on target (especially during the initial investment phase), help identify the need to reevaluate the project if the initial analysis was in error or significant environmental changes occur, and help improve the quality of investment proposals. When managers know they will be held accountable for the results of projects they initiate, they are likely to put more care into the development of capital expenditure proposals and take a greater interest in approved projects. Problems can occur when decision makers are rewarded for undertaking major projects but are not held responsible for the consequences that occur several years later. This problem is particularly acute in government organizations, such as the city of Denver's construction of a new airport, discussed in Management Accounting Practice 6-1.

A post-audit review of approved projects will also help the capital budgeting committee do a better job in evaluating new proposals. The committee may learn how to adjust proposals for the biases of individual managers; learn of new factors that should be considered in evaluating proposals; and

Emblem of Denver's Prosperity Becomes Financial Burden

In the 1980s, local economic growth, fueled by an oil and gas boom, led to frequent delays at Stapleton International Airport. City officials predicted continued growth, envisioning the number of passenger departures increasing from 16 million in 1985 to 26 million in 1995 with 36 daily flights to Europe. Against this background, city officials committed Denver to a new airport, selling it as an "emblem of Denver's prosperity." At a projected cost of $1.2 billion, the new facility, scheduled to open in October 1993, was to be one of the world's largest and most technologically advanced airports. To showcase state-of-the-art technology, plans called for the airport to have an automated baggage system with each bag being moved on an underground rail track in its own "telecar."

By October 1993, the projected costs of the new airport had increased to $3.1 billion, and the opening of the airport was delayed due to problems with fire, security, and baggage handling systems. In August 1994, the new mayor of Denver announced that the baggage handling system just "does not work" and that the city would have to spend an additional $50 million to install a manual baggage system utilizing conveyor belts and carts. By this time, the projected cost of the airport had risen to more than $4 billion, and delays in opening the airport were costing the city more than $2 million a day.

Meanwhile, the projected growth in air travel at Denver failed to materialize. In 1994, there was only one daily departure to Europe; and in 1993, there were only 16 million passenger departures, the same number as in 1985, the year the commitment to the new airport was made.

United Airlines, with a major hub at Denver, expressed concerns about increased landing fees and increased turnaround time at the new airport. The "new" low-tech baggage handling system would require so much time to move baggage between airplanes that United would have to lengthen passenger layovers between flights and keep aircraft on the ground longer, thereby reducing service and productivity.

Colorado Governor Roy Romer, who stumped hard for the new airport, was quoted as saying, "Had somebody told me the per passenger cost was going to be $18, I would not have supported the airport." Meanwhile, many passengers who frequently fly through Denver are sticking to carry-on baggage.

Based on: "Still Late for Arrival," *Newsweek* (August 22, 1994), pp. 38-40, "The Rocky Horror Airport Opening," *Business Week* (February 13, 1995), p. 50, and personal conversations with Denver-bound travelers.

avoid the routine approval of projects that appear desirable by themselves but are related to larger projects that are not meeting management's expectations.

CAPITAL BUDGETING MODELS THAT CONSIDER THE TIME VALUE OF MONEY

L O 2

The capital budgeting models presented in this chapter have gained wide acceptance by for-profit and not-for-profit organizations. You should have at least a rudimentary knowledge of the operation of these models and their strengths and weaknesses. Our primary focus is on the net present value and internal rate of return models, which are superior because they consider the time value of money. Later discussions will consider more traditional capital budgeting models, such as payback and the accounting rate of return that, while useful under certain circumstances, do not consider the time value of money. Although the cost of financing capital expenditures will be briefly considered, a detailed treatment of this topic, as well as a detailed examination of the sources of funds for financing investments, is left to books on financial management.

Organizing Expected Cash Flows

The focus of capital budgeting models that consider the time value of money is on future cash receipts and future cash disbursements that differ under decision alternatives. It is often convenient to distinguish between three phases of a project's cash flows:

- Initial investment
- Operation
- Disinvestment

All cash expenditures necessary to begin operations are classified as part of the project's initial investment. Expenditures to acquire property, plant, and equipment are clearly part of the initial investment. Less obvious, but equally important, are expenditures to acquire working capital such as inventories and to recruit and train employees. Although the initial investment phase often extends over many years, in most textbook examples and problems, we assume the initial investment takes place at a single point in time.

Cash receipts from sales of goods or services, as well as normal cash expenditures for materials, labor, and other operating expenses, occur during the operation phase. The operation phase is typically broken down into one-year periods; and for each period, operating cash expenditures are subtracted from operating cash receipts to determine the net operating cash inflow or outflow for the period.

The disinvestment phase occurs at the end of the project's life when assets are disposed of and any initial investment of working capital is recovered. Although this phase may also extend over many years, in textbook examples and problems, we frequently assume disinvestment takes place at a single point in time.

To illustrate the analysis of a project's cash flows, assume the management of Mobile Yogurt Shoppe is considering a capital expenditure proposal to operate a new Mobile Yogurt Shoppe in a resort community in the Ozark Mountains. Each Mobile Yogurt Shoppe is located in a specially constructed motor vehicle that moves on a regular schedule throughout the community it serves. The predicted cash flows associated with the project, which has an expected life of five years, are presented in Exhibit 6-1.

Ethics and Predicting Cash Flows

Accurately predicting the cash flows associated with a capital expenditure proposal is critical to proper evaluation of the proposal. Managers may be

EXHIBIT 6-1: ANALYSIS OF A PROJECT'S PREDICTED CASH FLOWS

Initial investment:		
Vehicle and equipment		$ 90,554
Inventories and other working capital		4,000
Total		$ 94,554
Operation (per year for 5 years):		
Sales		$175,000
Cash expenditures:		
Food	$ 47,000	
Labor	65,000	
Supplies	9,000	
Fuel and utilities	8,000	
Advertising	4,000	
Miscellaneous	12,000	-145,000
Net annual cash inflow		$ 30,000
Disinvestment (at the end of 5 years):		
Sale of vehicle and equipment		$ 8,000
Recovery of investment in inventories and		
other working capital		4,000
Total		$ 12,000

overly optimistic with their predictions, and they are sometimes tempted to modify predictions to justify capital expenditures. Perhaps they are interested in personal rewards. They may also want to avoid a loss of prestige or employment for themselves or to keep a local facility operating for the benefit of current employees and the local economy. Unfortunately, if a major expenditure does not work out, not only the local plant, but also the entire company may be forced out of business. Management Accounting Practice 6-2 examines the problems Nissan Motor Corp. experienced because of overly optimistic cash flow predictions.

Net Present Value

A project's **net present value**, usually computed as of the time of the initial investment, is the present value of the project's net cash inflows from operations and disinvestment less the amount of the initial investment. In computing a project's net present value, the cash flows occurring at different points in time are adjusted for the time value of money using a **discount rate** that is the minimum rate of return required for the project to be acceptable. Projects whose net present values are positive, or at least equal to zero, are acceptable and projects whose net present values are negative are unacceptable. Assuming management uses a 12 percent discount rate, the net present value of the proposed investment in a Mobile Yogurt Shoppe is shown in Exhibit 6-2 to be $20,400. Since the net present value is greater than zero, the investment in the Mobile Yogurt Shoppe is expected to be profitable, even when adjusted for the time value of money.

MANAGEMENT ACCOUNTING PRACTICE 6-2

Resale Values for Leased Infiniti Automobiles Are Very Finite

To increase demand for their products in the early 1990s, automobile companies began to aggressively encourage customers to lease new cars from the manufacturer. Important factors in determining the profitability of automobile leases include the cost of manufacturing the automobiles, the cost of financing the investment in leased automobiles, the monthly revenues from lease payments, and residual values of automobiles at the end of the leases.

The most difficult item to predict is the residual value at the end of the lease. That value (the selling price of the car) is a function of such things as the employment rate, the interest rate, and the actions of competitors at the time the lease expires. If, for example, the Federal Reserve increases the interest rate, the cost of financing the purchase of automobiles will increase, reducing sales and prices when leases expire.

The profitability of a lease and the monthly lease rate (the selling price of the lease) is influenced in part by predictions of residual value. If residual values are predicted to be high, the monthly lease can be set low enough to attract customers and still earn a profit.

In an effort to match monthly leases as low as $599 for competitive automobiles and still earn a profit on its investment in leased automobiles, Nissan Motor Corp. USA predicted that Infiniti automobiles could be sold for $32,500 at the end of a two-year lease. In 1993 and 1994 when the lease expired, the actual wholesale price for a two-year old Infiniti was $31,000. Because aggressive lease pricing left little room for error, industry analysts estimate that Nissan has lost millions of dollars on Infiniti leases.

....

Based on: David Woodruff and Larry Armstrong, "A High-Stakes Spin of the Wheel," *Business Week* (December 16, 1994), pp. 54-55.

EXHIBIT 6-2: NET PRESENT VALUE ANALYSIS OF A PROJECT'S PREDICTED CASH FLOWS

	Predicted Cash Inflows (Outflows)	Year(s) of Cash Flows	12% Present Value Factor	Present Value of Cash Flows
	(A)	(B)	(C)	(A) × (C)
Initial investment	$ (94,554)	0	1.000	$ (94,554)
Operation	30,000	1-5	3.605	108,150
Disinvestment	12,000	5	0.567	6,804
Net present value of all cash flows				$ 20,400

As an exercise, you should verify the amounts and computations in Exhibit 6-2. Start by tracing the cash flows back to Exhibit 6-1. Next, verify the 12 percent present value factors in Tables 6-1 and 6-2 on pages 307 and 308 at the back of this chapter. Note that the initial investment is assumed to occur at a single point in time, identified as time zero, the start of the project. In net present value computations, all cash flows are re-stated in terms of their value at time zero. Hence, time zero cash flows have a present value factor of one. To simplify computations, all other cash flows are assumed to occur at the end of years one through five, even if they occurred during the year. Although further refinements could be made to adjust for the fact that cash flows occur throughout each year, rather than at the end of the year, such adjustments are seldom necessary. Observe that the net operating cash inflows are treated as an annuity, whereas the cash flows for the initial investment and the disinvestment are treated as lump-sum amounts. If the net operating cash flows varied from year to year, we would have to treat each year's cash flow as a separate amount.

Internal Rate of Return

The **internal rate of return (IRR)**, often called the **time-adjusted rate of return**, is the discount rate that equates the present value of a project's cash inflows with the present value of the project's cash outflows. It is also described as:

1. The minimum rate that could be paid for the money invested in a project without losing money, or
2. The discount rate that results in a project's net present value equaling zero.

Computing IRR with Equal Cash Inflows

An investment proposal's internal rate of return is easily determined when a single investment is followed by a series of equal annual net cash inflows. The general relationship between the initial investment and the equal annual cash inflows is expressed as follows:

$$\frac{\text{Initial}}{\text{investment}} = \frac{\text{Present value factor}}{\text{for an annuity of \$1}} \times \frac{\text{Annual net}}{\text{cash inflow}}$$

We can solve for the appropriate present value factor as follows:

$$\frac{\text{Present value factor}}{\text{for an annuity of \$1}} = \frac{\text{Initial investment}}{\text{Annual net cash inflows}}$$

Once the present value factor is calculated, we enter Table 6-2 and go across the row corresponding to the expected life of the project until we find a table factor equal to the present value factor computed for the project. The corresponding percentage for the present value factor is the proposal's internal rate of return. If a table factor does not exactly equal the proposal's present value factor, a more accurate answer can be obtained by interpolation.

To illustrate, assume the Mobile Yogurt Shoppe's proposed investment has a zero disinvestment value. Using all information in Exhibit 6-1, except that for disinvestment, the proposal's present value factor is 3.152:

$$\frac{\text{Present value factor}}{\text{for an annuity of \$1}} = \frac{\text{Initial investment}}{\text{Annual net cash inflows}}$$

$$= \frac{\$94,554}{\$30,000}$$

$$= \underline{\underline{3.152}}$$

Entering Table 6-2, and going across the row for 5 periods, the closest table factor is 3.127, which corresponds to an internal rate of return of 18 percent. Because the proposal's present value factor is slightly larger than 3.127, interpolation can provide a more accurate answer:

	Present Value Factors	
16 percent	3.274	3.274
Internal rate of return	-3.152	
18 percent		-3.127
Difference	0.122	0.147

$$\text{True internal rate of return} = 0.16 + \left(\frac{0.122}{0.147} \times [0.18 - 0.16] \right)$$

$$= \underline{\underline{0.1766}}$$

Hence, the proposal's internal rate of return, ignoring any disinvestment value, is 17.66 percent.

The calculated internal rate of return should be compared to the discount rate established by management to evaluate investment proposals. If the proposal's IRR is greater than or equal to the discount rate, the project is acceptable; if the proposal's IRR is less than the discount rate, the project is unacceptable. Because Mobile Yogurt Shoppes has a 12 percent discount rate, the project is acceptable using the IRR model.

Computing IRR with Unequal Cash Inflows

If periodic cash flows subsequent to the initial investment are unequal, the simple procedure of determining a present value factor and looking up the closest corresponding factor in Table 6-2 cannot be used. Instead, if a calculator is not available, a trial-and-error approach must be used to determine the internal rate of return.

The first step is to select a discount rate estimated to be close to the proposal's IRR and to compute the proposal's net present value. If the resulting net present value is zero, the selected discount rate is the actual rate of return. However, it is unlikely that the first rate selected will be the proposal's IRR. If the resulting net present value is positive, this indicates the actual IRR is greater than the initially selected rate. In this case, the next step is to compute the proposal's net present value using a higher rate. If the second computation produces a negative net present value, the actual IRR is less than the selected rate. Therefore, the actual IRR is between the first and the second rates. This trial-and-error approach continues until a discount rate is found that equates the proposal's cash inflows and outflows. For the Mobile Yogurt Shoppe's investment proposal outlined in Exhibit 6-1, the details of the trial-and-error approach are presented in Exhibit 6-3.

EXHIBIT 6-3: COMPUTATIONS OF INTERNAL RATE OF RETURN WITH UNEQUAL CASH FLOWS

First trial with a 24 percent discount rate:

	Predicted Cash Inflows (Outflows)	Year(s) of Cash Flows	24% Present Value Factor	Present Value of Cash Flows
	(A)	(B)	(C)	(A) × (C)
Initial investment	$ (94,554)	0	1.000	$ (94,554)
Operation	30,000	1-5	2.745	82,350
Disinvestment	12,000	5	0.341	4,092
Net present value of all cash flows				$ (8,112)

Second trial with a 16 percent discount rate:

	Predicted Cash Inflows (Outflows)	Year(s) of Cash Flows	16% Present Value Factor	Present Value of Cash Flows
	(A)	(B)	(C)	(A) × (C)
Initial investment	$ (94,554)	0	1.000	$ (94,554)
Operation	30,000	1-5	3.274	98,220
Disinvestment	12,000	5	0.476	5,712
Net present value of all cash flows				$ 9,378

Third trial with a 20 percent discount rate:

	Predicted Cash Inflows (Outflows)	Year(s) of Cash Flows	20% Present Value Factor	Present Value of Cash Flows
	(A)	(B)	(C)	(A) × (C)
Initial investment	$ (94,554)	0	1.000	$ (94,554)
Operation	30,000	1-5	2.991	89,730
Disinvestment	12,000	5	0.402	4,824
Net present value of all cash flows				$ 0

Notice in Exhibit 6-3 that the first rate produced a negative net present value, indicating that the proposal's IRR is less than 24 percent. To produce a positive net present value, a smaller rate was selected for the second trial. Since the second rate produced a positive net present value, the proposal's true IRR must be between 16 and 24 percent. The 20-percent rate selected for the third trial produced a net present value of zero, indicating that this is the proposal's IRR.

Although manual calculation of an investment proposal's IRR is tedious, accurate results are easily obtained with a computer and appropriate software. Furthermore, many calculators contain IRR calculation functions. All you need to do is enter the predicted cash flows for each period. This computational ease does, however, increase the opportunity for inappropriate use. Being able to plug numbers into a computer or calculator and obtain a number labeled IRR may mislead the unwary user into believing it is easy to use this capital budgeting model. This simply is not true. Training and professional judgment are required to identify relevant costs, to implement procedures to obtain relevant cost information, and to make a good decision based on IRR information. Keep in mind that capital budgeting models are merely decision aids. People, not models, make decisions.

Cost of Capital

When discounting models are used to evaluate capital expenditure proposals, management must determine the discount rate (1) used to compute a proposal's net present value or (2) used as the standard for evaluating a proposal's IRR. An organization's cost of capital is often used as this discount rate.

The **cost of capital** is the average cost of obtaining the resources necessary to make investments. The cost of capital is the average rate an organization must pay for invested funds. This average rate takes into account such items as interest paid on notes or bonds, the effective dividend rate on preferred stock, and the discount rate that equates the present value of all dividends expected on common stock over the life of the organization to the current market value of the organization's common stock. The cost of capital for a company that has no debt or preferred stock is simply the cost of equity capital, computed as follows:

$$\text{Cost of equity capital} = \frac{\text{Current annual dividend per common share}}{\text{Current market price per common share}} + \frac{\text{Expected dividend growth rate}}{}$$

Procedures for determining the cost of capital for more complex capital structures are covered in finance textbooks. Investing in a project that has an internal rate of return equal to the cost of capital should not affect the market value of the firm's securities. Investing in a project that has a return greater than the cost of capital should increase the market value of a firm's securities. If, however, a firm invests in a project that has a return of less than the cost of capital, the market value of the firm's securities should fall.

The cost of capital is the minimum return that is acceptable for investment purposes. Any investment proposal not expected to yield this minimum rate should normally be rejected. Because of difficulties encountered in determining the cost of capital, many organizations adopt a discount rate or target rate of return without complicated mathematical analysis.

CAPITAL BUDGETING MODELS THAT DO NOT CONSIDER THE TIME VALUE OF MONEY

L O 3

For many years, capital budgeting models that do not consider the time value of money were more widely used than discounting models. Although their popularity has declined, nondiscounting models remain popular, especially as an initial screening device. We consider two nondiscounting models: payback period and the accounting rate of return.

Payback Period

The **payback period** is the time required to recover the initial investment in a project from operations. The payback decision rule states that acceptable projects must have less than some maximum payback period designated by management. Payback emphasizes management's concern with liquidity and the need to minimize risk through a rapid recovery of the initial investment. It is frequently used for small expenditures having such obvious benefits that the use of more sophisticated capital budgeting models is not required or justified. Management Accounting Practice 6-3 considers the use of payback to analyze an investment in computer memory.

When a project is expected to have equal annual operating cash inflows, its payback period is computed as follows:

$$\frac{\text{Payback}}{\text{period}} = \frac{\text{Initial investment}}{\text{Annual operating cash inflows}}$$

MANAGEMENT ACCOUNTING PRACTICE 6-3

With a Payback Period Less Than Two Months, Upgrading Computer Memory Is a "No Brainer"

To determine possible productivity gains from computer upgrades, such as that for additional random access memory (RAM), *PC Computing* performed a series of laboratory experiments. One of the experiments involved the time required to perform a set of tasks typically performed by an administrative assistant: create a letter, perform a mail merge, backup a directory, update an employee newsletter by cutting and pasting images, and printing. The experiment revealed that a 26 percent improvement in productivity could be obtained by upgrading from 4 megabytes to 16 megabytes of RAM.

Next, the researchers estimated that without the upgrade an administrative assistant would typically spend 100 hours per month performing similar tasks. With the upgrade providing a 26 percent gain in productivity, only 74 hours would be required, a savings of 26 hours. At a rate of pay of $13.50 per hour, this provides a savings of $351 per month or $4,212 per year.

The return on the investment depends on the cost of the additional memory. At a cost of $550, the payback period is approximately 1 1/2 months.

With payback results such as this, the investment in additional RAM appears justified without the need for discounting. Of course, as the researchers point out, the analysis is based on the assumption that the increased productivity gains will be used to perform additional value-added work, rather than freeing up time for visits at the water cooler.

Based on: Ron White, "Upgrades That Pay," *PC Computing* (November 1994), pp. 196-215.

For the Mobile Yogurt Shoppe's investment proposal, outlined in Exhibit 6-1, the payback period is 3.15 years:

$$\frac{\text{Payback}}{\text{period}} = \frac{\$94{,}554}{\$30{,}000}$$

$$= \underline{\underline{3.15}}$$

Determining the payback period for a project having unequal cash flows is slightly more complicated. Assume the Alderman Company is evaluating a capital expenditure proposal that requires an initial investment of $50,000 and has the following expected net cash inflows:

Year	Net Cash Inflow
1	$15,000
2	25,000
3	40,000
4	20,000
5	10,000

To compute the payback period, we must determine the net unrecovered amount at the end of each year. In the year of full recovery, the net cash inflows are assumed to occur evenly and are prorated based on the unrecovered investment at the start of the year. Full recovery of the Alderman Company's investment proposal is expected to occur in Year 3:

Year	Net Cash Inflow	Unrecovered Investment
0	$ 0	$50,000
1	15,000	35,000
2	25,000	10,000
3	40,000	

Therefore, $10,000 of $40,000 is needed in Year 3 to complete the recovery of the initial investment. This provides a proportion of 0.25 ($10,000/$40,000) and a payback period of 2.25 years (2 years plus 0.25 of Year 3). This project is acceptable if management specified a maximum payback period of 3 years. Because they occur after the payback period, the net cash inflows of Years 4 and 5 are ignored.

Accounting Rate of Return

The **accounting rate of return** is the average annual increase in net income that results from acceptance of a capital expenditure proposal divided by either the initial investment or the average investment in the project. This method differs from other capital budgeting models in that it focuses on accounting income rather than on cash flow. In most capital budgeting applications, accounting net income is approximated as net cash inflow from operations minus expenses not requiring the use of cash such as depreciation.

Consider the Mobile Yogurt Shoppe's capital expenditure proposal, whose cash flows are outlined in Exhibit 6-1. The vehicle and equipment cost $90,554 and have a disposal value of $8,000 at the end of 5 years, resulting in an average annual increase in net income of $13,489:

Annual net cash inflow from operations	$30,000
Less average annual depreciation ([$90,554 - $8,000]/5)	- 16,511
Average annual increase in net income	$13,489

Taking the investment in inventories and other working capital into account, the initial investment is $94,554 ($90,554 + $4,000), and the accounting rate of return *on initial investment* is 14.27 percent:

$$\text{Accounting rate of return} = \frac{\text{Average annual increase in net income}}{\text{Initial investment}} = \frac{\$13,489}{\$94,554} = 0.1427$$

The average investment, computed as the initial investment plus the expected value of any disinvestment, all divided by two, is $53,277 ([$94,554 + $12,000]/2). The accounting rate of return on *average* investment is 25.32 percent:

$$\text{Accounting rate of return} = \frac{\text{Average annual increase in net income}}{\text{Average investment}} = \frac{\$13,489}{\$53,277} = 0.2532$$

When using the accounting rate of return, management specifies some minimum acceptable rate of return. Capital expenditure proposals with a lower accounting rate of return are rejected, while acceptable proposals have an accounting rate of return greater than or equal to the minimum.

EVALUATION OF CAPITAL BUDGETING MODELS

L O 4

As a single criterion for evaluating capital expenditure proposals, capital budgeting models that consider the time value of money are superior to capital budgeting models that do not consider the time value of money. The payback model is merely concerned with how long it takes to recover the initial investment from a project. Yet, investments are not made with the objective of merely getting your money back. Indeed, not investing has a payback period of zero. Investments are made to earn a profit. Hence, what happens after the payback period is more important than the payback period itself. The payback model, when used as the sole investment criterion, has a fatal flaw in that it fails to consider cash flows after the payback period. Despite this flaw, payback is a rough-and-ready approach to getting a handle on investment proposals. Sometimes, a project is so attractive using payback that, when its life is considered, no further analysis is necessary.

For total life evaluations, the accounting rate of return is superior to the payback period in that it does consider the profitability of a capital expenditure proposal. Using the accounting rate of return, a project that merely returns the initial investment will have an average annual increase in net income of zero and an accounting rate of return of zero. The problem with the accounting rate of return is that it fails to consider the timing of cash flows. All cash flows within the life of an investment proposal are treated equally, despite that fact that cash flows occurring early in a project's life are more valuable than cash flows occurring late in a project's life. Early period cash flows can earn additional profits by being invested elsewhere. Consider the two investment proposals summarized in Exhibit 6-4. While both have an accounting rate of return of 5 percent, Proposal A is superior to Proposal B because most of its cash flows occur in the first two years. Because of the timing of the cash flows, when discounted at an annual rate of 10 percent, Proposal A has a net present value of $1,140, while Proposal B has a negative net present value of $(10,940).

The net present value and internal rate of return models both consider the time value of money and project profitability. They almost always provide the same evaluation of individual projects whose acceptance or rejection will not affect other projects.[1] There are, however, two basic differences between the net present value and the internal rate of return models that often lead to differences in the evaluation of competing investment proposals:

1. The net present value model gives explicit consideration to investment size. The internal rate of return model does not.
2. The net present value model assumes all net cash inflows are reinvested at the discount rate, while the internal rate of return model assumes all net cash inflows are reinvested at the project's internal rate of return.

These differences will be considered below when we discuss mutually exclusive investments.

ADDITIONAL ASPECTS OF CAPITAL BUDGETING

L O 5

The capital budgeting models discussed above do not make investment decisions. Rather, they help managers separate capital expenditure proposals that meet certain criteria from those that do not. Managers will then focus additional attention on those proposals that pass the initial screening performed using the capital budgeting models.

Multiple Investment Criteria

In performing this initial screening, management may use a single capital budgeting model, or they may use multiple models, including some we have not discussed. Management might specify that proposals must be in line with the organization's long-range goals and business strategy, have a maximum payback period of 3 years, have a positive net present value

---

[1] An exception often occurs when periods of net cash outflows are mixed with periods of net cash inflows. Under these circumstances, an investment proposal may have multiple internal rates of return. For a further discussion of this point, consult a financial management textbook.

EXHIBIT 6-4: EVALUATING CAPITAL BUDGETING MODELS WITH DIFFERENCES IN THE TIMING OF CASH FLOWS

Accounting rate of return analysis of Projects A and B:

	Project A	Project B
Predicted net cash inflow from operations:		
Year 1	$ 50,000	$ 10,000
Year 2	50,000	10,000
Year 3	10,000	50,000
Year 4	10,000	50,000
Total	$ 120,000	$ 120,000
Total depreciation	- 100,000	- 100,000
Total net income	$ 20,000	$ 20,000
Project life	÷ 4 years	÷ 4 years
Average annual increase in net income	$ 5,000	$ 5,000
Initial investment	÷ 100,000	÷ 100,000
Accounting rate of return on initial investment	0.05	0.05

Net present value analysis of Project A:

	Predicted Cash Inflows (Outflows)	Year(s) of Cash Flows	10% Present Value Factor	Present Value of Cash Flows
Initial investment	$(100,000)	0	1.000	$ (100,000)
Operation	50,000	1-2	1.736	86,800
	10,000	3-4	3.170 - 1.736	14,340
Net present value of all cash flows				$ 1,140

Net present value analysis of Project B:

	Predicted Cash Inflows (Outflows)	Year(s) of Cash Flows	10% Present Value Factor	Present Value of Cash Flows
Initial investment	$(100,000)	0	1.000	$ (100,000)
Operation	10,000	1-2	1.736	17,360
	50,000	3-4	3.170 - 1.736	71,700
Net present value of all cash flows				$ (10,940)

when discounted at 14 percent, and have an initial investment of less than $500,000. The maximum payback period might be intended to reduce risk, the present value criterion might be to ensure an adequate return to investors, and the maximum investment size might reflect the resources available for investment.

Nonquantitative factors are apt to play a decisive role in management's final decision to accept or reject a capital expenditure proposal that has passed the initial screening. As noted in Management Accounting Practice 6-4, market position, operational performance improvement, and strategy implementation are more important in making final investment decisions than quantitative factors developed using capital budgeting models. Also important at this point are top management's attitudes toward risk and financing alternatives, their confidence in the professional judgment of other managers making investment proposals, their beliefs about the future direction of the economy, and their evaluation of alternative investments. In the following sections, we will focus on the evaluation of risk, an approach to the differential analysis of project cash flows, predicting differential costs and revenues for high-tech investments, and evaluating mutually exclusive investments.

Evaluating Risk

All capital expenditure proposals involve many sources of risk, including risk related to:

- The cost of the initial investment
- The time required to complete the initial investment and begin operations
- Whether or not the new facilities will operate as planned
- The life of the facilities
- The customers' demand for the product or service
- The final selling price
- Operating costs
- Disposal values

Projected cash flows, such as those summarized for the Mobile Yogurt Shoppe proposal in Exhibit 6-1, are based on management's best prediction as to what will happen. Although these predictions are likely to reflect the professional judgment of economists, marketing personnel, engineers, and accountants, they are far from certain.

Many techniques have been developed to assist in the analysis of the risks inherent in capital budgeting. Suggested approaches include the following:

- The discount rate for individual projects may be adjusted based on management's perception of the risks associated with a project. A project perceived as being almost risk-free may be evaluated using a discount rate of 12 percent; a project perceived as having moderate risk may be evaluated using a discount rate of 16 percent; and a project perceived as having high risk may be evaluated using a discount rate of 20 percent.
- Several internal rates of return and/or net present values may be computed for a project. For example, a project's net present value might be computed three times: first assuming the most optimistic projections of cash flows; second assuming the most likely projections of cash flows; and third assuming the most pessimistic projections of

MANAGEMENT ACCOUNTING PRACTICE 6-4

Capital Budgeting in the U.S., Korea, and Japan

Surveys of accounting practices in the U.S., Korea, and Japan suggest that companies use multiple capital budgeting models, with payback being the most frequently used model in all three countries.

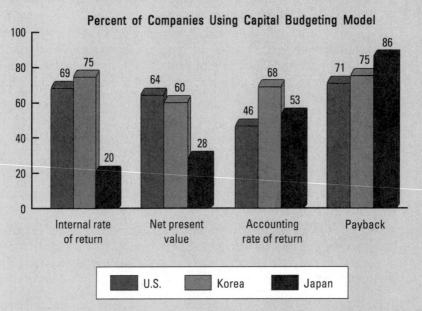

Percent of Companies Using Capital Budgeting Model

Until recently, investment funds were readily available, and the cost of capital was relatively low in Japan. This might partially explain the low use of models that consider the time value of money by Japanese companies. A tightening of investment funds and an increase in the cost of capital may lead to different results in future surveys.

Survey results also indicate that in making final investment decisions, other factors, such as providing an ability to compete in the marketplace, enhancing operational performance, and implementing manufacturing strategy, are even more important than the results of capital budgeting models. This is not surprising, given that capital expenditures should be made to support an organization's long-range goals and business strategy.

What was surprising in a survey of U.S. companies was that companies using payback expected a payback period of two to three years for most capital expenditures. This suggests a concern about risk, technological obsolescence (such as that experienced with personal computers), or an emphasis on short-term performance. The survey also indicated that firms most frequently used discount rates of between 15 and 20 percent.

Based on: Il-Woon Kim and Ja Song, "U.S., Korea, & Japan: Accounting Practices in Three Countries," *Management Accounting* (August 1990), pp. 26-30, and Robert A. Howell, James D. Brown, Stephen R. Soucy, and Allen Seed, *Management Accounting in the New Manufacturing Environment* (Montvale, NJ: Institute of Management Accountants (formerly National Association of Accountants), 1987), pp. 21-34.

cash flows. The final decision will then be based on management's attitudes toward risk. If the pessimistic outcome might lead to bankruptcy, a project whose most likely outcome is highly profitable would probably be rejected.

• A capital expenditure proposal may be subject to sensitivity analysis, which was defined in Chapter 2 as a study of the responsiveness of a model's dependent variable(s) to changes in one or more of its independent variables. Management might want to know, for example, the minimum annual net cash inflows that will provide an internal rate of return of 12 percent, other cost and revenue projections being as expected.

Consider the situation presented in Exhibit 6-1 and analyzed using net present value and internal rate of return models in Exhibits 6-2 and 6-3. This proposal has a positive net present value when its cash flows are discounted at 12 percent, and it has an expected IRR of 20 percent. Assuming Mobile Yogurt Shoppes has a 12 percent discount rate, management might wish to know the minimum annual net cash inflow that will meet this criterion.

In Exhibit 6-2, disinvestment cash inflows have a net present value of $6,804. When this amount is subtracted from the initial investment, $87,750 ($94,554 - $6,804) of the initial investment must be recovered from operations. If this amount is to be recovered over a 5-year period, with equal annual net cash inflows, and a 12 percent discount rate, the factor 3.605 (see Table 6-2) must equate the annual net cash inflows with the portion of the initial investment to be recovered from operations. Hence, the minimum annual net cash inflows must be $24,341:

$$\frac{\text{Minimum annual}}{\text{net cash inflow}} = \frac{\$87,750}{3.605}$$

$$= \underline{\underline{\$24,341}}$$

If management could then predict the probability of annual net cash inflows being greater than or equal to $24,341, they would have the probability of this project meeting a 12 percent discount rate. Again, the ultimate decision to accept or reject the proposal rests with management and their attitudes toward risk.

It is interesting to note the similarity of the analysis here, determining the minimum annual net cash inflows, and the determination of the break-even point in Chapter 2. In effect, $24,341 in annual net cash inflows is a time-adjusted break-even point.

Total and Differential Analysis of Cash Flows

All previous examples assume that capital expenditure proposals will produce additional net cash inflows. This is not always the case. Units of government and not-for-profit organizations may provide services that do not produce any cash inflows. For-profit organizations may be required to make capital expenditures to maintain product quality or to bring facilities up to environmental or safety standards. In these situations, it is impossible to compute a project's payback period, accounting rate of return, or internal rate of return. It is possible, however, to compute the present value of all life-cycle costs associated with alternative ways of providing the service or meeting the environmental or safety standard. Here, the alternative with the smallest negative net present value is preferred.

Capital expenditure proposals to reduce operating costs by upgrading facilities may not provide any incremental cash inflows. Again, we may use a total cost approach and calculate the present value of the costs associated with each alternative, with the low cost alternative being preferred. Alternatively, we may perform a differential analysis of cash flows and, treating any reduced operating costs as if they were cash inflows, compute the net present value or the internal rate of return of the cost reduction proposal. Recall from Chapter 3 that a differential cost analysis focuses on the costs that differ under alternative actions. Once the differential amounts are determined, they can be adjusted for the time value of money. To illustrate the differential approach, we consider an example introduced in Chapter 3.

The Ace Welding Company uses a Model I welding machine to produce 10,000 Mountain bicycle frames per year. The Model I welding machine is 2 years old and has a remaining useful life of 4 years. It cost $90,000 and has an estimated salvage value of zero dollars at the end of its useful life. Its current book value (original cost less accumulated depreciation) is $60,000, but its current disposal value is only $35,000.

Management is evaluating the desirability of replacing the Model I welding machine with a new Model II welding machine. The new machine costs $80,000, has a useful life of 4 years, and a predicted salvage value of zero dollars at the end of its useful life. Although the new machine has the same productive capacity as the old machine, its predicted operating costs are lower because it requires less electricity. Furthermore, because of a computer control system, the Model II machine will require less frequent and less expensive inspections and adjustments. Finally, the Model II machine requires less maintenance.

A differential analysis of the cash flows associated with this cost reduction proposal, broken down into the three phases of the project's life, are presented in Exhibit 6-5. Because the proposal does not have a disposal value, this portion of the analysis could have been omitted. Readers interested in a detailed explanation of the relevant costs included in this analysis are referred to Exhibit 3-1 and the accompanying Chapter 3 discussion of relevant costs. Assuming Ace Welding has a discount rate of 12 percent, the proposal's net present value, computed in Exhibit 6-6, is $2,681; and the proposal is acceptable.

Predicting Differential Costs and Revenues for High-Tech Investments

Special care must be taken when evaluating proposals for investments in the most current technological innovations such as flexible manufacturing systems (FMS) and computer integrated manufacturing (CIM). There are three types of errors to consider: (1) investing in unnecessary or overly complex equipment, (2) overestimating cost savings, and (3) underestimating incremental sales.

EXHIBIT 6-5: DIFFERENTIAL ANALYSIS OF PREDICTED CASH FLOWS

	Keep Old Model I Machine	Replace with New Model II Machine	Difference (Effect of Replacement on Income)
	(A)	(B)	(A) - (B)
Initial investment:			
Cost of new machine		$ 80,000	$ 80,000
Disposal value of old machine		(35,000)	(35,000)
Net initial investment			$ 45,000
Annual operating cash savings:			
Conversion:			
Mountain frames, Model I (10,000 units × $5)	$50,000		
Mountain frames, Model II (10,000 units × $4)		$ 40,000	$ 10,000
Inspection and adjustment:			
Mountain frames, Model I (10 × $500)	5,000		
Mountain frames, Model II (5 × $300)		1,500	3,500
Machine maintenance:			
Mountain frames, Model I ($200 × 12 months)	2,400		
Mountain frames, Model II ($200/year)		200	2,200
Net annual cost savings			$ 15,700
Disinvestment at end of life:			
Old	$ 0		
New		$ 0	

Differential Analysis of Predicted Cash Flows

EXHIBIT 6-6: NET PRESENT VALUE ANALYSIS OF DIFFERENTIAL CASH FLOWS

	Predicted Cash Inflows (Outflows)	Year(s) of Cash Flows	12% Present Value Factor	Present Value of Cash Flows
	(A)	(B)	(C)	(A) × (C)
Initial investment	$(45,000)	0	1.000	$(45,000)
Operation	15,700	1-4	3.037	47,681
Disinvestment	0	4	0.636	0
Net present value of all cash flows				$ 2,681

Investing in Unnecessary or Overly Complex Equipment

A basic error is to simply compare the cost associated with the current inefficient way of doing things with the predicted cost of performing the identical operations with more modern equipment. While capital budgeting models may suggest such investments are justifiable, the result could be the costly and rapid performance of nonvalue-added activities. Consider the following examples:

- A company invests in an automated system to speed the movement of work-in-process between workstations on the shop floor without first evaluating the plant layout. The firm is still unable to compete with other companies having better organized plants that allow lower cycle times, lower work-in-process inventories, and lower manufacturing costs. Management should have evaluated the plant layout before investing in new equipment. They may have found that rearranging the factory floor would have reduced materials movement and eliminated the need for the investment.
- A company invests in a large automated warehouse to permit the rapid storage and retrieval of goods while competitors work to eliminate excess inventory. The firm is left with large inventories and a large investment in the automated warehouse, while competitors, not having to earn a return on similar investments, are able to charge lower prices. Management should have evaluated the need for current inventory levels and perhaps shifted to a just-in-time approach to inventory management before considering the investment in an automated warehouse.
- A company invests in equipment to perform quality inspections, while competitors implement total quality management and work to eliminate the need for quality inspections. While defective products are now detected before shipment to customers, they are still being produced. Furthermore, the company has a higher capital investment than competitors. The result is, again, a less competitive cost structure. There may not have been a need for the inspection equipment if management shifted from inspecting all finished goods for conformance to an emphasis on "doing it right the first time."
- A company invests in automated welding equipment to more efficiently produce printer casings, while competitors simplify the product design and shift from welded to molded plastic casings. Although the cost of producing the welded casings may be lower, the company's cost structure is still not competitive.

All of these examples illustrate the limitations of capital budgeting models and the need for professional judgment. In the final analysis, people, not models, make decisions. Management must carefully evaluate the situations and determine if the proper alternatives and all important cash flows are considered.

Overestimating Cost Savings

When manufacturing overhead costs are driven by a number of activities, estimates of overhead cost savings based on a single activity cost driver may significantly overestimate cost savings. Assume, for example, that a company containing both machine-intensive and labor-intensive operations develops a cost estimating equation for manufacturing overhead with direct labor as the only independent variable. Because of this, all overhead costs are associated with direct labor. Here, the predicted cost savings may be computed as the sum of predicted reductions in direct labor plus predicted reductions in overhead, computed as the overhead per direct labor dollar or labor hour multiplied by the predicted reduction in direct labor dollars or labor hours. Because a major portion of the manufacturing overhead is driven by factors other than direct labor, reducing direct labor will not provide the predicted savings. While capital budgeting models may suggest the investment is acceptable, the models are based on inaccurate cost data.

Management should beware of overly simplistic computations of cost savings. This is an area where management needs the assistance of well-trained management accountants and engineers.

Underestimating Incremental Sales or Cost Savings

In evaluating proposals for investments in new equipment, management often assumes that the base line for comparison is the current sales level. This may not be the case. If competitors are investing in equipment to better meet customer needs and to reduce costs, a failure to make similar investments may result in uncompetitive prices and declining, rather than steady, sales. Hence, the base line for sales without the investment is over-stated, and the incremental sales of the investment is understated. Not considering the likely decline in sales understates the incremental sales associated with the investment and biases the results against the proposed investment.

Investments in the most advanced manufacturing technologies, such as flexible manufacturing systems (FMS) and computer integrated manufacturing (CIM), do more than simply allow the efficient production of current products. Such investments also make possible the rapid, low-cost switching to new products. The result is expanded sales opportunities.

Such investments may also produce cost savings further down the value chain, either within or outside the company. The Ace Welding Company's decision to acquire a new Model II welding machine might have the unanticipated consequence of reducing customer warranty claims or in-creasing sales because customers are attracted to a higher quality product. Management Accounting Practice 6-5 discusses how taking a value chain perspective might affect capital budgeting and other strategic decisions at Yakima-Olympia.

Unfortunately, because such opportunities are difficult to quantify, they are often ignored in the evaluation of capital expenditure proposals. The result is a bias against investments in FMS and CIM. The solution to this dilemma involves the application of management's professional judgment, a willingness to take risks based on professional judgment, and recognition that certain investments transcend capital budgeting models in that they involve strategic as well as long-range planning. At this level of planning, qualitative decisions concerning the nature of the organization are at least as important as quantified factors. Management Accounting Practice 6-6 examines the difficulty Aetna Life and Casualty Co. encountered in evaluating strategic investments in information technology.

Mutually Exclusive Investments

Two or more capital expenditure proposals are **mutually exclusive** if the acceptance of one automatically causes the rejection of the other(s). Perhaps a builder with a tract of land on the outskirts of Paris is trying to determine the most profitable use of the land. She is trying to choose among a shopping center, a housing development, and an office park. However, because of the size of the tract and zoning requirements, the land may only be used for one of these purposes.

MANAGEMENT ACCOUNTING PRACTICE 6-5

Value Chain Broadens Capital Budgeting Perspective for Yakima-Olympia

Yakima-Olympia (Y-O) is a vertically integrated forest product company whose activities range from developing and planting improved seedlings to the retail distribution of wood products. Nevertheless, like most forest product firms, Y-O (primarily for cost reasons such as nonunion wages) hires private logging contractors to cut trees. These contractors follow traditional procedures to fell all trees in an area, remove branches with chain saws, and drag trees to loading areas.

Y-O wanted its logging contractors in the Tidewater region of Virginia to switch to the use of harvesting machines that could selectively cut and trim mature trees to meet current production specifications. To do this, a logging contractor would have to make a capital investment of approximately $600,000 in new equipment. Over the harvesting machine's 5-year life, it would have annual cash operating costs of approximately $250,000. Following standard rates, the contractor would receive annual revenues of approximately $400,000 from Y-O. With a 12 percent time value of money, the proposed investment's net present value is minus $60,000. Consequently, Y-O met with little success in convincing contractors to switch to harvesting machines.

Analyzing the situation, John Shank and Vijay Govindarajan concluded that the proposal was being rejected because of a failure to analyze costs across Y-O's entire value chain. They noted that across the value chain, the use of harvesting machines would produce significant savings in land management, sorting, reduced waste, and reduced processing costs. Although the investment would produce major financial benefits, the stage in the value chain where the investment must be made, under traditional pricing policies, would receive none of the benefits. Shank and Govindarajan observed that Y-O will have to consider a gain-sharing mechanism to convince logging contractors to make the necessary investment. If this is not feasible, Y-O might decide that the economic gains from the investment are large enough to stop outside contracting and internalize logging operations.

Based on: John K. Shank and Vijay Govindarajan, "Strategic Cost Analysis of Technological Investments," *Sloan Management Review* (Fall 1992), pp. 39-51.

MANAGEMENT ACCOUNTING PRACTICE 6-6

Aetna Life and Casualty Doesn't Measure the Return on Information Technology

After spending a year trying to determine how to measure the return from investments in information technology, John Loewenberg, senior vice president of information and technology at Aetna Life & Casualty Co., gave up, calling it "an exercise in futility." Mr. Loewenberg observed that while there appears to be a correlation between investments in information technology and reductions in cost, it is difficult to say that one caused the other.

Aetna has a complex computer system that links a collection of central data bases with computer networks around the country. The system provides up-to-date information so that agents can immediately respond to customer questions. The complexity of the system makes it difficult to evaluate proposals for additional investments in the system. Mr. Loewenberg's frustration came from the fact that "once a business unit implemented a new technology solution, the [business and technology] became so integrated that you couldn't tell them apart."

Aetna managers now make the case for additional investments in technology on the basis of business objectives such as customer satisfaction and product improvements. Mr. Loewenberg focuses on delivering agreed-upon services as cost-effectively as possible.

Based on: "Magic Formula," *The Wall Street Journal* (November 14, 1994), p. R18.

When faced with mutually exclusive investments, management must determine which one to accept. The decision is relatively easy if only one of the proposals meets the organization's investment criteria. If, however, two or more proposals pass the initial screening performed by the investment criterion, management is faced with the task of selecting the best of the acceptable proposals. To help in the determination of the best investment proposal, management may request that the proposals be ranked on the basis of some criterion such as net present value or internal rate of return. Unfortunately, while these models almost always lead to identical decisions when used to evaluate individual investment proposals, they frequently produce different rankings of acceptable proposals. Assume three mutually exclusive investment proposals are being considered by a Japanese company. Relevant information is summarized in Exhibit 6-7. Note that the Japanese unit of currency is the yen, ¥.

Assuming the organization has a 12 percent cost of capital, all projects have positive net present values, and all projects have an internal rate of return in excess of 12 percent. Therefore, all are acceptable. The problem is to determine which of these acceptable proposals is most desirable. Ranking the proposals by their net present value indicates that Proposal B is best, while ranking by IRR indicates that Proposal C is best.

An often stated criticism of net present value, when used to rank investment proposals, is that it fails to adjust for the size of the proposed investment. To overcome this difficulty, managers may rank projects on the

EXHIBIT 6-7: RANKING CAPITAL BUDGETING PROPOSALS

	Proposal A	Proposal B	Proposal C
Predicted cash flows (in 000)*:			
Initial investment	¥ (26,900)	¥ (55,960)	¥ (30,560)
Operation:			
Year 1	10,000	20,000	20,000
Year 2	10,000	20,000	20,000
Year 3	10,000	20,000	0
Year 4	10,000	20,000	0
Disinvestment	0	0	0
Investment criterion:			
Net present value (in 000) at 12%	¥ 3,470	¥ 4,780	¥ 3,240
Internal rate of return	18%	16%	20%
Present value index	1.129	1.085	1.106
Ranking by investment criterion:			
Net present value	2	1	3
Internal rate of return	2	3	1
Present value index	1	3	2

*All monetary amounts are in thousands of Japanese yen, represented by ¥.

basis of each project's **present value index**, which is computed as the present value of the project's subsequent cash flows divided by the initial investment:

$$\frac{\text{Present value}}{\text{index}} = \frac{\text{Present value of subsequent cash flows}}{\text{Initial investment}}$$

For Proposal A, the present value of the subsequent cash flows, discounted at 12 percent, is ¥30,370,000 (¥10,000,000 × 3.037), and the present value index is 1.129:

$$\frac{\text{Present value}}{\text{index}} = \frac{¥30,370,000}{¥26,900,000}$$

$$= \underline{\underline{1.129}}$$

Using this criterion, projects that have a present value index of 1.0 or greater are acceptable, and the project with the highest present value index is preferred. Ranking the proposals in Exhibit 6-7 on the basis of their present value index results in Proposal A being ranked number 1.

We now have three acceptable proposals, three criteria, three different rankings, and the task of selecting only one of the three proposals. Many managers would select Proposal C because it has the highest IRR or Proposal A because it has the highest present value index. Either selection provides a satisfactory, but not an optimal, solution to the dilemma. If the true cost of capital is 12 percent and other investment opportunities only return 12 percent, the net present value criterion provides the proper choice.

This is illustrated in Exhibit 6-8 by evaluating the additional return earned on the differences between Proposals B and A and between Proposals B and C.

EXHIBIT 6-8: ANALYSIS OF INCREMENTAL INVESTMENTS

	Proposal B	Proposal A	Difference B - A
Predicted cash flows (in 000)*:			
Initial investment	¥ (55,960)	¥ (26,900)	¥ (29,060)
Operation:			
Year 1	20,000	10,000	10,000
Year 2	20,000	10,000	10,000
Year 3	20,000	10,000	10,000
Year 4	20,000	10,000	10,000
Disinvestment	0	0	0

Net present value of difference (B-A):

	Cash Inflows (Outflows)	Year(s) of Cash Flows	12% Present Value Factor	Present Value of Cash Flows
Initial investment	¥ (29,060)	0	1.000	¥ (29,060)
Operation	10,000	1-4	3.037	30,370
Disinvestment	0	4	0.636	0
Net present value				¥ 1,310

	Proposal B	Proposal C	Difference B - C
Predicted cash flows (in 000)*:			
Initial investment	¥ (55,960)	¥ (30,560)	¥ (25,400)
Operations:			
Year 1	20,000	20,000	0
Year 2	20,000	20,000	0
Year 3	20,000	0	20,000
Year 4	20,000	0	20,000
Disinvestment	0	0	0

Net present value of difference (B-C):

	Cash Inflows (Outflows)	Year(s) of Cash Flows	12% Present Value Factor	Present Value of Cash Flows
Initial investment	¥ (25,400)	0	1.000	¥ (25,400)
Operation	20,000	2-4	3.037 - 1.690	26,940
Disinvestment	0	4	0.636	0
Net present value				¥ 1,540

*All monetary amounts are in thousands of Japanese yen, represented by ¥.

The difference in the net present value and internal rate of return rankings results from differences in their reinvestment assumptions. The net present value model assumes all net cash inflows from a project are reinvested at the discount rate, while the internal rate of return model assumes all net cash inflows from a project are reinvested at the project's internal rate of return. If unlimited funds are available at the discount rate, then, marginal investments are made at this rate; and the assumption underlying the net present value model is the correct one. Returning to Exhibit 6-8, if all funds not invested in the chosen project and all funds recovered from the chosen project can only earn the discount rate, the firm is ¥1,540,000 better off selecting Proposal B rather than Proposal C.

The present value index eliminates the impact of size from net present value computations. However, size is an important consideration in evaluating investment proposals, especially if funds not invested in a project can only earn the discount rate. In Exhibit 6-8, we see that if funds not invested in the chosen project can only be invested at the discount rate, the firm is ¥1,310,000 better off by selecting Proposal B rather than Proposal A.

TAXES IN CAPITAL BUDGETING DECISIONS

L O 6

To focus on capital budgeting concepts, we deferred consideration of the impact of taxes on capital budgeting until the end of the chapter. Because income taxes affect cash flows and income, they are an important consideration in evaluating any business decision.

The cost of investments in plant and equipment is not deducted from taxable revenues in determining taxable income and income taxes at the time of the initial investment. Instead, the amount of the initial investment is deducted as depreciation over the operating life of an asset. To illustrate the impact of taxes on operating cash flows assume that:

- Revenues and operating cash receipts are the same each year.
- Depreciation is the only noncash expense of an organization.

Depreciation Tax Shield

While depreciation does not require the use of cash (the funds were spent at the time of the initial investment), depreciation is said to provide a "tax shield" because it reduces cash payments for income taxes. The **depreciation tax shield**, the reduction in taxes due to the deductibility of depreciation from taxable revenues, is computed as:

Depreciation tax shield = Depreciation × Tax rate

The value of the depreciation tax shield is illustrated using the Mobile Yogurt Shoppe's capital expenditure proposal summarized in Exhibit 6-1. Assuming a tax rate of 34 percent, the annual net income and after-tax cash flows for this investment without depreciation and with straight-line depreciation are shown in Exhibit 6-9. Examine this exhibit, paying particular attention to the lines for depreciation, income taxes, and net annual cash flow.

The Mobile Yogurt Shoppe's annual depreciation tax shield, using straight-line depreciation, is $6,158, computed as annual depreciation of $18,111 ($90,554 investment in depreciable assets/5-year life) multiplied by the tax rate of 34 percent. Without the depreciation tax shield, annual cash payments for income taxes would be $6,158 more, and after-tax cash flows would be $6,158 less.

The U.S. Tax Code contains guidelines concerning the depreciation of various kinds of assets. A detailed analysis of these guidelines is beyond the scope of this text. Tax guidelines allow organizations a choice in tax depreciation procedures between straight-line depreciation and an accelerated depreciation method detailed in the Tax Code. Because of the time

EXHIBIT 6-9: EFFECT OF DEPRECIATION ON TAXES, INCOME, AND CASH FLOW

Annual Taxes and Income Without Depreciation		Annual Taxes and Income with Depreciation	
Sales	$ 175,000	Sales	$ 175,000
Operating expenses (except depreciation)	(145,000)	Operating expenses (except depreciation)	(145,000)
Depreciation	-0-	Depreciation ($90,554/5 years)	(18,111)
Income before taxes without depreciation	$ 30,000	Income before taxes with depreciation	11,889
Income taxes (34%)	(10,200)	Income taxes (34%)	(4,042)
Net income	$ 19,800	Net income	$ 7,847

Depreciation reduces income taxes by the amount of depreciation times the tax rate. The difference in taxes, $6,158, ($10,200 - $4,042), is equal to the difference in depreciation multiplied by the tax rate, $6,158 ($18,111 × 0.34).

Annual Taxes and Cash Flow without Depreciation		Annual Taxes and Cash Flow with Depreciation	
Sales	$ 175,000	Sales	$ 175,000
Operating expenses (except depreciation)	(145,000)	Operating expenses (except depreciation)	(145,000)
Income taxes	(10,200)	Income taxes	(4,042)
Net annual cash inflow	$ 19,800	Net annual cash inflow	$ 25,958

The deductibility of depreciation for tax purposes reduces cash payments for taxes, thus increasing the net cash flow by the depreciation tax shield. The difference in cash flow, $6,158 ($25,958 - $19,800), is explained by the depreciation multiplied by the tax rate, $6,158 ($18,111 × 0.34). This is the depreciation tax shield.

value of money, profitable businesses should usually select the tax depreciation procedure that provides the earliest depreciation. To illustrate the effect of accelerated depreciation on taxes and capital budgeting, we will use double-declining balance depreciation (which most readers are familiar with) rather than the accelerated method detailed in the Code. When making capital expenditure decisions you should, of course, refer to the most current version of the Tax Code to determine the specific depreciation guidelines in effect at that time.

Exhibits 6-10 and 6-11 illustrate the effect of two alternative depreciation procedures, straight-line and double-declining balance, on the net present value of Mobile Yogurt Shoppe's proposed investment.

We assume the asset is fully depreciated for tax purposes during its 5-year life and sold for a taxable gain equal to its predicted salvage value. The cash flows for this investment were presented in Exhibit 6-1, and the effect of taxes on the investment's annual cash flows were examined in Exhibit 6-9. Ignoring taxes, the investment was shown, in Exhibit 6-2, to have a positive net present value of $20,400 at a discount rate of

EXHIBIT 6-10: ANALYSIS OF CAPITAL EXPENDITURES INCLUDING TAX EFFECTS: STRAIGHT-LINE DEPRECIATION

	Predicted Cash Inflows (Outflows)	Year(s) of Cash Flows	12% Present Value Factor	Present Value of Cash Flows
	(A)	(B)	(C)	(A) × (C)
Initial investment:				
Vehicle and equipment	$ (90,554)	0	1.000	$ (90,554)
Inventory and other working capital	(4,000)	0	1.000	(4,000)
Operations:				
Annual taxable income without depreciation	30,000	1-5	3.605	108,150
Taxes on income ($30,000 × 0.34)	(10,200)	1-5	3.605	(36,771)
Depreciation tax shield*	6,158	1-5	3.605	22,200
Disinvestment:				
Sale of vehicle and equipment	8,000	5	0.567	4,536
Taxes on gain on sale ($8,000 × 0.34)	(2,720)	5	0.567	(1,542)
Inventory and other working capital	4,000	5	0.567	2,268
Net present value of all cash flows				$ 4,287

*Computation of depreciation tax shield:
Annual straight-line depreciation ($90,554/5)	$ 18,111
Tax rate	× 0.34
Depreciation tax shield	$ 6,158

EXHIBIT 6-11: ANALYSIS OF CAPITAL EXPENDITURES INCLUDING TAX EFFECTS: DOUBLE-DECLINING BALANCE DEPRECIATION

	Predicted Cash Inflows (Outflows)	Year(s) of Cash Flows	12% Present Value Factor	Present Value of Cash Flows
	(A)	(B)	(C)	(A) × (C)
Initial investment:				
Vehicle and equipment	$ (90,554)	0	1.000	$ (90,554)
Inventory and other				
working capital	4,000	0	1.000	(4,000)
Operations:				
Annual taxable income				
without depreciation	30,000	1-5	3.605	108,150
Taxes on income				
($30,000 × 0.34)	(10,200)	1-5	3.605	(36,771)
Depreciation tax shield*:				
Year 1	12,315	1	0.893	10,997
Year 2	7,389	2	0.797	5,889
Year 3	4,434	3	0.712	3,157
Year 4	2,660	4	0.636	1,692
Year 5	3,990	5	0.567	2,262
Disinvestment:				
Sale of vehicle and equipment	8,000	5	0.567	4,536
Taxes on gain on sale				
($8,000 × 0.34)	(2,720)	5	0.567	(1,542)
Inventory and other				
working capital	4,000	5	0.567	2,268
Net present value of all cash flows				$ 6,084

*Computation of depreciation tax shield⁺:

Year	Depreciation Base	Annual Rate	Annual Depreciation	Tax Rate	Tax Shield
			(C)		(E)
	(A)	(B)	(A) × (B)	(D)	(C) × (D)
1	$90,554	2/5	$36,222	0.34	$12,315
2	54,332	2/5	21,733	0.34	7,389
3	32,599	2/5	13,040	0.34	4,434
4	19,559	2/5	7,824	0.34	2,660
5	11,735	balance	11,735	0.34	3,990

⁺The depreciation base is reduced by the amount of any previous depreciation. The annual rate is twice the straight-line rate. For simplicity, we depreciated the remaining balance in the fifth year and did not switch to straight-line depreciation when the straight-line amount exceeds the double-declining balance amount. This would happen in the fourth year, when $19,559 / 2 = $9,780.

12 percent. With taxes, the investment has a positive net present value of $4,287 using straight-line depreciation and $6,040 using double-declining balance depreciation. Although taxes over the entire life of the project are identical, the use of double-declining balance depreciation for taxes gives a higher net present value because it results in lower cash expenditures for taxes in the earlier years of an asset's life.

Investment Tax Credit

From time-to-time, for the purpose of stimulating investment and economic growth, the U.S. Federal Government has implemented an investment tax credit. An **investment tax credit** reduces taxes in the year a new asset is placed in service by some stated percent of the cost of the asset. Typically, this is done without reducing the depreciation base of the asset for tax purposes. An investment tax credit reduces cash payments for taxes and, hence, is treated as a cash inflow for capital budgeting purposes. This additional cash inflow increases the probability that a new asset will meet a taxpayer's capital expenditure criteria.

SUMMARY

Capital budgeting involves the identification of potentially desirable projects for capital expenditures, the subsequent evaluation of capital expenditure proposals, and the selection of proposals that meet certain criteria. In this chapter, we studied a number of capital budgeting models used to assist managers in evaluating capital expenditure proposals. We concluded that capital budgeting models that consider the time value of money, such as net present value and internal rate of return, are superior to capital budgeting models that do not consider the time value of money, such as the payback period and the accounting rate of return.

It is important to remember that capital budgeting models do not make investment decisions. Rather, they help managers separate capital expenditure proposals that meet certain criteria from those that do not. In making the final decision to accept or reject a capital expenditure proposal that has passed the initial screening, nonquantitative factors, such as management's attitude toward risk, are apt to play a decisive role.

In the latter portion of this chapter, we outlined some suggested approaches to analyzing risk, saw how differential analysis can aid in evaluating capital expenditure proposals that do not produce additional cash inflows, and studied the problems involved in selecting from among mutually exclusive investments. We concluded by considering the impact of taxes and the depreciation tax shield on capital expenditure proposals.

APPENDIX: TIME VALUE OF MONEY

When asked if they would rather have $500 today or Smith's IOU for $500 to be paid one year hence, rational decision makers respond that they would rather have $500 today. There are two reasons for this: first, the time value of money and, second, risk. A dollar today is worth more than a dollar tomorrow or at some future time. Having a dollar provides flexibility. It may be spent, buried, or invested in a number of projects. If invested in a savings account, it will amount to more than one dollar at some future time because of the effect of interest. The interest paid by a bank, or borrower, for the use of money is analogous to the rent paid for the use of land, buildings, or equipment. Furthermore, we live in an uncertain world; and, for a variety of reasons, the possibility exists that Smith may not pay his debts as they come due.

FUTURE VALUE

Future value is the amount a current sum of money earning a stated rate of interest will accumulate to at the end of a future period. Suppose you deposit $500 in a savings account at a financial institution that pays interest at the rate of 10 percent per year. At the end of the first year, the original deposit of $500 will have grown to $550 ($500 × 1.10). If you leave the $550 for another year, the amount will grow to $605 ($550 × 1.10). It can be stated that $500 today has a future value in one year of $550, or conversely, that $550 one year from today has a present value of $500. Note that interest of $55 ($605 × $550) was earned in the second year, whereas interest of only $50 was earned in the first year. This is because interest during the second year was earned on the principal plus interest from the first year ($550). When periodic interest is computed on principal plus prior periods' accumulated interest, the interest is said to be compounded. Compound interest is used throughout this text.

To determine future values at the end of one period (usually a year), multiply the beginning amount by 1 plus the interest rate. When multiple periods are involved, the future value is determined by repeatedly multiplying the beginning amount times 1 plus the interest rate for each period. When $500 is invested for 2 years at an interest rate of 10 percent per year, its future value is computed as $500 × 1.10 × 1.10. In general,

$$fv = pv(1 + i)^n$$

where:

$$fv = \text{future value amount}$$
$$pv = \text{present value amount}$$
$$i = \text{interest rate per period}$$
$$n = \text{number of periods}$$

For our $500 deposit, the equation becomes:

$$
\begin{aligned}
fv \text{ of } \$500 &= pv(1 + i)^n \\
&= \$500(1 + 0.10)^2 \\
&= \underline{\underline{\$605}}
\end{aligned}
$$

In a similar manner, once the interest rate and number of periods are known, the future value amount of any present value amount is easily determined.

Present value is the current worth of an amount of money to be received at some future date at some interest rate. Solving for *pv* in the future value equation, the new present value equation is determined as:

$$pv = \frac{fv}{(1 + i)^n}$$

Using the present value equation, the present value of $8,800 to be received in 1 year, discounted at 10 percent, is computed as follows:

$$pv \text{ of } \$8,800 = \frac{\$8,800}{(1 + 0.10)^1}$$

$$= \frac{\$8,800}{1.10}$$

$$= \underline{\underline{\$8,000}}$$

Thus, when the discount rate is 10 percent, the present value of $8,800 to be received in 1 year is $8,000.

The present value equation is often expressed as the future value amount times the present value of $1.00:

$$pv = fv \times \frac{\$1}{(1 + i)^n}$$

Using the equation for the present value of $1, the present value of $8,800 to be received in 1 year, discounted at 10 percent, is computed as follows:

$$pv \text{ of } \$8,800 = \$8,800 \times \frac{\$1}{(1 + 0.10)^1}$$

$$= \$8,800 \times 0.909$$

$$= \underline{\underline{\$8,000}}$$

The present value of $8,800 two periods from now is $7,273, computed as [$8,800/(1.10)^2] or [$8,800 × $1/(1.10)^2].

If a calculator is not available, present value computations can be done by hand. Tables, such as Table 6-1 for the present value of $1.00 at various interest rates and time periods, may be used to simplify hand computations. Using the factors in Table 6-1, the present values of any future amount can be determined. For example, with an interest rate of 10 percent, the present value of the following future amounts to be received in 1 period are as follows:

Future Value Amount		Present Value Factor of $1.00		Present Value
$ 100	×	0.909	=	$ 90.90
628	×	0.909	=	570.85
4,285	×	0.909	=	3,895.07
9,900	×	0.909	=	8,999.10

To further illustrate the use of Table 6-1, consider the following application. Alert Company wants to invest its surplus cash at 12 percent in order to have $10,000 to pay off a long-term note due at the end of 5 years. Table 6-1 shows that the present value factor for $1.00, discounted at 12 percent per year for 5 years, is 0.567. Multiplying $10,000 by 0.567, the present value is determined to be $5,670:

$$pv \text{ of } \$10,000 = \$10,000 \times \text{Present value factor for } \$1$$
$$= \$10,000 \times 0.567$$
$$= \underline{\underline{\$5,670}}$$

Therefore, if Alert invests $5,670 today, it will have $10,000 available to pay off its note in 5 years.

Present value tables are also used to make investment decisions. Assume that the Monroe Company can make an investment that will provide a cash flow of $12,000 at the end of 8 years. If the company demands a rate of return of 14 percent per year, what is the most it will be willing to pay for this investment? From Table 6-1, we find that the present value factor for $1.00, discounted at 14 percent per year for 8 years, is 0.351:

$$pv \text{ of } \$12,000 = \$12,000 \times \text{Present value factor for } \$1$$
$$= \$12,000 \times 0.351$$
$$= \underline{\underline{\$4,212}}$$

If the company demands an annual 14 percent return, the most it would be willing to invest today is $4,212.

ANNUITIES

Not all investments provide a single sum of money. Many investments provide periodic cash flows called annuities. An **annuity** is a series of equal cash flows received or paid over equal intervals of time. Suppose that $100 will be received at the end of each of the next 3 years. If the discount rate is 10 percent, the present value of this annuity can be determined by summing the present value of each receipt:

Year 1	$100 ×	$1/(1 + 0.10)^1$ =	$ 90.90
Year 2	$100 ×	$1/(1 + 0.10)^2$ =	82.65
Year 3	$100 ×	$1/(1 + 0.10)^3$ =	75.13
Total			$ 248.68

Alternatively, the following equation can be used to compute the present value of an annuity with cash flows at the end of each period:

$$pva = \frac{a}{i} \times \left[1 - \frac{1}{(1 + 0.10)^n} \right]$$

where:

pva = present value of an annuity (also called the annuity factor)
i = prevailing rate per period
n = number of periods
a = annuity amount

This equation was used to compute the factors presented in Table 6-2 for an annuity amount of $1.00. The present value of an annuity of $1.00 per period for 3 periods, discounted at 10 percent per period, is as follows:

$$pva \text{ of } \$1 = \frac{\$1}{0.10} \times \left[1 - \frac{1}{(1 + 0.10)^3} \right]$$

$$= 2.487$$

Using this factor, the present value of a $100 annuity can be computed as $100 × 2.487, which yields $248.70. To determine the present value of an annuity of any amount, the annuity factor for $1.00 can be multiplied by the annuity amount.

As an additional illustration of the use of Table 6-2, assume that the Red Kite Company is considering an investment in a piece of equipment that will produce net cash inflows of $2,000 at the end of each year for 5 years. If the company's desired rate of return is 12 percent, an investment of $7,210 will provide such a return:

$$pva \text{ of } \$2,000 = \$2,000 \times \text{Present value factor for an annuity of} \\ \$1 \text{ for 5 periods discounted at 12\%}$$

$$= \$2,000 \times 3.605$$

$$= \$7,210$$

Here, the $2,000 annuity is multiplied by 3.605, the factor for an annuity of $1.00 for 5 periods, discounted at 12 percent per period. This factor is found in Table 6-2.

Another use of Table 6-2 is to determine the amount that must be received annually to provide a desired rate of return on an investment. Assume the Burnsville Company invests $33,550 and desires a return of the investment plus interest of 8 percent in equal payments at the end of each year for 10 years. The minimum amount that must be received each year is determined by solving the equation for the present value of an annuity:

$$pva = a \times (pva \text{ of } \$1)$$

$$a = \frac{pva}{pva \text{ of } \$1}$$

From Table 6-2, we see that the 8 percent factor for 10 periods is 6.710. When the investment of $33,550 is divided by 6.710, the required annuity is computed to be $5,000:

$$a = \frac{\$33,550}{6.710}$$

$$= \$5,000$$

UNEQUAL FLOWS

Many investment situations do not produce equal periodic cash flows. When this occurs, the present value for each cash flow has to be determined independently because the annuity table can be used only for equal periodic cash flows. Table 6-1 is used to determine the present value of each future amount separately. To illustrate, assume the Atlanta Braves wish to acquire the contract of a popular baseball player who is known to attract large crowds. Management believes this player will return incremental cash flows to the team at the end of each of the next 3 years in the amounts of $2,500,000, $4,000,000, and $1,500,000. After 3 years, the player anticipates retiring. If the team's owners require a minimum return on their investment of 14 percent, how much would they be willing to pay for the player's contract?

To solve this problem, it is necessary to determine the present value of the expected future cash flows. Here we use Table 6-1 to find the $1.00 present value factors at 14 percent for periods 1, 2, and 3. The cash flows are then multiplied by these factors:

Year	Annual Cash Flow		Present Value of $1 at 14 Percent		Present Value Amount
1	$2,500,000	×	0.877	=	$2,192,500
2	4,000,000	×	0.769	=	3,076,000
3	1,500,000	×	0.675	=	1,012,500
Total					$6,281,000

The total present value of the cash flows for the three years, $6,281,000, represents the maximum amount the team would be willing to pay for the player's contract.

DEFERRED RETURNS

Many times, organizations make investments for which no cash is received until several periods have passed. The present value of an investment discounted at 12 percent per year, which has a $2,000 return only at the end of Years 4, 5, and 6, can be determined as follows:

Year	Amount		Present Value of $1 at 12 Percent		Present Value Amount
1	$ -0-	×	0.893	=	$ -0-
2	-0-	×	0.797	=	-0-
3	-0-	×	0.712	=	-0-
4	2,000	×	0.636	=	1,272
5	2,000	×	0.567	=	1,134
6	2,000	×	0.507	=	1,014
Total					$3,420

Computation of the present value of the deferred annuity can also be performed using the annuity tables if the cash flow amounts are equal for each period. The present value of an annuity for 6 years, minus the present value of an annuity for 3 years, yields the present value of an annuity for Years 4 through 6.

Present value of an annuity for 6 years at 12 percent: $2,000 × 4.111 = $8,222
Present value of an annuity for 3 years at 12 percent: 2,000 × 2.402 = - 4,804
Present value of the deferred annuity $3,418*

*The difference between the $3,420 above and the $3,418 is caused by rounding error.

Suggested Readings

Kaplan, Robert S. "Must CIM Be Justified by Faith Alone?" *Harvard Business Review* (March-April 1986), pp. 87-95.

Klammer, Thomas. *Managing Strategic and Capital Investment Decisions* (New York: Irwin, 1994).

Shank, John K., and Vijay Govindarajan. "Strategic Cost Analysis of Technological Investments," *Sloan Management Review* (Fall 1992), pp. 39-51.

Review Problem

Survey of Capital Budgeting Models
Consider the following investment proposal:

Initial investment:	
Depreciable assets	$27,740
Working capital	3,000
Operations (per year for 4 years):	
Cash receipts	$25,000
Cash expenditures	15,000
Disinvestment:	
Salvage value of plant and equipment	$ 2,000
Recovery of working capital	3,000

Required:
Determine each of the following:

(a) Net present value at a 10 percent discount rate.
(b) Internal rate of return.
(c) Payback period.
(d) Accounting rate of return on initial investment and on average investment.

The solution to the review problem is found at the end of Chapter 6 assignment material. To maximize your learning, you should make a serious attempt to develop a written solution to the review problem before looking at the solution. If there are errors in your solution, you should then attempt to determine the causes of the errors.

TABLE 6-1: PRESENT VALUE OF $1.00

Present Value of $1.00 $= \dfrac{1}{(1 + r)^n}$

Discount Rate (r)

Periods (n)	6%	8%	10%	12%	14%	16%	18%	20%	22%	24%	26%	28%	30%
1	0.943	0.926	0.909	0.893	0.877	0.862	0.847	0.833	0.820	0.806	0.794	0.781	0.769
2	0.890	0.857	0.826	0.797	0.769	0.743	0.718	0.694	0.672	0.650	0.630	0.610	0.592
3	0.840	0.794	0.751	0.712	0.675	0.641	0.609	0.579	0.551	0.524	0.500	0.477	0.455
4	0.792	0.735	0.683	0.636	0.592	0.552	0.516	0.482	0.451	0.423	0.397	0.373	0.350
5	0.747	0.681	0.621	0.567	0.519	0.476	0.437	0.402	0.370	0.341	0.315	0.291	0.269
6	0.705	0.630	0.564	0.507	0.456	0.410	0.370	0.335	0.303	0.275	0.250	0.227	0.207
7	0.665	0.583	0.513	0.452	0.400	0.354	0.314	0.279	0.249	0.222	0.198	0.178	0.159
8	0.627	0.540	0.467	0.404	0.351	0.305	0.266	0.233	0.204	0.179	0.157	0.139	0.123
9	0.592	0.500	0.424	0.361	0.308	0.263	0.225	0.194	0.167	0.144	0.125	0.108	0.094
10	0.558	0.463	0.386	0.322	0.270	0.227	0.191	0.162	0.137	0.116	0.099	0.085	0.073
11	0.527	0.429	0.350	0.287	0.237	0.195	0.162	0.135	0.112	0.094	0.079	0.066	0.056
12	0.497	0.397	0.319	0.257	0.208	0.168	0.137	0.112	0.092	0.076	0.062	0.052	0.043
13	0.469	0.368	0.290	0.229	0.182	0.145	0.116	0.093	0.075	0.061	0.050	0.040	0.033
14	0.442	0.340	0.263	0.205	0.160	0.125	0.099	0.078	0.062	0.049	0.039	0.032	0.025
15	0.417	0.315	0.239	0.183	0.140	0.108	0.084	0.065	0.051	0.040	0.031	0.025	0.020
16	0.394	0.292	0.218	0.163	0.123	0.093	0.071	0.054	0.042	0.032	0.025	0.019	0.015
17	0.371	0.270	0.198	0.146	0.108	0.080	0.060	0.045	0.034	0.026	0.020	0.015	0.012
18	0.350	0.250	0.180	0.130	0.095	0.069	0.051	0.038	0.028	0.021	0.016	0.012	0.009
19	0.331	0.232	0.164	0.116	0.083	0.060	0.043	0.031	0.023	0.017	0.012	0.009	0.007
20	0.312	0.215	0.149	0.104	0.073	0.051	0.037	0.026	0.019	0.014	0.010	0.007	0.005

TABLE 6-2: PRESENT VALUE OF AN ANNUITY OF $1.00

Present Value of an Annuity of $1.00 $= \dfrac{1}{r}\left(1 - \dfrac{1}{(1+r)^n}\right)$

Discount Rate (r)

Periods (n)	6%	8%	10%	12%	14%	16%	18%	20%	22%	24%	25%	26%	28%	30%
1	0.943	0.926	0.909	0.893	0.877	0.862	0.847	0.833	0.820	0.806	0.800	0.794	0.781	0.769
2	1.833	1.783	1.736	1.690	1.647	1.605	1.566	1.528	1.492	1.457	1.440	1.424	1.392	1.361
3	2.673	2.577	2.487	2.402	2.322	2.246	2.174	2.106	2.042	1.981	1.952	1.923	1.868	1.816
4	3.465	3.312	3.170	3.037	2.914	2.798	2.690	2.589	2.494	2.404	2.362	2.320	2.241	2.166
5	4.212	3.993	3.791	3.605	3.433	3.274	3.127	2.991	2.864	2.745	2.689	2.635	2.532	2.436
6	4.917	4.623	4.355	4.111	3.889	3.685	3.498	3.326	3.167	3.020	2.951	2.885	2.759	2.643
7	5.582	5.206	4.868	4.564	4.288	4.039	3.812	3.605	3.416	3.242	3.161	3.083	2.937	2.802
8	6.210	5.747	5.335	4.968	4.639	4.344	4.078	3.837	3.619	3.421	3.329	3.241	3.076	2.925
9	6.802	6.247	5.759	5.328	4.946	4.607	4.303	4.031	3.786	3.566	3.463	3.366	3.184	3.019
10	7.360	6.710	6.145	5.650	5.216	4.833	4.494	4.192	3.923	3.682	3.571	3.465	3.269	3.092
11	7.887	7.139	6.495	5.938	5.453	5.029	4.656	4.327	4.035	3.776	3.656	3.544	3.335	3.147
12	8.384	7.536	6.814	6.194	5.660	5.197	4.793	4.439	4.127	3.851	3.725	3.606	3.387	3.190
13	8.853	7.904	7.103	6.424	5.842	5.342	4.910	4.533	4.203	3.912	3.780	3.656	3.427	3.223
14	9.295	8.244	7.367	6.628	6.002	5.468	5.008	4.611	4.265	3.962	3.824	3.695	3.459	3.249
15	9.712	8.559	7.606	6.811	6.142	5.575	5.092	4.675	4.315	4.001	3.859	3.726	3.483	3.268
16	10.106	8.851	7.824	6.974	6.265	5.669	5.162	4.730	4.357	4.033	3.887	3.751	3.503	3.283
17	10.477	9.122	8.022	7.120	6.373	5.749	5.222	4.775	4.391	4.059	3.910	3.771	3.518	3.295
18	10.828	9.372	8.201	7.250	6.467	5.818	5.273	4.812	4.419	4.080	3.928	3.786	3.529	3.304
19	11.158	9.604	8.365	7.366	6.550	5.877	5.361	4.844	4.442	4.097	3.942	3.799	3.539	3.311
20	11.470	9.818	8.514	7.469	6.623	5.929	5.353	4.870	4.460	4.110	3.954	3.808	3.546	3.316

KEY TERMS

Accounting rate of return—the average annual increase in net income that results from acceptance of a capital expenditure proposal divided by either the initial investment or the average investment in the project.

Capital budgeting—the identification of potentially desirable projects for capital expenditures, the subsequent evaluation of capital expenditure proposals, and the selection of proposals that meet certain criteria.

Capital expenditures—investments of significant financial resources in projects to develop or introduce new products or services, to expand current production or service capacity, or to change current production or service facilities.

Cost of capital—the average cost of obtaining the resources necessary to make investments.

Depreciation tax shield—the reduction in taxes due to the deductibility of depreciation from taxable revenues.

Discount rate—the minimum rate of return required for the project to be acceptable.

Internal rate of return (IRR) (often called the **time-adjusted rate of return**)—the discount rate that equates the present value of a project's cash inflows with the present value of the project's cash outflows.

Investment tax credit—a reduction in income taxes of a percent of the cost of a new asset in the year the new asset is placed in service.

Mutually exclusive investments—the acceptance of one investment automatically causes the rejection of the other(s).

Net present value—the present value of a project's net cash inflows from operations and disinvestment less the amount of the initial investment.

Payback period—the time required to recover the initial investment in a project from operations.

Present value index—the present value of the project's subsequent cash flows divided by the initial investment.

Time-adjusted rate of return—see **internal rate of return**.

APPENDIX KEY TERMS

Annuity—a series of equal cash flows received or paid over equal intervals of time.

Future value—the amount a current sum of money earning a stated rate of interest will accumulate to at the end of a future period.

Present value—the current worth of a specified amount of money to be received at some future date at some interest rate.

REVIEW QUESTIONS

6-1

What is the relationship between long-range planning and capital budgeting?

6-2

What tasks are often assigned to the capital budgeting committee?

6-3

What purposes are served by a post-audit of approved capital expenditure proposals?

6-4

Into what three phases are a project's cash flows organized?

6-5

State three alternative definitions or descriptions of the internal rate of return.

6-6

Why is the cost of capital an important concept when discounting models are used for capital budgeting?

6-7

What weakness is inherent in the payback period when it is used as the sole investment criterion?

6-8

What weakness is inherent in the accounting rate of return when it is used as an investment criterion?

6-9

Why are the net present value and the internal rate of return models superior to the payback period and accounting rate of return models?

6-10

State two basic differences between the net present value and internal rate of return models that often lead to differences in the evaluation of competing investment proposals.

6-11

Identify several nonquantitative factors that are apt to play a decisive role in the final selection of projects for capital expenditures.

6-12

In what way does depreciation affect the analysis of cash flows for a proposed capital expenditure?

EXERCISES

6-1 Time Value of Money: Basics (Appendix)

Required:

Using the equations and tables in the appendix to this chapter, determine the answers to each of the following independent situations:

(a) The future value in 2 years of $1,000 deposited today in a savings account with interest compounded annually at 8 percent.
(b) The present value of $9,000 to be received in 5 years, discounted at 12 percent.
(c) The present value of an annuity of $2,000 per year for 5 years discounted at 16 percent.
(d) An initial investment of $32,010 is to be returned in 8 equal annual payments. Determine the amount of each payment if the interest rate is 10 percent.
(e) A proposed investment will provide cash flows of $20,000, $8,000, and $6,000 at the end of Years 1, 2, and 3, respectively. Using a discount rate of 20 percent, determine the present value of these cash flows.
(f) Find the present value of an investment that will pay $5,000 at the end of Years 10, 11, and 12. Use a discount rate of 14 percent.

6-2 Time Value of Money: Basics (Appendix)

Required

Using the equations and tables in the appendix to this chapter, determine the answers to each of the following independent situations:

(a) The future value in 2 years of $3,000 invested today in a certificate of deposit with interest compounded annually at 10 percent.
(b) The present value of $8,000 to be received in 5 years, discounted at 8 percent.
(c) The present value of an annuity of $10,000 per year for 4 years discounted at 12 percent.
(d) An initial investment of $14,740 is to be returned in 6 equal annual payments. Determine the amount of each payment if the interest rate is 16 percent.
(e) A proposed investment will provide cash flows of $6,000, $8,000, and $20,000 at the end of Years 1, 2, and 3, respectively. Using a discount rate of 18 percent, determine the present value of these cash flows.
(f) Find the present value of an investment that will pay $6,000 at the end of Years 8, 9, and 10. Use a discount rate of 14 percent.

6-3 NPV, IRR: Equal Annual Net Cash Inflows

The Sharp Company is evaluating a capital expenditure proposal that requires an initial investment of $8,002, has predicted cash inflows of $2,000 per year for 15 years, and has no salvage value.

Required:
(a) Using a discount rate of 14 percent, determine the net present value of the investment proposal.
(b) Determine the proposal's internal rate of return.

6-4 NPV, IRR: Equal Annual Net Cash Inflows

The Tack Company is evaluating a capital expenditure proposal that requires an initial investment of $28,590, has predicted cash inflows of $7,500 per year for 7 years, and has no salvage value.

Required:
(a) Using a discount rate of 16 percent, determine the net present value of the investment proposal.
(b) Determine the proposal's internal rate of return.

6-5 NPV, IRR: Unequal Annual Net Cash Inflows

The Lake Ski Company is evaluating a capital expenditure proposal that has the following predicted cash flows:

Initial investment	$(42,580)
Operation:	
Year 1	18,000
Year 2	25,000
Year 3	20,000
Salvage	0

Required:
(a) Using a discount rate of 12 percent, determine the net present value of the investment proposal.
(b) Determine the proposal's internal rate of return.

6-6 NPV, IRR: Unequal Annual Net Cash Inflows

The Alpine Ski Company is evaluating a capital expenditure proposal that has the following predicted cash flows:

Initial investment	$(40,860)
Operation:	
Year 1	20,000
Year 2	30,000
Year 3	10,000
Salvage	0

Required:
(a) Using a discount rate of 14 percent, determine the net present value of the investment proposal.
(b) Determine the proposal's internal rate of return.

6-7 Payback Period of a Cost Reduction Proposal

Northeast Insurance Company is considering the purchase of new software that can automatically estimate auto repair expenses. It is predicted that the software will save $4 off the cost of processing each claim and will improve customer service. The software and the 3,000 terminals needed for adjusters to use the software would cost $1.5 million. Additional costs of training adjusters to use the software will amount to $500,000. Northeast Insurance processes an average of 200,000 automobile repair claims per year.

Required:
Determine the payback period of the proposed capital expenditure.

6-8 Payback Period, Accounting Rate of Return
Presented is information pertaining to three capital expenditure proposals:

	Proposal A	Proposal B	Proposal C
Initial investment:			
Depreciable assets	$50,000	$100,000	$70,000
Working capital	0	0	10,000
Net cash inflow from operations			
(per year for 4 years)	20,000	35,000	25,000
Disinvestment:			
Depreciable assets	0	20,000	10,000
Working capital	0	0	10,000

Required:
(a) Determine each proposal's payback period.
(b) Determine each proposal's accounting rate of return on:
   (1) Initial investment.
   (2) Average investment.

6-9 Payback Period, IRR, Minimum Cash Flows
The management of Low Risk, Limited is currently evaluating the following investment proposal:

	Time 0	Year 1	Year 2	Year 3	Year 4
Initial investment	$120,000				
Net operating cash					
cash inflows		$50,000	$50,000	$50,000	$50,000

Required:
(a) Determine the proposal's payback period.
(b) Determine the proposal's internal rate of return. Do not interpolate.
(c) Given the amount of the initial investment, determine the minimum annual net cash inflows required to obtain an internal rate of return of 18 percent. Round the answer to the nearest dollar.

6-10 Time-Adjusted Cost-Volume-Profit Analysis
The Seventh Avenue Treat Shop is considering the desirability of producing a new chocolate candy called the "Pleasure Bomb." Before purchasing new equipment required to manufacture Pleasure Bombs, Tracy Smith, the proprietor of the Seventh Avenue Treat Shop, performed the following analysis:

Unit selling price	$ 1.25
Variable manufacturing and selling costs	- 1.15
Unit contribution margin	$ 0.10

Annual fixed costs:	
Depreciation (straight-line for 3 years)	$ 4,000
Other (all cash)	8,000
Total	$ 12,000

Annual break-even sales volume = $12,000 / $0.10 = 120,000 units

Because the expected annual sales volume is 130,000 units, Tracy Smith decided to undertake the production of Pleasure Bombs. This required an immediate investment of $120,000 in equipment that has a life of 3 years and no salvage value. After 3 years, the production of Pleasure Bombs will be discontinued.

Required:
(a) Evaluate the analysis performed by Tracy Smith.
(b) If the Seventh Avenue Treat Shop has a time value of money of 14 percent, should the investment be made with projected annual sales of 130,000 units?
(c) Considering the time value of money, what annual unit sales volume is required to break even?

6-11 Time-Adjusted Cost-Volume-Profit Analysis with Income Taxes (a continuation of 6-10)
Assume the same set of facts as given in Exercise 6-10.

Required:
With a 40 percent tax rate and a 14 percent time value of money, determine the annual unit sales required to break even on a time-adjusted basis.

PROBLEMS

6-12 Ranking Investment Proposals with Payback Period, Accounting Rate of Return, and Net Present Value
Presented is information pertaining to the cash flows of three mutually exclusive investment proposals:

	Proposal X	Proposal Y	Proposal Z
Initial investment	$45,000	$45,000	$45,000
Cash flows from operations:			
Year 1	40,000	22,500	45,000
Year 2	5,000	22,500	
Year 3	22,500	22,500	
Disinvestment	0	0	0
Life	3 years	3 years	1 year

Required:

(a) Rank these investment proposals using the payback period, the accounting rate of return on initial investment, and the net present value criteria. Assume the organization's cost of capital is 14 percent. Round calculations to four decimal places.

(b) Explain the difference in rankings. Which investment would you recommend if unlimited funds were available at the organization's cost of capital?

6-13 Ranking Investment Proposals Using NPV and Present Value Index

The Megabite Dog Food Company is considering the replacement of its traditional canned dog food with dog food packaged in either resealable plastic containers or in disposable foil-lined pouches. Although either alternative will produce significant cost savings and marketing benefits, limitations on available shelf space in stores require management to select only one alternative. Cash flow information on each alternative is presented below:

	Plastic Containers	Lined Pouches
Initial investment in necessary equipment	$50,000	$150,000
Increase in annual net cash flows	$20,000	$ 56,000
Life of equipment	5 years	5 years
Salvage value of equipment	$10,000	$ 12,000

Megabite has a 10 percent cost of capital.

Required:

(a) Evaluate the investment alternatives using the net present value and the present value index criteria.

(b) Explain the difference in rankings. Which investment would you recommend if unlimited funds were available at Megabite's cost of capital?

6-14 Ranking Investment Proposals Using NPV and Present Value Index

The Sea Breeze Cat Sand Company is considering the replacement of its traditional bag packaging of "cat sand" with either reusable plastic pails or reusable aluminum pails. Customers would make a refundable deposit on the container each time they purchased cat sand. Because the pails would be reusable, the net cost of cat sand to customers who returned the pail for a refund would be lower than the cost of cat sand sold in bags. Cash flow information on each alternative is presented below:

	Plastic	Aluminum
Initial investment	$80,000	$68,000
Increase in annual net cash flows	$35,000	$30,000
Life of equipment	4 years	4 years
Salvage value of equipment	$ 8,000	$ 9,000

Sea Breeze has a 16 percent cost of capital.

Required:
(a) Evaluate the investment alternatives using the net present value and the present value index criteria.
(b) Explain the difference in rankings. Which investment would you recommend if unlimited funds were available at Sea Breeze's cost of capital?

6-15 Cost Reduction Proposal: IRR, NPV, and Payback Period

The BJ Company currently discharges liquid waste into the Calgary Municipal Sewer System. However, the Calgary municipal government has informed BJ that a surcharge of $4 per thousand cubic liters will soon be imposed for the discharge of this effluent. This has prompted management to evaluate the desirability of treating its own liquid waste.

A proposed system consists of three elements. The first is a 7,500-liter retention basin, which would permit unusual discharges to be held and treated before entering the downstream system. The second is a continuous self-cleaning rotary filter where solids are removed. The third is an automated neutralization process where materials are added to control the alkalinity-acidity range.

The system is designed to process 500,000 liters a day. However, management anticipates that only about 200,000 liters of liquid waste would be processed in a normal workday. The company operates 300 days per year.

The initial investment in the system would be $400,000, and annual operating costs are predicted to be $150,000. The system has a predicted useful life of 10 years and a salvage value of $50,000.

Required:
(a) Determine the project's net present value at a discount rate of 18 percent.
(b) Determine the project's approximate internal rate of return.
(c) Determine the project's payback period.

6-16 NPV with Income Taxes: Straight-Line versus Accelerated Depreciation

John Paul Jones, Inc. is a conservatively managed boat company whose motto is, "The old ways are the good ways." Management has always used straight-line depreciation for tax and external reporting purposes. While they are reluctant to change, they are aware of the impact of taxes on a project's profitability.

Required:
For a typical $100,000 investment in equipment with a 5-year life and no salvage value, determine the present value of the advantage resulting from the use of double-declining balance depreciation as opposed to straight-line depreciation. Assume an income tax rate of 40 percent and a discount rate of 16 percent. Also assume that there will be a switch from double-declining balance to straight-line depreciation in the fourth year.

6-17 Payback Period, NPV, and PVI with Taxes and Straight-Line Depreciation

Spara is considering the various benefits that may result from the shortening of its production cycle time by changing from the company's present manual system to a computer-aided design/computer-aided manufacturing (CAD/CAM) system. The proposed system can provide productive time equivalency close to the 20,000 hours currently available with the manual system. The out-of-pocket costs of maintaining the manual system are $20 per hour.

The annual out-of-pocket costs of maintaining the CAD/CAM system are estimated to be $200,000, with an initial investment of $480,000. The estimated life of this system is 6 years with no salvage value. The tax rate is 30 percent and Spara will use straight-line depreciation for tax purposes. Spara requires a minimum after-tax return of 20 percent on projects of this type. Full capacity will be utilized.

Required:
(a) Compute the relevant annual after-tax cash flows related to investing in the CAD/CAM project.
(b) Based on the above computation, compute each of the following:
   (1) Payback period.
   (2) Net present value.
   (3) Present value index.   (CPA Adapted)

6-18 NPV with Taxes and Accelerated Depreciation
Assume the same set of facts as given in Exercise 6-17, except that Spara intends to use double-declining balance depreciation with a switch to straight-line depreciation, applied to any undepreciated balance, starting in Year 5.

Required:
Determine the project's net present value.

6-19 NPV Total and Differential Analysis of Replacement Decision
Gusher Petro is evaluating a proposal to purchase a new processor that would cost $120,000 and have a salvage value of $12,000 in 5 years. It would provide annual operating cash savings of $15,000, as detailed below:

	Old Processor	New Processor
Salaries	$34,000	$44,000
Supplies	6,000	5,000
Utilities	13,000	6,000
Cleaning and maintenance	22,000	5,000
Total cash expenditures	$75,000	$60,000

If the new processor is purchased, the old processor will be sold for its current salvage value of $30,000. If the new processor is not purchased, the old processor will be disposed of in 5 years at a predicted scrap value of $2,000. The old processor's present book value is $50,000. If kept, the old processor will require repairs predicted to cost $40,000 in one year.

Gusher's cost of capital is 16 percent.

Required:

(a) Use the total cost approach to evaluate the alternatives of keeping the old processor and purchasing the new processor. Indicate which alternative is preferred.

(b) Use the differential cost approach to evaluate the desirability of purchasing the new processor.

6-20 NPV Total and Differential Analysis of Replacement Decision

The White Snow Automatic Laundry must either have a complete overhaul of its current dry-cleaning system or purchase a new one. White Snow's accountant has developed the following cost projections:

	Present System	New System
Purchase cost new	$40,000	$50,000
Remaining book value	15,000	
Overhaul needed now	20,000	
Annual cash operating costs	35,000	20,000
Current salvage value	10,000	
Salvage value in 5 years	2,500	10,000

If White Snow keeps the old system, the system will have to be overhauled immediately. With the overhaul, the old system will have a useful life of 5 more years.

White Snow has a cost of capital of 20 percent.

Required:

(a) Use the total cost approach to evaluate the alternatives of keeping the old system and purchasing the new system. Indicate which alternative is preferred.

(b) Use the differential cost approach to evaluate the desirability of purchasing the new system.

6-21 NPV Differential Analysis of Replacement Decision

The management of Essen Manufacturing Company is currently evaluating a proposal to purchase a new and innovative drill press as a replacement for a less efficient piece of similar equipment, which would then be sold. The cost of the new equipment, including delivery and installation, is $175,000. If the equipment is purchased, Essen will incur costs of $5,000 in removing the present equipment and revamping service facilities. The present equipment has a book value of $100,000 and a remaining useful life of 10 years. Because of new technical improvements that have made the present equipment obsolete, it now has a disposal value of only $40,000.

Management has provided you with the following tabulation of comparative manufacturing costs:

	Present Equipment	New Equipment
Annual production (units)	400,000	400,000
Annual costs:		
Direct labor	$ 0.075/unit	$ 0.05/unit
Overhead:		
Depreciation (10% of asset's book value)	$ 20,000	$ 17,500
Other	$ 48,000	$ 20,000

Additional information:

- Management believes that if the current equipment is not replaced now, it will have to wait 10 years before replacement is justifiable.
- Both pieces of equipment are expected to have a negligible salvage value at the end of 10 years.
- Management expects to sell the entire annual production of 400,000 units.
- Essen's cost of capital is 14 percent.

Required:

Evaluate the desirability of purchasing the new equipment

DISCUSSION QUESTIONS AND CASES

6-22 Evaluating Data and Using Payback Period for an Investment Proposal

To determine the desirability of investing in a 17-inch super VGA monitor with a super VGA card (as opposed to the typical 14-inch monitor that comes with a new personal computer), the editors of *PC Computing* developed an experiment testing the time required to perform a set of tasks. The tasks included:

- Setting up a meeting using electronic mail
- Reviewing meeting requests
- Checking an on-line schedule
- Embedding a video file into a document
- Searching a customer data base to find a specific set of contracts
- Copying a data base into a spreadsheet
- Modifying a slide presentation

The editors assumed this was a typical set of tasks performed by a manager. They determined that there was a 9 percent productivity gain using the 17-inch monitor. One test manager commented that the largest productivity gain came from being able to have multiple applications open at the same time and from being able to view several slides at once.

Required:

(a) Accepting the 9 percent productivity gain as accurate, what additional information is needed to determine the payback period of an investment in one 17-inch super VGA monitor and a super VGA card that is to be used by a manager?

(b) Make any necessary assumptions and obtain whatever data you can (perhaps from computer component advertisements) to determine the payback period for the proposed investment.

6-23 IRR, NPV with Performance Evaluation Conflict

Pepperoni Pizza Company owns and operates fast-service pizza parlors throughout North America. The firm operates on a regional basis and provides almost complete autonomy to the manager of each region. Regional managers are responsible for long-range planning, capital expenditures, personnel policies, pricing, and so forth. Each year the performance of regional managers is evaluated by determining the accounting return on fixed assets in their regions. To accomplish this, regional net income is divided by the book value of fixed assets at the start of the year. A return of 14 percent is expected. Managers of regions earning a return of more than 16 percent are identified for possible promotion, and managers of regions with a return of less than 12 percent are subject to replacement.

Mr. Light, a hotel and restaurant school graduate, is manager of the Northeast region. He is regarded as a rising star and will be considered for promotion during the next 2 years. Mr. Light has been with Pepperoni for a total of 3 years. During that period, the return on fixed assets in his region, the oldest in the firm, has increased dramatically. He is currently considering a proposal to open 5 new parlors in the Boston area. The total project involves an investment of $640,000 and will double the number of Pepperoni pizzas sold in the Northeast region to a total of 600,000 per year. At an average price of $6 each, total sales revenue will be $3,600,000.

The expenses of operating each of the new parlors include variable costs of $4 per pizza and fixed costs (excluding depreciation) of $80,904 per year. Because each of the new parlors only has a 5-year life and no salvage value, yearly straight-line depreciation will be $25,600 ([$640,000/5 parlors] / 5 years).

Required:

(a) Evaluate the desirability of the $640,000 investment in new pizza parlors by computing the internal rate of return and the net present value. Assume a time value of money of 14 percent.

(b) If Mr. Light is bright, will he approve the expansion? Why or why not? Additional computations are suggested.

6-24 NPV, Project Reevaluation with Taxes, Straight-Line Depreciation

In 19X0, the Bayside Chemical Company prepared the following analysis of an investment proposal for a new manufacturing facility:

	Predicted Cash Inflows (Outflows)	Year(s) of Cash Flows	12% Present Value Factor	Present Value of Cash Flows
	(A)	(B)	(C)	(A) × (C)
Initial investment:				
Fixed assets	$(800,000)	0	1.000	$(800,000)
Working capital	(100,000)	0	1.000	(100,000)
Operations:				
Annual taxable income without depreciation	300,000	1-5	3.605	1,081,500
Taxes on income ($300,000 × 0.34)	(102,000)	1-5	3.605	(367,710)
Depreciation tax shield	54,400*	1-5	3.605	196,112
Disinvestment:				
Site restoration	80,000	5	0.567	(45,360)
Tax shield of restoration ($80,000 × 0.34)	27,200	5	0.567	15,422
Working capital	100,000	5	0.567	56,700
Net present value of all cash flows				$ 36,664

*Computation of depreciation tax shield:

Annual straight-line depreciation ($800,000/5)	$ 160,000
Tax rate	× 0.34
Depreciation tax shield	$ 54,400

Because the proposal had a positive net present value when discounted at Bayside's cost of capital of 12%, the project was approved; and all investments were made at the end of 19X0.

Shortly after production began in January 19X1, a government agency notified Bayside of additional expenditures totaling $200,000 required to bring the plant into compliance with new federal emission regulations. Bayside has the option of either complying with the regulations by December 31, 19X1, or selling the entire operation (fixed assets and working capital) for $250,000 on December 31, 19X1. The improvements will be depreciated over the remaining 4-year life of the plant using straight-line depreciation. The cost of site restoration will not be affected by the improvements.

If Bayside elects to sell the plant, any book loss may be treated as an offset against taxable income on other operations. This tax reduction is an additional cash benefit of selling.

Required:
(a) Should Bayside sell the plant or comply with the new federal regulations? To simplify calculations, assume any additional improvements are paid for on December 31, 19X1.
(b) Would Bayside have accepted the proposal in 19X0 if it was aware of the forthcoming federal regulations?
(c) Do you have any suggestions that might increase the project's net present value? No calculations are required.

6-25 NPV Analysis of Labor-Saving Investment: Cross-Subsidization

The Heavy Loading Company's plant has three production departments. Presented are the actual cost functions for each department:

$$D1: \text{Total annual overhead} = \$150,000 + \$5DLH + \$12MH$$
$$D2: \text{Total annual overhead} = \$185,000 + \$2DLH + \$10MH$$
$$D3: \text{Total annual overhead} = \$50,000 + \$10DLH$$

The direct labor rate is $12 per hour in all departments. Departments 1 and 2 are machine-intensive, while Department 3 is labor-intensive. The fixed overhead in Departments 1 and 2 is related to building occupancy, machine depreciation, and machine maintenance. The fixed overhead in Department 3 is related to building occupancy.

The following requirements are interrelated and concern a decision to introduce labor-saving equipment into Department 3.

Required:

(a) Management is not aware of the actual overhead cost functions. A plantwide overhead rate, based on the historic relationship between total annual overhead for the plant and total direct labor hours for the plant, is used to assign overhead to departments and products.

Presented are the actual number of direct labor hours (DLH) and machine hours (MH) for a typical year:

	Department 1	Department 2	Department 3
Direct labor hours	2,000	5,000	10,000
Machine hours	5,000	20,000	

Determine the plantwide overhead rate per direct labor hour. Also determine the annual overhead assigned to Department 3.

(b) Management, concerned about the high cost of products subject to Department 3 manufacturing operations, is evaluating a proposal to invest in a machine that would substantially reduce the labor content of Department 3 operations. The machine would require an initial investment of $500,000. In addition to fixed maintenance costs of $35,000 per year, the machine would have operating costs of $15 per machine hour. It is predicted that during a typical year the machine would operate 4,000 hours. Direct labor savings would amount to 7,000 hours per year. The machine is estimated to have a life of 5 years with no salvage value.

Heavy Loading's cost of capital is 16 percent. In evaluating the investment proposal, management included overhead cost savings at the plantwide rate per direct labor hour determined in requirement (a). Following management's procedures, determine the investment proposal's net present value. Based on this analysis, indicate whether or not management should accept the proposal.

(c) Assuming no change in costs, except in Department 3, determine the plantwide overhead rate per direct labor hour if the proposal is accepted. Why does the rate change from that computed in requirement (a)? Also determine the annual overhead now assigned to Department 3.

(d) Evaluate the decision to invest in the new machine. Was this the correct decision? Why or why not? Provide additional analysis as appropriate.

(e) Assume Heavy Loading did invest in the machine. Because the machine is special purpose, it does not have any resale value and its scrap value is exactly equal to removal costs. Based on your analysis in requirement (d), what should management do now?

6-26 NPV Analysis of Replacement and Expansion: Relevant Costs

Illinois Products Company manufactures several different products. One of the firm's principal products sells for $20 per unit. The sales manager of Illinois Products has stated repeatedly that he could sell more units of this product if they were available. In an attempt to substantiate his claim, the sales manager conducted a market research study last year at a cost of $44,000 to determine potential demand for this product. The study indicated that Illinois Products could sell 18,000 units of this product annually for the next 5 years.

The equipment currently in use has the capacity to produce 11,000 units annually. The variable production costs are $9 per unit. The equipment has a book value of $60,000 and a remaining useful life of 5 years. The salvage value is negligible now and will be zero in 5 years.

A maximum of 20,000 units could be produced annually on a new machine, which could be purchased for $300,000. The new machine has an estimated life of 5 years and no salvage value. Illinois Products' production manager has estimated that the new equipment would produce production efficiencies that would reduce the variable production costs to $7 per unit.

The sales manager felt so strongly about the need for additional capacity that he attempted to prepare an economic justification for the equipment even though this was not part of his responsibilities. His analysis, presented below, disappointed him because it did not justify acquiring the equipment.

Required investment:	
Purchase price of new equipment	$ 300,000
Loss on disposal of old equipment	60,000
Cost of market research study	44,000
Total investment	$ 404,000
Annual returns:	
Contribution from product:	
Using new equipment (20,000 x [$20 - $7])	$ 260,000
Using existing equipment (11,000 x [$20 - $9])	- 121,000
Increase in contribution	$ 139,000
Less depreciation ($300,000/5 years)	- 60,000
Increase in income	$ 79,000
Less 20 percent cost of capital on additional required investment (0.20 × $404,000)	- 80,800
Net annual return of proposed investment in new equipment	$ (1,800)

Illinois Products Company has a 20 percent cost of capital.

Required:

(a) The controller of Illinois Products Company plans to prepare a discounted cash flow analysis of this investment proposal and has asked you to prepare correct calculations of:

(1) The required investment in the new equipment.

(2) The recurring annual cash flows.

Explain the treatment of each item you treat differently from the original analysis prepared by the sales manager.

(b) Calculate the net present value of the proposed investment in the new equipment and indicate whether the investment proposal is acceptable.

(CMA Adapted)

6-27 Project Screening and Evaluation with Risk: Multiple Criteria

Transhemisphere uses a capital budgeting committee to evaluate and approve capital expenditure proposals. Because the committee is composed of busy executives, a staff has been assigned to assist the committee in the mechanical aspects of proposal evaluation. As a member of this staff, you have been requested to evaluate five mutually exclusive capital expenditure proposals.

Transhemisphere uses multiple criteria in the evaluation of capital expenditure proposals. The criteria are designed to consider the time period monies invested in a project are unavailable for other purposes, the maximum possible time-adjusted loss on a project, and the time-adjusted relative profitability of a project. To assist in monitoring accepted proposals, the committee also requests information regarding the minimum annual cash flows required for time-adjusted break-even. The criteria are applied on a sequential basis, with only proposals that meet the earlier criteria receiving further evaluation.

Specific procedures you are to follow are as follows:

1. Only proposals having an expected bailout and/or payback period of 3 years or less are subject to further evaluation. The bailout period is the time it takes to recover the investment in a project from any source, including disposal.

2. Evaluate the net present value of the pessimistic cash flows associated with each project using Transhemisphere's cost of capital of 16 percent. Projects whose pessimistic cash flows have a negative net present value of $50,000 or more are eliminated from further consideration.

3. Rank the remaining projects on the basis of the internal rate of return of their expected cash flows.

4. For the highest ranked project, determine the minimum annual net cash inflows needed to provide an internal rate of return equal to the company's cost of capital.

Information pertaining to the five capital expenditure proposals you have been asked to evaluate is presented below in thousands of dollars (000):

| Proposal | Initial Investment | Disposal Value at End of Year | | | Pessimistic | | Expected | |
		1	2	3	Annual Net Cash Inflow	Life	Annual Net Cash Inflow	Life
A	$196	$150	$100	$ 0	$ 40	7 years	$ 50	10 years
B	500	400	350	0	75	10 years	110	12 years
C	400	300	100	0	40	8 years	50	10 years
D	420	250	200	150	100	7 years	100	10 years
E	250	150	75	0	15	9 years	75	12 years

The nature of the investments is such that none of them has a disposal value after the end of its third year.

Required:

(a) Following Transhemisphere's capital budgeting procedures, evaluate the five proposals. Round calculations to the nearest dollar. Do not interpolate.

(b) Regardless of Transhemisphere's procedures, which proposal do you recommend and why?

6-28 Post-Audit and Reevaluation of Investment Proposal: NPV

The Anthony Company's capital budgeting committee is evaluating a capital expenditure proposal for the production of a stereo tuner to be sold as an add-on feature for television sets not equipped for stereophonic sound. The proposal calls for an independent contractor to construct the necessary facilities by 12/31/X0 at a total cost of $250,000. Payment for all construction costs will be made on that date, and an additional $50,000 in cash will be made available on 12/31/X0 for working capital to support sales and production activities.

Management anticipates that the stereo tuner has a limited market life because of the high probability that by 19X7 all quality television sets will have built-in stereo tuners. Accordingly, the proposal specifies that production will cease on 12/31/X6. The investment in working capital will be recovered on that date, and the production facilities will be sold for $30,000. Predicted net cash inflows from operations for 19X1 through 19X6 are as follows:

19X1	$100,000
19X2	100,000
19X3	100,000
19X4	40,000
19X5	40,000
19X6	40,000

The Anthony Company has a time value of money of 16 percent. For capital budgeting purposes, all cash flows are assumed to occur at the end of each year.

Required:

(a) Evaluate the capital expenditure proposal using the net present value method. Should Anthony accept the proposal?

(b) Assume the capital expenditure proposal is accepted, but construction delays caused by labor unrest and difficulties in obtaining the necessary construction permits delay the completion of the project. Payments totaling $200,000 were made to the construction company on 12/31/X0 for 19X0 construction. However, completion is now scheduled for 12/31/X1, and an additional $100,000 will be required to complete construction. If the project is continued, the additional $100,000 will be paid on 12/31/X1 and the plant will begin operations on 1/1/X2.

Because of the cost overruns, the capital budgeting committee requests a reevaluation of the project in early 19X1, before agreeing to any additional expenditures. After much effort, the following revised predictions of net operating cash inflows are developed:

19X2	$120,000
19X3	100,000
19X4	40,000
19X5	40,000
19X6	40,000

The working capital investment and disinvestment and the plant salvage values are not changed, except that the cash for working capital would now be made available on 12/31/X1.

Use the net present value method to reevaluate the initial decision to accept the proposal. Given the currently available information about the project, should it have been accepted in 19X0? (*Hint:* Determine the net present value as of 12/31/X0, assuming management has not committed Anthony to the proposal.)

(c) Given the situation that exists in early 19X1, should management continue or cancel the project? Assume the facilities have a current salvage value of $50,000. (*Hint:* Assume the decision is being made on 1/1/X1.)

6-29 Post-Audit and Reevaluation of Investment Proposal: IRR

Throughout his four years in college, Ronald King worked at the local Beef Burger Restaurant in College City. Although the working conditions were good and the pay was not bad, Ron believed he could do a much better job of managing the restaurant than the current owner-manager. In particular, Ron believed that the proper use of marketing campaigns and sales incentives, such as selling a second burger for a 25 percent discount, could increase annual sales by 50 percent.

Just before graduation in 19X2, when Ron inherited $500,000 from his great-uncle, he decided to give serious consideration to buying the restaurant. It seemed like a good idea because he liked the town and its college atmosphere, knew the business, and always wanted to work for himself. He also knew that the current owner wanted to sell the restaurant and retire to Florida.

As part of a small business management course, Ron developed the following income statement for the restaurant's 19X1 operations:

Beef Burger Restaurant: College City
Income Statement
For the Year Ending December 31, 19X1

Sales		$ 450,000
Expenses:		
Cost of food	$150,000	
Supplies	20,000	
Employee expenses	140,000	
Utilities	28,000	
Property taxes	20,000	
Insurance	10,000	
Advertising	8,000	
Depreciation	60,000	436,000
Net income		$ 14,000

Ron believed the cost of food and supplies were all variable, the employee expenses and utilities were half variable and half fixed in 19X1, and all other expenses were fixed.

If Ron purchased the restaurant and followed through on his plans, he believed there would be a 50 percent increase in unit sales volume and all variable costs. Of the fixed costs, only advertising would increase by $12,000. The use of discounts and special promotions would, however, limit the increase in sales revenue to only 40 percent even though sales volume increased 50 percent.

Required:
(a) Determine:
  (1) The current annual net cash inflow.
  (2) The predicted annual net cash inflow if Ron executes his plans and his assumptions are correct.
(b) Ron believes his plan would produce equal net cash inflows during each of the next 15 years, the period remaining on a long-term lease for the land the restaurant is built on. At the end of that time, the restaurant would have to be demolished at a predicted net cost of $80,000. Assuming Ron would otherwise invest the money in bonds expected to yield 12 percent, determine the maximum amount he could pay for the restaurant.
(c) Assume Ron accepts an offer from the current owner to buy the restaurant for $400,000. Unfortunately, while the expected increase in sales volume does occur, customers make much more extensive use of the promotions than Ron had anticipated. As a result, total sales revenues are 8 percent below projections. Furthermore, to improve employee attitudes, Ron gave a 10 percent raise immediately after purchasing the restaurant.
  Reevaluate the initial decision using the actual sales revenue and the increase in labor costs, assuming conditions will remain unchanged

over the remaining life of the project. Was the investment decision a wise one? Round calculations to the nearest dollar.

(d) Ron can sell the restaurant to a large franchise operator for $300,000. Alternatively, he believes that additional annual marketing expenditures and changes in promotions costing $20,000 per year can bring the sales revenues up to their original projections, *with no other changes in costs*. Should Ron sell the restaurant or keep it and make the additional expenditures? Round calculations to the nearest dollar. (*Hint:* Ron has just bought the restaurant.)

SOLUTION TO REVIEW PROBLEM

Basic computations:

Initial investment:

Depreciable assets	$27,740
Working capital	3,000
Total	$30,740

Operation:

Cash receipts	$25,000
Cash expenditures	- 15,000
Net cash inflow	$10,000

Disinvestment:

Sale of depreciable assets	$ 2,000
Recovery of working capital	3,000
Total	$ 5,000

(a)

Net present value at a 10 percent discount rate:

	Predicted Cash Inflows (Outflows)	Year(s) of Cash Flows	10% Present Value Factor	Present Value of Cash Flows
	(A)	(B)	(C)	(A) × (C)
Initial investment	$(30,740)	0	1.000	$(30,740)
Operation	10,000	1-4	3.170	31,700
Disinvestment	5,000	4	0.683	3,415
Net present value of all cash flows				$ 4,375

(b)

Internal rate of return:

Because the proposal has a positive net present value when discounted at 10 percent, its internal rate of return must be greater than 10 percent. Through a trial-and-error approach, the internal rate of return is determined to be 16 percent.

	Predicted Cash Inflows (Outflows)	Year(s) of Cash Flows	16% Present Value Factor	Present Value of Cash Flows
	(A)	(B)	(C)	(A) × (C)
Initial investment	$(30,740)	0	1.000	$ (30,740)
Operation	10,000	1-4	2.798	27,980
Disinvestment	5,000	4	0.552	2,760
Net present value of all cash flows				$ 0

(c)

Payback period = $30,740/$10,000

= 3.074 years

(d)

Accounting rate of return on initial and average investments:

Annual net cash inflow from operations	$10,000
Less average annual depreciation ([$27,740 - $2,000]/4)	- 6,435
Average annual increase in net income	$ 3,565

$$\text{Average investment} = (\$30,740 + \$5,000)/2$$

$$= \$17,870$$

$$\frac{\text{Accounting rate of return}}{\text{on initial investment}} = \frac{\$ 3,565}{\$30,740}$$

$$= 0.1160 \text{ or } 11.60\%$$

$$\frac{\text{Accounting rate of return}}{\text{on average investment}} = \frac{\$ 3,565}{\$17,870}$$

$$= 0.1995 \text{ or } 19.95\%$$

PART ▸ 3

▸ BUDGETING AND
PROFITABILITY ANALYSIS

OPERATIONAL BUDGETING

Budgets quantify future plans of action and are an integral part of the planning and control cycle of an organization. This cycle involves anticipating future activities before they happen and undertaking measures to ensure they occur in a way that is in the best interest of the organization. More than simply forecasting what will take place and reporting what actually did take place this cycle is an ongoing process of guiding, monitoring, and governing the organization. The cycle generally has the following phases:

1. Planning the activities of the organization as a whole and as subunits.
2. Providing a frame of reference and a set of specific expectations against which actual results are measured and compared.
3. Analyzing variations from plans and taking corrective action when needed.
4. Evaluating results, providing various forms of feedback, changing conditions, and setting the stage for the next planning period.

In this and the next three chapters, a structure for planning and controlling is developed, along with alternative procedures for reporting activities within this structure. Budgeting is an integral part of this planning and controlling process.

*The process of projecting the operations of an organization and their financial impact into the future is called operations budgeting. An **operating budget** is a set of formal financial documents that details expected revenues and expenses, as well as all other expected operating and financing transactions for a future period of time (usually one year). It is a plan of action. **The purpose of this chapter is to discuss the basic concepts and benefits of operating budgets, as well as alternative approaches to budget preparation.** An example of a complete operations budget is developed, starting with the forecasting of sales and concluding with the preparation of pro forma financial statements. Throughout the chapter, consideration is given to the behavioral implications of budgeting and the difficulties and problems often encountered in operations budgeting.*

JUSTIFICATIONS OF BUDGETING

L O 1

Budgets are a major component of the management control system. Budgeting requires making estimates about future needs and developments that may be difficult to predict and even more difficult to control. Many future events almost defy accurate prediction (e.g., a company trying to anticipate the cost of complying with union demands or federal regulations). Despite the difficulty and the inherent uncertainty involved in budgeting, numerous benefits normally accrue to firms whose managers engage in operations budgeting. These benefits include: improved planning, improved communications and coordination among organizational elements, and an improved basis of performance evaluation. The budget quantifies management's overall expectations of future income, cash flow, and financial position.

Budgeting is the process of planning for a future period and, as applied to the accounting aspects of an organization, requires management to systematically examine what is anticipated in their financial environment. Budgeting builds on historical information and performance to predict future performance. This look into the future invariably compels management to establish goals and objectives for the future; and, maybe more important, it helps management identify major problems that may develop later if corrective action is not taken. Managers prepare budgets that are both financial (expectations of revenues and expenses) and nonfinancial (expectations of physical needs such as equipment, space, personnel, and research). Note, however, that budgets of nonfinancial items have implications for financial expenditures (e.g., additional space needs must be paid for through either leasing or purchasing). This chapter concentrates on financial budgets.

Budgeting moves the organization from an informal "reactive" style to a formal "proactive" style of management. As a result, less time is spent solving unanticipated problems, and more time is spent on positive measures and preventative actions. The operating budget encompasses the entire organization; hence, its preparation requires the participation of all levels of management. The process of compiling, reviewing, and revising budget data requires managers to communicate with each other and with subordinates and superiors. Once completed, the operating budget becomes the plan of action for the entire organization and must, therefore, reflect the coordinated efforts of all components of the organization. The production and sales managers cannot make their plans independent of each other. The personnel department must know the needs of all other departments before it can budget its needs for new employees and training costs. The final version of the operating budget emerges after an extensive, often lengthy process of communication and coordination. It represents a synthesis of the experience and knowledge of management at every level of the organization.

Effective control requires a basis for evaluating performance. The traditional bases for evaluating performance are historical, industry, and budgeted data. The first two bases have some disadvantages. If *historical* data regarding the firm's performance are used for evaluating current performance, past inefficiencies may be allowed to continue as long as the organization operates at the same level. Also, changes in the organization's operating environment will not be reflected in the basis on which performance is evaluated. A properly developed budgeting system should require managers to examine the items under their control and detect any inefficiencies and changes in the operating environment.

Using *industry* data to evaluate performance has the disadvantage of comparing one organization to other companies that may be substantially different from it, thus leading to erroneous conclusions. Comparisons of one organization with others in an industry may be interesting, and they may provide a general perspective or benchmark of how well one organization is doing compared to similar ones; but this is usually a poor basis for evaluating management's performance for a particular operating period.

Budgeted data prepared for the period under review is a more realistic basis for evaluating performance than is historical data because the benchmarks are relevant and current. For example, sales this year may be higher than last year's, or utilities may be lower; but without additional information these items may not be favorable. Also, budgeted data allows consideration of future opportunities that would be ignored using historical data. Comparing actual and budgeted data produces variances that are meaningful measures of performance versus just saying that we were better or worse than we were last year.

MOTIVATIONAL ASPECTS AND HUMAN BEHAVIOR

L O 2

All organizations are composed of individuals who perform a wide variety of activities in pursuit of the organization's common goals. To accomplish these goals, it is important for management to recognize the effects that budgeting and performance evaluation methods and techniques may have on the behavior of the people in the organization.

Budgeting often produces strong reactions from employees. Some managers use budgets in such a way that employees perceive the budgets as a means of squeezing the last unit of productivity out of them. Budgets should serve as a means of identifying and rewarding good performance and identifying people and areas that need assistance. Because people inherently dislike restrictions on their behavior, we often hear only the negative aspects of budgeting. Budgeting can and should be used as a means of promoting productive behavior in people without threatening their security and self-esteem.

Properly used, an operating budget is an effective mechanism for motivating employees to higher levels of performance and productivity. Improperly developed and administered, it can foster feelings of animosity toward both management and the budget process. Behavioral research has generally concluded that when employees participate in the preparation of budgets and believe that the budgets represent fair standards for evaluating their performance, they receive personal satisfaction from accomplishing the goals set forth in the budgets. A specific example of such an application is found in Management Accounting Practice 7-1 where General Dynamics has implemented a management control system involving both managers and project team members.

Another important motivational aspect of operating budgets is related to management's recognition that budgets are not perfect. Mistakes in prediction and judgment are sometimes made, and unforeseen circumstances often develop, necessitating modification of the budget. Unless top management is willing to recognize when changes in the budget are needed, support for the budget at lower levels will quickly erode. If an organization is to receive maximum benefit from the budget process, support for the budget at the top management level, as well as at lower levels, must be maintained. Achieving this support may be the most difficult challenge facing an organization undertaking budgeting for the first time. Lower-level managers are not likely to respect the budget and the related performance reports if they perceive a lack of commitment by top management. Disregard for the budget by top management can quickly destroy the effectiveness of the budget throughout the organization.

In summary, managers who follow the suggestions below are more likely to be successful in using budgets as a positive motivational tool for accomplishing organizational goals through people.

1. Emphasize the importance of budgeting as a planning device.
2. Encourage wide participation in budget preparation at all levels of management.
3. Demonstrate through appropriate communications that the budget has the complete support of top management.
4. Recognize that the budget is not unalterable; that is, it may require modification if conditions change.
5. Use budget performance reports not just to identify poor performers, but also to recognize good performance.
6. Conduct programs in budget education to provide new managers with information about the purposes of budgets and to dispel erroneous misconceptions that may exist.

GENERAL APPROACHES TO BUDGETING

L O 3

Before an organization can develop operating budgets, management must decide which approaches to budgeting planning will be used for the various revenue and expenditure activities and organizational units. Widely used planning approaches to budgeting include: (1) the input/output approach, (2) the activity-based approach, (3) the incremental approach, and (4) the minimum level approach.

MANAGEMENT ACCOUNTING PRACTICE 7-1

Buying into Budgets at General Dynamics

General Dynamics uses a management control system called Cost Account Directive (CAD) as a means of securing both employee adherence to budgets and schedules and cooperation across functional lines—in an organization that pulls teams together from different functional groups. CAD can be used as a practical method of project management and control by almost any organization.

CAD describes the work to be completed (in a detailed task description) and helps build a project spreadsheet (the personnel, materials, expenses, computer time, and schedule necessary for the project). The four goals of each cost account directive are: (1) coordinating the goals of a project's manager with the goals of project team members from different functional groups; (2) motivating employees through specific goal setting; (3) monitoring the project's progress through budgeting; and (4) providing more accurate time and cost estimates. Although such a budget control process may appear time-consuming and complicated, it is a useful management tool when implemented correctly.

Based on: Terence J. Plaza and Mary M. K. Fleming, "Cost Account Directive—An Effective Man-

Input/Output Approach

The **input/output approach** budgets physical inputs and costs as functions of planned activity. This approach is often used for manufacturing and distribution activities where there are clearly defined relationships between effort and accomplishment. For example, if each unit produced requires 2 pounds of direct materials that cost $5 each, and the planned production volume is 25 units, then the budgeted inputs and costs for direct materials are 50 (25 units × 2 pounds per unit) and $250 (50 pounds × $5 per pound), respectively. Note that the budgeted inputs are a function of the planned outputs. The input/output approach starts with the planned outputs and works backward to budget the inputs. In evaluating the proposed budget, management would focus their attention on the physical and cost relationships between the inputs and the outputs. For variable costs, the input/output approach is most appropriate. This approach is seldom used for activities that do not have clearly defined input/output relationships such as advertising, research and development, and executive education.

Activity-Based Approach

The **activity-based approach** also budgets physical inputs and costs as functions of planned activity but reduces the distortions in the transformation through emphasis on the activity cost hierarchy. (See Chapter 4.) The focus is on determining the cost of planned activities for a process, department, service, product, or other budget objective of interest. Costs are budgeted on the basis of the cost objective's anticipated consumption of cost drivers.

The amount of each activity cost driver used by each budget objective product or service is determined and multiplied by the cost per unit of the activity cost driver. The result is an estimate of the costs of each product or service based on nonvolume-sensitive drivers such as assembly line setup or inspection, as well as the traditional volume-sensitive drivers such as direct material quantities. Activity-based budgeting predicts costs of budget objectives by adding all costs of the activity cost drivers that each product or service is budgeted to consume. In evaluating the proposed budget, management would focus their attention on identifying the optimal set of activities rather than just input/output relationships.

Incremental Approach

The **incremental approach** budgets costs for a coming period as a dollar or percentage change from the amount budgeted for (or spent during) some previous period. This approach is often used where the relationships between inputs and outputs are weak or nonexistent and particularly where discretionary fixed costs dominate. For example, it is difficult to establish a clear relationship between sales volume and advertising expenditures. Consequently, the budgeted amount of advertising for some coming period is often based on the budgeted or actual advertising expenditures in a previous period. If budgeted advertising expenditures for 19X1 were $200,000, the budgeted expenditures for 19X2 would be some increment, say 5 percent, above $200,000. In evaluating the proposed 19X2 budget, management would accept the $200,000 base and focus their attention only on a justification for the increment.

This approach to budgeting is widely used in government and other not-for-profit organizations. In seeking an annual budget appropriation, a manager operating under the incremental approach would be required to justify only proposed expenditures in excess of the previous budget appropriation. The primary advantage of the incremental approach is that it simplifies the budget process by considering only the increments in the various budget items. A major disadvantage is that existing waste and inefficiencies may escalate year after year without ever being discovered.

Minimum Level Approach

Using the **minimum level approach,** an organization establishes a base amount for all budget items and requires explanation or justification for any budgeted amount above the minimum. Under this method, some minimum amount of expenditures is presumed necessary to support ongoing activities in the organization. This method is very useful where many committed costs continue from period to period. Proponents of this approach maintain that requiring extensive justifications of budget items up to the minimum amount is an ineffective use of managerial time. Like the incremental approach, the minimum level approach is often used for activities that do not have clearly defined input/output relationships. For example, the corporate director of product development would need some minimum provision in the budget to support a minimum level of activity for ongoing projects. Additional increments might also be included, first, to support the current level of product development and, second, to undertake desirable new projects.

All four approaches are often used in the same organization. A manufacturing firm might, for example, use the input/output approach to budget distribution expenditures; the activity-based approach to budget its products and services; the incremental approach to budget administrative salaries, advertising, and contributions; and the minimum level approach to budget research and development, employee training, and computer operations.

BUDGET PREPARATION

L O 4

Budget preparation, while guided by the organization's general approach, must involve managers and other employees throughout the organization. Basic considerations of budget preparation must include one or a combination of the above mentioned approaches, a developmental procedure, some means of forecasting revenues or sales, and a department or committee to gather and formalize the budget.

Participation

There are probably no two organizations that use the same budget development procedures, but there are two approaches to budgeting that seem to characterize budget preparation in most organizations: the *imposed budget* and the *participation budget*. These are sometimes referred to as, respectively, the *top-down* approach and the *bottom-up* approach.

Under the **imposed budget, or top-down,** approach to budget preparation, top management decides on the primary goals and objectives for the whole organization and communicates these to lower management levels. This *nonparticipative* approach to budgeting can have serious motivational consequences. Personnel who do not participate in budget preparation are likely to lack a commitment to achieve their part of the budget. The prior section on motivational aspects of budgeting considered several problems when employees were ignored in the budgeting process. However, this approach can be a big timesaver because a minimum of people are involved in the process and because it minimizes the slack that managers at lower organizational levels are sometimes prone to build into their budgets.

The **participation budget** uses the benefits of improved communication, coordination, and motivation. The participation budget requires managers at all levels—and in some cases even nonmanagers—to become involved in budget preparation. This approach is sometimes referred to as the **bottom-up approach** and stresses employee empowerment. Budget proposals are made first at the lowest level of management and then are integrated into the proposals for the next level, and so on, until the proposals reach the top level of management where the budget is completed. Although the imposed budget approach was used quite frequently in the past, today most companies encourage greater participation in budget preparation, as discussed in Management Accounting Practice 7-2.

In the participative approach to budgeting, managers who are directly responsible for a given area have the initial input into the budgeting process for that area. This builds confidence into the budgeting process at the operating levels of the organization and is likely to promote a better budgeting system. Budget predictions are likely to be more accurate, and the person responsible for the budget is more likely to strive to accomplish its objectives. These *self-imposed budgets* reinforce the concept of participative management and should strengthen the overall budgeting process.

Participative budgeting approaches also have several disadvantages that must be considered. Because they require many people to become involved in the budgeting process, the period of preparation can often take several weeks or months. The further the budgeting process is from the beginning of the period being budgeted, the lower the confidence in the ability to predict what will happen. For example, if sales volume for the budget period starting in January has to be predicted in August, it is probably not as reliable as a sales forecast predicted in November. Continually changing events in the organization, in the economy, and with competitors during the additional months all combine to make predictions more difficult and less accurate.

Another potential disadvantage is padding the budget at different developmental stages to ensure that the budgeted amounts can be easily met during the period. Unless each successively higher management level is thoroughly familiar with the activities below it, padding can be easily accomplished. To overcome, or at least to minimize, budget padding, the management of the budgeting process must be carefully planned and executed.

MANAGEMENT ACCOUNTING PRACTICE 7-2

Bottom-Up Budgeting at Johnson & Johnson

Johnson & Johnson has an elaborate planning and budgeting process. "It encompasses every aspect of the business and requires managers to reassess constantly budget goals and action plans." The budget is detailed down to the expense center level for each operating division for each year. It also includes a second-year forecast in somewhat less detail.

In addition, "budget projections are prepared from the bottom up." The requirements for the budget are never issued by top management in advance of budget preparation. All initial inputs for the budget come from the operating departments. Final budgets are then developed with reference to the long-range plans of the company. After about six months of preparation and review at all levels, the budgets for the upcoming year and the second-year forecasts are presented and discussed at the corporate executive level.

Based on: Robert Simons, "Planning, Control, and Uncertainty: A Process View," in *Accounting and Management Field Study Perspective*, William J. Bruns, Jr., and Robert S. Kaplan, ed. (Boston: Harvard Business School Press, 1987), pp. 339-349.

Forecasts

Also important to budget preparation are the types of forecasts used. Though the sales forecast is primary to most organizations, other types of forecasts vary in importance. Other forecasts or predictions often used include: estimates of uncollectibles, production output as a ratio of resources input, production days available, employee turnover and subsequent training of new employees, and cash balance needs per month. Because of the diverse sources of these predictions, the preparation process requires coordination of most of the functions in an organization. Unfortunately, with the forecasts come new and additional demands by those providing input; for example, marketing wants to change the size of the product unit, production wants to operate only four days a week, and the treasurer wants a smaller daily cash balance.

Oversight

Obviously, all requests cannot be included in the budget. Someone must be responsible for deciding which requests are most important to the organization. Many organizations have a **budget committee** that is responsible for supervising budget preparation and serves as a review board for evaluating requests for discretionary cost items and new projects. The final responsibility for decisions rests with the budget committee, which is usually composed of top-level managers.

Larger companies sometimes have a **budget office**, responsible to the controller, that performs a staff function of assisting the budget committee. The budget office is responsible for the preparation, distribution, and processing of forms used in gathering budget data and handles most of the work of actually formulating the budget schedules and reports. The budget office staff may also assist the budget committee by preparing various analyses and special reports. Some large organizations even have a full-time budgeting staff who works year-round on the budget. This does not mean that it takes twelve months to prepare the budget or that once the annual budget is completed the budgeting staff has nothing else to do until the next year. Preparing a budget may take most of the year in some companies; also, the final budget is really never final—it may have to be revised several times during the course of the budget period. Furthermore, the multiyear, long-range plans of many companies are continuously updated to reflect changing conditions. Revisions and updating are part of the responsibility of the budget office.

Budgeting Periods

Up to this point, the normal budget period has been assumed to be one year. Although the annual budget period is certainly the most common, many organizations (ice cream vendors at the beach) budget for shorter periods (such as a month or a quarter of a year), while others (builders of hydroelectric power dams) budget for longer periods (such as two years, five years, or more). In addition to fixed-length budget periods, two other types of budget periods are commonly used, *cycle budgeting* and *continuous budgeting*.

For some businesses, a fixed time period is not particularly relevant to the planning of operations. A company engaged in large construction projects might find it more advantageous to prepare a budget for the project's entire life, which may be more than a year in some cases and less than a year in others. In these cases, the firm may use **life-cycle budgeting,** which is appropriate when the entire life of the project represents a more useful planning horizon than an artificial period of one year. Such cycles could be reduced to shorter planning periods by breaking the overall project into several components such as construction phases.

Under **continuous budgeting,** the budget is based on a moving time frame that extends over a fixed period. For example, an organization on a continuous four-quarter budget system adds a quarter to the budget at the end of each quarter of operations, thereby always maintaining a budget four quarters into the future. Under this system, plans for a full year into the future are always available; whereas under a fixed annual budget, operating plans for a full year ahead are available only at the beginning of the budget year. Because managers are constantly involved in this type of budgeting, the budget process becomes an active and integral part of the management process. Managers are forced to be future-oriented throughout the year, rather than just once each year. Continuous budgeting, which is now feasible with the aid of computers, helps to elevate the level of visibility and recognition of the planning function.

POTENTIAL PROBLEMS OF BUDGETING

L O 5

Like many other tools available to managers, budgeting offers the potential for vast benefits but also has potential pitfalls and problems. This section briefly mentions some of the more important problems that may be encountered in budgeting.

Preparation Time

Preparing a budget for a large organization can be a massive task, requiring hundreds, and perhaps thousands, of hours of valuable management time. Careful coordination and planning are required to keep budget preparation from becoming too onerous for managers or from interfering with their other responsibilities. This is particularly a problem for managers in large organizations that use participative (bottom-up) budgeting. To minimize the time required by each manager, the budget preparation calendar should be carefully planned, and easy-to-use forms should be provided.

Various types of budgeting models are in use today, thanks to the computer, that can save managers substantial amounts of time. Many of the models provide what-if and sensitivity analysis so that the manager can quickly examine the potential results of various cost objectives, cost drivers, and cost combinations. Even organizations with small computers and microcomputers can take advantage of the budgeting models as they have been adapted for all sizes of computers.

Accuracy

In some cases, the prediction ability of management is very limited. The more limited management's ability to make the accurate forecasts and predictions that are necessary for the budget, the more limited the usefulness of a single budget becomes. This is particularly true for newer businesses. Rapidly changing economic conditions also make budgeting difficult. Even then, however, managers who study the budgetary impact of possible changes can learn what factors to monitor most closely and how to develop contingency plans that can be implemented if needed. Many statistical and mathematical techniques, such as those discussed in Chapter 2, are available to improve the reliability of the budget data.

Budgetary Slack

Budgetary slack, sometimes referred to as "padding the budget," occurs when managers intentionally request more funds in the budget for their departments than they need to support the anticipated level of operations. If a department consistently produces large, favorable variances—or even small, favorable variances with little apparent effort—this may be a symptom of slack built into the budget. The desire by managers to pad their budgets may indicate poor relations between upper and lower management or poor administration of the budget.

Economy and Industry Factors

Although each organization is a unique entity whose peculiar characteristics are reflected in its operations budget, most organizations are also affected by general economic or industry conditions. Any inability to obtain accurate and reliable information about these conditions can pose serious problems for managers trying to make predictions about their own companies. For example, many organizations that depend on external sources of funds often find it very difficult to predict the cost and availability of funds.

Organizational Focus

Problems arise when organizations implement changes in operating procedures but fail to make supporting changes in budgeting and performance evaluation procedures. Companies often implement improvement programs such as total quality management, yet maintain their traditional hierarchical financial controls, including budgeting, in place. When this happens, budgetary units are still encouraged to meet short-run budget targets at the expense of doing what's best for the organization because they know their rewards and evaluations are based on what happened during the current period, not on what action they took to ensure the long-run success of the organization.

To overcome these problems, management should compile nonfinancial information to help plan and evaluate current operations. Reports that include customer satisfaction, product quality, and adherence to social and environmental issues can greatly assist in the overall evaluation of an organization's performance. These items do not ignore the variances from budget but simply provide assurances that everything the organization is attempting to achieve is somehow assessed in the overall evaluation process. According to H. Thomas Johnson, coauthor of *Relevance Lost* and author of *Relevance Regained: From Top-Down Control to Bottom Up,* "Companies should focus on goals that matter, not goals that count." Accounting and budgeting should not focus attention solely on short-run results, but also on the means of achieving the goals and objectives of the organization. New procedures must be implemented to improve the overall assessment process of management accounting.[1]

Ethics

The areas of budgeting and performance measurement are often prime targets of unethical practices. Because wrongful activities related to budgeting are unethical, rather than illegal, some organizations have difficulty dealing with them. However, when unethical actions cross that gray area into fraudulent actions, organizations are not reluctant to dismiss employees or even legally charge them with fraud.[2]

While wanting slack in a budget is natural, at some level building slack into a budget becomes unethical. Under some circumstances, budgetary slack is dishonest. It might even result in theft when favorable budget variances are rewarded with year-end bonuses or other rewards. Falsifying budgets, which may also include the concept of slack, occurs when managers include budget categories that are not needed in their operations. The funds allocated for such categories are used for other purposes or as another means of padding the budget's legitimate categories. Falsifying budgets is generally considered blatant and is grounds for dismissal in some organizations. Opposite to falsifying budgets is falsifying results. Oftentimes ethical issues surrounding budgets are not in the development of the budgets but in the reporting of the results. Examples include misclassification of expenses, inflating revenues or deflating expenses, postponing or accelerating the recording of activities at the end of an accounting period, or creating fictitious activities. See Management Accounting Practice 7-3 for an example.

ELEMENTS OF AN OPERATION BUDGET

L O 6

The types of budgets that must be prepared vary, depending on the nature of a business, its activities, and the needs of management. The overall budgeting process is designed to ensure the smooth operation of a business throughout its operating cycle. As shown in Exhibit 7-1, the operating cycle of a manufacturing or merchandising operation involves the conversion of cash into other assets, which are intended to produce revenues in excess of their costs. The cycle generally follows a path from cash, to inventories, to receivables, and back to cash. There are, of course, intermediate processes such as the purchase or manufacture of inventories, payments of accounts payable, and the collection of receivables. The operating budget is merely a detailed model of the firm's operating cycle that includes all aspects of the internal value chain.

---

1 Susan Jayson, "Focus on People—Not Costs," *Management Accounting* (September 1992), pp. 28-33.
2 See *Fraud Survey Results, 1993,* New York: KPMG Peat Marwick, 1993.

EXHIBIT 7-1: OPERATING CYCLE OF A MANUFACTURING OR MERCHANDISING OPERATION

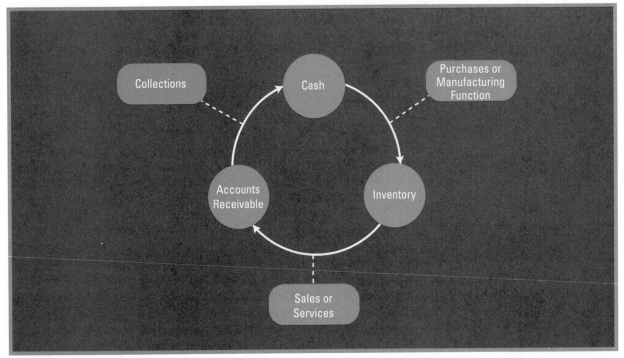

MANAGEMENT ACCOUNTING PRACTICE 7-3

Ethics: The Heart of Every Decision

Regarding the issue of ethics, C. J. Silas, retired CEO of Phillips Petroleum, states that, "What we are all called upon to do, whatever professional field we have chosen, is to make ethics the heart of every decision we make, from boardroom to the mailroom."

In his discussion of moral dilemmas, Silas cites several examples where managers made the wrong decisions, one including a budget-related situation. This particular person, a plant manager at a glass container plant, inflated the results of operations not slightly, but by 33 percent over actual levels. When the plant manager confessed to his wrongdoings, he stated that the actual results were so unfavorable, "that he was afraid the company would close the aging plant, throwing him and 300 employees out of work."

As Silas noted, "It's a lot harder to resist temptation when honesty and integrity could mean the end of your job, your company, even your town." Organizations should establish policies of operations that do not cause direct conflicts with managers' decisions, a concept Silas labeled "the moral dimension of competitiveness." An example would be an executive order to a manager to cut costs but not cut customer satisfaction. Organizations should provide guidelines and expectations of actions, not blatant orders where the means and goals seem to conflict.

Based on: C. J. Silas, "The Moral Dimension of Competitiveness," reprinted with permission of the Ethics Resource Center, Inc. by *Management Accounting* (December 1994), p. 72.

In most for-profit organizations, the budgeting process begins with the development of the sales budget and concludes with the development of pro forma financial statements. Exhibit 7-2 depicts the annual budget assembly process in a retail organization. Note how most of the budget data flow from sales toward cash and then toward the pro forma financial statements.

To illustrate the procedures involved in budget assembly, a quarterly operating budget will be developed for Backpacks Galore, Inc., (BGI), a retail organization that sells backpacks, for the year 19X5. The assembly sequence follows the overview illustrated in Exhibit 7-2. Each element of the budget process in Exhibit 7-2 is illustrated in a separate exhibit. Because of the numerous elements in the budget process illustrated for BGI, you will find it useful to refer to Exhibit 7-2 often.

The activities of a business can be summarized under three broad categories: operating activities, financing activities, and investing activities. To simplify our discussion, assume that Backpacks Galore engaged in no investing activities during the budget period and that the only financing activity was short-term borrowing. Normal profit-related activities performed in conducting the daily affairs of an organization are called **operating activities.** These, of course, are the major concern of management in preparing operating budgets. The operating activities of Backpacks Galore include:

1. Purchase of inventory for sale
2. Sales of goods or services
3. Purchase and use of goods and services classified as selling expenses
4. Purchase and use of goods and services classified as general and administrative expenses

In addition to preparing the budget for each operating activity, a cash budget is prepared to summarize the projected cash receipts and disbursements for the budget period. The importance of cash planning makes the cash budget a vital part of the total budget process. Management must, for example, be aware in advance of the need to borrow and have some idea when borrowed funds can be repaid.

The balance sheet at the end of 19X4, presented in Exhibit 7-3 (page 347), contains information to use as a starting point in preparing the various budgets. The input/output approach is used to budget the variable expenses. The budgets for other costs are developed using either the incremental approach or the minimum level approach. Budgets to be prepared include sales, purchases, selling expense, general and administrative expense, and cash.

Sales Budget

The **sales budget** contains a forecast of unit sales volume and sales revenue, and it may also contain a forecast of sales collections. The sales budget is a critical element in the overall operating budget process because so many of the other elements, such as purchases, labor needs, and other resource requirements, are based on projected sales. Managers use the best

EXHIBIT 7-2: OVERVIEW OF BUDGET ASSEMBLY PROCESS IN A MERCHANDISING FIRM

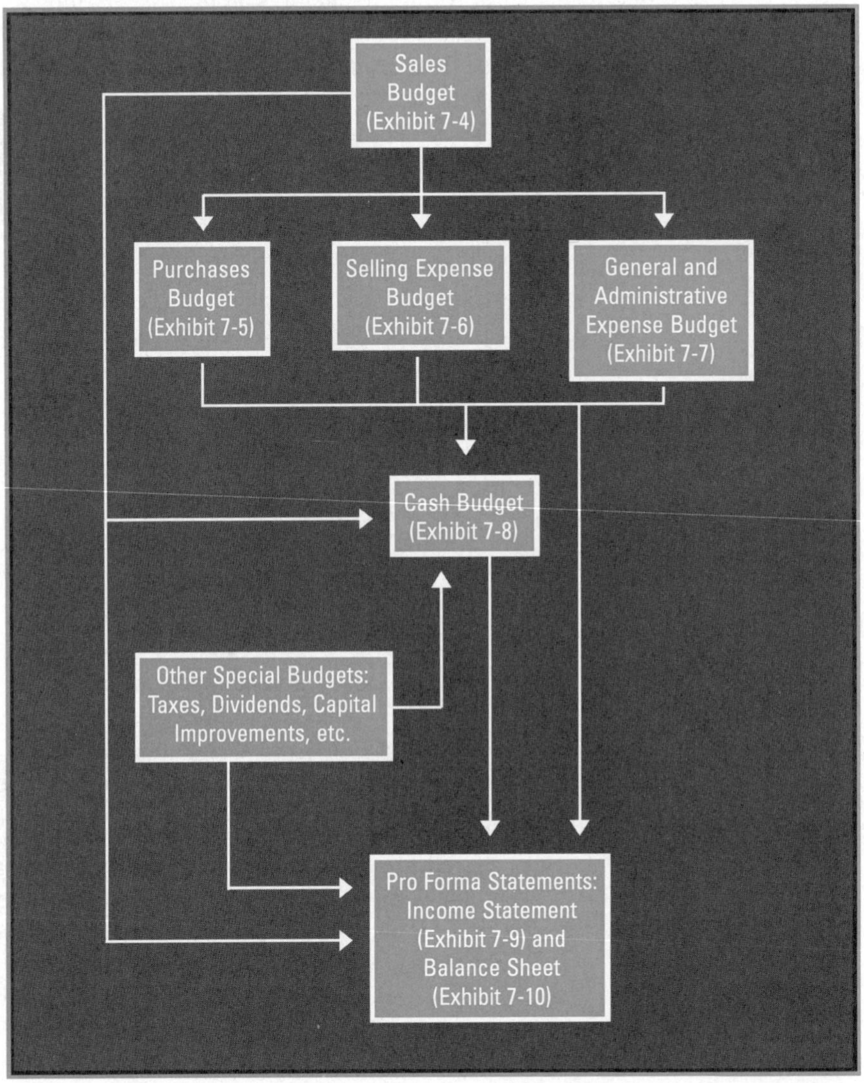

available information to forecast future market conditions accurately. These forecasts, when considered along with merchandise available, promotion and advertising plans, and expected pricing policies, should lead to the most dependable sales predictions. The sales budget of BGI for 19X5 is presented in Exhibit 7-4.

Purchases Budget

The **purchases budget** indicates the merchandise that must be acquired to meet sales needs and ending inventory requirements. It may be referred to as a merchandise budget if it contains only purchases of merchandise for sale. However, it often contains office and selling supplies. For simplicity, the purchases budget developed in this chapter includes only purchases of merchandise.

EXHIBIT 7-3: INITIAL BALANCE SHEET

Backpacks Galore, Inc.
Balance Sheet
December 31, 19X4

Assets

Current assets:			
Cash		$ 15,000	
Accounts receivable (net)		21,600	
Inventory:			
School bookpacks (5,000 × $10)	$ 50,000		
Hiking backpacks (1,600 × $60)	96,000	146,000	$182,600
Property and equipment:			
Land		$ 60,000	
Buildings and equipment	$260,000		
Less accumulated depreciation	124,800	135,200	195,200
Total assets			$377,800

Liabilities and stockholders' equity

Current liabilities:			
Accounts payable			$ 40,000
Stockholders' equity:			
Capital stock		$150,000	
Retained earnings		187,800	337,800
Total liabilities and stockholders' equity			$377,800

EXHIBIT 7-4: SALES BUDGET

Backpacks Galore, Inc.
Sales Budget
For the Year Ending December 31, 19X5

	First Quarter	Second Quarter	Third Quarter	Fourth Quarter	Year Total
Sales (units):					
School bookpacks	4,000	3,400	3,650	3,950	15,000
Hiking backpacks	1,100	1,600	2,500	1,300	6,500
Sales (dollars):					
School bookpacks × $20	$ 80,000	$ 68,000	$ 73,000	$ 79,000	$300,000
Hiking backpacks × $100	110,000	160,000	250,000	130,000	650,000
Total	$190,000	$228,000	$323,000	$209,000	$950,000

BGI's purchases budget is shown in Exhibit 7-5. Supplies are assumed to be immaterial and, therefore, are included in miscellaneous office expenses. Although there are many types of backpacks carried in inventory, for our purposes they are classified as either school or hiking. Purchase orders are sent to suppliers one quarter in advance of anticipated sales although delivery is not until the week before the new quarter begins. In case the shipment is delayed, the company carries an inventory cushion of 1,000 school bookpacks and 500 hiking backpacks.

From this budget, cash disbursements for purchases are predicted based on the expected timing of payments on account. This budget is critical to the overall budget process because it often contains the largest commitment of cash outflows from the organization.

To illustrate the purchase operations, let's examine the second quarter sales of school bookpacks. The inventory needs of the second quarter are determined to be 3,400 units (Exhibit 7-4). These anticipated sales are ordered during the first quarter (Exhibit 7-5). Assuming the goods arrive on time, the total beginning inventory of the second quarter will be 4,400 school bookpacks (1,000 units of base inventory plus the purchases of 3,400 units).

If BGI's suppliers were willing to make frequent deliveries, say weekly, BGI could then adopt an inventory system whereby it would no longer have to begin each quarter with the quarter's entire inventory levels. It might still place orders a quarter in advance with quicker payments in return for increased frequency of delivery. Although this would speed up the payments for the inventory, it would reduce the space needed to store the inventory, thereby freeing the space for other uses.

All purchases are made by a centralized purchasing department, and the quarterly purchases budget is very helpful in controlling the activities of this department. By using appropriate procedures for getting bids and placing orders, the department helps the organization to minimize the cost of carrying inventory.

Selling Expense Budget

The **selling expense budget** presents the costs and disbursements the organization plans to incur in connection with sales and distribution. Budgeted selling expenses include variable selling expenses and fixed selling expenses of $4,500 per quarter. Note in the selling expense budget, Exhibit 7-6 (page 350), that the budgeted variable selling expenses are based on budgeted sales as a percentage of budgeted sales dollars. The budgeted fixed selling expenses are based on amounts obtained from the manager of the sales department. Budgeted selling costs for BGI are paid in the quarter they are incurred.

General and Administrative Expense Budget

The **general and administrative expense budget** presents the expected costs and disbursements for the general administration of the organization such as the accounting department, the computer center, and the president's office. The depreciation of $2,000 per quarter is a noncash item and is not carried forward to the cash budget. Note in Exhibit 7-7 (page 351) that

EXHIBIT 7-5: PURCHASES BUDGET

Backpacks Galore, Inc.
Purchases Budget
For the Year Ending December 31, 19X5

	First Quarter	Second Quarter	Third Quarter	Fourth Quarter	Year Total
Purchase units:					
School bookpacks:					
Current quarter's sales	4,000	3,400	3,650	3,950	
Desired ending inventory*	4,400	4,650	4,950	5,100**	
Total needs	8,400	8,050	8,600	9,050	
Less beginning inventory	- 5,000	- 4,400	- 4,650	- 4,950	
Purchases	3,400	3,650	3,950	4,100	15,100
Hiking backpacks:					
Current quarter's sales	1,100	1,600	2,500	1,300	
Desired ending inventory*	2,100	3,000	1,800	1,700**	
Total needs	3,200	4,600	4,300	3,000	
Less beginning inventory	- 1,600	- 2,100	- 3,000	- 1,800	
Purchases	1,600	2,500	1,300	1,200	6,600
Total unit purchases	5,000	6,150	5,250	5,300	21,700
Purchase dollars:					
School bookpacks @ $10 each	$ 34,000	$ 36,500	$ 39,500	$ 41,000	$151,000
Hiking backpacks @ $60 each	96,000	150,000	78,000	72,000	396,000
Total	$130,000	$186,500	$117,500	$113,000	$547,000

*Next quarter's sales plus base inventory of 1,000 school bookpacks and 500 hiking backpacks.
**Projected sales for the first quarter of 19X6 are 4,100 school bookpacks and 1,200 hiking backpacks.

there are no variable general and administrative costs. This is because most expenditures categorized as general and administrative are related to top-management operations that do not vary with current sales. For BGI, all general and administrative costs, except depreciation, are assumed to be paid in the quarter they are incurred.

Cash Budget

The **cash budget** summarizes all cash receipts and disbursements expected to occur during the budget period. Almost all activities affect cash sooner or later. BGI's cash budget, presented in Exhibit 7-8 (page 352), is affected by credit policies, sales discounts taken by customers, collection experiences, payment policies, purchase and volume discounts taken, and myriad other factors.

Once the sales predictions are made, information on credit terms, collections policy, and past collection experience is used to develop a cash collections budget. Collections on sales normally include receipts from the

EXHIBIT 7-6: SELLING EXPENSE BUDGET

Backpacks Galore, Inc.
Selling Expense Budget
For the Year Ending December 31, 19X5

	First Quarter	Second Quarter	Third Quarter	Fourth Quarter	Year Total
Budgeted sales (from Exhibit 7-4)	$190,000	$228,000	$323,000	$209,000	$950,000
Selling costs and disbursements:					
Variable costs:					
Setup/Display (1% sales)	$ 1,900	$ 2,280	$ 3,230	$ 2,090	$ 9,500
Commissions (2% sales)	3,800	4,560	6,460	4,180	19,000
Miscellaneous (1% sales)	1,900	2,280	3,230	2,090	9,500
Total	$ 7,600	$ 9,120	$ 12,920	$ 8,360	$ 38,000
Fixed costs:					
Advertising	$ 2,250	$ 2,250	$ 2,250	$ 2,250	$ 9,000
Office expenses	1,250	1,250	1,250	1,250	5,000
Miscellaneous	1,000	1,000	1,000	1,000	4,000
Total	$ 4,500	$ 4,500	$ 4,500	$ 4,500	$ 18,000
Total selling costs and disbursements	$ 12,100	$ 13,620	$ 17,420	$ 12,860	$ 56,000

current period's sales and the collections from sales of prior periods. An allowance for bad debts, which reduces each period's collections, is also predicted. Other items often included are cash sales, sales discounts, allowances for volume discounts, and seasonal changes of sales prices and collections. For BGI, it is estimated that one-half of all sales are for cash and the other half are on the company's credit card.[3] Seventy-five percent of the credit sales are collected in the quarter of sale, and 24 percent are collected in the quarter after the sales take place. Bad debts are budgeted at 1 percent of credit sales. This resource flow is graphically illustrated as:

Sales
50 percent cash
50 percent credit
75 percent collected in current period
24 percent collected in next period
1 percent uncollected

For our cash budget, disbursements begin with purchases. An organization often delays cash disbursements as long as possible within any available discount period. For BGI, payments for purchases are assumed to be made 50 percent in the quarter purchased and 50 percent in the next

---

3 When sales are on bank credit cards, the collection will be immediate, less a bank user fee.

EXHIBIT 7-7: GENERAL AND ADMINISTRATIVE EXPENSE BUDGET

Backpacks Galore, Inc.
General and Administrative Expense Budget
For the Year Ending December 31, 19X5

	First Quarter	Second Quarter	Third Quarter	Fourth Quarter	Year Total
General and administrative costs and disbursements:					
Compensation	$20,000	$20,000	$20,000	$20,000	$ 80,000
Research and development	5,000	5,000	5,000	5,000	20,000
Insurance	2,000	2,000	2,000	2,000	8,000
Depreciation	2,000	2,000	2,000	2,000	8,000
Property taxes	3,000	3,000	3,000	3,000	12,000
Miscellaneous	1,000	1,000	1,000	1,000	4,000
Total general and administrative costs and disbursements	$33,000	$33,000	$33,000	$33,000	$132,000

quarter. This is predicated upon the payment terms and the staggered delivery of the goods.

Information on cash expenditures for selling expenses and for general and administrative expenses is based on budgets for each of these items. Note that the quarterly cash expenditures for general and administrative expenses are $31,000 rather than $33,000. The $2,000 difference relates to depreciation, which does not require the use of cash.

The tax information is furnished by BGI's external tax consultant, and the information for dividends is per the Board of Directors. Income taxes are determined on the basis of predicted taxable income following rules established by the Internal Revenue Service. The cash budget shows the cash operating deficiencies and surpluses expected to occur at the end of each quarter. This information is used to predict cash borrowing, loan payment, and cash investment needs.

The cash maintenance policy for Backpacks Galore requires that a minimum balance of $15,000 be maintained at all times. BGI has a line of credit with a major bank, with any interest on borrowed funds computed at the simple interest rate of 12 percent per year, or 1.0 percent per month. All necessary borrowing is assumed to occur at the start of each quarter in increments of $1,000. Repayments are assumed to occur at the end of the quarter. The cash budget presented in Exhibit 7-8 indicates that BGI will need to borrow $3,000 at the beginning of the first quarter and $22,000 at the beginning of the second. At the end of the third quarter, BGI will be able to repay the loan.

EXHIBIT 7-8: CASH BUDGET

Backpacks Galore, Inc.
Cash Budget
For the Year Ending December 31, 19X5

	First Quarter	Second Quarter	Third Quarter	Fourth Quarter	Year Total
Cash balance, beginning	$ 15,000	$ 15,750	$ 15,180	$ 56,155	$ 15,000
Collections on sales:					
Cash sales	$ 95,000	$114,000	$161,500	$104,500	$475,000
From credit sales:					
Current quarter	71,250	85,500	121,125	78,375	356,250
Prior quarter	21,600*	22,800	27,360	38,760	110,520
Total	187,850	222,300	309,985	221,635	941,770
Total available from operations	$202,850	$238,050	$325,165	$277,790	$956,770
Less budgeted disbursements:					
Purchasing (from Exhibit 7-5):					
Current quarter (50%)	$ 65,000	$ 93,250	$ 58,750	$ 56,500	$273,500
Previous quarter (50%)	40,000**	65,000	93,250	58,750	257,000
Total	$105,000	$158,250	$152,000	$115,250	$530,500
Selling (from Exhibit 7-6)	12,100	13,620	17,420	12,860	56,000
General and administrative					
(from Exhibit 7-7)***	31,000	31,000	31,000	31,000	124,000
Other:					
Income taxes	22,000	22,000	22,000	11,200	77,200
Dividends	20,000	20,000	20,000	30,000	90,000
Total	-190,100	-244,870	-242,420	-200,310	-877,700
Excess (deficiency) cash					
available over disbursements	$ 12,750	$ (6,820)	$ 82,745	$ 77,480	$ 79,070
Short-term financing#					
New loans	$ 3,000	$ 22,000	—	—	$ 25,000
Repayments	—	—	$(25,000)	—	(25,000)
Interest##	—	—	(1,590)	—	(1,590)
Net cash flow from financing	3,000	22,000	(26,590)	—	(1,590)
Cash balance, ending	$ 15,750	$ 15,180	$ 56,155	$ 77,480	$ 77,480
Budgeted bad debts					
(1% of credit sales)	$ 950	$ 1,140	$ 1,615	$ 1,045	$ 4,750

*This is based on the fourth quarter 19X4 credit sales.

**Unpaid balance at December 31, 19X4, reflects prior year payment terms.

#Short-term loans are obtained in increments of $1,000 to maintain cash at a minimum balance of $15,000 at all times. Accordingly, new loans required are budgeted for the beginning of the quarter, and repayments are budgeted for the end of the quarter. Loan repayments are made on a first-borrowed, first-repaid basis, and interest is paid only at the time of repayment.

##Interest computation for repayment of $25,000 is ($3,000 × 9 months × 0.01 = $270) + ($22,000 × 6 months × 0.01 = $1,320) = $1,590.

***Amounts for cash flow exclude depreciation.

Note: The Accounts Receivable balance on December 31, 19X5, is $25,080 ($209,000 × 0.50 × 0.24).

**Pro Forma
Financial
Statements**

The preparation of operating budgets culminates in the preparation of pro forma financial statements. **Pro forma financial statements** are hypothetical statements that reflect the "as if" effects of the budgeted activities on the actual financial position of the organization. That is, the statements reflect what the results of operations will be if all the predictions in the budget are correct. The preparation of pro forma financial statements has been simplified greatly by computer programs, especially financial spreadsheets that permit the user to immediately determine the impact of any assumed changes. The pro forma income statement may follow the functional format traditionally used for financial accounting or the contribution format introduced in Chapter 2. In either case, the balance sheet amounts reflect the corresponding entries.

Exhibit 7-9 presents the pro forma income statement for the year ending December 31, 19X5. If all the predictions made in the operating budget are correct, Backpacks Galore will produce a net income for the year of $138,460. Note that just about every item on the pro forma income statement comes from one of the budget schedules.

The pro forma balance sheet, presented in Exhibit 7-10, shows the anticipated financial position of BGI at the end of 19X5, assuming all the

EXHIBIT 7-9: PRO FORMA INCOME STATEMENT

Backpacks Galore, Inc.
Pro Forma Income Statement (Functional Format)
For the Year Ending December 31, 19X5

Sales (Exhibit 7-4)		$950,000
Expenses:		
Cost of goods sold:		
Beginning inventory (Exhibit 7-3)	$146,000	
Purchases (Exhibit 7-5)	547,000	
Cost of merchandise available	$693,000	
Ending inventory, 12/31/19X5*	-153,000	
Cost of goods sold	$540,000	
Selling operations (Exhibit 7-6)	56,000	
General and administrative (Exhibit 7-7)	132,000	
Bad debt expense (Exhibit 7-8)	4,750	-732,750
Income from operations		$217,250
Other expenses:		
Interest expense (Exhibit 7-8)		- 1,590
Net income before taxes		$215,660
Allowance for income taxes		- 77,200
Net income		$138,460

*(School bookpacks, 5,100 × $10 = $51,000) + (Hiking backpacks, 1,700 × $60 = $102,000) = $153,000 (Exhibit 7-5).

budget predictions are correct. Sources of the pro forma balance sheet data are included as part of the exhibit.

ACTIVITY-BASED BUDGETING

L O 7

While the operating budget provides an overview of an entire organization, management is sometimes interested in budgets for specific types of costs, products, or departments. If management wanted to obtain a better understanding and control of travel costs, they might develop an organiza-

EXHIBIT 7-10: PRO FORMA BALANCE SHEET

Backpacks Galore, Inc.
Pro Forma Balance Sheet
December 31, 19X5

Assets

Current assets:			
Cash (Exhibit 7-8)		$ 77,480	
Accounts receivable (net) (Exhibit 7-8)		25,080	
Merchandise inventory (Exhibit 7-9)		153,000	$255,560
Property and equipment:			
Land		$ 60,000	
Buildings and equipment	$260,000		
Less accumulated depreciation	-132,800	127,200	187,200
Total assets			$442,760

Liabilities and stockholders' equity

Current liabilities:			
Accounts payable (Exhibit 7-5)			$ 56,500
Stockholders' equity:			
Capital stock		$150,000	
Retained earnings		236,260	386,260
Total liabilities and stockholders' equity			$442,760

Sources of data:
1. The balance in accounts receivable is 24 percent of the fourth quarter credit sales ($104,500 × 0.24).
2. Land and buildings and equipment are the same as their respective balances at the end of 19X4.
3. Accumulated depreciation is equal to the balance at the end of 19X4 increased by the 19X5 depreciation ($124,800 + $8,000), Exhibit 7-7.
4. The balance in accounts payable is 50 percent of the fourth quarter purchases ($113,000 × 0.50).
5. Capital stock is the same as its balance at the end of 19X4.
6. Retained earnings is equal to the balance at the end of 19X4 plus pro forma net income of $138,460 less dividends of $90,000 reported in the cash budget.

tion-wide budget for travel costs. In a similar manner, specific budgets might be developed for telephone expenditures, quality costs, or any other item of interest. These specialized budgets typically cut across organizational boundaries. Their value as an analytic tool can be further enhanced if they focus on activities and activity costs.

Assume that Atlantic Magnetic, Inc., produces a variety of products, including magnetic tapes, components of hard disk drives, and 3 1/2-inch floppy disks. Because management is interested in examining the detailed costs of 3 1/2-inch floppy disks, perhaps as a starting point for a continuous improvement program, an activity-based budget is developed for this product. The 19X8 activity-based budget for floppy disks is shown in Exhibit 7-11.

To simplify the illustration we have omitted computational details, combined many activities, and clearly labeled the activities as unit, batch, or product level. This activity-based budget cuts across functional areas to bring all budgeted costs for 3 1/2-inch floppy disks together. Observe that it is based on activities, such as product development and design, procurement, setup, operations, inspection, and packaging, rather than on expense categories such as direct labor and overhead. Also note that the budget reflects an activity cost hierarchy, including unit level, batch level, and product level costs. Developing an activity-based budget requires a complete analysis of the internal value chain for 3 1/2-inch floppy disks. The analysis could be accomplished using the procedures discussed in Chapter 4.

EXHIBIT 7-11: ACTIVITY-BASED BUDGETING FOR A PRODUCT

Atlantic Magnetic, Inc.
Activity-Based Budget for 3 1/2-Inch Disks
For the Year Ending December 31, 19X8

Production and sales	500,000 units
Product development and design (product level)	$ 50,000
Product advertising (product level)	20,000
Procurement (batch level*)	10,000
Direct materials (unit level)	80,000
Production:	
Setup (batch level*)	10,000
Operations (unit level)	30,000
Inspection (one unit per batch, batch level*)	5,000
Packaging (per box, batch level*)	5,000
Distribution (per carton, batch level*)	10,000
Total	$ 220,000

*The size of the batches used for purchase orders, production, units per box, and boxes per carton may vary.

To illustrate another possible type of activity-based budget, the 19X8 activity-based budget for the Purchasing Department of Atlantic Magnetic is presented in Exhibit 7-12. Once again, to simplify the illustration, we have omitted computational details, combined many activities, and clearly labeled the activities as unit or product level. A more traditional budget for the Purchasing Department might be based on expense categories such as salaries, office supplies, and maintenance. Exhibit 7-12 reflects the activities performed by the department, including vendor screening and quality certification, placing orders, verifying orders, and receiving orders. Because the Purchasing Department conducts activities for several products, the procurement expenses in Exhibit 7-12 exceed those in Exhibit 7-11. Some Purchasing Department costs, such as those for vendor screening and quality certification and those classified as facility level, may not be assigned to any products.

Comparing Exhibits 7-11 and 7-12, note the different classifications of procurement as a batch cost from the viewpoint of the product, 3 1/2-inch floppy disks, and as a unit cost from the viewpoint of the Purchasing Department. From the perspective of the product, an order is placed for a batch of direct materials. From the perspective of the Purchasing Department, whose job is to acquire direct materials, each purchase order is a unit.

EXHIBIT 7-12: ACTIVITY-BASED BUDGETING FOR A DEPARTMENT

Atlantic Magnetic, Inc.
Activity-Based Budget for Purchasing Department
For the Year Ending December 31, 19X8

Budgeted activities:		
New vendors screened	130	
Orders placed	1,200	
Shipments received and inspected	1,400	
Budgeted costs:		
Vendor screening and quality certification		
(unit level per vendor)		$ 30,000
Procurement (unit level per purchase order):		
Placing orders	$50,000	
Verifying orders	25,000	
Receiving orders	16,000	
Inspecting orders	8,000	99,000
General administration and maintenance		
(facility level)		25,000
Total		$154,000

SUMMARY

Operating budgets are an integral part of the overall planning and control system. They represent management's expectations about the events and activities scheduled to occur during a specified future period. Budgets provide the basis for evaluating actual performance and modifying subsequent plans. Budgeting offers many potential benefits for organizations, including forcing managers to look at the future of the company, improving communication, improving coordination between various departments and functions in the organization, and motivating managers to achieve organizational objectives.

The input/output approach to budget planning is based on clearly defined relationships between effort and accomplishment. The activity-based approach focuses on determining the cost of planned activities for a process, department, service, or product. It views all costs as variable. The incremental approach requires budget review of proposals in excess of the budgeted (or actual) expenditures for the previous period. The minimum level approach requires review of any budgeted amounts in excess of some minimum amount. The budgeting process is usually implemented on an annual schedule, although companies in certain industries find the cyclical approach more appropriate. Continuous budgeting consists of adding a new time unit to the end of the budget period upon completing a unit of time.

Feedback is an essential part of budgeting. Without interpretation of actual performance, much of the benefit, including that of motivating people, would be lost. To receive maximum benefits from budgeting requires participation by all management levels, commitments by top management, and both positive and negative feedback.

Pitfalls of operations budgeting include placing excessive time demands on managers, expecting accurate and reliable predictions of all general economic and industry conditions, failure of top management to support the budget, poorly established organizational lines of authority and responsibility, and possible budget slack.

APPENDIX: MANUFACTURING BUDGETS

To facilitate the incorporation of budgeting into a manufacturing setting, the Backpacks Galore, Inc., example will be used, rather than developing an entire new illustration. The basic modification to the existing example is the assumption that the company must now manufacture the bookpacks and backpacks because the supplier's quality declined to an unacceptable level. Manufacturing budgets are further illustrated in the chapter's second Review Problem.

After the sales budget has been completed, the manufacturing manager(s) then decide(s) how much to produce, instead of how many finished units to order. The production budget, Exhibit 7-13, is based on the sales predictions from Exhibit 7-4 but has adjustments for beginning inventory and desired ending inventory.

EXHIBIT 7-13: PRODUCTION BUDGET

Backpacks Galore, Inc.
Production Budget
For the Year Ending December 31, 19X5

	First Quarter	Second Quarter	Third Quarter	Fourth Quarter	Year Total
School bookpacks, units:					
Budgeted sales (Exhibit 7-4)	4,000	3,400	3,650	3,950	15,000
Plus desired ending inventory	200	100	100	1,100	1,100
Total inventory requirements	4,200	3,500	3,750	5,050	16,100
Less beginning inventory	-1,000	- 200	- 100	- 100	- 1,000
Budgeted production	3,200	3,300	3,650	4,950	15,100
Hiking backpacks, units:					
Budgeted sales (Exhibit 7-4)	1,100	1,600	2,500	1,300	6,500
Plus desired ending inventory	100	50	50	600	600
Total inventory requirements	1,200	1,650	2,550	1,900	7,100
Less beginning inventory	- 500	- 100	- 50	- 50	- 500
Budgeted production	700	1,550	2,500	1,850	6,600

As with purchases of Backpacks Galore when it was just a retail organization, the purchases of materials and supplies for the manufacturing operation must still be coordinated with vendors on a frequent basis. Basically, the same purchasing assumptions apply for the manufacturing operations, except for direct materials delivery. Direct materials and supplies are ordered and delivered without a lead time. A basic purchases budget for the manufacturing operation of Backpacks Galore is shown in Exhibit 7-14.

Payment agreements for materials and supplies are the same as before—50 percent in quarter of purchase and 50 percent in the following quarter. However, all labor and other items, such as utilities and maintenance, are paid for in the quarter incurred. A summarized manufacturing disbursements budget is shown in Exhibit 7-15. This information is then used as input to the cash budget as is any other cash disbursements information. For Backpacks Galore, this would be included in Exhibit 7-8.

SUGGESTED READINGS

Cook, Donald. "Strategic Plan Creates a Blueprint for Budgeting," *Healthcare Financial Management* (May 1990), pp. 20-24.

Donaldson, Gordon. "Financial Goals and Strategic Consequences," *Harvard Business Review* (May-June 1985), pp. 56-66.

EXHIBIT 7-14: MANUFACTURING PURCHASES BUDGET

Backpacks Galore, Inc.
Manufacturing Purchases Budget
For the Year Ending December 31, 19X5

	First Quarter	Second Quarter	Third Quarter	Fourth Quarter	Year Total
Production budget units (Exhibit 7-13):					
School bookpacks	3,200	3,300	3,650	4,950	15,100
Hiking backpacks	700	1,550	2,500	1,850	6,600
Total production units	3,900	4,850	6,150	6,800	21,700
Purchases units:					
School, 1 sq. yard	3,200	3,300	3,650	4,950	15,100
Hiking, 1.5 sq. yards	1,050	2,325	3,750	2,775	9,900
Total sq. yards	4,250	5,625	7,400	7,725	25,000
Kits (zippers, straps, buckles), 1 each	3,900	4,850	6,150	6,800	21,700
Purchase dollars:					
School bookpack mat. at $7/yd.	$22,400	$ 23,100	$25,550	$34,650	$105,700
Hiking backpack mat. at $10/yd.	10,500	23,250	37,500	27,750	99,000
Kits (zippers, straps, buckles), 1 each at $5	19,500	24,250	30,750	34,000	108,500
Totals	$52,400	$ 70,600	$93,800	$96,400	$313,200

EXHIBIT 7-15: MANUFACTURING DISBURSEMENTS BUDGET

Backpacks Galore, Inc.
Manufacturing Disbursements Budget
For the Year Ending December 31, 19X5

	First Quarter	Second Quarter	Third Quarter	Fourth Quarter	Year Total
Materials:					
Current quarter (50%)	$26,200	$ 35,300	$ 46,900	$ 48,200	$156,600
Previous quarter (50%)	20,000*	26,200	35,300	46,900	128,400
Direct labor:					
School, 1/4 hr. at $20/hr.	16,000	16,500	18,250	24,750	75,500
Hiking, 1/3 hr. at $24/hr.	5,600	12,400	20,000	14,800	52,800
Manufacturing overhead:					
Variable, $2 per unit	7,800	9,700	12,300	13,600	43,400
Fixed per quarter	10,000	10,000	10,000	10,000	40,000
Total disbursements	$85,600	$110,100	$142,750	$158,250	$496,700

*Unpaid balance at December 31, 19X4, reflects prior year payment terms.

Gould, Gary R., and Edward W. Younkins. "Guidelines Help Managers Deal with Ethical Issues," *Healthcare Financial Management* (July 1992), pp. 35-40.

Jacob, Vernon K. "Sales Forecasting and Budgeting with 1-2-3," *Computers in Accounting* (October 1988), pp. 72-83.

Jayson, Susan. "Focus on People—Not Costs," *Management Accounting* (September 1992), pp. 28-33.

Ramey, Donald W. "Budgeting and Control of Discretionary Costs," *Journal of Cost Management* (Summer 1993), pp. 32-38.

Schiff, Michael, and Aerie Y. Lewin. "The Impact of People on Budgets," *The Accounting Review* (April 1970), pp. 259-268.

REVIEW PROBLEMS

7-1 Operating Budget for a Merchandising Organization

Stumphouse Cheese Company is a wholesale distributor of blue cheese and ice cream. The following information is available for April 19X4.

Estimated sales:

Blue cheese	160,000 hoops at $10 each
Ice cream	240,000 gallons at $5 each

Desired inventories:

	Beginning	Ending
Blue cheese	10,000	12,000
Ice cream	4,000	5,000

Estimated costs:

Blue cheese	$8 per hoop
Ice cream	$2 per gallon

Financial information:

- Beginning cash balance is $400,000.
- Purchases of merchandise are paid 60 percent in current month and 40 percent in following month. Purchases totaled $1,800,000 in March.
- Employee wages, salaries, and commissions are paid for in current month. Employee expenses for April totaled $156,000.
- Overhead expenses are paid in the next month. The accounts payable for these expenses from March is $80,000.
- Sales are on credit and are collected 70 percent in current period and 29 percent in the next period. March's sales were $3,000,000. Bad debts average 1 percent of sales.
- Selling and administrative expenses are paid monthly and total $450,000, including $40,000 of depreciation.

Required:

Prepare the following for April:

(a) Sales budget in dollars
(b) Purchases budget
(c) Cash budget
(d) Pro forma income statement

The solution to the review problem is found at the end of Chapter 7 assignment material. To maximize your learning, you should make a serious attempt to develop a written solution to the review problem before looking at the solution. If there are errors in your solution, you should then attempt to determine the causes of the errors.

7-2 Operating Budget for a Manufacturing Organization (requires Appendix)

Handy Company manufactures and sells two industrial products in a single plant. The new manager wants to have quarterly budgets and has prepared the following information for the first quarter of 19X1.

Estimated sales:

Drills	60,000 at $100 each
Saws	40,000 at $125 each

Predicted inventories:

	Beginning	Ending
Drills, finished	20,000	25,000
Saws, finished	8,000	10,000
Metal, direct materials	32,000 lbs.	36,000 lbs.
Plastic, direct materials	29,000 lbs.	32,000 lbs.
Handles, direct materials	6,000 each	7,000 each

Manufacturing requirements:

	Direct Materials	Direct Labor
Drills	Metal, 5 lbs. at $8 per lb.	2 hours at $12 per hour
	Plastic, 3 lbs. at $5 per lb.	
	Handles, 1 each at $3	
Saws	Metal, 4 lbs. at $8 per lb.	3 hours at $16 per hour
	Plastic, 3 lbs. at $5 per lb.	

Variable manufacturing overhead is applied at the rate of $1.50 per direct labor hour for each product. Fixed manufacturing overhead is $214,000 per quarter, including noncash expenditures of $156,000, and is allocated on total units completed.

Financial information:

- Beginning cash balance is $1,800,000.
- Purchases of direct materials and labor costs are paid for in quarter acquired.
- Overhead expenses are paid each quarter.
- Sales are on credit and are collected 50 percent in current period and the remainder the next period. Last quarter's sales were $8,400,000. There are no bad debts.

- Selling and administrative expenses are paid quarterly and total $340,000, including $90,000 of depreciation.
- All unit costs for the first quarter of 19X1 are the same as they were for the last quarter of 19X0.

Required:

For the first quarter of 19X1, prepare a:

(a) Sales budget in dollars
(b) Production budget in units
(c) Purchases budget
(d) Manufacturing disbursements budget
(e) Cash budget
(f) Budgeted income statement using the functional format *(Hint:* First determine the manufacturing costs per unit for drills and saws. These include direct materials, direct labor, variable manufacturing overhead, and the average fixed manufacturing overhead per unit completed.)

The solution to the review problem is found at the end of Chapter 7 assignment material. To maximize your learning, you should make a serious attempt to develop a written solution to the review problem before looking at the solution. If there are errors in your solution, you should then attempt to determine the causes of the errors.

KEY TERMS

Activity-based budget approach—budgets physical inputs and costs as a function of planned activity. Emphasis is on batches put into production and on the number of product lines. This approach traces costs to both volume-sensitive and nonvolume-sensitive driver costs.

Budget committee—a committee responsible for supervising budget preparation. It serves as a review board for evaluating requests for discretionary cost items and new projects.

Budget office—an organizational unit responsible for the preparation, distribution, and processing of forms used in gathering budget data. It handles most of the work of actually formulating the budget schedules and reports.

Budgetary slack—sometimes referred to as "padding the budget," occurs when managers intentionally request more funds in the budget for their departments than needed to support the anticipated level of operations.

Cash budget—summarizes all cash receipts and disbursements expected to occur during the budget period.

Continuous budgeting—budgeting based on a moving time frame that extends over a fixed period. A budget system adds an identical time period to the budget at the end of each period of operations, thereby always maintaining a budget of exactly the same time length.

General and administrative expense budget—indicates estimated expenses for the general administration of the organization such as the accounting department, the computer center, and the president's office.

Imposed, or **top-down, budget approach**—top management decides on the primary goals and objectives for the whole organization and communicates them to lower management levels.

Incremental budget approach—budgets costs for a coming period as a dollar or percentage change from the amount budgeted for (or spent during) some previous period. It is often used where the relationships between inputs and outputs are weak or nonexistent and particularly where fixed costs dominate.

Input/output budget approach—budgets physical inputs and costs as a function of planned activity. This approach is often used for manufacturing and distribution activities where there are clearly defined relationships between effort and accomplishment.

Life-cycle budgeting—is appropriate when the entire life of the project represents a more useful planning horizon than an artificial period of one year. Such cycles could be reduced to shorter planning periods by breaking the overall project into several components such as construction phases.

Minimum level budget approach—establishes a base amount for all budget items and requires explanation or justification for any budgeted amount above the minimum. An absolute minimum amount of expenditures is presumed necessary to support ongoing activities in the organization. It is very useful where many committed costs continue from period to period.

Operating activities—normal profit-related activities performed in conducting the daily affairs of an organization. These are the major concerns of management in preparing operating budgets.

Operating budget—a set of formal financial documents that details expected revenues and expenses, as well as all other expected operating and financing transactions for a future period of time (usually one year). It is a plan of action.

Participation, or **bottom-up, budget approach**—uses the benefits of improved communication, coordination, and motivation. The participation budget requires managers at all levels—and in some cases even nonmanagers—to become involved in budget preparation.

Pro forma financial statements—hypothetical statements that reflect the "as if" effects of the budgeted activities on the actual financial position of the organization. They reflect what the results of operations will be if all the predictions in the budget are correct.

Purchases budget—indicates the merchandise or materials that must be acquired to meet current needs and ending inventory requirements.

Sales budget—a forecast of unit sales volume and sales dollars. It may also contain a forecast of sales collections.

Selling expense budget—the costs and disbursements the organization plans to incur in connection with sales and distribution.

REVIEW QUESTIONS

7-1

Explain the relationship between budgeting and planning and control.

7-2

Does budgeting require formal planning? Identify and briefly describe three budget planning concepts.

Pg. 333

7-3

Discuss the three bases used for performance evaluation.

7-4

Why should motivational considerations be a part of budget planning and utilization?

7-5

Identify the types of organizations or situations for which the incremental approach to budgeting is best suited.

7-6

Identify the advantages and disadvantages of the incremental approach to budgeting.

7-7

Contrast the top-down and bottom-up approaches to budget preparation.

7-8

What is the role of the budget committee? Who should be on the budget committee?

7-9

Why are annual budgets not always desirable? What are some alternative budget periods?

7-10

Explain how continuous budgeting works.

7-11

Is budgetary slack a desirable feature? Can it be prevented? Why or why not?

7-12

Which budget brings together all other budgets? How is this accomplished?

7-13

What budgets are normally used to support the cash budget? What is the net result of cash budget preparations?

7-14

Define pro forma statements.

EXERCISES

7-1 Department Budget Using Input/Output Approach

The following data are from the general records of Department 16 for October 19X4.

- Each unit of product requires 6 direct labor hours, 20 liters of direct materials, and 1 container.
- Each liter of material processed requires $12 of manufacturing overhead.
- Average wages for direct laborers are $15 per hour.
- Direct materials currently costs $2 per liter.
- Containers cost $8 each.

Required:

Prepare a department budget for October 19X4 for Department 16 if planned production is 2,000 units of output.

7-2 Department Budgets Using Activity-Based Approach

The following data are from the general records of the Loading Department of St. Paul Transportation Company for November 19X5.

- Cleaning incoming trucks, 30 minutes.
- Obtaining and reviewing shipping documents for loading truck and instructing loaders, 20 minutes.
- Loading truck, 2 hours.
- Cleaning shipping dock and storage area after each loading, 15 minutes.
- Employees do both cleaning and loading tasks and are currently averaging $16 an hour in wages and benefits.
- The supervisor spends 10 percent of her time supervising the cleaning activities, 60 percent supervising various loading activities, and the remainder of her time in general planning and managing of the department. Her current salary is $4,000 per month.
- Other overhead of the department amounts to $10,000 per month and is allocated 20 percent to cleaning and 80 percent to loading.

Required:

Prepare an activities budget for cleaning and loading in the Loading Department for November 19X5, assuming there are 20 working days and an average of three trucks a day are loaded.

7-3 Sales Budget

Jennifer's T-Shirt Shop has very seasonal sales. For 19X7, Jennifer is trying to decide whether to establish a sales budget based on average sales or on sales estimated by quarter. The unit sales for 19X7 are expected to be 10 percent higher than 19X6 sales. Unit sales by quarter for 19X6 were as follows:

	Children's Shirts	Women's Shirts	Men's Shirts	Total Shirts
Winter quarter	200	200	100	500
Spring quarter	200	250	200	650
Summer quarter	400	300	200	900
Fall quarter	200	250	100	550
Total sales	1,000	1,000	600	2,600

Children's T-shirts sell for $4.00 each, women's sell for $8.00, and men's sell for $7.00.

Required:

Assuming a 10 percent increase in sales, prepare a sales budget for each quarter of 19X7 using:

(a) Average quarterly sales *(Hint:* Winter quarter children's shirts are 275 ([1,000 x 1.10]/4)).
(b) Actual quarterly sales *(Hint:* Winter quarter children's shirts are 220 (200 x 1.10)).
(c) Suggest advantages of each method.

7-4 Sales Budget

Quick Mix Company sells three products. The seasonal sales pattern for 19X6 is as follows:

	Products		
Quarter	Gravel	Limestone	Sand
1	10 %	25 %	20 %
2	20	25	30
3	30	25	40
4	40	25	10
	100 %	100 %	100 %

The annual sales budget shows forecasts of: Gravel, 150,000 tons; limestone, 120,000 tons; and sand, 180,000 tons. Next year's selling prices per ton will be: Gravel, $10; limestone, $5; and sand, $4.

Required:

Prepare a sales budget in units and dollars by quarters for the company for the coming year.

7-5 Purchases Budget in Units and Dollars

Budgeted sales of The Record Shop for the first six months of 19X3 are as follows:

Month	Unit Sales	Month	Unit Sales
January	120,000	April	210,000
February	160,000	May	180,000
March	200,000	June	240,000

Beginning inventory for 19X3 is 40,000 units. The budgeted inventory at the end of a month is 40 percent of units to be sold the following month. Purchase price per unit is $3.

Required:

Prepare a purchases budget in units and dollars for each month, January through May.

7-6 Purchases Budget in Units and Dollars (Appendix helpful)

Unit sales estimates for Snow King Plow Company for next year are as follows:

Month	Unit Sales	Month	Unit Sales
January	45,000	March	90,000
February	60,000	April	93,000

There were 10,000 units of finished goods in inventory at the beginning of January. Plans are to have an inventory of finished product equal to one-third of the sales for the next month.

Four hundred pounds of materials are required for each unit produced. Each pound of material costs $10. Inventory levels for materials are to be equal to one-fourth of the needs for the next month. Materials inventory on January 1 was 5.5 million pounds.

Required:

(a) Prepare a production budget for January, February, and March.
(b) Prepare a purchases budget in pounds and dollars for January and February.

7-7 Cash Budget

Wilson's Retail Company is planning a cash budget for the next three months. Estimated sales revenue is as follows:

Month	Sales Revenue	Month	Sales Revenue
January	$300,000	March	$200,000
February	225,000	April	175,000

All sales are on credit. Forty percent of the sales are collected during the month of sale, and 60 percent are collected during the next month.

Cost of goods sold is 70 percent of sales. Payments for merchandise sold are made in the month following the month of sale. Operating expenses to be paid amount to $41,000 each month and are paid during the month incurred.

The cash balance on February 1 is estimated to be $20,000.

Required:

Prepare monthly cash budgets for February, March, and April.

7-8 Cash Budget

Boston Tea Company began July with a cash balance of $142,000. A cash receipts and payments budget for each six-month period is prepared in advance. Sales have been estimated as follows:

Month	Sales Revenue	Month	Sales Revenue
May	$120,000	September	$ 80,000
June	140,000	October	100,000
July	80,000	November	100,000
August	60,000	December	120,000

All sales are on credit with 75 percent collected during the month of sale, 20 percent collected during the next month, and 5 percent collected during the second month following the month of sale.

Cost of goods sold averages 70 percent of sales revenue. Ending inventory is one-half of the next month's predicted cost of sales. The other half of the merchandise is acquired during the month of sale. All purchases are paid for in the month after purchase.

Operating costs are estimated at $18,000 each month and are paid for during the month incurred.

Required:
Prepare monthly cash budgets for the six months from July to December.

7-9 Cash Receipts

The sales budget for Cards, Inc., is forecasted as follows:

Month	Sales Revenue	Month	Sales Revenue
May	$60,000	July	$90,000
June	80,000	August	60,000·

To prepare a cash budget, the company must determine the budgeted cash collections from sales. Historically, the following trend has been established regarding cash collection of sales:

- 60 percent in month of sale
- 20 percent in month following sale
- 15 percent in second month following sale
- 5 percent uncollectible

The company gives a 2 percent cash discount for payments made by customers during the month of sale. The Accounts Receivable balance on April 30 is $24,000, of which $7,000 represents uncollected March sales and $17,000 represents uncollected April sales.

Required:
Prepare a schedule of budgeted cash collections from sales for May, June, and July. Include a three-month summary of estimated cash collections.

7-10 Cash Receipts

Chicago Metal Company is currently estimating cash receipts for the next six months. The Accounts Receivable balance is to be estimated at the end of each month also. Cash sales are estimated at 10 percent of sales for the month. The balance of sales should be collected as follows:

- 50 percent during the month of sale
- 40 percent during the following month
- 10 percent during the second month following month of sale

The Accounts Receivable balance at April 1 was $93,600. Budgeted and actual sales are as follows:

Month	Sales Revenue	Month	Sales Revenue
January	$200,000	April	$150,000
February	190,000	May	180,000
March	170,000	June	200,000

Required:

Prepare a schedule of budgeted cash collections for each month of the second quarter. Determine the estimated balance of Accounts Receivable at the end of each month.

7-11 Cash Disbursements

Oregon Timber Company is in the process of preparing its budget for next year. Cost of goods sold has been estimated at 70 percent of sales. Lumber purchases and payments are to be made during the month preceding the month of sale. Wages are estimated at 15 percent of sales and are paid during the month of sale. Other operating costs amounting to 10 percent of sales are to be paid in the month following the month of sales. Additionally, a monthly lease payment of $10,000 is paid to BMI for computer services. Sales revenue is forecast as follows:

Month	Sales Revenue	Month	Sales Revenue
February	$100,000	May	$210,000
March	160,000	June	180,000
April	180,000	July	230,000

Required:

Prepare a schedule of cash disbursements for April, May, and June.

7-12 Pro Forma Income Statement

Pendleton Company, a merchandising company, is developing its master budget for 19X2. The income statement for 19X1 is as follows:

Pendleton Company
Income Statement
For the Year Ending December 31, 19X1

Gross sales	$750,000
Less estimated uncollectible accounts	- 7,500
Net sales	$742,500
Cost of goods sold	- 430,000
Gross profit	$312,500
Operating expenses (including $25,000 depreciation)	- 200,500
Net income	$112,000

The following are management's goals and forecasts for 19X2:

1. Selling prices will increase by 8 percent, and sales volume will increase by 5 percent.
2. The cost of merchandise will increase by 4 percent.
3. All operating expenses are fixed and are paid in the month incurred. Price increases for operating expenses will be 10 percent.

4. The estimated uncollectibles are 1 percent of budgeted sales.

Required:
Prepare a budgeted traditional income statement for 19X2.

7-13 Pro Forma Income Statement

Big Burger Drive-In is planning a budget for the next fiscal year. Sales revenue has been estimated at $1,000,000. The cost of goods sold has been estimated at 70 percent of sales revenue. Depreciation on the office building and fixtures is budgeted at $50,000. Salaries and wages should amount to 15 percent of sales revenue. Advertising has been budgeted at $75,000, and utilities should amount to $20,000. Income tax is estimated at 40 percent of operating income.

Required:
Prepare a pro forma income statement for the next fiscal year.

7-14 Pro Forma Income Statement

Townville Orthodontist's accountant is planning a budget for the next fiscal year. Patient revenue is estimated by Dr. I. C. Klearly to be $2,000,000. Approximately 4 percent of revenue is uncollectible. Based on prior year's results, the cost of dental supplies is estimated to be 10 percent of gross revenue. Depreciation of equipment and fixtures is budgeted at $30,000 annually. Nurses' and office salaries should increase 5 percent over the current level of $250,000. Professional dues, fees, and meetings have been budgeted at $35,000. Utilities and other overhead items should amount to $20,000. Income tax is estimated at 30 percent of operating income.

Required:
Prepare a pro forma income statement for the next fiscal year.

7-15 Pro Forma Income Statement with Activity-Based Emphasis

Greenwood Company, a merchandising store, is developing its master budget for 19X2. The income statement for 19X1 is as follows:

Greenwood Company
Income Statement
For the Year Ending December 31, 19X1

Sales	$700,000
Less estimated uncollectible accounts	- 7,000
Net sales	$693,000
Cost of goods sold	-400,000
Gross profit	$293,000
Operating expenses (including $25,000 depreciation)	-175,000
Net income	$118,000

The following are management's goals and forecasts for 19X2:

1. Selling prices will increase by 5 percent, and sales volume will increase by 4 percent.

2. The cost of goods sold will increase by 4 percent.
3. All operating expenses are fixed and are paid in the month incurred. Price increases for operating expenses will be 9 percent.
4. The estimated uncollectibles are 1 percent of budgeted sales.
5. The company's activity cost categories are product development, manufacturing, marketing, and distribution.
6. Product development averages 10 percent of estimated cost of goods sold. The remaining estimate of cost of goods sold is for manufacturing.
7. Operating expenses are primarily composed of marketing and distribution efforts with marketing historically being 70 percent.

Required:
(a) Prepare a pro forma traditional income statement for 19X2.
(b) Prepare a pro forma income statement for 19X2 using the activity categories. (You may need to refer to Chapter 4.)

PROBLEMS

7-16 Cash Budget

Cash budgeting of Carolina Apple, a merchandising firm, is done on a monthly basis. The company is planning its cash needs for the third quarter of 19X1, and the following information is available to assist in preparing a cash budget.

Budgeted income statements for July through October 19X1 are as follows:

	July	August	September	October
Sales	$18,000	$24,000	$28,000	$36,000
Cost of goods sold	-10,000	-14,000	-16,000	-20,000
Gross profit	$ 8,000	$10,000	$12,000	$16,000
Less other expenses:				
Selling	$ 2,300	$ 3,000	$ 3,400	$ 4,200
Administrative	2,600	3,000	3,200	3,600
Total	- 4,900	- 6,000	- 6,600	- 7,800
Net income	$ 3,100	$ 4,000	$ 5,400	$ 8,200

Additional information:

1. Other expenses, which are paid monthly, include $1,000 a month of depreciation.
2. Sales are 30 percent for cash and 70 percent on credit.
3. Credit sales are collected 20 percent in the month of sale, 70 percent one month after sale, and 10 percent two months after sale.
4. May sales were $15,000, and June sales were $16,000. Merchandise is paid for 50 percent in the month of purchase. The remaining 50 percent is paid in the following month. Accounts payable for merchandise at June 30 totaled $6,000.

5. The company maintains its ending inventory levels at 25 percent of the cost of goods to be sold in the following month. The inventory at June 30 is $2,500.
6. An equipment note of $5,000 per month is being paid through August.
7. The company must maintain a cash balance of at least $5,000 at the end of each month. The cash balance on June 30 is $5,100.
8. The company can borrow from its bank as needed. Borrowings must be in multiples of $100. All borrowings take place at the beginning of a month, and all repayments are made at the end of a month. At the time the principal is repaid, interest is also paid on the portion of the principal repaid. The interest rate is 12 percent per annum.

Required:
(a) Prepare a monthly schedule of budgeted operating cash receipts for July, August, and September.
(b) Prepare a monthly purchases budget and a schedule of budgeted cash payments for purchases for July, August, and September.
(c) Prepare a monthly cash budget for July, August, and September. Show borrowings from the company's bank and repayments to the bank as needed to maintain the minimum cash balance.

7-17 Cash Budget

The Mobile Supply Company sells one product that is purchased for $20 and sold for $30. Budgeted sales in total dollars for next year are $720,000. The sales information needed for preparing the July budget is as follows:

Month	Sales Revenue	Month	Sales Revenue
May	$30,000	July	$48,000
June	42,000	August	60,000

Account balances at July 1 include:

Cash	$15,000
Merchandise Inventory	16,000
Accounts Receivable (sales)	23,000
Accounts Payable (purchases)	15,000

The company pays for one-half of its purchases in the month of purchase and the remainder in the following month. End-of-month inventory must be 50 percent of the budgeted sales in units for the next month.

A 2 percent cash discount on sales is allowed if payment is made during the month of sale. Experience indicates that 50 percent of the billings will be collected during the month of sale, 40 percent in the following month, 8 percent in the next following month, and 2 percent will be uncollectible.

Total budgeted selling and administrative expenses (excluding bad debts) for the fiscal year are estimated at $186,000, of which half is fixed expense (inclusive of a $20,000 annual depreciation charge). Fixed expenses are incurred evenly during the year. The other selling and administrative expenses vary with sales. Expenses are paid during the month incurred.

Required:

(a) Prepare a schedule of estimated cash collections for July.
(b) Prepare a schedule of estimated July cash payments for purchases. (Round calculations to the nearest dollar.)
(c) Prepare schedules of all July selling and administrative expenses and of those requiring cash payments.
(d) Prepare a cash budget in summary form for July.

7-18 Pro Forma Statements

Madison Butter Sales Company is preparing a budget for January and February of next year. The balance sheet as of December 31, 19X1, is given below:

Madison Butter Sales Company
Balance Sheet
December 31, 19X1

Assets		Liabilities and Equities	
Cash	$100,000	Accounts payable	$125,000
Accounts receivable	60,000	Operating expenses payable	10,000
Inventory	30,000	Miscellaneous payable	20,000
Equipment leasehold	60,000	Capital stock	25,000
		Retained earnings	70,000
Total assets	$250,000	Total liabilities and equities	$250,000

Monthly sales data for the current year and the budgeted data for next year are as follows:

November 19X1	$180,000	February 19X2	$250,000
December 19X1	100,000	March 19X2	260,000
January 19X2	240,000	April 19X2	280,000

For 19X2, the following conditions are expected to be present:

- Forty percent of the sales revenue is collected during the month of sale, with the balance collected during the following month.
- Cost of goods sold is 60 percent of sales. Merchandise inventory sufficient for 20 percent of next month's sales is to be maintained at the end of each month. All butter purchased for resale is paid for in the month following the month of purchase.
- Operating expenses for each month are estimated at 10 percent of sales revenue. All operating expenses are paid during the following month.
- Income taxes are estimated at 40 percent of income before taxes. Income taxes are paid 15 days after the end of the quarter. There were no taxes payable on December 31. The miscellaneous payables at December 31, 19X1, are to be paid during January 19X2.

Required:

(a) Prepare a contribution budgeted income statement for the quarter ending March 31, 19X2. Do not prepare monthly statements.

(b) Prepare a pro forma balance sheet as of March 31, 19X2.   *(Hint:* Prepare monthly purchases and cash budgets for January, February, and March.)

7-19 Budgets and Pro Forma Statements

The Peyton Department Store prepares budgets quarterly. The following information is available for use in planning the second quarter budgets for 19X1.

Peyton Department Stores
Balance Sheet
March 31, 19X1

Assets		Liabilities and Equities	
Cash	$ 3,000	Accounts payable	$26,000
Accounts receivable	25,000	Dividends payable	17,000
Inventory	30,000	Rent payable	2,000
Prepaid insurance	2,000	Stockholders' equity	40,000
Fixtures	25,000		
Total assets	$85,000	Total liabilities and equities	$85,000

Actual and forecasted sales for selected months in 19X1 are as follows:

Month	Sales Revenue	Month	Sales Revenue
January	$60,000	May	$60,000
February	50,000	June	70,000
March	40,000	July	90,000
April	50,000	August	80,000

Monthly operating expenses are as follows:

Wages and salaries	$25,000
Depreciation	100
Utilities	1,000
Rent	2,000

Cash dividends of $17,000 are paid during the first month of each quarter and declared during the third month of each quarter for the next quarter. Operating expenses are paid as incurred, except insurance, rent, and depreciation. Rent is paid during the following month. The prepaid insurance is for 5 more months. Cost of goods sold is equal to one half of sales.

Beginning inventories are sufficient for 120 percent of the next month's sales. Purchases during any given month are paid in full during the following month. All sales are on account, with 50 percent collected during the month of sale, 40 percent during the next month, and 10 percent during the month thereafter.

Money can be borrowed and repaid in multiples of $1,000 at an interest rate of 12 percent per annum. The company desires a minimum cash balance of $3,000 at the first of each month. At the time the principal is repaid, interest is paid on the portion of principal that is repaid. All borrowing is at the start of the month, and all repayment is at the end of the month. Money is never repaid at the end of the month it is borrowed.

Required:
(a) Prepare a purchases budget for each month of the second quarter ending June 30, 19X1.
(b) Prepare a cash receipts schedule for each month of the second quarter ending June 30, 19X1. Do not include borrowings.
(c) Prepare a cash disbursements schedule for each month of the second quarter ending June 30, 19X1. Do not include repayments of borrowings.
(d) Prepare a cash budget for each month of the second quarter ending June 30, 19X1. Do include budgeted borrowings and repayments.
(e) Prepare an income statement for each month of the second quarter ending June 30, 19X1.
(f) Prepare a pro forma balance sheet as of June 30, 19X1.

7-20 Inventory and Purchases Budgets (Appendix)

The Midwest Belt Company manufactures men's and boys' belts that are cut to order. Each foot or fraction thereof sells for $2.00. Small belts average 2 feet, and large belts average 3 feet in length. The leather is purchased from a local tannery for 90 cents per foot. The buckles are purchased at $2.00 for the small size and $2.50 for the large size. No changes are expected in any of the purchasing and selling prices.

Sales should increase 20 percent this year over last year. Last year the company sold 300 small belts and 140 large belts during January and February. The inventories are as follows:

December 31 Actual		February 28 Target	
Leather (feet)	900	Leather (feet)	800
Small buckles	200	Small buckles	200
Large buckles	300	Large buckles	250

Purchases are made to provide sufficient stock for each two-month period.

Required:
(a) Prepare a purchases budget in units for total January and February purchases of buckles and leather.
(b) Compute the budgeted cost of the direct materials to be used in manufacturing small and large belts during January and February.

7-21 Purchases Budget (Appendix)

Crown Candy Company manufactures various products to sell to retail stores. A sales budget for pecan turtles for the next several months is as follows:

Month	Budgeted Units in Boxes
June	20,000
July	24,000
August	30,000
September	36,000
October	40,000

There is no inventory of turtles on hand at June 1. During the summer, the company desires an ending finished goods inventory of 10 percent of the following month's sales. The direct materials must be purchased one month before they are needed in production. The June 1 direct materials inventory meets this requirement.

Pecan turtles require direct materials as follows:

	Pounds of Materials per Box of Product
Caramel	3
Pecans	2
Chocolate	5

Required:

Prepare a purchases budget in pounds of each ingredient for June and July. (*Hint:* A production budget for June, July, and August will be helpful.)

7-22 Production and Purchases Budgets (Appendix)

Topper Toys makes plastic riding tractors that require 3 pounds of material. The company wants raw materials on hand at the beginning of each month equal to one-half of the month's production needs. This requirement was met on April 1, the start of the second quarter. There are no work-in-process inventories. A sales budget in units for the next 4 months is given below:

Month	Unit Sales	Month	Unit Sales
April	15,000	June	24,000
May	18,000	July	26,000

Finished goods inventory at the end of each month must be equal to 40 percent of the next month's sales. On March 31, the finished goods inventory totaled 7,500 units.

Required:

(a) Prepare a production budget for April, May, and June.

(b) Prepare a purchases budget in pounds for April and May.

7-23 Comprehensive Budgets (Appendix)

Overton Products assembles computer terminals in a single plant. The controller has decided to begin a new evaluation system, which includes quarterly budgets. She has prepared the following information for the first quarter of 19X1:

Estimated sales:
20,000 units at $100 each

Predicted inventories:

	Beginning	Ending
Finished units	5,000	6,000
Frames, raw materials	2,000	3,000
Tubes, raw materials	1,000	1,200

Manufacturing requirements per unit:

Direct Materials	Direct Labor
1 frame at $16	2 hours at $15 per hour
1 tube at $20	

Variable manufacturing overhead is applied at the rate of $5 per direct labor hour. Fixed manufacturing overhead is $147,000 per quarter (including noncash expenditures of $30,000) and is allocated to total units completed.

Financial information:

- Beginning cash balance is $300,000.
- Purchases of direct materials and labor costs are paid for in the quarter acquired.
- Overhead expenses are paid in the next quarter. The accounts payable for these expenses from the last quarter of 19X0 is $320,000.
- Sales are on credit and are collected 40 percent in current period and the remainder the next period. Last quarter's sales were $1,800,000. There are no bad debts.
- Selling and administrative expenses are paid quarterly and total $240,000, including $70,000 of depreciation.
- All unit costs for the first quarter of 19X1 are the same as they are for the last quarter of 19X0.

Required:
For the first quarter of 19X1, prepare a:
(a) Sales budget in dollars
(b) Production budget in units
(c) Purchases budget
(d) Manufacturing disbursements budget
(e) Cash budget
(f) Budgeted income statement (*Hint:* First determine the total costs per unit.)

7-24 Comprehensive Budgets (Appendix)

Tuscaloosa Tire Company manufactures plastic tires for automated cleaning machines. It is completing its financial plans for 19X8 and is in need of assistance in the budgeting phase. You are provided the following information that may be useful in preparing the necessary budgets and schedules for 19X8:

Tuscaloosa Tire Company
Balance Sheet
December 31, 19X7

Assets

Current assets:

Cash	$200,000	
Accounts receivable (net)	294,000	$494,000

Plant, property, and equipment:

Land		$100,500	
Buildings and equipment	$350,000		
Less accumulated depreciation	-118,000	232,000	332,500
Total assets			$826,500

Liabilities and stockholder's equity

Current liabilities:

Accounts payable		$132,000
Stockholders' equity:		
Capital stock	$400,000	
Retained earnings	294,500	694,500
Total liabilities and stockholders' equity		$826,500

Estimated sales:

	First Quarter	Second Quarter	Third Quarter
Sales (units)	15,000	16,000	18,000
Sales ($30 each)	$450,000	$480,000	$540,000

All sales are on credit and are collected 30 percent in month of sale and 70 percent in month following sale. The company has a history of no bad debts. The sales from the last quarter of 19X7 were $420,000.

The company will have no inventories at the beginning of the year. Management desires 5,000 pounds of unmolded plastic at the end of the first quarter and 6,000 pounds of it at the end of the second quarter. Each wheel takes 2 pounds of plastic, including waste trimmings. There should be 2,000 wheel rims at the end of the first quarter and 2,500 at the end of the second quarter. Finished inventory should total 1,000 wheels at the end of the first quarter and 1,500 at the end of the second quarter.

Manufacturing requirements:

	Direct Materials	Direct Labor
Plastic	2 lbs. at $3 per lb.	One half-hour
Rims	1 each at $2	

Variable factory overhead is applied at the rate of $3 per direct labor hour for each finished unit. Fixed factory overhead is $170,000 per quarter, including noncash expenditures of $54,000, and is allocated on total units completed. Direct labor averages $20 per hour.

Additional information:

- Purchases of direct materials and labor costs are paid for in the quarter acquired.

- Overhead expenses are paid in the next quarter.
- The accounts payable on the balance sheet is for these expenses from the last quarter of 19X7.
- Selling and administrative expenses are paid quarterly and total $40,000, including $10,000 of depreciation.

Required:

For the first and second quarters of 19X8, prepare a:
(a) Sales budget in dollars
(b) Production budget in units
(c) Purchases budget
(d) Manufacturing disbursements budget
(e) Cash budget

DISCUSSION QUESTIONS

7-25 Behavioral Implications of Budgeting

Andrea Rawls, controller of Data Scientific, believes that effective budgeting greatly assists in meeting the goals and objectives of the organization. She argues that the budget serves as a blueprint for the operating activities during each reporting period and, as such, is an important control device. She believes that sound management evaluations can be based on the comparisons of performance and budgetary schedules and that employees respond more favorably when they participate in the budgetary process.

Jeff Cooke, treasurer of Data Scientific, agrees that budgeting is essential for overall organizational success, but he argues that human resources are too valuable to spend much time planning and preparing the budgetary process. He thinks that the roles people play in budgetary preparation are not important in the final analysis of a budget's effectiveness.

Required:

Contrast the participative versus imposed budgeting concepts and indicate how the ideas of Ms. Rawls and Mr. Cooke fit the two categories.

7-26 Behavioral Considerations and Budgeting

Scott Weidner, the controller in the Division of Social Services for the state, recognizes the importance of the budgetary process for planning, control, and motivation purposes. He believes that a properly implemented participative budgeting process for planning purposes and a management by exception reporting procedure based on the participative budget will motivate his subordinates to improve productivity within their particular departments. Based on this philosophy, Weidner has implemented the following budget procedures.

- An appropriation target figure is given to each department manager. This amount is the maximum funding that each department can expect to receive in the next fiscal year.
- Department managers develop their individual budgets within the following spending constraints as directed by the controller's staff.

1. Expenditure requests cannot exceed the appropriation target.
2. All fixed expenditures should be included in the budget. Fixed expenditures would include such items as contracts and salaries at current levels.
3. All government projects directed by higher authority should be included in the budget in their entirety.

- The controller's statement consolidates the departmental budget requests from the various departments into one budget that is to be submitted for the entire division.
- Upon final budget approval by the legislature, the controller's staff allocates the appropriation to the various departments on instructions from the division manager. However, a specified percentage of each department's appropriation is held back in anticipation of potential budget cuts and special funding needs. The amount and use of this contingency fund are left to the discretion of the division manager.
- Each department is allowed to adjust its budget when necessary to operate within the reduced appropriation level. However, as stated in the original directive, specific projects authorized by higher authority must remain intact.
- The final budget is used as the basis of control for a management by exception form of reporting. Excessive expenditures by account for each department are highlighted on a monthly basis. Department managers are expected to account for all expenditures over budget. Fiscal responsibility is an important factor in the overall performance evaluation of department managers.

Weidner believes his policy of allowing the department managers to participate in the budget process and then holding them accountable for their performance is essential, especially during these times of limited resources. He further believes that department managers will be motivated positively to increase the efficiency and effectiveness of their departments because they have provided input into the initial budgetary process and are required to justify any unfavorable performances.

Required:
(a) Explain the operational and behavioral benefits that generally are attributed to a participative budgeting process.
(b) Identify deficiencies in Scott Weidner's participative budgetary policy for planning and performance evaluation purposes. For each deficiency identified, recommend how the deficiency can be corrected.

(CMA Adapted)

7-27 Budgetary Slack with Ethical Considerations

Alene Adams was promoted to department manager of a production unit in Dallas Industries three years ago. She enjoys her job except for the evaluation measures, which are based on the department's budget. After three years of consistently poor annual evaluations based on a static budget, she has decided to improve the evaluation situation. At a recent budget meeting of junior-level managers, the topic of budgetary slack was discussed as a means to maintain some consistency in budgeting matters. As a result of this meeting, Ms. Adams decided to take the following steps in preparing the upcoming year's budget:

1. Use the top quartile for all wage and salary categories.
2. Select the optimistic values for the estimated production ranges for the coming year. These are provided by the marketing department.
3. Use the average of the three months in the current year with poorest production efficiency as benchmarks of success for the coming year.
4. Base equipment charges (primarily depreciation) on replacement values furnished by the purchasing department.
5. Base other fixed costs on current cost plus an inflation rate estimated for the coming year.
6. Use the average of the ten newly hired employees' performance as a basis of labor efficiency for the coming year.

Required:
(a) For each item on Ms. Adams's list, explain whether or not it will create budgetary slack. Use numerical examples as necessary to illustrate.
(b) Given the company's use of static budgets as one of the performance evaluation measures of its managers, can the use of built-in budgetary slack be justified by the managers?
(c) What would you recommend as a means for Ms. Adams to improve the budgeting situation in the company? Provide some specific examples of how the budgeting process might be improved.

7-28 Budgetary Slack with Ethical Considerations

Norton Company, a manufacturer of infant furniture and carriages, is in the initial stages of preparing the annual budget for 19X2. Scott Ford has recently joined Norton's accounting staff and is interested to learn as much as possible about the company's budgeting process. During a recent lunch with Marge Atkins, sales manager, and Pete Granger, production manager, Ford initiated the following conversation:

Ford: Since I'm new around here and am going to be involved with the preparation of the annual budget, I'd be interested to learn how the two of you estimate sales and production numbers.

Atkins: We start out very methodically by looking at recent history, discussing what we know about current accounts, potential customers, and the general state of consumer spending. Then, we add that usual dose of intuition to come up with the best forecast we can.

Granger: I usually take the sales projections as the basis for my projections. Of course, we have to make an estimate of what this year's closing inventories will be, which is sometimes difficult.

Ford: Why does that present a problem? There must have been an estimate of closing inventories in the budget for the current year.

Granger: Those numbers aren't always reliable since Marge makes some adjustments to the sales numbers before passing them on to me.

Ford: What kind of adjustments?

Atkins: Well, we don't want to fall short of the sales projections, so we generally give ourselves a little breathing room by lowering the initial sales projection anywhere from 5 to 10 percent.

Granger: So, you can see why this year's budget is not a very reliable starting point. We always have to adjust the projected production rates as the year progresses; and, of course, this changes the ending inventory estimates. By the way, we make similar adjustments to expenses by adding at least 10 percent to the estimates; I think everyone around here does the same thing.

Required:
(a) Marge Atkins and Pete Granger have described the use of budgetary slack.
   (1) Explain why Atkins and Granger behave in this manner, and describe the benefits they expect to realize from the use of budgetary slack.
   (2) Explain how the use of budgetary slack can adversely affect Atkins and Granger.
(b) As a management accountant, Scott Ford believes that the behavior described by Marge Atkins and Pete Granger may be unethical and that he may have an obligation not to support this behavior. By citing specific standards of competence, confidentiality, integrity, and/or objectivity from Statements on Management Accounting Number 1C, *Standards of Ethical Conduct for Management Accountants*, book Appendix A, explain why the use of budgetary slack may be unethical.

(CMA Adapted)

SOLUTIONS TO REVIEW PROBLEMS

Review Problem 7-1
(a)
Stumphouse Cheese Company
Sales Budget
April 19X4

	Units	Price	Sales
Blue cheese	160,000	$10	$1,600,000
Ice cream	240,000	5	1,200,000
Total			$2,800,000

(b)

Stumphouse Cheese Company
Purchases Budget
April 19X4

	Blue Cheese	Ice Cream	Total
Units:			
Sales needs	160,000	240,000	
Desired ending inventory	12,000	5,000	
Total	172,000	245,000	
Less beginning inventory	- 10,000	- 4,000	
Purchases needed	162,000	241,000	
Dollars:			
Sales needs	$1,280,000	$480,000	
Desired ending inventory	96,000	10,000	
Total	$1,376,000	$490,000	
Less beginning inventory	- 80,000	- 8,000	
Purchases needed	$1,296,000	$482,000	$1,778,000

(c)

Stumphouse Cheese Company
Cash Budget
April 19X4

Cash balance, beginning		$ 400,000
Collections on sales:		
Current month's sales (70% × $2,800,000)	$1,960,000	
Previous month's sales (29% × $3,000,000)	870,000	2,830,000
Cash available from operations		$3,230,000
Less budgeted disbursements:		
March purchases ($1,800,000 × 40%)	$ 720,000	
April purchases ($1,778,000 × 60%)	1,066,800	
Wages, Salaries, and Commissions	156,000	
Overhead (March)	80,000	
Selling and administrative		
($450,000 - $40,000 depreciation)	410,000	- 2,432,800
Cash balance, ending		$ 797,200

(d)

Stumphouse Cheese Company
Pro Forma Income Statement
April 19X4

Sales (sales budget)		$2,800,000
Allowance for bad debts		28,000
Net sales		$2,772,000
Costs of merchandise sold:		
Blue cheese (160,000 × $8)	$1,280,000	
Ice cream (240,000 × $2)	480,000	$1,760,000
Wages and salaries		156,000
Overhead		80,000
Selling and administrative		450,000	-2,446,000
Net income		$ 326,000

Review Problem 7-2

(a)

> **Handy Company**
> **Sales Budget**
> **First Quarter 19X1**

	Units	Price	Sales
Drills	60,000	$100	$ 6,000,000
Saws	40,000	125	5,000,000
Total			$11,000,000

(b)

> **Handy Company**
> **Production Budget**
> **First Quarter 19X1**

	Drills	Saws
Budget sales	60,000	40,000
Plus desired ending inventory	25,000	10,000
Total inventory requirements	85,000	50,000
Less beginning inventory	-20,000	- 8,000
Budgeted production	65,000	42,000

(c)

> **Handy Company**
> **Purchases Budget**
> **First Quarter 19X1**

	Drills	Saws	Total
Metal purchases:			
Production units (from production budget)	65,000	42,000	
Metal	× 5 lbs.	× 4 lbs.	
Production needs	325,000 lbs.	168,000 lbs.	493,000 lbs.
Desired ending inventory			36,000
Total metal needs			529,000 lbs.
Less beginning inventory			- 32,000
Purchases needed			497,000 lbs.
Cost per lb.			× $8
Total purchases			$3,976,000

	Drills	Saws	Total
Plastic purchases:			
Production units (from production budget)	65,000	42,000	107,000
Plastic			× 3 lbs.
Production needs			321,000 lbs.
Desired ending inventory			32,000
Total plastic needs			353,000 lbs.
Less beginning inventory			- 29,000
Purchases needed			324,000 lbs.
Cost per lb.			× $5
Total purchases			$1,620,000
Handle purchases:			
Production units (from production budget)	65,000		65,000
Handles			× 1
Production needs			65,000
Desired ending inventory			7,000
Total handle needs			72,000
Less beginning inventory			- 6,000
Purchases needed			66,000
Cost per handle			× $3
Total purchases			$ 198,000
Total purchases:			
Metal			$3,976,000
Plastic			1,620,000
Handles			198,000
Total			$5,794,000

(d)

Handy Company
Manufacturing Disbursements Budget
First Quarter 19X1

	Drills	Saws	Total
Purchases			$5,794,000
Budgeted production	65,000	42,000	
Direct labor hours per unit	× 2	× 3	
Total direct labor hours	130,000	126,000	
Labor rate	× $12	× $16	
Labor expenditures	$1,560,000	$2,016,000	3,576,000
Direct labor hours	130,000	126,000	
Variable factory overhead rate	× $1.50	× $1.50	
Total variable overhead	$ 195,000	$ 189,000	384,000
Fixed factory overhead ($214,000 - $156,000)			58,000
Total			$9,812,000

(e)

Handy Company
Cash Budget
First Quarter 19X1

Cash balance, beginning		$ 1,800,000
Collections on sales:		
Current quarter's sales (50%)	$5,500,000	
Previous quarter's sales (50%)	4,200,000	9,700,000
Cash available from operations		$11,500,000
Less budgeted disbursements:		
Manufacturing	$9,812,000	
Selling and administrative		
($340,000 - $90,000 depreciation)	250,000	10,062,000
Cash balance, ending		$ 1,438,000

(f)

Schedule of Manufacturing Costs per Unit

		Drills	Saws
Metal:	5 lbs. at $8/lb.	$40.00	
	4 lbs. at $8/lb.		$ 32.00
Plastic:	3 lbs. at $5/lb.	15.00	15.00
Handles:	1 each at $3	3.00	
Direct labor:	2 hrs. at $12/hr.	24.00	
	3 hrs. at $16/hr.		48.00
Variable factory overhead:	2 hrs. at $1.50/labor hr.	3.00	
	3 hrs. at $1.50/labor hr.		4.50
Fixed factory overhead:	$214,000/107,000*	2.00	2.00
Total unit costs		$87.00	$101.50

*From production budget; 65,000 drills and 42,000 saws

Handy Company
Pro Forma Income Statement
First Quarter 19X1

Sales (sales budget)		$11,000,000
Less costs of goods sold:		
Drills (60,000 × $87)	$5,220,000	
Saws (40,000 × $101.50)	4,060,000	- 9,280,000
Gross profit		$ 1,720,000
Selling and administrative expenses		- 340,000
Net income		$ 1,380,000

After completing this chapter, you should be able to:

LO 1

Explain the concept of responsibility accounting.

LO 2

Identify the different types of reporting for cost centers.

LO 3

Determine and interpret variable cost variances.

LO 4

Determine fixed overhead variances.

LO 5

Develop cost variance reports.

LO 6

Prepare a performance report for a revenue center.

RESPONSIBILITY ACCOUNTING AND PERFORMANCE ASSESSMENT

In organizations around the world, there is growing recognition that current systems of encouraging and rewarding improvement in employee performance do not apply to the full range of managerial positions. For most organizations, systems for evaluating nonmanagerial performance are accepted and entrenched, even if they are not defined. In contrast, systems for recognizing effectiveness of managerial performance are not as well developed and subject to continual skepticism.

One explanation for this difference in assessment is the supposed ease of evaluating nonmanagerial activities and the acknowledged complexity of appraising effective managing. A second explanation rests in the traditional education and experience of managers. Before they were managers, these people were engineers, accountants, production employees, or some other technical job holder. While they developed a strong professional identity in their premanagement position, they did not have formal training as managers. Finally, perhaps the most important reason for the failure to define and recognize effective managing is the dramatic variation among the different areas that must be managed. Managing an engineering department with all college graduates is quite different from managing a receiving department in the warehouse with mostly high school graduates. The variation exists in areas of employee motivation, amount and degree of supervision needed, planning, and budgeting, to name a few.

One of the ways management accounting can address the problems of assessing the job of managing is through feedback. Because not everything can be measured, it is important to provide timely feedback for those things that are being measured. Also, proper measures are situation specific; and what works in the production department may not work, or even be appropriate, in the customer services department. As related to accounting, feedback in the form of performance reports is essential if the benefits of budgeting and other types of planning are to be fully realized. Managers need to know how actual results compare with the current budget in order to control current operations and to improve operations in future periods.

Consider a relatively simple situation where the unit cost of raw materials exceeds the cost allowed in the budget. A performance report addressed to the appropriate manager indicates the existence of the disparity, and the manager initiates an investigation to determine its cause. The manager may find that a new employee doing purchasing is buying from unauthorized vendors or in small lots. In this case, the manager will take action to bring performance into line with plans, perhaps by having the new employee work closely with a more experienced colleague. Alternatively, the investigation may reveal unanticipated price increases. In this case, the budget possibly should be revised to reflect the price increases, and the new prices should also be used in future budgets.

*Performance reports should be prepared in accordance with the concept of **responsibility accounting,** which is the structuring of performance reports addressed to individual or group members of an organization in a manner that emphasizes the factors controllable by them. The organizational units that these managers manage are called* responsibility centers. *Ideally, the reports show only revenues and expenses controllable by the responsibility center managers.*

The purpose of this chapter is to examine the nature of financial performance reports and the concepts that underlie their development, assessment, and use. *This includes performance reports for revenue and cost centers and how standard costs are established for direct materials, direct labor, and variable manufacturing overhead.[1] The relationship between performance reports and organization structure, as well as the types of financial performance reports that are best suited to various activities, are discussed.*

RESPONSIBILITY ACCOUNTING

L O 1

Performance reports that contain comparisons of actual results with plans or budgets serve as assessment tools and attention-directors to help managers determine and control the organization's activities. In accordance with the concept of management by exception, the absence of significant differences indicates that activities are proceeding as planned, whereas the presence of significant differences indicates a need either to take corrective action or to revise plans.

In responsibility accounting, the focus is on specific units within the organization that are responsible for the accomplishment of specific activities or objectives. Performance reports are customized to emphasize the activities of each specific organizational unit. For example, a financial performance report addressed to the head of a production department contains manufacturing costs controllable by the department head; it does not contain costs (such as advertising, sales commissions, or the president's salary) that the head of the production department cannot control. Including non-

---

1 Standard unit costs ordinarily are not calculated for fixed manufacturing overhead costs for performance evaluation purposes because these costs are incurred based on production capacity provided, not production capacity used. Accordingly, they are not controlled on a per unit of production basis.

controllable costs in the report distracts the manager's attention from controllable costs and, thereby, dilutes a manager's efforts to deal with controllable items. Lower-level managers may also become frustrated with the entire performance reporting system if they believe upper-level managers expect them to control costs they cannot influence. However, some companies insist on reporting all related revenues and expenses in the same report. When this is the case, the noncontrollable items should be clearly labeled.

Responsibility accounting can lead to unethical practices by managers in key positions. If too much pressure is placed on the managers to perform and meet the requirements of the responsibility accounting system, they sometimes take actions that are not in the best interest of the organization. An example of such an action is presented in Management Accounting Practice 8-1 where a vice president of Bausch & Lomb forced sales in one year to the detriment of the company's sales the following year. The designers of an organization's responsibility accounting system need to be aware of the potential pressures that performance evaluation can place upon managers. The reward system of the organization should be such that managers are not influenced to make undesirable decisions just to receive bonuses or promotions.

Financial Planning Feedback

The importance of feedback to financial planning is illustrated in Exhibit 8-1. Here, budgeting and performance evaluation are presented as a continuous cycle. As the accounting period passes, actual operating data are accumulated and compared with the current budget in the form of performance reports. The appropriate managers receive these reports and then obtain additional information to explain significant deviations from the budget. Based on this information, management attempts to improve current operations and plans for the future, which are summarized in the new budget. The new budget then becomes the current budget, and the cycle continues.

EXHIBIT 8-1: THE BUDGETING-PERFORMANCE EVALUATION CYCLE

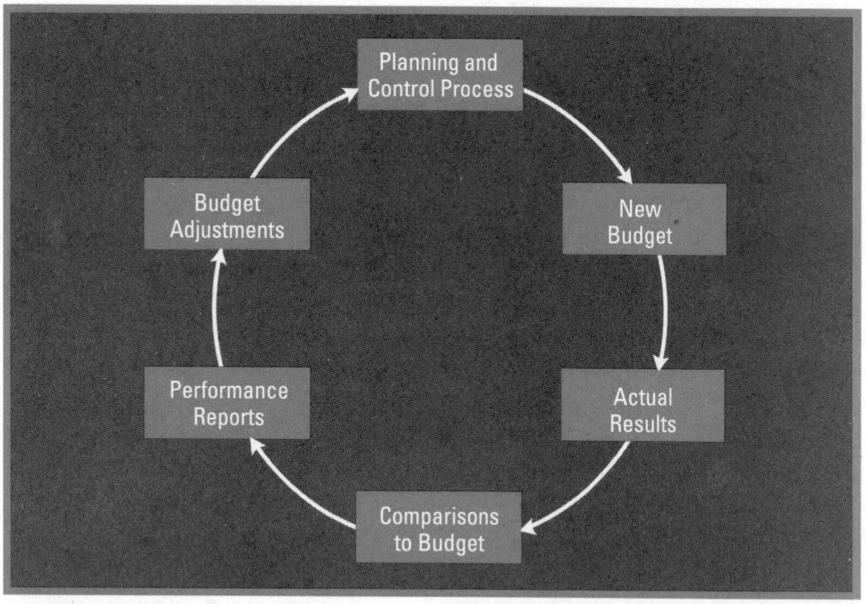

Performance Reporting and Organizational Structures

Before implementing a responsibility accounting system, all areas of authority and responsibility within an organization must be clearly defined. Organization charts and other documents should be examined to determine an organization's authority and responsibility structure. As part of defining an organization's responsibility accounting system, an examination of the organizational structure should be made. **Organizational structure** is the arrangement of lines of responsibility within the organization. However, organizational structures vary widely. Some companies have functional-based structures along the lines of marketing, production, research, and the like; while other companies use products, services, customers, or geography as the basis of organization. When an attempt is made to implement a responsibility accounting system, management may find instances of overlapping duties, of authority not commensurate with responsibility, and of expenditures for which no one appears responsible. These circumstances can make the development of a responsibility accounting system difficult.

MANAGEMENT ACCOUNTING PRACTICE 8-1

Ethics and Responsibility Accounting

In late 1993, the contact lens division of Bausch & Lomb, Inc., was experiencing lower than anticipated sales levels. In December, the head of the division called a meeting of its independent distributors and told them that the company had changed its sales strategy. Effective immediately, each distributor would have to boost its inventory of contact lenses if it wanted to remain a distributor of Bausch & Lomb products.

The strategy: Distributors could only buy in very large quantities (some as much as a two-year supply). Even though increased quantities usually mean lower prices, not so with Bausch & Lomb; the prices being charged increased by amounts up to 50 percent. And finally, if a distributor wanted to maintain its relationship with the company, it had to place these large orders by December 24, 1993. As one distributor stated, "When your No. 1 vendor says you'd better take it or else, what're you going to do?" All but two of Bausch & Lomb's distributors complied with the new sales strategy demands. In January, those two distributors were dropped by the company.

The results: Initially the strategy paid off; the sales in the last few days of December totalled about $25 million and amounted to half of the division's profit for the entire year. The division manager was delighted of course, sales and profits soared, and his operations were in great shape. However, the long-term results were not favorable. By June 1994, the company announced that high inventories by its distributors would severely reduce sales and profits for the year. The profit decline—approximately 37 percent.

The ending: The manager got what he wanted—increased sales and a nice profit for the year. But the company and its stockholders paid the price of one manager's poor decision. In the summer of 1994, after the company made the announcement about the sales decline, the company's stock fell from $50 to $32. After this disclosure, the manager was forced to step down from his position and a class-action lawsuit was filed by stockholders accusing the company of falsely inflating sales and earnings.

Based on: "Numbers Game at Bausch & Lomb?" *Business Week* (December 19, 1994), pp. 108-110.

Though performance reports can be developed for areas of responsibility as narrow as a single worker, the basic responsibility unit in most organizations is the department. In manufacturing plants, separate responsibility centers are set up for individual production and service departments. In large universities, separate responsibility centers are set up for individual academic departments (e.g., accounting, psychology, and mathematics) and staff and service departments (e.g., human resources, cafeteria, and maintenance). When a large department performs a number of diverse and significant activities, responsibility accounting may be further refined so that a single department contains several responsibility centers with performance reports prepared for each.

An abbreviated organization chart for a company that owns and leases space in shopping malls is presented in Exhibit 8-2. The short-run objective of the firm is to earn a profit by renting space in company-owned shopping malls. The president and the executive vice president are responsible for overall operations and profitability. The authority to set rents and to incur marketing costs involved with the rental units is delegated to the vice president of marketing, who in turn delegates a portion of this authority to each of two district marketing managers. The authority to incur costs in connection with the actual rental spaces (stores) is delegated to the vice president of operations, who in turn delegates a portion of this authority to each mall manager. Finally, each mall manager delegates the authority to incur costs, in connection with specific rental activities, to department heads.

Commensurate with their authority, individual department heads have quite narrow responsibility. And, commensurate with greater authority, responsibility is broader at higher levels in the organization. A series of financial performance reports, illustrating expanding authority for operating costs, is presented in Exhibit 8-3 (page 393). A mall manager is responsible for more costs than is a department head, and the vice president of operations is responsible for more costs than is a single mall manager. Note how the performance reports tie together. The totals for the head of the Security Department are included as one line in the mall manager's report, and the totals for the manager of Mall 2 are included as one line in the report for the vice president of operations. This aggregation takes place because the managers closest to actual activities need detailed information to control day-to-day activities, whereas upper-level managers spend less time controlling activities and more time planning them.

Financial Performance Measures

All product and service activities result in financial measures. The common financial performance measures are income statements, variance reports of actual to budget, variance reports of actual to standard, and return on investment. The variance measures, in particular, are usually available at all levels in the organization. A department head needs to know if the department's labor costs are within acceptable ranges; a plant manager needs to know if the plant labor costs are within acceptable ranges; and a division manager needs to know if division labor costs are within acceptable ranges.

Basic performance reports are almost always stated in terms of dollars, a common, additive unit of measure for all activities. Once the dollar

EXHIBIT 8-2: PARTIAL ORGANIZATION CHART OF A SHOPPING MALL RENTAL COMPANY

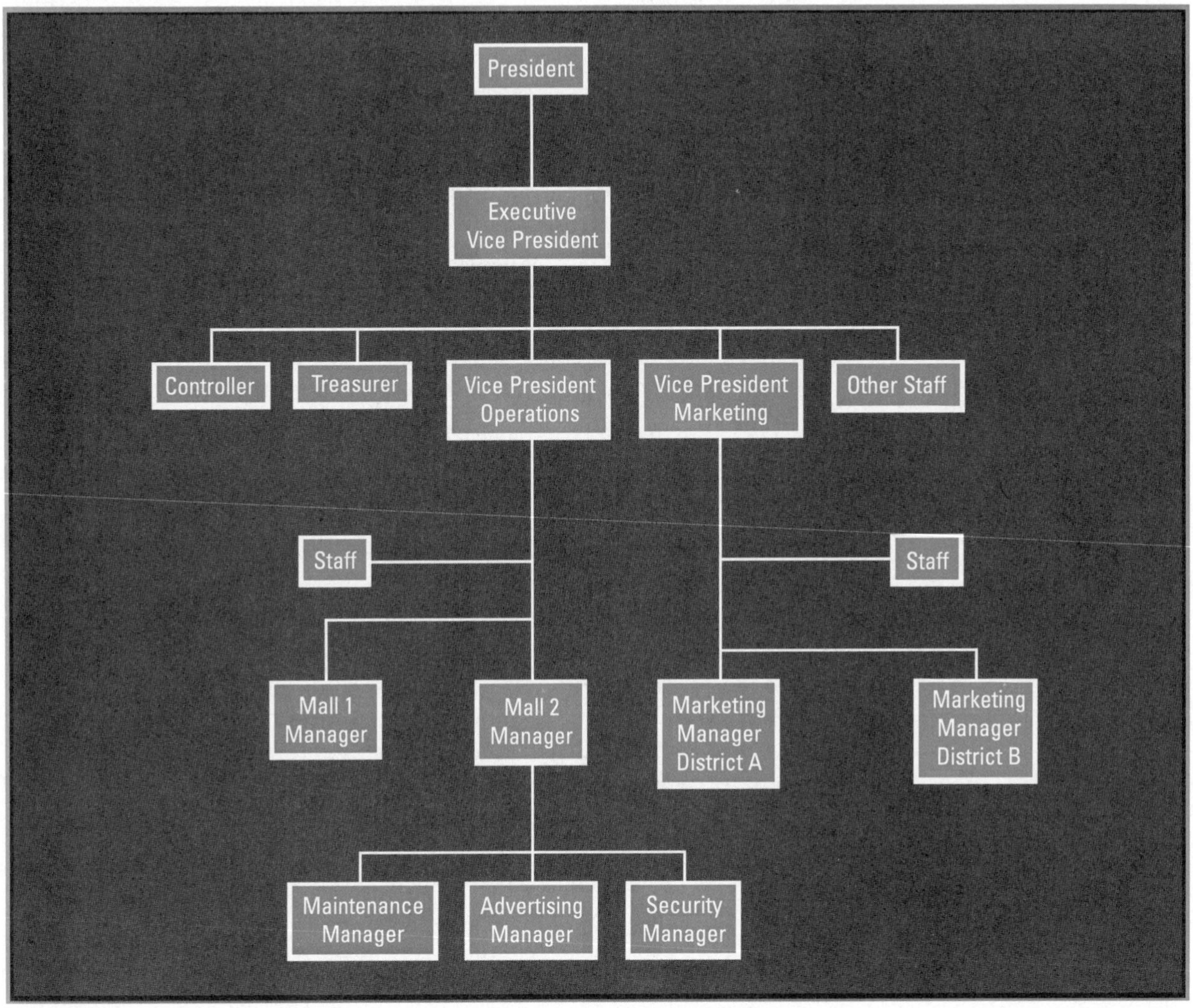

impact of each activity is determined, the dollar measures can be summarized and reported up the corporate ladder. Furthermore, both the immediate supervisor of an activity and managers far removed from the activity can understand the impact of dollars on cash flow and income.

Nonfinancial Performance Measures

Limited nonfinancial information is routinely collected and reported along with financial information in most cost accounting systems. Examples of traditionally reported nonfinancial information include: sales volume in units, production output in units, reporting bases such as labor and machine hours, and various quantity measures of materials used (i.e., pounds, liters, etc.). Often times organizations select measures based on their ability to aid in explaining the successes and failures of the organizations' activities. Typically, measures for selected industries might include the following:

EXHIBIT 8-3: RESPONSIBILITY ACCOUNTING REPORTS FOR MULTIPLE LEVELS

	Actual Cost	Allowed Cost	Variance*
Vice President Operations			
Mall 1	$ 55,000	$ 54,800	$ 200 U
> Mall 2	69,600	68,400	1,200 U
Vice pres.'s office (itemized)	10,900	12,000	1,100 F
Total	$135,500	$135,200	$ 300 U
Manager: Mall 2			
Maintenance Department	$ 25,400	$ 24,700	$ 700 U
Advertising Department	17,500	18,000	500 F
>> Security Department	20,500	19,900	600 U
Mall mgr.'s office (itemized)	6,200	5,800	400 U
< Total	$ 69,600	$ 68,400	$1,200 U
Head: Security Department			
Supplies	$ 3,000	$ 2,000	$1,000 U
Staff wages	9,500	10,000	500 F
General overhead (itemized)	8,000	7,900	100 U
<< Total	$ 20,500	$ 19,900	$ 600 U

*F = Favorable, if actual costs are less than allowed costs.
U = Unfavorable, if actual costs are greater than allowed costs.

Industry	Measurement Unit
Consulting	Hours billed
Restaurant	Customers served
Social agency of government	Clients served per day
Telephone company	Minutes of use
University	Student credit-hours per term

In most situations, dollars should not be used to the exclusion of nondollar performance measures. A favorable financial variance that resulted from an unethical or illegal action should not be rewarded. Short-sighted managers may also take actions that appear favorable in the short run but are detrimental to the organization in the long run. Excessive pressures for employee productivity may result in strikes and employee turnover, and bargain purchases of raw materials may result in excess waste. These examples illustrate the need for upper-level management to inquire about the causes of favorable as well as unfavorable variances. Variances of any substantial amount should be indicators (red flags) that something in the process is not operating as it should, and nonfinancial measures can often identify causes of variances outside the norm.

As the next century approaches, organizations must be prepared to meet the competitive global environment with a competitive reporting system. Responsibility accounting reports must be expanded to include productivity, quality, and innovative assessments. Productivity must be assessed via accurate measures of efficient resource utilization. Dollars of resources used must be supplemented—and in many cases replaced—by reporting schemes measuring material movements, setup times and frequencies, energy consumed, and administrative resources employed. As illustrated in Management Accounting Practice 8-2, companies are making increased use of nonfinancial measures of performance. Additional productivity measures may include value-added per employee or machine hour and output to input ratios of materials (resources) used.

Frequency of Performance Reports

Performance reports must be provided frequently enough to allow managers to take timely, corrective action. Although annual performance reports may assist in developing plans and evaluating a manager's performance,

---

MANAGEMENT ACCOUNTING PRACTICE 8-2

Performance Measurement

Internal performance measures of a nonfinancial nature are constantly being sought by corporate executives. Top executives believe that such measures will help their managers improve the evaluation of job performance. They will also help the executives evaluate the managers.

A major research study conducted for the Boston University Manufacturing Roundtable resulted in the development of the Performance Measurement Questionnaire (PMQ). The questionnaire reportedly assists organizations in evaluating the effectiveness and efficiency of existing performance measures and in determining the congruence of the organization's strategies and actions.

Through the use of the questionnaire, an organization's areas needing improvement can be identified, its current evaluation measures can be adjusted to better capture needed information, and it provides a framework for aligning measures with desired improvements. It also provides the management with a list of common attributes that a good performance measurement system contains as related to their industry. It takes into account the organization's culture, level of abilities and competencies, and access to available resources.

A couple of sample questions, with related headings, provide some insights as to how the information is gathered about the organization:

Long-Run Importance of Improvement	Improvement Areas	Effect of Current Performance Measures on Improvement
None . . . . Great		Inhibit . . . . Support
1 2 3 4 5 6 7	Labor efficiency	1 2 3 4 5 6 7
1 2 3 4 5 6 7	Product technology	1 2 3 4 5 6 7
	Performance Factors	
1 2 3 4 5 6 7	Inventory turnover	1 2 3 4 5 6 7
1 2 3 4 5 6 7	Manufacturing lead times	1 2 3 4 5 6 7

Based on: Paul McMann and Alfred J. Nanni, Jr., "Is Your Company Really Measuring Performance?" *Management Accounting* (November 1994) pp. 55-58.

they are of no use in adjusting operations during the year. On the other hand, daily or hourly performance reports may be of great value to some managers but a distraction to others. The solution to this dilemma is to recognize that different levels of management and different personnel at each level have differing needs for performance information. The head of a production department may require daily, hourly, or continuous information about operations under his or her control, whereas a plant manager may need only weekly reports from each department head. Similarly, the vice president of production may require only monthly performance reports from each plant. The further a manager is from actual operations, the less the manager's need for frequent feedback. Higher-level managers spend more time planning operations and motivating personnel to execute these plans, and lower-level managers spend more time executing plans. Hence, lower-level managers have greater need for frequent and timely feedback.

Types of Responsibility Centers

each only worries about their resp.

Under responsibility accounting, performance reports are prepared for departments, segments of departments, or groupings of departments that operate under the control and authority of a responsible manager. Each organizational unit for which performance reports are prepared is identified as a responsibility center. For the purpose of evaluating their financial performance, responsibility centers may be classified as cost centers, revenue centers, profit centers, and investment centers.

Cost Center

A **cost center** is a responsibility center whose manager is responsible only for managing costs; there is no revenue responsibility. A cost center may be as small as a segment of a department or large enough to include a major aspect of the organization such as all manufacturing activities. The financial performance reports in Exhibit 8-3 illustrate an increasing responsibility for cost management. Each department head is responsible only for costs incurred for his or her department, but each mall manager is responsible for all mall operating costs. Cost centers are established for operating as well as nonoperating activities. In Exhibit 8-2, each of the staff departments, such as the Controller, is evaluated as a cost center. Cost centers are also established in manufacturing, merchandising, service, and not-for-profit organizations. Typical examples of these cost centers include the following:

Organization	Cost Center
Manufacturing plant	Tooling Department Assembly Department
Retail store	Inventory control function Maintenance Department
TV station	Audio/video engineering Buildings and grounds
College	History Department Power plant
City government	Public safety (police and fire) Road Maintenance

Revenue Center *Only*

A **revenue center** is a responsibility center whose manager is responsible for the generation of sales revenues. In Exhibit 8-2, there are three revenue centers: District A, District B, and the Vice President of Marketing. A performance report is prepared for each district and for the Vice President of Marketing. Even though the basic performance report of a revenue center emphasizes sales, revenue centers are likely to be assigned responsibility for the controllable costs they incur in generating revenues. If revenues and costs are evaluated separately, the center has dual responsibility as a revenue center and as a cost center. If controllable costs are deducted from revenues to obtain some bottom-line contribution, the center is, in fact, being treated more like a profit center than a cost center.

Profit Center

both Cost & Revenue

A **profit center** is a responsibility center whose manager is responsible for revenues, costs, and resulting profits. It may be an entire organization, but it is more frequently a segment of an organization such as a product line, marketing territory, or store. In the context of performance evaluation, the word "profit" may not refer to the bottom line of an income statement; instead, it is likely to refer to the profit center's contribution to common corporate costs and profit. Profit is computed as the center's revenues less all costs identified with operating the center. In addition to a center's profits, other measures of performance may include quality assessments, service ratings, and operating efficiencies.

A large retail organization might evaluate each of its stores as a profit center, with the store manager being the administrative officer. The store manager, who has responsibility for the overall operation of the store, accepts the store's physical structure and the organization's investment in the store as givens. Having limited authority regarding the size of the store's total assets, the store manager is not held responsible for the relationship between profits and assets. Profit centers are discussed further in Chapter 9.

Investment Center

Acquiring of Assets

Profit Cost Revenue

An **investment center** is a responsibility center whose manager is responsible for the relationship between its profits and the total assets invested in the center. Investment center managers have a high degree of organizational autonomy. In general, the management of an investment center is expected to earn a target profit per dollar invested. Investment center managers are evaluated on the basis of how well they use the total resources entrusted to their care to earn a profit. An investment center is the broadest and most inclusive type of responsibility center. The entire organization depicted in Exhibit 8-2 would be regarded as an investment center, with the president and the executive vice president being the investment center's management. They have more authority and responsibility than other managers and are primarily responsible for planning, organizing, and controlling firm activities. Because of their authority regarding the size of corporate assets, they are held responsible for the relationship between profits and assets. Investment centers are discussed further in Chapter 9.

PERFORMANCE REPORTING FOR COST CENTERS

L O 2

Financial performance reports for cost centers should always include a comparison of actual and budgeted (or allowed) costs and should always identify the difference as a variance. "Allowed costs" are used in performance reports as the flexible budget amounts for the actual level of activity. The variance is favorable if actual costs are less than budgeted (or allowed) costs and unfavorable if actual costs are greater than budgeted (or allowed) costs. These comparisons are made in total and for each type of controllable cost assigned to the cost center.

Development of Flexible Budgets

A budget that is based on a single prediction of sales and production is called a **static budget**. The operating budget explained in Chapter 7 is a static budget. Budgets may also be drawn up for a series of possible production and sales volumes, or budgets may be adjusted to a particular level of production after the fact. These budgets, based on cost-volume or cost-activity relationships, are called **flexible budgets**; they are used to determine what costs should have been for an attained level of activity.

Before developing a flexible budget, management must understand how costs respond to changes in activity. Some costs respond to unit or volume activity; others, to batch activity. Assume the Store-It Company, which produces compact disk carrying cases for home, car, and office, has three departments: Production, Sales, and Administration. The focus in this section is on the development of financial performance reports for the Production Department. The flexible budget cost estimating equation for total monthly production costs of carrying cases is based on the production standards and is as follows:

Flexible budget for variable items:

Direct materials	2 pounds per unit at $5 per pound, or $10 per unit
Direct labor	1/4 hour per unit at $24 per hour, or $6 per unit
Manufacturing overhead:	
Group A	0.4 machine hour at $3.60 per hour, or $1.44 per unit
Group B	2 pounds per unit at $3 per pound, or $6 per unit

Flexible budget for fixed overhead: $52,000

Flexible budget equation for monthly production costs:

		Fixed Costs		Variable Costs
Direct materials				$10.00X
Direct labor				6.00X
Manufacturing overhead:				
Variable:				
Group A				1.44X
Group B				6.00X
Fixed		$52,000		
Total cost equation	=	$52,000	+	$23.44X

where:

Group A = the overhead items that are closely
related to machine hours

Group B = the overhead items that are closely
related to direct materials

X = the number of units produced

It should be noted that the variable overhead items are based on cost drivers and do not add any quantity amounts. For example, the Group B overhead items are closely related to the use of direct materials for the product and do not add another two pounds to the product. The base of budgeting the Group B overhead costs is simply stated on a per unit basis, which happens to allow two pounds of direct materials per unit. Therefore, for every two pounds of direct materials used, an allowance of Group B overhead is made of $6 (2 pounds × $3).

If management plans to produce 10,000 cases in July 19X7, requiring 4,000 machine hours and 20,000 pounds of materials, the budgeted Production Department costs for the month will amount to $286,400:

Store-It Company
Production Department Budget
For the Month of July 19X7

Manufacturing costs:	
Direct materials (20,000* pounds × $5)	$100,000
Direct labor (2,500** hours × $24)	60,000
Variable manufacturing overhead:	
Group A (4,000# machine hours × $3.60)	14,400
Group B (20,000## pounds of materials × $3)	60,000
Fixed overhead	52,000
Total	$286,400

  *10,000 units × 2 pounds per unit
**10,000 units × 0.25 hour per unit
  #10,000 units × 0.40 machine hours
##10,000 units × 2 pounds of materials

**Flexible
Budgets
Emphasize
Efficiency**

If actual production happened to equal 10,000 units, the performance of the Production Department in controlling costs could be based on a comparison of actual and budgeted manufacturing costs. But, if production were at some volume other than that planned in the original manufacturing budget, it would be inappropriate to compare actual manufacturing costs with the costs predicted in the original static budget. Doing so would intermix two separate Production Department responsibilities—namely, the manufacturing responsibility for production volume and the financial responsibility for cost control.

The original budget for production volume was set on the basis of predicted needs for sales and inventory requirements, taking into consideration materials, labor, and facilities constraints. In the absence of any changes in these needs, the Production Department's manufacturing responsibility for production volume is evaluated by comparing the actual and budgeted production volumes. If, however, production needs change, perhaps due to an unexpected increase or decrease in sales volume, the Production Department should attempt to make appropriate changes in its production volume. And, when the actual production volume is anything other than the originally budgeted amount, the Production Department's financial responsibility for cost control should be based on the actual level of production.

For the purpose of evaluating the financial performance of cost centers, a flexible budget is tailored, after the fact, to the actual level of activity. A **flexible budget variance** is computed for each cost as the difference between the actual cost and the flexible budget cost of producing a given quantity of product or service. Assume that actual production for July totalled 11,000 units, rather than the 10,000 units that were budgeted. Examples of a performance report for July manufacturing costs, based on static and flexible budgets, are presented in Exhibit 8-4. When the Production Department's financial performance is evaluated using the static budget, the actual cost of producing 11,000 units is compared to the budgeted cost of producing 10,000 units. The result is a series of unfavorable static budget variances totaling $26,600.

EXHIBIT 8-4: FLEXIBLE BUDGETS AND PERFORMANCE EVALUATION

Store-It Company
Production Department Performance Report
For the Month of July 19X7

	Based on Static Budget			Based on Flexible Budget		
	Actual	Original Budget	Static Budget Variance	Actual	Flexible Budget*	Flexible Budget Variance
Volume	11,000	10,000		11,000	11,000	
Manufacturing costs:						
Direct materials	$108,000	$100,000	$ 8,000 U	$108,000	$110,000	$2,000 F
Direct labor	70,000	60,000	10,000 U	70,000	66,000	4,000 U
Variable overhead:						
Group A		$ 14,400			$ 15,840	
Group B		60,000			66,000	
Total	82,000	74,400	7,600 U	82,000	81,840	160 U
Fixed overhead	53,000	52,000	1,000 U	53,000	52,000	1,000 U
Totals	$313,000	$286,400	$26,600 U	$313,000	$309,840	$3,160 U

*Flexible budget manufacturing costs: (Actual level × Budgeted unit cost)
  Direct materials (11,000 units × 2 pounds × $5)
  Direct labor (11,000 units × 0.25 labor hours × $24)
  Variable overhead:
   Group A (11,000 units × 0.4 machine hours × $3.60)
   Group B (11,000 units × 2 pounds × $3)

However, when the Production Department's financial performance is evaluated by comparing actual costs with costs allowed in a flexible budget drawn up for the actual production volume, the results are mixed. Direct materials have a $2,000 favorable flexible budget variance. Direct labor has a $4,000 unfavorable flexible budget variance. The total variable overhead variance is $160 unfavorable. The fixed overhead has a $1,000 unfavorable variance. The net unfavorable flexible budget variance is $3,160, a substantial change from the static variance of $26,600 unfavorable. Notice that there are no variable overhead flexible budget variances for individual Group A and Group B items because they are not tracked individually. Although many companies track all overhead groupings, the added complexity to our example would be distracting.

It should be obvious that the flexible budget variances are a much better indicator of performance than are the static budget variances, which do not take into account the increased level of production, 11,000 units, not 10,000 units. Almost anyone could have guessed that when production increases by 10 percent, the static budget variances would be unfavorable. Likewise, when actual production is substantially below the planned level of activity, the static variances are usually favorable.

Standard Costs

A **standard cost**, a budget for one batch or unit of product, indicates what it should cost to produce one batch or unit of product under efficient operating conditions. In a standard costing environment, the flexible budget is based on standard batch or unit costs. Traditionally, standard costs have been developed from an engineering analysis or from an analysis of historical data adjusted for expected changes in the product, production technology, or costs. When standards are developed using historical data, management must be careful to ensure that past inefficiencies are excluded from current standards. Target costing and continuous improvement costing, which were discussed in Chapter 5, may also be used to set standard costs. In target costing, an allowance for profit is subtracted from a desired selling price to determine the maximum allowable cost. In continuous improvement costing, the maximum allowable cost is set as the current cost less a target reduction in cost. Management Accounting Practice 8-3 examines performance reports based on continuous improvement costing.

To obtain the full benefit of standard costs, the standards must be based on realistic expectations and accepted by employees. The standard variable product cost for direct labor for the Store-It Company is $6 per unit. Some organizations intentionally set "tight" standards to motivate employees toward higher levels of production. The management of Store-It Company might set their standards for direct labor at 0.22 hours per unit, rather than at the expected 0.25 hours per unit, hoping that employees will strive toward the lower time and, consequently, the lower cost of $5.28. The use of tight standards often causes planning and behavioral problems. Management expects them to result in unfavorable variances. Accordingly, tight standards should not be used to budget input requirements and cash flows— management expects to incur more labor costs than the standards allow. The use of tight standards can have undesirable behavioral effects if lower-level managers and employees find that a second set of standards is used in the

---

MANAGEMENT ACCOUNTING PRACTICE 8-3

Continuous Improvement (Kaizen) Costing

Continuous improvement costing, also known as Kaizen costing, takes target costing one step further in that it provides a means of ensuring continuous improvement activities after the target costs have been developed. It aims at reducing the actual costs below the standard costs. Kaizen costing activities are defined as those activities that sustain the current level of existing production and are very specific with respect to each department and each accounting period.

The actual production costs of the prior period serves as the cost base of the current period. The target of the Kaizen method seeks to reduce the cost base during the current period. The ratio of the target reduction amount to the base amount is the target reduction rate. After the target reduction amount for each activity is determined, the actual cost of the activity is then compared to the target amounts for the computation of variances. For each activity being controlled, the process flows as follows (with example):

Item	Cost Base	→	Continuous Improvement Target Ratio	→	Continuous Improvement Target Costs	→	Actual Costs	→	Variance
Indirect labor (per day)	$14,000	×	0.92	=	$12,880	–	$13,100	=	$220 U

The key is the selection of the target ratio by members of management and the area or department involved with the activity. Once Kaizen costing is established for a period, it becomes a very aggressive tool in the process of cost reduction.

....

Based on: Yasuhiro Monden and John Lee, "How a Japanese Auto Maker Reduces Costs," *Management Accounting* (August 1993), pp. 22-26.

"real" budget or if they are constantly subject to unfavorable performance reports. They may come to distrust the entire budgeting and performance evaluation system, or they may quit trying to achieve any of the organization's standards.

Tight standards are more likely to occur in an imposed budget and less likely to occur in a participation budget where employees are actively involved in budget preparation. In a participation budget, the problems may be to avoid loose standards that are easily attained and to avoid overstating the costs required to produce a product. Loose standards may fail to properly motivate employees and may make the company uncompetitive due to costs and prices that are higher than those of competitors.

Standard and Discretionary Cost Centers A distinction is often made between standard and discretionary cost centers. A **standard cost center** is a cost center that has clearly defined relationships between effort and accomplishment. A **discretionary cost center** is a cost center that does not have clearly defined relationships between effort and accomplishment.

The financial performance of standard cost centers is evaluated with the aid of flexible budgets drawn up for the actual level of activity. A production department is the most obvious example of a standard cost center. However, the growth of services and service industries—and the resultant need to control service costs—has led to an expanding use of standard cost centers in these types of organizations. Standard cost centers can be established for any segment of a business for which it is possible to develop input/output relationships and standard cost per unit or batch of activity. Possible applications include the costs of packaging, transportation, commissions, utilities, room cleaning, residential fire inspection, laundry, automobile repair, and processing loan applications.

Discretionary costs are set at a fixed amount at the discretion of management. Changing these costs does not affect production or service capacity in the near-term. Because a relationship between effort and accomplishment is absent, the financial performance of a discretionary cost center cannot be evaluated with the aid of a flexible budget. Indeed, it is difficult to evaluate the performance of a discretionary cost center by any financial assessment means. The best monetary evaluation is based on a comparison of the actual and budgeted costs for a given period, with the results identified as being over budget or under budget. This is an area where nonfinancial measures are generally the best indicators of success. In a research and development department, the best assessments may be the number of successful new products developed, quality improvements in existing products, and number of new ideas generated (even though some may have failed).

If a research and development budget for 19X9 contained authorized expenditures of $1.5 million, but the actual 19X9 expenditures amounted to $1.2 million, the $300,000 difference is not necessarily favorable. Research and development was $300,000 under budget. Whether this is good or bad depends on what was accomplished during the year. If the money was saved by canceling a program critical to the organization's future, the net result is hardly favorable. Again, all the variance does is inform management that actual results were not in line with plans. Management must investigate further to determine the significance of the variance.

Though it is difficult to evaluate the under-budget performance of a discretionary cost center, an over-budget performance has an undesirable implication, regardless of the results achieved. If, after the budget is approved, the manager of a discretionary cost center realizes the center's budget is inadequate, the manager should request additional funds or notify his or her supervisor of the need to reduce activity. Going over budget implies that the manager is unable to operate within the budgeted resources. Obviously, a manager should not be allowed unlimited use of the organization's resources. Also, a cost center that was initially established as a discretionary cost center may be changed to a standard cost center once management determines the relationships between the center's operating costs and measures of its activity. A management that desires to better plan and control costs will encourage the evolution from discretionary to standard cost centers wherever practical.

VARIANCE ANALYSIS FOR VARIABLE COSTS

[handwritten margin notes: 2 types / Price & Quantity]

To use and interpret standard cost variances properly, managers must understand both the standard-setting process and the framework for computing and analyzing standard cost variances. While these are preliminary tools for decision analysis regarding activities and operations, they nevertheless give managers a starting point as to the general movement toward efficiency, or lack thereof, of the defined activities being evaluated. However, the variances alone do not explain why the activity is different from expectations. Underlying causes of variances must always be investigated before final judgment is passed on the effectiveness and efficiency of an operation or activity. The following sections on variances consider possible explanations as to why variances occur in each area.

Standard cost variance analysis provides a system for examining the flexible budget variance, which is the difference between the *actual cost* and *flexible budget cost* of producing a given quantity of product or service. Actual cost is determined by multiplying actual quantities of materials, labor, and overhead inputs used in producing goods and services times the actual prices paid for the inputs at actual production levels. Flexible budget cost is determined by multiplying standard input quantities allowed for materials, labor, and overhead times the standard price per input unit. In other words, the flexible budget may also be computed as actual output times standard unit cost. Recall that standard unit cost represents what it should cost to produce a completed unit of product or service under efficient operating conditions. To determine standard unit cost, management establishes separate quantity and price (or rate) standards for each input production component. Following activity-based costing (ABC) concepts, each manufacturing activity might have its own standard costs that focus on underlying concepts and cost drivers. However, to provide a more defined focus, our illustrations use only materials, labor, and overhead as the major production components.

Standard cost variance analysis identifies the general causes for the total flexible budget variance by breaking it down into separate price and quantity variances for each production component. Two possible reasons why actual cost may differ from flexible budget cost for a given amount of output produced are: (1) there was a difference between actual and standard prices paid for the production components, the **price variance**, and (2) there was a difference between the actual quantity and the standard quantity allowed for the production components, the **quantity variance**. These are illustrated in detail in the following sections dealing with direct materials, direct labor, and variable overhead. It should be noted that the variances have different names for different cost categories, as follows:

Cost Component	Price Variance Name	Quantity Variance Name
Direct materials	Materials price variance	Materials quantity variance
Direct labor	Labor rate variance	Labor efficiency variance
Variable overhead	Variable overhead spending variance	Variable overhead efficiency variance

Fixed overhead is excluded from the unit standard costs because, within the relevant range of normal activity, it does not vary with the volume of production. For the purpose of internal planning and control, fixed costs are budgeted and evaluated for total capacity, rather than on a per unit basis. However, for external reporting, fixed overhead costs are normally assigned to products on a per unit basis. Also, to facilitate product costing, many organizations develop a standard fixed overhead cost per unit. In the following sections, we analyze the flexible budget cost variances for each of the variable cost components and compute the appropriate price (rate) and quantity (efficiency) variances. Control of the fixed manufacturing overhead flexible budget variance is also discussed. Our illustration of variance analysis is based on the July 19X7 activity and costs of the Store-It Company's Production Department.

Store-It Company Production Department Actual Manufacturing Costs For the Month of July 19X7	
Actual units completed	11,000
Manufacturing costs:	
Direct materials (24,000 pounds × $4.50)	$108,000
Direct labor (2,800 hours × $25)	70,000
Variable manufacturing overhead:	82,000
Group A (4,100 machine hours)	
Group B (24,000 pounds)	
Fixed overhead	53,000
Total	$313,000

Material Standards and Variances

There are two basic elements contained in the standards for direct materials: the standard price and the standard quantity. Materials standards indicate:

1. How much should be paid for each input unit of direct materials.
2. The quantity of direct materials allowed to produce one unit of output.

The standard price per unit of direct materials should include all reasonable costs necessary to acquire the materials. These costs include the invoice price of materials, less planned discounts, plus freight, insurance, special handling, and any other costs related to the acquisition of the materials. The standard quantity represents the number of units of raw materials allowed for the production of one unit of finished product. The standard quantity of raw materials allowed to produce a unit of finished product should include the amount dictated by the physical characteristics of the process and the product, plus a reasonable allowance for normal spoilage, waste, and other inefficiencies. The quantity standard may be determined by engineering analysis, professional judgment, or by averaging the actual amount used for several periods. An average of actual past materials usage may not be a good standard because it could include excessive wastes and inefficiencies in the standard quantity.

Store-It Company has a direct materials quantity standard of 2.0 pounds per finished unit produced. In fact, each unit may physically contain only 1.8 pounds of raw materials, with the additional 0.2 pound representing the amount allowed by the standards for normal spoilage, waste, and other inefficiencies. This is an area where the company may consider implementing quality cost analysis to see if the situation can be improved.

The **materials price variance** is the difference between the actual materials cost and the standard cost of actual materials inputs. The **materials quantity variance** is the difference between the standard cost of actual materials inputs and the flexible budget cost for materials. The direct materials variances for Store-It Company are shown below:

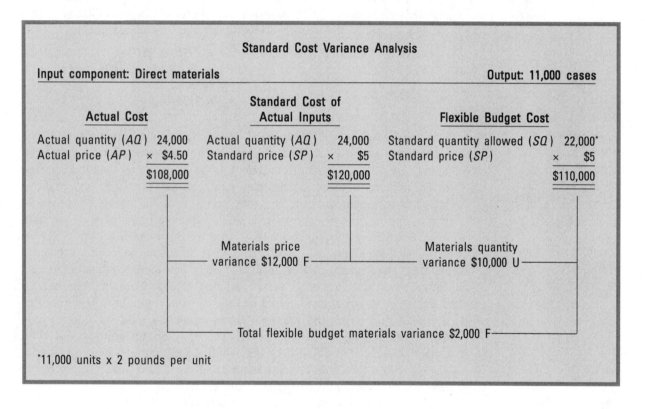

Store-It Company had a favorable materials price variance of $12,000 because the actual cost of materials used ($108,000) was less than the standard cost of actual materials used ($120,000). Stated another way, for the materials actually used, the total price paid was $12,000 less than the price allowed by the standards. The price variance can also be viewed as the actual quantity (AQ) used times the difference between the actual price (AP) and the standard price (SP). Store-It Company paid $0.50 per pound below the standard price for 24,000 pounds for a total savings of $12,000. This is readily shown using the formula approach:

$$\begin{aligned} \text{Materials price variance} &= AQ\,(AP - SP) \\ &= 24{,}000\ (\$4.50 - \$5.00) \\ &= 24{,}000 \times \$0.50 \\ &= \$12{,}000\ \text{F} \end{aligned}$$

The unfavorable quantity variance of $10,000 occurred because the standard cost of actual materials used, $120,000 (24,000 × $5), was greater than the cost of materials allowed by the flexible budget, $110,000 (22,000 × $5). A total of 22,000 pounds of materials is allowed to produce 11,000 units of finished outputs. This is computed as 11,000 finished units times 2 pounds of direct materials per unit. The materials quantity variance may also be computed as the standard price (*SP*) per pound times the difference between the number of pounds actually used (*AQ*) and the number of pounds allowed (*SQ*). The use of 2,000 pounds of materials more than the standard quantity allowed at a standard price of $5 per pound resulted in an additional cost of $10,000. This is also readily shown using the formula approach:

$$\begin{aligned} \text{Materials quantity variance} &= SP\,(AQ - SQ) \\ &= \$5\ (24{,}000 - 22{,}000) \\ &= \$5 \times 2{,}000 \\ &= \$10{,}000\ \text{U} \end{aligned}$$

Interpreting Materials Variances

While it is necessary to understand how variances are computed, it is even more important to know what to do with the variances after they are computed. A *favorable materials price variance* indicates that the manager responsible for materials purchases paid less per unit than the price allowed by the standards. This may result from receiving discounts for purchasing larger than normal quantities, effective bargaining by the manager, purchasing substandard quality materials, purchasing from a distress seller, or other factors. Ordinarily when a favorable price variance is reported, the manager's performance will be interpreted as favorable. However, if the favorable price variance results from the purchase of materials of lower than standard quality or from a purchase in larger than desirable quantities, the manager's performance would be questionable. Consistent and highly favorable variances may be an indication of situations that are undermining the responsibility accounting system by building slack into the standards or using incorrect data. These situations should be investigated thoroughly for causes and corrections.

An *unfavorable materials price variance* means that the purchasing manager paid more per unit for materials than the price allowed by the standards. This may be caused by failure to buy in sufficient quantities to get normal discounts, purchase of higher quality materials than called for in the product specifications, failure to place materials orders on a timely basis, thereby requiring a more expensive shipping alternative, uncontrollable price changes in the market for direct materials, failure to bargain for the best available prices, or other factors. It should be emphasized that an unfavorable variance does not always mean that the manager performed unfavorably, and a favorable variance does not always indicate favorable performance. There are many noncontrollable factors surrounding the purchasing function due to timing problems, changing vendors, and changing materials demands from production.

A *favorable materials quantity variance* means that the actual quantity of raw materials used was less than the quantity allowed for the units produced. This may result from factors such as less materials waste than allowed by the standards, better than expected machine efficiency, direct materials of higher quality than required by the standards, and more efficient use of direct materials by employees.

An *unfavorable materials quantity variance* occurs when the quantity of raw materials used exceeds the quantity allowed for the units produced. This may result from incurring more waste than provided for in the standards, poorly maintained machinery requiring larger amounts of raw materials, raw materials of lower quality than required by the standards, or poorly trained employees who were unable to use the materials at the level of efficiency required by the standards.

The above example of materials variances assumes an inventory system where the amount of materials awaiting use in the production facilities is minimal. For those situations where managers need a closer association with purchased materials and their variances, a split materials variance is used. This method computes the materials price variance at the time of purchase, rather than at the time of usage. The timing difference provides the manager with an immediate valuation of the purchasing function. The split method has no effect on the materials quantity variance; it is still computed at the time of usage.

The split method is generally preferred when materials purchases are not closely tied to a period's production because of scarce supply, fluctuating prices, special purchase opportunities, or other types of special situations. The purchasing manager may need to receive price variance information as soon as possible after the actual purchase of materials. If the price variance is measured when materials are used (which may be weeks or months after materials are purchased), the price variance information may be received too late to be useful in controlling materials prices. Timely reporting of price variance information is often as necessary for making pricing decisions as it is for making other decisions based on current replacement costs.

Labor Standards and Variances

Direct labor standards consist of two components: *rate* and *efficiency*. To evaluate management performance in controlling labor costs by using a standard cost system, it is necessary to determine the *standard labor rate* for each hour of labor allowed and the *standard labor time allowed* to produce a unit.

Setting labor rate standards may be quite simple or extremely complex, depending on the particular circumstances. If only one class of employee is used to make each product and if all employees have the same wage rate, determination of the standard cost is relatively easy: Simply adopt the normal wage rate as the standard labor rate. If several different classes of employees are used in making each unit of product, separate efficiency and rate standards must be established for each class.

If wage rates vary for a given class of employees because of seniority or other differences, an average wage rate is ordinarily used for the labor rate standard. In these cases, any variance caused by using an average rate should be negligible, unless there are large variations in wage rates within a particular employee class. To simplify our Store-It Company examples, an average wage rate is assumed.

The standard labor time per unit can be determined by an engineering approach or an empirical observation approach. When using an engineering approach, industrial engineers ascertain the amount of labor required to produce a unit of finished product by applying time and motion methods or other available techniques. Normal operating conditions are assumed in arriving at the labor efficiency standard. Therefore, allowances must be made for normal machine downtime, employee personal breaks, and so forth. Under the empirical approach, the long-run average time required in the past to produce a unit under normal operating conditions is used as a basis for the standard. By using normal operating conditions, inefficiencies such as machine downtime and employee breaks are automatically factored into the standard.

Using the general variance model for materials, we can compute the labor rate and efficiency variances. The **labor rate variance** is the difference between the actual cost and the standard cost of actual labor inputs. The **labor efficiency variance** is the difference between the standard cost of actual labor inputs and the flexible budget cost for labor.

Store-It Company's direct labor standards provide for 1/4 hour of direct labor per unit produced. During July 19X7, 2,800 hours were worked at a cost of $25 per hour. Using these data, the labor rate (price) variance and labor efficiency (quantity) variance can be computed as shown in the following illustration:

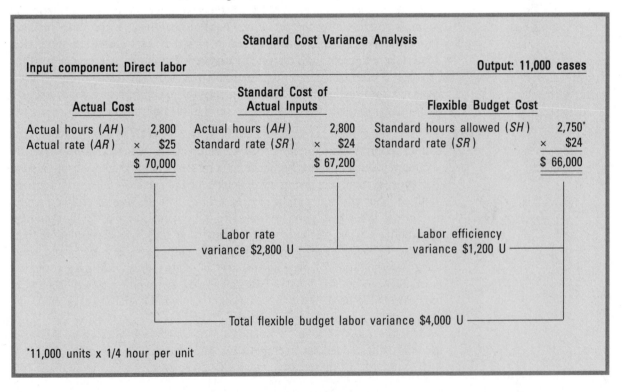

Standard Cost Variance Analysis

Input component: Direct labor   Output: 11,000 cases

Actual Cost			Standard Cost of Actual Inputs			Flexible Budget Cost		
Actual hours (AH)		2,800	Actual hours (AH)		2,800	Standard hours allowed (SH)		2,750*
Actual rate (AR)	×	$25	Standard rate (SR)	×	$24	Standard rate (SR)	×	$24
		$ 70,000			$ 67,200			$ 66,000

Labor rate variance $2,800 U   Labor efficiency variance $1,200 U

Total flexible budget labor variance $4,000 U

*11,000 units x 1/4 hour per unit

The labor rate variance can also be computed in formula form as the actual hours used times the difference between the actual labor rate and the standard labor rate. The symbols are the same as in the diagram.

$$\begin{aligned} \text{Labor rate variance} &= AH\,(AR - SR) \\ &= 2{,}800\,(\$25 - \$24) \\ &= 2{,}800 \times \$1 \\ &= \underline{\$2{,}800}\ U \end{aligned}$$

This computation of the labor rate variance shows that the company paid $1.00 above the standard rate for each of the 2,800 hours worked. Stated another way, the labor actually used was $2,800 more than allowed by the standards.

Since 11,000 units of product were finished during the period, and 1/4 hour of labor was allowed for each unit, the total standard hours allowed was 2,750. The labor efficiency variance can also be computed as the standard rate times the difference between the actual direct labor hours and the standard hours allowed for the output achieved:

$$\begin{aligned} \text{Labor efficiency variance} &= SR\,(AH - SH) \\ &= \$24\,(2{,}800 - 2{,}750) \\ &= \$24 \times 50 \\ &= \underline{\$1{,}200}\ U \end{aligned}$$

This computation of the labor efficiency variance indicates that the company used 50 more direct labor hours than the budget permitted and that each of these hours costs $24, or a total of $1,200 more than allowed by the standard.

Interpreting Labor Variances

The possible explanations for labor rate variances are rather limited. An *unfavorable labor rate variance* may be caused by the use of higher paid laborers than provided for by the standards. Also, a new labor union contract increasing wages may have been implemented after the standards were set. In this case, the standards should have been revised to account for the wage rate change. In a nonunion situation where wages are not controlled by negotiated contract, there is the possibility that a manager may arbitrarily increase employee wages above the standard rate. This will also give rise to an unfavorable labor rate variance.

A *favorable labor rate variance* occurs if lower paid workers were used or if actual wage rates were below standard labor rates. As an example of falling wage rates, in the early 1990s, economic problems in the computer industry forced some union negotiators to relinquish previously awarded employee benefits. Such adjustments, however, should be reflected in the standards before the variances are reported.

Unfavorable labor efficiency variances occur whenever workers require more than the number of hours allowed by the standards to produce a given amount of product. This may be caused by a management decision to use poorly trained workers or poorly maintained machinery, or it may be caused by downtime resulting from the use of low-quality materials. Low employee morale and generally bad working conditions may also adversely affect the efficiency of workers, resulting in an unfavorable labor efficiency variance.

A *favorable labor efficiency variance* occurs when fewer labor hours are used than are allowed by the standards. This above-normal efficiency may be caused by the company's use of higher skilled (and higher paid) workers, better machinery, or raw materials of higher quality than provided for by the standards. High employee morale, improved job satisfaction, or generally improved working conditions may also account for the above-normal efficiency of the workers.

Variable Overhead Standards and Variances

Overhead costs are usually separated into fixed and variable elements for control purposes. Such a division is necessary because the variance between actual costs and expected costs is caused by different factors for fixed and variable costs. This section is limited to a discussion of the standards and variances related to variable manufacturing overhead costs. Fixed overhead costs are discussed later in the chapter.

Unlike direct labor and direct materials costs, which represent specific cost components, manufacturing overhead represents *groups* of different costs. Consequently, setting standards is often more difficult for overhead costs than it is for labor or materials costs. Because of the difficulty of tracing overhead costs to cost objectives and then to the finished product, the engineering approach to setting overhead standards is seldom used. For mixed manufacturing overhead costs (those that have variable and fixed components), an estimation technique, such as high-low, regression analysis (least-squares), or scatter diagram, is often used to separate the fixed and variable overhead components. These techniques were discussed in Chapter 2. If management concludes that the observations used in estimating variable costs reflect normal operating conditions, the estimate will probably be adopted as the standard variable cost. Additional constraints or problems may require the company to consider basing overhead variance analysis on a hierarchy of costs as is done in activity-based costing. This approach, although somewhat complex, allows the manager to analyze a three-level approach: unit level, batch level, and product level.[2]

Because it includes many heterogeneous costs, variable manufacturing overhead poses a unique problem in measuring standard quantity and standard price. Direct materials have a natural physical measure of quantity such as tons, barrels, pounds, and liters. Similarly, direct labor is measurable in hours. However, no single quantity measure is common to all variable overhead items. Variable overhead is a cost group that may simultaneously include costs measurable in hours, pounds, liters, kilowatts, and gallons.

To deal with the problem of multiple quantity measures in variable manufacturing overhead, most companies use an artificial, or substitute, measure of quantity for all items in a given group. Typical substitute measures are *machine hours, units of finished product, direct labor hours*, and *direct labor dollars*. The variable overhead standard is then stated in terms of this

---

2 For a detailed discussion of this topic, refer to an article by Jack M. Ruhl, "Activity-Based Variance Analysis," *Journal of Cost Management* (Vol. 8, No. 4), pp. 38-47.

single-factor base, and the amount of variable overhead budgeted is based on this artificial activity measure. To illustrate, assume that Store-It Company's standard variable overhead rates consist of the following:

Variable Overhead Cost Item	Quantity Consumed per Cost Driver	Standard Cost per Measurement Unit
	Group A per Machine Hour*	
Indirect materials:		
Hand cutting tools	1 each	$1.10
Cleaning agents	1 fluid ounce	0.15
Cleaning supplies	1 hand towel	0.25
Indirect labor:		
Maintenance workers	5 minutes	1.50
Fringe benefits	1 direct labor hour	0.60
Total variable factory overhead cost per machine hour		$3.60
	Group B per Pound of Direct Materials**	
Indirect materials:		
Sealant coating	2 fluid ounces	$0.30
Hinge lubricants	3 milliliters	0.25
Cleaning supplies	4 fluid ounces	0.15
Indirect labor:		
Inspection workers	6 minutes	2.25
Electricity	0.2 kilowatt-hour	0.05
Total variable factory overhead cost per pound of direct materials		$3.00

* Each unit requires 1/4 machine hour; standard cost per unit equals $0.90 ($3.60 × 1/4).
** Each unit requires 2 pounds of direct materials; standard cost per unit equals $6.

Store-It Company budgets variable manufacturing overhead in terms of two cost drivers: machine hours and pounds of direct materials. Management has determined that hours and pounds are better measures than units of finished product as to how much variable overhead cost is expected because these costs tend to vary in relation to machine hours worked and pounds of direct materials used, whether or not the production activities are producing at the standard level of one finished unit per 1/4 labor hour.

The general model for computing standard cost variances for direct labor and materials can also be used in computing variable overhead variances. However, the actual costs of inputs, such as indirect materials, indirect labor, and utilities, are ordinarily obtained directly from the accounting records rather than being computed as quantity times price.

The **variable overhead spending variance** is the difference between the actual variable overhead cost and the standard variable overhead cost for the actual inputs (machine hours and pounds of direct materials in this example). The **variable overhead efficiency variance** is the difference between the standard variable overhead cost for the actual inputs and the flexible budget cost allowed for variable overhead based on outputs.

For Store-It Company, the actual variable overhead is given at $82,000. This represents the actual cost of indirect materials, indirect labor, and utilities recorded during the period. Since actual variable overhead is expected to vary with machine hours worked and pounds of direct materials used, the standard cost of actual activity-based inputs is calculated as actual machine hours (AMH) and pounds of materials (AP) times the standard variable overhead rate per machine hour ($SMHR$) and pound (SRP) respectively:

$$
\begin{aligned}
\text{Standard cost of actual inputs} &= (AMH \times SMHR) + (AP \times SRP) \\
&= (4{,}100 \times \$3.60) + (24{,}000 \times \$3) \\
&= \$14{,}760 + \$72{,}000 \\
&= \underline{\underline{\$86{,}760}}
\end{aligned}
$$

The flexible budget cost for variable overhead allowed for the actual outputs is based on the 4,400 machine hours allowed (SMH) for the units produced during the period (11,000 units × 0.4 hour) and on 22,000 pounds of materials allowed (SP) for the units produced during the period (11,000 units × 2 pounds). The allowed quantities are multiplied by the standard prices, ($SMHR$) and (SRP), respectively. The resulting variable overhead flexible budget cost is $81,840:

$$
\begin{aligned}
\text{Flexible budget cost} &= (SMH \times SMHR) + (SP \times SRP) \\
&= (4{,}400 \times \$3.60) + (22{,}000 \times \$3) \\
&= \$15{,}840 + \$66{,}000 \\
&= \underline{\underline{\$81{,}840}}
\end{aligned}
$$

Using these data, the variable overhead spending (price) variance and the variable overhead efficiency (quantity) variance are shown on the next page.

An alternative to the computation of the variable overhead efficiency variance is as follows:

$$
\begin{aligned}
\text{Variable overhead} &= SMHR\,(AMH - SMH) + SRP\,(AP - SP) \\
\text{efficiency variance} &= \$3.60\,(4{,}100 - 4{,}400) + \$3\,(24{,}000 - 22{,}000) \\
&= (\$3.60 \times -300) + (\$3 \times 2{,}000) \\
&= -\$1{,}080 + \$6{,}000 \\
&= \underline{\underline{\$4{,}920 \text{ U}}}
\end{aligned}
$$

where:

$$
\begin{aligned}
SMHR &= \text{standard machine hour rate} \\
AMH &= \text{actual machine hours} \\
SMH &= \text{standard machine hours} \\
SRP &= \text{standard rate per pound} \\
AP &= \text{actual pounds used} \\
SP &= \text{standard pounds allowed}
\end{aligned}
$$

This approach emphasizes that the 300 machine hours saved should have produced a variable overhead savings of $1,080, at the standard rate of $3.60 per machine hour, while the 2,000 extra pounds should have

Standard Cost Variance Analysis

Input component: Variable overhead   **Output: 11,000 cases**

Actual Costs	Standard Cost of Actual Inputs		Flexible Budget cost	
$82,000	Actual machine hours (*AMH*)	4,100	Machine hours allowed (*SMH*)	4,400
	Standard rate (*SMHR*)	× $3.60	Standard rate (*SMHR*)	× $3.60
	Driver total	$14,760	Driver total	$15,840
	Actual pounds (*AP*)	24,000	Pounds allowed (*SP*)	22,000
	Standard rate (*SRP*)	× $3	Standard rate (*SRP*)	× $3
	Driver total	72,000	Driver total	66,000
	Total	$86,760	Total	$81,840

Variable overhead spending variance
$4,760 F

Variable overhead efficiency variance
$4,920 U

Total flexible budget variable overhead variance $160 U

produced an unfavorable variance of $6,000. Once netted, however, the efficiency variance is $4,920 unfavorable.

Interpreting Variable Overhead Variances

Why did Store-It Company spend $4,760 less than expected for the actual machine hours and pounds? Was it caused by decreasing prices for indirect materials, by lower than expected wage rates for indirect labor, or by lower than expected kilowatt rates for electricity? Or was it caused by use of smaller quantities of indirect materials, indirect labor, and utilities for the cost drivers: machine hours and material pounds? The answer is that the favorable spending variance could have resulted *both* from decreasing prices for variable overhead goods and services used *and* from less than expected consumption of these goods and services or from a combination of increases and decreases. Thus, the term *spending* variance is used instead of the term *price* variance.

For variable overhead, an *unfavorable spending variance* encompasses all factors that cause actual expenditures to exceed the amount expected for the actual hours and actual pounds, including consuming excessive quantities of variable overhead items, as well as paying too much for the variable overhead items consumed. Conversely, a *favorable spending variance* results when the actual expenditures are less than expected for the hours worked and pounds used. This is caused by consuming fewer overhead items than expected, or by paying less than the expected amount for overhead items consumed, or by both of these.

The key to understanding the variable overhead spending variance is recognizing that the amount of variable overhead cost allowed is determined by the actual level of the activity bases. For Store-It Company, actual machine hours and pounds of materials used determine the spending budget for variable overhead. Any deviation from this spending budget—due to uncontrolled or mismanaged variable overhead price or quantity variables—causes a spending variance to occur.

The variable overhead efficiency variance measures the difference between the standard variable overhead cost for the actual use of the activity base and the standard variable overhead cost for the allowed use of the activity base. This variance measures the amount of variable overhead that should have been incurred or saved because of the efficient or inefficient use of the activity base. It provides no information about the degree of efficiency in using variable overhead items such as indirect materials and indirect labor. This information is reflected in the spending variance. When overhead is being measured and budgeted on the basis of machine or labor hours, it is logical to expect overhead costs to be affected by the degree of machine or labor efficiency. This effect is measured by the variable overhead efficiency variance. Because of the connection of this variance to machine or labor efficiency, it will always be in the same direction as the machine or labor efficiency variance; favorable machine efficiency results in favorable overhead efficiency, and vice versa.

In the Store-It Company illustration of variable overhead variances, the activity bases selected for budgeting variable overhead cost were machine hours and pounds of materials used. Observations similar to those made for hours and pounds could also be made for other activity bases such as number of jobs run or number of units produced. However, as the utilization of multiple cost drivers increases, the ability to analyze the total overhead variance becomes complicated. As in our illustration, the use of two drivers causes additional explanation because one driver was favorable for the period and one was unfavorable. Advantages of multiple drivers can often be realized when only one or two drivers do not properly explain what is taking place. Management Accounting Practice 8-4 (page 416) is a case in point.

It is important to understand the potential interactive effect of the use of direct labor, direct materials, and machinery on the overall efficiency of the production process. These three factors must be combined efficiently to produce a unit of finished product of optimal quality. The quality of one factor usually affects the efficiency in using the other two components. For example, low-quality materials ordinarily reduce the efficiency of workers and machinery. Likewise, poorly maintained machinery reduces the efficiency of the workers and causes excessive waste of raw materials. And use of poorly trained workers often results in lower than normal output from the use of materials and machinery. Because of these interactive relationships, the interpretation of one variance is often interrelated with the interpretation of other variances. Seldom are there clear-cut and isolated explanations for each variance reported. Because of complexities of this sort, *using* variances is far more challenging than *computing* them.

FIXED OVERHEAD STANDARDS AND VARIANCES

L O 4

By definition, the quantity of goods and services purchased by fixed expenditures is not expected to change in proportion to short-run changes in the level of production. For example, in the short run the production level does not affect the amount of depreciation on buildings, the number of fixed salaried employees, or the amount of real property subject to property taxes. Whether 10,000 or 15,000 cases are produced, the same quantity of fixed overhead is expected to be incurred so long as the production level is within the relevant range of activity provided by the current fixed overhead items. Therefore, an efficiency variance is ordinarily not computed for fixed overhead costs.

Even though the components of fixed overhead are not expected to be affected by the production activity level in the short run, the actual amount spent for fixed overhead items can differ from the amount budgeted by management. For example, higher than budgeted supervisors' salaries may be paid, longer than normal working shifts can cause heating or cooling costs to exceed budget, and price increases can cause the amounts paid for equipment maintenance costs to be higher than expected. Fixed overhead costs in excess of the amount budgeted are reflected in the fixed overhead budget variance. The **fixed overhead budget variance** is the difference between budgeted and actual fixed overhead:

$$\frac{\text{Fixed overhead}}{\text{budget variance}} = \frac{\text{Actual fixed}}{\text{overhead}} - \frac{\text{Budgeted fixed}}{\text{overhead}}$$

Using the fixed overhead data for Store-It Company, the fixed overhead budget variance is computed as $1,000 unfavorable in Exhibit 8-4 (page 399). This is $53,000 of actual fixed overhead costs minus $52,000 of budgeted fixed overhead costs. The fixed overhead budget variance is always the same as the total fixed overhead flexible budget variance. Because budgeted fixed overhead is the same for all outputs within the relevant range, the budget variance explains the total flexible budget variance between actual and allowed fixed overhead. Additional information on fixed overhead variances is provided in Appendix A of this chapter.

REPORTING COST VARIANCES

L O 5

Two critical factors in the operation of a responsibility accounting system are: (1) the reporting of variances to the appropriate managers and (2) the response of management with explanations and control decisions. The method and format used to report variances to managers should be tailored to the specific needs of each situation. Exhibit 8-5 (page 417) illustrates, for Store-It Company, one possible approach for reporting performance

---

MANAGEMENT ACCOUNTING PRACTICE 8-4

Overhead Denominator Selection

Organizations, or operating departments, are often confused about how actual operations are related to the assignment of overhead costs. In one large equipment manufacturer, the machining shop was operating under such confusion. The managers could not understand how they kept getting bids for simple, low-volume parts that made heavy demands of the support resources when the facility had been designed to be competitive on bidding for complex, high-volume products and parts. The company's traditional standard cost accounting system had been used in the machining department and used a three-level base composed of direct materials dollars, direct labor dollars, and machine hours.

Upon investigation of actual cost drivers, it was found that 40 percent of the department's support resources were not used to produce individual product units. To be more reflective of the processes, the company developed five new cost drivers: setup time, number of production runs, materials movements, active parts numbers maintenance, and facility management. The first three related to how many batches were produced; the fourth, to the number of different types of products produced; and the fifth, to the facility as a whole. The five new drivers provided the managers with a completely different view of how the department operated. The former system had failed to show the widely different demands that the products placed on the resources, whereas the new system was much closer to the reality of how the products and parts utilized the resources.

Based on: Robin Cooper and Robert S. Kaplan, "Profit Priorities From Activity-Based Costing," *Harvard Business Review* (May-June 1991), pp. 130-135.

---

results and standard cost. In this example, Store-It's production manager is assumed to be responsible for direct materials usage and purchases, a normal situation for organizations where materials are ordered by production personnel for immediate use. If purchases had not been the responsibility of the production manager, the materials price variance would not have been included in the production manager's performance report.

Managers receiving performance reports are usually required to respond to their immediate supervisors within a designated period of time with explanations for variances that are significant in amount. Ordinarily, it is not economically feasible to investigate all variances. Each company must determine what constitutes a significant variance warranting managerial attention. All significant variances, both *favorable* and *unfavorable*, should be investigated. As previously stated, a favorable variance does not necessarily indicate favorable managerial performance, nor does an unfavorable variance indicate things are going poorly. Each significant variance must be evaluated for cause and followed with appropriate, corrective action.

EXHIBIT 8-5: STANDARD COST PERFORMANCE REPORT

Store-It Company
Production Department Standard Cost Performance Report
For the Month of July 19X6

	Actual Costs	Flexible Budget Cost	Flexible Budget Variances	Variance Analysis	
Direct materials	$108,000	$110,000	$ 2,000 F	$12,000 F	Materials price variance
				10,000 U	Materials quantity variance
Direct labor	70,000	66,000	4,000 U	2,800 U	Labor rate variance
				1,200 U	Labor efficiency variance
Variable overhead:					
Group A		$ 15,840			
Group B		66,000			
Total	82,000	81,840	160 U	4,760 F	Variable overhead spending variance
				4,920 U	Variable overhead efficiency variance
Fixed overhead	53,000	52,000	1,000 U	1,000 U	Fixed overhead budget variance
Totals	$313,000	$309,840	$ 3,160 U	$ 3,160 U	

L O 6

PERFORMANCE REPORTS FOR REVENUE CENTERS

The financial performance reports for revenue centers (defined earlier) include a comparison of actual and budgeted revenues, with the difference identified as a variance similar to those of the cost centers. Controllable costs may be deducted from revenues to obtain some bottom-line contribution. If the center is then evaluated on the basis of this contribution, it is being treated as a profit center.

If the organization is to meet its budgeted profit goal for a period, with its budgeted fixed and variable costs, the organization's revenue centers must meet their original revenue budgets. Consequently, the original budget (a static budget), rather than a flexible budget, is used to evaluate the financial performance of revenue centers.

Assume the Store-It Company's July 19X7 sales budget for carrying cases called for the sale of 10,000 units at $40 each. If Store-It Company actually sold 11,000 units at $39 each, the total revenue variance would be $29,000 favorable:

Actual revenues (11,000 × $39)	$ 429,000
Budgeted revenues (10,000 × $40)	- 400,000
Revenue variance	$ 29,000 F

Because actual revenues exceeded budgeted revenues, the revenue variance is favorable. Note that two distinct events occurred to create the $29,000 favorable variance: the selling price declined from $40 to $39, and the sales volume increased from 10,000 to 11,000 units. These two causes of the total revenue variance are identified as the sales price variance and the sales volume variance.

The **sales price variance** indicates the impact on revenues of a change in selling price, given the actual sales volume. It is computed as the change in selling price times the actual sales volume:

$$\begin{array}{c}\text{Sales}\\\text{price}\\\text{variance}\end{array} = \left(\begin{array}{c}\text{Actual}\\\text{selling}\\\text{price}\end{array} - \begin{array}{c}\text{Budgeted}\\\text{selling}\\\text{price}\end{array}\right) \times \begin{array}{c}\text{Actual}\\\text{sales}\\\text{volume}\end{array}$$

The **sales volume variance** indicates the impact on revenues of the change in sales volume, assuming there was no change in selling price. It is computed as the difference between the actual and the budgeted sales volumes times the budgeted selling price:

$$\begin{array}{c}\text{Sales}\\\text{volume}\\\text{variance}\end{array} = \left(\begin{array}{c}\text{Actual}\\\text{sales}\\\text{volume}\end{array} - \begin{array}{c}\text{Budgeted}\\\text{sales}\\\text{volume}\end{array}\right) \times \begin{array}{c}\text{Budgeted}\\\text{selling}\\\text{price}\end{array}$$

The July sales price and volume variances for Store-It Company are $11,000 U and $40,000 F, respectively:

Sales price variance	= ($39 - $40) × 11,000	= $11,000 U
Sales volume variance	= (11,000 - 10,000) × $40	= 40,000 F
Total revenue variance		= $29,000 F

The interpretation of these variances is subjective. In this case, we might say that if the increase in sales volume had not been accompanied by a decline in selling price, revenues would have increased $40,000. The $1 per unit decline in selling price cost the company $11,000 in revenues. Alternatively, we might note that a $1 reduction in the unit selling price was more than offset by an increase in sales volume.

In any case, variances are merely signals that actual results are not proceeding according to plan. They help managers identify potential problems and opportunities. An investigation into their cause(s) may even indicate that a manager who received a favorable variance was doing a poor job, whereas a manager who received an unfavorable variance was doing an outstanding job. Consider Store-It Company's favorable sales volume variance. This occurred because actual sales exceeded budgeted sales by 1,000 units or 10 percent, which on the surface indicates good performance. But what if the total market for the company's products exceeded the company's forecast by 15 percent? In this case, Store-It Company's sales volume falls below its expected percentage share of the market, and the favorable variance may occur, despite a poor marketing effort, because of strong customer demand that competitors could not fill.

Inclusion of Controllable Costs

Controllable costs should also be considered when evaluating the overall performance of revenue centers. A failure to consider costs might encourage uneconomic selling practices, such as excessive advertising and entertaining, and spending too much time on small accounts. The controllable costs of revenue centers include variable and fixed selling costs. These costs are sometimes further classified into order getting and order filling costs. **Order getting costs** are costs incurred to obtain customers' orders (for example, advertising, salespersons' salaries and commissions, travel, telephone, and entertainment). **Order filling costs** are costs incurred to place finished goods in the hands of purchasers (for example, storing, packaging, and transportation).

The performance of a revenue center in controlling costs can be evaluated with the aid of a flexible budget drawn up for the actual level of activity. Assume the Store-It Company's July 19X7 budget for the Sales Department calls for fixed costs of $10,000 and variable costs of $5 per unit sold. If the actual fixed and variable selling expenses for July are $9,500 and $65,000, respectively, the total cost variances assigned to the Sales Department are $9,500 unfavorable, as shown in Exhibit 8-6. In evaluating the performance of the Sales Department as both a cost center and a revenue center, management would consider these cost variances, as well as the revenue variances.

Revenue Centers as Profit Centers

Even though we have computed revenue and cost variances for Store-It Company's Sales Department, we are still left with an incomplete picture of the performance of this revenue center. Is the Sales Department's performance best represented by the $29,000 favorable revenue variance, by the $9,500 unfavorable cost variance, or by the net favorable variance of $19,500 ($29,000 F - $9,500 U)? Actually, it is inappropriate to attempt to obtain an overall measure of the Sales Department's performance by combining these separate revenue and cost variances. The combination of

EXHIBIT 8-6: SALES DEPARTMENT PERFORMANCE REPORT

Store-It Company
Sales Department Performance Report for Costs
For the Month of July 19X7

	Flexible Budget Formula	Actual	Flexible Budget	Flexible Budget Variance
Volume		11,000	11,000	
Selling expenses:				
Variable	$5/unit	$65,000	$55,000	$10,000 U
Fixed	$10,000/month	9,500	10,000	500 F
Total		$74,500	$65,000	$ 9,500 U

revenue and cost variances is only appropriate for a profit center; and, so far, we have left out one important cost that must be assigned to the Sales Department before it can be treated as a profit center.   That cost is the standard variable cost of goods sold.

As a profit center, the Sales Department acquires units from the Production Department and sells them outside the firm. Its total responsibilities include revenues, the standard variable cost of goods sold, and actual selling expenses. Note that the Sales Department is assigned the standard, rather than the actual, variable cost of goods sold. Because the Sales Department does not control production activities, it should not be assigned actual production costs. Doing so would result in the Production Department's variances being passed on to the Sales Department. Fixed manufacturing costs are not assigned to the Sales Department because short-run variations in sales volume do not normally affect the total amount of these costs.

To evaluate the Sales Department as a profit center, the computation of the sales volume variance must be adjusted for the corresponding variations in allowed costs. In its current form, the sales volume variance does not consider that costs or revenues respond to changes in sales volume. To evaluate the performance of a profit center, this variance must be stated net of its impact on the flexible budgets for manufacturing and selling costs. The standard variable costs that respond to changes in sales volume are as follows:

Direct materials	$ 10.00
Direct labor	6.00
Manufacturing overhead	7.44*
Selling	5.00
Total	$ 28.44

*$1.44 for Group A overhead items and $6.00 for Group B overhead items

In general, the **net sales volume variance** indicates the impact of a change in sales volume on the contribution margin, given the budgeted selling price *and* the standard variable costs. It is computed as the difference between the actual and the budgeted sales volumes times the budgeted unit contribution margin.

$$\begin{matrix} \text{Net sales} \\ \text{volume} \\ \text{variance} \end{matrix} = \begin{pmatrix} \text{Actual} & & \text{Budgeted} \\ \text{sales} & - & \text{sales} \\ \text{volume} & & \text{volume} \end{pmatrix} \times \begin{matrix} \text{Budgeted unit} \\ \text{contribution} \\ \text{margin} \end{matrix}$$

The budgeted unit contribution margin is the budgeted selling price minus the standard variable costs per unit:

Budgeted unit selling price	$40.00
Standard unit variable costs	- 28.44
Budgeted unit contribution margin	$11.56

Using the formula presented above, the net sales volume variance is computed as follows:

$$\text{Net sales volume variance} = (11,000 - 10,000) \times \$11.56$$
$$= \underline{\underline{\$11,560}} \text{ F}$$

As a profit center, the Sales Department has responsibility for the sales price variance, the net sales volume variance, and any cost variances associated with its operations. The company's sales price variance was previously computed to be $11,000 U, the $1 reduction in selling price times the actual sales volume of 11,000 units. The net sales volume variance was determined to be $11,560 F, the 1,000 unit increase in sales volume times the budgeted unit contribution margin of $11.56. The cost variances assigned to the Sales Department net to $9,500 U, the difference between $74,500 in actual selling costs and $65,000 in selling costs allowed for the actual sales volume. As a profit center, the Sales Department's net variances are $8,940 unfavorable:

Sales price variance	$11,000 U
Net sales volume variance	11,560 F
Selling expense variance	9,500 U
Net Sales Department variances	$ 8,940 U

In an attempt to improve their overall performance, managers often commit themselves to unfavorable variances in some areas, believing these variances will be more than offset by other favorable variances. In the case above, it appears that the favorable net sales volume variance was not sufficient to offset the price reductions and the higher selling expenses. Also note that the more complete evaluation of the Sales Department as a profit center (with an $8,940 unfavorable variance) gives a very different impression than the evaluation of the Sales Department as a revenue center (with a $29,000 favorable variance) or as a dual revenue and cost center (with a $19,500 net favorable variance).

SUMMARY

Responsibility accounting is the structuring of performance reports addressed to individual members of an organization in a manner that emphasizes the factors controllable by them. Each organizational unit for which performance reports are prepared is identified as a responsibility center. Each of these units has a manager who is responsible for the activities and performance of the unit. For the purpose of evaluating their financial performance, responsibility centers are classified as investment centers, profit centers, revenue centers, or cost centers. An investment center manager is responsible for the relationship between its profits and the total assets invested in the center. A profit center manager is responsible for the difference between revenues and costs. Although a revenue center manager is responsible for the generation of sales revenue, he/she is often assigned responsibility for the controllable costs incurred in generating revenues. If controllable costs are deducted from revenues, the center is, in fact, being treated as a profit center. A cost center manager is financially responsible only for the occurrence of costs, which is often further classified as either a standard or discretionary cost center.

Cost centers that have a predictable relationship between production inputs and outputs often use standard costs for controlling costs and evaluating manager performance. Standard cost systems require that cost standards be developed for each type of product (or service provided) and that they include standard unit costs for materials, labor, and overhead. Periodically, actual costs are compared with standard costs, and cost variances are reported to managers for possible corrective action. The performance of a standard cost center is evaluated by comparing actual costs with the costs allowed in a flexible budget drawn up for the actual level of activity.

A discretionary cost center is a cost center that does not have clearly defined relationships between activity and accomplishment. Discretionary cost centers are evaluated, for accounting purposes, by comparing the actual and budgeted costs for a given period. The difference is identified as over budget or under budget.

Variance analysis involves breaking down flexible budget variances into specific variances caused by price and quantity departures from standards. Both price and quantity variances are reported for labor, materials, and overhead. In financial performance reports, most companies measure the quantity of variable overhead consumed in terms of a substitute activity base, such as machine hours or direct labor hours, rather than in terms of the quantity of specific overhead goods and services consumed. Therefore, the variable overhead efficiency variance measures the impact on overhead cost of the efficiency with which the activity base is used. The variable overhead spending variance measures the combined impact of price and quantity deviations from standards for variable overhead goods and services used. While this is acceptable if variance analysis is used as a preliminary evaluation tool, additional inputs are needed for analysis if there are multiple cost drivers.

In financial performance reports, fixed overhead is often budgeted and reported in a lump sum and, therefore, is not affected by the level of activity achieved during the period. The fixed overhead budget variance is the difference between actual fixed overhead and budgeted fixed overhead.

Financial performance reports for revenue centers should include a comparison of actual and budgeted revenues, with related variances. Controllable costs may be deducted from revenues to obtain the center's contribution to corporate profits.

APPENDIX A: A CLOSER LOOK AT FIXED OVERHEAD VARIANCES

Organizations that use standard costing typically desire to have separate overhead rates for fixed and variable costs. Standard overhead rates are computed by dividing the budgeted overhead costs for the period by the budgeted activity for the period. The motivation for using standard rates for fixed and variable costs include rapid product costing and smoothing the workload of the cost accountants. Furthermore, the use of a standard fixed overhead rate results in identical fixed costs being assigned to identical products, regardless of when they are produced during the year.

When a standard fixed overhead rate is used, total fixed overhead costs assigned to production behave as variable costs. As production increases, the total fixed overhead assigned to production increases. Because total budgeted fixed overhead does not vary, differences arise between budgeted and assigned fixed overhead; and managers often inquire about the cause of the differences.

The standard fixed overhead rate is computed as the budgeted fixed costs divided by some budgeted standard level of activity. Since budgeted fixed overhead is the same for all levels of output (within the relevant production range), the standard fixed overhead rate varies, depending on the budgeted level of activity. In our example of Store-It Company, the budgeted monthly fixed manufacturing overhead is $52,000. (See Exhibit 8-4.) To simplify the illustration, assume Store-It develops its standard fixed overhead rate monthly, instead of annually, and that it bases the rate on a budgeted activity level of 4,000 machine hours per month. The standard fixed overhead rate per machine hour is $13.

$$\text{Standard fixed overhead rate} = \frac{\text{Budgeted total}}{\text{fixed overhead}} \div \frac{\text{Budgeted}}{\text{activity level}}$$
$$= \$52,000 \,/\, 4,000 \text{ hours}$$
$$= \underline{\underline{\$13}} \text{ per machine hour}$$

The total fixed overhead assigned to production is computed as the standard rate of $13 multiplied by the standard machine hours allowed for the units produced. Therefore, the assigned fixed overhead cost equals the budgeted monthly fixed overhead cost only if the allowed activity is equal to the budgeted activity of 4,000 hours. If the company operates less than 4,000 allowed hours, the fixed overhead assigned to production is less than the $52,000 budgeted; if it operates more than 4,000 allowed hours, the fixed overhead assigned to production is more than the amount budgeted.

Even though total fixed overhead is not affected by production below or above the standard activity level, the fixed overhead assigned to production increases at the rate of $13 per allowed machine hour. The difference between total budgeted fixed overhead and total standard fixed overhead assigned to production is called the **fixed overhead volume variance.** This variance is sometimes referred to as the **denominator variance**, a term that emphasizes the accounting origin of the variance. The fixed overhead volume variance indicates neither good nor bad performance by the production personnel. Instead, it merely indicates a difference between the activity allowed for the actual output and the activity level used as the denominator in computing the standard fixed overhead rate.

To explain the difference between actual fixed overhead and standard fixed overhead assigned to production, two fixed overhead variances are computed: the budget variance and the volume variance. These variances are illustrated for Store-It, assuming the following data:

Budgeted fixed overhead	$52,000
Actual fixed overhead	53,000
Budgeted activity level	4,000 hours for 10,000 units
Actual activity level	4,100 hours for 11,000 units

Because actual and budgeted fixed overhead costs do not vary for activities within the relevant range, their amounts are stated as totals, rather than computed as a function of some activity volume. The amount of fixed overhead assigned to production does vary with activity and is computed as the standard hours allowed for the actual outputs times the standard fixed overhead rate per hour. The fixed overhead budget variance represents the difference between actual fixed overhead and budgeted fixed overhead. The budget variance is caused by a combination of price and quantity factors related to the use of fixed overhead goods and services (e.g., heating or cooling costs, indirect labor, etc.). The $1,000 unfavorable budget variance for Store-It was caused either by using excessive quantities of fixed overhead goods and services, or by paying higher prices than expected for those items, or both.

The volume variance represents the difference between budgeted and assigned fixed overhead and is caused by a difference between the activity level allowed for the actual output and the budgeted activity used in computing the fixed overhead rate. The $5,200 favorable volume variance for Store-It indicates that the activity level allowed for the actual output was more than the budgeted activity level. As previously stated, this variance ordinarily cannot be used to control costs. If the budgeted activity is based on production capacity, this variance can be used only to alert management that facilities are under utilized or that they are utilized above management's expectations.

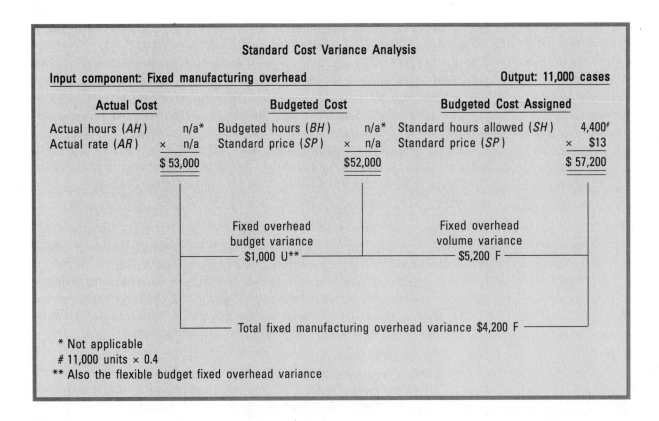

APPENDIX B: RECONCILING BUDGETED AND ACTUAL INCOME

It is possible to reconcile the difference between budgeted and actual net income for an entire organization. This can be done either by (1) assigning all costs and revenues to responsibility centers and summarizing the financial performance of each responsibility center or (2) developing a detailed reconciliation of actual and budgeted costs and revenues for the organization as a whole. The Store-It Company's budgeted and actual income statements, in a contribution format, for July 19X7 are presented in Exhibit 8-7.

EXHIBIT 8-7: BUDGETED AND ACTUAL INCOME STATEMENTS: CONTRIBUTION FORMAT

Store-It Company
Budgeted Income Statement
For the Month of July 19X7

Sales (10,000 units x $40)			$400,000
Less variable costs:			
Variable cost of goods sold:			
Direct materials (10,000 units x $10)	$100,000		
Direct labor (10,000 units x $6)	60,000		
Manufacturing overhead*	74,400	$234,400	
Selling (10,000 units x $5)		50,000	- 284,400
Contribution margin			$115,600
Less fixed costs:			
Manufacturing overhead		$ 52,000	
Selling		10,000	
Administrative		4,000	- 66,000
Net income			$ 49,600

* Group A (4,000 machine hours x $3.60) + Group B (20,000 pounds of materials x $3) = $74,400

Store-It Company
Actual Income Statement
For the Month of July 19X7

Sales (11,000 units x $39)			$429,000
Less variable costs:			
Variable cost of goods sold:			
Direct materials	$108,000		
Direct labor	70,000		
Manufacturing overhead	82,000	$260,000	
Selling		65,000	- 325,000
Contribution margin			$104,000
Less fixed costs:			
Manufacturing overhead		$ 53,000	
Selling		9,500	
Administrative		3,800	- 66,300
Net income			$ 37,700

Following the first reconciliation approach, assume that the Store-It Company contains three responsibility centers: a Production Department, a Sales Department, and an Administration Department. Because actual sales are in units and not batches, all computations are shown with per unit prices and costs. Further assume that the Production and the Administration Departments are cost centers and that the Sales Department is a profit center. The Production Department's variances, as itemized in Exhibit 8-4, net to $3,160 U. The Sales Department's variances are shown on page 421 to net to $8,940 U. The only variance for the Administration Department is the $200 difference between actual and budgeted fixed administrative costs ($3,800 actual - $4,000 budget). Because the Administration Department is a discretionary cost center, this variance is best identified as under budget. For consistency in the performance reports, however, it is labeled favorable. By assigning all variances to these three responsibility centers, the reconciliation of budgeted and actual income is as follows:

Budgeted net income		$ 49,600
Sales Department variances:		
Sales price variance*	($39 - $40) × 11,000 = $ 11,000 U	
Net sales volume variance	(11,000 - 10,000) x ($40 - $28.44) = 11,560 F	
Variable expense variance	(11,000 x $5) - $65,000 = 10,000 U	
Fixed expense variance	$9,500 - $10,000 = 500 F	8,940 U
Production Department variances:		
Variable expenses	$260,000 - $257,840 = 2,160 U	
Fixed expenses	$53,000 - $52,000 = 1,000 U	3,160 U
Administration Department variances:		
Fixed expenses	$3,800 - $4,000 = 200 F	200 F
Actual net income		$ 37,700

*Actual amounts on left and flexible budget or budget amounts on right where appropriate.

Following the second approach, a detailed reconciliation of budgeted and actual costs and revenues for the organization as a whole is presented in Exhibit 8-8. The actual results for the year are presented in column (1). The information in this column is based on the actual sales volume, the actual selling prices, and the actual costs. The original budget for the year is presented in column (7). The information in this column is based on the budgeted volume, the budgeted selling prices, and the budgeted costs. The three possible sources of variation between the original budget and the actual results (costs, selling prices, and volume) are analyzed in columns (2), (4), and (6).

The cost variances in column (2) reconcile the difference between the actual costs in column (1) and the costs allowed for the actual volume in column (3). Included in column (2) are the manufacturing cost variances (direct materials, direct labor, variable manufacturing overhead, and fixed manufacturing overhead, totaling $3,160 U), the selling expense variances (variable and fixed, totaling $9,500 U), and the administrative cost variances (all fixed, totaling $200 F). The sales revenues in columns (1) and (3) are based on actual volume at actual prices. Hence, no sales variances are included in column (2).

EXHIBIT 8-8: RECONCILIATION OF BUDGETED AND ACTUAL INCOME

	(1) Actual Volume at Actual Selling Prices and Actual Costs (Actual Results)	(2) Cost Variances	(3) Actual Volume at Actual Selling Prices and Standard Costs	(4) Price Variance	(5) Actual Volume at Budgeted Prices and Standard Costs (Flexible Budget)	(6) Net Sales Volume Variance	(7) Budgeted Volume at Budgeted Selling Prices and Standard Costs (Original Budget)
Volume (units)	11,000		11,000		11,000	1,000 F	10,000
Sales	$429,000		$429,000	$11,000 U	$440,000	$40,000 F	$400,000
Less variable costs:							
Direct materials	$108,000	$ 2,000 F	$110,000		$110,000	$10,000 U	$100,000
Direct labor	70,000	4,000 U	66,000		66,000	6,000 U	60,000
Manufacturing overhead	82,000	160 U	81,840		81,840	7,440 U	74,400
Selling	65,000	10,000 U	55,000		55,000	5,000 U	50,000
Total	- 325,000	12,160 U	-312,840		- 312,840	- 28,440 U	- 284,400
Contribution margin	$104,000		$116,160		$127,160	$11,560 F	$115,600
Less fixed costs:							
Manufacturing overhead	$ 53,000	1,000 U	$ 52,000		$ 52,000		$ 52,000
Selling	9,500	500 F	10,000		10,000		10,000
Administration	3,800	200 F	4,000		4,000		4,000
Total	- 66,300	300 U	- 66,000		- 66,000		- 66,000
Net income	$ 37,700	$12,460 U	$ 50,160	$11,000 U	$ 61,160	$11,560 F	$ 49,600

The sales price variance in column (4) reconciles the difference between the actual volume at actual selling prices in column (3) and the actual volume at budgeted selling prices in column (5). Note that the allowed costs for the actual volume, first computed in column (3), are restated in column (5). This means that column (5) is the flexible budget for both revenues and costs at the actual volume of production and sales. The differences between the actual results in column (1) and the flexible budget in column (5) are explained by the cost and price variances in columns (2) and (4).

Finally, the net sales volume variance in column (6) reconciles the difference between the flexible budget for revenues and costs based on actual volume and the original budget for revenues and costs based on budgeted sales. The differential effects of the production and sales volume on revenues and costs are disclosed in this column and totaled to determine the net sales volume variance of $11,560 F.

SUGGESTED READINGS

Cooper, Robin, and Robert S. Kaplan. "Flexible Budgeting in an Activity-Based Costing Framework," *Accounting Horizons*, Vol. 8., No. 2 (June 1994), pp. 104-109.

Cooper, Robin and Robert S. Kaplan. "Profit Priorities From Activity-Based Costing," *Harvard Business Review* (May-June 1991), pp. 130-135.

Cotton, William D. J. "Relevance Regained Downunder," *Management Accounting* (May 1994), pp. 38-42.

Mak, V. T., and Melvin L. Roush. "Flexible Budgeting and Variance Analysis in an Activity-Based Costing Environment," *Accounting Horizons*, Vol. 8. No. 2 (June 1994), pp. 93-103.

Ruhl, Jack M. "Activity-Based Variance Analysis," *Journal of Cost Management*, Vol. 8., No. 4 (Winter 1995), pp. 38-47.

Shank, John K., and Vijay Govindarajan. *Strategic Cost Management* (New York: The Free Press, 1993).

Yang, Gilbert Y., and Roger C. Wu. "Strategic Costing and ABC," *Management Accounting* (May 1993), pp. 33-37.

REVIEW PROBLEM

Standard Cost Variance Analysis

The flexible budget performance report for Sunset Enterprises, Inc., for March 19X5 is presented below. The company manufactures folding chairs, its only product.

	Flexible Budget Formula	Actual Costs	Flexible Budget Cost	Flexible Budget Variances
Output units		5,000	5,000	
Direct materials	$5/pound × 4 pounds	$104,125	$100,000	$ 4,125 U
Direct labor	$12/hour × 1.25 hours	82,400	75,000	7,400 U
Variable manufacturing overhead:				
Category 1	$4.80/hour × 1.25 direct labor hours	31,000	30,000	1,000 U
Category 2	$4/unit	18,000	20,000	2,000 F
Fixed manufacturing overhead	$40,000/month	42,000	40,000	2,000 U
Totals		$277,525	$265,000	$12,525 U

The standard unit cost for folding chairs is as follows:

Direct materials (4 pounds × $5 per pound)	$ 20
Direct labor (1.25 hours × $12 per hour)	15
Variable overhead, Category 1 ($4.80 per direct labor hour [$4.80 × 1.25 hr.])	6
Variable overhead, Category 2 ($4 per finished unit)	4
Total standard variable cost per unit	$ 45

Actual cost of materials is based on 21,250 pounds of direct materials purchased and used at $4.90 per pound, and actual cost of direct labor is based on 7,000 direct labor hours. Variable overhead is applied on direct labor hours for Category 1 and finished units for Category 2.

Required:

(a) Calculate all standard cost variances for direct materials, direct labor, and variable manufacturing overhead.

(b) Prepare a March 19X5 standard cost performance report for the Production Department.

The solution to this problem is found at the end of the Chapter 8 assignment materials. To maximize your learning, you should make a serious attempt to develop a written solution to the review problem before looking at the solution. If there are errors in your solution, you should then attempt to determine the causes of the errors.

KEY TERMS

Cost center—a responsibility center whose manager is responsible only for managing costs.

Discretionary cost center—a cost center that does not have clearly defined relationships between effort and accomplishment.

Fixed overhead budget variance—the difference between budgeted and actual fixed overhead.

Flexible budgets—budgets that are adjusted to a particular level of production after the fact. These budgets, based on cost-volume or cost-activity relationships, are used to determine what costs should have been for an attained level of activity.

Flexible budget variance—computed for each cost as the difference between the actual cost and the flexible budget cost of producing a given quantity of product or service.

Investment center—a responsibility center whose manager is responsible for the relationship between its profits and the total assets invested in the center. In general, the management of an investment center is expected to earn a target profit per dollar invested.

Labor efficiency variance—the difference between the standard cost of actual labor inputs and the flexible budget cost for labor.

Labor rate variance—the difference between the actual cost and the standard cost of actual labor inputs.

Materials price variance—the difference between the actual materials cost and the standard cost of actual materials inputs.

Materials quantity variance—the difference between the standard cost of actual materials inputs and the flexible budget cost for materials.

Net sales volume variance—indicates the impact of a change in sales volume on the contribution margin, given the budgeted selling price and the standard variable costs. It is computed as the difference between the actual and the budgeted sales volumes times the budgeted unit contribution margin.

Order filling costs—costs incurred to place finished goods in the hands of purchasers (for example, storing, packaging, and transportation). Many of these costs are fixed; others are variable.

Order getting costs—costs incurred to obtain customers' orders (for example, advertising, salespersons' salaries and commissions, travel, telephone, and entertainment).

Organizational structure—the arrangement of lines of responsibility within the organization.

Price variance—the difference between actual and standard prices paid for resources and components times the quantity purchased.

Profit center—a responsibility center whose manager is responsible for revenues, costs, and resulting profits. It may be an entire organization, but it is more frequently a segment of an organization such as a product line, marketing territory, or store.

Quantity variance—the difference between the actual quantity and the standard quantity allowed for the production components times the standard cost.

Responsibility accounting—the structuring of performance reports addressed to individual or group members of an organization in a manner that emphasizes the factors controllable by them. The focus is on specific units within the organization that are responsible for the accomplishment of specific activities or objectives.

Revenue center—a responsibility center whose manager is responsible for the generation of sales revenues.

Sales price variance—the impact on revenues of a change in selling price, given the actual sales volume. It is computed as the change in selling price times the actual sales volume.

Sales volume variance—the impact on revenues of the change in sales volume, assuming there was no change in selling price. It is computed as the difference between the actual and the budgeted sales volumes times the budgeted selling price.

Standard cost—a budget for one batch or unit of product. Standard costs indicate what it should cost to produce one batch or unit of product under efficient operating conditions.

Standard cost center—a cost center that has clearly defined relationships between effort and accomplishment.

Standard cost variance analysis—a system for examining the flexible budget variance, which is the difference between the actual cost and flexible budget cost of producing a given quantity of product or service.

Static budget—a budget based on a prior prediction of expected sales and production.

Variable overhead efficiency variance—the difference between the standard variable overhead cost for the actual activity-based inputs and the flexible budget cost for variable overhead based on outputs.

Variable overhead spending variance—the difference between the actual variable overhead cost and the standard variable overhead cost for the actual activity-based inputs.

APPENDIX KEY TERMS

Denominator variance—see fixed overhead volume variance.

Fixed overhead volume variance—the difference between total budgeted fixed overhead and total standard fixed overhead assigned to production.

REVIEW QUESTIONS

8-1
What is responsibility accounting? Why should noncontrollable costs be excluded from performance reports prepared in accordance with responsibility accounting?

8-2
Why does a production supervisor often need more frequent performance measurements than the vice president of production?

8-3
Responsibility accounting reports must be expanded to include what nonfinancial areas? Give some examples of nonfinancial measures.

8-4
Distinguish between investment and profit centers.

8-5
How is a cost center different from either an investment or profit center?

8-6

What problems can result from the use of tight standards?

8-7

Distinguish between a standard cost center and a discretionary cost center.

8-8

What is a standard cost variance, and what is the objective of variance analysis?

8-9

Standard cost variances can usually be broken down into two basic types of variances. Identify and describe these two types of variances.

8-10

Identify possible causes for (1) a favorable materials price variance, (2) an unfavorable materials price variance, (3) a favorable materials quantity variance, and (4) an unfavorable materials quantity variance.

8-11

What is the appropriate treatment in the standard cost system of a change in wage rates in the contract with the labor union?

8-12

How is the variable overhead spending variance computed, and what factors may cause it to occur?

8-13

If prices of indirect materials exceed the prices used in budgeting variable overhead, which variance is likely to be affected? Explain.

8-14

Explain the net sales volume variance and list its components.

EXERCISES

8-1 Flexible Budgets and Performance Evaluation

Presented is the January 19X1 performance report for the Production Department of the Thompson Company.

Thompson Company
Production Department Performance Report
For the Month of January 19X1

	Actual	Budget	Variance
Volume	30,000	28,000	
Manufacturing costs:			
Direct materials	$ 89,600	$ 84,000	$ 5,600 U
Direct labor	165,000	140,000	25,000 U
Variable overhead	64,000	56,000	8,000 U
Fixed overhead	27,500	28,000	500 F
Total	$346,100	$308,000	$38,100 U

Required:

(a) Evaluate the performance report.

(b) Prepare a more appropriate performance report.

8-2 Materials Variances

Fisher Company uses standard costs to control materials costs. The standards call for 2 pounds of materials for each finished unit produced. The standard cost per pound of materials is $1.50. During May, 4,800 finished units were manufactured, and 8,800 pounds of materials were used. The price paid for the materials was $1.52 per pound. There were no beginning or ending materials inventories.

Required:

(a) Determine the flexible budget materials cost for the manufacture of 4,800 finished units.

(b) Determine the actual materials cost incurred for the manufacture of 4,800 finished units, and compute the total materials variance.

(c) How much of the difference between the answers to requirements (a) and (b) was related to the price paid for the purchase of materials?

(d) How much of the difference between the answers to requirements (a) and (b) was related to the quantity of materials used?

8-3 Materials Price Variance Based on Purchases and on Usage

The Charleston Company manufactures decorative weather vanes that have a standard cost of $1.50 per pound for direct materials used in the manufacturing process. During September, 11,000 pounds of materials were purchased for $1.55 per pound, and 10,000 pounds were actually used in making weather vanes. There were no beginning inventories.

Required:

(a) Determine the materials price variance assuming that materials costs are the responsibility of the materials purchasing manager.

(b) Determine the materials price variance assuming that materials costs are the responsibility of the production manager.

(c) Discuss the issues involved in determining the price variance at the point of purchase versus the point of consumption.

8-4 Direct Labor Variances

Dolex Company manufactures specialty electronic circuitry through a unique photoelectronic process. One of the primary products, Model ZX40, has a standard labor time of 1/2 hour and a standard labor rate of $13.50 per hour. During February, the following activities pertaining to direct labor for ZX40 were recorded:

Direct labor hours used	2,200
Direct labor cost	$34,000
Units of ZX40 manufactured	4,600

(a) Determine the labor rate variance.
(b) Determine the labor efficiency variance.
(c) Determine the total flexible budget labor cost variance.

8-5 Variable Overhead Variances

Tea Leaf Company bases standard variable overhead cost on direct labor hours as the cost driver. Standard variable overhead cost has been set at $15 per unit of output, based on $5 of variable overhead per direct labor hour for 3 hours allowed to produce 1 finished unit. Last month, 4,300 direct labor hours were used, and 1,400 units of output were manufactured. The following actual variable overhead costs were incurred:

Indirect materials	$ 4,500
Indirect labor	8,200
Utilities	5,800
Miscellaneous	3,500
Total variable overhead	$22,000

Required:
(a) Determine the variable overhead spending variance.
(b) Determine the variable overhead efficiency variance.
(c) How is the variable overhead efficiency variance related to labor efficiency?
(d) If the company used smaller quantities of indirect materials than those reflected in the standards, in which variance would the resulting cost savings be reflected? Explain.

8-6 Fixed Overhead Variances (Appendix A)

The Gainesville Company uses standard costs for cost control and internal reporting. Fixed costs are budgeted at $7,500 per month at a normal operating level of 10,000 units of production output. During October, actual fixed costs were $7,900, and actual production output was 9,500 units.

Required:
(a) Determine the fixed overhead budget variance.
(b) Assume the company applied fixed overhead to production on a per unit basis. Determine the fixed overhead volume variance.
(c) Was the fixed overhead budget variance from requirement (a) affected because the company operated below the normal activity level of 10,000 units? Explain.
(d) Explain the possible causes for the volume variance computed in requirement (b). How is reporting of the volume variance useful to management?

8-7 Causes for Variances

During January, the Mayday Company reported the following variances in the production of flagpoles, its only product.

1. Materials price variance
2. Materials quantity variance
3. Labor rate variance
4. Labor efficiency variance
5. Variable overhead spending variance
6. Variable overhead efficiency variance
7. Fixed overhead budget variance

Required:

(a) Identify the variances that are caused primarily by price factors.
(b) Identify the variances that are caused primarily by quantity usage factors.
(c) Identify the variances that are caused by both price and quantity factors.

8-8 Standard Costs of Services

The President of Guinnett Dekalb Bank has decided that his bank should be using a standard cost system to evaluate management's efficiency in controlling costs of various services that the bank performs for its customers.

Required:

(a) Identify five typical services that banks perform for their retail customers for which it would be practical to use standards costs.
(b) What major obstacles is the bank likely to encounter in developing standard costs for its services and using them in performance evaluation and variance analysis?

8-9 Sales Variances

Presented is information pertaining to an item sold by the Winding Creek General Store:

	Actual	Budget
Unit sales	150	125
Unit selling price	$ 26	$ 25
Unit standard variable costs	- 20	- 20
Unit contribution margin	$ 6	$ 5
Revenues	$ 3,900	$ 3,125
Standard variable costs	- 3,000	- 2,500
Contribution margin at standard costs	$ 900	$ 625

Required:

(a) Compute the sales price and the sales volume variances.
(b) Use the variances computed in requirement (a) to reconcile the budgeted and the actual revenues.
(c) Compute the net sales volume variance.
(d) Use the sales price and the net sales volume variances to reconcile the difference between the budgeted and the actual contribution margins at standard costs.

8-10 Reconciling Budgeted and Actual Income (Appendix B)

The Fromer Company is a merchandising firm that buys and sells a single product. Presented is information from Fromer's 19X4 and 19X3 income statements.

	19X4	19X3
Unit sales	220,000	250,000
Sales revenue	$770,000	$750,000
Cost of goods sold	- 506,000	- 500,000
Gross profit	$264,000	$250,000

Required:

(a) Reconcile the variation in sales revenue using appropriate sales variances. Treat 19X3 as the base or standard.

(b) Reconcile the variation in gross profit using appropriate sales and cost variances. Treat 19X3 as the base or standard.

PROBLEMS

8-11 Multiple Product Performance Report

Creative Products manufactures two models of cassette tape storage cases: regular and deluxe. Presented is standard cost information for each model:

Regular		**Deluxe**	
Direct materials:			
Lumber (2 board feet × $3) = $ 6.00		(3 board feet × $3) = $ 9.00	
Assembly kit = 2.00		= 2.00	
Direct labor (1 hour × $4) = 4.00		(1.25 hours × $4) = 5.00	
Variable overhead			
(1 labor hour × $2) = 2.00		(1.25 labor hours × $2) = 2.50	
Total $14.00		$18.50	

Budgeted fixed manufacturing overhead is $15,000 per month. During July 19X1, Creative Products produced 5,000 regular and 3,000 deluxe storage cases while incurring the following manufacturing costs:

Direct materials	$ 80,000
Direct labor	34,000
Variable overhead	16,000
Fixed overhead	17,500
Total	$147,500

Required:

Prepare a flexible budget performance report for July 19X1 manufacturing activities.

8-12 Computation of Variable Cost Variances

Information pertaining to the standard costs and actual activity for the Tyler Company for September is presented on next page:

Standard cost per unit:

Direct materials	4 units of material A at $2 per unit
	1 unit of material B at $3 per unit
Direct labor	3 hours at $8 per hour
Variable overhead	$1.50 per direct labor hour

Activity for September:

Materials purchased:	
Material A	4,500 units at $2.05 per unit
Material B	1,100 units at $3.10 per unit
Materials used:	
Material A	4,150 units
Material B	1,005 units
Direct labor used	2,950 hours at $8.20 per hour
Variable overhead costs	$3,800
Production output	1,000 units

There were no beginning direct materials inventories.

Required:

(a) Based on materials used, determine the materials price and quantity variances.
(b) Determine the labor rate and efficiency variances.
(c) Determine the variable overhead spending and efficiency variances.

8-13 Variance Computations and Performance Report

The Outdoor Company manufactures camping tents from a lightweight synthetic fabric. Each tent has a standard materials cost of $20, consisting of 4 yards of fabric at $5 per yard. The standards call for 2 hours of direct labor at $12 per hour and variable overhead at the rate of $2.50 per direct labor hour. Fixed costs are budgeted at $10,000 per month.

The following data were recorded for October 19X5, the first month of operations:

Fabric purchased	9,000 yards at $4.90 per yard
Fabric used in production of 1,700 tents	7,000 yards
Direct labor used	3,600 hours at $12.50 per hour
Variable overhead costs incurred	$ 8,900
Fixed overhead costs incurred	$13,000

Required:

(a) Compute all standard cost variances for variable costs (materials, labor, and overhead). Base the materials price variance on use.
(b) Determine the fixed overhead budget variance.
(c) Determine the standard variable cost of the 1,700 tents produced, broken down into direct materials, direct labor, and variable overhead.
(d) Prepare a standard cost performance report using the format illustrated in Exhibit 8-5.
(e) Give one possible reason for each of the variances computed above.

8-14 Determining Unit Costs, Variance Analysis, and Interpretation

The Harmon Company, a manufacturer of dog food, produces its product in 1,000-bag batches. The standard cost of each batch consists of 8,000 pounds of direct materials at $0.30 per pound, 48 direct labor hours at $8.50 per hour, and variable overhead cost (based on machine hours) at the rate of $10 per hour for 16 machine hours per batch.

The following variable costs were incurred for the last 1,000-bag batch produced:

Direct materials	8,200 pounds costing $2,378 were purchased and used
Direct labor	45 hours costing $450
Variable overhead	$200
Machine hours used	18

Required:

(a) Determine the actual and standard variable costs per bag of dog food produced, broken down into direct materials, direct labor, and variable overhead.
(b) For the last 1,000-bag batch, determine the standard cost variances for direct materials, direct labor, and variable overhead.
(c) Explain the possible causes for each of the variances determined in requirement (b).

8-15 Computation of Variances and Other Missing Data

The following data for the O'Keefe Company pertain to the production of 300 units of product X during December. Selected data items are omitted.

Direct materials: (All materials purchased were used during period.)
   Standard cost per unit: (a) pounds at $3.20 per pound
   Total actual cost: (b) pounds costing $5,673
   Standard cost allowed for units produced: $5,760
   Materials price variance: (c)
   Materials quantity variance: $96 U
Direct labor:
   Standard cost: 2 hours at $7.00
   Actual cost per hour: $7.25
   Total actual cost: (d)
   Labor rate variance: (e)
   Labor efficiency variance: $140 U
Variable overhead:
   Standard costs: (f) hours at $4 per direct labor hour
   Actual cost: $2,250
   Variable overhead spending variance: (g)
   Variable overhead efficiency variance: (h)

Required:

Fill in the missing amounts in the blanks lettered (a) through (h).

8-16 Measuring the Effects of Decisions on Standard Cost Variances

Below are five unrelated situations that affect one or more standard cost variances for materials, labor, and overhead:

1. Lois Jones, a production worker, announced her intentions to resign in order to accept another job paying $1.20 per hour more. To keep from losing her, the production manager agreed to raise her salary from $7.00 to $8.50 per hour. Lois works an average of 175 regular hours per month.

2. At the beginning of the month, a supplier of a component used in our product notified us that, because of a minor design improvement, the price will be increased by 15 percent above the current standard price of $100 per unit. As a result of the improved design, we expect the number of defective components to decrease by 80 units per month. On average, 1,200 units of the component are purchased each month. Defective units are identified prior to use and are not returnable. The standards do not include an allowance for defective components.

3. In an effort to meet a deadline on a rush order in Department A, the plant manager reassigned several higher skilled workers from Department B, for a total of 300 labor hours. The average salary of the Department B workers was $1.85 more than the standard $7.00 per hour rate of the Department A workers. Since they were not accustomed to the work, the average Department B worker was able to produce only 36 units per hour, instead of the standard 48 units per hour. (Consider only the effect on Department A labor variances.)

4. Rob Celiba is an inspector who earns a base salary of $700 per month, plus a piece rate of 20 cents per bundle inspected. His company accounts for inspection costs as manufacturing overhead. Because of a payroll department error in June, Rob was paid $500, plus a piece rate of 30 cents per bundle. He received gross wages totaling $1,100.

5. The materials purchasing manager purchased 5,000 units of component K2X from a new source at a price $12 below the standard unit price of $200. These components turned out to be of extremely poor quality with defects occurring at three times the standard rate of 5 percent. Defective materials are identified prior to use.

   The higher rate of defects reduced the output of workers (who earn $8 per hour) from 20 units per hour to 15 units per hour on the units containing the discount components. Each finished unit contains one K2X component. To appease the workers, who were irate at having to work with inferior components, the production manager agreed to pay the workers an additional 25 cents for each of the components (good and bad) in the discount batch. Variable manufacturing overhead is applied at the rate of $4 per direct labor hour. The defective units also caused a 20-hour increase in total machine hours. The actual cost of electricity to run the machines is $2 per hour.

Required:

For each of the above situations, determine which standard cost variance(s) will be affected, and compute the amount of the effect for one month on each variance. Indicate whether the effect is favorable or unfavorable. Assume the standards are not changed in response to these situations. (Round calculations to two decimal places.)

8-17 Variance Analysis: Manufacturing Overhead Based on Labor Costs

Armando Corporation manufactures a product with the following standard costs:

Direct materials (20 yds. × $1.35 per yd.)	$ 27
Direct labor (4 hrs. × $9 per hr.)	36
Variable manufacturing overhead costs	20
Total variable standard cost per unit of output	$ 83
Total budgeted fixed manufacturing overhead per month	$6,000

The following information pertains to July 19X1:

Direct materials purchased (18,000 yds. × $1.38 per yd.)	$24,840
Direct materials used (9,500 yds. × $1.38 per yd.)	13,110
Direct labor (2,100 hrs. × $9.15 per hour)	19,215
Total manufacturing overhead ($6,800 fixed)	16,650

500 units of product were actually produced in July 19X1.

Required:

(a) Determine the standard variable overhead rate per direct labor hour.
(b) Compute the following variances:
  (1) Materials price variance, based on materials used
  (2) Materials quantity variance
  (3) Labor rate variance
  (4) Labor efficiency variance
  (5) Variable overhead spending variance
  (6) Variable overhead efficiency variance
  (7) Fixed overhead budget variance
(c) Prepare a Production Department performance report showing actual costs, flexible budget costs, total flexible budget variances, and standard cost variances for July.

(CPA Adapted)

8-18 Fixed Overhead Budget and Volume Variance (Appendix A)

The Starling Company assigns fixed overhead costs to inventory for external reporting purposes by using a predetermined standard overhead rate based on direct labor hours. The standard rate is based on a normal (or denominator) activity level of 10,000 standard allowed direct labor hours per year. There are 5 standard allowed hours for each unit of output. Budgeted fixed overhead costs are $200,000 per year. During 19X8, the Starling Company produced 2,100 units of output, and actual fixed costs were $205,000.

Required:

(a) Determine the standard fixed overhead rate used to assign fixed costs to inventory.
(b) Determine the amount of fixed overhead assigned to inventory in 19X8.
(c) Determine the fixed overhead budget variance.
(d) Determine the fixed overhead volume variance.

(e) Even though the cost of security guards is controlled as a fixed cost, the number of hours worked by the guards may fluctuate somewhat. If the number of hours worked by the guards in 19X8 had been smaller, which fixed overhead variance would have been affected? Explain. If the wage rate for security guards had increased during the year (with no revision of the standard), which variance would have been affected? Explain.

(f) What information does the fixed overhead volume variance computed above convey to management?

8-19 Profit Center Performance Report (Appendix B)

The Record Rack is a store that specializes in the sale of recordings of classical music. Due to a recent upsurge in the popularity of J. S. Bach's works, the Record Rack has established a separate room, Bach's Concert Room, dealing only in recordings of Bach's music. The albums are purchased from a wholesaler for $4.25 each. Though the standard retail price is $7.75 per album, the manager of Bach's Concert Room may undertake price reductions and other sales promotions in an attempt to increase sales volume. With the exception of the cost of albums, the operating costs of Bach's Concert Room are fixed.

Presented are the budgeted and the actual August 19X3 contribution statements of Bach's Concert Room.

Record Rack: Bach's Concert Room
Budgeted and Actual Contribution Statements
For the Month of August 19X3

	Actual	Budget
Unit sales	4,200	4,000
Unit selling price	$ 7.25	$ 7.75
Sales revenue	$30,450	$31,000
Cost of goods sold	- 17,850	- 17,000
Gross profit	$12,600	$14,000
Operating costs	- 5,000	- 6,000
Contribution to corporate costs and profits	$ 7,600	$ 8,000

Required:
Compute variances to assist in evaluating the performance of Bach's Concert Room as a profit center. Use these variances to reconcile the budgeted and actual contribution to corporate costs and profits.

8-20 Reconciling Budgeted and Actual Income (Appendix B)

Presented are the budgeted and actual contribution income statements of Queen's Encyclopedia, Limited, for October 19X8.

Queen's Encyclopedia contains three responsibility centers: a Production Department, a Sales Department, and an Administration Department. The Production and Administration Departments are cost centers, and the Sales Department is a profit center.

Queen's Encyclopedia, Limited
Budgeted Contribution Income Statement
For the Month of October 19X8

Sales (900 × $300)			$270,000
Less variable costs:			
Variable cost of goods sold:			
Direct materials (900 × $50)	$45,000		
Direct labor (900 × $20)	18,000		
Manufacturing overhead (900 × $30)	27,000	$90,000	
Selling (900 × $70)		63,000	-153,000
Contribution margin			$117,000
Less fixed costs:			
Manufacturing overhead		$40,000	
Selling		50,000	
Administrative		10,500	-100,500
Net income			$ 16,500

Queen's Encyclopedia, Limited
Actual Contribution Income Statement
For the Month of October 19X8

Sales (1,000 × $320)			$ 320,000
Less variable costs:			
Cost of goods sold:			
Direct materials	$50,000		
Direct labor	22,000		
Manufacturing overhead	35,000	$107,000	
Selling		100,000	- 207,000
Contribution margin			$ 113,000
Less fixed costs:			
Manufacturing overhead		$ 38,000	
Selling		65,000	
Administrative		12,000	- 115,000
Net income (loss)			$ (2,000)

Required:

(a) Prepare a performance report for the Production Department that compares actual and allowed costs.

(b) Prepare a performance report for selling expenses that compares actual and allowed costs.

(c) Determine the sales price and the net sales volume variances.

(d) Prepare a report that summarizes the performance of the Sales Department.

(e) Determine the amount by which the Administration Department was over or under budget.

(f) Prepare a report reconciling budgeted and actual net income. Your report should focus on the performance of each responsibility center.

8-21 Reconciling Budgeted and Actual Income (Appendix B)

The budgeted and the actual income statements of Queen's Encyclopedia, Limited, for October 19X8 are presented in Problem 8-20.

Required:

Prepare a detailed reconciliation of actual and budgeted costs, revenues, and income for the organization as a whole. Use a format similar to that of Exhibit 8-8 (page 427).

DISCUSSION QUESTIONS AND CASES

8-22 Discretionary Cost Center Performance Reports

Buggywhip Products had been extremely profitable at the turn of the twentieth century, but the company had been "whipped" in recent years by competition and a failure to introduce new consumer products. In 19X2, Tom Bright became head of the Consumer Products Research (CPR) department and began a number of product development projects. Although the department produced several good ideas that led to the introduction of several promising products at the start of 19X6, Mr. Bright was criticized for poor cost control. The financial performance reports for CPR under Mr. Bright's leadership were consistently unfavorable. Management was quite concerned about cost control because profits were low, and the company's cash budget indicated that additional borrowing would be required throughout 19X6 to cover out-of-pocket costs.

Because of his inability to exert proper cost control, Mr. Bright was relieved of his responsibilities in 19X6, and John Tight became head of Consumer Products Research. Mr. Tight vowed to improve the performance of CPR and scaled back CPR's development activities to obtain favorable financial performance reports.

By the end of 19X7, Buggywhip Products had improved its market position, profitability, and cash position. At this time, the Board of Directors promoted Mr. Tight to President, congratulating him for the contribution CPR made to the revitalization of the company, as well as his success in improving the financial performance of CPR. Mr. Tight assured the Board that the company's financial performance would improve even more in the future as he applied the same cost reducing measures that had worked so well in CPR to the company as a whole.

Required:

(a) For the purpose of evaluating financial performance, classify the Consumer Products Research department as a responsibility center. What unique problems are associated with evaluating the financial performance of this type of responsibility center?

(b) Compare the performances of Mr. Bright and Mr. Tight in their role as head of Consumer Products Research. Did Mr. Tight do a much better job, thereby making him deserving of the promotion? Why or why not?

8-23 Discretionary Cost Center Performance Reports

The budget for the Literature Department of Classic University is set by the Dean of the School of Liberal Arts in consultation with the Chairperson of the Literature Department. It is a line item budget with separate appropriations for such things as faculty salaries, secretarial support, travel, research, equipment, and instructional supplies. The budget for each year is a function of the budget for the previous year, with an adjustment for certain items that were funded at an excess or inadequate level during the previous year.

While the Chairperson of the Literature Department has done a good job in controlling most departmental costs, the Dean is concerned about the Chairperson's inability to keep instructional supplies in line with the budget. Prior to meeting with the Dean to discuss the 19X8 departmental budget, the Chairperson developed the following summary of the financial performance of the Literature Department in controlling the cost of instructional supplies:

Classic University
Literature Department
Summary of Financial Performance for Instructional Supplies
For the Years 19X3-19X7

	Student Enrollment	Actual	Budget	Budget Variance
19X3	4,500	$15,500	$12,000	$3,500 U
19X4	6,000	20,000	13,750	6,250 U
19X5	5,250	17,750	16,875	875 U
19X6	6,300	20,900	16,438	4,462 U
19X7	5,500	18,500	18,669	169 F

Required:

Comment on the financial performance of the Literature Department. What budgetary planning and control problem is illustrated by the above data?

8-24 Evaluating a Sales Compensation Plan

Prior to 19X3, the Carbon Chemical Company paid its sales representatives a straight salary plus selling expenses. In an attempt to better motivate them, the company changed their basis of compensation from salary to commissions based on gross sales. The commission rate was computed as 19X2 sales salaries divided by 19X2 gross sales revenues.

Early in 19X4, Martha Childs, the company president, was reviewing Carbon Chemical's 19X3 performance, as compared to its 19X2 performance. She became concerned that the commissions are not motivating the sales representatives to work in the company's best interest, and she wants your advice.

Presented is comparative 19X2 and 19X3 information:

	19X2	19X3
Gross sales	$ 648,000	$ 934,000
Less sales returns and allowances	- 8,000	- 34,000
Net sales	$ 640,000	$ 900,000
Variable costs:		
Cost of goods sold	$ 388,800	$ 560,400
Commissions	0	74,720
Total	- 388,800	- 635,120
Contribution margin	$ 251,200	$ 264,880
Fixed costs:		
Sales salaries	$ 51,840	$ 0
Other selling	20,000	55,000
Administrative	80,000	90,000
Total	- 151,840	- 145,000
Net income	$ 99,360	$ 119,880

Required:

Evaluate the sales compensation plan, and suggest some alternative plans that might better motivate the sales representatives to work in the company's interest.

8-25 Causes of Standard Cost Variances

Below are ten unrelated situations that would ordinarily be expected to affect one or more standard cost variances:

1. A salaried production supervisor is given a raise, and no adjustment is made in the labor cost standards.
2. The materials purchasing manager gets a special reduced price on raw materials by purchasing a train carload. A warehouse had to be rented to accommodate the unusually large amount of raw materials. The rental fee was charged to Rent Expense, a fixed overhead item.
3. An unusually hot August caused the company to use 25,000 kilowatts more electricity than provided for in the variable overhead standards.
4. The local electric utility company raised the charge per kilowatt-hour. No adjustment was made in the variable overhead standards.
5. The plant manager traded in his leased company car for a new one in July, increasing the monthly lease payment by $150.
6. A machine malfunction on the assembly line caused by using cheap and inferior raw materials resulted in decreased output by the machine operator and higher than normal machine repair costs. Repairs are treated as variable overhead costs.
7. The production maintenance supervisor decreased routine maintenance checks, resulting in lower maintenance cost and lower machine production output per hour. Maintenance costs are treated as fixed costs.
8. An announcement that vacation benefits had been increased resulted in improved employee morale. Consequently, raw materials pilferage and waste declined, and production efficiency increased.

9. The plant manager reclassified her secretary to administrative assistant and gave him an increase in salary.
10. A union contract agreement was signed calling for an immediate 5 percent increase in production worker wages. No changes were made in the standards.

Required:

For each of the above situations, indicate by letter which of the following standard cost variances would be affected. More than one variance will be affected in some cases.

(a) Materials price variance
(b) Materials quantity variance
(c) Labor rate variance
(d) Labor efficiency variance
(e) Variable overhead spending variance
(f) Variable overhead efficiency variance
(g) Fixed overhead budget variance

8-26 Developing Cost Standards for Materials and Labor

After several years of operating without a formal system of cost control, the Carlsen Company, a tools manufacturer, has decided to implement a standard cost system. The system will be established first for the department that makes lug wrenches for automobile mechanics. The standard production batch size is 100 wrenches. The actual materials and labor required for 8 batches selected randomly from last year's production are as follows:

Batch	Materials Used (in Pounds)	Labor Used (in Hours)
1	504	10
2	508	9
3	506	9
4	521	5
5	516	8
6	518	7
7	520	6
8	515	8
Average	513.5	7.75

Management has obtained the following recommendations concerning what the materials and labor quantity standards should be:

- The manufacturer of the equipment used in making the wrenches advertises in the toolmakers' trade journal that the machine Carlsen uses can produce 100 wrenches with 500 pounds of direct materials and 5 labor hours. Carlsen's engineers believe the standards should be based on these facts.
- The Accounting Department believes more realistic standards would be 504 pounds and 5 hours.

- The production supervisor believes the standards should be 513.5 pounds and 7.75 hours.
- The production workers argue for standards of 525 pounds and 8 hours.

Required:

(a) State the arguments for and against each of the recommendations and the probable effects of each recommendation on the quantity variance for materials and labor.

(b) Which recommendation provides the best combination of cost control and motivation to the production workers? Explain.

8-27 Behavioral Effect of Standard Costs

The Delaware Corp. has used a standard cost system for evaluating the performance of its responsibility center managers for three years. Top management believes that standard costing has not produced the cost savings or increases in productivity and profits promised by the accounting department. Large unfavorable variances are consistently reported for most cost categories, and employee morale has fallen since the system was installed. To help pinpoint the problem with the system, top management asked for separate evaluations of the system by the plant department manager, the accounting department manager, and the personnel department manager. Their responses are summarized below:

Plant Manager: The standards are unrealistic. They assume an ideal working environment that does not allow materials defects or errors by the workers or machines. Consequently, morale has gone down and productivity has declined. Standards should be based on expected actual prices and recent past averages for efficiency. Thus, if we improve over the past, we receive a favorable variance.

Accounting Manager: The goal of accounting reports is to measure performance against an absolute standard and the best approximation of that standard is ideal conditions. Cost standards should be comparable to "par" on a golf course. Just as the game of golf uses a handicap system to allow for differences in individual players' skills and scores, it may be necessary for management to interpret variances based on the circumstances that produced the variances. Accordingly, in one case, a given unfavorable variance may represent poor performance; whereas, in another case, it may represent good performance. The managers are just going to have to recognize these subtleties in standard cost systems and depend on upper management to be fair.

Personnel Manager: The key to employee productivity is employee satisfaction and a sense of accomplishment. A set of standards that can never be met denies managers of this vital motivator. The current standards would be appropriate in a laboratory with a controlled environment, but not in the factory with its many variables. If we are to recapture our old "team spirit," we must give the managers a goal that they can achieve through hard work.

Required:

Discuss the behavioral issues involved in the Delaware Corp.'s standard cost dilemma. Evaluate each of the three responses (pros and cons) and recommend a course of action.

8-28 Evaluating a Company-Wide Performance Report (Appendix B)

Mr. Micawber, the production supervisor, bursts into your office, carrying the Crupp Company's 19X2 performance report:

"There is villainy here, sir! And I shall get to the bottom of it. I will not stop searching until I have found the answer! Why is Mr. Heep so down on my department? I thought we did a good job last year. But Heep claims I and my production people cost the company $31,500! I plead with you, sir, explain this performance report to me."

Trying to calm Mr. Micawber, you take the report from him and ask to be left alone for 15 minutes. The report is as follows:

Crupp Company, Limited
Performance Report
For the Year 19X2

	Actual	Budget	Variance
Unit sales	7,500	5,000	
Sales	$262,500	$225,000	$37,500 F
Less manufacturing costs:			
Direct materials	$ 55,500	$ 47,500	$ 8,000 U
Direct labor	48,000	32,500	15,500 U
Manufacturing overhead	40,000	32,000*	8,000 U
Total	-143,500	-112,000	-31,500 U
Gross profit	$119,000	$113,000	$ 6,000 F
Less selling and administrative expenses:			
Selling (all fixed)	$ 60,000	$ 40,000	$20,000 U
Administrative (all fixed)	55,000	50,000	5,000 U
Total	-115,000	-90,000	-25,000 U
Net income	$ 4,000	$ 23,000	$19,000 U

Performance Summary:

Budgeted net income				$23,000
Sales Department variances:				
Sales revenue		$ 37,500 F		
Selling expenses		20,000 U	$17,500 F	
Administration Department variances			5,000 U	
Production Department variances			31,500 U	19,000 U
Actual net income				$ 4,000

*Includes fixed manufacturing overhead of $22,000.

Required:

(a) Evaluate the performance report. Is Mr. Heep correct? Or, is there "villainy here"?

(b) Assume that the Sales Department is a profit center and that the Production and Administration Departments are cost centers. Determine the responsibility of each for cost, revenue, and income variances, and prepare a report reconciling budgeted and actual net income. Your report should focus on the performance of each responsibility center.

8-29 Evaluating Company-Wide Performance: The Case of Multiple Profit Centers (Appendix B)

Computeraid produces a variety of computer accessories. To improve financial incentives, the Production Department and the Sales Department are both treated as profit centers, with all goods produced in the Production Department being "sold" to the Sales Department at 150 percent of variable cost. The costs of the Administrative Department are allocated equally to the Production and Sales Departments. The following performance reports (shown below and on page 450) are for the Production and Sales Departments for the year 19X8.

Management congratulated the Production Department supervisor for another outstanding performance and offered him a raise. The manager of the Sales Department, on the other hand, was called to a special meeting of the Board of Directors and told that unless she provided an adequate explanation of her department's performance, she would be terminated.

Computeraid
Production Department Performance Report
For the Year 19X8

	Actual	Budget	Variance
Unit sales	10,000	7,000	
Sales revenue	$241,500	$147,000	
Less variable manufacturing costs:			
Direct materials	$ 69,000	$ 35,000	
Direct labor	32,000	21,000	
Manufacturing overhead	60,000	42,000	
Total	- 161,000	- 98,000	
Contribution margin	$ 80,500	$ 49,000	
Less fixed costs:			
Manufacturing overhead	$ 24,000	$ 25,000	
Administrative	15,000	10,000	
Total	- 39,000	- 35,000	
Manufacturing profit	$ 41,500	$ 14,000	$ 27,500 F

Computeraid
Sales Department Performance Report
For the Year 19X8

	Actual	Budget	Variance
Unit sales	10,000	7,000	
Sales revenue	$310,000	$217,000	
Less variable costs:			
Cost of goods sold	$241,500	$147,000	
Selling and distribution	50,000	35,000	
Total	- 291,500	- 182,000	
Contribution margin	$ 18,500	$ 35,000	
Less fixed costs:			
Selling and distribution	$ 8,000	$ 8,000	
Administrative	15,000	10,000	
Total	- 23,000	- 18,000	
Selling profit (loss)	$ (4,500)	$ 17,000	$ 21,500 U

Required:

Extremely concerned about her future with the organization, the manager of the Sales Department has asked you to (1) evaluate the 19X8 performance reports for each department and (2) assist in preparing revised 19X8 performance reports for each department and Computeraid as a whole.

8-30 Evaluating Cost Center Performance Reports

Berwin Inc., is a manufacturer of small industrial tools with an annual sales volume of $3.5 million. Sales growth has been steady during the year, and there is no evidence of cyclical demand. Production has increased gradually during the year and has been distributed evenly throughout each month. The company employs a sequential processing system with all production activities located in the same building. Fixed manufacturing overhead is applied to all products using a single rate.

Berwin has always been able to compete with other manufacturers of small industrial tools. However, its market has expanded only in response to product innovations. Thus, research and development are very important and have helped Berwin to expand as well as to maintain demand.

Carl Viller, controller, has designed and implemented a new budget system in response to concerns voiced by George Berwin, president. An annual budget that has been divided into 12 equal segments has been prepared to assist in the timely evaluation of monthly performance. Berwin was visibly upset upon receiving the May performance report for the Machining Department (shown on next page). Berwin exclaimed, "How can they be efficient enough to produce nine extra units every working day and still miss the budget by $300 a day?" Jean Jordan, Machining Department supervisor, could not understand "all the red ink" when she knew the department had operated more efficiently in May than it had in the preceding months. Jordan stated, "I was expecting a pat on the back, and instead the boss tore me apart. What's more, I don't even know why!"

Berwin, Inc.
Machining Department Performance Report
For the Month Ended May 31, 19X4

	Actual	Budget	(Over) Under Budget
Volume in units	3,180	3,000	(180)
Variable manufacturing costs:			
Direct materials	$ 24,843	$ 24,000	$ (843)
Direct labor	29,302	27,750	(1,552)
Manufacturing overhead	35,035	33,300	(1,735)
Total	$ 89,180	$ 85,050	$(4,130)
Fixed manufacturing overhead:			
Indirect labor	$ 3,334	$ 3,300	$ (34)
Depreciation	1,500	1,500	
Taxes	300	300	
Insurance	240	240	
Other	1,027	930	(97)
Total	6,401	6,270	(131)
Corporate overhead:			
Research and development	$ 3,728	$ 2,400	$(1,328)
Selling and administrative	4,075	3,600	(475)
Total	7,803	6,000	(1,803)
Total costs assigned to Department	$103,384	$ 97,320	$(6,064)

Required:
(a) Review the May performance report for the Machining Department. Based on the information presented in the report:
  (1) Discuss the strengths of the new budget system in general.
  (2) Identify the weaknesses of the performance report and explain how the report should be revised to eliminate each weakness.
(b) Prepare a revised May performance report for the Machining Department. (CMA Adapted)

8-31 Evaluating Cost Center Performance Reports with Behavioral Implications
Denny Daniels is production manager of the Alumalloy Division of WRT, Inc. Alumalloy has limited contact with outside customers and has no sales staff. Most of its customers are other divisions of WRT. All sales

and purchases with outside customers are handled by other corporate divisions. Therefore, Alumalloy is treated as a cost center for reporting and evaluation purposes, rather than as a revenue or profit center.

Daniels perceives accounting as an historical number generating process that provides little useful information for conducting his job. Consequently, the entire accounting process is regarded as a negative motivational device that does not reflect how hard or how effectively he works as a production manager. Daniels tried to discuss these perceptions and concerns with John Scott, the controller for the Alumalloy Division. Daniels told Scott, "I think the cost report is misleading. I know I've had better production over a number of operating periods, but the cost report still says I have excessive costs. Look, I'm not an accountant; I'm a production manager. I know how to get a good quality product out. Over a number of years, I've even cut the raw materials used to do it. But the cost report doesn't show any of this. Basically, it's always negative, no matter what I do. There's no way you can win with accounting or the people at corporate headquarters who use those reports."

Scott gave Daniels little consolation. "The accounting system and the cost reports generated by headquarters," Scott stated, "are just part of the corporate game and almost impossible for an individual to change. Although these accounting reports are pretty much the basis for evaluating the efficiency of your division and the means corporate management uses to determine whether you have done the job they want, you shouldn't worry too much. You haven't been fired yet! Besides, these cost reports have been used by WRT for the last twenty-five years."

Daniels perceived from talking to the production manager of the Zinc Division that most of what Scott said was probably true. However, some minor cost reporting changes for Zinc had been agreed to by corporate headquarters. He also knew from the trade grapevine that the turnover of production managers was considered high at WRT, even though relatively few were fired. Most seemed to end up quitting, usually in disgust, because of beliefs that they were not being evaluated fairly. Typical comments of production managers who have left WRT are:

- "Corporate headquarters doesn't really listen to us. All they consider are those misleading cost reports. They don't want them changed, and they don't want any supplemental information."
- "The accountants may be quick with numbers, but they don't know anything about production. As it was, I either had to ignore the cost reports entirely or pretend they are important even though they didn't tell how good a job I had done. No matter what they say about not firing people, negative reports mean negative evaluations. I'm better off working for another company."

A recent copy of the cost report prepared by corporate headquarters for the Alumalloy Division is shown below. Daniels does not like this report because he believes it fails to reflect the division's operations properly, thereby resulting in an unfair evaluation of performance.

Alumalloy Division
Cost Report
For the Month of April 19X0

	Original Budget	Actual Cost	Excess Cost
Aluminum	$ 400,000	$ 437,000	$37,000
Labor	560,000	540,000	
Overhead	100,000	134,000	34,000
Total	$1,060,000	$1,111,000	

Required:

(a) Comment on Denny Daniels' perceptions of John Scott, the controller; corporate headquarters; the cost report; and himself as a production manager. Discuss how his perceptions affect his behavior and probable performance as a production manager and employee of WRT.

(b) Identify and explain three changes that could be made in the cost information presented to the production managers that would make the information more meaningful and less threatening to them.

(CMA Adapted)

8-32 Evaluating Alternative Sales Compensation Plans

Pre-Fab Corporation, a relatively large company in the manufactured housing industry, is known for its aggressive sales promotion campaigns. Pre-Fab's innovative advertising and sales strategies have resulted in generally satisfactory performance in the last few years.

One of Pre-Fab's objectives is to increase sales revenue by at least 10 percent annually. This objective has been obtained. Return on investment is considered good and had increased annually until last year when net income decreased for the first time in nine years. The latest economic recession could be the cause of the change, but other factors, such as sales growth, discount this reason.

A significant portion of Pre-Fab's administrative expenses are fixed, but the majority of the manufacturing expenses are variable in nature. The increases in selling prices have been consistent with the 12 percent increase in manufacturing expenses. Pre-Fab has consistently been able to maintain a company-wide contribution margin of approximately 30 percent. However, the contribution margin on individual product lines varies from 15 to 45 percent.

Sales commission expenses increased 30 percent over the past year. The prefabricated housing industry has always been sales-oriented, and Pre-Fab's management has believed in generously rewarding the efforts of its sales personnel. The sales force compensation plan consists of three segments:

- A guaranteed annual salary, which is increased annually at about a 6 percent rate. The salary is below industry average.
- A sales commission of 9 percent of total sales dollars. This is higher than the industry average.

• A year-end bonus of 5 percent of total sales dollars to each salesperson when his or her total sales dollars exceed the prior year by at least 12 percent.

The current compensation plan has resulted in an average annual income of $62,500 per sales employee, compared with an industry annual average of $50,000. The compensation plan has been effective in generating increased sales. Further, the Sales Department employees are satisfied with the plan. Management, however, is concerned about the financial implications of the current plan. They believe the plan has caused higher selling expenses and a lower net income relative to the sales revenue increase.

At the last staff meeting, the controller suggested that the sales compensation plan be modified so that sales employees could earn an annual average income of $57,500. The controller believed that such a plan still would be attractive to its sales personnel and, at the same time, allow the company to earn a more satisfactory profit.

The vice president for sales voiced strong objection to altering the current compensation plan because employee morale and incentive would drop significantly if there were any change. Nevertheless, most of the staff believed that the area of sales compensation merited a review. The president stated that all phases of a company operation can benefit from a periodic review, no matter how successful they have been in the past.

Several compensation plans known to be used by other companies in the manufactured housing industry are:

• Straight commission as a percentage of sales
• Straight salary
• Salary plus compensation based on sales to new customers
• Salary plus compensation based on contribution margin
• Salary plus compensation based on unit sales volume

Required:
(a) Discuss the advantages and disadvantages of Pre-Fab Corporation's current sales compensation plan with respect to (1) the financial aspects of the company and (2) the behavioral aspects of the sales personnel.
(b) For each of the alternative compensation plans known to be used by other companies in the manufactured housing industry, discuss whether the plan would be an improvement over the current plan in terms of (1) the financial performance of the company and (2) the behavioral implications for the sales personnel.

(CMA Adapted)

8-33 Variance Analysis and Evaluating Traditional Activity Bases

Uncle Henry's Old Fashioned Cookies bakes cookies for retail stores. The company's best selling cookie is chocolate nut supreme, which is marketed as a gourmet cookie and regularly sells for $8 per pound. The standard cost per pound of chocolate nut supreme, based on Uncle Henry's normal monthly production of 400,000 pounds is shown below:

Cost Item	Quantity	Standard Unit Cost	Total Cost
Direct materials:			
Cookie mix	10 oz.	$ 0.02 per oz.	$0.20
Milk chocolate	5 oz.	0.15 per oz.	0.75
Almonds	1 oz.	0.50 per oz.	0.50
Direct labor:			
Mixing	1 min.	14.40 per hr.	0.24
Baking	2 min.	18.00 per hr.	0.60
Variable overhead*	3 min.	32.40 per hr.	1.62
Total standard cost per pound			$3.91

*Applied on the basis of direct labor hours

Uncle Henry's management accountant, Karen Blair, prepares monthly budget reports based on these standard costs. Presented below is April's contribution report that compares budgeted and actual performance:

Uncle Henry's Old Fashioned Cookies
Contribution Report
April 19X5

	Actual	Budget	Variance
Units (in pounds)	450,000	400,000	50,000 F
Revenue	$3,555,000	$3,200,000	$355,000 F
Direct materials	$ 865,000	$ 580,000	$285,000 U
Direct labor	348,000	336,000	12,000 U
Variable overhead	750,000	648,000	102,000 U
Total variable costs	-1,963,000	-1,564,000	-399,000 U
Contribution margin	$1,592,000	$1,636,000	$ 44,000 U

Justine Molly, president of the company is disappointed with the results. Despite a sizeable increase in the number of cookies sold, the product's expected contribution to the overall profitability of the firm decreased. Molly has asked Ms. Blair to identify the reasons why the contribution margin decreased. Blair has gathered the information presented below to help her analyze the decrease:

Cost Item	Quantity	Actual Cost
Direct materials:		
Cookie mix	4,650,000 oz.	$ 93,000
Milk chocolate	2,660,000 oz.	532,000
Almonds	480,000 oz.	240,000
Direct labor:		
Mixing	450,000 min.	108,000
Baking	800,000 min.	240,000
Variable overhead		750,000
Total variable costs		$1,963,000

Required:
(a) Prepare an explanation of the $44,000 unfavorable variance between the budgeted and actual contribution margin for the chocolate nut supreme cookie product line during April 19X5 by calculating the following variances. Assume that all materials are used in the month of purchase.
   (1) Sales price variance
   (2) Materials price variance
   (3) Materials quantity variance
   (4) Labor efficiency variance
   (5) Variable overhead efficiency variance
   (6) Variable overhead spending variance
   (7) Net sales volume variance
(b) (1) Explain the problems that might arise in using direct labor hours as the basis for budgeting overhead.
   (2) How might activity-based costing solve the problems described above?   (CMA Adapted)

SOLUTION TO REVIEW PROBLEM

(a)

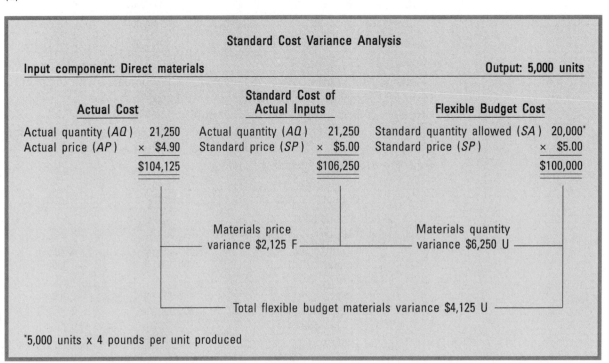

Standard Cost Variance Analysis

Input component: Direct materials   Output: 5,000 units

Actual Cost		Standard Cost of Actual Inputs		Flexible Budget Cost	
Actual quantity (AQ)	21,250	Actual quantity (AQ)	21,250	Standard quantity allowed (SA)	20,000*
Actual price (AP)	× $4.90	Standard price (SP)	× $5.00	Standard price (SP)	× $5.00
	$104,125		$106,250		$100,000

Materials price variance $2,125 F   Materials quantity variance $6,250 U

Total flexible budget materials variance $4,125 U

*5,000 units x 4 pounds per unit produced

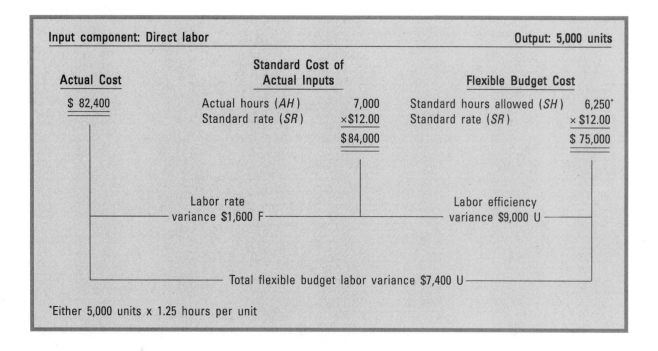

Input component: Direct labor   **Output: 5,000 units**

Actual Cost	Standard Cost of Actual Inputs		Flexible Budget Cost	
$ 82,400	Actual hours (AH)	7,000	Standard hours allowed (SH)	6,250*
	Standard rate (SR)	×$12.00	Standard rate (SR)	× $12.00
		$84,000		$ 75,000

Labor rate variance $1,600 F   Labor efficiency variance $9,000 U

Total flexible budget labor variance $7,400 U

*Either 5,000 units x 1.25 hours per unit

Input component: Variable overhead   **Output: 5,000 units**

	Actual Costs	Standard Cost of Actual Inputs		Flexible Budget Cost	
Category 1	$31,000	Actual labor hours	7,000	Standard hours allowed	6,250
Category 2	18,000	Standard rate	× $4.80	Standard rate	× 4.80
Total	$49,000	Driver total	$33,600	Driver total	$30,000
		Finished units	5,000	Finished units	5,000
		Standard rate	× $4	Standard rate	× $4
		Driver total	20,000	Driver total	20,000
		Total	$53,600	Total	$50,000

Variable overhead spending variance $4,600 F   Variable overhead efficiency variance $3,600 U

Total flexible budget variable overhead variance $1,000 F

(b)

Sunset Enterprises, Inc.
Production Department Standard Cost Performance Report
For the Month of March 19X6

	Actual Costs	Flexible Budget Cost	Flexible Budget Variances	Variance Analysis	
Direct materials	$104,125	$100,000	$ 4,125 U	$ 2,125 F	Materials price variance
				6,250 U	Materials quantity variance
Direct labor	82,400	75,000	7,400 U	1,600 F	Labor rate variance
				9,000 U	Labor efficiency variance
Variable factory overhead	49,000	50,000	1,000 F	4,600 F	Variable overhead spending variance
				3,600 U	Variable overhead efficiency variance
Fixed factory overhead	42,000	40,000	2,000 U	2,000 U	Fixed overhead budget variance
Totals	$277,525	$265,000	$12,525 U	$12,525 U	

After completing this chapter, you should be able to:

L O 1

Recognize a strategic business segment.

L O 2

Discuss the advantages and disadvantages of both centralization and decentralization.

L O 3

Understand the development and use of segment reports.

L O 4

Evaluate and select proper transfer pricing techniques.

L O 5

Discuss the issues that cause difficulty in evaluating decentralized operations.

L O 6

Calculate and explain return on investment and residual income measures for divisional performance.

PROFITABILITY ANALYSIS OF STRATEGIC BUSINESS SEGMENTS

As organizations become large and complex entities that maintain many product lines, operate in several countries, or overlap different industries, they need financial and nonfinancial reporting that addresses each unique operating unit. Organizations with multiple products, multiple plants, or multiple markets for their products often find it desirable to determine the profits of each segment of the organization. Segment reporting allows a company's internal profitability reports to be prepared by products, territories, divisions, or on some other basis. Although a centralized organizational structure is appropriate for many organizations, it has several limitations and is often replaced by a decentralized structure in diverse and complex organizations.

The purpose of this chapter is to examine techniques used to measure and evaluate the financial performance of segments of decentralized organizations. Illustrations are provided in the areas of financial analysis and segment reporting. The various ways in which such operations can be evaluated, how they interact with each other financially (through transfer pricing), and the problems large organizations with decentralized operations encounter are all discussed.

STRATEGIC BUSINESS SEGMENTS

L O 1

Organizations may develop many different types of business segments for reporting purposes. Recall from Chapter 8 that the basic responsibility reporting units are cost centers, revenue centers, profit centers, and investment centers. An organization may choose any one or a combination of these as the starting point for its strategic segment reporting. If responsibility centers provide the best means of controlling segments, they should be used unless strong arguments prevail for other types of reporting.

It is also important to note that the types of responsibility centers are not necessarily related to the level of centralization or decentralization. Although most decentralized organizations use segment reporting, it may be equally useful in other organizations. Many centralized organizations use segment reporting with either cost, revenue, or profit centers as the base. Most investment centers are found in decentralized organizations.

The type of organizational structure selected by an organization may influence the types of business segments used. In decentralized organizations, for example, the reporting units (generally called divisions) normally become quasi-independent, often having their own computer system, cost accounting system, and administrative and marketing staffs. When this occurs, top management must closely monitor the possibility of problems in keeping the units properly functioning for the benefit of the entire organization. These problem areas are discussed later in this chapter.

A strategic business segment is generally one that has its own mission and set of goals to be achieved. The mission of the segment influences the decisions that its top managers make in both short-run and long-run situations. The resulting environment provides the segment with its place in the organizational structure and controls to a great extent the type of financial reporting and evaluation measures used by the segment. The initial influence is the type of organizational structure currently in existence because this dictates the freedom of the segment managers to make decisions. This chapter begins with a discussion of the management philosophies of operating the organization and then provides several measures of evaluation of the various types of organizational units.

MANAGEMENT PHILOSOPHIES OF DECENTRALIZED OPERATIONS

L O 2

Decentralization is the delegation of decision-making authority to successively lower management levels in an organization. The lower in the organization the authority is delegated, the greater the decentralization. The most compelling arguments for decentralization are based on the need for management to be more responsive to the various operating units and segments of the organization. The advantages of decentralization include:

- Firsthand decision making. Personnel closely associated with problems and situations are allowed to make decisions. Experience in decision making at low management levels results in having managers trained for higher level positions when they become available.
- Timely decisions. Most decisions are made locally without having to feed information up the chain of command and then wait for a response.
- Specialization. Corporate management can concentrate on strategic planning and policy, and divisional management can concentrate on operating decisions.
- Motivation. Managers who actively participate in decision making are more committed to the success of programs and are more willing to accept responsibility for the consequences of their actions.
- Focus. Smaller organizational units have fewer objectives, are more flexible to changing conditions, and are better able to keep their focus on the tasks at hand than are larger units.

Before accepting decentralization as the answer to organizational problems, management must consider its disadvantages. The primary problems associated with this type of organizational structure include:

- Lack of competent personnel. Division management may not be able to carry out and control its operations in accordance with company policy because of a lack of competent personnel.
- Performance measurement. In organizations with many decentralized units, it is difficult to keep all operating units on the same measurement system. This includes reporting periods, methods of reporting, and consistency of data collection.
- Suboptimization. It is difficult to keep each unit operating for the benefit of the entire organization rather than for its own selfish benefit.
- Duplication. Multiple units may be performing the same functions because of increased autonomy allowed by decentralization. This increases the cost of operations especially in such areas as payroll processing, employee hiring and training, and legal work.

To establish a proper framework and point of reference for *decentralization*, it is necessary to examine some of the issues surrounding *centralization*. **Centralization** exists when top management controls the major functions of an organization (such as manufacturing, sales, accounting, computer operations, marketing, research and development, and management control). A centralized organizational structure normally includes the following advantages:

- Economies of scale. Centralized resources can be more fully utilized than can the same resources divided into smaller groupings.
- Sophistication of applications. By combining the firm's resources, greater efficiency may be achieved and more complex tasks performed.
- Improved control. Direct lines of authority provide better control of resources. Improved control permits the organization to rapidly shift resources to achieve changing corporate goals. Centralization also

permits a greater perspective by top managers because they are in contact with a larger proportion of activities than if they were decentralized.

However, like decentralization, centralization has limitations, the most significant of which are:

- Span of control.   After the size of a given function increases to a certain level, it becomes difficult to control from the top of an organization.
- Complexity. Combining activities into large centralized functions may create organizations of such complexity that they become unmanageable.
- Diseconomies of scale.   When functions become too large, problems of control and efficiency begin to occur. Almost every organizational function has a point of diminishing returns where adding another employee, work task, or manager does little toward reaching the overall organizational objectives.

As organizations expand in size and complexity, centralized control becomes more difficult. Planning, organizing, and controlling may eventually overwhelm top management in a large centralized organization. The solution to this problem is the decentralization of the organization into smaller operating units as Dial Corporation did, as described in Management Accounting Practice 9-1 (page 464). With proper planning and staffing of each unit or division, the organization may overcome the disadvantages of decentralization and improve overall organizational performance.

In most large, decentralized organizations, the primary operating units are called *divisions*. Each division is largely autonomous, with the division manager being responsible for sales, production, and administration of the unit. Division managers frequently have control over all activities, although capital budgeting and long-range planning activities may be limited. These two activities are often centralized within corporate headquarters, with the various division managers given control over the investments once they are made. As generally organized, divisions are the most common example of investment centers.

A decentralized organizational structure is illustrated in Exhibit 9-1. The theory behind this structure is to delegate enough responsibility to each division and to let each division operate as a quasi-independent business. You might want to contrast this with the centralized organizational chart in Exhibit 8-2.

The division management group usually includes managers from the computer center, personnel, marketing, controller's office, production, and other necessary functions. One potential problem of such a structure is the conflict of two superiors. The dashed lines in Exhibit 9-1 represent each staff's responsibility to corporate headquarters, whereas the solid lines connect each staff to the division vice president who has day-to-day authority. For example, the Division Controller (the division's chief accountant) has a dual responsibility: (1) to Vice President Division B who

EXHIBIT 9-1: ORGANIZATION CHART WITH DECENTRALIZATION

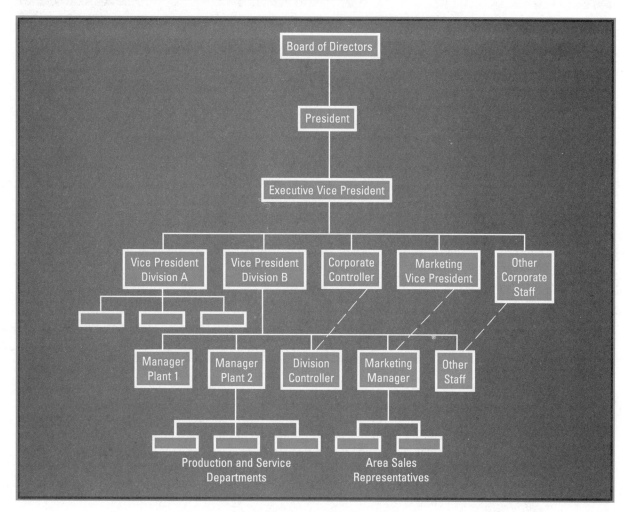

Production and Service Departments

Area Sales Representatives

exercises line authority and (2) to the Corporate Controller (the company's chief accountant) who exercises functional authority. The Division Controller must follow certain firm-wide accounting procedures specified by the Corporate Controller. Sometimes the Division Controller is regarded as an extension of the Corporate Controller, or as a "front-office employee." In this case, the Division Controller has a direct-line relationship with the Corporate Controller and a staff-line relationship with Vice President Division B.

DECENTRALIZATION (SEGMENT) REPORTING

L O 3

Recall from Chapter 8 that responsibility accounting is the structuring of performance reports addressed to individual members of an organization in a manner that emphasizes the factors controllable by them. Responsibility

MANAGEMENT ACCOUNTING PRACTICE 9-1

Dial Decentralizes

Until 1989, Dial Corporation was a highly centralized organization even though it had many diverse operations and numerous plants and distribution centers. Beginning in late 1988 and continuing through 1989, the company began a decentralizing phase that reduced the number of management levels and dramatically decentralized decision-making authority and accountability. The new structure also included increased empowerment to business-unit work groups and key management personnel. Each unit or manager was charged with improving the related operating function through self-assessment.

Evaluation groups were responsible for evaluating the company's management information system as it affected their individual environments. After completing the evaluation phase, top managers decided to change the overall operating environment to meet the strategic business needs of the operating unit managers. These changes eventually led to an information system that could rapidly respond to changing customer needs, including new product development, faster product delivery, more reliance on electronic data interchange, and an on-line system for customer order status.

Based on: Michael A. Robinson, "Decentralize and Outsource: Dial's Approach to MIS Improvement," *Management Accounting* (September 1991), pp. 27-31.

accounting reports may be prepared for cost centers, revenue centers, profit centers, or investment centers. Cost centers are evaluated by comparing actual with allowed costs, and revenue centers are evaluated by comparing actual with budgeted revenues. Because divisions operate as quasi-independent businesses with significant authority over their activities and the size of their investments, they are evaluated as either profit or investment centers.

When the investment center concept is implemented, the use of net income as a performance measure is not sufficient because different centers may have substantially different asset bases. In these situations, net income does not properly reflect the efficient use of the assets employed. The *return on investment* ratio is often used as the primary basis for evaluating investment centers. This concept is more relevant than traditional net income because investment center performance should consider both the investment center's income and the size of its asset base used to generate the income. A closely related concept, *residual income*, is also frequently used. Both of these evaluation methods are discussed in a later section. In this section of the chapter, emphasis is on cost classification and the evaluation reports of individual segments.

Segment reports are income statements that show operating results for portions or segments of a business. When the reporting of operating activities is presented for product lines, it is often labeled *product reporting*. Segment reporting is used primarily for internal purposes, although generally accepted accounting principles also require some disclosure of segment information for some public corporations.

Segment reporting is very common in organizations where there are distinct divisions of product lines, geographic territories, or organizational units. The segments or products of the organization for which reports are prepared depend on the information needs of management. Examples of segment reports are:

1. Income statements for each retail store, district, or division.
2. Income statements for each product line or service.
3. Income statements for each sales territory or customer category.
4. Cost reports for cost centers (segments without sales or revenue).

Although there are many different types of segment reports, three functions are basic to the preparation of every report:

1. Identification of the reporting objective segment.
2. Assignment of direct costs to the reporting objective segment.
3. Allocation of indirect costs to the reporting objective segment.

Segment reporting requires careful control over data collection and storage because of the different reporting formats. To effectively report the activities of a business segment, management should use the contribution approach, which focuses on the contribution made by each segment to cover common costs and to provide for a profit.

A company with a single product or a homogeneous activity has little difficulty defining the activities to be included in its operating report, but the reporting structure of a multisegment business is not so easily defined. For example, if management wants to know the profit contributed by a certain product in a particular sales region, cost determination may be complicated in that certain marketing efforts promote several products within the sales region, whereas others overlap different sales regions. Each reporting objective must be identified and described as precisely as possible to ensure that all relevant revenues and costs—but only relevant revenues and costs—are assigned to each reporting segment. Multisegmented businesses may also want to consider the use of activity-based contribution margin statements. These can be very beneficial for companies with numerous products, product lines, and business segments.

Contribution Margin

Segment reports should emphasize a segment's contribution to corporate profit. To compute the contribution margin by segments, sales and variable expenses must be assigned to each reporting segment. Since records are generally kept by segments, the accumulation of these data is relatively easy.

The nature and extent of segmentation of operating reports depend on the organizational structure of the company. The reporting needs of large organizations may not be met with just one segment report, whether segmented by territory, product, division, or other reporting objective. A highly decentralized multilevel organization with different levels of operations may use a reporting structure similar to that presented for Offshore

Refining Company. The Exhibit 9-2 series (pages 467-469) illustrates how a company with multiple levels can provide various reporting schemes. Offshore Refining has two divisions, four products, and two territories. Division A has two products, Oil and Gas, and Division B has two products, Chemical and Saline. The two sales territories, Atlantic and Gulf, overlap the two divisions.

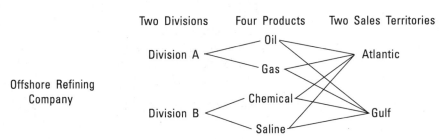

The accounting information system of Offshore Refining is designed to allow for three categorizations of segment reporting, in addition to consolidating the data for total company reporting. Generally, the possibilities of segment reporting are limited only by the availability of detailed data supplied by the accounting information system and the system's ability to combine records of the different segments. Segment reports can have as many levels as management finds useful. Segment reporting configurations typically follow a scheme similar to the one given below where reporting relationships are established between each level of reporting and the next lower level, with management deciding which order reveals the most relevant information for decision making. In fact, some companies provide segment reports to managers with different ordered segments. One report may have products as the primary level and with territories as the second level, and another report may reverse the roles with territories as the primary level and with products as the secondary level.

	Segments								Company Totals
Primary		A			B		C		
Second level	1	2	3	1	2	1	2	3	
Third level	a b c	a c	a b c	a b c	a b c	a b c	a b c	a b c	

A primary (first-level) report shows the company's total operating results along with one other reporting objective. In Exhibit 9-2(a), the primary reporting objective is division. The company could also use territories or products as primary reporting segments. Exhibit 9-2(a) shows the primary reporting segments first, followed by Exhibit 9-2(b), which further segments one of these divisions in terms of the product lines sold within the division. Exhibit 9-2(c) further divides one of these product lines into the territories where it is sold. As each segment is further divided, the report shows more detailed aspects of the company.

The *first-level statements* for Offshore Refining show the company totals and a set of income statements segmented by its major reporting

EXHIBIT 9-2: REPORT CONFIGURATIONS SEGMENTED BY DIVISION, PRODUCTS OF DIVISION, AND TERRITORIES OF PRODUCT

(a) Segment margins by divisions of Offshore Refining Company (first level) (in thousands)

| | Segments | | Company Totals |
	Division A	Division B	
Sales	$100,000	$200,000	$ 300,000
Less:			
Variable manufacturing expenses	- 20,000	- 50,000	- 70,000
Manufacturing margin	$ 80,000	$150,000	$ 230,000
Less:			
Variable selling expenses	$ 10,000	$ 15,000	$ 25,000
Variable administrative expenses	25,000	30,000	55,000
Total	- 35,000	- 45,000	- 80,000
Contribution margin	$ 45,000	$105,000	$ 150,000
Less direct fixed expenses:			
Manufacturing	$ 15,000	$ 50,000	$ 65,000
Selling	5,000	17,000	22,000
Administrative	10,000	18,000	28,000
Total	- 30,000	- 85,000	- 115,000
Division margin	$ 15,000	$ 20,000	$ 35,000
Less common expenses:			
Manufacturing			$ 6,000
Selling			2,000
Administrative			4,000
Total			- 12,000
Net income			$ 23,000

objective: operating divisions. For Exhibit 9-2(a), sales and expense data are presented for the two reporting divisions of Offshore Refining. The direct manufacturing costs (variable costs) are deducted from division sales to determine the **manufacturing margin.** The variable expenses of nonmanufacturing activities are then deducted to obtain the contribution margin. All direct fixed expenses identifiable with each division are subtracted from the contribution margin to arrive at the **division margin**. This is the amount that each division contributes toward covering common corporate expenses and generating corporate profits. Common corporate expenses include the general administrative expenses of operating the corporate offices and conducting corporate activities. These expenses are necessary in the operations of the company but not identifiable within specific divisions.

Second-level statements may be presented for each first-level reporting objective. In our illustration, a product line contribution statement is presented for each product of Division A. These reports, in Exhibit 9-2(b), are useful to management in making decisions related to product pricing, sales

EXHIBIT 9-2 (CONTINUED)

(b) Segment margins by products within Division A of Offshore Refining Company (second level)
(in thousands)

| | Segments | | Division A |
	Oil Products	Gas Products	Totals
Sales	$40,000	$60,000	$100,000
Less:			
Variable manufacturing expenses	- 5,000	- 15,000	- 20,000
Manufacturing margin	$35,000	$45,000	$ 80,000
Less:			
Variable selling expenses	$ 5,000	$ 5,000	$ 10,000
Variable administrative expenses	12,000	13,000	25,000
Total	- 17,000	- 18,000	- 35,000
Contribution margin	$18,000	$27,000	$ 45,000
Less direct fixed expenses:			
Manufacturing	$ 4,000	$ 8,000	$ 12,000
Selling	1,000	3,000	4,000
Administrative	4,000	4,000	8,000
Total	- 9,000	- 15,000	- 24,000
Product margin	$ 9,000	$12,000	$ 21,000
Less common expenses:			
Manufacturing			$ 3,000
Selling			1,000
Administrative			2,000
Total			- 6,000
Division margin			$ 15,000

strategy, inventory levels, break-even analysis, and production scheduling. The decision to continue or discontinue a product may also be based, in part, on information provided by these statements.

In Exhibit 9-2(b), the computations of the manufacturing margin and the contribution margin follow the same format as the divisional contribution statement. However, the computation of the **product margin** (product sales less direct product costs) is somewhat different from the computation of the divisional contribution. This difference occurs because some of the fixed expenses regarded as direct at the divisional segment level are not regarded as direct at the product level. These fixed expenses include such items as divisional office salaries and plant security, which pertain to the general operation of the division rather than to the products. Therefore, only part of the fixed expenses of the division is assigned to products, with the balance of $6,000,000 reported as common costs. These divisional expenses are similar to the common fixed expenses of the company in the divisional contribution statement.

The next set of reports, *third-level statements*, is a breakdown of a second-level reporting objective. Exhibit 9-2(c) shows the amount of

EXHIBIT 9-2 (CONTINUED)

(c) Segment margins by sales territories of Oil Products within Division A of Offshore Refining Company (third level)(in thousands)

| | Segments | | Oil Products |
	Atlantic	Gulf	Totals
Sales	$12,000	$28,000	$40,000
Less:			
Variable manufacturing expenses	- 1,500	- 3,500	- 5,000
Manufacturing margin	$10,500	$24,500	$35,000
Less:			
Variable selling expenses	$ 2,000	$ 3,000	$ 5,000
Variable administrative expenses	4,000	8,000	12,000
Total	- 6,000	- 11,000	- 17,000
Contribution margin	$ 4,500	$13,500	$18,000
Less direct fixed expenses:			
Selling	$ 100	$ 400	$ 500
Administrative	1,000	2,000	3,000
Total	- 1,100	- 2,400	- 3,500
Territory margin	$ 3,400	$11,100	$14,500
Less common expenses:			
Manufacturing			$ 4,000
Selling			500
Administrative			1,000
Total			- 5,500
Product margin			$ 9,000

contribution margin of Oil Products in Division A generated by each sales region. The **territory margin** is the contribution margin less direct fixed expenses associated with a given market area. The margins for the same product often vary because of different environments. For example, the company office that serves the Atlantic area may experience significantly higher marketing and distribution costs than will the office serving the Gulf area. Though the Atlantic area is more populated, it is farther from the refineries. Additionally, the company may have a better reputation in the Gulf area, thereby making sales easier.

Note from the Exhibit 9-2 series that fewer fixed expenses are allocated to segments as the reporting process is separated into specific segments. Because the allocation would be very subjective, none of the fixed manufacturing expense is assignable to the sales territories in Exhibit 9-2(c), and smaller amounts of the selling and administrative expenses are allocated at this level. Each level has certain costs that can be defined as direct or indirect; and at each subsequent level, the total expenses are smaller because the indirect expenses are not carried forward from the previous level. This reduction is evident for the Atlantic and Gulf areas where the territorial margins totaled $14,500,000, whereas the total product margin was $9,000,000.

Other segment configurations are used by organizations to meet different management needs. Although reports segmented by division, product line, and territory are the most common, segment reports can also be based on plants, single products, industries (for conglomerates), and domestic and foreign operations. Because segment reporting allows a company to examine itself from various perspectives, management will select the types of segment reports that are most beneficial for decision making. Reporting efficiency, however, depends upon a sound accounting information system. All data to be used in segment reporting should be coded in a way that allows revenues and expenses to be appropriately classified for each segment reporting format and for consolidated corporate reports.

Direct Versus Common Segment Costs

The **segment margin** represents the amount that a segment contributes toward the common (indirect) costs of the organization and toward profits.[1] It is generally considered one of the best gauges of profitability for a given segment of a company. At the operating management level, segment margins are helpful in making decisions related to production such as those pertaining to capacity changes and long-range pricing policies. The contribution margin is most useful in those situations involving short-run operating decisions such as pricing of special orders and accepting or rejecting special projects.

It may be difficult to distinguish between direct and common segment costs. **Direct segment costs** are often defined as costs that would not be incurred if the segment being evaluated were to be discontinued. They are specifically identifiable with a particular segment. For example, if the Gas Products segment in Exhibit 9-2(b) were discontinued, Gas Product advertising would probably be discontinued; therefore, it should be classified as a direct cost of Gas Products. Other examples include equipment depreciation and segment management salaries. On the other hand, the Division A vice president would probably not be terminated even if the Gas Products segment was discontinued. Therefore the vice president's salary is common to both product lines.

Common segment costs, also called **indirect segment costs,** are related to more than one segment and are not directly traceable to a particular segment. These costs are referred to as common costs because they are incurred at one level for the benefit of two or more segments at a lower level. Nonmanufacturing activities often have numerous indirect costs. A large organization, for example, may provide a centralized computer operation to serve all its production and marketing activities. Other examples of common costs include salaries of corporate management, company-wide sales promotions, and expenses of the corporate accounting department.

Note from Exhibit 9-2(a) that when segments are defined as divisions, Division A has $30,000,000 in direct fixed costs. In Exhibit 9-2(b), only

---

1 Segment margin can also be used to assist in measuring the segment return on investment.

$24,000,000 of this amount remains direct when the definition of a segment is narrowed from divisions to that of product lines in a division. The other $6,000,000 becomes a common cost of Division A product lines.

There are several possible reasons that the $6,000,000 of direct fixed costs is a common cost when the division is broken down into product line segments; for example, the amount could include the monthly salary of the division manager. The division manager's salary is a direct cost when considering the division as a whole, but it is common to the separate product lines within the divisions. Other items that might be treated the same way include plant depreciation, security costs, computer costs, and office equipment.

The $24,000,000 of fixed costs that remain direct ($9,000,000 for Oil and $15,000,000 for Gas) after the division is separated into product line segments consist of items that can be assigned to the products. These might include product research, equipment rental, and product advertising.

Common segment costs should not be allocated; they should simply be deducted from the segment margin in total to arrive at the net income for the company or deducted from the segment income of the next higher level segment. Nothing is added to the usefulness of segment reports by allocating common costs to the various segments; in fact, allocations of this sort may significantly reduce the usefulness of the information. These arbitrary allocations will draw attention away from direct segment costs toward those items that are not directly traceable to a given segment.

Segment Decisions

Decisions to continue or to drop a segment may be based, at least partially, on segment reports. A problem (similar to that previously discussed in comparing direct and common segment costs) arises when determining whether a cost is relevant to a segment or to a product being considered for continuation or noncontinuation. When a company is able to identify relatively small segments, accountants generally find that the smaller the segments used for reporting, the more the costs tend to be common and, therefore, irrelevant to most short-term decisions.

The isolation of direct costs is complicated in that accounting reports often show allocations of common costs among various segments as expenses in the segment reports. To illustrate, if common facilities are used by a dairy processor in the manufacture of various milk products, the income statement for each product would probably include a portion of the depreciation on the facilities. In Exhibit 9-3(a), Yogurt appears unprofitable, and management might be tempted to discontinue it. If the depreciation is $100,000 per year and a total of 1,000,000 liters of all products are made, each liter of product could be charged with $0.10. Suppose that Yogurt, with current sales of 200,000 liters, is dropped. The $20,000 depreciation expense formerly allocated to Yogurt will not be avoided in the short run. The remaining 800,000 liters of the other products must now be charged with $0.125 per liter, an increase of $0.025. As a result, the apparent profitability of the remaining products would be reduced, and company profits would decline, as shown in Exhibit 9-3(b). In fact, the profit decline is due to the decision to drop Yogurt. When a segment is dropped, there may be no short-run reduction in common costs. For this reason, allocated common costs are generally irrelevant to a decision about whether a particular segment should be dropped. In making these decisions, managers must be careful to identify any sunk costs. Even if they are direct costs of a segment, they should be ignored in the decision analysis.

TRANSFER PRICING

Transfer pricing is used when products or services are exchanged between quasi-independent segments of an organization. A **transfer price** is the internal value assigned a product or service that one division provides to another. Transfer-pricing transactions normally occur between profit or investment centers rather than between cost centers of an organization.

The objective of transfer pricing is to transmit financial data between departments or divisions of a company as they use each other's goods and services. Transfer-pricing systems are normally used in decentralized operations to determine whether organizational objectives are being achieved in each division. For division managers to be accountable for all transactions, both external and internal, transfer prices must be determined for the internal transfers of goods and services.

EXHIBIT 9-3: CONTINUING OR DISCONTINUING A PRODUCT: INCORRECT ALLOCATION OF COMMON COSTS

(a) Current period product income statements (partial)

	Cream	Ice Cream	Yogurt	Company Totals
Sales (liters)	500,000	300,000	200,000	
	× $0.22	× $0.30	× $0.40	
	$110,000	$ 90,000	$ 80,000	$280,000
Variable costs	- 40,000	- 30,000	- 65,000	-135,000
Contribution margin	$ 70,000	$ 60,000	$ 15,000	$145,000
Depreciation expense	- 50,000	- 30,000	- 20,000	-100,000
Segment and company income	$ 20,000	$ 30,000	$ (5,000)	$ 45,000

(b) Pro forma product income statements (partial)

	Cream	Ice Cream	Company Totals
Sales	$110,000	$90,000	$200,000
Variable costs	- 40,000	- 30,000	- 70,000
Contribution margin	$ 70,000	$60,000	$130,000
Depreciation expense	- 62,500	- 37,500	-100,000
Segment and company income	$ 7,500	$22,500	$ 30,000

**Management
Considerations**

The desire of the selling and buying divisions of the same company to maximize their individual performance measures often creates transfer-pricing problems. Acting as independent units, the divisions may take actions that are not in the best interest of the organization as a whole. The three examples that follow illustrate the need for the organization to maintain a corporate profit-maximizing viewpoint while attempting to allow divisional autonomy and responsibility.

Rex Manufacturing has five divisions that interchange products and product components with each other. Assume that Division 6 manufactures two products: Alpha and Beta. Alpha is sold externally for $50 per unit, and Beta is transferred to Division 13 for $60 per unit. The costs associated with the two products are shown below:

	Product	
	Alpha	Beta
Direct materials	$15	$14
Direct labor	5	10
Variable manufacturing overhead	5	16
Fixed manufacturing overhead	6	15
Variable selling	4	0
Total	$35	$55

A proposal has just been received from another company to supply Division 13 with a substitute product similar to Beta at a price of $52. From the company's viewpoint, this is merely a make or buy decision. The relevant costs are the differential outlay costs of the alternative actions. If the fixed manufacturing costs of Division 6 cannot be reduced, the relevant costs from the company's perspective are as follows:

Buy		$52
Make:		
Direct materials	$14	
Direct labor	10	
Variable manufacturing overhead	16	- 40
Difference favors making		$12

The decision for Division 13's management is basically one of cost minimization: Buy from the source that charges the lowest price. If Division 6 is not willing to transfer Beta at a price of $52 or less, the management of Division 13 may go to the external supplier so that the division's profits can be maximized. Although Division 13's managers are concerned about the cost of Beta, they are also concerned about the quality of the goods. If the $52 product is inferior in quality, Division 13's management may decide to buy from Division 6 at the higher price.

Prior to Division 13's receipt of the external offer to buy Beta for $52 per unit, Division 6 had been transferring Beta for $60. For Division 6, this is a decision to reduce the contribution margin of Beta and, therefore, lower divisional profits or to find an alternative use of its resources. Of course, corporate management may intervene and require the internal transfer.

For the second example, assume that Division 6 can either transfer Beta to Division 13 or sell an equivalent amount externally for $60 per unit. Now the decision for Division 6's management is simple: Sell to the buyer willing to pay the most.

To examine a slightly different transfer-pricing conflict, assume that Division 6 can sell all the Alpha that it can produce (it is operating at capacity). While there is no external market for Beta, there is a one-to-one trade-off between the production of Alpha and Beta. They both use equal amounts of the limited capacity of Division 6.

The corporation still regards this as a make or buy decision, but the costs of producing Beta have changed. Beta now includes an outlay cost and an opportunity cost. The outlay cost is the variable cost of $40 ($14 + $10 + $16) computed above. The opportunity cost is the net benefit foregone if the limited capacity of Division 6 is used to produce Beta rather than Alpha:

Selling price of Alpha		$50
Outlay costs of Alpha:		
Direct materials	$15	
Direct labor	5	
Variable manufacturing overhead	5	
Variable selling	4	-29
Opportunity cost of making Beta		$21

Accordingly, the relevant costs in the make or buy decision are as shown below:

Make:		
Outlay cost of Beta	$40	
Opportunity cost of Beta	21	$61
Buy		$52

Product Beta should be purchased from the outside supplier. If there were no outside suppliers, the relevant cost of manufacturing Beta would still be $61. This is another way of saying that Beta should not be produced and processed further in Division 13 unless the resultant revenues cover all outlay costs (including the $40 in Division 6) and provide a contribution of at least $21 ($61 - $40). From the viewpoint of the corporation, the relevant costs in make or buy decisions are *the external price, the outlay costs of manufacture, and the opportunity cost to manufacture*. The opportunity cost is zero if there is excess capacity.

Determining Transfer Prices

As illustrated above, the transfer price of goods or services may be subject to much controversy. Although a price must be agreed upon for each item or service transferred between divisions, the selection of the pricing method is dependent upon many factors. The conditions surrounding the transfer determines which of the alternative methods discussed below is selected.

In considering each method, observe that each transfer results in a revenue entry on the supplier's books and a cost entry on the receiver's books. Transfers may be considered as sales by the supplier and as purchases by the receiver. Although no method is likely to be ideal, one must be selected if the profit or investment center concept is used.

Market Price

When there is an existing market with established prices for an intermediate product and the transfer actions of the company will not affect prices, market prices are ideal transfer prices. See Management Accounting Practice 9-2 for a discussion about the popularity of transfer-pricing methods.

If divisions are free to buy and sell outside the firm, the use of market prices preserves divisional autonomy and leads divisions to act in a manner that maximizes corporate goal congruence. Unfortunately, not all product transfers have established external markets. Furthermore, the divisions should carefully evaluate whether the market price is competitive or controlled by one or two large companies. When there are substantial selling expenses associated with outside sales, many firms specify the transfer price as market price less selling expenses. The internal sale may not require the incurrence of costs to get and fill the order.

To illustrate, assume that product Alpha of Division 6 can be sold competitively at $50 per unit or transferred to Division 24 for additional processing. Under most situations, Division 6 will never sell Alpha for less than $50, and Division 24 will likewise never pay more than $50 for it. However, if any variable expenses related to marketing and shipping can be eliminated by divisional transfers, these costs are generally subtracted from the competitive market price. In our illustration, where variable selling expenses are $4 for Alpha, the transfer price could be reduced to $46 ($50 - $4). A price between $46 and $50 would probably be better than either extreme price. To the extent that these transfer prices represent a near competitive situation, the profitability of each division can then be evaluated fairly.

Variable Costs

If excess capacity exists in the supplying division, establishing a transfer price equal to variable costs leads the purchasing division to act in a manner that is optimal from the corporation's viewpoint. The buying division has the corporation's variable cost as its own variable cost as it enters the external market. Unfortunately, establishing the transfer price at variable cost causes the supplying division to report zero profits or a loss equal to any fixed costs. If excess capacity does not exist, establishing a transfer price at variable cost may not lead to optimal action because the supplying division may have to forego sales that include a markup for fixed costs and profits. If Beta could be sold externally for $60, Division 6 would not want to transfer Beta to Division 13 for a $40 transfer price based on the following variable costs:

Direct materials	$14
Direct labor	10
Variable manufacturing overhead	16
Total variable costs	$40

Division 6 would much rather sell outside the company for $60, which covers variable costs and provides for a profit contribution margin of $20:

Selling price of Beta	$ 60
Variable costs	- 40
Contribution margin	$ 20

Variable Costs Plus Opportunity Costs

From the viewpoint of the organization, variable costs plus any opportunity cost is the optimal transfer price. Because all relevant costs are included in the transfer price, the purchasing division is led to act in a manner optimal for the company overall whether or not excess capacity exists.

MANAGEMENT ACCOUNTING PRACTICE 9-2

Transfer Pricing in the 1990s

During the 1980s, the United States and several other countries introduced transfer-pricing guidelines through their taxing agencies. These changes were an attempt to provide a sound base when goods or services were transferred from one country to another by the same company. In the United States, all companies with foreign divisions and subsidiaries are required to maintain extensive documentation supporting intracompany transactions, and all transfer prices must be determined in advance. This is to minimize shifting income to a country with favored tax rates at the end of the tax year.

A recent survey of the *Fortune* 500 industrial companies (143 respondents) revealed that most of them (92 percent of those responding) use transfer pricing. The methods used differed among companies and also varied as to whether the transfer of goods and services took place domestically or internationally. A summary of the methods used indicates that market-based transfer prices were preferred with domestic transfers, while cost-based transfer prices were slightly preferred for international transfers. Of all the methods given, the most popular for domestic transfers was market price without any adjustment at 25.1 percent. The leader for international transfers was full cost plus markup at 26.8 percent, closely followed by market price without adjustment at 26.1 percent. For domestic transfers, there was no close second choice.

Citing a previous study, the authors did a comparison of methods and found that companies have slowly shifted from cost-based to market-based methods for both domestic and international transfers. Also, there was a shift away from negotiated prices between 1977 and 1990.

Based on: Roger Y. W. Tang, "Transfer Pricing in the 1990s," *Management Accounting* (February 1992), pp. 22-26.

With excess capacity in the supplying division, the transfer price is the variable cost per unit. Without excess capacity, the transfer price is the sum of the variable and opportunity costs. Following this rule in the previous example, if Division 6 had excess capacity, the transfer price of Beta would be set at Beta's variable costs of $40 per unit. At this transfer price, Division 13 would buy Beta internally, rather than externally, at $52 per unit. If Division 6 cannot sell Beta externally, but can sell all the Alpha it can produce, and is operating at capacity, the transfer price per unit would be set at $61, the sum of Beta's variable and opportunity costs ($40 + $21). (Refer back to page 474.) At this transfer price, Division 13 would buy Beta externally for $52. In both situations, the management of Division 13 has acted in accordance with the profit-maximizing goal of the organization.

However, there are two problems with this method. First, when the supplying division has excess capacity, establishing the transfer price at variable cost causes the supplying division to report zero profits or a loss equal to any fixed costs. Second, it is difficult to determine opportunity costs when the supplying division produces several products. If the problems with the previously mentioned transfer-pricing methods are too great, three other methods are available: absorption cost plus markup, negotiated prices, and dual prices.

Absorption Cost Plus Markup

According to absorption costing, all variable and fixed manufacturing costs are product costs. Pricing internal transfers at absorption cost eliminates the supplying division's reported loss on each product that may occur using a variable cost transfer price. Absorption cost plus markup provides the supplying division with a contribution toward unallocated costs. In "cost-plus" transfer pricing, "cost" should be defined as standard cost rather than as actual cost. This prevents the supplying division from passing on the cost of inefficient operations to other divisions, and it allows the buying division to know its cost in advance of purchase. Even though "cost-plus" transfer prices may not maximize company profits, they are widely used. Their popularity stems from several factors, including ease of implementation, justifiability, and perceived fairness. Once everyone agrees on absorption cost plus markup pricing rules, internal disputes are minimized.

Negotiated Prices

Negotiated transfer prices are used when the supplying and buying divisions independently agree on a price. As with market-based transfer prices, negotiated transfer prices are believed to preserve divisional autonomy. Negotiated transfer prices may lead to some suboptimal decisions, but this is regarded as a small price to pay for other benefits of decentralization. When negotiated transfer prices are used, some corporations establish arbitration procedures to help settle disputes between divisions. However, the existence of an arbitrator with any real or perceived authority reduces divisional autonomy.

Negotiated prices should have market prices as their ceiling and variable costs as their floor. Although frequently used where an external market for the product or component exists, the most common use of negotiated prices is where no identical-product external market exists. Negotiations may start with a floor price plus add-ons such as overhead and profit markups, or they may start with a ceiling price less adjustments for selling and administrative expenses and allowances for quantity discounts. Where no identical-product external market exists, the market price for a similar completed product may be used, less the estimated cost of completing the product from the transfer stage to the completed stage.

Assume that the Financial Consulting Division performs the service Customer Billing for the Engineering Consulting Division. There is no comparable external market service, but the Financial Consulting Division provides a similar service, Financial Consult, which is billed externally for $132 an hour. The cost to the Financial Consulting Division for service Customer Billing is a follows:

Direct labor	$35
Direct materials	10
Variable overhead	30
Direct costs	$75
Fixed overhead (estimated)	20
Total	$95

The managers of the Financial and Engineering Consulting divisions decide to negotiate a fee for the service using a ceiling of $132. Financial Consulting's management recognizes that the additional direct labor of the service Financial Consult is $12 per hour more than for the service Customer Billing and, thereby, offers the service Customer Billing for $120 per hour to Engineering. Engineering's manager argues that the fixed overhead needs to be adjusted or maybe even eliminated. Financial Consulting finally agrees to reduce the fixed overhead by 20 percent. The final transfer price (fee) of the service the Customer Billing to Engineering is $109 based on the following analysis:

Direct labor	$ 35
Direct materials	10
Variable overhead	30
Fixed overhead	16
Total costs	$ 91
Profit margin (20%)	18
Transfer price	$109

The transfer price of $109 is between the variable cost to produce, $75, and the adjusted external fee of $120. Engineering accepts the fee because it appears fair, and Financial Consulting accepts the price because it exceeds variable costs and provides an adequate contribution margin. If the Financial Consulting Division has idle capacity, Engineering should also argue that some or all of the fixed items be eliminated because they will not change if the service is provided.

Dual Prices

Dual prices exist when a company allows a difference in the supplier's and receiver's transfer prices for the same product. This method allegedly minimizes internal squabbles of division managers and problems of conflicting divisional goals. The supplier's price normally approximates market price, which allows the selling division to show a "normal" profit on items that it transfers internally. The receiver's price is usually the internal cost of the product or service. Dual prices eliminate the receiver's need for covering internally transferred profits when the final external price is established. The receiver is also allowed to make a profit from the final product that was transferred in.

Applying Transfer Pricing

Once transfer prices have been determined, they can be used to record interdivisional sales. Although most divisional income statements are more detailed, the following illustrations concentrate only on the elements related to the transfer of goods and services. Leigh Ann's Fashions, a dress manufacturer, has two divisions, Sewing and Sales. The Sewing Division sells to the Sales Division and to other distributors. The Sales Division buys from no one but the Sewing Division. During the first quarter of 19X7, the Sewing Division incurred the following unit costs:

Direct materials	$ 8
Direct labor	5
Variable manufacturing overhead	3
Variable selling	1
Total	$17

Total production for the quarter was 30,000 dresses for the Sewing Division, of which 20,000 were sold to the Sales Division for $20 each. The external selling price for each dress was $25. There were no beginning or ending inventories. Fixed manufacturing overhead for the quarter totaled $60,000.

After the Sales Division receives the dresses, it affixes private labels where necessary and then packages and ships dresses to retail customers. The variable unit costs are $4, and the Sales Division incurs $40,000 in fixed costs each quarter. The Sales Division sold all dresses received during the first quarter for $30 each.

Exhibit 9-4 provides a simple illustration of how transfer pricing affects each division's income statement and the company as a whole. The 20,000 units transferred from Sewing to Sales shows up as $400,000 of internal sales for Sewing and as $400,000 of transferred-in cost to Sales. Note that both amounts are ignored for the overall company income statement. The reason for this elimination at the company level is the desire to provide external users of financial statements information related to economic activities with outside parties, not with internal transfers.

Now assume Sales is allowed to buy from outside suppliers. An outside supplier has offered to sell the Sales Division dresses of similar style and quality for $18. The Sewing Division's management is offered the option

EXHIBIT 9-4: DIVISIONAL AND COMPANY INCOME STATEMENTS, INTERNAL TRANSFER

Leigh Ann's Fashions
Divisional and Company Income Statements
First Quarter 19X7

	Sewing Division	Sales Division	Company
Sales:			
External*	$ 250,000	$ 600,000	$ 850,000
Internal**	400,000	-	-
Total	$ 650,000	$ 600,000	$ 850,000
Variable costs:			
Incurred#	$ 510,000	$ 80,000	$ 590,000
Transferred-in##	-	400,000	-
Total	- 510,000	- 480,000	- 590,000
Contribution margin	$ 140,000	$ 120,000	$ 260,000
Fixed costs	- 60,000	- 40,000	- 100,000
Net income	$ 80,000	$ 80,000	$ 160,000

*10,000 units × $25 = $250,000, and 20,000 units × $30 = $600,000
**20,000 units × $20 = $400,000
#30,000 units × $17 = $510,000, and 20,000 units × $4 = $80,000
##Transferred-in costs are the same as internal sales.

of reducing its transfer price to $18, but it refuses even though Sewing has no other use for the production capacity. The Sales Division's management contends that Sewing will have a markup of $2 on each dress because its variable selling cost is not necessary for internal sales, but Sewing's management disagrees. Note in Exhibit 9-5 that the company and the Sewing Division had a lower net income when the Sales Division purchased outside, but the Sales Division increased its income by $40,000 when it bought externally.

Finally, assume that Sewing is willing to negotiate a transfer price with Sales for $18. The resulting income statements for each division and the company as a whole are illustrated in Exhibit 9-6 (page 482). Comparing Exhibits 9-4 and 9-6, note that the income to the company remains the same when there are internal transfers even though the transfer price changes from $20 to $18. However, the divisional incomes change by increasing one and reducing the other. No doubt, the management of Sales is pleased to have the outside competition because its income increases under each alternative.

These examples illustrate that transfer prices affect the profitability of divisions and the evaluations of the division managers. By simply adjusting the transfer price, the Sewing Division's income is reduced from $80,000 to $40,000, a substantial difference for evaluation purposes.

It is often necessary to determine the impact of transfer prices on a company to fully assess the results of decisions involving transfer pricing.

EXHIBIT 9-5: DIVISIONAL AND COMPANY INCOME STATEMENTS, EXTERNAL SUPPLIER

Leigh Ann's Fashions
Divisional and Company Income Statements
First Quarter 19X7

	Sewing Division	Sales Division	Company
Sales:			
External*	$ 250,000	$ 600,000	$ 850,000
Internal	-	-	-
Total	$ 250,000	$ 600,000	$ 850,000
Variable costs:			
Incurred**	$ 170,000	$ 80,000	$ 250,000
External purchases#	-	360,000	360,000
Total	- 170,000	- 440,000	- 610,000
Contribution margin	$ 80,000	$ 160,000	$ 240,000
Fixed costs	- 60,000	- 40,000	- 100,000
Net income	$ 20,000	$ 120,000	$ 140,000

*10,000 units × $25 = $250,000, and 20,000 units × $30 = $600,000
**10,000 units × $17 = $170,000, and 20,000 units × $4 = $80,000
#20,000 units × $18 = $360,000

Depending on how these types of decision are resolved, divisional managers may be pleased or displeased with the reporting system and responsibility accounting.

SUBOPTIMIZATION

L O 5

A transfer-pricing problem, **suboptimization**, exists when divisions, acting in their own best interest, set transfer prices or make decisions based on transfer prices that are not in the best interest of the organization as a whole. The seriousness of the transfer-pricing problem depends on the extent to which the affairs of divisions are intertwined. Assuming full capacity when intermediate products have established markets and divisions are free to buy and sell outside the firm, the use of market prices avoids the transfer-pricing problem.

A potential transfer-pricing problem exists when divisions exchange goods or services for which there is no established market. See Management Accounting Practice 9-3 (page 483) for an example. If the actual or potential amount of such transfers is relatively small, the use of cost-plus or negotiated prices seems most appropriate. Some managers believe the benefits of decentralization more than offset any loss of profit on individual products.

EXHIBIT 9-6: DIVISIONAL AND COMPANY INCOME STATEMENTS

Leigh Ann's Fashions
Divisional and Company Income Statements
First Quarter 19X7

	Sewing Division	Sales Division	Company
Sales:			
External*	$ 250,000	$ 600,000	$ 850,000
Internal**	360,000	-	-
Total	$ 610,000	$ 600,000	$ 850,000
Variable costs:			
Incurred#	$ 510,000	$ 80,000	$ 590,000
Transferred-in##	-	360,000	-
Total	- 510,000	- 440,000	- 590,000
Contribution margin	$ 100,000	$ 160,000	$ 260,000
Fixed costs	- 60,000	- 40,000	- 100,000
Net income	$ 40,000	$ 120,000	$ 160,000

*10,000 units x $25 = $250,000, and 20,000 units x $30 = $600,000
**20,000 units x $18 = $360,000
#30,000 units x $17 = $510,000, and 20,000 units x $4 = $80,000
##Transferred-in costs are the same as internal sales.

Though suboptimization may be tolerated on some products to obtain the benefits of decentralization, the transfer-pricing problem sometimes becomes so severe that cost and revenue centers should be used in place of investment or profit centers. Consider a single-product firm that attempts to operate its manufacturing and marketing activities as separate profit or investment centers. The affairs of these two divisions cannot be disentangled, and any attempt to do so will reduce the profits of the entire business.

The ideal solutions for the supplying division and for the buying division generally conflict. From the organization's perspective, the desired transfers may not occur because the division managers, pursuing their own best interests, could decide against a transfer. These conflicts sometimes are overcome by having a higher ranking manager impose a transfer price and insist that a transfer be made. But the managers of divisions in an organization that has a policy of decentralization often regard these orders as undermining their autonomy. So the imposition of a price may solve the goal congruence and incentive problem but reduce autonomy. Transfer pricing thus becomes a problem with no ideal solutions.

Seldom does a single transfer price meet all the criteria for inducing top management's desired decisions. The best transfer price depends on the circumstances at hand. Furthermore, the optimal price for either division may differ from that employed for external needs, including tax requirements.

MANAGEMENT ACCOUNTING PRACTICE 9-3

Simple Adjustments Can Make a Big Difference

Bellcore (Bell Communications Research) designed a state-of-the-art transferring pricing system in 1983. However, with the passing of time, defects in the system began to appear. Engineering was spending time performing word processing, graphics, technical publications, and secretarial duties because they couldn't afford the high prices those in-house departments were charging with their fancy transfer prices. The word processing, graphics, technical publications, and secretarial departments were unable to contain their costs even with a large work volume and were losing corporate customers because of their high prices.

After a careful review, it was determined that part of the reason for the high costs was because these departments were paying more than their share for overhead and rent. Nonusage-based services (travel planning, libraries, purchasing, and so on) were charged on a headcount basis. These in-house departments accounted for 12 percent of the company's employment and were charged for 12 percent of the nonusage-based services. However, their actual usage was considerably less. A change in allocation methods reduced the service centers' total costs by 19 percent. Bellcore is committed to its transfer pricing system and believes that by making necessary adjustments the system will continually improve.

Based on: Edward J. Kovac and Henry P. Troy, "Getting Transfer Price Right: What Bellcore Did," *Harvard Business Review* (September-October 1989), pp. 148-154.

EVALUATION
MEASURES

L O 6

Two of the most common measures used to evaluate profitability of investment centers, return on investment and residual income, are discussed in the following sections. Several supporting components of these two measures, which help clarify the applications, are also presented.

Return on
Investment

Return on investment (ROI) is a measure of the earnings per dollar of investment.[2] The return on investment of an investment center is computed by dividing the income of the center by its asset base (usually total assets):

$$\text{ROI} = \frac{\text{Investment center income}}{\text{Investment center asset base}}$$

---

2 Other similar concepts that are often used to supplement or replace ROI, but are not discussed here, include return on assets, return on net assets, and return on production assets.

It can also be computed as investment turnover times the return-on-sales ratio (also called *margin, income percentage of revenue*, and *income-sales ratio*):

$$\text{ROI} = \text{Investment turnover} \times \text{Return-on-sales ratio}$$

where:

$$\text{Investment turnover} = \frac{\text{Sales}}{\text{Investment center asset base}}$$

and

$$\text{Return-on-sales ratio} = \frac{\text{Investment center income}}{\text{Sales}}$$

When investment turnover is multiplied by the return-on-sales ratio, the product is the same as investment center income divided by investment center asset base:

$$\text{ROI} = \frac{\text{Sales}}{\text{Investment center asset base}} \times \frac{\text{Investment center income}}{\text{Sales}}$$

$$= \frac{\text{Investment center income}}{\text{Investment center asset base}}$$

Once ROI is computed, it is compared to some previously identified performance criteria. These include the investment center's previous ROI, overall company ROI, the ROI of similar divisions, or the ROI of nonaffiliated companies that operate in similar markets. The breakdown of ROI into investment turnover and return-on-sales ratio is useful in determining the source of variance in overall performance.

To illustrate the computation and use of ROI, the following information is available concerning the 19X3 operations of the Maine Division of North American Steel:

Sales	$1,200,000
Income	144,000
Asset base	800,000

From these facts, ROI can be computed as:

$$\text{ROI} = \frac{\text{Investment center income}}{\text{Investment center asset base}}$$

$$= \$144{,}000/\$800{,}000$$

$$= 0.18 \text{ or } 18 \text{ percent}$$

or as:

$$\text{ROI} = \frac{\text{Sales}}{\text{Investment center asset base}} \times \frac{\text{Investment center income}}{\text{Sales}}$$

$$= \frac{\$1{,}200{,}000}{\$800{,}000} \times \frac{\$144{,}000}{\$1{,}200{,}000}$$

$$= 1.5 \times 0.12 = 0.18 \text{ or } 18 \text{ percent.}$$

During 19X3, Maine Division earned a return on its investment base of 18 percent, consisting of an investment turnover of 1.5 times and a return-on-sales ratio of 0.12. Using such an analysis, the company has three measurement criteria with which to evaluate the performance of Maine Division: (1) ROI, (2) investment turnover, and (3) return-on-sales ratio.

For 19X3, North American chose to evaluate its divisions based on company ROI and its interrelated components of investment turnover and return-on-sales ratio. The information for each division is shown in Exhibit 9-7. Because each division is different in size, the company evaluation standard is not a simple average of the divisions but is based on desired levels of company sales, assets, and income.

Based on ROI, the Tijuana Division had the best performance, Alberta Division excelled in investment turnover, and Missouri Division had the highest return-on-sales ratio. From Exhibit 9-7, it is obvious that Tijuana Division had the best year because it was the only division that exceeded all three of the company's performance criteria. For 19X3, each division equaled or exceeded the minimum ROI established by the company, even though the component criteria of ROI were not always achieved. For example, Maine Division achieved the minimum ROI even though its return-on-sales ratio was below 0.15. It accomplished this by having an investment turnover that exceeded the minimum by 0.3 (1.5 less 1.2).

To properly evaluate each division, the company should study the underlying components of ROI. For the Maine Division, management would want to know why the minimum investment turnover was exceeded, while the return-on-sales ratio minimum was not. The Maine Division may have incurred unfavorable cost variances by producing inefficiently. As a result of inefficient production, the return-on-sales ratio declined to a point below the minimum desired level. It is difficult to evaluate a large operating division based on one financial figure. Management should select several key indicators of performance when conducting periodic reviews of its operating segments.

EXHIBIT 9-7: PERFORMANCE EVALUATION DATA

North American Steel
Performance Measures
For the Year Ending June 30, 19X3

		Performance Measures	
	ROI	Investment Turnover	Return-on-Sales Ratio
Operating unit:			
Maine Division	0.18	1.5	0.12
Alberta Division	0.24	3.0	0.08
Missouri Division	0.22	1.1	0.20
Tijuana Division	0.27	1.5	0.18
Average (company)	0.21	1.4	0.15
Company performance criteria:			
Projected minimums	0.18	1.2	0.15

A similar analysis of ROI and its components can be made when planning for future periods. In developing plans for 19X4, management wants to know the possible effect of changes in the major elements of ROI for Maine Division. Sensitivity analysis can be used to predict the impact of changes in sales, the investment center asset base, or investment center income.

Assuming the investment base is unchanged, a projected ROI can be determined for Maine Division for a sales goal of $1,600,000 and an income goal of $160,000:

$$\text{ROI} = \frac{\text{Sales}}{\text{Investment center asset base}} \times \frac{\text{Investment center income}}{\text{Sales}}$$

$$= \frac{\$1,600,000}{\$800,000} \times \frac{\$160,000}{\$1,600,000}$$

$$= 2.0 \times 0.10$$

$$= \underline{\underline{0.20}} \text{ or 20 percent.}$$

Note that ROI increased from 18 to 20 percent, even though the return-on-sales ratio decreased from 12 to 10 percent. The change in turnover from 1.5 to 2.0 more than offset the reduced return-on-sales ratio.

Starting from Maine's 19X3 performance, now assume that projected operating efficiencies reduce expenses by $12,000 and that sales remain constant, thereby increasing income to $156,000. The ROI increases from 18 percent to 19.5 percent:

$$\text{ROI} = \frac{\text{Sales}}{\text{Investment center asset base}} \times \frac{\text{Investment center income}}{\text{Sales}}$$

$$= \frac{\$1,200,000}{\$800,000} \times \frac{\$156,000}{\$1,200,000}$$

$$= 1.5 \times 0.13$$

$$= \underline{\underline{0.195}} \text{ or 19.5 percent.}$$

Sensitivity analysis may involve changing only one factor or a combination of factors in the ROI model. When more than one factor is changed, the user must be careful to properly analyze exactly how much change is caused by each factor.

Management may desire a minimum ROI. In this case, the major elements of the ROI model can be manipulated to determine the best way to meet this minimum. If, for example, ROI is set at 24 percent, it may be obtained by changing only the investment base (from $800,000 to $600,000):

$$\text{ROI} = \frac{\text{Sales}}{\text{Investment center asset base}} \times \frac{\text{Investment center income}}{\text{Sales}}$$

$$= \frac{\$1,200,000}{\$600,000} \times \frac{\$144,000}{\$1,200,000}$$

$$= 2.0 \times 0.12$$

$$= \underline{\underline{0.24}} \text{ or 24 percent.}$$

Or it may be obtained by changing a combination of the investment base (from \$800,000 to \$900,000) and income (from \$144,000 to \$216,000):

$$\text{ROI} = \frac{\text{Sales}}{\text{Investment center asset base}} \times \frac{\text{Investment center income}}{\text{Sales}}$$

$$= \frac{\$1,200,000}{\$900,000} \times \frac{\$216,000}{\$1,200,000}$$

$$= 1.333 \times 0.18$$

$$= \underline{0.24} \text{ or 24 percent.}$$

It may also be obtained by changing any combination of the three factors, together or separately.

Statistics such as ROI, investment turnover, and return-on-sales ratio, mean little by themselves. They take on meaning only when compared with an objective, a trend, another division, a competitor, or an industry average. Many businesses establish minimum ROIs for each of their divisions, which are expected to attain or exceed this minimum return. The salaries, bonuses, and promotions of division managers may be tied directly to the ROI of their divisions. Without other evaluation techniques, managers often strive for ROI maximization, sometimes to the long-run detriment of the entire organization.

Investment Base

Despite the relevance and conceptual simplicity of ROI, a division's ROI cannot be computed until management determines how divisional investment and income are to be measured. Because the primary purpose for computing ROI is to evaluate the effectiveness of a division's operating management in using the assets entrusted to them, most organizations define investment as the average total assets of a division during the evaluation period.

For most companies, the investment base is limited to each division's operating assets. These normally include those assets held for productive use, such as cash, accounts receivable, inventory, and plant and equipment. Nonproductive assets, such as land for a future plant site, would not be included in the investment base of a division, only for the company.

Corporate cash and receivables are sometimes held by corporate headquarters, which permits more efficiency in billings and collections. This enables the corporation to hold a smaller total amount of cash than would be required if each division had its own bank account. Although it is relatively easy to assign receivables held by corporate headquarters to divisions (on the basis of their origin) for ROI computations, the assignment of cash presents some problems. Because of operating economies, the total cash requirements of the entire organization are less than the cash requirements of all divisions acting as independent units. However, assigning cash on the basis of the division's independent cash needs is likely to raise objections. The best approach seems to be to allocate cash based on the amount of incremental cash needed to support each division as compared to the company as a whole; nevertheless, cash allocations are most frequently based on relative sales or cash expenditures.

The next problem relates to general corporate assets. It is not advisable to allocate the cost of physical assets utilized by corporate headquarters to the operating divisions. Though the divisions might need additional administrative facilities if they were truly independent, they have no control over the headquarters' facilities. Additionally, the joint nature and use of these facilities make any allocation arbitrary.

Investment Center Income

Divisional income is equal to divisional revenues less divisional operating expenses. Except for service expenses that can be clearly identified with the activities of individual divisions (such as the variable costs of processing accounts receivable), the expenses of operating corporate headquarters should not be allocated to the division for ROI purposes. Some managers advocate not allocating even if the absence of corporate headquarters would cause divisions to incur additional expenses. In many decentralized operations, corporate general and administrative expenses are often allocated to divisions for internal reporting purposes, but they are excluded when computing divisional ROI.

Some companies allocate all expenses in determining ROI based on management's belief that these expenses represent the value of services rendered by the home office. Other managers believe that allocated expenses should not be included because division management has no control over the incurrence or allocation of headquarters' expenses. Also, the allocations are often for items of questionable value to the division, such as the corporation's legal costs.

Generally, such allocations are not included in the computation of divisional ROI. Only expenses directly associated with the division should be included in ROI computations. An example of a directly associated cost is the advertising expense of products only produced by the division. The amount of expenses allocated should be approximately the same as it would be if the division had incurred the services on its own. If allocated corporate costs are substantially greater than a division's independently incurred costs would be, costs are allocated in excess of benefits received—a very undesirable situation.

Asset Measurement

Once divisional investment and income have been operationally defined and ROI computations have been made, the significance of the resulting ratios may still be questioned. Return on investment may be overstated in terms of constant dollars because inflation and arbitrary depreciation procedures cause an undervaluation of the inventory and fixed assets included in the investment center asset base. Asset measurement is particularly troublesome if inventories are valued at last-in, first-out (LIFO) cost and fixed assets were acquired many years ago. A division manager may hesitate to replace an old, inefficient asset with a new, efficient one because the replacement may lower income and ROI through an increased investment base and increased depreciation.

To improve the comparability between divisions' old and new assets, some firms value assets at original cost, rather than at net book value (cost less accumulated depreciation), in ROI computations. This procedure does not reflect inflation, however. An old asset that cost $120,000 ten years ago is still being compared with an asset that costs $200,000 today. A better solution might be to value old assets at their replacement cost, although obtaining replacement cost data can be a problem. This raises issues about the cost and value of information and about whether or not the old asset would be replaced in kind at today's prices.

One of the problems with the comparisons of ROI among divisions is the difference in the historical cost of each division's assets. It is somewhat difficult to compare a division whose asset base is measured in 1996 dollars with one that has most of its asset base measured in 1974 dollars. To overcome this problem, many companies require all divisions to use some common dollar base. This problem is particularly acute when divisions are located in different countries and adjustments have to be made for variations in exchange rates, as well as variations in the price level.

Residual Income

Residual income is an often-mentioned alternative to return on investment for measuring investment center performance. **Residual income** is the excess of investment center income over the minimum rate of return set by top management. The minimum rate of return represents the rate that can be earned on alternative investments of similar risks.

The minimum dollar return is computed as a percentage of the investment center's asset base. When residual income is the primary basis of evaluation, the management of each investment center is encouraged to maximize residual income rather than ROI. To illustrate the computation, assume a company requires a minimum return of 12 percent on each division's investment base. The residual income of a division of the company that has an annual net operating income of $200,000 and an investment base of $1,500,000 is $20,000:

Division income	$200,000
Minimum return ($1,500,000 x 0.12)	-180,000
Residual income	$ 20,000

Although it is generally agreed that residual income provides a useful evaluation of profitability, there are several approaches as to how the deduction is computed. In recent years a variation of residual income, referred to as economic value-added, has gained in popularity. The most significant feature of economic value-added is the use of an organization's cost of capital as the minimum return. See Management Accounting Practice 9-4 for a description of this approach.

Many executives view residual income as a better measure of performance than ROI. They believe that residual income encourages managers to make profitable investments that would otherwise be rejected by managers who are being measured by ROI. To illustrate, assume that two divisions of Color Company have an opportunity to make an investment of $100,000 that will generate a return of 20 percent. The manager of Green

MANAGEMENT ACCOUNTING PRACTICE 9-4

Economic Value-Added: It's Catching on at Quaker Oats and Coca-Cola

To better evaluate their companies, financial managers at Quaker Oats, Coca-Cola, and other corporate giants are looking at a modified method of determining residual income. Advocates claim that it is the best evaluation measure to come along in decades. Its simplicity also makes it a favorite of companies with less sophisticated financial measurement models.

Because residual income has been defined in numerous ways, evaluators of financial statements have often sought to stabilize the computation by defining the terms and concepts being used. The most recent attempt at stabilizing the model is economic value-added (EVA), a variation of the residual income computation with differently defined parameters.

EVA defines the base as total operating capital, meaning all fixed assets (equipment, computers, buildings, etc.) used to create the income plus the working capital (cash, inventories, and receivables). EVA is the after-tax operating income less the annual cost of capital.

Additionally, EVA defines what is meant by cost of capital. According to Tully, it is "what your shareholders could be getting in price appreciation and dividends if they invested instead in a portfolio of companies about as risky as yours." As used in this text, it would be the opportunity cost expressed in terms of a percentage. For a corporation to be successful and add economic value, it must at least match its investors' opportunity cost of the next best alternative.

After the investment base, income, and cost of capital rate have been determined, the EVA is computed the same way as residual income. However, EVA cannot always replace residual income because companies often have segments that they want to measure that do not have easily determined capital and income as measured by EVA.

Based on: Shawn Tully, "The Real Key to Creating Wealth," *Fortune* (September 20, 1993), pp. 38-50.

Division is evaluated using ROI, and the manager of Orange Division is evaluated using residual income. The current ROI of each division is 24 percent, and each division has a current income of $120,000 and a minimum rate of 18 percent on invested capital. If each division has a current investment base of $500,000, the effect of the proposed investment on each division's performance is as follows:

	Current	+	Proposed	=	Total
Green Division:					
Investment center income	$120,000		$ 20,000		$140,000
Asset base	$500,000		$100,000		$600,000
ROI	0.24 or		0.20 or		0.233 or
	24 percent		20 percent		23.3 percent
Orange Division:					
Asset base	$500,000		$100,000		$600,000
Investment center income	$120,000		$ 20,000		$140,000
Minimum return (0.18 x base)	- 90,000		- 18,000		-108,000
Residual income	$ 30,000		$ 2,000		$ 32,000

Since the performance of the Green Division is being measured according to the best rate of return that can be generated, the manager will not want to make the new investment because it reduces the current ROI of 24 percent to 23.3 percent. This is true, even though the company's minimum return is only 18 percent. Not wanting to explain a decline in the division's ROI, the manager will probably reject the opportunity even though it may have benefited the company as a whole.

The Orange Division manager will probably be happy to accept the new project because it increases residual income by $2,000. Any investment that provides a return greater than the required minimum of 18 percent will be acceptable to the Orange Division manager. Given a profit maximization goal for the organization, the residual income method is preferred because it encourages division managers to accept all projects with returns above the 18 percent cutoff.

The primary disadvantage of the residual income method is that it measures performance in dollars. It cannot be used to compare the performance of divisions of different sizes; for example, the residual income of a multimillion dollar sales division would be expected to be larger than that of a half-million dollar sales division.

SUMMARY

When an organization expands in size, management must decide whether to adopt a centralized or decentralized structure. As individual units within an organization become large enough to be separately evaluated as quasi-independent businesses, management generally decides to decentralize its operations into investment centers. During such a change, sound practices of responsibility accounting must be developed.

The selection of the evaluation method to be used for each responsibility center is generally determined by what the center can realistically be responsible for in its operations. Centers that receive no revenues can hardly be labeled profit centers, but centers that have unique product lines sold externally can be considered profit or investment centers.

Segment reports are income statements that show operating results for portions or segments of a business. The format and frequency of segment reports are limited only by management's needs and willingness to incur the cost for these reports.

The distinction between direct segment costs and indirect, or common, segment costs is very important in segment reporting. Direct segment costs are costs specifically identifiable with a particular segment of a business. By subtracting a segment's direct costs from its revenues, segment margin is obtained. Indirect, or common, segment costs are costs that are not directly traceable to a particular segment but are necessary to support the activities of two or more segments. Indirect segment costs may be allocated to segments for a variety of reporting purposes, but unavoidable indirect segment costs should not be allocated in internal reports that are to be used for management decisions such as whether to continue or discontinue a segment.

Organizations that have internal transfers between profit or investment centers are faced with using transfer pricing and its related problems of goal congruence. Seldom does a single transfer price meet all the criteria for inducing top management's desired decisions. The best transfer price depends on the circumstances at hand. Furthermore, the optimal price for either division may differ from that employed for external needs, including tax requirements.

To properly evaluate each responsibility center, management must select some type of measurement system. The two most popular methods of evaluating investment center performance are return on investment (ROI) and residual income. In most situations, it is recommended that both methods be used if feasible.

SUGGESTED READINGS

Ali, Hamdi F. "A Multicontribution Activity-Based Income Statement," *Journal of Cost Management* (Fall 1994), pp. 45-54.

Benke, Ralph L., Jr., and Ashton C. Bishop. "Transfer Pricing in an Oligopolistic Market," *The Journal of Cost Analysis,* Vol. 4, No. 2 (Fall 1986), pp. 69-82.

Bloomfield, Brian P., and Rod Coombs. "Information Technology, Control and Power: The Centralization and Decentralization Debate Revisited," *Journal of Management Studies*, Vol. 19, No. 4 (July 1992), pp. 459-484.

Cooper, Robin, and Robert S. Kaplan. "Profit Priorities From Activity-Based Costing," *Harvard Business Review* (May-June 1991), pp. 130-135.

Corr, Paul J., and Donald D. Bourque. "Managing in a Reorganization," *Management Accounting* (January 1988), pp. 33-37.

Dearden, John. "Measuring Profit Center Managers" *Harvard Business Review* (September-October 1987), pp. 84-88.

Dorkey, Frank C. "Calculating Proper Transfer Prices," *Public Utilities Fortnightly*, Vol. 127, No. 1 (January 1, 1991), pp. 25-28.

Edwards, James B. *Uses of Performance Measures* (Montvale, NJ.: National Association of Accountants, 1986).

Hansen, Don R., Rick L. Crosser, and Doug Laufer. "Moral Ethics versus Tax Ethics: The Case of Transfer Pricing Among Multinational Corporations," *Journal of Business Ethics*, Vol. 11 (1992), pp. 679-686.

Langrehr, Virginia, and Frederick W. Langrehr. "Measuring the Ability to Repay: The Residual Income Ratio," *Journal of Consumer Affairs*, Vol. 23, No. 2 (Winter 1989), pp. 393-407.

Lesser, Fredrick E. "Does Your Transfer Pricing Make Cents?" *Management Accounting* (December 1987), pp. 43-47.

McConville, Daniel J. "All About EVA (Economic Value-Added)," *Industry Week* (April 18, 1994), pp. 55-58.

Nanni, Alfred J., Jr., Robb Dixon, and Thomas E. Vollman. "Strategic Control and Performance Measurement," *Journal of Cost Management*, Vol. 4, No. 2 (1990), pp. 33-42.

Sah, Raaj K., and Joseph E. Stiglitz. "The Quality of Managers in Centralized versus Decentralized Organizations," *Quarterly Journal of Economics*, Vol. 106, No. 1 (February 1991), pp. 289-296.

Schroeder, Douglas A. "Organizational Structure and Intrafirm Transfer Prices for Interdependent Products," *Journal of Business, Finance, and Accounting*, Vol. 20, No. 3 (April 1993), pp. 441-456.

REVIEW PROBLEM

Measures for Divisional Performance

Parent Company, a decentralized organization, has three divisions, X, Y, and Z. Corporate management desires a minimum return of 15 percent on its investments.

The divisions' 19X8 results were as follows:

Division	Income	Investment
X	$30,000	$200,000
Y	50,000	250,000
Z	22,000	100,000

The company is planning an expansion project in 19X9 that will cost $50,000 and return $9,000 per year.

Required:

(a) Compute the ROI for each division for 19X8.
(b) Compute the residual income for each division for 19X8.
(c) Rank the divisions according to their ROI and residual income.
(d) Assume other income and investments will remain unchanged. Determine the effect of adding the new project on each division's ROI and residual income for 19X9.

The solution to the review problem is found at the end of the Chapter 9 assignment material. To maximize your learning, you should make a serious attempt to develop a written solution to the review problem before looking at the solution. If there are errors in your solution, you should then attempt to determine the causes of the errors.

KEY TERMS

Centralization—when top management controls the major functions of an organization (such as manufacturing, sales, accounting, computer operations, marketing, research and development, and management control).

Common segment costs (also called **indirect segment costs**)—costs related to more than one segment and not directly traceable to a particular segment. These costs are referred to as common costs because they are incurred at one level for the benefit of two or more segments at a lower level.

Decentralization—the delegation of decision-making authority to successively lower management levels in an organization. The lower in the organization the authority is delegated, the greater the decentralization.

Direct segment costs—costs that would not be incurred if the segment being evaluated were discontinued. They are specifically identifiable with a particular segment.

Division margin—the amount each division contributes toward covering common corporate expenses and generating corporate profits. It is computed by subtracting all direct fixed expenses identifiable with each division from the contribution margin.

Indirect segment costs—see **Common segment costs**.

Manufacturing margin—the result when direct manufacturing costs (variable costs) are deducted from division sales.

Product margin—computed as product sales less direct product costs.

Residual income—the excess of investment center income over the minimum rate of return set by top management. The minimum dollar return is computed as a percentage of the investment center's asset base.

Return on investment (ROI)—a measure of the earnings per dollar of investment. The return on investment of an investment center is computed by dividing the income of the center by its asset base (usually total assets). It can also be computed as investment turnover times the return-on-sales ratio.

Segment margin—the amount that a segment contributes toward the common (indirect) costs of the organization and toward profits. It is segment sales less direct segment costs.

Segment reports—income statements that show operating results for portions or segments of a business. Segment reporting is used primarily for internal purposes, although generally accepted accounting principles also require disclosure of segment information for some public corporations.

Suboptimization—when managers or operating units, acting in their own best interest, make decisions that are not in the best interest of the organization as a whole.

Territory margin—the result when all direct fixed expenses identifiable with each territory are subtracted from the contribution margin. It is the amount that each territory contributes toward covering common corporate expenses and generating corporate profits.

Transfer price—the internal value assigned a product or service that one division provides to another.

REVIEW QUESTIONS

9-1

What are the primary advantages of having a decentralized organizational structure?

9-2

How can the problems of decentralization be minimized?

9-3

What is the relationship between segment reports and product reports?

9-4

What is a reporting objective? How is it determined?

9-5

Can a company have more than one type of first-level statement in segment reporting?

9-6

Explain the relationships between any two levels of statements in segment reporting.

9-7

How do you distinguish between direct and indirect segment costs?

9-8

What types of information are needed before management should decide on dropping a segment?

9-9

In what types of organizations and for what purpose are transfer prices used?

9-10

What problems arise when transfer pricing is used?

9-11

When do transfer prices lead to suboptimization? How can suboptimization be minimized? Can it be eliminated? Why or why not?

9-12

For what purpose do organizations use return on investment? Why is this measure preferred to net income?

9-13

How is an investment center's asset base determined?

9-14

How does residual income assist in the evaluation process?

9-15

What information does residual income provide that ROI does not?

9-1 Centralization Versus Decentralization

For each of the following activities, characteristics, and applications, tell whether they are generally found in a centralized organization, in a decentralized organization, or in both types of organizations.

(a) Cost centers
(b) Profit centers
(c) Maximization of benefits over costs
(d) Minimization of duplication of functions
(e) Few interdependencies among divisions
(f) Very little suboptimization
(g) Faster responsiveness to user needs
(h) Greater freedom for managers at lower organizational levels to make decisions

9-2 Centralization Versus Decentralization

For each of the following activities, characteristics, and applications, tell whether they are generally found in a centralized organization, in a decentralized organization, or in both types of organizations.

(a) Investment centers
(b) Revenue centers
(c) Greater decisions made by top management
(d) Minimization of responsibility centers
(e) Provision of information to corporate headquarters at greater expense
(f) Greater sophistication of operations
(g) Slower responsiveness to user needs
(h) Greater specialization of operations to meet users' needs

9-3 Multiple Levels of Segment Reporting

Abraham Appliances manufactures four different lines of household appliances: cooking, cleaning, convenience, and safety. Each of the product lines is produced in all of the company's three plants: Abbeyville, Bakersville, and Charlottesville. Marketing efforts of the company are divided into five regions: East, West, South, North, and Central.

Required:

Develop a segment reporting schematic that has three different levels. Be sure to identify each segment's level. Briefly explain why you chose the primary-level segment.

9-4 Income Statements Segmented by Territory

The Dual Manufacturing Company has two product lines. The 19X1 income statements of each product line and the company are as follows:

Dual Manufacturing Company
Product Line and Company Income Statements
For the Year Ending December 31, 19X1

| | Product Lines | | Company Total |
	Pens	Pencils	
Sales	$20,000	$30,000	$50,000
Less variable expenses	- 8,000	- 12,000	- 20,000
Contribution margin	$12,000	$18,000	$30,000
Less direct fixed expenses	- 8,000	- 7,000	- 15,000
Product margin	$ 4,000	$11,000	$15,000
Less common fixed expenses			- 6,000
Net income			$ 9,000

The pens and pencils are sold in two territories, Alaska and Alabama, as follows:

	Alaska	Alabama
Pen sales	$12,000	$ 8,000
Pencil sales	9,000	21,000
Total sales	$21,000	$29,000

The common fixed expenses above are traceable to each territory as follows:

Alaska fixed expenses	$2,000
Alabama fixed expenses	3,000
Home office administration fixed expenses	1,000
Total common fixed expenses	$6,000

The direct fixed expenses of pens, $8,000, and of pencils, $7,000, cannot be identified with either territory.

Required:
(a) Prepare income statements segmented by territory for 19X1. Include a column for the entire firm.
(b) Why are direct expenses of one type of segment report not necessarily direct expenses of another type of segment report?

9-5 Income Statements Segmented by Products

Clayton Consulting Firm provides three types of client services. The income statement for 19X2 is as follows:

Clayton Consulting Firm
Income Statement
For the Year Ending December 31, 19X2

Sales		$800,000
Less variable costs		-535,000
Contribution margin		$265,000
Less fixed expenses:		
Service	$70,000	
Selling and administrative	65,000	-135,000
Net income		$130,000

The sales, contribution margin ratios, and direct fixed expenses for the three types of services are as follows:

	Service 14	Service 28	Service 33
Sales	$250,000	$250,000	$300,000
Contribution margin ratio	30%	40%	30%
Direct fixed expenses of services	$ 20,000	$ 18,000	$ 16,000

Required:

Prepare income statements segmented by products. Include a column for the entire firm in the statement.

9-6 Transfer Pricing and Divisional Profit

Leitch Consulting Company has two divisions: Tax Consultants and Financial Consultants. In addition to its external sales, each division performs work for the other division. The external fees earned by each division in 19X0 were $400,000 for Tax Consultants and $700,000 for Financial Consultants. Tax Consultants worked 3,000 hours for Financial Consultants, and Financial Consultants worked 1,200 hours for Tax Consultants. The costs of services performed were $220,000 for Tax Consultants and $480,000 for Financial Consultants.

Required:

(a) Determine the gross profit for each division and for the company as a whole if the transfer price from Tax to Financial is $30 per hour and the transfer price from Financial to Tax is $25 per hour.

(b) Determine the gross profit for each division and for the company as a whole if the transfer price for each division is $30 per hour.

(c) What are the gross profit results for the divisions and the company as a whole if the two divisions net their hours and charge a transfer fee of $25 per excess hour? Which division manager would favor this arrangement?

9-7 Transfer Pricing and Divisional Gross Profit

Greenwood Paper Company has two divisions. The Pulp Division prepares the wood for processing. The Paper Division processes the pulp into paper. No inventories exist in either division at the beginning of 19X3. During the year, the Pulp Division prepared 40,000 cords of wood at a cost of $240,000. All the pulp was transferred to the Paper Division where additional operating costs of $5 per cord were incurred. The 400,000 pounds of finished paper were sold for $1,000,000.

Required:

(a) Determine the gross profit for each division and for the company as a whole if the transfer price from Pulp to Paper is at cost, $6 per cord.

(b) Determine the gross profit for each division and for the company as a whole if the transfer price is $5 per cord.

(c) Determine the gross profit for each division and for the company as a whole if the transfer price is $7 per cord.

9-8 Internal or External Acquisitions: No Opportunity Costs

The Van Division of the CP Corporation has offered to purchase 180,000 wheels from the Wheel Division for $52 per wheel. At a normal volume of 500,000 wheels per year, production costs per wheel for the Wheel Division are as follows:

Direct materials	$ 20
Direct labor	10
Variable overhead	6
Fixed overhead	20
Total	$ 56

The Wheel Division has been selling 500,000 wheels per year to outside buyers at $68 each. Capacity is 700,000 wheels per year. The Van Division has been buying wheels from outside suppliers at $65 per wheel.

Required:

(a) Should the Wheel Division manager accept the offer? Show computations.

(b) From the standpoint of the company, will the internal sale be beneficial?

9-9 Appropriate Transfer Prices: Opportunity Costs

The Plains Peanut Butter Company recently acquired a peanut processing company that has a normal annual capacity of 4,000,000 pounds and that sold 2,800,000 pounds last year at a price of $2 per pound. The purpose of the acquisition is to furnish peanuts for the peanut butter plant. The peanut butter plant needs 1,600,000 pounds of peanuts per year. It has been purchasing peanuts from suppliers at the market price.

Production costs of the peanut processing company per pound are as follows:

Direct materials	$0.50
Direct labor	0.25
Variable overhead	0.12
Fixed overhead at normal capacity	0.20
Total	$1.07

Management is trying to decide what transfer price to use for sales from the newly acquired Peanut Division to the Peanut Butter Division. The manager of the Peanut Division argues that $2, the market price, is appropriate. The manager of the Peanut Butter Division argues that the cost price of $1.07 or perhaps even less should be used, since fixed overhead costs should be recomputed.

Any output of the Peanut Division, up to 2,800,000 pounds, not sold to the Peanut Butter Division could be sold to regular customers at $2 per pound.

Required:

(a) Compute the annual gross profit for the Peanut Division using a transfer price of $2.

(b) Compute the annual gross profit for the Peanut Division using a transfer price of $1.07.

(c) What transfer price(s) will lead the manager of the Peanut Butter Division to act in a manner that will maximize company profits?

9-10 Negotiating a Transfer Price with Excess Capacity

The Weaving Division of Carolina Textiles, Inc., produces cloth that is sold to the company's Dyeing Division and to outside customers. Operating data for the Weaving Division for 19X3 are as follows:

	To the Dyeing Division	To Outside Customers
Sales:		
300,000 yards at $5	$1,500,000	
200,000 yards at $6		$1,200,000
Variable expenses at $2	- 600,000	- 400,000
Contribution margin	$ 900,000	$ 800,000
Fixed expenses*	- 750,000	- 500,000
Net income	$ 150,000	$ 300,000

*Allocated on the basis of unit sales

The Dyeing Division has just received an offer from an outside supplier to supply cloth at $4.30 per yard. The manager of the Weaving Division is not willing to meet the $4.30 price. She argues that it costs her $4.50 per yard to produce and sell to the Dyeing Division, so she would show no profit on the Dyeing Division sales. Sales to outside customers are at a maximum, 200,000 yards.

Required:

(a) Verify the Weaving Division's $4.50 unit cost figure.

(b) Should the Weaving Division meet the outside price of $4.30 for Dyeing Division sales? Explain.

(c) Could the $4.30 price be met and still show a profit for the Weaving Division sales to the Dyeing Division? Show computations.

9-11 Dual Transfer Pricing

The Greek Company has two divisions: Beta and Gamma. Gamma Division produces a product at a variable cost of $6 per unit and sells 150,000 units to outside customers at $10 per unit and 40,000 units to Beta Division at variable cost plus 40 percent. Under the dual transfer price system, Beta Division pays only the variable cost per unit. The fixed costs of Gamma Division are $250,000 per year.

Beta Division sells its finished product to outside customers at $23 per unit. Beta has variable costs of $5 per unit, in addition to the costs from Gamma Division. The annual fixed costs of Beta Division are $170,000. There are no beginning or ending inventories.

Required:

(a) Prepare the income statements for the two divisions and the company as a whole.

(b) Why is the income for the company less than the sum of the profit figures shown on the income statements for the two divisions? Explain.

9-12 Transfer Prices at Full Cost with Excess Capacity: Divisional Viewpoint

The Dairy Company has a Cheese Division that produces cheese that sells for $12 per unit in the open market. The cost of the product is $8 (variable manufacturing of $5, plus fixed manufacturing of $3). Total fixed manufacturing costs are $210,000 at the normal annual production volume of 70,000 units.

The Overseas Division has offered to buy 15,000 units at the full cost of $8. The Producing Division has excess capacity, and the 15,000 units can be produced without interfering with the current outside sales of 70,000 units. The total fixed cost of the Cheese Division will not change.

Required:

Explain whether the Cheese Division should accept or reject the offer. Show calculations.

9-13 Transfer Pricing with Excess Capacity: Divisional and Corporate Viewpoints

The Boyett Art Company has a Print Division that is currently producing 100,000 prints per year but has a capacity of 150,000 prints. The variable costs of each print are $30, and the annual fixed costs are $900,000. The prints sell for $40 in the open market.

The Retail Division of the company wants to buy 50,000 prints at $28 each. The Print Division manager refuses the order because the price is below variable cost. The Retail Division manager argues that the order should be accepted because it will lower the fixed cost per print from $9 to $6.

Required:

(a) Should the order from the Retail Division be accepted? Why or why not?
(b) From the viewpoints of the Print Division and the company, should the order be accepted if the manager of the Retail Division intends to sell each print in the outside market for $42 after incurring additional costs of $10 per print?
(c) What action should the company take, assuming it believes in divisional autonomy?

9-14 ROI and Residual Income: Basic Computations

Salmon Company uses return on investment and residual income as two of the evaluation tools for division managers. The company has a minimum desired rate of return on investment of 12 percent.

Selected operating data for three divisions of the company are given below.

	East Division	West Division	Central Division
Sales	$600,000	$750,000	$900,000
Operating assets	300,000	250,000	350,000
Net operating income	51,000	56,000	59,000

Required:

(a) Compute the return on investment for each division. (Round answers to three decimal places.)

(b) Compute the residual income for each division.

(c) Which divisional manager is doing the best job based on ROI? Based on residual income? Why?

9-15 ROI and Residual Income: Impact of a New Investment

The Firebird Division of Central Motors had an operating income of $90,000 and net assets of $400,000. Central Motors has a target rate of return of 16 percent.

Required:

(a) Compute the return on investment.

(b) Compute the residual income.

(c) Firebird has an opportunity to increase operating income by $20,000 with an investment in assets of $85,000.

    (1) Compute the Firebird Division's return on investment if the project is undertaken. (Round your answer to three decimal places.)

    (2) Compute the Firebird Division's residual income if the project is undertaken.

9-16 ROI: Fill in the Unknowns

Provide the missing data in the following situations:

	Division K	Division L	Division M
Sales	$?2,500,000	$5,000,000	$? 1,200,000
Net operating income	$100,000	$ 200,000	$144,000
Operating assets	$?625,000	$? 2,000,000	$800,000
Return on investment	16 %	10 %	? .18
Return-on-sales ratio	0.04	? .04	0.12
Investment turnover	?4	? 2.5	1.5

9-17 ROI and Residual Income with Different Bases

Basic Company requires a return on capital of 12 percent. The following financial information is available for 19X8:

	Division 200 Value Base		Division 300 Value Base		Division 400 Value Base	
	Book	Current	Book	Current	Book	Current
Sales	$100,000	$100,000	$200,000	$200,000	$800,000	$800,000
Income	12,000	10,000	16,000	17,000	50,000	52,000
Assets	60,000	80,000	90,000	100,000	600,000	580,000

Required:

(a) Compute return on investment using both book and current values for each division. (Round answers to three decimal places.)

(b) Compute residual income for both book and current values for each division.

(c) Does book value or current value provide the better basis for performance evaluation? Which division do you consider the most successful?

PROBLEMS

9-18 Segment Reporting

Protection Company has provided you with the following information about its operations:

1. There are two products: umbrellas and hats.
2. There are two sales territories: Southeast and Northwest.
3. Monthly traceable direct fixed costs are $15,000 in the Southeast territory and $14,000 in the Northwest territory.
4. During January of 19X3, Southeast sold $40,000 of umbrellas and $20,000 of hats, and Northwest sold $10,000 of umbrellas and $30,000 of hats.
5. Variable cost of sales and selling expenses total 40 percent for umbrellas and 70 percent for hats.
6. Of Northwest's direct fixed costs, $5,000 is traceable to umbrellas and $5,000 to hats.
7. Of Southeast's direct fixed costs, $4,000 is traceable to umbrellas and $2,000 to hats.
8. Total fixed costs of the Protection Company were $40,000 during January.
9. Total variable costs of the Protection Company were $55,000 during January.

Required:

(a) Prepare January segment income statements for both territories. Include a column for the entire firm.
(b) Prepare income statements segmented by product within each territory. Include a column for the entire firm.

9-19 Multiple Segment Reports

Earth Products, Incorporated, sells throughout the world in three sales territories: Europe, the East, and the West. For July 19X3, all $50,000 of administrative expense is allocated, except $10,000, which is common to all units and cannot be traced to the sales territories. The percentage of product line sales made in each of the sales territories and the allocations of traceable fixed expenses are shown below:

| | Sales Territory | | | |
	Europe	East	West	Total
Cookware sales	40 %	50 %	10 %	100 %
China sales	40	40	20	100
Vases sales	20	20	60	100
Fixed administrative expense	$15,000	$15,000	$10,000	$40,000
Fixed selling expense	30,000	60,000	60,000	150,000

The manufacturing takes place in one large facility with three distinct manufacturing operations. Selected cost data are shown below.

| | Product Line | | | |
	Cookware	China	Vases	Total
Variable costs	$ 9	$ 9	$ 5	
Depreciation and supervision	15,000	15,000	12,000	$ 45,000*
Other mfg. overhead (common)				10,000
Fixed administrative expense (common)				50,000
Fixed selling expense (common)				150,000

*Includes common costs of $3,000

The unit sales and selling price for each product are shown below:

	Unit Sales	Selling Price
Cookware	10,000	$10
China	20,000	15
Vases	15,000	20

Required:
(a) Prepare an income statement for July 19X3 segmented by product line. Include a column for the entire firm.
(b) Prepare an income statement for July 19X3 segmented by sales territories. Include a column for the entire firm.

9-20 Segment Reporting and Analysis

Neighborhood Bakery, Incorporated, bakes three products: donuts, pies, and cakes. It sells them in the cities of Irmo and Jackson. For March 19X4, the following income statement was prepared:

Neighborhood Bakery, Incorporated
Territory and Company Income Statements
For the Month of March 19X4

| | City | | Company Total |
	Irmo	Jackson	
Sales	$2,100	$500	$2,600
Cost of goods sold	-1,500	-300	-1,800
Gross profit	$ 600	$200	$ 800
Selling and administrative expenses	- 400	- 100	- 500
Net income	$ 200	$100	$ 300

Sales and selected variable expense data are as follows:

| | Products | | |
	Donuts	Pies	Cakes
Fixed baking expenses	$200	$140	$100
Variable baking expenses as a percentage of sales	50%	50%	60%
Variable selling expenses as a percentage of sales	4%	4%	5%
City of Irmo, sales	$800	$900	$400
City of Jackson, sales	$200	$100	$200

The fixed selling expenses were $260 for March, of which $210 was a direct expense of the Irmo market and $50 a direct expense of the Jackson market. Fixed administrative expenses were $130, which management has decided not to allocate when using the contribution approach.

Required:

(a) Prepare a segment income statement for each sales territory for March. Include a column for the entire firm.
(b) Prepare segment income statements for each product. Include a column for the entire firm.
(c) Should any products or territories be dropped?

9-21 Segment Reporting and Analysis

The Hardback Book Company has prepared income statements segmented by divisions, but management is still uncertain about actual performance. Financial information for 19X8 is given as follows:

| | Segments | | |
	Textbook Division	Professional Division	Total Company
Sales	$180,000	$410,000	$590,000
Less variable expenses:			
Manufacturing	$ 32,000	$205,000	$237,000
Selling and administrative	4,000	20,500	24,500
Total	- 36,000	-225,500	-261,500
Contribution margin	$144,000	$184,500	$328,500
Less direct fixed expenses	- 15,000	-220,000	-235,000
Net income	$129,000	$ (35,500)	$ 93,500

The Professional Division concerns management and needs additional analysis. Additional information regarding the 19X8 operations of the Professional Division is as follows:

	Accounting	Executive	Management
Sales	$140,000	$140,000	$130,000
Variable manufacturing expenses as a percentage of sales	60%	40%	50%
Other variable expenses as a percentage of sales	5%	5%	5%
Direct fixed expenses	$ 50,000	$ 75,000	$ 50,000

The professional accounting books are sold to auditors and controllers. The current information on these markets is as follows:

| | Sales Market | |
	Auditors	Controllers
Sales	$ 30,000	$110,000
Variable manufacturing expenses as a percentage of sales	60%	60%
Other variable expenses as a percentage of sales	16%	2%
Direct fixed expenses	$ 20,000	$ 25,000

Required:

(a) Prepare an income statement segmented by products of the Professional Division. Include a column for the division as a whole.

(b) Prepare an income statement segmented by markets of the accounting books of the Professional Division.

(c) Evaluate which accounting books the Professional Division should keep or discontinue.

9-22 Segment Reports

The Justa Corporation produces and sells three products. The three products, A, B, and C, are sold in a Local Market and in a Regional Market. After the end of the first quarter of 19X2, the following income statement was prepared:

Justa Corporation
Territory and Company Income Statements
First Quarter of 19X2

	Local	Regional	Company
Sales	$1,000,000	$300,000	$1,300,000
Cost of goods sold	- 775,000	- 235,000	1,010,000
Gross profit	$ 225,000	$ 65,000	$ 290,000
Selling expenses	$ 60,000	$ 45,000	$ 105,000
Administrative expenses	40,000	12,000	52,000
Total	- 100,000	- 57,000	- 157,000
Net income	$ 125,000	$ 8,000	$ 133,000

Management has expressed special concern with the Regional Market because of the extremely poor return on sales. This market was entered a year ago because of excess capacity. It was originally believed that the return on sales would improve with time, but after a year, no noticeable improvement can be seen from the results as reported in the above quarterly statement.

In attempting to decide whether to eliminate the Regional Market, the following information has been gathered:

	Products		
	A	B	C
Sales	$500,000	$400,000	$400,000
Variable manufacturing expenses as a percentage of sales	60 %	70 %	60 %
Variable selling expenses as a percentage of sales	3 %	2 %	2 %

Sales by Markets

Product	Local	Regional
A	$400,000	$100,000
B	300,000	100,000
C	300,000	100,000

All administrative expenses and fixed manufacturing expenses are common to the three products and the two markets and are fixed for the period. The remaining selling expenses are fixed for the period and separable by market. All fixed expenses are based on a prorated yearly amount.

Required:

(a) Prepare the quarterly income statement showing contribution margins by markets (territories). Include a column for the company as a whole.

(b) Assuming there are no alternative uses for the Justa Corporation's present capacity, would you recommend dropping the Regional Market? Why or why not?

(c) Prepare the quarterly income statement showing contribution margins by products. Include a column for the company as a whole.

(d) It is believed that a new product can be ready for sale next year if the Justa Corporation decides to go ahead with continued research. The new product can be produced by simply converting equipment now used in producing Product C. This conversion will increase fixed costs by $10,000 per quarter. What must be the minimum contribution margin per quarter for the new product to make the changeover financially feasible?

(CMA Adapted)

9-23 Segment Reports and Cost Allocations

Clive Mathews and Sons has three sales divisions. One of the key evaluation inputs for each division manager is the performance of his/her division based upon divisional income. The divisional statements for 19X4 are as follows:

	Division Kiwi	Division Queensland	Division Hawaiian	Company Total
Sales	$400,000	$500,000	$450,000	$1,350,000
Cost of sales	$200,000	$240,000	$230,000	$ 670,000
Division overhead	100,000	110,000	110,000	320,000
Divisional expenses	-300,000	-350,000	-340,000	- 990,000
Division contribution	$100,000	$150,000	$110,000	$ 360,000
Corporate overhead	- 70,000	- 90,000	- 80,000	- 240,000
Division income	$ 30,000	$ 60,000	$ 30,000	$ 120,000

The Hawaiian manager is unhappy that his profitability is the same as that of the Kiwi Division and half that of the Queensland Division when his sales are halfway between these two divisions. The manager knows that his division must carry more product lines because of customer demands, and many of these additional product lines are not very profitable. He has not dropped these marginal product lines because of idle capacity; all of them cover their own variable costs.

After analyzing the product lines with the lowest profit margins, the divisional controller for Hawaiian provided the manager with the following:

Sales of marginal products		$90,000
Cost of sales	$50,000	
Avoidable fixed costs	20,000	- 70,000
Product margin		$20,000
Proportion of corporate overhead		- 16,000
Product income		$ 4,000

Although these products were 20 percent of Hawaiian's total sales, they contributed only about 13 percent of the division's profits. The controller also noted that the corporate overhead allocation was based on a formula of sales and divisional contribution margin.

Required:

(a) Prepare a set of segment statements for 19X5 assuming all facts remain the same, except that the weak product lines of Hawaiian are dropped and corporate overhead is allocated as follows: Kiwi, $80,000; Queensland, $95,000; and Hawaiian, $65,000. Does the Hawaiian Division appear better after this action? What will be the responses of the two other division managers?

(b) Suggest improvements to Mathews and Sons' reporting process that will better reflect the actual operations of the divisions. Keep in mind the utilization of the reporting process to assist in the evaluation of the managers. What other changes might be made to improve the manager evaluation process?

9-24 Transfer Pricing

The International Building Company owns its own clay mine, which supplies clay for the Brick Division. The clay is charged to the Brick Division at market price. Income statements for 19X5 were as follows:

International Building Company
Divisional Income Statements
For the Year Ending December 31, 19X5

	Clay Mine	Brick Division
Sales	$800,000	$2,000,000
Production costs:		
Materials	$ -	$ 800,000
Labor	380,000	500,000
Overhead	160,000	300,000
Total	- 540,000	-1,600,000
Gross profit	$260,000	$ 400,000
Selling and administrative costs	- 120,000	- 300,000
Income of division	$140,000	$ 100,000

In 19X5 and 19X6, the clay mine sold 20,000 tons of clay. In 19X6, the market prices of clay increased 50 percent, and conversion costs increased 10 percent, whereas the Brick Division increased its price by 10 percent. Income statements for 19X6 were as follows:

International Building Company
Divisional Income Statements
For the Year Ending December 31, 19X6

	Clay Mine	Brick Division
Sales	$1,200,000	$2,200,000
Production costs:		
Materials	$ -	$1,200,000
Labor	418,000	550,000
Overhead	176,000	330,000
Total	- 594,000	-2,080,000
Gross profit	$ 606,000	$ 120,000
Selling and administrative costs	- 120,000	- 330,000
Income (loss) of division	$ 486,000	$ (210,000)

Corporate management is concerned about the Brick Division's 19X6 loss.

Required:
(a) Prepare income statements for the company in 19X5 and 19X6.
(b) Evaluate the company's performance in 19X6.
(c) What should be the transfer price for clay? Discuss.

9-25 ROI and Residual Income: Impact of a New Investment

Office Equipment, Inc., is a decentralized organization with four autonomous divisions. The divisions are evaluated on the basis of the change in their return on invested assets. Operating results in the Modern Division for 19X1 are given below:

Office Equipment, Inc.
Modern Division
Income Statement
For the Year Ending December 31, 19X1

Sales	$2,500,000
Less variable expenses	-1,250,000
Contribution margin	$1,250,000
Less fixed expenses	- 900,000
Net operating income	$ 350,000

Operating assets for Modern Division currently average $1,800,000. The Modern Division can add a new product line for an investment of $300,000. Relevant data for the new product line are as follows:

Sales	$800,000
Variable expenses	0.60 of sales
Fixed expenses	$300,000

Required:
(a) Determine the effect on ROI of accepting the new product line. (Round calculations to three decimal places.)
(b) If a return of 6 percent is the minimum that should be earned by any division, and residual income is used to evaluate managers, would this

encourage the division to accept the new product line? Explain and show computations.

9-26 Decentralization and Autonomy

Edwin Hall, chairman of the board and president of Arrow Works Products Company, founded the company in the mid-1970s. He is a talented and creative engineer. Arrow Works was started with one of his inventions, an intricate die-cast item that required a minimum of finish work. The item was manufactured for Arrow Works by a Gary, Indiana, foundry. The product sold well in a wide market.

The company issued common stock in 1982 to finance the purchase of the Gary foundry. Additional shares were issued in 1985 when Arrow purchased a fabricating plant in Cleveland to meet the capacity requirement of a defense contract.

The company now consists of five divisions. Each division is headed by a manager who reports to Hall. The Chicago Division contains the product development and engineering department and the finishing (assembly) operation for the basic products. The Gary Plant and Cleveland Plant are the other two divisions engaged in manufacturing operations. All products manufactured are sold through two selling divisions. The Eastern Sales Division is located in Pittsburgh and covers the country from Chicago to the East Coast. The Western Sales Division, which covers the rest of the country, is located in Denver. The Western Sales Division is the newer operation and was established just eight months ago.

Hall, who still owns 53 percent of the outstanding stock, actively participates in the management of the company. He travels frequently and regularly to all the company's plants and offices. He says, "Having a business with locations in five different cities spread over half the country requires all of my time." Despite his regular and frequent visits, he believes the company is decentralized, with the managers having complete autonomy. "They make all the decisions and run their own shops. Of course, they don't understand the total business as I do, so I have to straighten them out once in a while. My managers are all good people, but they can't be expected to handle everything alone. I try to help all I can."

The last two months have been a period of considerable stress for Mr. Hall. During this period, John Staple, manager of the fabricating plant, was advised by his physician to request a six-month sick leave to relieve the work pressures that had made him nervous and tense. This request had followed by three days a phone call in which Hall had directly and bluntly blamed Staple for the lagging production output and increased rework and scrap of the fabricating plant. Hall made no allowances for the pressures created by the operation of the plant at volumes in excess of normal and close to its maximum rated capacity for the previous nine months.

Hall thought Staple and he had had a long and good relationship before this event. Hall attributed his loss of temper in this case to his frustration with several other management problems that had arisen in the past two months. The sales manager of the Denver office had resigned shortly after a visit from Hall. The letter of resignation stated he was seeking a position with greater responsibility. The sales manager in Pittsburgh asked to be reassigned to a sales position in the field; he did not believe he could cope with the pressure of management.

Required:
(a) Explain the difference between centralized and decentralized management.
(b) Is Arrow Works Products Company decentralized as Edwin Hall believes? Explain your answer.
(c) Could the events that have occurred over the past two months in Arrow Works Products Company have been expected? Explain your answer.   (CMA Adapted)

9-27 Transfer Pricing at Average Manufacturing Cost
Division 23 of Numbers Company produces large metal numbers that are sold to Division 86. This Division uses numbers in constructing signs that are sold to highway departments of local governments.

Division 23 contains two operations: stamping and finishing. The unit variable cost of materials and labor used in the stamping operation is $100. The fixed stamping overhead is $800,000 per year. Current production of 20,000 units is at full capacity.

The variable cost of labor used in the finishing operation is $12 per number. The fixed overhead in this operation is $340,000 per year.

The company uses average manufacturing cost as a transfer price. The price data for each operation presented to Division 86 by Division 23 are shown below:

Stamping:		
Variable cost per unit	$100	
Fixed overhead cost per unit ($800,000/20,000 units)	40	$140
Finishing:		
Labor cost per unit	$ 12	
Fixed overhead cost per unit ($340,000/20,000 units)	17	29
Total cost per unit		$169

An outside company has offered to lease Division 86 machinery that would perform the finishing part of the number manufacturing. The lease is $200,000 per year. With the new machinery, the labor cost per frame would remain at $12. If Division 23 transfers the units for $140, the following analysis can be made:

Current process:		
Finishing process costs (20,000 x $29)		$580,000
New process:		
Machine rental cost per year	$200,000	
Labor cost ($12 x 20,000 units)	240,000	-440,000
Savings		$140,000

The manager of Division 86 wants approval to acquire the new machinery.

Required:

(a) How would you advise the company concerning the proposed lease?

(b) How could the transfer-pricing system be modified or the transfer-pricing problem eliminated?

9-28 Transfer Pricing with and Without Capacity Constraints

The National Carpet Company has just acquired a new Backing Division. The Backing Division produces a rubber backing, which it sells for $2 per square yard. Sales are about 1,200,000 square yards a year. Since the Backing Division has a capacity of 2,000,000 square yards a year, top management is thinking that it might be wise for the company's Tufting Division to start purchasing from the newly acquired Backing Division.

The Tufting Division now purchases 600,000 square yards of backing a year from an outside supplier at a price of $1.80 per square yard. That the current price is lower than the competitive $2 price is a result of the large quantity discounts.

The Backing Division's cost per square yard is shown below:

Direct materials	$1.00
Direct labor	0.20
Variable overhead	0.25
Fixed overhead (1,200,000 level)	0.10
Total cost	$1.55

Required:

(a) If both divisions are to be treated as investment centers and their performance evaluated by the ROI formula, what transfer price would you recommend? Why?

(b) What will be the effect on the profits of the company using your transfer price?

(c) Based on your transfer price, would you expect the ROI in the Backing Division to increase, decrease, or remain unchanged? Explain.

(d) What would be the effect on the ROI of the Tufting Division using your transfer price? Explain.

(e) Assume that the Backing Division is now selling 2,000,000 square yards a year to retail outlets. What transfer price would you recommend? Explain what will happen between Backing and Tufting.

(f) If the Backing Division is at capacity and decides to sell to the Tufting Division for $1.80 per square yard, what will be the effect on the profits of the company?

9-29 Transfer Pricing and Special Orders

Atlantic Telephone Company has several manufacturing divisions. The Pacific Division produces a component part that is used in the manufacture of electronic equipment. The cost per part for July is as follows:

Variable cost	$ 90
Fixed cost (at 2,000 units per month capacity)	60
Total cost per part	$150

Some of Pacific Division's output is sold to outside manufacturers, and some is sold internally to the Electronics Division. The price per part is $175.

The Electronics Division's cost and revenue structure is shown below:

Selling price per unit		$1,000
Less variable costs per unit:		
Cost of parts from the Pacific Division	$175	
Other variable costs	400	
Total variable costs		- 575
Contribution margin per unit		$ 425
Less fixed costs per unit (at 200 units per month)		- 100
Net income per unit		$ 325

The Electronics Division received an order for 10 units. The buyer wants to pay only $500 per unit.

Required:

(a) From the perspective of the Electronics Division, should the $500 price be accepted? Explain.

(b) If both divisions have excess capacity, would the Electronics Division's action benefit the company as a whole? Explain.

(c) If the Electronics Division has excess capacity, but the Pacific Division does not and can sell all its parts to outside manufacturers, what would be the advantage or disadvantage to the Electronics Division of accepting the 10-unit order at the $500 price?

(d) To make a decision that is in the best interest of Atlantic Telephone, what transfer-pricing information is needed by the Electronics Division?

9-30 An Evaluation of Market-Based Transfer Prices

World Wide Products, a large diversified corporation, operates its divisions on a decentralized basis. Division Alpha makes Product X, which can be sold either to Division Beta or to outside customers.

At current levels of production, the variable cost of making Product X is $3.50 per unit, the fixed cost is 50 cents, and the market price is $7.00 per unit. There are no separate selling costs.

Division Beta processes Product X into Product Y. The additional variable cost of producing Product Y is $4.00 per unit.

Top management is developing a corporate transfer-pricing policy. The bases for setting transfer prices being reviewed are average manufacturing cost, unit variable costs, and market price.

Required:

(a) In order to maximize company profits, which of the transfer price bases being reviewed should be used and why?

(b) Which of the transfer price bases in the short run would tend to encourage the best use of the corporation's productive capacity? Why would this not be true in the long run?

(c) Identify two possible advantages that Division Beta might expect if it purchased Product X from Division Alpha at the current market price.

(d) What possible disadvantage might accrue to Division Alpha if it was committed to sell all its production of X to Division Beta at the current market price?

9-31 Evaluating ROI

The Independent Consulting Company has several decentralized divisions. Each division manager is responsible for service revenue, cost of operations, acquisition and financing of divisional assets, and working capital management.

The vice president of general operations is considering changing from annual to multiyear evaluations of division managers. Currently, a review of the performance, attitudes, and skills of management is undertaken annually. As a trial run, two managers will be selected for the new evaluation procedure. The selection has been narrowed to the managers of Divisions 11 and 14.

Both managers became division managers in 19X1. Their divisions have the following operating results for the last three years:

(in thousands)	Division 11			Division 14		
	19X1	19X2	19X3	19X1	19X2	19X3
Estimated industry sales	$1,000,000	$1,200,000	$1,300,000	$500,000	$600,000	$650,000
Division sales	$ 100,000	$ 110,000	$ 121,000	$ 45,000	$ 60,000	$ 75,000
Variable costs	$ 30,000	$ 32,000	$ 34,500	$ 13,500	$ 17,500	$ 21,000
Fixed operating costs	40,000	40,500	42,000	17,000	20,000	23,000
Fixed administrative costs	27,500	32,500	32,500	14,000	20,000	25,000
Total costs	- 97,500	- 105,000	- 109,000	- 44,500	- 57,500	- 69,000
Net income	$ 2,500	$ 5,000	$ 12,000	$ 500	$ 2,500	$ 6,000
Net assets	$ 22,700	$ 23,500	$ 24,500	$ 12,300	$ 14,000	$ 17,000
Return on investment	?	?	?	?	?	?

Required:

(a) Determine ROI for each year for each manager.
(b) Is ROI an appropriate measurement for manager evaluation? Why?
(c) What additional measures might be used?
(d) Per year, which manager performed better?
(e) Over three years, which manager performed better?

(CMA Adapted)

9-32 A Transfer Pricing Dispute

MBR, Inc., consists of three divisions that formerly were three independent manufacturing companies. Bader Corporation and Roper Company merged in 19X5, and the merged corporation acquired Mitchell Company in 19X6. The name of the corporation was subsequently changed to MBR, Inc., and each company became a separate division retaining the name of its former company.

The three divisions have operated as if they were still independent companies. Each division has its own sales force and production facilities. Each division management is responsible for sales, cost of operations, acquisition and financing of divisional assets, and working capital management. The corporate management of MBR evaluates the performance of the divisions and division managements on the basis of return on investment.

Mitchell Division has just been awarded a contract for a product that uses a component manufactured by the Roper Division, as well as by outside suppliers. Mitchell used a cost figure of $3.80 for the component manufactured by Roper in preparing its bid for the new product. This cost figure was supplied by Roper in response to Mitchell's request for the average variable cost of the component and represents the standard variable manufacturing cost and variable selling and distribution expenses.

Roper has an active sales force that is continually soliciting new prospects. Roper's regular selling price for the component Mitchell needs for the new product is $6.50. Sales of this component are expected to increase. However, the Roper management has indicated that it could supply Mitchell with the required quantities of the component at the regular selling price less variable selling and distribution expenses. Mitchell's management has responded by offering to pay standard variable manufacturing cost plus 20 percent.

The two divisions have been unable to agree on a transfer price. Corporate management has never established a transfer price policy because interdivisional transactions have never occurred. As a compromise, the corporate vice president of finance suggested a price equal to the standard full manufacturing cost (i.e., no selling and distribution expenses) plus a 15 percent markup. This price has also been rejected by the two division managers because each considered it grossly unfair.

The unit cost structure for the Roper component and the three suggested prices are shown below:

Standard variable manufacturing cost	$3.20
Standard fixed manufacturing cost	1.20
Variable selling and distribution expenses	0.60
	$5.00
Regular selling price less variable selling and distribution expenses ($6.50 - $0.60)	$5.90
Standard full manufacturing cost plus 15% ($4.40 x 1.15)	$5.06
Variable manufacturing plus 20% ($3.20 x 1.20)	$3.84

Required:

(a) What should be the attitude of the Roper Division's management toward the three proposed prices?

(b) Is the negotiation of a price between the Mitchell and Roper Divisions a satisfactory method of solving the transfer price problem? Explain your answer.

(c) Should the corporate management of MBR, Inc., become involved in this transfer price controversy? Explain your answer.

(CMA Adapted)

9-33 Segmented Reports by Revenue Center

Music Teachers, Inc., is an educational association for music teachers that had 20,000 members during 19X5. The association operates from a central headquarters but has local membership chapters throughout the United States and Canada. Monthly meetings are held by the local chapters to discuss recent developments on topics of interest to music teachers. The association's journal, *Teachers' Forum*, is issued monthly with features about recent developments in the field. The association publishes books and reports and sponsors professional courses that qualify for continuing professional education credit. The statement of revenues and expenses follows:

Music Teachers, Inc.
Statement of Revenues and Expenses
For the Year Ending November 30, 19X5

Revenues		$3,275,000
Expenses:		
Salaries	$920,000	
Personnel costs	230,000	
Occupancy costs	280,000	
Reimbursement to local chapters	600,000	
Other membership services	500,000	
Printing and paper	320,000	
Postage and shipping	176,000	
Instructors' fees	80,000	
General and administrative	38,000	-3,144,000
Excess of revenues over expenses		$ 131,000

The board of directors has requested that a segmented statement of operations be prepared showing the contribution of each revenue center (i.e., Membership, Magazine Subscriptions, Books and Reports, and Continuing Education). Mickie Doyle, who has been assigned this responsibility, has gathered the following data prior to statement preparation:

- Membership dues are $100 per year, of which $20 is considered to cover a one-year subscription to the association's journal. Other benefits include membership in the association and chapter affiliation. The portion of the dues covering the magazine subscription ($20) should be assigned to the Magazine Subscriptions revenue center.
- One-year subscriptions to *Teachers' Forum* were sold to nonmembers and libraries at $30 each. A total of 2,500 of these subscriptions were sold. In addition to subscriptions, the magazine generated $100,000 in advertising revenue. The costs per magazine subscription were $7 for printing and paper and $4 for postage and shipping.
- A total of 28,000 technical reports and professional texts were sold by the Books and Reports Department at an average unit selling price of $25. Average costs per publication were as follows:

Printing and paper	$4
Postage and shipping	2

- The association offers a variety of continuing education courses to both members and nonmembers. During 19X5, the one-day course, which cost participants $75 each, was attended by 2,400 people. A total of 1,760 people took two-day courses at a cost of $125 per person. Outside instructors were paid to teach some courses.
- Salary and occupancy data were as follows:

	Salaries	Square Footage
Membership	$210,000	2,000
Magazine Subscriptions	150,000	2,000
Books and Reports	300,000	3,000
Continuing Education	180,000	2,000
Corporate Staff	80,000	1,000
Totals	$920,000	10,000

- The Books and Reports Department also rents warehouse space at an annual cost of $50,000.
- Personnel costs for such employee benefits as health insurance and retirement are 25 percent of salaries.
- Printing and paper costs other than for magazine subscriptions, books, and reports relate to the Continuing Education Department.
- General and administrative expenses include all other costs incurred by the corporate staff to operate the association.

Doyle has decided she will assign all revenues and expenses to the revenue centers that can be: (1) traced directly to a revenue center or (2) allocated on a reasonable and logical basis to a revenue center. The expenses that can be traced or assigned to corporate staff, as well as any other expenses that cannot be assigned to revenue centers, will be grouped with the general and administrative expenses and not allocated to the revenue centers. She believes that allocations often tend to be arbitrary and are not useful for management reporting and analysis. She believes that any further allocation of the general and administrative expenses associated with the operation and administration of the association would be arbitrary.

Required:

(a) Prepare a segmented statement of revenues and expenses that presents the contribution of each revenue center and includes the common costs of the organization that are not allocated to the revenue centers.

(b) If segmented reporting is adopted by the association for continuing usage, discuss the ways the information provided by the report can be utilized by the association.

(c) Mickie Doyle decided not to allocate some indirect or nontraceable expenses to revenue centers because she believes that allocations tend to be arbitrary.
   (1) Besides the arbitrary argument, what reasons are often presented for not allocating indirect or nontraceable expenses to revenue centers?
   (2) Under what circumstances might the allocation of indirect or nontraceable expenses to revenue centers be acceptable?

(CMA Adapted)

SOLUTION TO REVIEW PROBLEM

(a)

$$\text{Return on investment} = \frac{\text{Investment center income}}{\text{Investment center asset base}}$$

Division X = $30,000/$200,000
= 0.15 or 15 percent

Division Y = $50,000/$250,000
= 0.20 or 20 percent

Division Z = $22,000/$100,000
= 0.22 or 22 percent

(b)

$$\text{Residual income} = \text{Investment center income} - \left(\text{Minimum return} \times \text{Investment center asset base}\right)$$

Division X = $30,000 - (0.15 × $200,000)
        = $0.00

Division Y = $50,000 - (0.15 × $250,000)
        = $12,500

Division Z = $22,000 - (0.15 × $100,000)
        = $7,000

(c)

ROI ranks Division Z first, Division Y second, and Division X third. Residual income ranks Division Y first, Division Z second, and Division X third.

Because the investments for each division are different, it is difficult to rank the divisions by residual income. Division Y had the largest residual income, but it also had the largest investment. Division Z's residual income was 56 percent of Division Y's income, but only 40 percent of the investment of Division Y.

(d)

Return on investment:

Investment = $9,000/$50,000
         = 0.18 or 18 percent

Division X = ($30,000 + $9,000)/($200,000 + $50,000)
         = 0.156 or 15.6 percent

Division Y = ($50,000 + $9,000)/($250,000 + $50,000)
         = 0.1967 or 19.67 percent

Division Z = ($22,000 + $9,000)/($100,000 + $50,000)
         = 0.2067 or 20.67 percent

ROI will increase for Division X but decrease for Divisions Y and Z, even though the project's ROI of 18 percent exceeds the company's minimum return of 15 percent.

Residual income:

Division X = ($30,000 + $9,000) - (0.15 × [$200,000 + $50,000])
         = $1,500

Division Y = ($50,000 + $9,000) - (0.15 × [$250,000 + $50,000])
         = $14,000

Division Z = ($22,000 + $9,000) - (0.15 × [$100,000 + $50,000])
         = $8,500

Because the project's ROI exceeds the company's minimum return, the residual income of all divisions will increase.

▶ INVENTORY AND
SERVICE COSTING

JOB COSTING AND THE MANUFACTURING ENVIRONMENT

Throughout this text, we discuss how to determine the cost of various types of cost objectives such as products, activities, departments, geographic regions, divisions, customers, etc. An overarching theme is that cost measurements must be appropriate for the purposes for which the cost measurements will be used. For example, if the cost objective is a product, its relevant cost as part of an ongoing product line may be quite different from its relevant cost as a close-out item. Further, if the purpose is to evaluate a manager's effectiveness in managing the costs of producing the product, still another cost measurement might be necessary.

*In this chapter, we discuss the systems used to measure the cost of producing inventories and services for sale to customers. Although there are numerous managerial benefits from determining the cost of inventories, an important reason for product costing for many companies is to provide information for use in financial accounting reports. **Financial reporting** is the process of preparing financial statements (income statement, balance sheet, and statement of cash flows) for the firm in accordance with generally accepted accounting principles. Product cost measurements are essential for reporting the cost of inventories held at the end of the period in the balance sheet and the cost of goods sold during the period in the income statement. Companies that produce products are required to have cost systems, which are often very elaborate and expensive to maintain, to provide these inventory costs. For example, the Coca-Cola Company's 1993 financial statements reported "Cost of Goods Sold" of over $5 billion on the income statement and over $1 billion of "Inventories" on the balance sheet. These measurements were outputs of Coke's product costing system.*

Although the costs provided by product costing systems are sometimes designed primarily to satisfy financial reporting needs, often these inventory cost measurements can be used or modified for other purposes to meet management information needs. For instance, managers at the Coca-Cola Company may need to know how much it costs to produce and deliver a

12-ounce serving of Diet Coke to the local McDonald's in Plains, Georgia (USA), as well as how much it costs to produce and deliver a half-liter serving in Tbilisi, Georgia (in Eastern Europe). They may also need to know the cost of providing Coke concentrate in stainless steel returnable containers versus disposable containers. Hence, it is important for managers to have a clear understanding of the basic design and capabilities of their organization's product costing system. One of the most serious mistakes a manager can make is to assume that inventory costs provided by the cost system for financial accounting purposes may also be used without any modifications for managerial purposes. Management Accounting Practice 10-1 provides some insight into how some managers perceive the benefits of using financial reporting information for managerial purposes.

The purpose of this chapter is to provide an overview of product costing systems and a framework for understanding costs in a production environment. *We discuss the differences between measuring product costs in production and nonproduction environments and examine costing issues related to producing physical products versus producing services. We also discuss aspects of the manufacturing environment that may affect the product costing system.*

MANAGEMENT ACCOUNTING PRACTICE 10-1

Do Cost Systems Designed for Financial Reporting Satisfy Managers' Needs?

Professors McKinnon and Bruns, of Northeastern and Harvard Universities, respectively, interviewed 73 top managers in 12 manufacturing companies to determine the usefulness of accounting information to operating managers. One of their findings—which was not new or surprising—was that the primary characteristics about information that makes it useful is timeliness, accuracy, and relevance. They also found that most of the managers believed that the information they were receiving from the financial accounting system did not satisfy these requirements and that they have constructed their own information networks to supplement those created by management accountants. The result is a partial or complete severance of the link between the financial reports and the operations that forms their genesis. McKinnon and Bruns indicated that the failure of management accountants to break from financial reporting paradigms has led to separate management information departments in some firms, which is further isolating management accountants from operating decisions. Their admonition is for management accountants to become better informed in information technology so they can better bridge the gap that exists between financial reporting and the day-to-day need for managerial information.

Based on: Sharon M. McKinnon and William J. Bruns, Jr., "What Production Managers Really Want to Know, Management Accountants Are Failing to Tell Them," *Management Accounting* (January 1993), pp. 29-35.

Inventory Costs in Different Organizations

L O 1

Organizations may be classified generally as service, merchandising, or manufacturing organizations. **Service organizations** perform work for others. Included in this category are Bank of America, SuperCuts hair salons, The Shriner's Children's Hospital, Pizza Hut restaurants, United Artists movie theaters, Consolidated Edison electric utility, Princeton University, the City of New York, CSX Railroad, Delta Airlines, and the international accounting firm of Price Waterhouse. **Merchandising organizations** buy and sell goods and include companies such as Nordstom's department stores, Safeway grocery stores, L. L. Bean, Ace Hardware, and Wal-Mart. **Manufacturing organizations** process raw materials into finished products and include Mercedes Benz, Birmingham Steel, Compaq Computer, Reebok, and Henredon Furniture.

In general, service organizations have a low percentage of their total assets invested in inventory, which usually consists only of the supplies needed to facilitate their operations. Merchandising organizations usually have a high percentage of their total assets invested in inventory. Their most significant inventory investment is in merchandise purchased for resale, but they also have supplies inventories.

Manufacturing organizations convert raw materials into finished products for sale to other organizations and, like merchandisers, often have a high percentage of their total assets invested in inventories. However, rather than just one major inventory category, manufacturing organizations typically have three: raw materials, work-in-process, and finished goods. **Raw materials inventories** contain the physical ingredients and components that will be converted by machines and/or human labor into a finished product. **Work-in-process inventories** are the partially completed goods that are in process of being converted into a finished product. **Finished goods inventories** are the completed manufactured products held for sale to customers.

Manufacturing organizations also have investments in supplies inventories. Some of these supplies are used to facilitate production. Others are used in selling and administrative activities. Exhibit 10-1 illustrates the flow of inventory costs in service, merchandising, and manufacturing organizations. Note that in all three types of organizations, the financial accounting system initially records the costs of inventories as assets; but when they are eventually consumed or sold, inventories become expenses.

Inventory Costing and Service Costing

L O 2

Inventory costing systems were initially developed in the late eighteenth and early nineteenth centuries (as large manufacturing companies began to emerge both in Europe and America) to provide accountants the necessary

EXHIBIT 10-1: INVENTORY COSTS IN VARIOUS ORGANIZATIONS

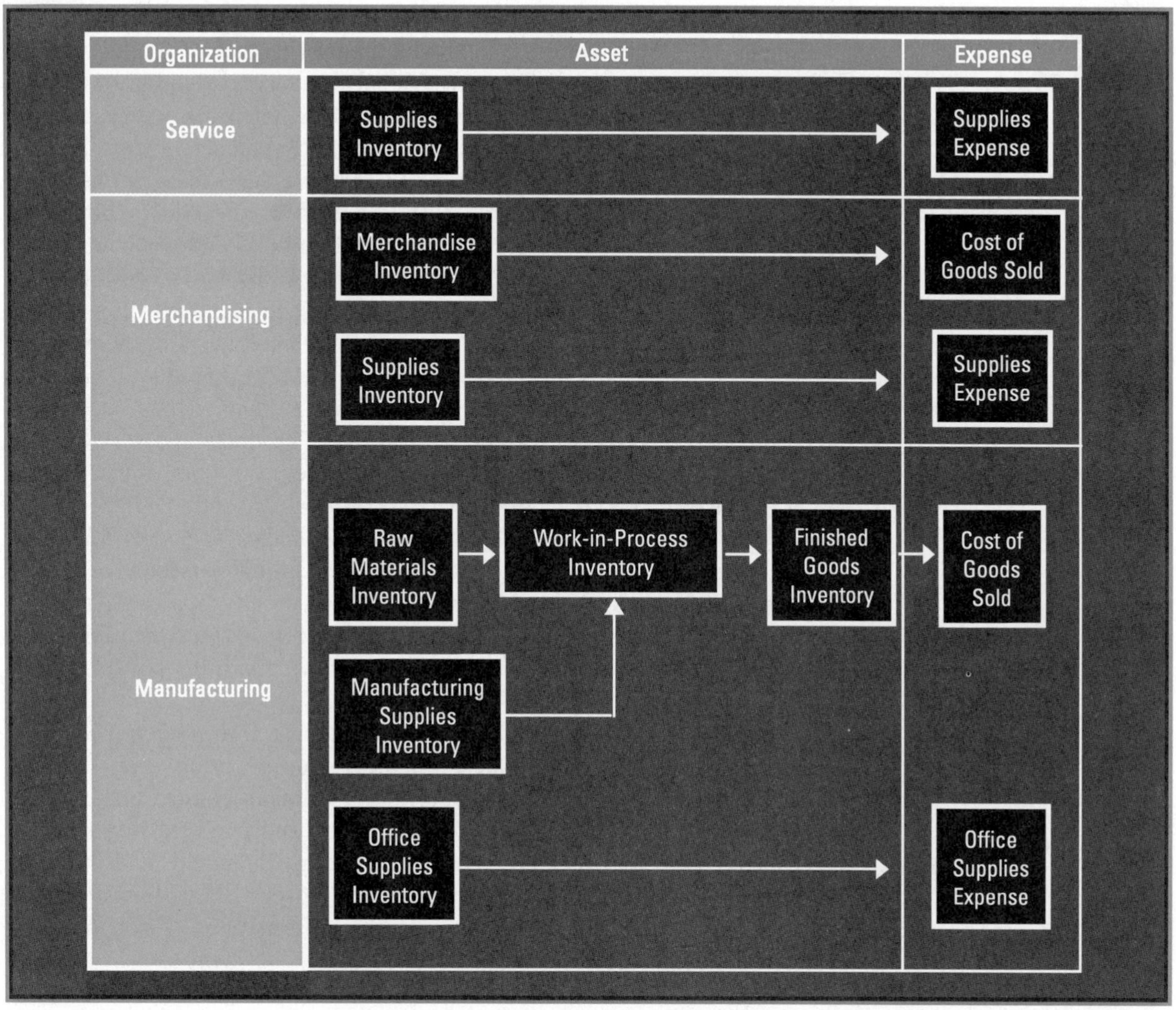

Organization	Asset	Expense
Service	Supplies Inventory →	Supplies Expense
Merchandising	Merchandise Inventory →	Cost of Goods Sold
	Supplies Inventory →	Supplies Expense
Manufacturing	Raw Materials Inventory → Work-in-Process Inventory → Finished Goods Inventory →	Cost of Goods Sold
	Manufacturing Supplies Inventory →	
	Office Supplies Inventory →	Office Supplies Expense

information for preparing company financial statements. Before the balance sheet and income statement could be prepared, accountants needed to know the cost of inventory on hand at the end of the year and the cost of inventory sold during the year.

As large, industrialized companies emerged, the need for outside capital grew. Originally, this need was satisfied by banks and other lenders; and, later, equity markets developed, allowing businesses to raise large amounts of capital by selling stocks in their companies to outside investors. Throughout this evolution, inventory has played an important role in the financial reporting process. Inventory valuations have often been the basis for loans to companies; and over the past 50 to 75 years, the stock markets have been influenced by profits possibly more than by any other factor—and profits are directly affected by the cost of inventory sold.

As the profit motive of managers has become dominant, product costing systems have become crucial to business success in many companies. Product cost is a key number by which managers manage businesses. It is often an important factor in evaluating the profitability of products (since price minus cost equals profit), it drives performance evaluation of managers (since lower costs mean higher profit and higher profit means a better evaluation), and it drives the product mix (since managers must choose which products to offer, and low-profit products are often replaced by high-profit products). Unreliable cost information can lead to disastrous results (noncompetitive pricing of goods and services, wrong conclusions about performance, and bad decisions regarding product mix).

Although costing systems were developed first in manufacturing organizations, over the past 25 years, costing systems have become increasingly important to service organizations. Whereas the term "product" was once used only to indicate a physical, inventoriable product, it has taken on a much broader meaning to include both physical products and services. In many cases, it is now difficult to determine whether a company is primarily a producer of goods or services. Is McDonald's producing food products or providing a service? Is AT&T, which makes and sells telephone switching equipment and sells long-distance calling services, a service company or a manufacturing company? Does it really matter? Do managers in service companies have any less need for cost information about the services they produce than manufacturers have about the physical products they produce?

The answer is that all organizations need cost information about the goods and services they produce, not only for preparing their external financial reports, but also because they want to make good decisions on a day-to-day basis that ultimately lead to a strong and progressively improving balance sheet and income statement. The profit motive and the need to produce favorable financial statements are closely linked with the need for managers to have reliable and timely cost information. Throughout the remainder of this and the next three chapters, we will discuss various costing systems found in manufacturing and service organizations, pointing out strengths and potential pitfalls of these systems in meeting the need for managerial cost information.

INVENTORY COSTING FOR FINANCIAL REPORTING

LO 3

Financial reporting for manufacturing organizations makes an important distinction between the cost of producing products and the cost of all other activities such as selling and administration. In general, inventory values for financial reporting purposes include only the costs of *producing* products. Information about costs related to *selling* inventories, such as marketing, distribution, customer service, and so forth, are all important for managerial decision-making purposes, but they are specifically excluded from product costs in the corporate financial statements. Therefore, the distinction between product and period costs is necessary.

**Product
Costs and
Period Costs**

For financial reporting, all costs incurred in *manufacturing* products are called **product costs** and are carried in the accounts as an asset (inventory) until the product is sold, at which time they are recognized as an expense (cost of goods sold). Inventoriable product costs include the costs of raw materials, plant employee salaries and wages, and all other *manufacturing* costs incurred to transform raw materials into finished products. Expired costs, other than those related to manufacturing inventory, are called **period costs** and are recognized as expenses when incurred. Noninventoriable period costs include the president's salary, sales commissions, advertising costs, and all other *nonmanufacturing* costs. Product and period costs are illustrated in Exhibit 10-2.

Costs such as research and development, marketing, distribution, and customer service are important for strategic and value chain analyses; how-

EXHIBIT 10-2: PRODUCT COSTS AND PERIOD COSTS FOR FINANCIAL REPORTING

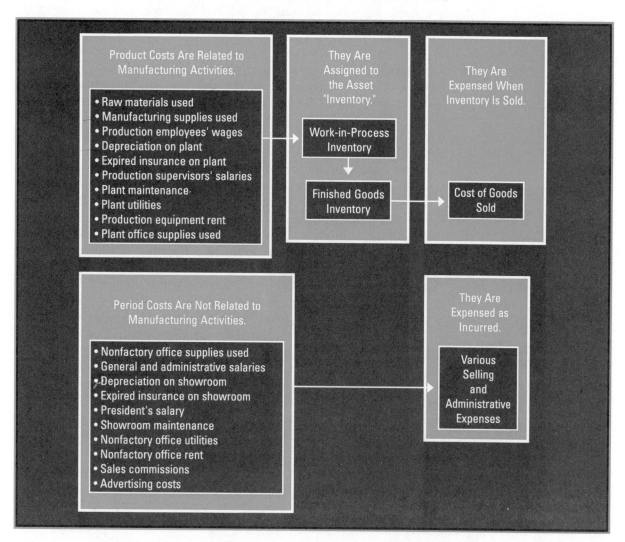

ever, since these costs are not incurred in the production process, they are not product costs for *financial reporting purposes*. For *internal managerial purposes*, accountants and managers often use the term "product costing" to embrace all costs incurred in connection with a product or service throughout the value chain.

To summarize, in the "product cost" versus "period cost" framework of *financial reporting*, costs are classified based on whether or not they are related to the manufacturing process. If they are related to the manufacturing process, they are product costs; otherwise, they are period costs. In this framework, costs that seem very similar may be treated quite differently. For example, note in Exhibit 10-2 that the expired cost of insurance on the *plant* is a *product cost*, but the expired cost of insurance on the *showroom* is a *period cost*. The reason is that the plant is used in manufacturing, but the showroom is not. This method of accounting for inventory that assigns all manufacturing costs to inventory is sometimes referred to as the **absorption cost,** or **full absorption cost** method, because all manufacturing costs are said to be *fully absorbed* into the cost of the product.

Three Components of Product Cost

The manufacture of even a simple product, such as a small wooden table, requires three basic ingredients: materials (wood), labor (the skill of a worker), and production facilities (a building to work in, a saw, and other tools). Corresponding to these three basic ingredients of any product are three basic categories of product costs: direct materials, direct labor, and manufacturing overhead.

Direct materials are the costs of the primary raw materials converted into finished goods. Examples of primary raw materials include iron ore to a steel mill, coiled aluminum to a manufacturer of aluminum siding, cow's milk to a dairy, logs to a sawmill, and lumber to a builder. Note that the finished product of one firm may be the raw materials of another firm down the value chain. For example, rolled steel is a finished product of Bethlehem Steel Company, but it is the raw material of the Maytag Company for the manufacture of washers and dryers. **Direct labor** consists of wages earned by production employees *for the time they actually spend working on a product*, and **manufacturing overhead** includes all manufacturing costs other than direct materials and direct labor.[1] **Conversion cost** consists of the combined costs of direct labor and manufacturing overhead incurred to convert raw materials into finished goods.

Examples of manufacturing overhead are manufacturing supplies, depreciation on manufacturing buildings and equipment, and the costs of plant taxes, insurance, maintenance, security, and utilities. Also included are production supervisors' salaries and all other manufacturing-related labor

---

[1] Manufacturing overhead is also called *factory overhead, burden, manufacturing burden,* and just *overhead*. All but the last of these terms are acceptable. The word "overhead" by itself does not indicate the type of overhead. Merchandising organizations occasionally refer to administrative costs as overhead.

costs for workers who do not work directly on the product (such as maintenance, security, and janitorial personnel). Although direct materials and direct labor are often the dominant product costs, today it is not uncommon for manufacturing overhead to comprise the largest percentage of total product cost. Consider the case of the "$7 aspirin" in Management Accounting Practice 10-2, where overhead costs make up the vast majority of the cost of providing an aspirin to a hospital patient.

Just as raw materials, labor, and production facilities are combined to produce a finished product, direct materials costs, direct labor costs, and manufacturing overhead costs are accumulated to obtain the total cost of goods produced. Exhibit 10-3 illustrates that these product costs are accumulated in the general ledger in Work-in-Process Inventory[2] (or just Work-in-Process) as production takes place and then transferred to Finished Goods Inventory when production is completed. Product costs are finally assigned to Cost of Goods Sold when the finished goods are sold.

EXHIBIT 10-3: THREE PRODUCT COSTS

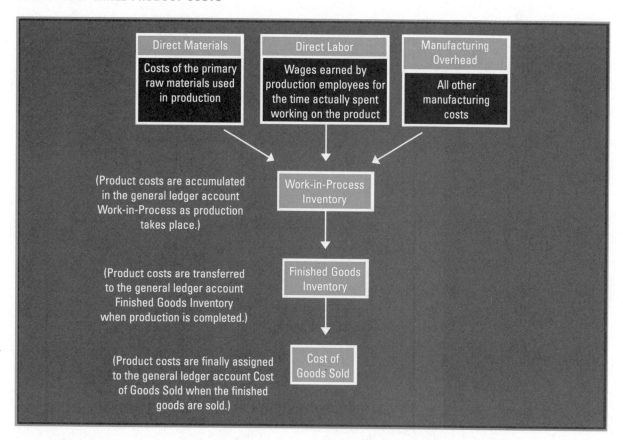

---

2 Account titles are capitalized to make it easier to determine when reference is being made to a physical item, such as work-in-process inventory, or to the account, Work-in-Process Inventory, in which costs assigned to the work-in-process inventory are accumulated.

MANAGEMENT ACCOUNTING PRACTICE 10-2

Product Costing for a $7 Aspirin

The furor over the government being charged $600 for a toilet seat was overshadowed only by a California hospital patient who was charged $7 on her hospital bill for each aspirin taken during her hospital stay. This patient wrote Ann Landers for an explanation of how such a high cost could be justified. Ann Landers explained that it was probably because the $7 included appropriate costs for the attending physician's time to prescribe the aspirin, the dispensing pharmacist's time to fill the prescription, the cost of the records department for maintaining records on the prescription, and the unreimbursed costs of the hospital that are "shifted" to other goods and services rendered by the hospital.

A corporate controller, picking up on this story, provided the following likely breakdown of the direct and indirect costs of the $7 aspirin:

Direct materials cost:	
Aspirin	$0.012
Direct labor cost:	
Physician	0.500
Pharmacist	0.603
Nurse	0.111
Overhead:	
Indirect labor:	
Orderly	0.200
Recordkeeping	0.200
Supplies:	
Cup	0.020
Shared and shifted costs:	
Unreimbursed Medicare	0.200
Indigent care	0.223
Uncollectible receivables	0.084
Malpractice insurance	0.068
Excess bed capacity	0.169
Other operating costs	0.056
Other administrative costs	0.112
Excess time elements	0.074
Product cost	$2.632
Other hospital overhead costs (32.98%)	.868
Full cost	$3.500
Profit	3.500
Selling price	$7.000

The controller explains that "in an effort to remain within the cost guidelines of reasonable and customary amounts of charges for such items as semiprivate room rates, operating room, recovery room, and intensive care units, hospitals have begun to 'unbundle' their charges into a variety of smaller-dollar, innocuous units of charges that can be multiplied across the spectrum of the patient population on a daily or multiple-daily basis under the general category of 'ancillary' charges. Aspirin is one of these items . . . ." This is an example of how a poor cost system can distort product cost measurements.

Based on: David W. McFadden, "The Legacy of the $7 Aspirin," *Management Accounting* (April 1990), pp. 38-41.

A Closer Look at Manufacturing Overhead

Possibly the biggest challenge in measuring the cost of a product is determining the amount of overhead incurred to produce it. Direct materials cost is driven by the number of raw materials units used; hence, its cost is simply the number of units of raw materials used multiplied by the related cost per unit. Direct labor cost is driven by the number of direct labor hours worked on the product; so, its cost is the number of direct labor hours used times the appropriate rate per direct labor hour. But what about manufacturing overhead? Manufacturing overhead often consists of dozens of different cost elements, potentially with many different cost drivers. Electricity cost is based on kilowatt-hours and water cost on gallons used; depreciation is usually measured in years of service and insurance in premium dollars per thousand dollars of coverage; and supervisors' salaries are a fixed amount per month.

Historically, accountants have believed that, even when possible, it is not cost-effective to try to measure separately the cost incurred for each manufacturing overhead item to produce a unit of finished product. Instead of identifying separate cost drivers for each individual cost component in manufacturing overhead, a single cost driver is often assumed for assigning total manufacturing overhead to the products. This process of spreading indirect manufacturing overhead cost to finished inventory is referred to as "applying" overhead to the product.

If a company produced only one product, it would be simple to apply overhead to the units produced because it would involve merely dividing total manufacturing overhead cost incurred by the number of units produced to get a cost per unit. For example, if total manufacturing overhead cost was $100,000 for the period and 20,000 units of product were produced during the period, the overhead cost applied to each unit would be $5.

Selecting a Basis (or Cost Driver) for Overhead Application

Since most companies produce different products in the same manufacturing facilities and since the amount of work required to produce each product is not equal, using a simple average of manufacturing overhead cost per unit does not provide a good estimate of the actual manufacturing overhead costs incurred to produce each unit of product. Some units that require extensive manufacturing activity have too little cost assigned to them, and others that require only a small amount of manufacturing effort have too much cost assigned to them. In these cases, units produced is not an appropriate cost driver for manufacturing overhead.

To solve this problem, an overhead application base, or cost driver, other than number of units produced, is usually used. The overhead application base selected is some activity that is common to all products but varies in quantity for each product, depending on the amount of manufacturing effort that went into making the product. For example, *machine hours* may be used to apply manufacturing overhead costs if the *number of machine hours used* is believed to be the primary cause of *manufacturing overhead cost incurred*. If so, products that require more machine hours to produce are assigned a higher manufacturing overhead cost.

Using Predetermined Overhead Rates

Although some organizations assign actual manufacturing overhead to products at the end of the period (normally the end of each month), three problems often result from measuring product cost using "actual" manufacturing overhead costs:

(1) Actual manufacturing overhead cost may not be known until several days or weeks after the end of the period, delaying the calculation of unit product cost.

(2) Some costs that are seasonal, such as annual insurance premiums or employee bonuses, are not incurred each period, thus making the actual cost of a product produced in one month of the year greater than that of another, even though nonseasonal costs may have been identical for both months.

(3) When there is a significant amount of fixed manufacturing overhead, the costs assigned to products will vary from period to period, depending on the overall volume of activity for the period.

To overcome these problems, most firms use a **predetermined manufacturing overhead rate** to assign manufacturing overhead costs to products. A predetermined rate is established at the start of each year by dividing the *predicted overhead costs* for the year by the *predicted volume of activity in the overhead base* for the year. A predetermined manufacturing overhead rate based on direct labor hours is computed as:

$$\text{Predetermined manufacturing overhead rate per direct labor hour} = \frac{\text{Predicted total manufacturing overhead cost for the year}}{\text{Predicted total direct labor hours for the year}}$$

Using a predetermined manufacturing overhead rate based on direct labor hours, we compute the assignment of overhead to Work-in-Process Inventory as:

$$\text{Manufacturing overhead assigned to Work-in-Process Inventory} = \text{Actual direct labor hours} \times \text{Predetermined manufacturing overhead rate per direct labor hour}$$

To illustrate, late in 19X6, Harmon Manufacturing Company predicted a 19X7 activity level of 25,000 direct labor hours with manufacturing overhead totaling $187,500. Using this information, its 19X7 predetermined overhead rate per direct labor hour was computed:

$$\frac{\text{Predetermined}}{\text{overhead rate}} = \frac{\$187,500}{25,000}$$

$$= \$7.50 \text{ per direct labor hour}$$

If 2,000 direct labor hours were used in September 19X7, the applied overhead would be $15,000:

$$2,000 \times \$7.50 = \underline{\underline{\$15,000}}$$

When a predetermined rate is used based on annual predictions of overhead costs and activity in the overhead applications base, monthly variations between actual and applied manufacturing overhead are expected because of the seasonality of certain costs and variations in monthly activity. Hence, in some months, overhead will be "overapplied" as applied overhead exceeds actual overhead; in other months, overhead will be "underapplied" as actual overhead exceeds applied overhead. If the beginning-of-the-year estimates are accurate for annual overhead costs and annual activity in the application base, monthly over- and underapplied amounts during the year should offset each other by the end of the period. During the year, the cumulative over- or underapplied balance should be monitored to identify an excessive over- or underapplied balance and to determine if the estimate of the overhead rate should be revised before year-end. Later in this chapter, we consider methods for accounting for any over- or underapplied manufacturing overhead balance that may exist at the end of the year.

Limitations of a Single Manufacturing Overhead Rate

In the discussions above, a single overhead rate, based either on actual or predetermined overhead cost and activity, was used to apply manufacturing costs to products. This approach to assigning manufacturing overhead to products *assumes* that all costs are caused by one cost driver, such as machine hours or direct labor hours, which is selected as the basis for applying overhead. Historically, a single plant-wide overhead application rate based on direct labor hours was widely used when direct labor was the predominant cost factor in production and when manufacturing overhead costs were often related to direct labor.

Technological progress over the past 25 years has caused significant changes in the factors of manufacturing costs, resulting in major shifts in costs in many industries from direct labor to manufacturing overhead. A good example of this shift is the worldwide automobile industry in which firms like Chrysler, Toyota, and Volvo have spent billions of dollars on robotics and other technologies, thereby reducing the significance of direct labor in the production process. In many cases, these technological changes mean that direct labor hours are no longer an appropriate basis for assigning manufacturing costs to products. In others, these changes mean there is no longer a single allocation basis, or cost driver, appropriate for assigning manufacturing overhead to products.

Although some companies continue to use a single (actual or predetermined) manufacturing overhead rate because it is convenient, many companies no longer use this approach. Instead, they have adopted multiple overhead rates based on cost categories for either major departments or activities within the organization.

THE MANUFACTURING ENVIRONMENT

L O 4

In Chapter 7, which dealt with operating budgets, quarterly production budgets are developed for an entire year. Although quarterly production budgets are important in planning overall operations, they are not detailed enough to run a factory. Manufacturing personnel need to know what specific products to produce on specific machines on a daily or even hourly basis. The detailed scheduling of products on machines is performed by production scheduling personnel. Exactly how production is scheduled depends on whether process or job production is used and whether job production is in response to a specific customer sales order or for speculative inventory.

In **process production**, a single product is produced on a continuous basis. Here, a production facility may be devoted exclusively to one product or to a closely related set of products. Companies where you would likely find a process production environment are Snapple Beverage Company, the Western Electric Division of AT&T, which makes fiber optic cables, Burlington Mills, and Bowater Paper Company, which makes continuous rolled paper for the printing of daily newspapers such as the *Chicago Tribune*. When continuous production involves only a single product, the costing issues are relatively straightforward. Product costing for process production is discussed in Chapter 11.

In **job production**, also called **job-order production**, products are produced in single units or in batches of identical units; however, the products included in different jobs may vary considerably. Examples of single-unit jobs can be found at Hallco Builders, a builder of custom-designed homes, at Lockheed-Martin Company, which makes the world's largest cargo planes for military use, at Metric Construction Company, which builds skyscrapers, and at Sally Industries, Inc., which makes animated robots for theme parks. (See Management Accounting Practice 10-3.) Batch jobs would be more common at companies such as HartMarx, a clothing manufacturer, and at Steelcase Furniture Company, a large producer of office furnishings. A job may be produced in response to a customer's order for intermediate components that are to go into a final product, such as when Ford Motor Company purchases engine blocks from the Internet Corporation, a foundry company that makes precision parts for the automobile industry. When a job results from a customer's order, marketing personnel forward the order to production scheduling personnel, who determine when and how the products specified in the order are to be produced. Important scheduling considerations include the overall workload, raw materials availability, specific equipment or labor requirements, and the delivery date or dates of the finished product.

Important staff groups involved in production planning and control include engineering, scheduling, expediting, quality control, and accounting. Engineering is primarily concerned with determining how a product should be produced. On the basis of an engineering analysis, aided by cost data,

MANAGEMENT ACCOUNTING PRACTICE 10-3

Sally Industries Uses Job Costing to Track Costs of Making Magic

If you've ever been to Disney World, MCA Universal Studios, Euro Disney, or any of the other major theme parks that have sprung up in Florida, California, or other parts of the world, you have probably seen the bigger-than-life examples of historic and prehistoric characters that move and talk like living creatures. Many of these robotic-driven creations are manufactured by Sally Industries, Inc., which uses a job-cost system to account for the thousands of dollars that go into building each model. This is an example of where job costing is necessary, because no two products are alike and each must be designed and built to precise specifications. A detailed job-cost sheet may include as many as 20 different modules for the model, each broken down into materials, labor, and manufacturing overhead. Since Sally Industries normally sells its products on a fixed-price contract, having an accurate measurement of cost is important to evaluate how actual costs compare with predicted costs and to determine how profitable each job is.

Based on: Thomas Barton and Frederick M. Cole, "Accounting for Magic," *Management Accounting* (January 1991), pp. 27-31.

engineering develops manufacturing specifications for each product. These manufacturing specifications are often summarized in two important documents: a bill of materials and an operations list. Each product's **bill of materials** specifies the kinds and quantities of raw materials required to produce one unit of product. Each product's **operations list** specifies the manufacturing operations and related times required to produce one unit or batch of product. The operations list should also include information on any machine setup time required before production of the product can begin.

Production scheduling prepares a production order for each job. The **production order** assigns a unique identification number to a job and specifies such details as the quantity to be produced in the job, the total raw materials requirements of the job, the manufacturing operations to be performed on the job, and perhaps even the time when each manufacturing operation should be performed. In preparing a production order, scheduling uses the product's bill of materials and operations list to determine the materials and the manufacturing times required to complete the job. Scheduling also uses information concerning production deadlines and available manufacturing capabilities. When a job consists of several units, the materials and time requirements are determined by making appropriate computations. The production order serves as authorization for manufacturing personnel to requisition raw materials and to utilize manufacturing facilities.

A **job-cost sheet** is a document used to accumulate the costs for a specific job in a job-cost system. The job-cost sheet serves as the basic record for recording actual progress on the job. As production takes place, materials, labor, and machine resources utilized are recorded on the job-cost sheet along with the related job costs.

Production Files and Records

A **file** is simply a collection of related records, and a **record** is a related set of alphabetic and/or numeric data items. Both records and files may be maintained electronically on a computer or manually in a paper-based system. Important files in any product cost system include files of inventory records for raw materials, work-in-process, and finished goods, as well as files for bills of materials and operations lists. Sample records from a manual system for raw materials, finished goods, bill of materials, and operations list are illustrated in Exhibit 10-4.

Certain files in the cost system provide the necessary detail for amounts maintained in total in the general ledger. For example, the raw materials inventory file contains separate raw materials records for each type of raw materials, indicating increases, decreases, and the available balance for both units and costs. Every time there is a change in the Raw Materials general ledger account, there must be an accompanying, equal change in one or more individual inventory records. Therefore, at any given time, the total of the balances for all raw materials inventory records should equal the balance in the Raw Materials general ledger account. Because of this relationship between the raw materials inventory file and the Raw Materials Inventory account in the general ledger, we refer to the Raw Materials Inventory account as a *control account* and the raw materials file of detailed records as a *subsidiary ledger*. Other general ledger accounts related to the product cost system that have subsidiary files of records are Work-in-Process, Finished Goods, and Cost of Goods Sold.

Each product produced has a record in the bill of materials and the operations list files, indicating the resources required to produce one unit of the product. These files do not have related general ledger accounts. Hence, they are not subsidiary ledgers.

Other records required to operate a job-cost system include production orders, job-cost sheets, materials requisition forms, and work tickets. These records are illustrated in Exhibit 10-5 (pages 536-538).

Production orders and job-cost sheets were discussed previously. The job number assigned in the production order is also recorded on a job-cost sheet. The production order serves as authorization for production supervisors to obtain materials from the storeroom and to issue work orders to production employees. A **materials requisition form** indicates the type and quantity of each raw material issued to the factory. This form is used to record the transfer of responsibility for materials and to make appropriate notations on raw materials and job-cost sheet records. The materials requisition form has a field to record the job number, and the job-cost sheet has a field to record the requisition number. If a question arises regarding the issuance of materials, the requisition number and job number provide a trail for tracing the destination and the source of the materials. The materials requisition form also identifies the materials warehouse employee who issued the materials and the production employee who received them.

EXHIBIT 10-4: BASIC PRODUCTION RECORDS

Raw Materials Inventory Record
Part No. _____   Description _____

	Purchased			Issued			Balance		
Date	Units	Unit Cost	Total Cost	Units	Unit Cost	Total Cost	Units	Unit Cost	Total Cost

Finished Goods Inventory Record
Product No. _____   Description _____

	Received from Factory			Sold			Balance		
Date	Units	Unit Cost	Total Cost	Units	Unit Cost	Total Cost	Units	Unit Cost	Total Cost

Bill of Materials
Raw Materials Requirements per Unit of Product

Product No. _____   Description _____

Part Number	Description	Quantity per Unit

Operations List
Production Operations and Time Usage per Unit of Product

Product No. _____   Description _____

Department Number	Operation Description	Machine/Labor Requirements	Setup Time	Operating Time

EXHIBIT 10-5: JOB COST SYSTEM RECORDS

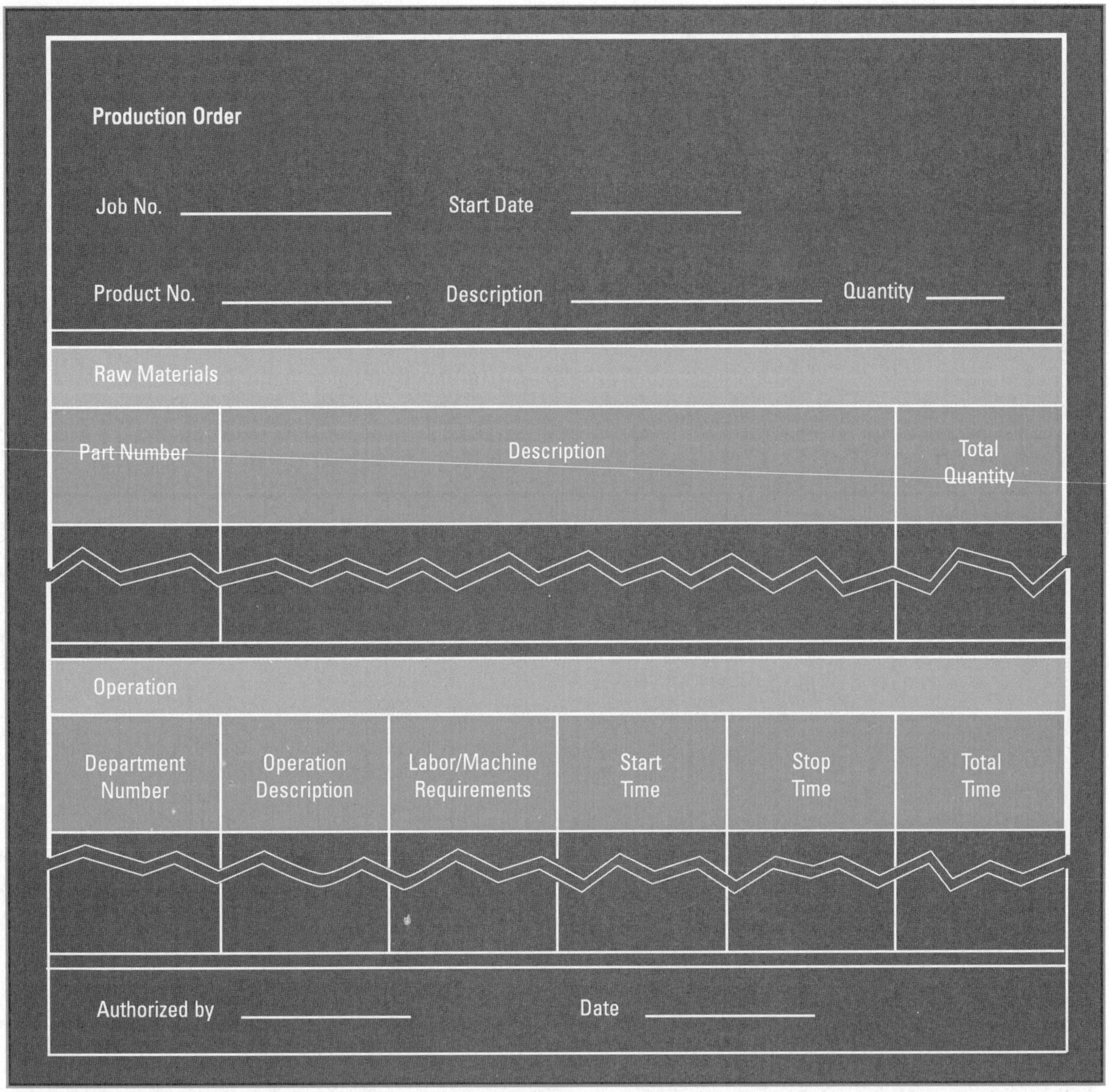

Production Order

Job No. _____   Start Date _____

Product No. _____   Description _____   Quantity _____

Raw Materials

Part Number	Description	Total Quantity

Operation

Department Number	Operation Description	Labor/Machine Requirements	Start Time	Stop Time	Total Time

Authorized by _____   Date _____

A **work ticket** is used to record the time a job spends in a specific manufacturing operation. Each manufacturing operation performed on a job is documented by a work ticket. The work tickets completed for a job should correspond to the operations specified on the job's production order. Time information on the work tickets is used by production scheduling or expediting personnel to determine whether the job is on schedule. When production times are multiplied by appropriate rates in the lower portion, the work ticket is used to assign costs to the job.

EXHIBIT 10-5 (CONTINUED)

Job-Cost Sheet

Job No. _____

Product No. _____ Description _____ Quantity _____

Raw Materials Cost

Date	Department	Requisition Number	Description	Total Cost

Conversion Costs: Direct Labor or Machine

Date	Department	Work Ticket Number	Description	Total Time	Total Cost

Applied Overhead

Date	Department	Basis of Application	Total Cost

Total Cost of Job

Unit Cost

_____

_____

EXHIBIT 10-5 (CONTINUED)

Materials Requisition Form

Requisition No. ______ Job No. ______ Date ______

Department ____________________

Part Number	Description	Total Quantity	Unit Cost	Total Cost

Issued by __________ Received by __________

Work Ticket

Work Ticket No. ______ Date __________

Department ______________ Job No. ____

Time Started ______ Time Completed ____

Employee/Machine Operator __________

Office Use

Total Time ____ Rate ____ Total Cost ____

A manufacturing operation may involve a single direct labor employee, a group of direct labor employees, a machine, or even a heating, cooling, or aging process. When the operation involves a single employee, the rate recorded on the work ticket is simply the employee's wage rate. When it involves a group of employees, the rate is composed of the wage rates of all employees in the group. When the work involves a machine operation, the rate includes a charge for machine time, as well as the time of any machine operators. Other operations, such as heating, cooling, or aging, will also have a rate for each unit of time.

Impact of Computers on Manufacturing

Significant changes are taking place in production planning and control procedures. Perhaps the most significant changes involve the increasing use of computers for scheduling, monitoring, and costing. Just a few years ago, the files and records illustrated in Exhibits 10-4 and 10-5 were maintained manually, making data collection and analysis costly and time-consuming. With centralized data processing, the original transactions were still manually recorded on materials requisitions or work tickets and then entered into the computer. Today, computer terminals are often spread throughout the factory. As each operation on a job is started and completed, the job's status is entered into a computer terminal.

Many firms have implemented bar coding and **automatic identification systems (AIS)** that allow inventory and production information to be entered into a computer without writing or keying. In an AIS, laser scanners connected to a computer data base "read" bar codes attached to production orders, materials, machines, or employee badges. The bar codes may be read as materials pass by a fixed laser scanner, or they may be read by a hand-held laser scanner such as those used at major retailers such as Macy's and Home Depot. In this environment, managers can keep information at almost any level of detail they wish. And production supervisors have the capability of continuously monitoring inventory levels, the status of all personnel and machines, the location of each job in the plant, the on-time status of each job, and the costs assigned to each job. Exception reports are easily developed to alert appropriate personnel when operations are not proceeding according to schedule. Computer programs are even used to adjust production schedules when necessary.

In addition to being used to monitor production and rapidly process data, computers aid in designing new products, controlling machine operations, and even automating machine setups. **Computer-aided design (CAD)** involves the use of computers to design products. Using high-resolution computer monitors with graphics software, custom products can be rapidly designed. Engineering drawings for the product, as well as a bill of materials and an operations list, can be developed when needed.

Computer-aided manufacturing (CAM) involves the use of computers to control the operation of machines. Although few firms have operations that are completely controlled by computers, many have "islands of automation" for some operations existing alongside more traditional labor- and machine-intensive manufacturing techniques. See Management Accounting Practice 10-4 for an example of how computers are used in movements of materials and products.

Flexible manufacturing systems (FMS) are an extension of computer-aided manufacturing techniques through a series of manufacturing operations, including the automatic movement of units between operations and the automatic and rapid setup of machines to produce each product. An FMS virtually eliminates all direct labor in the manufacturing process.

Computer-integrated manufacturing (CIM) is the ultimate extension of the CAD, CAM, and FMS concepts to a completely automated and computer-controlled factory where production is automatic once a product is designed and the decision to produce is made. In their advanced stages, factories utilizing flexible manufacturing systems and computer-integrated manufacturing are sometimes referred to as "lights-out factories" because they can be operated in the dark and without people. Obviously, CIM represents a seldom encountered extreme point on a continuum that begins with paper, pencil, and hand tools.

The attractions of these computer-based monitoring, design, and production techniques are lower production times, higher quality products, and

MANAGEMENT ACCOUNTING PRACTICE 10-4

Lights-Out Warehouse Improves Product Delivery Time at South-Western Publishing

Before publishing this text on management accounting, the authors were invited to South-Western Publishing Company's corporate headquarters in Cincinnati to meet the editorial staff. During the visit, we were given a tour of South-Western's facilities, including the warehouse and order-filling departments. One of the most fascinating aspects of the tour was the "lights-out" warehouse where textbooks are stored on pallets held by steel racks about 20 to 30 feet tall. A totally automated, computer-controlled system stores and retrieves books from the warehouse without the intervention of human hands. When the order was received by South-Western from your college or university bookstore for the book you are reading, equipment was directed electronically to go to the appropriate location in the warehouse, to retrieve the correct number of boxes of this text, and to deliver them to the Shipping Department for addressing and delivery. This illustrates how companies are using computer-controlled equipment to improve the manufacturing, storage, and movement of products.

lower product cost. With lower production times, a firm obtains a competitive advantage by being able to fill customers' orders quickly, thereby providing better service. Lower production times also reduce the need for speculative inventories that provide for variability in the demand for products or components. Again, there is less need for speculative inventories when an unexpected demand can be filled quickly. Lower inventories result in lower inventory holding costs such as spoilage, theft, warehousing, and obsolescence. High quality arises from better design, rapid identification of defects, and correction of the cause of defects before large numbers of defective units are produced. Higher quality production, with few defects, reduces the cost of good units. Hence, both speed and quality improvements make it possible to reduce costs. Lower costs mean greater profits at a given price or an increased ability to compete on the basis of price.

JOB COSTING FOR PRODUCTS AND SERVICES

LO 5

Inventory costs in a manufacturing organization flow in a logical pattern through the accounting system. The costs of purchased raw materials are recorded in the Raw Materials account, and the cost of other incidental supplies are recorded as Manufacturing Supplies. As primary raw materials are requisitioned to the factory, direct materials costs are transferred from Raw Materials to Work-in-Process. Direct labor costs are added to Work-in-Process on the basis of the time devoted to processing raw materials. All other costs are accumulated initially in the Manufacturing Overhead account and periodically assigned (applied) to Work-in-Process.

When products are completed, their accumulated product costs are transferred from Work-in-Process to Finished Goods Inventory. Later when the products are sold, their costs are transferred from Finished Goods Inventory to Cost of Goods Sold. This general pattern of manufacturing cost flows is shown in Exhibit 10-6.

The numbered journal entries posted to the accounts in Exhibit 10-6 are presented in journal entry form in Exhibit 10-7. Before the journal entries can be recorded, the supporting data (materials requisition slips, work tickets, and so forth) must be completed, collected, and summarized. Although data can be processed using either a manual or computerized accounting system, accounting procedures are best illustrated within the context of a paper-based manual accounting system. Before proceeding, take a few minutes to review the transactions in Exhibits 10-6 and 10-7 carefully to make sure you understand the general flow of costs.

A possible pattern of cost flows for a factory containing only machine-intensive manufacturing operations is shown in Exhibit 10-8 (page 543). The major difference between Exhibits 10-6 and 10-8 is the combining of direct labor and manufacturing overhead into a single conversion cost pool. Note especially journal entry number 3. Although manufacturing overhead

EXHIBIT 10-6: BASIC MANUFACTURING COST FLOWS

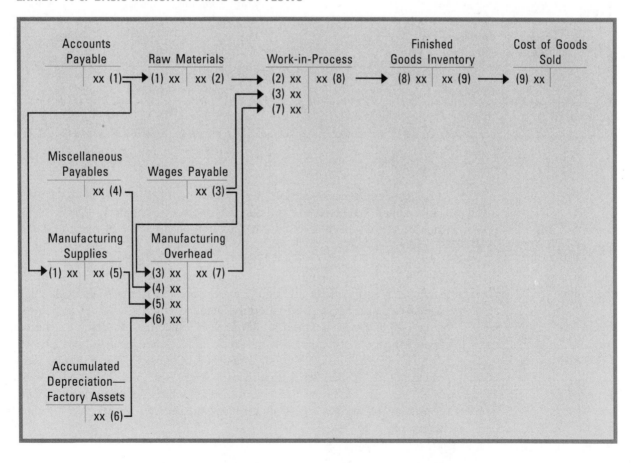

EXHIBIT 10-7: BASIC MANUFACTURING JOURNAL ENTRIES

(1) Raw Materials   xx
    Manufacturing Supplies   xx
      Accounts Payable   xx
  To record purchase of raw
  materials and manufacturing
  supplies on account.

(2) Work-in-Process   xx
    Raw Materials   xx
  To record requisition and transfer
  of raw materials to the factory
  from materials stores.

(3) Work-in-Process   xx
    Manufacturing Overhead   xx
    Wages Payable   xx
  To assign direct labor cost
  incurred to Work-in-Process
  and indirect labor cost to
  Manufacturing Overhead.

(4) Manufacturing Overhead   xx
    Miscellaneous Payables*   xx
  To record incurrence of various
  manufacturing overhead costs
  such as repairs and maintenance
  and property taxes.

(5) Manufacturing Overhead   xx
    Manufacturing Supplies   xx
  To record supplies used in
  manufacturing.

(6) Manufacturing Overhead   xx
    Accumulated Depreciation
    —Factory Assets   xx
  To recognize depreciation on
  factory assets.

(7) Work-in-Process   xx
    Manufacturing Overhead   xx
  To assign manufacturing overhead
  costs to Work-in-Process.

(8) Finished Goods Inventory   xx
    Work-in-Process   xx
  To record transfer of finished goods
  from work-in-process inventory to
  finished goods inventory.

(9) Cost of Goods Sold   xx
    Finished Goods Inventory   xx
  To record the cost of finished
  goods sold.

*The account Miscellaneous Payables is used for convenience in this example to record any liability other than that for wages and inventory purchases. Miscellaneous payables include utilities payable, taxes payable, rent payable, etc.

in a labor-intensive operation is most often applied on the basis of direct labor hours or direct labor dollars, it is more appropriate to apply conversion costs in a machine-intensive operation on the basis of machine hours.

**Job Costing
Illustrated**

Fox Brothers, Inc., manufactures a line of wool sports jackets for men and women. Because there are significant differences in materials costs and a need to control inventories carefully, detailed records are kept of the raw materials assigned to specific jobs. Raw materials consist of different styles of wool fabric, interfacing fabric, liner fabric, and button sets.

Total inventories at the beginning of August 19X7 included Raw Materials, $36,100; Work-in-Process, $109,900; and Finished Goods, $75,000. In addition, there were Manufacturing Supplies of $1,600, consisting of various items such as thread, needles, shears, and machine lubricant.

EXHIBIT 10-8: BASIC MANUFACTURING COST FLOWS FOR MACHINE-INTENSIVE OPERATIONS

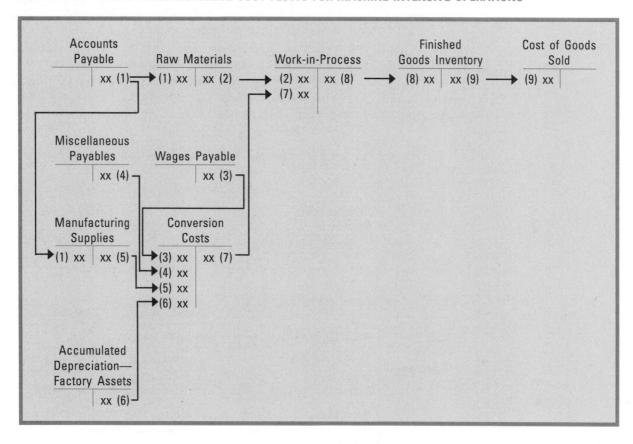

Raw Materials			
Description	Quantity	Unit Cost	Total Cost
Wool fabric W09	3,000 yards	$ 7	$21,000
Wool fabric W12	500 yards	12	6,000
Interfacing	1,500 yards	1	1,500
Liner	2,000 yards	3	6,000
Buttons	400 sets	4	1,600
Total			$36,100

Manufacturing Supplies		Finished Goods Inventory	
	Total Cost	Job	Total Cost
Various	$1,600	424	$75,000

Work-in-Process	
Job	Total Cost
425	$ 58,600
426	51,300
Total	$109,900

To illustrate manufacturing cost flows in a job-cost system, summary manufacturing-cost journal entries recorded by Fox Brothers, Inc., during August 19X7 are presented below. In reality, there would be a number of journal entries of each type. Included are the entries recorded in the general journal and the procedures performed in the cost system records. Cost system procedures consist of supporting documentation recorded in subsidiary records and other records related to recognizing changes in Raw Materials, Work-in-Process, and Finished Goods Inventory.

1. Purchased raw materials and manufacturing supplies on account.

JOURNAL ENTRY	Raw Materials	30,000	
	Manufacturing Supplies	1,000	
	Accounts Payable		31,000

COST SYSTEM PROCEDURES	Recorded purchases on raw materials inventory records:
	Wool fabric W12 1,000 yards × $12 = $12,000
	Liner 2,000 yards × $3 = 6,000
	Buttons 3,000 sets × $4 = 12,000
	Note: Separate inventory records are not maintained for manufacturing supplies such as thread, needles, etc., because their costs are small.

2. Requisitioned materials needed to complete Jobs 425 and 426. Started two new jobs, 427 and 428, and requisitioned direct materials for them.

| JOURNAL ENTRY | Work-in-Process | 54,300 | |
| | Raw Materials | | 54,300 |

COST SYSTEM PROCEDURES	(a) Prepare production orders and job-cost sheets for Jobs 427 and 428.
	(b) Prepare materials requisition forms.
	(c) Record issuances on raw materials inventory records and assign cost to jobs on job-cost sheets.

(continued)

	Job 425	Job 426	Job 427	Job 428	Total
Buttons:					
1,200 sets × $4	$4,800				$ 4,800
900 sets × $4		$3,600			3,600
500 sets × $4			$ 2,000		2,000
Wool fabric W12:					
1,500 yds. × $12			18,000		18,000
Wool fabric W09:					
2,400 yds. × $7				$16,800	16,800
Interfacing:					
500 yds. × $1			500		500
800 yds. × $1				800	800
Liner:					
1,000 yds. × $3			3,000		3,000
1,600 yds. × $3				4,800	4,800
Total	$4,800	$3,600	$23,500	$22,400	$ 54,300

3. Recorded August payroll liability for direct labor of $34,450 and indirect labor of $7,200.

JOURNAL ENTRY			
Work-in-Process		34,450	
Manufacturing Overhead		7,200	
Wages Payable			41,650

COST SYSTEM PROCEDURES

(a) Prepare work tickets.
(b) Assign direct labor costs to jobs.

	Job 425	Job 426	Job 427	Job 428	Total
Labor hours	600	900	1,000	945	
Labor rate	× $10	× $10	× $10	× $10	
Total	$6,000	$9,000	$10,000	$9,450	$ 34,450

Note: The $7,200 of indirect labor costs is not assigned directly to the jobs. It is recorded as Manufacturing Overhead, which is assigned to products in item 5.

4. Recorded additional manufacturing overhead costs.

JOURNAL ENTRY		
Manufacturing Overhead	7,090	
Manufacturing Supplies		950
Accumulated Depreciation—Factory Assets		1,500
Utilities Payable		2,400
Property Taxes Payable		1,200
Miscellaneous Payables		1,040

COST SYSTEM PROCEDURES	Manufacturing Overhead is a control account with a subsidiary ledger (file) containing a record for each type of overhead cost. Each manufacturing cost is recorded on the appropriate record.

Manufacturing supplies used	$ 950
Factory depreciation	1,500
Utilities	2,400
Property taxes	1,200
Miscellaneous	1,040
Total	$7,090

5. Applied manufacturing overhead of $13,780 to jobs using a predetermined rate of $4 per direct labor hour.

JOURNAL ENTRY	Work-in-Process	13,780	
	Manufacturing Overhead		13,780

COST SYSTEM PROCEDURES	Record overhead on job-cost sheets.

	Job 425	Job 426	Job 427	Job 428	Total
Labor hours	600	900	1,000	945	
Overhead rate	× $4	× $4	× $4	× $4	
Total	$2,400	$3,600	$4,000	$3,780	$13,780

6. Completed Jobs 425, 426, and 427.

JOURNAL ENTRY	Finished Goods Inventory	176,800	
	Work-in-Process		176,800

COST SYSTEM PROCEDURES	(a) Complete job-cost sheets to determine total cost of finished jobs.

	Job 425	Job 426	Job 427	Total
Beginning balance	$58,600	$51,300	$ 0	$109,900
Current costs:				
Direct materials (entry # 2)	4,800	3,600	23,500	31,900
Direct labor (entry # 3)	6,000	9,000	10,000	25,000
Applied overhead (entry # 4)	2,400	3,600	4,000	10,000
Total cost of jobs	$71,800	$67,500	$37,500	$176,800

(b) Transfer job-cost sheets for completed jobs to finished goods subsidiary file.

(c) Perform any additional analysis desired for completed jobs, such as unit costs.

	Job 425	Job 426	Job 427
Total cost of jobs	$71,800	$67,500	$37,500
Units in job	÷ 1,200	÷ 900	÷ 500
Unit cost	$ 59.83	$ 75.00	$ 75.00

7. Delivered Jobs 424, 425, and 426 to customers for a sales price of $400,000.

JOURNAL ENTRIES			
	Accounts Receivable	400,000	
	Sales Revenue		400,000
	Cost of Goods Sold	214,300	
	Finished Goods Inventory		214,300

COST SYSTEM PROCEDURES		
Transfer job-cost sheets for Jobs 424, 425, and 426 from finished goods subsidiary file to a file for jobs completed and shipped.		
	Job 424	$ 75,000
	Job 425	71,800
	Job 426	67,500
	Total	$214,300

Exhibit 10-9 shows the various manufacturing inventory accounts, Cost of Goods Sold, and the cost system records reflecting the above transactions. Note how the cost system records provide supporting documentation for the ending balances in the inventory accounts.

Fox Brothers' product costing system is probably adequate for determining the cost for each job for purposes of valuing ending inventories and cost of goods sold. For example, the system recognizes the differences in materials costs by carefully tracking each type of material as a separate cost pool. Because all direct labor employees are paid the same rate, it is necessary to maintain only one labor cost pool. Although there are three distinct operations in making sports coats (cutting, sewing, and finishing), the various styles of coats are assumed to be homogeneous, with the same proportionate time spent on each operation for each product. Hence, with only one manufacturing overhead cost pool applied on the basis of direct labor hours, individual product costs are probably reasonably accurate. As mentioned earlier, in future chapters, we will discuss how greater accuracy may be achieved in some cases by using multiple overhead cost pools.

Even though the Fox Brothers' costing system is adequate for inventory costing for financial statement purposes, it has rather severe limitations for

EXHIBIT 10-9: GENERAL LEDGER ACCOUNTS AND SUBSIDIARY JOB COST SYSTEM RECORDS FOR FOX BROTHERS, INC.

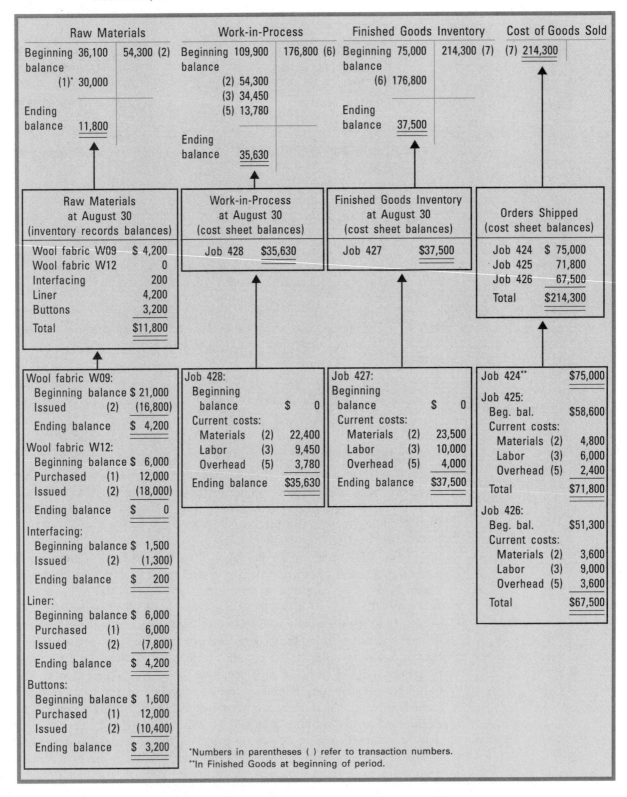

Raw Materials

Beginning balance	36,100	54,300	(2)
(1)*	30,000		
Ending balance	11,800		

Work-in-Process

Beginning balance	109,900	176,800	(6)
(2)	54,300		
(3)	34,450		
(5)	13,780		
Ending balance	35,630		

Finished Goods Inventory

Beginning balance	75,000	214,300	(7)
(6)	176,800		
Ending balance	37,500		

Cost of Goods Sold

(7)	214,300

Raw Materials at August 30 (inventory records balances)

Wool fabric W09	$ 4,200
Wool fabric W12	0
Interfacing	200
Liner	4,200
Buttons	3,200
Total	$11,800

Work-in-Process at August 30 (cost sheet balances)

Job 428	$35,630

Finished Goods Inventory at August 30 (cost sheet balances)

Job 427	$37,500

Orders Shipped (cost sheet balances)

Job 424	$ 75,000
Job 425	71,800
Job 426	67,500
Total	$214,300

Wool fabric W09:

Beginning balance		$ 21,000
Issued	(2)	(16,800)
Ending balance		$ 4,200

Wool fabric W12:

Beginning balance		$ 6,000
Purchased	(1)	12,000
Issued	(2)	(18,000)
Ending balance		$ 0

Interfacing:

Beginning balance		$ 1,500
Issued	(2)	(1,300)
Ending balance		$ 200

Liner:

Beginning balance		$ 6,000
Purchased	(1)	6,000
Issued	(2)	(7,800)
Ending balance		$ 4,200

Buttons:

Beginning balance		$ 1,600
Purchased	(1)	12,000
Issued	(2)	(10,400)
Ending balance		$ 3,200

Job 428:

Beginning balance		$ 0
Current costs:		
Materials	(2)	22,400
Labor	(3)	9,450
Overhead	(5)	3,780
Ending balance		$35,630

Job 427:

Beginning balance		$ 0
Current costs:		
Materials	(2)	23,500
Labor	(3)	10,000
Overhead	(5)	4,000
Ending balance		$37,500

Job 424** $75,000

Job 425:

Beg. bal.		$58,600
Current costs:		
Materials	(2)	4,800
Labor	(3)	6,000
Overhead	(5)	2,400
Total		$71,800

Job 426:

Beg. bal.		$51,300
Current costs:		
Materials	(2)	3,600
Labor	(3)	9,000
Overhead	(5)	3,600
Total		$67,500

*Numbers in parentheses ( ) refer to transaction numbers.
**In Finished Goods at beginning of period.

other purposes. For example, for pricing purposes, the Sales Department would need to take into account the costs of marketing and selling the product and customer service, which are not considered in a product cost system. Also, this system does not provide information for decisions concerning individual operations. Although the system does track total labor hours for the plant, it does not, for example, allow a comparison of budgeted and planned cutting hours. This information may be useful in evaluating the cutting operation. Nor does the system provide the detailed information required to make special decisions such as subcontracting cutting operations rather than performing them internally. To answer these questions, Fox Brothers' accountants would have to perform a special cost study. In spite of these limitations, this system may be adequate for the purposes it was designed; and management might continue to operate the current system if the costs of improving and modifying the cost system exceed the perceived benefits.

Statement of Cost of Goods Manufactured

The income statement for a merchandising organization, which purchases products ready to sell, normally includes the following calculation of cost of goods sold:

Sales		xxxx
Less cost of goods sold:		
Beginning inventory	xxx	
Plus purchases	xxx	
Goods available	xxx	
Less ending inventory	-xxx	-xxxx
Gross profit		xxxx
Less selling and administrative expenses		-xxxx
Net income		xxxx

Manufacturing organizations modify only one line of this income statement format, changing "Purchases" to "Cost of goods manufactured." A manufacturer acquires finished goods from the factory; hence, its cost of finished goods completed during the period is the total cost transferred from Work-in-Process to Finished Goods during the period.

For internal reporting purposes, most companies prepare a separate **statement of cost of goods manufactured**, which summarizes the cost of goods completed and transferred into finished goods inventory during the period. A cost of goods manufactured statement and an income statement for Fox Brothers, Inc., are presented in Exhibit 10-10 for August 19X7.

Overapplied and Underapplied Overhead

Assume that in the Fox Brothers' example the predetermined manufacturing overhead rate of $4 per direct labor hour was based on predicted manufacturing overhead for the year of $100,000 and predicted direct labor hours of 25,000. Assume further that at year-end it was determined that the company actually incurred $100,000 in manufacturing overhead during the year and that actual direct labor hours for the year were 25,000. Summary entries (1) to record actual overhead and (2) to apply overhead to Work-in-Process for the year are as follows:

EXHIBIT 10-10: STATEMENT OF COST OF GOODS MANUFACTURED AND INCOME STATEMENT FOR FOX BROTHERS, INC.

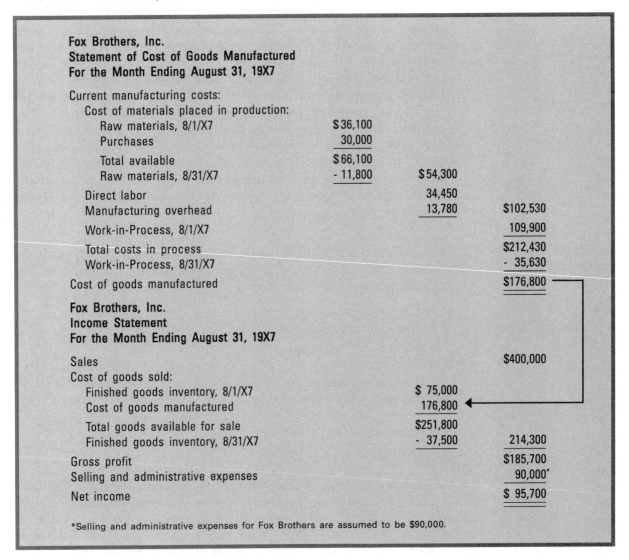

Fox Brothers, Inc.
Statement of Cost of Goods Manufactured
For the Month Ending August 31, 19X7

Current manufacturing costs:			
Cost of materials placed in production:			
Raw materials, 8/1/X7	$36,100		
Purchases	30,000		
Total available	$66,100		
Raw materials, 8/31/X7	- 11,800	$54,300	
Direct labor		34,450	
Manufacturing overhead		13,780	$102,530
Work-in-Process, 8/1/X7			109,900
Total costs in process			$212,430
Work-in-Process, 8/31/X7			- 35,630
Cost of goods manufactured			$176,800

Fox Brothers, Inc.
Income Statement
For the Month Ending August 31, 19X7

Sales			$400,000
Cost of goods sold:			
Finished goods inventory, 8/1/X7		$ 75,000	
Cost of goods manufactured		176,800	
Total goods available for sale		$251,800	
Finished goods inventory, 8/31/X7		- 37,500	214,300
Gross profit			$185,700
Selling and administrative expenses			90,000*
Net income			$ 95,700

*Selling and administrative expenses for Fox Brothers are assumed to be $90,000.

JOURNAL ENTRIES			
(1) Manufacturing Overhead		100,000	
Various balance sheet accounts			100,000
(2) Work-in-Process		100,000	
Manufacturing Overhead			100,000

Because the actual cost recorded equals the applied cost, there is no balance in Manufacturing Overhead at the end of the year. However, if either the actual overhead cost or the actual level of the production activity base differed from its predicted value, there would have been a balance in Manufacturing Overhead, representing overapplied or underapplied overhead.

Now assume that the prediction of 25,000 direct labor hours was correct but that actual overhead cost was $105,000. In this case, Manufacturing Overhead shows a $5,000 debit balance representing underapplied manufacturing overhead:

Manufacturing Overhead	
Actual 105,000	100,000 Applied
Underapplied factory overhead 5,000	

If actual manufacturing overhead were only $98,000, Manufacturing Overhead would be overapplied and show a $2,000 credit balance:

Manufacturing Overhead	
Actual 98,000	100,000 Applied
	2,000 Overapplied manufacturing overhead

It is apparent that if the *prediction* of total manufacturing overhead cost is not accurate, there will be an underapplied or overapplied balance in Manufacturing Overhead at the end of the year. A similar result occurs when the actual production activity level is different from the predicted activity level used in computing the predetermined rate. Any balances in Manufacturing Overhead during the year representing overapplied or underapplied overhead are usually allowed to accumulate from month to month. In the absence of evidence to the contrary, it is assumed that differences during the year result from variations in production or in seasonal cost differences or in both. Any balance in Manufacturing Overhead at the end of the year is usually disposed of by one of the two methods discussed below.

Disposition of Manufacturing Overhead Balances

To illustrate the disposition of a Manufacturing Overhead balance at the end of the accounting period, assume the following year-end account balances (all debits) for a manufacturing company:

Work-in-Process	$300,000
Finished Goods Inventory	200,000
Cost of Goods Sold	500,000
Manufacturing Overhead (underapplied)	8,000

A common method for disposing of the $8,000 debit balance in Manufacturing Overhead at the end of the period is merely to write it off to Cost of Goods Sold by the following journal entry:

JOURNAL ENTRY	Cost of Goods Sold	8,000	
	Manufacturing Overhead		8,000

The effect of this entry is to close out the Manufacturing Overhead account and to charge the underapplied balance to Cost of Goods Sold, thus increasing total expenses on the income statement and reducing net income. If Manufacturing Overhead has a credit balance, representing overapplied overhead, Manufacturing Overhead would be debited, and Cost of Goods Sold would be credited, reducing total expenses and increasing net income.

Another method of disposing of an end-of-period balance in Manufacturing Overhead is to allocate it among Work-in-Process, Finished Goods Inventory, and Cost of Goods Sold. This allocation is frequently made on the basis of the relative total cost in each account at the end of the period. The following computations show how the $8,000 would be disposed of under the allocation method:

	Account Balance	Relative Portion of Total		Underapplied Factory Overhead		Allocation
Work-in-Process	$ 300,000	0.30	×	$8,000	=	$2,400
Finished Goods Inventory	200,000	0.20	×	8,000	=	1,600
Cost of Goods Sold	500,000	0.50	×	8,000	=	4,000
Total	$1,000,000	1.00				$8,000

The entry to record the assignment of the Manufacturing Overhead balance to Work-in-Process, Finished Goods Inventory, and Cost of Goods Sold is shown in the following journal entry:

JOURNAL ENTRY	Work-in-Process	2,400	
	Finished Goods Inventory	1,600	
	Cost of Goods Sold	4,000	
	Manufacturing Overhead		8,000

The rationale for writing over- or underapplied overhead off to Cost of Goods Sold is that it is convenient and simple. If the predicted amounts used in calculating the predetermined rate are relatively accurate, the underapplied or overapplied amount should be relatively small, thereby justifying the use of the most convenient method. Also, if inventory balances are small, the costs assigned to Work-in-Process and Finished Goods Inventory would be insignificant in any case.

The allocation method, however, is more desirable if the over- or underapplied Manufacturing Overhead balance is relatively large and the organization has large balances in Work-in-Process and Finished Goods Inventory. An overapplied or underapplied balance in Manufacturing Overhead is always caused by the use of a predetermined overhead rate that differs from the actual overhead rate. If we waited until the end of the period to apply overhead, an accurate overhead rate based on actual cost could be used. Therefore, it is logical to allocate the ending balance in Manufacturing Overhead to the accounts affected by the inaccurate predetermined rate; that is, to Work-in-Process, Finished Goods Inventory, and Cost of Goods Sold. After the allocation, the balance in each account should be approximately the same as it would have been had an actual rate been used.

JOB COSTING FOR SERVICES

L O 6

Service costing, the assignment of costs to services, makes extensive use of job costing concepts to determine the cost of filling customer service orders in organizations such as automobile repair shops, charter airlines, CPA firms, hospitals, and law firms. Many of these organizations bill clients on the basis of resources consumed. Consequently, they maintain detailed job records for billing purposes. On the invoice sent to the client, the organization will itemize any materials consumed on the job at a selling price per unit, the labor hours worked on the job at a billing rate per hour, and the time special facilities were used at a billing rate per unit of time. Employees with different capabilities and experience often have different billing rates. In a CPA firm, for example, a partner or a senior manager has a higher billing rate than a staff accountant.

The prices and rates must be high enough to cover costs not assigned to specific jobs and, in for-profit organizations, to provide for a profit. To evaluate the contribution to common costs and profit from a job, a comparison must be made between the price charged the customer and the actual cost of the job. This is easily done when the actual cost of resources itemized on the customer's invoice is presented on a job-cost sheet. A CPA firm, for example, should accumulate the actual hardware and software costs of an accounting system installed for a client, along with the actual wages earned by employees while working on the job and any related travel costs. Comparing the total of these costs with the price charged the client indicates the total contribution of the job to common costs and profit.

Although service organizations may identify costs with individual jobs for management accounting purposes, there is considerable variation in the way job-cost information is presented in financial statements. Some organizations report the cost of jobs completed in their income statements using an account such as Cost of Services Provided. Accomplishing this requires accounting procedures similar to those outlined in Exhibits 10-6 and 10-7. The only major change involves replacing "Cost of Goods Sold" with "Cost of Services Provided."

More often, however, service organizations do not formally establish detailed financial accounting procedures to trace the flow of service costs. Instead, service job costs are left in their original cost categories such as materials expense, salaries and wages expense, travel expense, and so forth.

Because all service costs are typically regarded as period rather than product costs, either procedure is acceptable for financial reporting.

Regardless of the formal treatment of service costs in financial accounting records and statements, the managers of a well-run service organization have a need for information regarding job cost and contribution. Management Accounting Practice 10-5 illustrates how one hospital used product cost information to improve managerial decisions.

The above examples of service costing all involve situations where the order is filled in response to a specific customer request. Job costing can also be used to determine the cost of making services available even when the names of specific customers are not known in advance and the service is being provided on a speculative basis. A regularly scheduled airline flight, for example, could be regarded as a job. Management is interested in knowing the cost of the job in order to determine its profitability. This is but another example of the versatility of job costing.

SUMMARY

Product costing involves determining the cost assignable to goods and/or services as they flow through the production process. Product costing may be necessary for a variety of reasons such as pricing, cost control, performance evaluation, etc. However, for a firm that produces inventoriable products, a primary purpose of the product costing system is to assign

MANAGEMENT ACCOUNTING PRACTICE 10-5

Thomas Jefferson University Hospital Uses Cost Accounting System to Evaluate Financial Impact of New Treatments

Thomas Jefferson University Hospital (TJUH) uses its "costing" system to determine the relative costs of different treatments for a given illness. In effect, the system is a job-cost system with each patient being a separate job. One objective of the system is to evaluate the financial impact of new treatments simultaneously with evaluating the clinical impact of those new treatments. For example, TJUH used the system to evaluate the cost of using a new pharmaceutical product, Zofran, developed to prevent severe episodes of nausea and vomiting associated with cancer chemotherapy treatments. Chemotherapy patients were divided into three different groups (job-cost categories) for the study: those who received Zofran therapy, those who received traditional antiemetic therapy, and those who received both.

The results showed that even though Zofran was a more expensive drug, it did not cost more to use Zofran because patients using it had shorter hospital stays. As health care cost containment pressures increase, the need for this type of cost analysis will become more critical; and good cost accounting systems can help hospitals produce more reliable cost data for these studies.

Based on: Carly E. Carpenter, Linda C. Weitzel, Nelda E. Johnson, and David B. Nash, "Cost Accounting Supports Clinical Evaluations," *Healthcare Financial Management* (April 1994), pp. 40-45.

costs in the financial statements to inventories on hand at the end of the period and to inventories sold during the period. Cost information generated by the product costing system *may* be useful for other purposes, so long as the user of the information understands clearly the underlying assumptions on which the costs were developed and is able to make any necessary modifications to suit the purpose for which the cost data are being used.

A cost framework differentiates costs into product or period costs. Product costs are related to producing a product or service; whereas, period costs are related to nonmanufacturing activities such as selling and general administration. In the financial statements, product costs are carried as an asset until the product is sold, but period costs are deducted as an expense as they are incurred.

The two most widely used product costing methods are job costing and process costing. Process costing is used primarily in situations where a continuous process produces homogeneous products such as petroleum or newsprint paper. Job costing, or some variation of it, is used in all other production situations. Job costing is particularly useful where a company produces a variety of products in discrete batches, as illustrated for the production of garments. It is also well suited where each job is a single, unique product such as in constructing commercial buildings or oceanliners.

In both job and process costing, the primary objective is to identify all product costs—direct materials, direct labor, and overhead—and to assign them systematically and equitably to the jobs or to the process departments. Once product costs are assigned to the job or department, they follow the physical inventory through Work-in-Process, Finished Goods Inventory, and, finally, into Cost of Goods Sold.

Although most product costing applications involve physical products, in recent years many applications of product costing, job and process, have been developed for organizations that produce services rather than inventoriable products. In these situations, the primary purpose is to provide information useful to managers as opposed to aiding financial reporting. The major issues in designing the cost system in a service environment still relate to identifying direct costs (primarily labor) and determining how to assign overhead costs to the units of service. The key to developing a good cost system is understanding the particular production environment and tailoring the system to reflect the characteristics of that environment and to meet the needs of its managers.

SUGGESTED READINGS

Banker, Rajiv D., and John S. Hughes. "Product Costing and Pricing," *Management Accounting* (July 1994), pp. 479-494.

Bennett, Robert E., James A. Hendricks, David E. Keys, and Edward J. Rudnicki. *Cost Accounting for Factory Automation* (Montvale, NJ: National Association of Accountants, 1987).

Cooper, Robin, and Robert S. Kaplan. "How Cost Accounting Distorts Product Cost," *Management Accounting* (April 1988), pp. 20-27.

Martinson, Otto B. *Cost Accounting in the Service Industry* (Montvale, NJ: Institute of Management Accountants, 1994).

REVIEW PROBLEM

Job-Cost System: Journal Entries and Statement of Cost of Goods Manufactured
Tri-Star Printing Company prints sales fliers for retail and mail-order companies. Production costs are accounted for using a job-cost system. At the beginning of June 19X5, raw materials inventories totaled $7,000, manufacturing supplies amounted to $800, two jobs were in process—Job 225 with assigned costs of $13,750 and Job 226 with assigned costs of $1,800—and there were no finished goods inventories. The following information summarized June manufacturing activities:

- Raw materials costing $40,000 were purchased on account.
- Manufacturing supplies costing $9,000 were purchased on account.
- Requisitioned materials needed to complete Job 226. Started two new jobs, 227 and 228, and requisitioned direct materials for them as follows:

Direct materials:	
Job 226	$ 2,600
Job 227	18,000
Job 228	14,400
Total	$35,000

- June salaries and wages were as follows:

Direct labor:	
Job 225 - 500 hours × $10 per hour	$ 5,000
Job 226 - 1,500 hours × $10 per hour	15,000
Job 227 - 2,050 hours × $10 per hour	20,500
Job 228 - 800 hours × $10 per hour	8,000
Total direct labor	$48,500
Indirect labor	5,000
Total	$53,500

- Used manufacturing supplies costing $5,500.
- Depreciation on factory fixed assets totaled $5,000.
- Miscellaneous factory overhead cost of $8,750 was incurred on account.
- Factory overhead was applied at the rate of $5 per direct labor hour.
- Jobs 225, 226, and 227 were completed.
- Jobs 225 and 226 were delivered to customers.

Required:

(a) Prepare summary journal entries to record June 19X5 manufacturing activities. Number journal entries.

(*Hint*: Prepare cost sheets for completed jobs.)

(b) Prepare T-accounts for all inventory accounts (except manufacturing supplies) and Cost of Goods Sold. Record all beginning balances, post June transactions, and determine ending balances in these accounts.

(c) Show the job-cost details to support the June 30, 19X5, balance in Work-in-Process.

(d) Prepare a statement of cost of goods manufactured for June 19X5.

The solution to the review problem is found at the end of Chapter 10 assignment material. To maximize your learning, you should make a serious attempt to develop a written solution to the review problem before looking at the solution. If there are errors in your solution, you should then attempt to determine the causes of the errors.

KEY TERMS

Absorption cost—a method of inventory accounting that assigns all manufacturing costs, both variable and fixed, to inventory.

Automatic identification systems (AIS)—the use of bar coding of products and production processes that allows inventory and production information to be entered into a computer without writing or keying.

Bill of materials—a document that specifies the kinds and quantities of raw materials required to produce one unit of product.

Computer-aided design (CAD)—a concept that involves the use of computers to design products.

Computer-aided manufacturing (CAM)—a concept that involves the use of computers to control the operation of machines.

Computer-integrated manufacturing (CIM)—the ultimate extension of the CAD, CAM, and FMS concepts to a completely automated and computer-controlled factory where production is automatic once a product is designed and the decision to produce is made.

Conversion cost—the combined costs of direct labor and manufacturing overhead incurred to convert raw materials into finished goods.

Direct labor—wages earned by production employees for the time they actually spend working on a product.

Direct materials—the costs of primary raw materials converted into finished goods.

File—a collection of related records.

Financial reporting—the process of preparing financial statements (income statement, balance sheet, and statement of cash flows) for the firm in accordance with generally accepted accounting principles.

Finished goods inventories—the completed manufactured products held for sale to customers.

Flexible manufacturing systems (FMS)—an extension of computer-aided manufacturing techniques through a series of manufacturing operations, including the automatic movement of units between operations and the automatic and rapid setup of machines to produce each product.

Full absorption cost—see **absorption cost**.

Job-cost sheet—a document used to accumulate the costs for specific jobs in a job-cost system.

Job-order production—a production environment where products are produced in single units or in batches of identical units.

Job production—see **job-order production**.

Manufacturing organizations—organizations that process raw materials into finished products for sale to others.

Manufacturing overhead—all manufacturing costs other than direct materials and direct labor.

Materials requisition form—a document used to record the type and quantity of each raw material issued to the factory.

Merchandising organizations—organizations that buy and sell goods without performing manufacturing operations.

Operations list—a document that specifies the manufacturing operations and related times required to produce one unit or batch of product.

Period costs—expired nonproduct costs; they are recognized as expenses when incurred.

Predetermined manufacturing overhead rate—an overhead rate established at the start of each year by dividing the predicted overhead costs for the year by the predicted volume of activity in the overhead base for the year.

Process production—a manufacturing environment where a single product is produced on a continuous basis.

Product costs—costs that are assigned to products as they are produced that are carried in the accounts as an asset (inventory) until the product is sold, at which time they are recognized as an expense (cost of goods sold).

Production order—a document that assigns a unique identification number to a job and specifies such details as the quantity to be produced in the job, the total raw materials requirements of the job, the manufacturing operations to be performed on the job, and perhaps even the time when each manufacturing operation should be performed.

Raw materials inventories—the physical ingredients and components that will be converted by machines and/or human labor into a finished product.

Record—a related set of alphabetic and/or numeric data items.

Service costing—the process of assigning costs to services performed.

Service organizations—nonmanufacturing organizations that perform work for others, including banks, hospitals, and real estate agencies.

Statement of cost of goods manufactured—a report that summarizes the cost of goods completed and transferred into finished goods inventory during the period.

Work-in-process inventories—partially completed goods consisting of raw materials that are in process of being converted into a finished product.

Work ticket—a document used to record the time a job spends in a specific manufacturing operation.

REVIEW QUESTIONS

10-1

Distinguish among service, merchandising, and manufacturing organizations on the basis of the importance and complexity of inventory cost measurement.

10-2

Distinguish between product costing and service costing.

10-3

When is depreciation a product cost? When is depreciation a period cost?

10-4

What are the three major product cost elements?

10-5

What are the characteristics of a good basis of overhead application?

10-6

How are predetermined overhead rates developed? Why are they widely used? *at start of year. (estimate)*

10-7

Briefly distinguish between process and job production. Provide examples of products typically produced under each system.

10-8

Briefly describe the role of engineering and production scheduling personnel in the production planning process.

10-9

Identify the primary records involved in the operation of a job-cost system.

10-10

Describe the flow of costs through the accounting system of a labor-intensive manufacturing organization.

10-11

Briefly describe two methods of disposing of underapplied or overapplied manufacturing overhead.

10-12

Identify two reasons why a service organization should maintain detailed job-cost information.

EXERCISES

10-1 Classification of Product and Period Costs

Required:

Classify the following costs incurred by an automobile manufacturer as product costs or periods costs. Further classify the product costs as direct materials or conversion.

(a) Salaries of legal staff
(b) Automobile window glass
(c) Depreciation on word processor in president's office
(d) Plant fire department
(e) Automobile tires
(f) Automobile bumpers
(g) Wages paid assembly line maintenance workers
(h) Salary of corporate controller
(i) Automobile engines
(j) Subsidy of plant cafeteria
(k) Wages paid assembly line production workers
(l) National sales meeting in Detroit
(m) Overtime premium paid assembly line workers
(n) Advertising on national television
(o) Depreciation on assembly line

10-2 Analyzing Activity in Inventory Accounts

Selected data concerning the past fiscal year's operations of the Hull Manufacturing Company are presented below:

Raw materials used	$290,000
Total manufacturing costs charged to production during the year (includes raw materials, direct labor, and manufacturing overhead applied at a rate of 60 percent of direct labor costs)	686,000
Cost of goods available for sale	826,000
Selling and general expenses	25,000

	Inventories	
	Beginning	**Ending**
Raw materials	$70,000	$ 80,000
Work-in-process	80,000	30,000
Finished goods	90,000	110,000

Required:

Determine each of the following:

(a) Cost of raw materials purchased
(b) Direct labor costs charged to production
(c) Cost of goods manufactured
(d) Cost of goods sold

10-3 Statements: Cost of Goods Manufactured, Income

Information from the records of the Alexandria Manufacturing Company is given below for August 19X4:

Sales	$205,000
Selling and administrative expenses	83,000
Purchases of raw materials	20,000
Direct labor	15,000
Manufacturing overhead	32,000

	Inventories	
	August 1	**August 31**
Raw materials	$ 7,000	$ 5,000
Work-in-process	14,000	11,000
Finished goods	15,000	19,000

Required:

Prepare a statement of cost of goods manufactured and an income statement for August.

10-4 Statement of Cost of Goods Manufactured from Percent Relationships

Information about the Portion Company for the year ending December 31, 19X1, is given below:

- Sales equal $400,000.
- Direct materials total $64,000.
- Manufacturing overhead is 150 percent of direct labor.
- The beginning inventory of finished goods is 20 percent of the cost of goods sold.
- The ending inventory of finished goods is twice the beginning inventory.
- The gross profit is 20 percent of sales.
- There is no beginning or ending work-in-process.

Required:

Prepare a statement of cost of goods manufactured for 19X1. *(Hint:* Prepare an analysis of changes in Finished Goods Inventory.)

10-5 Income Statement and Statement of Cost of Goods Manufactured from Percent Relationships

Information about the Lots-O-Luck Company for the year ending December 31, 19X1, is as follows:

Sales	$350,000
Net income	5,000
Ending inventories:	
Raw materials	18,000
Work-in-process	8,000
Finished goods	67,000

- Inventory changes:
  - Ending raw materials are twice beginning raw materials.
  - Ending work-in-process is one-third larger than beginning work-in-process.
  - Finished goods inventory increased by $15,000 during the year.
- Selling and administrative expenses are 5 times net income.
- Prime costs are 60 percent of manufacturing costs.
- Conversion costs are 80 percent of manufacturing costs.

Required:

Prepare an income statement and a statement of cost of goods manufactured for 19X1. *(Hint:* Set up the statement formats and start the solution from known information.)

10-6 Developing and Using a Predetermined Overhead Rate

The following predictions were made for 19X2:

Total manufacturing overhead for the year	$380,000
Total machine hours for the year	20,000

Actual results for February 19X2 were as follows:

Manufacturing overhead	$ 55,200
Machine hours	3,100

Required:

(a) Determine the 19X2 predetermined overhead rate per machine hour.
(b) Using the predetermined overhead rate per machine hour, determine the manufacturing overhead applied to Work-in-Process during February.
(c) As of February 1, actual overhead was underapplied by $4,000. Determine the cumulative amount of any overapplied or underapplied overhead at the end of February.

10-7 Developing and Using a Predetermined Overhead Rate: High-Low Cost Estimation

The Wesley Company used an actual plant-wide overhead rate and based its prices on cost, plus a markup of 25 percent. Recently the marketing manager, Gardner James, and the production manager, Alice Smith, confronted the controller with a common problem.

The marketing manager expressed a concern that Wesley's prices seem to vary widely throughout the year. According to Mr. James, "It seems irrational to charge higher prices when business is bad and lower prices when business is good. While we get a lot of business during high volume months because we charge less than our competitors, it is a waste of time to even call on customers during low volume months because we are raising prices while our competitors are lowering them."

Ms. Smith also believed that it was "folly to be so pushed that we have to pay overtime in some months and then lay employees off in others." She commented, "While there are natural variations in customer demand, the accounting system seems to amplify this variation."

Required:

(a) Evaluate the arguments presented by James and Smith. What suggestions do you have for improving the accounting and pricing procedures?

(b) Assume the Wesley Company has the following total manufacturing overhead costs and direct labor hours in 19X1 and 19X2:

	19X1	19X2
Total manufacturing overhead	$200,000	$237,500
Direct labor hours	20,000	27,500

Use the high-low method to develop a cost estimating equation for total manufacturing overhead.

(c) Develop a predetermined rate for 19X4, assuming 25,000 direct labor hours are budgeted for 19X4.

(d) Assume that the actual level of activity in 19X4 amounted to 30,000 direct labor hours and that the total 19X4 manufacturing overhead was $240,000. Determine the underapplied or overapplied manufacturing overhead at the end of 19X4.

(e) Describe two ways of handling any underapplied or overapplied manufacturing overhead at the end of the year.

10-8 Under- and Overapplied Manufacturing Overhead

Presented are selected account balances of the Mouser Company at the end of 19X4:

Work-in-Process	$ 55,000 debit
Finished Goods Inventory	75,000 debit
Cost of Goods Sold	370,000 debit
Manufacturing Overhead	32,000 credit

Required:

(a) Does Mouser Company use a predetermined overhead rate, or does it assign actual overhead to Work-in-Process? Explain.

(b) Were manufacturing overhead costs underapplied or overapplied in 19X4? Explain.

(c) Prepare the journal entry to dispose of the Manufacturing Overhead balance, assuming it is written off to Cost of Goods Sold.

(d) Prepare the journal entry to dispose of the Manufacturing Overhead balance, assuming it is allocated to Work-in-Process, Finished Goods Inventory, and Cost of Goods Sold.

(e) Which method of disposing of underapplied or overapplied manufacturing overhead is more accurate? Explain.

10-9 Under- and Overapplied Manufacturing Overhead

The management of the Norcross Company decided to use a predetermined rate to assign manufacturing overhead. The following predictions were made for 19X4:

Manufacturing overhead costs	$270,000
Direct labor hours	30,000 hours
Direct labor costs	$300,000
Machine hours	45,000 hours

Required:

(a) Compute the predetermined manufacturing overhead rate under three different bases:
   (1) Direct labor hours
   (2) Direct labor dollars
   (3) Machine hours

(b) Assume actual manufacturing overhead was $268,000 and that management elected to apply manufacturing overhead to Work-in-Process on direct labor hours. If 32,000 direct labor hours were used in 19X4, determine the amount manufacturing overhead was underapplied or overapplied.

(c) The Norcross Company follows a policy of writing off any underapplied or overapplied Manufacturing Overhead to Cost of Goods Sold at the end of the year. Make the entry necessary at the end of 19X4 to dispose of the balance determined in requirement (b).

(d) Describe an alternative procedure that might be used to dispose of underapplied or overapplied manufacturing overhead.

10-10 Manufacturing Cost Flows with Machine Hours Allocation: Journal Entries

Fork Manufacturing Company's November 1, 19X6, Work-in-Process balance was $5,000. During November, Fork Manufacturing completed the following manufacturing transactions:

- Purchased raw materials costing $60,000 and manufacturing supplies costing $3,000 on account.

- Requisitioned raw materials costing $40,000 to the factory.
- Incurred direct labor costs of $27,000 and indirect labor costs of $4,800.
- Used manufacturing supplies costing $3,000.
- Recorded manufacturing depreciation of $15,000.
- Miscellaneous payables for manufacturing overhead totaled $3,600.
- Applied manufacturing overhead at a predetermined rate of $10 per machine hour with 2,250 machine hours.
- Completed jobs costing $85,000.
- Finished goods costing $96,000 were sold.

Required:

(a) Prepare summary journal entries to record November 19X6 manufacturing activities. Number all journal entries.
(b) Prepare a T-account for Work-in-Process, record the beginning balance, post all transactions, and determine the November 30, 19X2, balance.

10-11 Manufacturing Cost Flows with Labor Hours Allocation: Journal Entries

Malone Manufacturing Company's June 1, 19X2, Work-in-Process balance was $4,000. During June, Malone Manufacturing completed the following manufacturing transactions:

- Purchased raw materials costing $24,000 and manufacturing supplies costing $2,000 on account.
- Requisitioned raw materials costing $28,000 to the factory.
- Manufacturing payroll for the month consists of 2,200 hours of direct labor and 400 hours of indirect labor, both at $11 per hour.
- Used manufacturing supplies costing $800.
- Recorded manufacturing depreciation of $12,000.
- Miscellaneous payables for manufacturing overhead totaled $2,800.
- Applied manufacturing overhead at a predetermined rate of $8 per direct labor hour.
- Completed jobs costing $72,000.
- Finished goods costing $81,500 were sold.

Required:

(a) Prepare summary journal entries to record June 19X2 manufacturing activities. Number all journal entries.
(b) Prepare a T-account for Work-in-Process, record the beginning balance, post all transactions, and determine the June 30, 19X2, balance.

10-12 Service Cost Flows: Journal Entries

Video Marketing, Ltd., produces television advertisements for businesses marketing products in the western provinces of Canada. To achieve cost control, Video Marketing uses a job-cost system similar to that found in a manufacturing organization. Some different account titles are used:

Account	Replaces
Videos-in-Process	Work-in-Process
Production Supplies Inventory	Manufacturing Supplies Inventory
Cost of Videos Completed	Cost of Goods Sold
Studio Overhead	Manufacturing Overhead

Video Marketing does not maintain Raw Materials or Finished Goods Inventory accounts. Materials, such as props needed for videos, are purchased as needed from outside sources and charged directly to Videos-in-Process and the appropriate job when received. Videos are delivered directly to clients upon completion. The October 1, 19X2, Videos-in-Process balance was $1,000. During October, Video Marketing completed the following production transactions:

- Purchased production supplies costing $1,500 on account.
- Purchased materials chargeable to specific jobs costing $27,000 on account.
- Incurred direct labor costs of $65,000 and indirect labor costs of $32,000.
- Used production supplies costing $850.
- Recorded studio depreciation of $3,000.
- Miscellaneous payables for studio overhead totaled $1,800.
- Applied studio overhead at a predetermined rate of $9.50 per studio hour, with 480 studio hours.
- Completed jobs costing $97,000 and delivered them directly to clients.

Required:

(a) Prepare summary journal entries to record October production activities. Number all journal entries.
(b) Prepare a T-account for Videos-in-Process, record the beginning balance, post all transactions, and determine the October 31, 19X2, balance.

10-13 Manufacturing T-Accounts: Missing Data

Presented are partially completed manufacturing T-accounts:

Raw Materials			
6/1/X5	7,000	DM? (3)	
(1)	P?		
6/30/X5	12,000		

Work-in-Process			
6/1/X5	BWIP?	CGM? (7)	
(3)	DM?		
(4)	DL?		
(6)	75,000		
6/30/X5	24,000		

Finished Goods Inventory			
(7)	CGM?	110,000	(8)
6/30/X5	20,000		

Cost of Goods Sold	
(8) 110,000	

Additional information:

- Ending Work-in-Process is three times as large as the beginning Work-in-Process.
- Manufacturing overhead is applied at 150 percent of direct materials.

Required:

Determine each of the following amounts:

(a) Purchases (P)
(b) Direct materials (DM)
(c) Beginning Work-in-Process (BWIP)
(d) Direct labor (DL)
(e) Cost of goods manufactured (CGM)

10-14 Construction T-Accounts: Missing Data

Presented are partially completed T-accounts of a construction company:

Raw Materials				Contracts-in-Process		
2/1/X8	4,000	DM? (3)		2/1/X8	12,000	CCC? (7)
(1)	80,000			(3)	DM?	
2/28/X8	9,000			(4)	DL?	
				(6)	ACOH?	
				2/28/X8	ECIP?	

Cost of Completed Contracts		
(7)	CCC?	

Additional information:

- Ending Contracts-in-Process is half as large as the beginning Contracts-in-Process.
- Conversion costs amount to two-thirds of the total current construction costs.
- Construction overhead is applied at 50 percent of direct labor dollars.

Required:

Determine each of the following amounts:

(a) Direct materials (DM)
(b) Direct labor (DL)
(c) Applied construction overhead (ACOH)
(d) Ending contracts-in-process (ECIP)
(e) Cost of completed contracts (CCC)

10-15 Analyzing a Job-Cost Sheet of a Service Company

Accounting Software Solutions assigns all direct costs to jobs. When jobs are completed, their costs are transferred from Work-in-Process to Cost of Completed Service Contracts. The following information pertains to Job 385, completed on December 31, 19X1.

Job No. *385*
Description *Install accounting software package*
Raw materials costs

Date	Description	Units	Cost
11/20/X1	Oak Tree Accounting Complete	1	$1,200

Direct labor costs

Date	Description	Units	Cost
11/15/X1	Needs assessment (manager)	16 hours	800
11/30/X1	Installation (staff)	24 hours	840
12/15/X1	Training (staff)	16 hours	560
12/31/X1	Review and acceptance (partner)	4 hours	400

Other direct costs

Date	Description	Cost
11/12/X1	Travel expense reimbursement #x1-1107	126
11/27/X1	Travel expense reimbursement #x1-1123	250
12/13/X1	Travel expense reimbursement #x1-1213	130
12/29/X1	Travel expense reimbursement #x1-1227	65
Total cost of job		$4,371

Additional information:

- The company maintains an inventory of accounting software and assigns software to jobs at cost.
- Travel expense reimbursements for such items as mileage, food, and lodging are paid directly to employees upon receipt of a completed expense form.
- Employees are paid twice a month.
- Transactions are journalized on the date indicated on the related job-cost sheet.

Required:

(a) Prepare chronological journal entries, with a date column, to record the costs assigned to Job 385. Also prepare the journal entry to record the completion of the job.
(b) Prepare chronological journal entries, with a date column, for Job 385, assuming management elected to expense job costs as incurred rather than to assign them to specific jobs.
(c) Why might a service company assign costs to jobs for internal purposes even if it immediately expenses job costs for financial reporting?

10-16 Analyzing the Job-Cost Sheet of a Machine-Intensive Manufacturing Company

The following information is taken from the records of the Flexible Machine Shop for Job 1432, completed on February 27, 19X9.

Job No. *1432*

Description *Complete 100 motor housings*

Raw materials costs

Date	Description	Units	Cost
2/25/X9	Medium gauge sheet metal	200 sq. ft.	$ 420

Conversion costs

Date	Description	Units	Cost
2/26/X9	Cutting	0.5 hours	200
2/26/X9	Welding	2.0 hours	600
2/27/X9	Tempering	3.0 hours	450

Applied overhead

Date	Description	Units	Cost
2/26/X9	Plant-wide overhead, cutting	0.5 hours	25
2/26/X9	Plant-wide overhead, welding	2.0 hours	100
2/27/X9	Plant-wide overhead, tempering	3.0 hours	150

Total cost of job $1,945

Additional information:

- All materials are added in the cutting operation.
- The company maintains separate Work-in-Process and Conversion Cost accounts for each operation.
- Common, plant-wide overhead costs are accumulated in a separate Plant Manufacturing Overhead account and assigned on the basis of work hours as jobs are worked on in each operation.
- Transactions are journalized on the date indicated on the related job-cost sheet.

Required:

(a) Prepare chronological journal entries, with a date column, to record the costs assigned to Job 1432, the transfer of Job 1432 between operations, and the completion of the job.

(b) Prepare a set of chronological journal entries, with a date column, for Job 1432 and the completion of the job, assuming the company does not maintain separate Work-in-Process and Conversion Cost accounts for each operation.

(c) Why might a company producing a homogeneous product line desire to accumulate conversion costs for each major operation rather than simply accumulating and assigning them on a plant-wide basis?

PROBLEMS

10-17 Statements: Cost of Goods Manufactured, Income

Presented below is information from the records of the Saskatchewan River Production Company for July 19X3.

Purchases:	
Raw materials	$ 70,000
Manufacturing supplies	3,500
Office supplies	1,200
Sales	425,700
Administrative salaries	12,000
Direct labor	117,500
Production employees' fringe benefits	4,000*
Sales commissions	50,000
Production supervisors' salaries	7,200
Depreciation on plant	14,000
Depreciation on office	20,000
Plant maintenance	10,000
Plant utilities	35,000
Office utilities	8,000
Office maintenance	2,000
Production equipment rent	6,000
Office equipment rent	1,300

	Inventories	
	July 1	July 31
Raw materials	$17,000	$15,000
Manufacturing supplies	1,500	3,000
Office supplies	600	1,000
Work-in-process	51,000	40,000
Finished goods	35,000	27,100

*Classified as manufacturing overhead

Required:

Prepare a statement of cost of goods manufactured and an income statement. Actual overhead costs are assigned to products.

10-18 Correcting Erroneous Statements: Cost of Goods Manufactured, Income

Presented are two reports prepared by the former accountant of Misclassification Manufacturing Corporation:

Misclassification Manufacturing Corporation
Statement of Cost of Goods Manufactured and Income
For the Month Ending December 31, 19X5

Sales		$200,000
Less direct materials		- 40,000
Gross profit		$160,000
Less other expenses:		
Cost of goods sold (computed below)	$89,000	
Office supplies	500	
Manufacturing utilities	2,000	
Office utilities	500	- 92,000
Net income		$ 68,000

Misclassification Manufacturing Corporation
Statement of Cost of Goods Sold
For the Month Ending December 31, 19X5

Finished goods inventory 12/1/X5			$30,000
Work-in-process 12/1/X5			6,000
Total			$36,000
Current manufacturing costs:			
Salaries and wages:			
Direct labor	$10,000		
Other manufacturing	4,000		
Sales	8,000		
Administrative	6,000	$28,000	
Other:			
Manufacturing supplies	$ 3,000		
Manufacturing depreciation	7,000		
Insurance on showroom	2,000		
Miscellaneous manufacturing			
overhead	13,000	25,000	53,000
Total work-in-process			$89,000
Work-in-process 12/31/X5			- 0
Cost of goods sold			$89,000

Additional information:

- The 12/31/X5 finished goods inventory was $4,000.
- Dividends of $10,000 were declared and paid during December.
- All amounts, except those specifically computed in the presented statements, are correct.

Required:

Prepare a statement of cost of goods manufactured and an income statement in good form.

10-19 Account Interrelationships: Missing Data
Required:

Supply the missing data in each independent case.

	Case 1	Case 2	Case 3	Case 4
Sales	$50,000	$?	$?	$?
Raw materials, beginning	10,000	13,000	?	5,300
Purchases	?	13,000	2,500	31,400
Raw materials, ending	8,000	?	500	6,200
Direct materials	?	20,000	2,000	?
Direct labor	20,000	25,000	6,000	?
Manufacturing overhead	10,000	8,000	?	29,200
Current manufacturing costs	55,000	?	12,000	?
Work-in-process, beginning	?	8,000	8,000	5,300
Work-in-process, ending	5,000	7,000	?	4,000
Cost of goods manufactured	55,000	?	19,000	82,000
Finished goods, beginning	?	6,000	1,500	8,000

(continued)

Finished goods, ending	25,000	?	500	10,000
Cost of goods sold	?	55,000	?	?
Gross profit	10,000	9,000	?	10,500
Other expenses	8,000	?	5,000	3,500
Net income (loss)	?	(4,000)	1,000	?

10-20 Statements: Cost of Goods Manufactured, Income with Predetermined Overhead and Labor Cost Classifications

Presented is information pertaining to Big Bear, Incorporated, for April 19X9.

Sales	$200,000
Purchases:	
Raw materials	35,000
Manufacturing supplies	800
Office supplies	500
Salaries (including fringe benefits):	
Administrative	6,000
Production supervisors	3,600
Sales	15,000
Depreciation:	
Plant and machinery	8,000
Office and office equipment	4,000
Utilities:	
Plant	5,250
Office	890

	Inventories	
	April 1	April 30
Raw materials	$5,000	$3,500
Manufacturing supplies	1,000	1,100
Office supplies	900	800
Work-in-process	2,000	2,300
Finished goods	8,000	9,000

Additional information:

- Manufacturing overhead is applied to products at 80 percent of direct labor dollars.
- Employee base wages are $12 per hour.
- Employee fringe benefits amount to 40 percent of the base wage rate. They are classified as manufacturing overhead.
- During April, production employees worked 5,600 hours, including 4,800 regular hours and 200 overtime hours spent working on products. There were 600 indirect labor hours.
- Employees are paid a 50 percent overtime premium. Any overtime premium is treated as manufacturing overhead.

Required:

(a) Prepare a statement of cost of goods manufactured and an income statement.

(b) Determine underapplied or overapplied overhead for April.

(c) Recompute direct labor and actual manufacturing overhead assuming employee fringe benefits for direct labor hours are classified as direct labor.

10-21 Actual and Predetermined Overhead Rates

Note: Predetermined overhead rates are used throughout the chapter. An alternative is to accumulate actual overhead costs for the period in Manufacturing Overhead and apply actual costs at the close of the period to all jobs in-process during the period.

Al's Job Shop started operations on January 1, 19X2. During the month, the following events occurred:

- Materials costing $8,000 were purchased on account.
- Direct materials costing $3,000 were placed in-process.
- A total of 400 direct labor hours was charged to individual jobs at a rate of $6 per hour.
- Overhead costs for the month of January were as follows:

Depreciation on plant and equipment	$ 500
Indirect labor	1,500
Utilities	600
Property taxes on plant	650
Insurance on plant	550

- Only one job, B42, with materials costs of $600, direct labor charges of $300 for 50 direct labor hours, and applied overhead was in process on January 31.
- The plant and equipment were purchased before operations began. The insurance was prepaid. All other costs will be paid during the following month.

Required:

(a) Assuming Al's Job Shop assigned actual monthly overhead costs to jobs on the basis of actual monthly direct labor hours, prepare summary journal entries for the month of January.

(b) Assuming Al's Job Shop uses a predetermined overhead rate of $10 per direct labor hour, prepare summary journal entries for the month of January. Describe the appropriate treatment of any overapplied or underapplied overhead for the month of January.

(c) Review the overhead items and classify each as fixed or variable in relation to direct labor hours. Next, predict the actual overhead rates for months when 200 and 1,000 direct labor hours are used. Assuming jobs similar to B42 were in process at the end of each month, determine the costs assigned to these jobs. (*Hint:* Determine a variable overhead rate.)

(d) Why do you suppose predetermined overhead rates are preferred to actual overhead rates?

10-22 Job Costing Journal Entries: Predetermined Overhead Rate

Top Drawer Office Equipment manufactures desks, chairs, file cabinets, and similar office products in batches for speculative inventories. Production costs are accounted for using a job-cost system. At the beginning of April 19X3, raw materials inventories totaled $8,500, manufacturing supplies amounted to $1,200, and two jobs were in process: Job 522 with assigned costs of $5,640 and Job 523 with assigned costs of $2,400. Finished goods inventories totaled $6,000. The following information summarizes April manufacturing activities:

- Raw materials costing $25,000 were purchased on account.
- Manufacturing supplies costing $3,000 were purchased on account.
- Requisitioned materials needed to complete Job 523. Started two new jobs, 524 and 525, and requisitioned direct materials for them.

Direct materials:	
Job 523	$ 3,400
Job 524	12,500
Job 525	9,600
Total	$ 25,500

- April salaries and wages were as follows:

Direct labor:		
Job 522	300 hours × $12/hour	$ 3,600
Job 523	800 hours × $12/hour	9,600
Job 524	1,200 hours × $12/hour	14,400
Job 525	1,000 hours × $12/hour	12,000
Total direct labor		$ 39,600
Indirect labor		6,400
Total		$ 46,000

- Used manufacturing supplies costing $2,250.
- Depreciation on factory fixed assets totaled $4,000.
- Miscellaneous manufacturing overhead costs of $5,500 were incurred on account.
- Manufacturing overhead was applied at the rate of $6 per direct labor hour.
- Jobs 522, 523, and 524 were completed.

Required:

(a) Prepare summary journal entries to record April 19X3 manufacturing activities. Number all journal entries. (*Hint:* Prepare cost sheets for completed jobs.)

(b) Prepare T-accounts for Raw Materials and Work-in-Process. Record beginning balances, post April transactions, and determine ending balances in these accounts.

(c) Show the job-cost details to support the April 30, 19X3, balance in Work-in-Process.

10-23 A Comprehensive Financial Accounting Extension to Problem 10-22

This is a continuation of Problem 10-22. Completion of this problem may require you to review material contained in your financial accounting text.

Presented is a condensed version of Top Drawer Office Equipment's April 1, 19X3, balance sheet, as well as information regarding administrative, marketing, and financial transactions for the month of April.

Top Drawer Office Equipment
Balance Sheet
As of April 1, 19X3
Assets

Cash	$ 12,880
Accounts receivable	125,000
Raw materials	8,500
Manufacturing supplies	1,200
Work-in-process	8,040
Finished goods	6,000
Manufacturing overhead (overapplied)	(500)
Office supplies	1,700
Prepaid office rent	3,600
Net plant equipment	340,000
Total	$506,420

Liabilities and stockholders' equity

Accounts payable	$ 20,000
Wages payable	21,000
Miscellaneous payables	3,000
Capital stock	400,000
Retained earnings	62,420
Total	$506,420

Additional information:

- Sold finished goods costing $69,000 on account for $120,000.
- Purchased office supplies costing $280 on account.
- Used office supplies costing $350.
- Wages earned by administrative and marketing employees were as follows:

Administrative	$3,800
Selling	8,400

- Miscellaneous expenses were as follows:

Administrative	$ 3,500
Selling	12,390

- Expired prepaid office rent for April amounted to $1,200.
- Paid accounts payable totaling $26,000.
- Paid wages payable of $61,000.

- Paid miscellaneous payables totaling $21,500.
- Collected $130,000 on account.
- Recorded profit or loss for the month in Expense and Revenue Summary and closed account to Retained Earnings.

Required:

(a) Prepare summary journal entries for all additional transactions.
(b) Prepare the following financial statements:
    (1) Statement of cost of goods manufactured for the month of April 19X3
    (2) Income statement for the month of April 19X3
    (3) Balance sheet as of April 30, 19X3

(*Hint:* Use previously determined balances for inventory accounts. Determine the effect of posting other journal entries to permanent accounts. Post net effect of all transactions affecting temporary accounts to Retained Earnings.)

10-24 Job Costing Journal Entries: Predetermined Overhead Rate

Neatlawn Mower Company manufactures a variety of gasoline-powered mowers for discount hardware and department stores. Neatlawn uses a job-cost system and treats each customer's order as a separate job.

The primary mower components (motors, chassis, and wheels) are purchased from three different suppliers under long-term contracts that call for the delivery of raw materials as needed directly to the production floor. When a customer's order is received, a raw materials purchase order is electronically placed with suppliers. The purchase order specifies the scheduled date production is to begin on the customer's order as the delivery date for motors and chassis and specifies the scheduled date production is to be completed as the delivery date for the wheels. As a consequence, there are no raw materials inventories, and raw materials are charged directly to Work-in-Process upon receipt.

Upon completion, goods are shipped directly to customers rather than transferred to finished goods inventory.

At the beginning of July 19X8, Neatlawn had the following work-in-process inventories:

Job 365	$20,000
Job 366	16,500
Job 367	15,000
Job 368	9,000
Total	$60,500

During July, the following activities took place:

- Started Jobs 369, 370, and 371.
- Ordered and received the following raw materials for specified jobs:

Job	Motors	Chassis	Wheels	Total
366	$ 0	$ 0	$ 800	$ 800
367	0	0	1,200	1,200
368	0	0	1,600	1,600
369	12,000	4,000	1,000	17,000
370	9,000	3,500	900	13,400
371	8,500	3,800	0	12,300
Total	$29,500	$11,300	$5,500	$46,300

- July manufacturing payroll is summarized below:

Direct labor:
Job 365	$ 500
Job 366	3,200
Job 367	3,400
Job 368	4,160
Job 369	1,300
Job 370	2,620
Job 371	2,000
Total	$17,180
Indirect labor	3,436
Total	$20,616

- Additional July manufacturing overhead costs were:

Manufacturing supplies purchased on account and used	$ 2,800
Depreciation on factory fixed assets	6,000
Miscellaneous payables	5,100
Total	$13,900

- Manufacturing overhead was applied using a predetermined rate based on predicted annual overhead of $180,000 and predicted annual direct labor of $200,000.
- Jobs 365 through 370 were completed and shipped.

Required:
(a) Prepare summary journal entries to record July 19X8 manufacturing activities. Number all journal entries. (*Hint:* Prepare cost sheets for completed jobs.)
(b) Prepare a T-account for Work-in-Process. Record the beginning balance, post July transactions, and determine ending balance in this account.
(c) Show the job-cost details to support the July 31, 19X8, balance in Work-in-Process.

10-25 A Comprehensive Financial Accounting Extension to Problem 10-24
This is a continuation of Problem 10-24. Completion of this problem may require you to review material contained in your financial accounting text.

Presented is a condensed version of Neatlawn Mower Company's July 1, 19X8, balance sheet, as well as information regarding administrative, marketing, and financial transactions for the month of July.

Neatlawn Mower Company
Balance Sheet
As of July 1, 19X8

Assets

Cash	$ 21,900
Accounts receivable	80,000
Work-in-process	60,500
Manufacturing overhead (underapplied)	1,200
Office supplies	950
Net plant and equipment	280,000
Net office and equipment	190,000
Total	$634,550

Liabilities and stockholders' equity

Accounts payable	$ 47,000
Wages payable	14,000
Miscellaneous payables	6,500
Capital stock	350,000
Retained earnings	217,050
Total	$634,550

- Sold Jobs 365 through 370 on account for $175,000.
- Purchased office supplies costing $300 on account.
- Used office supplies costing $290.
- Wages earned by administrative and marketing employees were as follows:

Administrative	$4,900
Selling	2,500

- Recorded depreciation of $4,000 on office and equipment.
- Miscellaneous expenses were as follows:

Administrative	$2,750
Selling	5,800

- Paid accounts payable totaling $51,000.
- Paid wages payable of $41,000.
- Paid miscellaneous payables totaling $8,000.
- Collected $190,000 on account.
- Recorded profit or loss for the month in Expense and Revenue Summary and closed account to Retained Earnings.

Required:
(a) Prepare summary journal entries for all additional transactions.
(b) Prepare the following financial statements:
   (1) Statement of cost of goods manufactured for the month of July 19X8.

(2) Income statement for the month of July 19X8.

(3) Balance sheet as of July 31, 19X8.

(*Hint*: Use previously determined balances for inventory accounts. Determine the effect of posting other journal entries to permanent accounts. Post net effect of all transactions affecting temporary accounts to Retained Earnings.)

DISCUSSION QUESTIONS AND CASES

10-26 Cost Data for Financial Reporting, Cost-Volume-Profit Analysis, and Sell or Process Further Decisions

Completion of this question may require you to review material contained in Chapters 2 and 3 of this text.

The Tall Pines Furniture Company manufactures a single product, unassembled and unpainted wooden chairs, sold through direct mail. Presented are a statement of cost of goods manufactured and an income statement for 19X2, when 8,000 units were manufactured and sold. Beginning and ending inventories were 1,000 units of finished goods.

Tall Pines Furniture Company
Statement of Cost of Goods Manufactured
For the Year Ending December 31, 19X2

Current manufacturing costs:			
Cost of materials placed in production		$120,000	
Direct labor		40,000	
Manufacturing overhead:			
Variable	$24,000		
Fixed	30,000	54,000	$214,000
Work-in-process, 1/1/X2			0
Total costs in process			$214,000
Work-in-process, 12/31/X2			- 0
Cost of goods manufactured			$214,000

Tall Pines Furniture Company
Income Statement
For the Year Ending December 31, 19X2

Sales (8,000 units × $60)		$480,000
Cost of goods sold:		
Finished goods inventory, 1/1/X2 (1,000 units × $26.75)	$ 26,750	
Cost of goods manufactured	214,000	
Total goods available for sale	$240,750	
Finished goods inventory, 12/31/X2 (1,000 units × $26.75)	- 26,750	-214,000
Gross profit		$266,000
Selling and administrative expenses:		
Variable	$ 80,000	
Fixed	40,000	-120,000
Net income		$146,000

Required:

(a) Determine Tall Pines' annual break-even point in units.

(b) Determine the annual sales volume required to obtain an annual profit of $160,000.

(c) Explain why the unit cost used in determining the break-even point and the sales volume required to achieve a desired profit differs from the unit cost of goods sold and the unit cost of the ending inventory used for financial reporting.

(d) What type of an income statement would be more useful to management in making decisions? Why?

(e) Management is contemplating assembling and painting the chairs for sale through outdoor furniture stores rather than selling the unassembled and unpainted chairs by direct mail. At an annual volume of 8,000 units, this will increase manufacturing costs by $160,000, while reducing selling and administrative costs by $20,000. Including a 40 percent markup on Tall Pines' selling price, the outdoor furniture stores will list the chairs for $112 each. Should Tall Pines finish the chairs or continue selling them unassembled and unpainted by direct mail? Why?

(f) Assuming Tall Pines finishes the chairs, for financial reporting purposes, what unit cost should it assign to any ending inventory of finished goods?

(g) Explain why the inventory value used in requirement (f) differs from the costs used in requirement (e).

10-27 Cost Data for Financial Reporting and Special Order Decision

Completion of this question may require you to review material contained in Chapters 2 and 3 of this text.

The Friendly Greeting Card Company produces a full range of greeting cards sold through drugstores and department stores. Each card is designed by independent artists. Following the design, a production master is prepared. The production master has an indefinite life. Product designs for popular cards are deemed to be valuable assets. If a card sells well, many batches of the design will be manufactured over a period of years. Hence, Friendly Greeting maintains an inventory of production masters so that cards may be reissued from time-to-time.

Cards are produced in batches that vary in sizes of 1,000 units. An average batch consists of approximately 10,000 cards. Producing a batch requires placing the production master on the printing press, setting the press for the appropriate size paper, and making other adjustments for colors and so forth.

Presented are facility, product, batch, and unit level cost information:

Product design and production master per new card	$1,500
Batch setup (typically per 10,000 cards)	150
Materials per 1,000 cards	100
Conversion per 1,000 cards	80

Shipping:	
Batch	20
Per card	0.01
Selling and administrative:	
Company-wide	200,000
Per product design marketed	500

Information from last year:

Product designs and masters prepared for new cards	90
Product designs marketed	120
Number of batches manufactured	500
Cards manufactured and sold	5,000,000

Required:

(a) Describe how you would determine the cost of goods sold and the value of any ending inventory for financial reporting purposes. No computations are required.

(b) You have just received an inquiry from Mall-Mart department stores to develop and manufacture 20 special designs for sale exclusively in Mall-Mart stores. The cards would be sold for $1.50 each, and Mall-Mart would pay Friendly Greeting $0.40 per card. The initial order is for 20,000 cards of each design. If the cards sell well, Mall-Mart plans to place additional orders for these and other designs. Because of the preestablished sales relationship, there would not be any marketing costs associated with the cards sold to Mall-Mart. How would you go about evaluating the desirability of the Mall-Mart proposal?

(c) Explain any differences between the costs considered in your answer to requirement (a) and the costs considered in your answer to requirement (b).

10-28 Continue or Discontinue: Plant-Wide Overhead with Unit and Batch Level Cost Drivers

Completion of this case may require you to review material in Chapters 2, 3, and 4 of this text.

Good Buddy Electronics is the producer of the popular "Good Buddy" citizens band (CB) radio. Although Good Buddy Electronics was one of the early producers of CB radios, in recent years, the profitability of CB radios has declined because of market saturation and foreign price competition. To fully utilize its production capacity, Good Buddy has started producing a variety of consumer electronic appliances to order. This additional business necessitated a change in the firm's accounting system.

When a single product was produced on a continuous basis, product costs were computed as current manufacturing costs divided by the number of units produced. With the expansion of activities to include products made to customer specifications, Good Buddy instituted a job-cost system. The system assigns actual direct materials costs to jobs. Because production operations make extensive use of machine assembly operations, direct labor and overhead costs are combined into a single conversion rate per machine hour.

Last year, Good Buddy produced 100,000 Good Buddy CB radios and 250 other jobs to customer order. These additional jobs averaged 200 units each. Presented is unit selling price and cost information for last year:

	Good Buddy CB Radio	Other Products
Selling price	$90.00	$125.00
Manufacturing costs:		
Direct materials	$60.00	$ 60.00
Conversion	25.20	50.40
Total	-85.20	-110.40
Gross profit	$ 4.80	$ 14.60
Selling and distribution costs	- 2.00	- 2.00
Profit	$ 2.80	$ 12.60

Godfrey (Good Buddy) Beckles, the president, is concerned about the declining profitability of CB radios in comparison with specialty products and is considering a proposal to discontinue the production of CB radios to specialize on other products. Even though other products have a relatively low volume and require additional selling and manufacturing effort, they are more profitable due to the premium prices they command.

Prior to finalizing his recommendation, Mr. Beckles has asked his bright young assistant—you—to take a final look at the situation and prepare a written report by noon tomorrow. You eagerly talk with personnel in sales, accounting, and production where you acquire the following additional information:

- CB radios require 0.1 machine hours each, while the custom products require an average of 0.2 machine hours each.
- All products are produced using similar types of equipment that have similar original costs and hourly operating costs.
- To avoid excess finished goods inventory levels, CB radios are produced in 10 equal sized batches throughout the year, rather than in 1 batch of 100,000 units. Each of the 250 other jobs is manufactured in a separate batch.
- Regardless of the product or the length of the production run, machine setup time is approximately 20 machine hours per batch. The cost of machine setup is treated as manufacturing overhead.
- Variable operating costs are the same per unit of time, regardless of whether machines are operating or being set up.
- Conversion costs are assigned to jobs on the basis of machine hours.
- Last year's selling and distribution costs for CB radios included a fixed element of $50,000 and a variable element of $0.50 per unit.
- Selling and distribution costs for other products average $800 per order.

- In preparing the analysis of product profitability, selling and administrative costs were placed in a single cost pool and assigned on the basis of units sold.

Required:

Determine the actual unit profitability of CB radios and other products, and prepare a report recommending whether or not the production of CB radios should be discontinued.

10-29 Continue or Discontinue: Plant-wide Overhead with Labor- and Machine-Intensive Operations

Completion of this case may require you to review material in Chapters 2, 3, and 4 of this text.

When Cornell Products started operation five years ago, its only product was a radar detector known as the Bear Detector. The production system was simple, with Bear Detectors manually assembled from purchased components. With no ending work-in-process inventories, unit costs were calculated once a month, dividing current manufacturing costs by units produced.

Last year, Cornell Products began to manufacture a second product: code-named the Lion Tamer. The production of Lion Tamers involved both machine-intensive fabrication and assembly.

The introduction of the second product necessitated a change in the firm's simple accounting system. Cornell Products now separately assigns direct material and direct labor costs to each product using information contained on materials requisitions and work tickets. Manufacturing overhead is accumulated in a single cost pool and assigned on the basis of direct labor hours, which is common to both products.

Presented are last year's financial results by product:

	Bear Detector	Lion Tamer
Sales:		
Units	5,000	2,000
Dollars	$500,000	$300,000
Cost of goods sold:		
Direct materials	$100,000	$ 60,000
Direct labor	150,000	45,000
Applied overhead	270,000	81,000
Total	-520,000	-186,000
Gross profit	$(20,000)	$114,000

Management is concerned about the mixed nature of last year's financial performance. It appears that the Lion Tamer is a roaring success. The only competition, the Nittney Company, which has been selling a competing product for considerably more than Cornell's Lion Tamer, is in financial difficulty and likely to file for bankruptcy. The management of Cornell Products attributes the Lion Tamer's success to excellent production management.

Management is concerned, however, about the future of the Bear Detector and is likely to discontinue that product unless its profitability can be improved.

Required:

You have been asked to evaluate the profitability of Cornell's two products and to make any recommendations you believe appropriate. You obtain the following information:

- The labor rate is $15 per hour.
- Cornell has two separate production operations: fabrication and assembly. Bear Detectors only undergo assembly operations. Lion Tamers undergo both fabrication and assembly. Bear Detectors require 2 assembly hours per unit. Lion Tamers require 1 fabrication hour and 1/2 assembly hour per unit.
- The annual Fabricating Department cost function is:
  $200,000 + $5(labor hours)
- The annual Assembly Department overhead cost function is:
  $20,000 + $11(labor hours)

SOLUTION TO REVIEW PROBLEM

(a)

JOURNAL ENTRIES	June 19X5		
	(1) Raw Materials	40,000	
	Accounts Payable		40,000
	(2) Manufacturing Supplies	9,000	
	Accounts Payable		9,000
	(3) Work-in-Process	35,000	
	Raw Materials		35,000
	(4) Work-in-Process	48,500	
	Manufacturing Overhead	5,000	
	Wages Payable		53,500
	(5) Manufacturing Overhead	19,250	
	Manufacturing Supplies		5,500
	Accumulated Depreciation—Factory Assets		5,000
	Miscellaneous Payables		8,750
	(6) Work-in-Process	24,250	
	Manufacturing Overhead (4,850 × $5)		24,250
	(7) Finished Goods Inventory	96,900	
	Work-in-Process		96,900

	Job 225	Job 226	Job 227	Total
Beginning balance	$13,750	$ 1,800	$ 0	$15,550
Current costs:				
Direct materials	0	2,600	18,000	20,600
Direct labor	5,000	15,000	20,500	40,500
Manufacturing overhead	2,500	7,500	10,250	20,250
Total cost	$21,250	$26,900	$48,750	$96,900
(8) Cost of Goods Sold			48,150	
Finished Goods Inventory				
($21,250 + $26,900)				48,150

(b)   Accounts:

Raw Materials		
6/1/X5 7,000	35,000 (3)	
(1) 40,000		
6/30/X5 12,000		

Work-in-Process		
6/1/X5 15,550	96,900 (7)	
(3) 35,000		
(4) 48,500		
(6) 24,250		
6/30/X5 26,400		

Finished Goods Inventory		
6/1/X5 -0-	48,150 (8)	
(7) 96,900		
6/30/X5 48,750		

Cost of Goods Sold		
(8) 48,150		

(c)   Job 228

Direct materials	$14,400
Direct labor	8,000
Applied manufacturing overhead (800 × $5)	4,000
Total	$26,400

(d)

Tri-Star Printing Company
Statement of Cost of Goods Manufactured
For the Month Ending June 30, 19X5

Current manufacturing costs:			
Cost of materials placed in production:			
Raw materials, 6/1/X5	$ 7,000		
Purchases	40,000		
Total available	$47,000		
Raw materials, 6/30/X5	- 12,000	$ 35,000	
Direct labor		48,500	
Manufacturing overhead		24,250	$107,750
Work-in-process, 6/1/X5			15,550
Total costs in process			$123,300
Work-in-process, 6/30/X5			- 26,400
Cost of goods manufactured			$ 96,900

After completing this chapter, you should be able to:

L O 1

Explain the distinctions between job and process product costing systems.

L O 2

Prepare a cost of production report and journal entries for manufacturing transactions for a process costing system.

L O 3

Discuss how process costing procedures can be used to determine the cost of units produced in service organizations.

L O 4

Explain the problem of cost cross-subsidization that may occur when multiple products are produced and how it may be avoided.

L O 5

Identify and discuss the primary issues to consider in designing a product costing system.

PROCESS COSTING FOR GOODS AND SERVICES

In this chapter, we continue the discussion of product costing begun in Chapter 10. Recall that product costing serves two primary purposes: (1) to provide inventory valuations for financial reporting purposes and (2) to provide information to managers about the cost of goods and services produced to help them to make decisions regarding their products.

Chapter 10 laid the foundation for the discussion of product costing by introducing the manufacturing environment and by defining the two basic types of product costing systems found in practice today—job costing and process costing. Job costing procedures were illustrated for Fox Brothers, Inc., an apparel manufacturer. A job costing system works well when products are made one at a time (building houses) or in batches of identical items (making blue jeans). However, if products are produced in a continuous manufacturing environment, where production does not have a distinct beginning and end (refining fossil fuels such as gasoline or diesel), it is necessary to accumulate cost information for the entire manufacturing process for each time period (usually a month) using a process costing system.

The purpose of this chapter is to analyze the differences between job and process costing systems and to illustrate basic process costing procedures. *The use of process costing systems to measure the cost of goods and services and the use of hybrid job/process costing systems will be discussed. In addition, we will examine the problem of product cross-subsidization that may occur when a company produces multiple products. The chapter ends with a discussion of the key considerations in designing a product costing system.*

THE DISTINCTIONS BETWEEN JOB AND PROCESS COSTING

L O 1

As resources are used in production, a job costing system accumulates costs for each "job" or "batch"; whereas, a process costing system accumulates costs for the manufacturing "process" (or "department" or "cost center"). In job costing, the unit cost is the total cost of the "job" divided by the units produced in the job; but in process costing, the cost of a single unit is equal to the total accumulated product cost for the "process" or "department" divided by the number of units produced. Therefore, if a job at Metric Construction Company consists of a high-rise office building, the total job cost is also the unit cost; but if a job at General Dynamics Company consists of a batch of 100 airplane engines, the unit cost is equal to the total job cost divided by 100 parts. Further, if a continuous process is being operated at Sherwin Williams Paint Company, and during the month 400,000 gallons of paint are produced, the cost per gallon is equal to the total process cost for the month divided by 400,000 gallons. To recap, job costing systems accumulate costs for each job or batch; whereas, process costing systems accumulate costs for each manufacturing process or department.

Another distinction between job and process costing is related to the time period for which manufacturing costs are accumulated. In a job costing system, job costs are accumulated for each job on a job-cost sheet, and those costs remain in Work-in-Process *until the job is completed*, irrespective of how long the job is in progress. Each job is discrete and is not considered completed until all units in the job are finished. The cost of the completed job (and the units in the job) is determined when the job is finished, which will not necessarily coincide with the end of an accounting period. Jobs frequently overlap two or more accounting periods—especially in organizations like Metric Construction Company—with the costs of any unfinished jobs at the end of a period included in ending Work-in-Process.

In a process costing system, the manufacturing process consists of a continuous stream of homogeneous goods entering and leaving the production process. For example, pulp wood enters and newsprint exits a paper manufacturing process on an uninterrupted basis. During each accounting period, the goods worked on usually consist of three groups: (1) unfinished goods carried over from the previous period that were completed during the current period, (2) goods both started and completed in the current period, and (3) goods started in the current period but unfinished at the end of the period.[1]

---

1 A possible, but uncommon, fourth category of units in continuous processes are units that were unfinished at both the beginning and end of the current period. An example would be the production of certain alcoholic beverages that involve an aging process extending over several periods.

In a process costing system, costs are accumulated for each accounting period (normally a month) and assigned to the units produced during the period. Since some goods are only partially processed during the period, it is necessary to determine the total production for the period in terms of the equivalent number of completed units. For example, if 300 units were started and completed through 40 percent of the process during the period, then the *equivalent* of 120 (300 units × 0.40) fully completed units was processed. The total number of equivalent units is divided into the total costs for the period to determine the average cost per unit produced.

A good example of a process costing environment involving continuous production is the soft drink bottling process. At Coca-Cola Enterprises's Atlanta bottling facility, more than 2,000 twelve-ounce cans of Coca-Cola are produced per minute in a continuous process. The process adds the ingredients (concentrate syrup, water, sweetener, and the carbonation agent) in the cans at various points in the process and blends the ingredients in the can. At the end of the process, the cans are automatically wrapped in either 6-pack or 12-pack sizes. For another example, see Management Accounting Practice 11-1 for a discussion of the process costing environment at a large Japanese chemicals producer.

PROCESS COSTING PROCEDURES

L O 2

Unlike a job costing system in which job-cost sheets are used to collect cost information for each job, in a process costing system, cost accumula-

---

MANAGEMENT ACCOUNTING PRACTICE 11-1

Process Costing in a Japanese Dyestuffs Plant

Nippon Kayaku is a large industrial company in Japan and produces a wide range of products, including industrial explosives, pharmaceuticals, agrochemicals, sophisticated products (resins, flame retardants, etc.) and dyestuffs. Nippon Kayaku's dyestuff division produces dyes particularly targeted to the polyester and cotton-blended textiles market.

The Fukuyama Plant manufactures about 600 products for the sophisticated products and dyestuffs divisions, some of which are produced in continuous processes and others in batches. The costing system accumulates costs separately for the more than 1,000 processes, and product costs are determined for a particular product merely by adding the unit costs of the processes used to make that product. For example, the cost of the dyestuff product, Kayaset, consists of the costs of five processes: condensation, filtration, drying, grinding, and packaging. Nippon Kayaku uses these product costs for inventory valuation purposes and for managerial decision-making purposes.

Based on: Robin Cooper, "Nippon Kayaku," Harvard Business School Case #9-195-068, pp. 1-7.

tion is simpler because each department's production is treated as though it were the only job worked on during the period. In a department that has just one manufacturing process, process costing is particularly straightforward because the Work-in-Process account is, in effect, the departmental cost record. As discussed later in the chapter, if a department has more than one manufacturing process, separate records should be maintained for each process.

To illustrate process costing procedures, consider Micro Systems Co., which manufactures memory chips for microcomputers using sophisticated machinery in a one-step process. Each finished unit requires one unit of raw materials added at the beginning of the manufacturing process. The production and cost data for the month of July 19X8 for Micro Systems are as follows:

July Production Data

Units in process, beginning of period (75% converted)	4,000
Units started	36,000
Completed and transferred to finished goods	35,000
Units in process, end of period (20% converted)	5,000

July Cost Data

Beginning Work-in-Process:		
Materials costs		$ 16,000
Conversion costs (direct labor and		
manufacturing overhead)		9,000
Total		$ 25,000
Raw materials purchased and transferred to		
processing (36,000 × $4)		$144,000
Conversion costs for July:		
Direct labor	$62,200	
Manufacturing overhead applied	46,700	108,900
Current manufacturing costs		$252,900

The Cost of Production Report

The key to using process costing procedures is understanding the **cost of production report**, which summarizes unit and cost data for each department or process for each period. It consists of the following sections:

- Summary of units in process
- Equivalent units
- Total cost to be accounted for and cost per equivalent unit
- Accounting for total cost

The cost of production report for Micro Systems Co. is shown in Exhibit 11-1, and its four sections are discussed below.

Summary of Units in Process

This section of the cost of production report provides a summary of all units in the department during the period—both from an *input* and an *output* perspective. From an *input* perspective, total units in process during the period consisted of:

- Units in process at the beginning of the period, plus
- Units started during the period.

From an *output* perspective, these units in process during the period were either:

- Completed and transferred out of the department, or
- Still on hand at the end of the period.

In the *summary of units in process*, all units are treated the same, regardless of the amount of processing that took place on them during the period. The objective here is to account for all discrete units of product in process at any time during the period. Note in Exhibit 11-1 in the *summary of units in process* that 40,000 individual units were in process during July

EXHIBIT 11-1: COST OF PRODUCTION REPORT FOR PROCESS COSTING SYSTEM

Micro Systems Co.
Cost of Production Report
For the Month Ending July 31, 19X8

Summary of units in process:

Beginning	4,000
Units started	36,000
In process	40,000
Completed	-35,000
Ending	5,000

Equivalent units in process:

	Materials	Conversion
Units completed	35,000	35,000
Plus equivalent units in ending inventory	5,000	1,000*
Equivalent units in process	40,000	36,000

Total cost to be accounted for and cost per equivalent unit in process:

	Materials	Conversion	Total
Work-in-Process, beginning	$ 16,000	$ 9,000	$ 25,000
Current cost	144,000	108,900**	252,900
Total cost in process	$160,000	$117,900	$277,900 ←
Equivalent units in process	÷ 40,000	÷ 36,000	
Cost per equivalent unit in process	$ 4.00	$ 3.275	$ 7.275

Accounting for total costs:

Transferred out (35,000 × $7.275)		$254,625
Work-in-Process, ending:		
Materials (5,000 × $4.00)	$20,000	
Conversion (1,000 × $3.275)	3,275	23,275
Total cost accounted for		$277,900 ←

*5,000 units 20% converted
**Includes direct labor of $62,200 and applied manufacturing overhead of $46,700

19X8, of which 4,000 units were in beginning inventory, partially completed, and 36,000 new units were started during the month. During the period, 35,000 (of the 40,000 units in process) were completed, and the remaining 5,000 were still in process at the end of the month.

Equivalent Units in Process

In this section of the cost of production report, the objective is to translate the number of units in process during the period into equivalent completed units of production. **Equivalent completed units** is the number of completed units that is equal, in terms of production cost, to a given number of partially completed units. For example, 80 units for which 50 percent of the expected total processing cost has been incurred, is the equivalent of 40 completed units (80 × 0.50).

Frequently, direct materials costs are incurred largely, if not entirely, at the beginning of the process; and direct labor and manufacturing overhead costs are added throughout the production process. If direct labor and manufacturing costs are added to the process simultaneously, it is common to treat them jointly as *conversion costs.* For example, Micro Systems Co. adds all materials at the beginning of the process, and all conversion costs—direct labor and manufacturing overhead—are added evenly throughout the manufacturing process. Therefore, separate computations are made for equivalent units of *materials* and equivalent units of *conversion.* Although the department worked on 40,000 units during the period, the total number of *equivalent units completed* with conversion costs was only 36,000 units, consisting of 35,000 finished units plus 1,000 equivalent units in ending inventory (5,000 units 20 percent converted). Because all materials are added at the start of the process, the 40,000 units (35,000 finished and 5,000 in process) were completed with materials costs.

It is often helpful to examine the physical flow of the units in equation form. To ensure that all units have been accounted for, the following physical-flow equation can be used:

$$\text{EU in process} = \text{Units completed} + \text{EU in ending inventory}$$

where:

$$\text{EU} = \textit{equivalent units}$$

For *materials,* the equation is:

$$\text{EU in process (materials)} = 35,000 + 5,000$$
$$= \underline{\underline{40,000}}$$

For *conversion,* the equation is:

$$\text{EU in process (conversion)} = 35,000 + 1,000$$
$$= \underline{\underline{36,000}}$$

Total Cost to Be Accounted for and Cost per Equivalent Unit in Process

This section of the report summarizes total costs assigned to the department during the period and calculates the *cost per equivalent unit* for materials, conversion, and in total. Total cost assigned to the department consists of the beginning Work-in-Process balance (if any) plus *current costs* incurred. For Micro Systems, the total cost to be accounted for during July was $277,900, consisting of $25,000 in Work-in-Process at the beginning of the period, plus current costs of $252,900 incurred in July. Notice in Exhibit 11-1 that these amounts are broken down between *materials* costs and *conversion* costs.

To compute *cost per equivalent unit,* total cost in process is divided by the equivalent units in process. This is done separately for materials cost and conversion cost. Note that the *total* cost per equivalent unit is the sum of the unit costs for materials and conversion. It is not possible to get the total cost per unit by dividing total costs of $277,900 by some equivalent unit amount, because the number of equivalent units in process was different for materials and conversion. Review Exhibit 11-1 carefully to make sure you understand the calculation of unit cost for materials and conversion and the calculation of total unit cost.

Accounting for Total Costs

This section shows the disposition of the total costs charged to the department during the period. In the previous section, we saw that total cost charged to Work-in-Process for the period was $277,900, consisting of the beginning balance and current costs. The purpose of the *accounting for total costs* section of the cost of production report is to show how total cost for the period is divided between units completed (and sent to finished goods) and units still in process at the end of the period. From the previous section, note that each fully processed unit has $4.00 of materials cost and $3.275 of conversion costs, for a total unit cost of $7.275.

The first step in assigning total cost is to calculate the cost of units transferred out by multiplying the units completed during the period times the total cost per unit—35,000 units times $7.275. This assigns $254,625 of the total cost of $277,900 to units transferred out, leaving the difference, or $23,275, to be assigned to ending Work-in-Process. To verify that $23,275 is the correct amount of cost to leave in ending Work-in-Process, the materials and conversion costs in ending Work-in-Process are calculated separately. Recall that the 5,000 units in process at the end of the period are 100 percent completed with materials costs but only 20 percent completed with conversion costs. Therefore, in ending Work-in-Process, the materials cost component is $20,000 (or 5,000 × 100% × $4.00), the conversion cost component is $3,275 (or 5,000 × 20% × $3.275), and the total cost of ending Work-in-Process is $23,275 ($20,000 + $3,275). The following equation can be used to verify that all the costs assigned to the department during the period have been accounted for:

$$\text{Total cost to be accounted for} = \text{Total cost accounted for}$$

$$\underset{\text{in-Process}}{\text{Beginning Work}} + \underset{\text{costs}}{\text{Current}} = \underset{\text{(or transferred)}}{\underset{\text{manufactured}}{\text{Cost of goods}}} + \underset{\text{in-Process}}{\text{Ending Work-}}$$

$$\$25,000 + \$252,900 = \$254,625 + \$23,275$$

$$\underline{\$277,900} = \underline{\$277,900}$$

Important Assumptions About Beginning Inventories in Process Costing

Because the costs of materials, labor, and overhead are constantly changing, unit costs are seldom exactly the same from period to period. Hence, if a unit is manufactured partially in one period and partially in the following period, its actual cost is probably not equal to the unit cost of units produced in either period. For instance, if the precise cost per unit manufactured in one period is $4.00, and in the subsequent period it is $4.10, a unit produced 50 percent in each period would have an accurate unit cost of $4.05 (assuming all materials and conversion costs are added evenly over the production process).

Each company that operates a process costing system must assess how beneficial it is for its managers to know the precise cost of units both started and completed during the current period versus those that overlap two periods and whether the benefits exceed the costs of measuring this cost. Suppose a company completed 10,000 units during the period and the production of 200 of these units overlapped the previous and current periods. Does the company gain much from calculating a different unit cost for the 9,800 units produced entirely in the current period and the 200 units that overlapped two periods? If the primary purpose of the inventory cost system is to measure costs for the financial statements, it may not be worth the additional costs to refine the costs so precisely. However, if the purpose is cost control, pricing, or performance evaluation, calculating precise cost information for each period may be very important and may justify calculating unit costs more precisely.

In the cost of production report in Exhibit 11-1, we made no attempt to account separately for the completed units that came from beginning inventory and those that were started during the current period. The method illustrated in Exhibit 11-1 is called the **weighted average method,** and it simply spreads the combined beginning inventory cost and current manufacturing costs (for materials, labor, and overhead) over the units completed and in ending inventory on an average basis. For example, the total cost in process for conversion of $117,900 included both beginning inventory cost and current costs, and the 36,000 equivalent units in process for conversion included both units from beginning inventory and units started during the current period. Hence, the average cost per unit of $3.275 (or $117,900 / 36,000) is a *weighted average* cost of units in beginning inventory and units started during the current period. It is not the precise cost per unit for the current period's production activity, but rather an average cost that includes the cost of partially completed units in beginning inventory carried over from the previous period.

First-In, First-Out Process Costing

An alternative, more precise process costing method to the weighted average method is the **first-in, first-out (FIFO) method**. It accounts for unit costs of beginning inventory units separately from the cost of units started during the current period. Under this assumption, the first costs incurred each period are assumed to have been used to complete the unfinished units carried over from the previous period. Hence, those units are costed partially based on the prior period's unit costs and partially based on the current period's unit costs.

If unit costs are changing significantly from period to period, and if beginning inventories are large relative to total production for the period, it would likely be beneficial to have the more precise unit cost for each period that the FIFO method provides. However, with the current trend toward maintaining smaller inventories, the additional effort and cost of measuring FIFO inventory costs may not be justifiable in many cases. Detailed coverage of the FIFO method is included in cost accounting textbooks.

Journal Entries for Process Costing Systems

The cost of production report summarizes manufacturing costs assigned to Work-in-Process during the period and provides information for preparing the journal entry to record the cost of goods completed and transferred to finished goods inventory (or to another department) during the period. The journal entries and the supporting documents to record the assignment of costs to Work-in-Process are essentially the same as those discussed for job costing. Summary July 19X8 journal entries for Micro Systems Co. are as follows:

JOURNAL ENTRIES		
(1) Raw Materials	144,000	
Accounts Payable		144,000
To record cost of raw materials purchases. (This illustration assumed that the costs of materials purchased and materials transferred to the factory for the month were the same amounts.)		
(2) Work-in-Process	144,000	
Raw Materials		144,000
To record materials requisitioned to the factory.		
(3) Work-in-Process	62,200	
Wages Payable		62,200
To record wages for the period.		
(4) Work-in-Process	46,700	
Manufacturing Overhead		46,700
To apply manufacturing overhead to Work-in-Process.		
(5) Finished Goods Inventory	254,625	
Work-in-Process		254,625
To record transfer of completed units to finished goods.		

Note: Actual manufacturing overhead costs incurred would be recorded the same for process and job costing systems; therefore, they are not included in this illustration. See Chapter 10 for further discussion of actual overhead costs.

After the above entries have been posted to the ledger, the Work-in-Process account for Micro Systems Co. appears as follows:

Work-in-Process			
7/1/X8 balance	25,000	254,625 (5)	
(2) Direct materials	144,000		
(3) Direct labor	62,200		
(4) Manufacturing overhead	46,700		
7/31/X8 balance	23,275		

Note in Exhibit 11-1 that the $254,625 assigned to 35,000 units transferred out is equal to the amount credited to Work-in-Process for costs transferred to Finished Goods Inventory. Also, the $23,275 balance in Work-in-Process is equal to the amount assigned to units in ending work-in-process on the cost of production report.

Process Costing for Multiple Processes or Departments

The Micro Systems Co. illustration above involved only one process; however, many process costing applications include multiple processes or departments. (See Management Accounting Practice 11-1.) How would the cost system have differed if Micro Systems had two departments—a Molding Department and a Finishing Department? In that case, costs would have been accumulated separately for each department and recorded in separate Work-in-Process accounts as products moved through the departments. As products were completed in the Molding Department and transferred to the Finishing Department, costs of completed units would be transferred by the following entry:

JOURNAL ENTRY	Work-in-Process, Finishing	xxx	
	Work-in-Process, Molding		xxx

On its cost of production report, the Finishing Department would treat the transferred-in costs received from the Molding Department as they treat materials costs added at the beginning of the process. **Transferred-in costs** include the combined cost of materials, labor, and overhead transferred in to a department as goods are received from the previous department. If the Finishing Department also added materials to the units, the transferred-in costs from Molding would probably be reported in a separate column from materials costs on the cost of production report. Total unit cost at the end of the finishing process would consist of transferred-in Molding Department costs, plus Finishing Department costs for materials and conversion. The following T-accounts show how manufacturing costs flow through the Work-in-Process accounts into Finished Goods Inventory for Micro Systems, assuming all direct materials costs are incurred in the Molding Department:

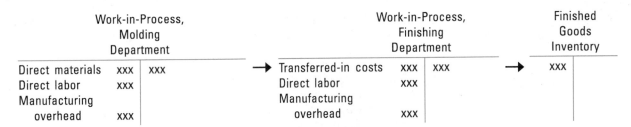

Work-in-Process, Molding Department			Work-in-Process, Finishing Department			Finished Goods Inventory	
Direct materials	xxx	xxx	→ Transferred-in costs	xxx	xxx	→	xxx
Direct labor	xxx		Direct labor	xxx			
Manufacturing overhead	xxx		Manufacturing overhead	xxx			

As direct materials and direct labor costs are incurred by each department, they are debited to the respective Work-in-Process accounts. When goods are transferred from Molding to Finishing, the costs accumulated for those goods in Molding are credited to Work-in-Process, Molding, and debited to Work-in-Process, Finishing. When goods are completed in Finishing and transferred into finished goods inventory, their total costs (including those incurred in both departments) are credited to Work-in-Process, Finishing, and debited to Finished Goods Inventory.

PROCESS COSTING IN SERVICE ORGANIZATIONS

L O 3

There are many applications of process costing for service organizations. Process costing in service organizations is similar to that of manufacturing organizations—the primary purpose being to assign costs to cost objectives. Generally, the use of process costing techniques for service organizations is easier than for manufacturing organizations because the raw materials element is not necessary. The applications for the labor and overhead costs are similar, if not identical, to those of a manufacturing firm.

Process costing for services is similar to job costing for batches in that an average cost for similar or identical services is determined. There are important differences, though, between batch and process costing. In a batch environment, a discrete group of services is identified and costed; but in a process environment, services are performed on a continuous basis. Batch costing accumulates the cost *for a specific group* of services as the batch moves through the various activities that make up the service. Process service costing measures the average cost of identical or similar services performed *each period* (each month) in a department. An example of batch service costing is determining the cost of registering a student at your college during the fall term registration period, and an example of process service costing is determining the cost each month of processing a check by a bank. If continuously performed services involved multiple processes, the total cost of the service would be the sum of the unit costs for each process.

There are several important considerations before using process costing in the service organization. The difficulty in many service situations is defining the appropriate cost objective. For manufacturing applications, the normal cost objective is inventory, or units thereof. Inventory does not exist in most service applications; so, the selection of the cost objective becomes a major management decision. Is the cost objective a general activity (check processing in a bank), a specific activity (sorting only letters, as opposed to letters and packages), or a mission activity (patient care in a hospital as opposed to individual patients)?

General activities should be used when the service process is identical for all processing even though some of the items processed are different. A bank processes many types of checks (personal, business, cashiers, and travelers), but all checks go through the same chain of activities. Specific activity cost objectives should be used when the items processed take different activity paths. Although the mail center processes all mail via the same steps (receiving, sorting, bundling, etc.), the handling operations are different. Letters can be sorted and handled by machine, but packages must be sorted and grouped by hand.

Using mission activity as the cost objective is another approach to applying process costing to service situations. Rather than tracking the cost of each service rendered per unit or batch (a job processing approach), a company can assign costs over a longer period of time to another reasonable objective—for example, all patient care. At the end of a set period, all costs assigned to patient care are divided by the total number of patient-days during the period to obtain the evaluation data, cost per patient-day. This approach assumes that all processed units (patients in this example) receive approximately the same activity (patient care); and, therefore, the average cost per unit (patient-day) is sufficient for evaluation purposes.

After it is determined that process costing would be appropriate for a service activity, the actual decision to use it is generally contingent on two important factors about the items being evaluated. First, is average cost per unit acceptable as an input item to the decision process? For some activities, the answer is obvious. For instance, tracking the actual cost of processing each check through a bank would probably not be as useful as determining the average cost of processing checks for a given period; therefore, average cost is acceptable. For other activities, the answer is more difficult to determine. Should the decision model include average cost per patient-day or actual cost per individual patient?

The second item to be considered relates to the benefits versus the costs of the resulting information. Normally, it is easier to track and record the cost of an activity or process than it is to track and record the cost of each individual item in the activity. Often actual cost tracking is impossible for practical reasons (the actual cost of processing a check through a banking system, for example).

With appropriate planning, every service organization can establish a means of proper reporting through cost assignment. Although process costing will not work in every situation, it has many applications in service organizations. And, as illustrated in this text, there are many possibilities for applying either job or process costing to activities in service organizations.

COSTING FOR
MULTIPLE
PRODUCTS

L O 4

Production is the ultimate cost driver in a manufacturing facility. When all units produced in a plant are identical, a simple division of total production costs by total units produced provides accurate unit costs. When the products produced in a plant differ significantly, it is necessary to recognize many cost drivers to reflect the extent to which different products use different resources with different costs. Hence, as products become more heterogeneous, it is necessary to perform an increasingly detailed analysis of cost drivers.

Recall the Fox Brothers, Inc., example from Chapter 10, which concerned a homogeneous product line of sports jackets and which used seven cost pools and related cost drivers:

Cost Pool	Cost Driver
Direct materials:	
Wool fabric W09	Yards
Wool fabric W12	Yards
Interfacing	Yards
Liner	Yards
Buttons	Sets
Direct labor	Direct labor hours
Manufacturing overhead	Direct labor hours

Fox Brothers has five separate cost pools for materials because of differing materials costs and handling characteristics. With a single labor rate of $10 per hour, only one direct labor cost pool is required. Assuming manufacturing overhead is caused by and highly correlated with the use of direct labor, direct labor hours is an acceptable basis of overhead allocation. However, the addition of a new product with different production characteristics from sports jackets could result in product cross-subsidization if Fox Brothers continued to recognize only one cost driver for manufacturing overhead.

The Problem of Cross-Subsidization

Assume that Fox Brothers installed a new, fully automated flexible manufacturing system (FMS) used exclusively to manufacture a new product line of designer jeans, in addition to sports coats. To accommodate this addition of the new product, the cost accounting system could be modified simply by adding cost pools for the new raw materials items and adding all costs of operating the new equipment to manufacturing overhead. (In a FMS, virtually all labor costs are classified as indirect labor.) With manufacturing overhead assigned on the basis of direct labor hours, the predetermined overhead rate per direct labor hour would probably increase significantly. Although this modified system would account for costs in a systematic manner, sports jackets would continue to be assigned all overhead costs because they use all the direct labor hours, and the designer jeans would be assigned no overhead costs because they use no direct labor hours.

With this costing system, sports jackets are said to be cross-subsidizing designer jeans because a portion of the cost of manufacturing designer jeans (manufacturing overhead costs) are assigned to sports jackets. This could lead Fox Brothers' management into believing erroneously that designer jeans are very profitable and sports jackets are unprofitable. Clearly, this could be a serious error. The culprit is a bad cost accounting system. Even if overhead costs are allocated on some other basis (such as the number of units produced) in order to assign some overhead costs to jeans, the resulting costs are unlikely to be sufficiently accurate for such decisions as pricing or evaluating Fox Brothers' ability to compete.

When products are heterogeneous and require varying degrees of attention in operations that have different cost drivers, significant cost assignment errors may result from the use of a single, plant-wide overhead rate. With sports jackets produced in a labor-intensive operation and designer jeans produced using a fully automated flexible manufacturing system, Fox Brothers' cost system should contain at least nine cost pools and should recognize machine hours as an additional cost driver:

Cost Pool	Cost Driver
Direct materials:	
Wool fabric W09	Yards
Wool fabric W12	Yards
Interfacing	Yards
Liner	Yards
Buttons	Sets
Denim	Yards
Labor-intensive operations:	
Direct labor	Direct labor hours
Manufacturing overhead	Direct labor hours
Flexible manufacturing system operations:	
Conversion	Machine hours

This is an extreme, but not unusual, example because many companies that started with focused factories producing a single product have failed to modernize their accounting system as new products and production procedures have been added. The resulting cross-subsidization of costs hinders the organization's ability to compete as competition intensifies and becomes more global. *The more varied the production alternatives and the product mix, the greater the need for a costing system that recognizes a diverse set of detailed cost drivers.* It is no longer adequate to perform detailed costing of direct materials and direct labor while lumping overhead into an amorphous blob. See Management Accounting Practice 11-2 for a discussion of how Boeing Aircraft adapted its costing system as its product line evolved.

Overhead must be analyzed in detail and divided into a number of homogeneous cost pools. Cost drivers must be identified for each cost pool. And the costs in each cost pool must be assigned to products using the

MANAGEMENT ACCOUNTING PRACTICE 11-2

Boeing Improves Product Costing with Modified Process Costing System

Aircraft manufacturers traditionally have used job costing methods, but recently Boeing Aircraft has been moving toward implementing a modified process cost accounting system. The old system, developed when Boeing was primarily a military aircraft manufacturing company, has become inadequate as its production methods, the makeup of cost, and the need for information have changed.

Under the old system, costs that could not be directly traced to jobs—an amount that had risen to almost 70 percent to 80 percent of total production costs—were assigned to jobs based on direct labor cost. This meant that production managers were almost powerless to affect total product cost other than by reducing head count of direct laborers.

Even though Boeing still produces multiple products in a particular "process" center, under the new system, a unit weighting for different products (or parts) is used to convert these parts to common production units. For example, one part may be equal to 2.10 production units, whereas another part may be equal to 3.30 production units. After the process cost per production unit is calculated, the cost for a particular part is determined by multiplying the cost per production unit times the number of units assigned to that part.

The primary benefit of this modified process costing system is that it allows overhead costs to be assigned to processes where managers have direct responsibility for the incurrence of those costs, and it produces costs more closely connected with the activities that produced those costs.

Based on: Robert J. Bowlby, "How Boeing Tracks Costs, A to Z," *Financial Executive* (November/ December 1994), pp. 20-23.

most appropriate cost driver. Although such detailed analysis would not have been possible a few years ago, the rapid changes in the manufacturing environment related to the increasing use of computers make the detailed tracing of costs possible as a by-product of ongoing planning and control operations required for other purposes. The development of activity-based costing (introduced in Chapter 4) has contributed significantly to the process of product costing for heterogeneous products. The use of multiple overhead cost pools is discussed in more detail in Chapter 12, and activity-based costing to improve product costing is discussed in Chapter 13.

DESIGNING AN INVENTORY COSTING SYSTEM

L O 5

The product costing system—job-order or process—is actually a component of the accounting information system that is, in turn, part of the overall management information system. The design of any part of the management information system should be driven primarily by the information output needs and objectives and the environment in which the system operates. So the key questions are: "What environmental characteristics must be considered in the system design?" and "How will the information from the system be used?"

In Chapters 10 and 11, we have discussed costing systems for conventional job and process applications using simple, straightforward situations for Fox Brothers and Micro Systems. Although there are a vast number of companies that use systems very similar to these, many other companies have production environments that do not lend themselves entirely to using either a conventional product costing system or a conventional process costing system. Such companies design systems customized to their particular production environment, and usually these systems contain elements of both job and process costing systems. They are often called *hybrid systems*. It is not our purpose to go into detail illustrating hybrid systems, but a good example can be seen in Management Accounting Practice 11-3 for Kunde Estate Winery.

A simple information system is always easier to design than is a complex one. Accordingly, it is much easier to build an inventory costing system based on simplistic assumptions that will be used only to support the financial reporting process, but will not be used directly for planning and control, pricing, or other purposes. One notion sometimes held by

---

MANAGEMENT ACCOUNTING PRACTICE 11-3

California Winery Uses Hybrid Costing System to Measure the Cost of a Bottle of Wine

Kunde Estate Winery, located in California's Sonoma Valley, is typical of the many small family-owned wineries found in the Northern California wine region. At Kunde, a hybrid costing system that has characteristics of both job and process costing is used to determine the cost of a bottle of wine produced from each lot of grapes harvested each year. Because each lot in a given vintage may be processed differently, each lot is a separate job (or batch). Hence, costs are traced through the various wine-making processes (or departments) for each job. The cost of initial harvested grape lots is allocated to jobs based on the amount of grapes assigned to the various types of wine to be produced, since a particular lot may be used to produce different types of wine. After this allocation, costs are accumulated by departments and are then allocated to each wine batch based on the amount of time the wine spends in each department. Thus, a red wine that requires more aging than a white wine would be assigned a greater amount of "wine aging" department costs. The result of this hybrid job/process costing system is that Kunde Estate Winery has a very accurate measurement of the cost differentials for producing different types of wine. This information can be particularly helpful in the decision each year of how to use the grapes harvested to produce different wines. Of course, it is also very helpful in assigning costs to wines in process and in finished goods at the end of the year for financial reporting purposes.

....

Based on: John Y. Lee and Brian Gray Jacobs, "Kunde Estate Winery: A Case Study in Cost Accounting," *CMA Magazine* (April 1993), pp. 15-18.

accountants is that product costing systems do not need to be too reliable since they are merely part of the financial reporting system. This is fallacious reasoning because external users of financial statements, no less than internal managers, need reliable information about earnings and net worth. Even if this reasoning were valid for financial reporting, the problem is that once an inventory system begins producing cost data, it invariably will be used directly or indirectly for other purposes. Consequently, one cannot overstate the importance of designing inventory costing systems that produce reliable information.

Probably the best approach to designing an inventory costing system is to view its basic purpose as that of providing reliable inventory valuation data for financial reporting purposes. However, the design must also recognize that information coming from the system may be only partially useful for other purposes or that the information will need to be modified or augmented for certain other purposes. For example, the cost per unit of inventory that the costing system produces is probably not very useful for assessing managerial performance from period to period because a manager may be able to decrease the cost per unit merely by producing and stockpiling more inventory (thus, spreading fixed costs over more units). However, more inventory on hand means more costs of carrying inventory.

Also, cost data produced by the costing system is generally inadequate as a basis for evaluating prices and profitability because the cost data take into account only manufacturing costs. Reliable costing system output is a good starting point in determining total cost to produce a good or service, but the price ultimately must cover not only inventoriable production costs, but also other costs related to getting the product to market and to servicing customers. Hence, in this case, we must augment manufacturing cost information with additional information.

Another critical issue in costing systems design is determining how accurate the output of the system must be to be reliable. Perfection is normally not the goal in designing information systems (unless, for example, you are designing the systems for controlling the space shuttle). The goal in most systems generally is to perfect the system up to the point where costs exceed the benefits of additional improvements. As long as the incremental benefits equal or exceed the incremental costs, the system should be improved. For example, as illustrated for Fox Brothers, as long as it was producing only sports coats by a uniform production process, it was not cost beneficial to have more than one overhead cost pool based on direct labor hours. However, when Fox Brothers added the flexible manufacturing system to make designer jeans, it became necessary to add a second cost pool based on machine hours. In some cases, activity-based costing with numerous cost pools may be justified in terms of the additional reliability of the data produced, whereas in other cases, the additional cost pools may not produce significantly different results from a single cost pool allocated based on direct labor or machine hours. What's important is to always be alert to the possibility of improvements in the system that may offer valuable payoffs to the company and to constantly monitor the system design to make sure it optimally meets current needs.

SUMMARY

Product costing involves the determination of the cumulative cost of inventories as they flow through the manufacturing process using either individual jobs or manufacturing processes as the cost objective. Process costing involves the determination of the cost per unit of a homogeneous product as units pass continuously from one production operation to another.

This chapter examined the process costing method, including calculation of equivalent units, the cost of production report, and related journal entries. Process costing assigns costs to units completed and to units in work-in-process based on the number of equivalent whole units worked on during the period. The chapter illustrated the weighted average method of process costing and described the FIFO method. The weighted average method combines the costs of beginning inventory with current costs and assigns the resulting total costs to all units in process during the period using an average cost calculation. The FIFO method assigns costs separately for units in beginning inventory from those started during the period. Units started during the period are not affected by beginning inventory costs, and units in beginning inventory are costed partially based on prior period costs and partially based on current period costs.

Process costing has many applications in service organizations. Service organizations use process costing techniques for managerial purposes, rather than for financial reporting purposes, since service organizations are not concerned with inventories. Although this chapter illustrated process costing in a manufacturing setting, the only major change required to apply process costing to a service setting is likely to be the elimination of direct materials costs. Direct labor and manufacturing overhead—or its equivalent—exist in all organizations.

In designing a costing system, it is important to determine the appropriate number of cost drivers that determine the various components of costs. This is particularly important when multiple products are produced. Failure to properly identify cost drivers for overhead may result in product cost cross-subsidization, where manufacturing cost is overassigned to one product and underassigned to another. The most important considerations in designing a cost system are making sure its design is consistent with the use that will be made of the system outputs and making sure the total system benefits exceed their costs.

APPENDIX A: JOINT PRODUCTS AND BY-PRODUCTS

Joint products are two or more products produced simultaneously by a common manufacturing process. The costs of producing joint products are called **joint costs.** An example of joint products is crude oil products (such as gasoline, diesel, and kerosene) that are produced by a common refining process. Similarly, various chemical products are often produced by a single process. A **by-product** is a product with insignificant value that is produced jointly with one or more other products.

JOINT PRODUCT COST ALLOCATION

For product costing purposes, it is necessary to allocate joint product costs to the respective joint products. Joint cost allocation occurs at the split-off point in the production process. The **split-off point** is the point in the process where the joint products emerge as separate, identifiable products. Any costs incurred in further processing of a joint product after split-off are product specific costs, not joint costs.

To illustrate joint cost allocation, assume Aem Enterprises manufactures two automotive fuel additives, Speedo and Econo, from a common manufacturing process. In August 19X7, Aem incurred joint costs of $24,000 to produce 8,000 liters of Speedo and 12,000 liters of Econo as shown below:

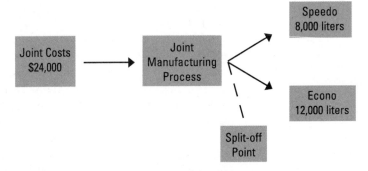

Two methods commonly used to allocate joint costs are the physical quantity method and the sales value allocation method. Under the **physical quantity method**, joint costs are allocated on the basis of relative quantities of a common physical characteristic possessed by the joint products. Physical characteristics used for joint cost allocation are varied and include number of units of product, weight measures, and volume measures. For Aem Enterprises, the unit measure (a liter) is also a volume measure because 1 physical unit of product consists of 1 liter of volume. Under the physical quantity method, using liters of production as the allocation base, the allocated costs are $9,600 for Speedo and $14,400 for Econo; computed as follows:

Product	Quantity (Liters)	Relative Quantity		Joint Cost		Allocation
Speedo	8,000	0.40	×	$24,000	=	$ 9,600
Econo	12,000	0.60	×	$24,000	=	14,400
	20,000	1.00				$24,000

Each product has a cost of $1.20 per liter ($9,600 / 8,000 and $14,400 / 12,000) at the split-off point. If there are no costs following split-off and if Speedo sells for $3 per liter and Econo sells for $1 per liter, the gross profit for Speedo is $14,400, whereas Econo has a negative $2,400 gross profit.

	Speedo	Econo	Total
Unit sales (liters)	8,000	12,000	20,000
Sales price per unit	$3	$1	
Sales	$24,000	$12,000	$36,000
Cost of goods sold	- 9,600	- 14,400	- 24,000
Gross profit	$14,400	$(2,400)	$12,000

Allocating joint costs on the basis of physical quantities produces a distortion in the gross profit calculations any time the selling price per unit of quantity is not the same for all joint products. The reason for this distortion is that the physical quantity method assigns an *equal amount of cost* to each unit *of physical measure*—in this case, to each liter—regardless of its selling price. If joint costs are allocated on the basis of physical quantity, the cost per liter is $1.20 for both Speedo and Econo; but the selling price of Speedo is three times as much as Econo's selling price. Since together the products generate a total gross profit of $12,000 and one product cannot be produced without the other, does it seem reasonable to assume that one is produced at a profit while the other is produced at a loss?

If selling prices vary significantly between the joint products, sales value is a better basis for allocating joint costs. Under the **sales value allocation method,** each dollar of sales value for all products is assigned an equal amount of cost. The sales value method allocations for Speedo and Econo are as follows:

Product	Sales Value Computation	Sales Value Amount	Relative Sales Value	Joint Cost	Allocation
Speedo	8,000 × $3 =	$24,000	0.667 ×	$24,000 =	$16,000
Econo	12,000 × $1 =	12,000	0.333 ×	$24,000 =	8,000
		$36,000	1.000		$24,000

Speedo has a cost of $2 per liter ($16,000 / 8,000), and Econo has a cost of $0.667 per liter ($8,000 / 12,000). Using the costs for Speedo and Econo determined by the sales value allocation method, the respective gross profits are $8,000 and $4,000, as shown in the partial income statement below:

	Speedo	Econo	Total
Units sales (liter)	8,000	12,000	20,000
Sales price per unit	$3	$1	
Sales	$24,000	$12,000	$36,000
Cost of goods sold	- 16,000	- 8,000	-24,000
Gross profit	$ 8,000	$ 4,000	$12,000

Under the sales value allocation method, the gross margin ratio is the same (one-third of selling price) for both products.

Additional processing may be required after split-off on some joint products. In this case, the sales value allocation method must be modified to allocate joint costs on the basis of net realizable value at the point of split-off, rather than on the basis of sales value for completed units. Net realizable value is computed as ultimate sales value less additional processing costs incurred beyond the split-off point. For example, if $4,000 of additional processing costs were required after split-off before the 8,000 liters of Speedo could be sold for $24,000, the joint cost allocation would be made on the basis of relative net realizable values of $20,000 ($24,000 - $4,000) for Speedo and $12,000 for Econo.

If the joint products can be sold at the split-off point, the sales value at the split-off point should be used to allocate joint costs. This is true even if joint products are processed further.

The decision of whether to continue with additional processing after split-off is unrelated to the cost allocation procedure. Sometimes additional processing is necessary before the product can be sold, in which case further processing ordinarily must be done. In other cases, the product may be sold either at split-off or after additional processing. The decision of whether to continue processing is based entirely on relevant cost analysis. If the additional revenue from processing exceeds the additional cost of processing, the product should be processed further; otherwise, the product should be sold at split-off. These relevant cost issues are discussed and illustrated in Chapter 3.

ACCOUNTING FOR BY-PRODUCTS

By-products are products with relatively low sales value that are obtained incidental to producing other products. Production of by-products is not a major objective of the manufacturing process; it is a result of production of the main products. For example, a furniture factory primarily manufactures furniture, but it produces sawdust (which is salable) as an inevitable and natural result.

A by-product is not treated as a joint product and, therefore, is not allocated costs in the joint cost allocation procedure. If by-products do not generate revenues—which is the case for many waste by-products—there is no special accounting required other than recording any disposition costs as additional manufacturing expense. If by-products can be sold and if their selling prices are insignificant, revenues from the sale of by-products are usually recorded as other income, and no cost is assigned to the by-products.

In other cases where by-product costs and revenues are more significant, joint-product costs are allocated to the by-products equal to their selling prices, resulting in no profit or loss being recognized when they are sold. The remaining joint processing costs after subtracting by-product costs are allocated to the main products by either the physical quantity or sales value allocation method. This is the procedure used for costing by-products at Nippon Kayaku, discussed in Management Accounting Practice 11-1.

Products initially considered to be by-products may later become main products as new uses and applications for them are discovered. When this occurs, the accounting treatment should be revised to reflect a change in assumptions and to begin allocating costs to the products as joint products.

APPENDIX B: PRODUCT COSTING USING STANDARD COSTS

In Chapter 8, we discussed the use of standard costs and flexible budgets as a means for reporting the performance of responsibility cost center managers. The objectives of standard costing for performance evaluation purposes are to identify the difference (or variance) between actual costs and standard costs allowed by the flexible budget and to elicit managers' explanations for variances that are significant—both favorable and unfavorable variances.

Standard costs can also be used to greatly simplify the recording of product costs in the financial accounting system. Recall from Chapter 10 that the Manufacturing Overhead account is used to record actual costs, but many companies use a predetermined overhead rate to record overhead costs in the inventory accounts. A standard costing system for recording product costs functions similarly to the predetermined overhead method, except it uses a predetermined, or standard, cost for *all* elements of production—direct materials, direct labor, and manufacturing overhead. Hence, the first and most critical step in operating a standard product costing system is establishing the standard costs for these three components of production costs.

The key steps in using a standard product costing system are summarized as follows:

1. All increases and decreases in the inventory accounts for Raw Materials, Work-in-Process, and Finished Goods are recorded based only on *standard costs*. Actual costs are not entered in the inventory accounts.
2. The Standard Cost Variances account is used to record differences between actual costs and standard costs.
3. Any balance in the Standard Cost Variances account at the end of the period is disposed of either by charging it to Cost of Goods Sold or by allocating it to the inventory accounts and Cost of Goods Sold in proportion to their year-end balances.

The flow of manufacturing costs through the accounts using a standard costing system is illustrated in Exhibit 11-2, with the balance in the Standard Cost Variances account charged to Cost of Goods Sold.

The journal entries corresponding to the cost flows illustrated in Exhibit 11-2 are as follows (assuming all variances are unfavorable):

EXHIBIT 11-2: FLOW OF MANUFACTURING COSTS IN A STANDARD COST SYSTEM

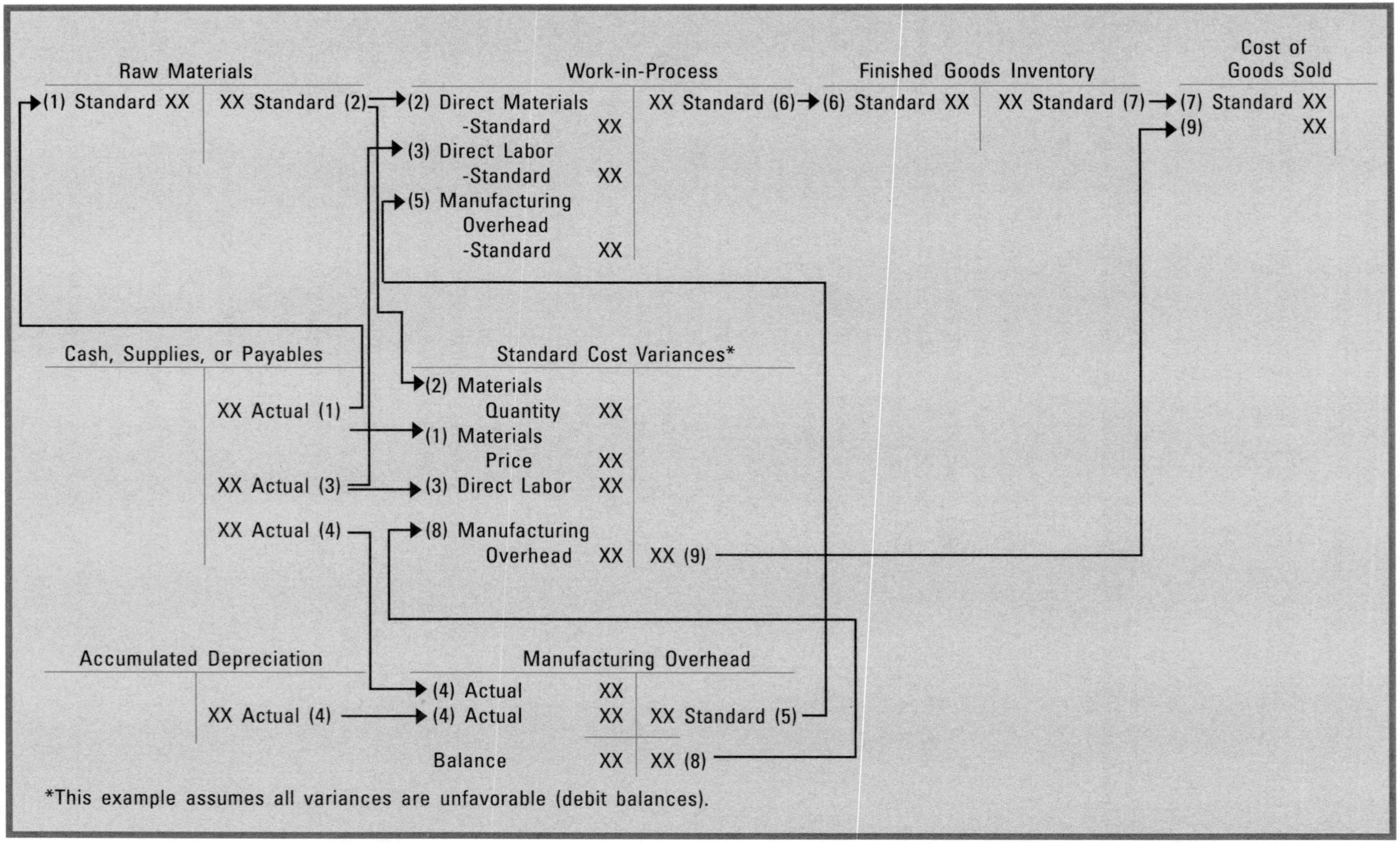

*This example assumes all variances are unfavorable (debit balances).

JOURNAL ENTRIES	(1) When raw materials are purchased, they are recorded at standard unit cost.		

Raw Materials (standard)	xxx	
Standard Cost Variances	xxx	
Cash (actual)		xxx

(2) When materials are requisitioned to the factory, they are added to Work-in-Process at standard cost for the standard quantity allowed, with any quantity variance recognized.

Work-in-Process (standard)	xxx	
Standard Cost Variances	xxx	
Raw Materials (standard)		xxx

(3) When direct labor wages are paid, direct labor costs are added to Work-in-Process based on standard quantity allowed and standard price.

Work-in-Process (standard)	xxx	
Standard Cost Variances	xxx	
Wages Payable (actual)		xxx

(4) Actual manufacturing overhead costs are recorded as incurred.

Manufacturing Overhead (actual)	xxx	
Wages Payable (actual)		xxx
Cash or Payables (actual)		xxx
Supplies (actual)		xxx
Accumulated Depreciation (actual)		xxx

(5) Manufacturing overhead costs are assigned to Work-in-Process at standard cost when the quantity of the overhead allocation base is determined.

Work-in-Process (standard)	xxx	
Manufacturing Overhead (standard)		xxx

(6) Standard cost of goods completed is transferred to Finished Goods at standard unit cost when goods are completed.

Finished Goods Inventory (standard)	xxx	
Work-in-Process (standard)		xxx

(7) Cost of goods sold is recorded at standard costs at the time inventory is sold.

Cost of Goods Sold (standard)	xxx	
Finished Goods Inventory (standard)		xxx

(8) The underapplied manufacturing overhead cost balance is closed to the Standard Cost Variances account.

Standard Cost Variances	xxx	
Manufacturing Overhead		xxx

> (9) The Standard Cost Variances balance for materials, labor, and overhead is closed to Cost of Goods Sold.
>
> | Cost of Goods Sold | xxx | |
> | Standard Cost Variances | | xxx |

When standard costs are used to record inventory transactions, it is not necessary to wait until actual costs are known to assign costs to units completed and/or sold. Therefore, for financial reporting purposes, a standard production costing system is convenient because it speeds up the recording of costs in the inventory accounts. For managerial accounting purposes, it is still necessary to measure actual costs to determine the actual cost of a completed job or the actual cost of a unit processed. It is not sufficient to know only how much it should have cost to produce a unit of service or product, but managers also need to know how much it actually cost and the reason for any variance.

Although most manufacturing companies have used some type of standard costing system to account for product costs, there is some evidence that with increased automation and real-time access to information, there may be good reason to revert to using only actual costs in the product costing system. Evidence discussed in Management Accounting Practice 11-4 indicates that the use of standard costing systems in certain types of manufacturing environments may be declining.

SUGGESTED READINGS

Cooper, Robin. "Does Your Company Need a New Cost System?" *Journal of Cost Management* (Spring 1987), pp. 45-49.

Cooper, Robin and Robert S. Kaplan. *The Design of Cost Management Systems* (Englewood Cliffs, NJ: Prentice Hall, 1991).

Falhaber, Thomas A., Fred A. Coad, and Thomas J. Little. "Building a Process Cost Management System From the Bottom Up," *Management Accounting* (May 1988), pp. 58-62.

Sandretto, Michael J. "What Kind of Cost System Do You Need?" *Harvard Business Review* (January-February 1985), pp. 110-118.

REVIEW PROBLEM

Process Costing System: Cost of Production Report and Journal Entries

Magnetic Media, Inc., manufactures magnetic data disks that are used in the computer industry. Since there is very little product differentiation between Magnetic's products, it uses a process costing system to determine inventory costs. Production and manufacturing cost data for 19X7 are as follows:

MANAGEMENT ACCOUNTING PRACTICE 11-4

Standard Cost Systems May Not Be Necessary in Automated Manufacturing Environments

A survey to determine trends in the design of product costing systems indicates that the increased use of automated manufacturing systems may be causing companies to convert their product costing systems back to actual costs from standard costs. The traditional argument against using actual costs is that they are more difficult to obtain for current production and that waiting for actual costs delays the product costing process.

With the growth of flexible manufacturing systems, which are virtually hands-free, actual data can be obtained on a real-time basis, overcoming the disadvantage of using actual costs. A criticism of using standard costs in an automated environment is that standard costs tend to include a "fudge factor" (an allowance for inefficiency), which may not be necessary in a fully automated environment.

This study reported that 42 percent of respondents at companies using process costing systems believed that running actual costs clearly provided better information; however, for companies using job-order costing systems, the percentage increased to 100 percent. As the researchers indicated, "This may suggest that discrete product companies are more likely to incorporate running actuals in lieu of standards because of the stronger relationship between product cost and selling price."

Based on: Thomas Tyson, Leslie Weisenfeld, and David Stout, "Running Actual Costs vs. Standard Costs," *Management Accounting* (August 1989), pp. 54-56.

Production data (units)

Units in process, beginning of period (60% converted)	3,000,000
Units started	27,000,000
Completed and transferred to finished goods	25,000,000
Units in process, end of period (30% converted)	5,000,000

All materials are added at the start of the production process.

Manufacturing costs

Work-in-Process, beginning of period	
(materials, $468,000; conversion, $252,000)	$ 720,000
Current manufacturing costs:	
Raw materials transferred to processing	6,132,000
Direct labor for the period	1,550,000
Manufacturing overhead applied for the period	3,498,000

Required:

(a) Prepare a cost of production report for Magnetic Media, Inc., for 19X7 using the weighted average approach to process costing illustrated in the chapter.

(b) Prepare journal entries to record current manufacturing costs assigned to Work-in-Process and to record inventory completed and transferred to Finished Goods Inventory during the period.

The solution to the review problem is found at the end of Chapter 11 assignment material. To maximize your learning, you should make a serious attempt to develop a written solution to the review problem before looking at the solution. If there are errors in your solution, you should then attempt to determine the causes of the errors.

KEY TERMS

Cost of production report—a document that summarizes total unit and cost data for each department or process for each period in a process costing system.

Equivalent completed units—the number of completed units that is equal, in terms of production effort (cost), to a given number of partially completed units.

First-in, first-out (FIFO) method—a process costing method that accounts for unit costs of beginning inventory separately from the cost of units started during the current period. The first costs incurred each period are assumed to have been used to complete the incomplete units carried over from the previous period.

Transferred-in costs—the combined cost of materials, labor, and overhead transferred in to a department as goods are received from the previous department.

Weighted average method—a method of inventory costing that spreads the combined cost of beginning inventory and current manufacturing costs (for materials, labor, and overhead) over the units completed and in ending inventory on an average basis.

APPENDIX A KEY TERMS

By-product—a product with insignificant value that is produced jointly with one or more other products.

Joint costs—the costs of producing joint products.

Joint products—two or more products produced simultaneously by a common manufacturing process.

Physical quantity method—a joint cost allocation method that allocates joint costs to joint products based on the relative quantities of a common physical characteristic possessed by the joint products.

Sales value allocation method—a joint cost allocation method that allocates costs to joint products based on the relative sales value of the joint products produced.

Split-off point—the point in a joint product manufacturing process where joint products emerge as separate, identifiable products.

REVIEW QUESTIONS

11-1
Describe the difference between job-order and process costing in terms of the primary cost objective and time period for which costs are accumulated.

11-2
What are the four major elements of a cost of production report?

11-3
What are equivalent completed units?

11-4
Under what conditions will equivalent units in process be different for materials and conversion costs?

11-5
Describe the calculation of the cost of units completed and transferred to finished goods.

11-6
Under what circumstances might the FIFO method be preferred to the weighted average method of process costing?

11-7
Which record in a process costing system provides cost data used to record the transfer of completed goods from Work-in-Process to Finished Goods?

11-8
When process costing involves multiple departments, what cost element must be considered in all departments except the first one?

11-9
What is product cost cross-subsidization and when is it most likely to occur?

11-10
Why is it important to have an accurate and reliable product costing system?

11-11
Even if inventory cost information used for financial reporting is accurate, it is generally an inadequate basis for evaluating the profitability of individual products. Why?

EXERCISES

11-1 Job-Order Costing and Process Costing Applications

Required:
For each of the following manufacturing situations, indicate whether job-order or process costing is more appropriate and why.

(a) A manufacturer of peanut butter
(b) A chemical plant that produces household cleaners
(c) A shoe manufacturer
(d) A modular home builder
(e) A company that makes only original equipment front windshields for automobile manufacturers

11-2 Job-Order Costing and Process Costing Applications

Required:
For each of the following situations, indicate whether job-order or process costing is more appropriate and why:

(a) A building contractor for residential dwellings
(b) A manufacturer of nylon yarn that sells to textile companies that make fabric
(c) A clothing manufacturer that makes suits in several different fabrics, colors, styles, and sizes
(d) A hosiery mill that manufactures one product that fits all sizes
(e) A vehicle battery manufacturer that has just received an order for 500,000 identical batteries to be delivered as manufactured over the next 12 months

11-3 Costing Work-in-Process and Finished Goods

King Manufacturing Company makes one product that is produced on a continuous basis in one department. All materials are added at the beginning of production. The total cost per equivalent unit in process in March 19X4 was $4.60, consisting of $3.00 for materials and $1.60 for conversion. During the month, 8,000 units of product were transferred to finished goods inventory; and on March 31, 4,000 units were in process, 10 percent converted. King uses weighted average costing.

Required:
(a) Determine the cost of goods transferred to finished goods inventory.
(b) Determine the cost of the ending work-in-process inventory.
(c) What was the total cost of the beginning work-in-process inventory, plus the current manufacturing costs?

11-4 Costing Work-in-Process and Finished Goods Without Beginning Inventories

Kiwi Manufacturing makes glue in a continuous process in one department. All materials are added at the beginning of the process, and labor and overhead are incurred evenly throughout the process. The unit cost for 19X3 was $35 per drum, consisting of $21 for materials and $14 for conversion. During the year, 4,800 drums of glue were produced; and on December 31, 19X3, 12 drums were in process, 40 percent completed as to conversion. There was no beginning inventory.

Required:
(a) Determine the cost of goods transferred to finished goods inventory.
(b) Determine the cost of the ending work-in-process inventory.
(c) What was the total cost in process?

11-5 Equivalent Unit Computations

During April 19X6, Four Corners Manufacturing placed 220,000 kilograms of horse feed in its Mixing Department. At the end of the month, 10,000 kilograms were still in process, 30 percent completed as to conversion. All raw materials are placed in Mixing at the beginning of the process. Four Corners uses weighted average costing.

Required:
(a) Determine the equivalent units in process for materials and conversion costs assuming there was no beginning inventory.
(b) Determine the equivalent units in process for materials and conversion costs assuming that 12,000 kilograms of feed, 40 percent completed, were in process prior to the addition of the 220,000 kilograms.

11-6 Equivalent Unit Computations

During February 19X5, Apex Co. had 15,000 units of product in process in its Mixing Department, of which 3,000 were still in process (25 percent converted) at the end of the period.

Required:
(a) Determine the equivalent units in process for conversion assuming there was no beginning inventory.
(b) Determine the equivalent units in process for conversion assuming that 2,800 of the 15,000 units were in beginning work-in-process, 30 percent converted, and that Apex uses weighted average costing.
(c) Determine the equivalent units in process for conversion assuming that 2,800 of the 15,000 units were in beginning work-in-process, 30 percent converted, that 5,000 units were in ending inventory, 50 percent completed, and that Apex uses weighted average costing.

11-7 Cost of Production Report: No Beginning Inventories

Fisk Manufacturing Company is a new company that produces newsprint paper through a special recycling process that uses scrap paper products. Production and cost data for October 19X7, the first month of operations for the company, are presented below:

Units of product started in process during October	90,000
Units completed and transferred to finished goods	75,000
Machine hours operated	10,000
Direct materials costs incurred	$243,000
Direct labor costs incurred	$ 95,265

Raw materials are added at the beginning of the process for each unit of product produced, and labor and manufacturing overhead are added evenly throughout the manufacturing process. Manufacturing overhead is applied to Work-in-Process at the rate of $12 per machine hour. Units in process at the end of the period were 65 percent converted.

Required:

Prepare a cost of production report for Fisk Manufacturing Company for October 19X7.

11-8 Cost of Production Report: No Beginning Inventories

Rodeway Paving Products Company manufactures asphalt paving materials for highway construction through a single-step process in which all materials are added at the beginning of the process. During October 19X4, Rodeway accumulated the following data in its process costing system:

Production data:	
Work-in-process, 10/1/X4	0 tons
Raw materials transferred to processing	25,000 tons
Work-in-process, 10/30/X4 (75% converted)	5,000 tons
Cost data:	
Raw materials transferred to processing	$300,000
Conversion costs:	
Direct labor cost incurred	19,000
Manufacturing overhead applied	?

Manufacturing overhead is applied at the rate of $1 per equivalent unit (ton) processed.

Required:

Prepare a cost of production report for October 19X4.

11-9 Joint Cost Allocation: Physical Quantity Method (Appendix A)

Chemco, Inc., processes two products, Bugoff and Weedout, used in the control of weeds and pests in lawn care. These products begin from a unique joint refining process in batches of 10,000 liters of mixture. At split-off, one-fourth of the mixture emerges as Bugoff and three-fourths as Weedout. Both products require further processing after split-off. The following cost and production data from August 19X1 were determined:

Total joint costs per batch	$15,000
Cost of further processing of Bugoff	5,000
Cost of further processing of Weedout	10,000
Beginning inventories	None

Required:

(a) Determine the joint cost allocation per batch of each product using the physical quantity method.
(b) Determine the total cost per liter for each product. (Round answer to the nearest cent.)

11-10 Joint Cost Allocation: Physical Quantity and Relative Sales Value Allocation Methods (Appendix A)

Hills and Dales Farms is a large poultry producer that processes and sells various grades of packaged chicken to grocery chains. Chickens are grown and accounted for in groups of 50,000. At the end of the standard growing period, the chickens are separated and sold by grades. Grades A and B are sold to grocery chains, and grades C and D are sold for other uses. For costing purposes, Hills and Dales treats each batch of newly hatched chicks as a joint product. The following data pertain to the last batch of 50,000 chicks:

Grade	Number of Chickens	Average Pounds of Chickens	Selling Price per Pound
A	25,000	4	$0.50
B	15,000	3	0.40
C	6,000	2 1/2	0.30
D	4,000	1 1/4	0.20

Total joint costs for this batch were $40,000.

Required:

(a) Compute the cost allocations for each product using the physical quantity number of chickens.
(b) Compute the cost allocations for each product using physical quantity if measured in pounds of chicken.
(c) Compute the cost allocations for each product using the relative sales value allocation method.

PROBLEMS

11-11 Weighted Average Process Costing with Beginning Inventories: Production Report and Journal Entries

Chamblee Processing Company manufactures a product on a continuous basis in two departments: Processing and Finishing. All materials are added at the beginning of work on the product in the Processing Department. During December 19X5, the following events occurred in the Processing Department:

Units started	16,000 units
Units completed and transferred to Finishing	15,000 units
Costs assigned to Processing:	
Raw materials (one unit of raw materials for each unit of product started)	$142,000
Manufacturing supplies used	18,000
Direct labor costs incurred	51,000
Supervisors' salaries	12,000
Other production labor costs	14,000
Depreciation on equipment	6,000
Other production costs	18,000

Additional information:

- Chamblee uses weighted average costing and applies manufacturing overhead to Work-in-Process at the rate of 100 percent of direct labor cost.
- Ending inventory in the Processing Department consists of 3,000 units that are one-third converted.
- Beginning inventory contained 2,000 units, one-half converted, with a cost of $27,300 ($17,300 for materials and $10,000 for conversion).

Required:

(a) Prepare a cost of production report for the Processing Department for December.
(b) Prepare all journal entries to record costs incurred by the Processing Department in December and to record the transfer of units to the Finishing Department. Overapplied or underapplied manufacturing overhead is written off to Cost of Goods Sold at the end of each month.

11-12 Weighted Average Process Costing with Beginning Inventories: Production Report and Journal Entries

Hillsborough, Inc., processes its only product in a single process and uses weighted average process costing to account for inventory costs. The following inventory, production, and cost data are provided for June 19X8:

Production data:		
Beginning inventory (25% converted)	210,000 units	
Units started	650,000 units	
Ending inventory (50% converted)	180,000 units	
Manufacturing costs:		
Beginning inventory in process:		
Materials cost	$146,000	
Conversion cost	88,000	$234,000
Raw materials cost added at beginning of process		739,800
Direct labor cost incurred		410,000
Manufacturing overhead applied		333,600

Required:

(a) Prepare a cost of production report for Hillsborough for June.
(b) Prepare journal entries to record costs incurred during the month for raw materials and direct labor and to record manufacturing overhead applied. Also prepare the entry to record the cost of goods completed and transferred to Finished Goods Inventory.
(c) Prepare a cost of goods manufactured report for Hillsborough for June.

11-13 Process Costing, Work-in-Process Analysis, Weighted Average Costing

Karkare Products, Inc., manufactures automobile polish through a process involving two departments: Mixing and Bottling. All materials are added at the beginning of the Mixing Department process. Manufacturing overhead is applied at the rate of 125 percent of direct labor costs. The Work-in-Process account for the Mixing Department for May 19X5 is presented below:

	Work-in-Process, Mixing		
5/1/X5 balance (100,000 units, 40% converted)	240,200	(c) ?	Finished and transferred to Bottling Department (a) ? units
May costs assigned:			
Raw materials (400,000 units)	460,000		
Direct labor	(b) ?		
Manufacturing overhead	100,000		
5/31/X5 balance (60,000 units, 45% converted)	(d) ?		

The beginning Work-in-Process balance consists of materials, $140,000, and conversion cost, $100,200.

Required:

Determine the values for the missing items lettered (a) through (d) in the Mixing Department's Work-in-Process account. Assume the company uses weighted average costing (*Hint:* You may want to prepare a cost of production report.)

11-14 Process Costing Production Reports for Two-Department Process: A Challenge Problem

The Dexter Production Company manufactures a single product. Its operations are a continuing process carried on in two departments: Machining and Finishing. In the production process, materials are added to the product in each department without increasing the number of units produced. For June 19X5, the company records indicated the following production statistics for each department:

	Machining	Finishing
Units in process, 6/1/X5	—	—
Units transferred from previous department	—	60,000
Units started in production	80,000	—
Units in process, 6/30/X5	20,000	10,000
Percent of completion of units in process at 6/30/X5:		
Materials	100%	100%
Conversion	50%	70%
Cost records showed the following charges for June:		
Materials	$240,000	$ 88,500
Labor	140,000	141,500
Overhead	65,000	25,700

Required:

Prepare separate cost of production reports for the Machining and Finishing Departments for June 19X5. In preparing the report for the Finishing

Department, the cost of the units transferred in from the Machining Department is treated the same as raw materials added at the beginning of the process.

(CPA Adapted)

11-15 Process Costing: Two Departments' Cost of Production Reports

Atlantic Paper Company manufactures paper used in printing newspapers. The process involves two departments: Processing and Bleaching. Raw materials are added at the beginning of the Processing Department. Goods are transferred from the Processing Department to the Bleaching Department and from Bleaching to finished goods inventory. Production and cost data for Atlantic Paper Company are presented below for the month of January 19X5:

	Processing	Bleaching
Production data (units):		
In process, 1/1/X5 (33 1/3% converted in Processing, 25% converted in Bleaching)	150,000	80,000
Raw materials transferred to Processing	450,000	
Transferred to Bleaching from Processing	500,000	500,000
Transferred to finished goods		520,000
Cost data:		
Raw materials	$3,600,000	
Conversion costs:		
Direct labor costs	2,000,000	$3,000,000
Manufacturing overhead applied (210% of direct labor cost for Processing and 120% of direct labor cost for Bleaching)	4,200,000	3,600,000

Additional information:

- Assume that 1 unit of raw materials is required to produce 1 unit of product.
- Ending work-in-process inventory was 50 percent converted in the Processing Department and 20 percent converted in the Bleaching Department.
- The company uses weighted average costing.
- Beginning work-in-process consisted of the following:

	Processing	Bleaching
Raw materials	$1,125,000	
Transferred-in costs		$1,520,000
Conversion costs	575,000	242,400
Total	$1,700,000	$1,762,400

Required:

(a) Prepare cost of production reports for the Processing and Bleaching Departments.
(b) Prepare the journal entries to record (1) transfer of units from the Processing Department to the Bleaching Department and (2) the

transfer of units from the Bleaching Department to Finished Goods Inventory.

(c) Determine the total materials cost and total conversion cost in the final product.

11-16 Joint Cost Allocation: Physical Quantity and Sales Value Allocation Methods (Appendix A)

Vreeland, Inc., manufactures products X, Y, and Z from a joint process. Joint product costs were $120,000 during September. Additional information is as follows:

| | | | Sales Value and Additional Costs if Processed Further | |
Product	Units Produced	Sales Value at Split-Off	Sales Value	Additional Costs
X	6,000	$40,000	$55,000	$9,000
Y	4,000	35,000	45,000	7,000
Z	2,000	25,000	30,000	5,000

Required:

(a) Determine the amount of joint product costs to be allocated to each of the products during September assuming the company uses the physical quantity method of joint cost allocation.

(b) Determine the amount of joint product costs to be allocated to each of the products during September assuming the company uses the sales value method of joint cost allocation. (Round calculations to four decimal places.)

(c) Should any of the products be processed further? Explain.

(CPA Adapted)

11-17 Joint Cost Allocation: Net Realizable Sales Value Allocation Method (Appendix A)

Doe Corporation grows, processes, cans, and sells three main pineapple products: sliced pineapple, crushed pineapple, and pineapple juice. The outside skin is cut off in the Cutting Department and processed as animal feed. The skin is treated as a by-product. Doe's production process is as follows:

- Pineapples are first processed in the Cutting Department. The pineapples are washed, and the outside skin is cut away. Then, the pineapples are cored and trimmed for slicing. The three main products (sliced, crushed, and juice) and the by-product (animal feed) are recognized after processing in the Cutting Department. Each product is then transferred to a separate department for final processing.

- The trimmed pineapples are forwarded to the Slicing Department, where the pineapples are sliced and canned. Any juice generated during the slicing operation is packed in the cans with the slices.

- The pieces of pineapple trimmed from the fruit are diced and canned in the Crushing Department. Again, the juice generated during this operation is packed in the can with the crushed pineapple.

- The core and surplus pineapple generated from the Cutting Department are pulverized into a liquid in the Juicing Department.
- The outside skin is chopped into animal feed in the Feed Department.

The Doe Corporation uses the relative sales value allocation method (based on net realizable value) to assign costs of the joint process to its main products. The by-product is inventoried at its market value. A total of 270,000 pounds entered the Cutting Department during May. The schedule below shows the costs incurred in each department, the proportion by weight transferred to the four final processing departments, and the selling price of each product.

Department	Costs Incurred	Percent of Product by Weight Transferred to Departments	Selling Price per Pound of Final Product
Cutting	$60,000	—	None
Slicing	4,700	35	$0.60
Crushing	10,580	28	0.55
Juicing	3,250	27	0.30
Animal feed	700	10	0.10
Total	$79,230	100	

Required:
(a) Calculate the number of pounds of pineapple that result as output for pineapple slices, crushed pineapple, pineapple juice, and animal feed.
(b) Calculate the net realizable value at the split-off point of the three main products.
(c) Calculate the amount of the cost of the Cutting Department assigned to each of the three main products and to the by-product in accordance with corporate policy.
(d) Calculate the gross profits for each of the three main products.

(CMA Adapted)

11-18 Standard Cost Journal Entries (Appendix B)

Konrad Company uses a standard costing system in accounting for the production of its only product: a gadget called "de-slicer" that attaches to golf clubs to help golfers hit the ball straighter. The standard cost of producing one de-slicer is $7.70. During a recent month, the following activities occurred:

- Raw materials with a standard cost of $73,000 were purchased on account for $75,000.
- 20,000 units were started and completed.
- 18,500 units were sold.
- Actual raw materials issued to processing had a standard cost of $71,000. The direct materials flexible budget for the units produced during the period was $69,000.
- The direct labor flexible budget for the units produced during the period was $50,000, whereas actual direct labor was $47,500.

- Actual manufacturing overhead was as follows:

Indirect labor	$12,000
Manufacturing supplies	8,000
Depreciation on plant and equipment	14,000
Utilities bill received but not paid	4,000

- The manufacturing overhead flexible budget for the units produced was $35,000.

Required:

Prepare standard cost journal entries for the month, including the entry to close the Standard Cost Variances account. Number your entries.

11-19 Standard Cost Journal Entries (Appendix B)

The Greenwich Clock Company manufactures clocks with movements purchased from a Swiss company and with housings purchased from a British Company.

The standard cost per finished unit of model AJ9 is $40:

Movement	$ 15
Housing	10
Labor (0.5 hours × $16 per labor hour)	8
Applied variable overhead (per completed unit)	4
Applied fixed overhead (per completed unit)	3
Total	$ 40

During a recent month, the following activities related to the production of model AJ9 occurred:

- Purchased 2,200 movements for $31,200 and 3,000 housings for $32,500.
- 3,000 units were completed.
- 2,900 units were sold.
- At the end of the month, actual manufacturing activities were summarized as follows:
  - Actual raw materials issued to production consisted of 3,000 movements and 3,050 housings.
  - Actual direct labor costs consisted of 1,450 hours at $16 per hour.
  - Actual indirect labor amounted to $5,000.
  - Used manufacturing supplies costing $3,000.
  - Monthly depreciation on plant and equipment was $10,000.
  - Received bills for miscellaneous overhead costing $4,500.

Required:

Prepare standard cost journal entries for the month, including the entry to close the Standard Cost Variances account. Number your entries.

DISCUSSION QUESTIONS AND CASES

11-20 Costing System Design in a Changing Environment

Massey Lawn Products has been in business for four years. The company initially implemented a job-cost system for its production operations.

Separate job-cost systems were implemented for the production of lawn mowers, garden tillers, and leaf mulchers. The company had one assembly line, and each batch operation produced only 30 to 45 units. The amounts of time, labor, materials and parts, and equipment usage were easily monitored. Manufacturing supplies were also tracked and charged per batch. Other factory overhead items were charged using a predetermined overhead rate that was set each quarter. The job-cost data for a typical job is as follows:

Product Name	8HPTiller	Job No.	613
Product No.	11	Date	12-11-X7

	Hours	Dollars
Direct labor @ $16 per hour	200	$3,200
Assembly line time @ $42 per hour	16	672
Components and parts:		
Motors (32 × $100 each)		3,200
Component sets (32 × $70 each)		2,240
Overhead @ $24 per assembly line hour	16	384
Total costs		$9,696
Units completed		32
Cost per unit ($9,696/32)		$ 303

During the past year, the demand for each of the products has grown rapidly; and the job costing accountant has encountered much difficulty in tracking and recording the cost for every batch. The plant now has three assembly lines, one for each product line. Within each product line, there are three models, the only major difference between them being the horsepower size of the motors. The assembly line workers are trained for all three lines; and many of the component parts, such as handles and wheels, are interchangeable between products.

Required:
(a) What arguments can be made for maintaining the job costing system?
(b) What arguments can be made for changing to process costing?
(c) Make a recommendation as to which system you prefer and explain how your system will meet the demands now placed upon the production system.

11-21 Costing System Design: Evaluating a Job Costing System with Multiple Manufacturing Steps

The Lawrence Windo Company manufactures standard and custom windows. The standard windows are manufactured for stock in lot sizes of 100 units. The custom windows are made-to-order in lot sizes that typically range between 1 and 50 units. The main difference between the standard and the custom windows is the available sizes. While the standard windows are available in only a limited number of sizes, the custom windows are made in any size customers request. Both products conform to

Lawrence's high standards and go through identical manufacturing steps using common facilities:

- Glass cutting
- Wood and vinyl cutting
- Gluing and assembly
- Pressing
- Varnishing
- Drying
- Inspection and repair
- Packaging

Although the production time to produce a single window is less than 5 hours, scheduling considerations typically result in standard windows taking 2 to 3 weeks to produce. Because they receive scheduling priority, the custom windows are normally produced in 2 days. The two cutting operations and the pressing operation are major bottlenecks because the setup times before each lot can be processed are 30 minutes for each operation.

Costs are assigned to each lot on the basis of actual materials costs, plus a standard markup for conversion. The conversion markup is applied on the basis of actual materials cost. It is computed each year based on total conversion costs and total materials costs during the previous year.

Prices for standard windows are set at 150 percent of manufacturing costs. Recognizing the additional sales and design effort required for custom windows, the prices for custom windows are set at 180 percent of manufacturing costs.

Required:
(a) Briefly comment on Lawrence Windo's cost accounting system. Will it produce accurate product costs? Why or why not? What will be the direction and likely result of any costing errors?
(b) Identify the basic records Lawrence Windo should have to initiate production and to accumulate information for product costing purposes.
(c) Describe a costing system that will provide accurate cost information for Lawrence Windo.

11-22 Cross-Subsidization: Plant-Wide and Departmental Overhead Rates

Gauche Company manufactures two products, A and B, and incurs overhead costs in two production departments, I and II. The equation for annual overhead costs in each production department is as follows:

$$\text{Department I overhead} = \$400{,}000 + \$20 \text{ per machine hour}$$

$$\text{Department II overhead} = \$400{,}000 + \$50 \text{ per machine hour}$$

Each unit of A requires 2 machine hours in Department I and 3 hours in Department II. Each unit of B requires 7.5 hours in Department I and 1.25 hours in Department II. During 19X8, 50,000 units of A and 40,000 units of B were produced.

Required:

(a) Use the information on resource consumption for each product and the equations for total overhead to determine the total 19X8 overhead costs in each production department.

(b) Assuming departmental overhead rates based on machine hours are used, determine the total overhead costs assigned to each product and to each unit of A and B.

(c) Assuming a plant-wide overhead rate based on machine hours is used, determine the total overhead costs assigned to each product and to each unit of A and B.

(d) For each product in total and for each unit of A and B, determine the cross-subsidization involved in using a plant-wide rate.

(e) Mention several erroneous decisions management may make if costs are assigned using the plant-wide rate.

11-23 Cross-Subsidization: Plant-Wide and Departmental Overhead Rates

Droit Company manufactures two products, Alpha and Beta, and incurs overhead costs in two departments, Purchasing and Manufacturing. The equation for annual overhead costs in each department is as follows:

Purchasing overhead = $72,000 + $0.10 per dollar of raw materials issued

Manufacturing overhead = $500,000 + $4 per labor hour

Each unit of Alpha requires raw materials costing $20 and 4 labor hours. Each unit of Beta requires raw materials costing $80 and 2 labor hours. During 19X9, 10,000 units of Alpha and 20,000 units of Beta were produced.

Required:

(a) Use the information on resource consumption for each product and the equations for total overhead to determine the total 19X9 overhead costs in the Purchasing and Manufacturing Departments.

(b) Assuming Purchasing uses a departmental overhead rate based on the dollar value of raw materials issued and Manufacturing uses an overhead rate based on labor hours, determine the total overhead costs assigned to each product and to each unit of Alpha and Beta.

(c) Assuming a plant-wide overhead rate based on labor hours is used, determine the total overhead costs assigned to each product and to each unit of Alpha and Beta.

(d) Determine the cross-subsidization involved in using a plant-wide rate for each product and each unit of Alpha and Beta.

(e) Mention several erroneous decisions management may make if costs are assigned using the plant-wide rate.

11-24 Production Planning and Job Costing with Multiple Cost Centers

Adirondack Cedar Products manufactures wooden furniture in three production operations: sawing/beveling, drilling, and assembling/sanding. Each operation is treated as a cost center with a combined predetermined conversion rate for direct labor and overhead. Presented are bills of materials and operations lists for two styles of wooden bookcases, standard and deluxe, produced by the firm:

Bill of Materials

Product _Standard bookcase_

Product No. _201_

Part	Quantity
1" cedar	26 board feet
1 1/2" screw	24

Bill of Materials

Product _Deluxe bookcase_

Product No. _202_

Part	Quantity
1" cedar	55 board feet
1/4" cedar	20 board feet
Brackets	2 sets
Handle	2
1 1/2" screw	40

Operations List

Product _Standard bookcase_

Product No. _201_

Operation	Operating time
Saw	5 minutes
Drill	5 minutes
Assemble/sand	20 minutes

Operations List

Product _Deluxe bookcase_

Product No. _202_

Operation	Operating time
Saw/bevel	20 minutes
Drill	10 minutes
Assemble/sand	30 minutes

Cost information is as follows:

1" cedar	$0.50 per board foot
1/4" cedar	0.20 per board foot
1 1/2" screws	0.015 each
Bracket	0.75 per set
Handles	0.25 each
Sawing/beveling conversion rate	24.00 per hour
Drilling conversion rate	15.00 per hour
Assembling/sanding conversion rate	10.00 per hour

Required:

(a) Prepare a production order, including start and stop times, for the manufacture of 20 deluxe bookcases. Production is to begin at 10:00 A.M. on Tuesday morning, April 4, 19X4, and continue during normal business hours until completed. Units are not to be passed from saw/bevel until 75 percent of the units are completed. At that time, units will be passed directly from one operation to the next as they are completed. Normal business hours are 8:00 A.M.-12:00 P.M. and 1:00 P.M.-5:00 P.M. Identify the production order as Job 387.

(b) Prepare materials requisitions for Job 387. All wood is added at the start of operations in sawing/beveling and all other parts are added during assembling/sanding. The next materials requisition is number 1093.

(c) Prepare work tickets for Job 387 assuming operations proceed exactly according to plan. The next work ticket is number 2413.

(d) Prepare a cost sheet for Job 387.

(e) Prepare all journal entries to assign costs to Job 387 as it passes from one operation to the next and as it is completed.

(f) Using T-accounts for inventory and conversion cost accounts, prepare a diagram illustrating the flow of costs through the costing system.

(g) Evaluate Adirondack Cedar Products' costing system. Is it appropriate for the firm's product mix and production operations? Suggest any specific changes that might result in more accurate product costs. Suggest any simplifications that might be implemented without reducing the accuracy of cost information.

11-25 Designing a Job Costing System for Heterogeneous Products

The Montana Machine Shop is organized by function; that is, each type of machine or activity is grouped together. The plant layout is presented below:

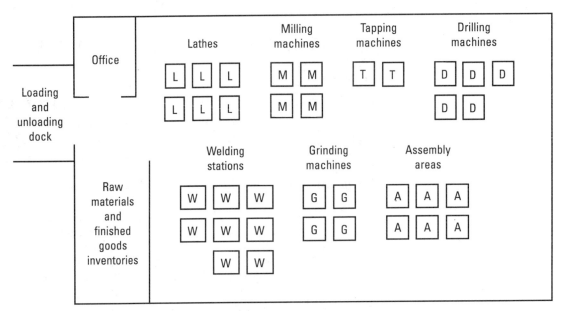

Each square represents a machine or work area. The six lathes operate with little operator assistance once they are set up and a unit of product is loaded. Consequently, there is one operator for every two machines. Each of the four milling, two tapping, five drilling, and four grinding machines has one operator. Each welding station has two operators, and each assembly area has two employees. The welding and assembly operations are labor-intensive, while all other operations are machine-paced. The original cost and the operating costs of each type of machine differ significantly.

The shop produces a variety of metal products for speculative inventory. The products are quite heterogeneous, requiring varying amounts of raw materials and attention in each production operation. Jobs follow a jumbled path from start to finish. Parts of a job, for example, might require work on the lathes and milling machines, followed by welding, drilling, assembly, and then more welding.

Required:

(a) Identify the basic records required to plan and initiate production and to accumulate information for product costing purposes.

(b) Describe a costing system that will provide accurate job-cost information for the Montana Machine Shop. Your answer should consider the number and names of cost centers and how materials, labor, and overhead costs are to be assigned to jobs worked on in each cost center. Do not be overly concerned about developing information to evaluate individual machines and their operators. Do be concerned about the cost and complexity of the costing system.

11-26 Designing a Job Costing System for Heterogeneous Products: Changes in Manufacturing Procedures

This is a continuation of Problem 11-25.

In an effort to reduce the cycle time between starting and completing a product and work-in-process inventories, the management of the Montana Machine Shop performed a detailed analysis of the firm's products and production procedures. They found that although there was considerable diversity in finished products, all products underwent one of two standard production sequences. At the end of these sequences, some products went directly to finished goods inventory, while others underwent some additional welding, grinding, or assembly operations. Basically, the company produced two products, with some units of each undergoing additional manufacturing operations to meet particular product specifications.

Management believed that this information would help them look at their products in a new way. Organizing manufacturing to produce two primary products would greatly simplify bills of materials, operations lists, and production orders. Other products based on these two products could then have product specifications starting with the appropriate intermediate product. On the manufacturing floor, most operations could be rearranged around the two primary products, rather than by function. What's more, with proper line balancing, there would be no need to change machine settings for the machines dedicated to the production of the two primary products. The proposed plant layout is as follows:

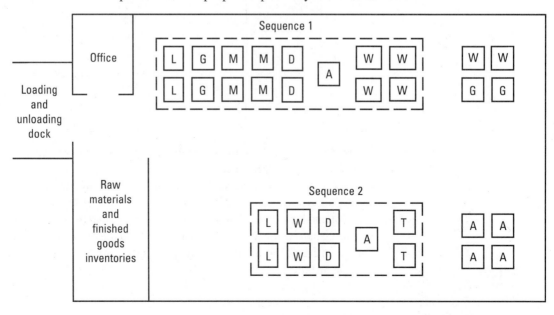

Sequences 1 and 2 refer to the homogeneous set of activities required to produce Products 1 and 2. The other operations on the right are only used for products that undergo additional manufacturing activities. Because of increased productivity due to the reduction in the number of machine setups, management was able to eliminate two lathes and one drill press.

Required:

Describe how the costing system proposed for Problem 11-25 should be modified. The primary purpose of the system is to provide accurate job-cost information. Your answer should consider the number and names of cost centers and how materials, labor, and overhead costs are to be assigned to jobs worked on in each cost center. Do not be overly concerned about developing information to evaluate individual machines and their operators. Do be concerned about the cost and complexity of the costing system.

11-27 Designing a Product Costing System: Changes in Manufacturing Procedures from Batch to Continuous Production

Carolina Wood Products manufactures a single product, bookcases, in a series of four manufacturing operations: sawing, drilling, sanding, and assembly. All units are identical in all respects. The plant layout is as follows:

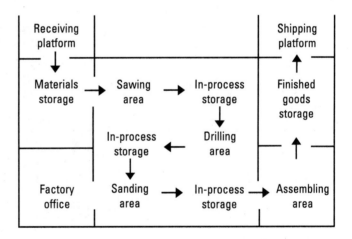

The flow of work is indicated by the arrows. All operations are either labor-intensive or labor-paced.

Bookcases are produced for speculative inventory, rather than in response to specific customer orders, in batches of 30 units. A job-cost sheet is maintained for each batch. All work on a batch is completed at each operation before the batch is placed in either in-process or finished goods storage. All units in a batch are then taken to the next operation for further manufacturing.

Required:

(a) Identify the basic records required to plan and initiate production and to accumulate information for product costing purposes.

(b) For the purpose of obtaining accurate product costs only, identify the number of cost centers that should be established, indicate why this number of cost centers is required, and describe how labor and overhead costs should be assigned to each job.

(c) To reduce in-process inventories, management has decided to change from batch to continuous production. Under continuous production, units will move continuously from one operation to the next without being placed in in-process storage.

   (1) Is it possible to continue to utilize a job costing system with batches of 30 units?

   (2) Briefly describe a more efficient approach to product costing under the new manufacturing environment.

   (3) What is the minimum number of cost centers required for accurate product costing under the costing system that you described above?

   (4) Identify one major subjective judgment that would likely be made each period under the costing system that you described above.

11-28 Designing a Costing System for Heterogeneous Products: Changes in Production Procedures[2]

Rantoul Tool, Inc., is a medium-sized producer of custom machine tools. The company's single production facility is located just west of Pittsburgh, Pennsylvania. Last year's sales totaled $93 million. Rantoul's 115 employees include 7 sales representatives, 4 industrial and mechanical engineers, 16 office employees (order entry, accounting, scheduling, secretarial services, and health), 5 corporate officers, and 83 plant employees (supervisors, expediters, machine operators, materials handlers, and maintenance).

Rantoul's products are used as manufacturing supplies by large manufacturers. Products vary considerably in their raw materials and manufacturing requirements. Because of competitive pressures, accurate product cost information is required for pricing and cost control.

Until about 5 years ago, Rantoul's factory contained a total of 35 machines of 8 different types, distributed as follows:

Type	Number	Type	Number
A	5	E	8
B	6	X	1
C	4	Y	1
D	9	Z	1

The machines differed significantly in their original cost, operating life, power consumption, and maintenance requirements.

2 Adapted with permission from "Instructional Case: Rantoul Tool, Inc." by Wayne J. Morse, *Issues in Accounting Education* 5, no.1 (Spring 1990): pp. 78-87. Copyrighted by the American Accounting Association.

Production Flows: Plant Layout

Rantoul's machines were laid out and organized into departments by machine type with a supervisor in charge of each department. Although each was unique, the 3 specialty machines (X, Y, and Z) were placed in 1 department. Hence, there were a total of 6 departments. The layout of the 35 machines is diagrammed in Exhibit 11-3. Each department's work area is enclosed in dashed lines.

The firm's products, produced in batches of identical units referred to as a job, were quite heterogeneous. Some required work on only three machines but others required work on as many as seven machines. Nor was there a consistent work flow among machines. Some jobs, for example, went from a B to a D to a Z, while others went from an A to a Z to a D to a C, and so forth.

A work team of one or more employees was assigned to each machine center. In general, each operator worked on only the machine to which he or she was assigned and worked on only one job at a time. A worker would occasionally help another operator who was having difficulty.

At the start of each morning and afternoon, each department supervisor received information on job assignments for the next four hours. Employees obtained materials for jobs from either the raw materials storage area or the in-process storage area, located as shown in Exhibit 11-3. After performing the required operation, employees placed the job in either the in-process storage area or the inspection/packing/shipping area.

EXHIBIT 11-3: RANTOUL TOOL, INC., ORIGINAL PLANT LAYOUT

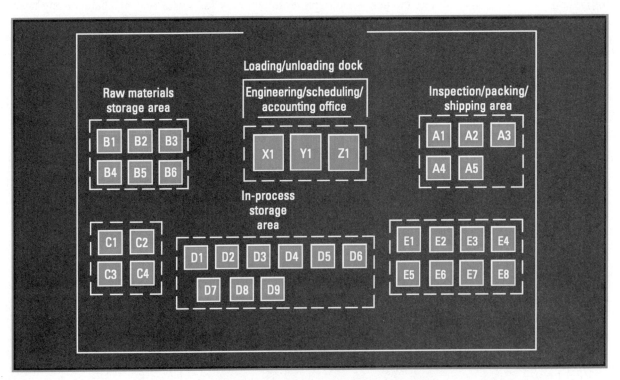

Systems Redesign: Dedicated Production Lines

The production system described above served management well for many years. But beginning in the early 1980s, as competitive pressures increased, management became concerned about the high storage cost of in-process inventories and the amount of time production employees spent on activities that did not add value to the final product.

About seven years ago, management instituted a special study of work flows with the goal of reducing in-process inventories and nonvalue-added activities. Only activities that physically changed materials were classified as value-added. All other activities, including receiving instructions, moving inventories, looking for jobs in the in-process storage area, and setting up machines to work on jobs, were classified as nonvalue-added.

The study revealed that although the products were quite heterogeneous, approximately 50 percent of the company's products could be placed in one of two homogeneous categories. Products in each of these categories required work on the same types of machines, in the same sequence, and with the same proportion of work time on each machine in the sequence. What's more, the machine settings for products in each category were similar; so, virtually no additional setup time was required in the changeover from one job to another within the same product category.

Management believed that significant improvements in productivity and reductions in inventory could be obtained by changing the plant layout so the jobs in these two homogeneous categories would never enter the in-process storage area. Instead, employees would move the units in each job directly from one machine to the next.

Management anticipated that shorter production times and reduced selling prices, made possible by increased productivity, would result in an increase in sales. Consequently, management elected to maintain the current number of machines. Management also anticipated a reduction in the complexity of machine setups and the need to expedite orders. This made possible a reduction in the number of departments and production supervisors from six to five. The new departments were: Category 1 products; Category 2 products; Machine Groups B, E, and C; Machine Group D; and Machine Groups X, Z, and A.

The number of machines placed in the first two departments were selected to achieve balanced flows within the departments, given the varying speeds of individual machines. The redesigned plant layout is presented in Exhibit 11-4. Each department's work area is enclosed in dashed lines.

The Flexible Manufacturing System

Rantoul's management was delighted with the results obtained from the plant reorganization. As a result of reduced materials movement and less in-process inventory in storage, manufacturing and storage costs fell, while production times decreased. Even more welcome was a decline in the percentage of Category 1 and Category 2 products identified as defective. The increase in quality appeared to result from (1) an increased ability to spot quality problems when there is less inventory to deal with and (2) the immediate identification of quality problems by subsequent machine

EXHIBIT 11-4: RANTOUL TOOL, INC., REDESIGNED PLANT LAYOUT

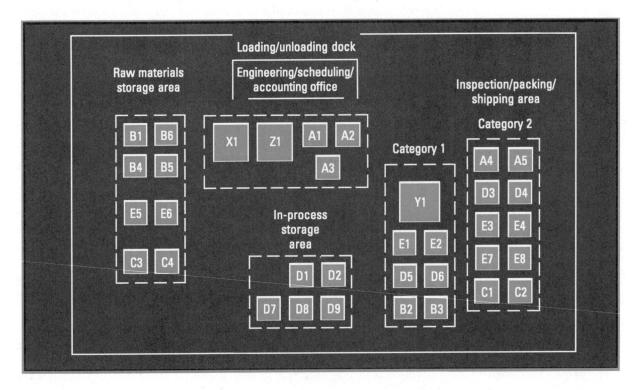

operators. The immediate identification of problems facilitated corrective action before many units were spoiled.

Management has now turned its attention to correcting the problem of high setup costs and in-process inventories of products not in Categories 1 or 2. These products are now called Category 3 products. In an attempt to reduce the cost of Category 3 products, management has decided to replace all machines used to manufacture them, installing in their place a flexible manufacturing system (FMS). The lines for Category 1 and Category 2 products will not be changed. As before, each Category 3 product will follow its own production path; each will require its own combination of operations.

In the new FMS line for Category 3 products, jobs will be subdivided into individual units. Employees will place all materials for each unit on a portable platform. Subsequent movements to appropriate machines and all machine work will be automatic and computer-controlled. Because each of the new machines will be highly flexible, labor setup time will be virtually nil. The work platforms will be of identical size. Each platform will contain coded information about the operations to be performed at each workstation and the materials or partially completed units required for those operations. As the platform arrives at a machine, the coded information will be used to verify the job, and the specified work will be performed. If materials are misplaced or if the coding is incorrect, a call for manual assistance will be sent automatically.

Computers will monitor all operations and keep detailed records on job status and the amount of time each unit spends on each machine. Maintenance employees will continually inspect machines and make needed adjustments. As units are completed, employees will remove the units from the portable platforms, inspect the units, assemble the units by job, and pack the jobs for shipment. The in-process storage area will be eliminated.

The redesigned plant layout, with the FMS line, is presented in Exhibit 11-5. The computer-controlled machines in Category 3 are identified as H1 through L1. There is only one machine of each type, and the operating costs of each machine differ significantly. The broad lines around and to the machines represent the computer-controlled movement system.

The redesigned factory will have only three production departments for Category 1, 2, and 3 products. The number of direct labor employees will be significantly reduced, but those left will have an increase in their responsibilities. Support activities will expand to include two new service departments: Computer Control and Maintenance.

Required:

(a) For a job costing system, identify the basic records required to plan and initiate production and to accumulate information for product costing purposes.

EXHIBIT 11-5: RANTOUL TOOL, INC., REDESIGNED PLANT LAYOUT WITH A FLEXIBLE MANUFACTURING SYSTEM

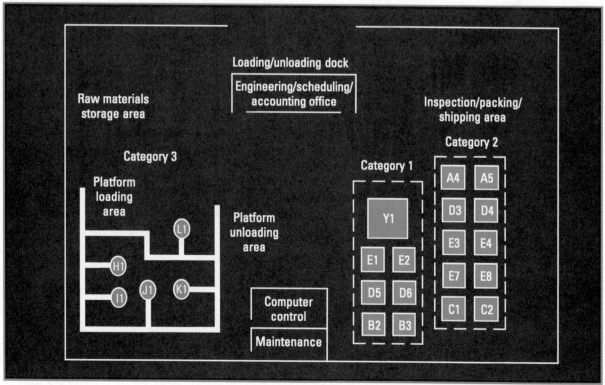

(b) Describe a costing system that would have provided accurate job cost information for Rantoul's management when the original plant layout was used. Do not be overly concerned about developing information to evaluate individual machines and their operators. Do be concerned about the cost and complexity of the costing system.
(c) Describe a costing system that would have provided accurate cost information for Rantoul's management when it changed its plant layout to accommodate products in Categories 1 and 2.
(d) Describe a costing system that will provide accurate product cost information for the new flexible manufacturing system.

SOLUTION TO REVIEW PROBLEM

(a)

Magnetic Media, Inc.
Cost of Production Report
For the Month Ending December 31, 19X7

Summary of units in process:

Beginning	3,000,000
Units started	27,000,000
In process	30,000,000
Completed	-25,000,000
Ending	5,000,000

Equivalent units in process:	Materials	Conversion
Units completed	25,000,000	25,000,000
Plus equivalent units in ending inventory	5,000,000	1,500,000*
Equivalent units in process	30,000,000	26,500,000

Total cost to be accounted for and cost per equivalent unit in process:	Materials	Conversion	Total
Work-in-Process, beginning	$ 468,000	$ 252,000	$ 720,000
Current cost	6,132,000	5,048,000**	11,180,000
Total cost in process	$ 6,600,000	$ 5,300,000	$11,900,000
Equivalent units in process	÷30,000,000	÷26,500,000	
Cost per equivalent unit in process	$0.22	$0.20	$0.42

Accounting for total costs:

Transferred out (25,000,000 × $0.42)		$10,500,000
Work-in-Process, ending:		
Materials (5,000,000 × $0.22)	$1,100,000	
Conversion (1,500,000 × $0.20)	300,000	1,400,000
Total cost accounted for		$11,900,000

*5,000,000 units 30% converted
**Includes direct labor of $1,550,000 and applied manufacturing overhead of $3,498,000

(b)

JOURNAL ENTRIES	Work-in-Process Raw Materials To record requisition of raw materials to factory.	6,132,000	6,132,000
	Work-in-Process Wages Payable To record wages for the month and assign direct labor cost to Work-in-Process.	1,550,000	1,550,000
	Work-in-Process Manufacturing Overhead To apply manufacturing overhead to Work-in-Process.	3,498,000	3,498,000
	Finished Goods Inventory Work-in-Process To transfer cost of units completed to Finished Goods Inventory.	10,500,000	10,500,000

12

ALLOCATING INDIRECT COSTS AND INVENTORY VALUATION APPROACHES

In this chapter, we continue our discussion of topics related to cost measurement and inventory valuation. All cost measurements involve assigning costs to a cost objective or reassigning them from one cost objective to another. For various reasons, it is not always possible or feasible to make a direct association between a cost objective and all of its costs. For instance, in the illustrations of job and process costing in Chapters 10 and 11, direct materials and direct labor costs were assigned directly to products, whereas indirect manufacturing costs were assigned to products on the basis of some volume-related factor common to all products such as machine hours or direct labor hours.

Consider the following cost measurement situation. Assume the management of a company wants to know the total cost for the year of operating the personnel department (which is one of several staff departments located in the company's main administration building). Many costs, including salaries of personnel department employees, long-distance telephone charges, travel, and other personnel costs, can be assigned directly to the department. On the other hand, other costs, such as the cost of electricity and building space, may not be measured directly for the personnel department, especially if there is only one meter recording the electricity used in the building and if the lease contract stipulates only a monthly rental for the whole building. Obviously, a portion of both the electricity and lease costs is incurred for the benefit of the personnel department, but neither is incurred or recorded in a way that identifies the amounts attributable to each of the departments located in the building.

Since electricity and lease costs cannot be directly determined for the personnel department, the only way a portion of these costs can be attributed to that department is by indirect assignment *or, as some call it,* cost allocation. *Just as manufacturing overhead may be assigned to products based on direct labor hours, electricity cost may be allocated to the personnel and other departments in the building based on the number of electrical outlets and lights, the amount of cubic feet of heated space, or some other logical basis; and lease costs might be allocated based on square footage used.*

Unfortunately, indirect cost assignment, or allocation, is an inexact process because it involves making judgments such as what allocation base to use for making the assignment and whether to allocate all indirect costs using the same allocation base. If poor judgments are made, significant errors in total cost measurements may result. Consequently, caution must always be exercised in making indirect cost assignments. **One purpose of this chapter is to explore the nature of indirect costs. We will consider the uses and limitations of cost allocation and examine some of the alternative methods of assigning indirect costs to cost objectives.** *Although much of this discussion is presented from the perspective of product costing, keep in mind that indirect costs and the tracing of indirect costs to cost objectives are relevant to virtually all cost objectives. Indeed, it would be a rare occurrence for all costs associated with any cost objective to be* directly *traceable to it.*

The discussions of inventory costing systems in Chapters 10 and 11 were based on the absorption costing *approach, which treats all manufacturing costs as* product costs *and all other costs as* period costs. *This general approach to product costing is required for external financial reporting; however, an alternative approach often used for internal reporting and managerial decision making purposes is* variable costing. *The only difference between absorption and variable costing is the treatment of* fixed manufacturing overhead costs such as depreciation and fixed salaries. *Under absorption costing, fixed costs are included in the cost of inventory (a product cost); but under variable costing, they are recorded as a current operating expense (a period cost).* **Another purpose of this chapter is to present a comparison and analysis of absorption and variable costing.** *Both methods are illustrated showing their effects, respectively, on inventory valuation and income. The advantages and disadvantages of each method are also discussed.*

ALLOCATING INDIRECT COSTS

LO 1

A major theme of this text is cost measurement, which involves determining the costs appropriately assigned to or associated with a particular cost objective. Costs are generally assumed to be assignable to a particular cost objective if they were incurred for its benefit or if the costs were caused by the existence of that cost objective. Going back to our example of the personnel department, the department employees' salaries, clearly, are costs of the department because they can be directly traced to or associated with that department. They were incurred for the direct benefit of the personnel department.

On the other hand, the cost of electricity was incurred for the common benefit of all occupants of the building; hence, electricity is an indirect, or **common cost**, for all the departments occupying the building. Other indirect costs of activities that benefited the personnel department include security, maintenance of the grounds and parking areas, and the cost of the building receptionist. But what about the cost of operating the payroll department or the computer processing department or the legal department? Should some of these costs be allocated to the personnel department if it receives services or benefits from these departments? What about the president's salary? Since the president is responsible for the whole company, should her/his salary be allocated to all the different departments in the company? What about the cost of operating the company jet? Should it, combined with the president's salary, be allocated to the other departments, since the president is the primary user of the plane?

These are just a few examples of the many difficult questions concerning the allocation of indirect costs. To provide some structure to the discussion of these and other important questions, it is necessary to examine the three basic elements of any indirect cost allocation system:

- Cost objectives
- Cost pools
- Allocation bases

Cost Objectives

As noted previously, a **cost objective** is anything to which costs are assigned. Although the most traditional cost objectives are departments, products, and services, managers' needs for cost information are quite varied. In serving management, accountants must think beyond these traditional cost objectives. Likewise, it is important for managers to seek the advice of their management accountants when they need nontraditional cost information. A cost objective can be anything for which management desires cost information.

As noted in Chapter 5, management might desire information on the total costs associated with the failure to produce products that conform to quality specifications. In this case, information concerning such costs as rework, spoiled or defective units, and warranty claims could be gathered from throughout the organization for each product and totaled for the cost objective "cost of quality failure." This information might be useful in justifying expenditures for better product design, simplified manufacturing procedures, training, or new equipment. Other examples of useful cost objectives include: (1) the cost of moving materials between workstations (used in evaluating the desirability of rearranging equipment), (2) the cost of inspecting incoming raw materials and returning raw materials that do not meet quality specifications (used in rating and negotiating with vendors), and (3) the firm-wide cost of long-distance telephone service (used in evaluating the desirability of switching carriers and/or subscribing to wide-area telephone service).

Cost Pools

A **cost pool** is a collection of related costs, such as manufacturing overhead, that is assigned to other cost objectives. As a practical matter, it is not feasible in many situations to assign each item of cost (such as the plant manager's salary) separately. Instead, several similar costs are combined into a cost pool, and the entire pool is allocated as a single item. Indirect costs are often pooled along departmental lines such as costs for the payroll department, computing center, or maintenance department. Pooling all building-related costs or the cost for any other natural function is also frequently done. Sometimes these functional cost pools are referred to as departments even though they may not exist as such on the organization chart. For example, all building-related costs (depreciation, insurance, repairs, etc.) are often pooled together to form building department costs, which are then allocated to the departments that use the building. The key consideration in establishing cost pools is that the items pooled together should be relatively homogeneous and have a logical cause-and-effect relation to the allocation base. For instance, a building cost pool would include all costs related to the maintenance and operation of the building and might be allocated on the basis of square footage occupied. The costs in this pool, such as insurance, property taxes, and depreciation, have a logical cause-and-effect relation to the amount of square footage provided. As the square footage increases, these costs are usually expected to increase.

Within functional cost pools, it may be useful to provide separate pools for fixed costs and variable costs. This will result in cost allocations that more accurately reflect the factors that drive costs. Fixed costs are often driven by capacity, whereas variable costs are driven by actual activity.

To illustrate the allocation of fixed and variable costs, assume that Alco Manufacturing Company has one factory with three producing departments: Stamping, Assembly, and Inspection. There is also a Maintenance Department that provides services to the producing departments. Costs incurred by the Maintenance Department are placed in separate fixed and variable cost pools and allocated to the producing departments. Fixed costs consist of maintenance staff salaries, depreciation, insurance, and utilities for the maintenance shop facilities. Variable costs consist of supplies and parts used in performing maintenance services for the producing departments. Maintenance Department costs for 19X8 were as follows:

Fixed costs	$60,000
Variable costs	37,500
Total Maintenance Department costs	$97,500

Five hundred hours of service were performed for the three producing departments as follows:

Stamping Department	250
Assembly Department	200
Inspection Department	50
Total standard service hours	500

In setting up the Maintenance Department, Alco's management decided on a maintenance service capacity of 800 standard service hours per year. This capacity was based on a maximum need of 400 hours for the Stamping Department and 200 hours each for the Assembly and Inspection Departments. It was also determined that *fixed costs* should be allocated on the basis of *capacity provided* to each production department and that *variable costs* should be allocated on the basis of *actual usage* of Maintenance Department services. Exhibit 12-1 shows the allocation computations for fixed and variable Maintenance Department costs. The fixed costs percentages (50%, 25%, and 25%) reflect the cost of the capacity provided for each department, whereas the variable costs percentages (50%, 40%, and 10%) reflect the variable costs actually incurred on behalf of each department during the period.

Allocation Bases

The allocation base is the connecting link between cost objectives and cost pools. The indirect **cost allocation base** is the factor or characteristic common to the cost objectives that determines how much of the cost pool is assigned to each cost objective. The allocation base selected varies, depending on the nature of the indirect costs and the nature of the cost objectives. For example, labor-related costs may be allocated according to some measure (or estimate) of the labor time devoted to the various cost objectives. Depreciation and other building-related costs are often allocated on the basis of square footage occupied. Other examples of indirect costs and frequently used allocation bases include the following:

Cost Category	Allocation Base
Employee health services	Number of employees or calls
Personnel	Number of employees or new hires
Plant and grounds	Square footage occupied
Maintenance and repairs	Number of repair orders or service hours
Purchasing	Number of orders placed
Warehouse	Square footage used or value of materials stored

The most important consideration in selecting an allocation base is making sure there is a logical cause-and-effect association between the base selected and the costs incurred. For instance, it is logical to allocate personnel department costs according to the number of employees because the function of the personnel department is to provide employee-related services to the various departments. Thus, personnel costs are incurred as these services are provided. It follows that departments with a large number of employees should receive a larger allocation of personnel department costs than do departments with fewer employees.

Selecting allocation bases may not always be simple and straightforward. For example, it may be necessary in some cases in allocating building costs to differentiate among various areas of the building. Some areas of the building may be more costly to operate than other spaces; or some space, because of location within the building, may be more valuable because of its preferred location. For the allocation of indirect costs to be fair, these kinds of differences must be reflected in the choice of the allocation base, as illustrated by Management Accounting Practice 12-1 for Bellcore (page 644).

Another consideration in selecting an allocation base is whether to reflect the service capacity provided or only the actual services used. Refer to Exhibit 12-1, where we use different bases for allocating fixed and

EXHIBIT 12-1: ALLOCATION OF FIXED AND VARIABLE COSTS

Fixed cost allocation:

Department	Capacity Provided			Total Fixed Cost		Fixed Cost Allocation
	Service Hours	Percent				
Stamping	400	50	×	$60,000	=	$30,000
Assembly	200	25	×	60,000	=	15,000
Inspection	200	25	×	60,000	=	15,000
Total	800	100				$60,000

Variable cost allocation:

Department	Capacity Used			Total Variable Cost		Variable Cost Allocation
	Service Hours	Percent				
Stamping	250	50	×	$37,500	=	$18,750
Assembly	200	40	×	37,500	=	15,000
Inspection	50	10	×	37,500	=	3,750
Total	500	100				$37,500

Total Maintenance Department cost allocation:

Department	Fixed Cost	Variable Cost	Total Allocation
Stamping	$30,000	$18,750	$48,750
Assembly	15,000	15,000	30,000
Inspection	15,000	3,750	18,750
Total	$60,000	$37,500	$97,500

variable costs. Fixed costs are allocated based on the capacity provided, and variable costs are allocated according to the actual services used. Basing fixed costs on capacity provided eliminates the possibility that the amount of the cost allocation to one department is affected by the level of services utilized by other departments.

In Exhibit 12-1, the Assembly Department uses 200 service hours during the year, equaling the capacity provided for it. The 200 hours represent 25 percent (200 hours / 800 hours) of the total capacity of the service department, but they represent 40 percent (200 hours / 500 hours) of the total actual services rendered. If fixed costs had been allocated based on actual services *used,* rather than on capacity *provided*, $24,000 (40 percent of $60,000 fixed costs), instead of $15,000 (25 percent of $60,000 fixed costs), of fixed costs would have been assigned to the Assembly Department. This additional charge of $9,000 would have resulted from other producing departments failing to use the capacity provided for them. When fixed service department costs are allocated according to capacity provided, managers of producing departments are charged for the capacity provided whether they use it or not, and their use of services has no effect on the amount of costs allocated to other departments. A benefit of this allocation system is that it reduces the temptation for managers to avoid or delay services in order to minimize fixed cost allocations to their departments.

MANAGEMENT ACCOUNTING PRACTICE 12-1

Bellcore Corrects Unfair Service Cost Allocations

Bellcore (which stands for Bell Communications Research) is a joint venture organization that was created by the breakup of AT&T in 1983 to provide scientific and engineering research services to the seven new regional telephone companies. Bellcore was set up to provide services on a cost charge-back basis to these seven companies; hence, it was necessary for all support costs incurred at Bellcore to be assigned, along with direct costs, to the services performed by Bellcore engineers and scientists for the various telephone companies. This created a classic support service cost allocation problem.

Cost cross-subsidization was strictly forbidden at Bellcore, making it even more important to have equitable bases for allocated support function costs to the primary operating departments. A problem emerged almost immediately after Bellcore's establishment when both service and operating departments were allocated unusually large costs for support services such as Graphics, Word Processing, Technical Publications, and Secretarial/Clerical. Believing that support service costs were being unfairly allocated, some managers declined to use such services, either foregoing them entirely or going outside Bellcore to less expensive vendors.

A task force set up to study the problem of unfair support service cost allocations discovered that, even though cross-subsidization was strictly forbidden among services to client companies, there was a high degree of cross-subsidization of support services within Bellcore. It was discovered that because of inappropriate cost allocation bases, the costs of services among support departments were not being properly assigned. For example, Landlord (or building) Services costs were being assigned based on square footage without regard to the nature of the space occupied, causing Secreterial/Clerical to be assigned the same square footage cost for very basic building space as was charged to the Applied Research Department, which occupied much more technically sophisticated space. In effect, Secretarial/Clerical was subsidizing Applied Research.

A thorough study of the cost allocation system at Bellcore resulted in significant changes in the allocation of support services costs, causing allocations for some services to decrease and others to increase. Those departments hit the hardest have slowly accepted the changes because both the support service department managers and the operating department managers recognize that the revised system is fairer in terms of reflecting the actual costs of services used.

Based on: Edward J. Kovac and Henry P. Troy, "Getting the Transfer Prices Right: What Bellcore Did," *Harvard Business Review* (September-October 1989), pp. 148-154.

DIRECT AND INDIRECT DEPARTMENT COSTS

L O 2

As stated in Chapter 11, it may be desirable in some cases to accumulate costs by departments if there are multiple processes involved in producing products. In addition to multiple production departments, many companies have production support departments such as maintenance, facilities, engineering, and administration. These departments, which provide support services to the production and/or other support departments, are called **service departments.**

It is important in a responsibility accounting system to assign costs to managers who have responsibility for them. Hence, both production and service departments are normally cost centers because the responsible departmental managers are held accountable for costs they incur directly and for costs that benefit them indirectly. In addition to assigning costs to cost centers, it is necessary for product costing purposes to ultimately assign all production costs to products. Therefore, companies often assign manufacturing overhead costs initially to a variety of cost centers, both production and service departments, and subsequently reassign or allocate them to products.

It is not uncommon for companies to have several levels of allocations in their cost allocation procedures. As illustrated in Exhibit 12-2, a company could have three different levels of allocation if its manufacturing overhead costs were incurred in and initially assigned to the following *cost centers*: plant administration, plant services (such as maintenance or computer support), and the production departments. To assign all of its manufacturing related costs to products, the following procedures would allocate plant administration and plant services costs to the production departments so they could ultimately be assigned to the products:

Step 1. Plant administration department costs are allocated to the *service and production departments.*

Step 2. Service department costs (including indirect costs allocated from plant administration) are subsequently allocated to the *production departments.*

Step 3. Production department costs (including indirect costs allocated from plant administration and service departments) are assigned to *products.*

In this example, for purposes of controlling costs and evaluating managerial performance of administrative and service departments, the costs of plant administration and plant services are *direct department costs.* For product costing purposes, they are *indirect department costs* of the production departments.

To summarize, a **direct department cost** is assigned to a department upon the cost's incurrence, and an **indirect department cost** is reassigned or allocated to a department from another cost objective. It is possible for a cost to be a direct cost of more than one cost objective. For example, direct materials and direct labor costs are at the same time direct *department* costs of the production departments that initially incurred them and direct *product* costs with respect to the specific production jobs or processes for which they were incurred. Management Accounting Practice 12-2 (page 647) discusses how Hewlett-Packard has used a sequential allocation of cost pools to get more reliable product cost data.

EXHIBIT 12-2: DIRECT AND INDIRECT COSTS IN A THREE-LEVEL COST ALLOCATION SYSTEM

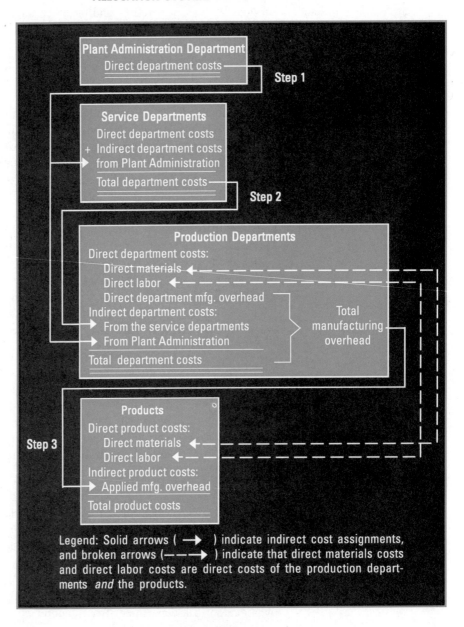

Plant Administration Department
Direct department costs

Step 1

Service Departments
Direct department costs
+ Indirect department costs from Plant Administration
Total department costs

Step 2

Production Departments
Direct department costs:
　Direct materials
　Direct labor
　Direct department mfg. overhead
Indirect department costs:
→ From the service departments
→ From Plant Administration
Total department costs

Total manufacturing overhead

Products
Direct product costs:
　Direct materials
　Direct labor
Indirect product costs:
→ Applied mfg. overhead
Total product costs

Step 3

Legend: Solid arrows (——→) indicate indirect cost assignments, and broken arrows (———→) indicate that direct materials costs and direct labor costs are direct costs of the production departments *and* the products.

SERVICE DEPARTMENT COST ALLOCATION

L O 3

Service departments provide a wide range of support functions, primarily for one or more production departments. Examples of service departments are maintenance, personnel, payroll, security, grounds, data processing, food services, and health services. These departments, which are considered essential elements in the overall manufacturing process, do not work

MANAGEMENT ACCOUNTING PRACTICE 12-2

Creating Multiple Cost Allocation Pools Improves Cost Data at Hewlett-Packard

Roseville Networks Division of Hewlett-Packard was producing over 250 different circuit board assemblies and other products in the mid-1980s when it decided that its old costing system was not providing reliable and useful cost data. Over a period of several years, the system was redesigned to include two different types of cost pools: (1) procurement and production and (2) support. The new system entails first allocating support cost pools (such as engineering, data processing, and manufacturing management) to the procurement and production cost pools. Procurement and production cost pools are then assigned to products using activity cost drivers.

By pooling together costs that have similar cost drivers and assigning them to products through a multilevel allocation process, the Roseville Division now has a costing system that managers believe better represents the accurate costs of products.

Based on: Debbie Berlant, Reese Browning, and George Foster, "How Hewlett-Packard Gets Numbers It Can Trust," *Harvard Business Review* (January-February 1990), pp. 178-183.

directly on the "product," but they do provide auxiliary support to the producing departments. In addition to providing support for the various producing departments, some service departments also provide services to *other service departments*. For example, the payroll and personnel departments may provide services to all departments, both production and service, and maintenance may provide services to the producing departments as well as limited services to health and food services. Services provided by one service department to other service departments are called **interdepartmental services**.

To illustrate service department cost allocations, consider the Krown Kola Company, which has two producing departments, Mixing and Bottling, and three service departments. The service departments and their respective service functions and cost allocation bases are as follows:

Department	Service Functions	Allocation Base
Administrative Services	Accounting, audit, payroll, and inventory control	Total department capital investment
Human Resources	Personnel, training, and health services	Number of employees
Plant and Facilities	Maintenance, security, depreciation, and insurance	Square footage occupied

Difficulty in choosing an allocation base for service department costs is not uncommon. For example, Krown Kola may have readily determined the appropriate allocation bases for the Human Resources and Plant and Facilities Departments but may have found the choice for Administrative Services to be less clear. Perhaps after conducting correlation studies, it was determined that the most equitable base for allocating Administrative Services costs to other departments was total capital investment in the departments.

Direct departmental costs and allocation base information used to illustrate Krown Kola's July 19X8 service department cost allocations are summarized as follows:

	Direct Department Costs	Number of Employees		Square Footage Occupied		Department Capital Investment	
Service departments:							
Administrative Services	$ 27,000	15	15%	4,000	8%	$ —	—
Human Resources	20,000	—	—	2,000	4	45,000	8%
Plant and Facilities	10,000	5	5	—	—	50,000	9
Producing departments:							
Mixing	40,000*	24	24	11,000	22	180,000	33
Bottling	90,000*	56	56	33,000	66	270,000	50
	$187,000	100	100%	50,000	100%	$545,000	100%

*Direct department overhead

Note that the information above omitted the number of employees in the Human Resources Department, square footage used by the Plant and Facilities Department, and the amount of capital investment in the Administrative Services Department. These data were omitted because a department normally does not allocate costs to itself; it allocates costs only to the departments it serves. Consequently, the number of employees in the Human Resources Department is not useful information for allocating Human Resources costs, since all such costs will be allocated only to the *other* departments. Three methods commonly used for service department cost allocations—direct, step, and linear algebra— are discussed below. To simplify the illustrations and focus on the direct, step, and linear algebra allocation methods, we will not perform separate allocations for fixed and variable costs.

Direct Method

The **direct method** allocates all service department costs based only on the amount of services provided to the producing departments. Exhibit 12-3 shows the flow of costs using the direct method. Note that all arrows depicting the cost flows extend directly from service departments to producing departments; there are no cost allocations among the service departments.

Exhibit 12-4 (page 650) shows the service department cost allocations for the direct method. Notice the allocation base used to allocate Human Resources costs: Only the employees in the producing departments are considered in computing the allocation percentages—24 in Mixing and 56 in Bottling, for a total of 80 employees in the allocation base. Thirty percent (24/80) of the producing department employees work in Mixing; therefore, 30 percent of Human Resources costs are allocated to Mixing.

EXHIBIT 12-3: FLOW OF COSTS—DIRECT METHOD

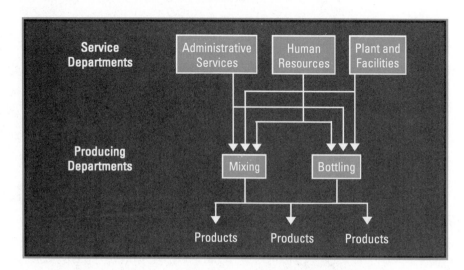

Applying the same reasoning, 70 percent of Human Resources costs are allocated to Bottling. Similar logic is followed in computing the cost allocations for Plant and Facilities and Administrative Services.

The cost allocation summary at the bottom of Exhibit 12-4 shows that all service department costs have been allocated, decreasing the service department costs to zero and increasing the producing department overhead balances by the amounts of the respective allocations. Also, note that total costs are not affected by the allocations—the total $187,000 was merely redistributed so that all costs are assigned to the producing departments. Total departmental overhead costs of the producing departments after allocation of service costs are $59,300 for Mixing and $127,700 for Bottling.

Evaluation of the Direct Method

The advantage of the direct method of allocating service department costs is that it is easy and convenient to use (see Management Accounting Practice 12-3, page 651). Its primary disadvantage is that it does not recognize the costs for interdepartmental services provided by one service department to another. Instead, any costs incurred to provide services to other service departments are passed directly to the producing departments. To illustrate the problem that may result from using the direct method, assume that Rambo Company has two service departments, S1 and S2, and two producing departments, P1 and P2, that provide services as follows:

Percent of Services Provided from	Percent of Services Provided to			
	S1	S2	P1	P2
S1	0%	0%	70%	30%
S2	50%	0%	25%	25%

If the direct method is used to allocate service department costs to the producing departments, S2 total costs will be allocated equally to the producing departments because they use the same amount of S2 services

EXHIBIT 12-4: SERVICE DEPARTMENT COST ALLOCATIONS—DIRECT METHOD

	Total	Mixing	Bottling
Administrative Services Department:			
Allocation base (capital investment)	$450,000	$180,000	$270,000
Percent of total base	100%	40%	60%
Cost allocations	$ 27,000	$ 10,800	$ 16,200
Human Resources Department:			
Allocation base (number of employees)	80	24	56
Percent of total base	100%	30%	70%
Cost allocations	$20,000	$ 6,000	$14,000
Plant and Facilities Department:			
Allocation base (square footage occupied)	44,000	11,000	33,000
Percent of total base	100%	25%	75%
Cost allocations	$10,000	$ 2,500	$ 7,500

Cost allocation summary:

	Administrative Services	Human Resources	Plant and Facilities	Mixing	Bottling	Total
Departmental cost before allocations	$ 27,000	$ 20,000	$ 10,000	$40,000	$ 90,000	$187,000
Cost allocations:						
Administrative Services	(27,000)			10,800	16,200	—
Human Resources		(20,000)		6,000	14,000	—
Plant and Facilities			(10,000)	2,500	7,500	—
Departmental costs after allocations	$ 0	$ 0	$ 0	$59,300	$127,700	$187,000

MANAGEMENT ACCOUNTING PRACTICE 12-3

Cost Allocations for Services in a University

A typical case of service department cost allocation using the direct method can be found in most large colleges and universities. The producing departments of a university are its academic departments and professional schools, and its support service departments are those such as student services (which includes housing, dining, and student life activities), facilities management (which is responsible for the physical campus), academic support (such as libraries and university computing centers), and administration (such as the president's office, fund-raising activities, and the legal department). Commonly used bases for allocating these service department costs are: number of students for student services and academic support, square footage of space occupied for facilities management, and total revenues for administration.

The allocation of these support service costs are often major budget line items in the deans' and department heads' operating budgets, affecting the amount of money left for direct operating needs such as faculty salaries, research support, and academic travel. Hence, it is important that the cost allocation method be perceived as fair and appropriate by those whose budgets are charged with these allocated costs. Using the direct allocation method might be appropriate in allocating some university service costs, such as student services, but would probably not be appropriate in allocating others, such as computer services, which are used by both the academic departments and the other service departments.

(25 percent each). Is this an equitable allocation of S2 costs? S2 actually provides half of its services to the other service department (S1), which, in turn, provides the majority of its services to P1. Assume that S2 has total direct department costs of $100,000. If the direct method is used to allocate service department costs, the entire $100,000 will be divided equally between the two producing departments, each being allocated $50,000, with no allocation to S1.

Consider the following alternative allocation of the $100,000 of S2 costs that takes into account interdepartmental services. First, allocate 25 percent, or $25,000, to each of the producing departments and 50 percent, or $50,000, to S1. Next, reallocate the $50,000 allocated to S1 from S2 to the producing departments in proportion to the amount of services provided to them by S1—70 percent and 30 percent, respectively. In this scenario, the $100,000 of S2 costs is ultimately allocated, $60,000 to P1 and $40,000 to P2, as follows:

	S1	S2	P1	P2
Step 1:				
Allocate S2 costs to S1, P1, and P2	$50,000	$(100,000)	$25,000	$25,000
Step 2:				
Reallocate S1 costs to P1 and P2	(50,000)	—	35,000	15,000
Final allocation of S2 costs	$ 0	$(100,000)	$60,000	$40,000

This calculation shows only the ultimate allocation of S2 costs. Of course, any S1 direct department costs would also have to be allocated to P1 and P2 on a 70/30 basis. If interdepartmental services are ignored, P1 is allocated only $50,000 of S2 costs; but by taking into account interdepartmental services, P1 is allocated $60,000. Certainly, a more accurate measure of the services received both *directly* and *indirectly* by P1 from S2 is $60,000, not $50,000.

As long as all producing departments use approximately the same percentage of services of each of the service departments, the direct method will provide a close approximation of the accurate costs that should be assigned to the producing departments. In this example, the percentages of services used by the producing departments were quite different—70 percent and 30 percent for S1, and 50 percent and 50 percent for S2. As illustrated, in such situations, the direct method can result in significant allocation errors.

Other Allocation Methods

In situations where it is desirable to take interdepartmental services into account, two other methods, *step* and *linear algebra*, are often used in the allocation of service department costs. The **step method** gives partial recognition of interdepartmental services by using a methodology, similar to that illustrated above for the Rambo Company, that allocates the service departments *sequentially* both to the remaining service departments and the producing departments. Any indirect costs allocated to a service department in this process are added to that department's direct department costs for allocation to the remaining departments. After the last service department is allocated, all service department costs are indirect department costs of the producing departments. These indirect department costs, combined with direct departmental overhead, will be applied to the products. The step method is illustrated graphically in Exhibit 12-5 for the Krown Kola Company. Notice the sequence of the allocations: Human Resources (first), Administrative Services (second), and Plant and Facilities (third).

When using the step method, the sequence of allocation is typically based on the relative percentage of services provided to other service departments, with the largest provider of interdepartmental services allocated first and the smallest provider of interdepartmental services allocated last. For Krown Kola, Human Resources is allocated first because, of the three service departments, it provides the largest percentage (20 percent) of its services to other service departments (15 percent to Administrative Services and 5 percent to Plant and Facilities). (See original data on page 648.) Plant and Facilities is allocated last because it provides the least amount (12 percent) of its services to other service departments (8 percent to Administrative Services and 4 percent to Human Resources). The service department cost allocations for Krown Kola using the step method are given in Exhibit 12-6 (page 654).

The disadvantage of the step method is that it provides only partial recognition of interdepartmental services. For Krown Kola, the step method

EXHIBIT 12-5: FLOW OF COSTS—STEP METHOD

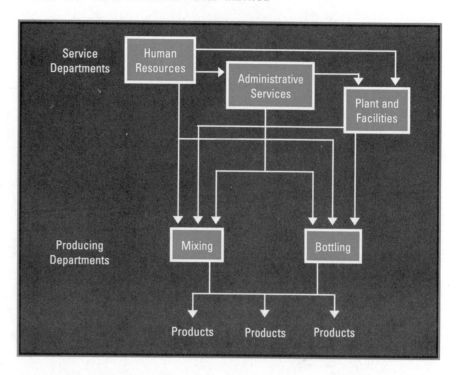

recognizes Human Resources services provided to the other two service departments; however, no services received by Human Resources from the other two departments are recognized. Similarly, services from Administrative Services to Plant and Facilities are recognized, but not the reverse. To achieve the most accurate service department cost allocation, there should be full recognition of services among service departments as well as among service and producing departments. This requires using the linear algebra method, sometimes called the *reciprocal method*. The **linear algebra method** uses a series of linear algebraic equations, which are solved simultaneously, to allocate service department costs both interdepartmentally and to the producing departments. This method is illustrated graphically in Exhibit 12-7 (page 655) for a company that has two service departments and two producing departments. Notice that the cost allocation arrows go from each service department to the other service department as well as to the producing departments.

As stated previously, whether a company should use the direct method, step method, or linear algebra method depends on the extensiveness of interdepartmental services and how evenly services are used by the producing departments. In some cases, the direct method, which was illustrated in detail, provides accurate allocations; but in other cases, it is necessary to use the step or linear algebra methods to get accurate cost allocations. Both the step method and the linear algebra method are discussed and illustrated in more depth in most cost accounting texts.

EXHIBIT 12-6: SERVICE DEPARTMENT COST ALLOCATIONS—STEP METHOD

	Total	Administrative Services	Plant and Facilities	Mixing	Bottling
Human Resources Department:					
Allocation base (number of employees)	100	15	5	24	56
Percent of total base	100%	15%	5%	24%	56%
Cost allocations	$ 20,000	$3,000	$ 1,000	$ 4,800	$ 11,200
Administrative Services Department:					
Allocation base (capital investment)	$500,000		50,000	$180,000	$270,000
Percent of total base	100%		10%	36%	54%
Cost allocations	$ 30,000		$ 3,000	$ 10,800	$ 16,200
Plant and Facilities Department:					
Allocation base (square footage occupied)	44,000			11,000	33,000
Percent of total base	100%			25%	75%
Cost allocations	$ 14,000			$ 3,500	$ 10,500

Cost allocation summary:

	Human Resources	Administrative Services	Plant and Facilities	Mixing	Bottling	Total
Departmental cost before allocations	$ 20,000	$ 27,000	$ 10,000	$40,000	$ 90,000	$187,000
Cost allocations:						
Human Resources	(20,000)	3,000	1,000	4,800	11,200	—
Administrative Services		(30,000)	3,000	10,800	16,200	—
Plant and Facilities			(14,000)	3,500	10,500	—
Departmental costs after allocations	$ 0	$ 0	$ 0	$59,100	$127,900	$187,000

EXHIBIT 12-7: FLOW OF COSTS—LINEAR ALGEBRA METHOD

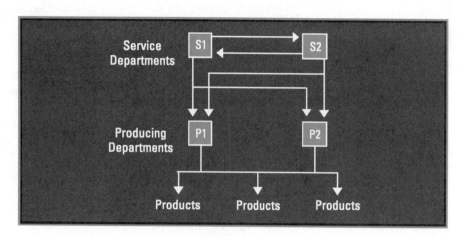

**APPLYING
MANUFACTURING
OVERHEAD USING
DEPARTMENTAL RATES**

Once service department costs are allocated to the producing departments, the next step in the product costing process is to apply those costs to Work-in-Process as discussed and illustrated in Chapters 10 and 11. Suppose that the manufacturing process at Krown Kola is labor-intensive in the Mixing Department but machine-intensive in the Bottling Department and that manufacturing overhead is applied to products as follows:

Department	Manufacturing Overhead Application Base
Mixing Department	Direct labor hours
Bottling Department	Machine hours

During the month of July 19X8, there were 500 direct labor hours worked in the Mixing Department and 800 machine hours used in the Bottling Department. Using the total production department overhead costs calculated by the step method, the manufacturing overhead rates based on actual costs for July are calculated as follows:

	Mixing	Bottling
Total departmental manufacturing overhead (direct departmental plus allocated) (Exhibit 12-6)	$59,100	$127,900
Quantity of overhead application base:		
Direct labor hours	÷ 500	
Machine hours		÷ 800
Departmental manufacturing overhead rates	$ 118.2	$159.875
	Per direct labor hour	Per machine hour

These rates are used to assign manufacturing overhead to Work-in-Process for July. This example assumes Krown Kola applies *actual* overhead to products on a monthly basis. As we discussed in Chapter 10, companies often use *predetermined* overhead rates throughout the year to average seasonal differences in costs. In that case, using a calculation similar to the above, the predetermined rates would reflect service department cost allocations based on *predicted* (instead of actual) data for costs and the allocation base quantity.

By creating separate manufacturing overhead cost allocation pools, allocation bases, and overhead application rates for Mixing and Bottling, it is possible to recognize overhead cost differences in various products based on differences in Mixing Department labor hours used and Bottling Department machine hours used for each product. This represents a cost system improvement in most multiproduct manufacturing environments over using a single, plant-wide overhead rate, and it reduces the likelihood of cost cross-subsidization. For quite a number of years, many companies have used departmental overhead rates to improve their product costing results; however, in recent years, many of these companies have further refined and improved their costing systems by implementing activity-based costing concepts into their product costing systems. ABC was introduced in Chapter 4, and its application to product costing is discussed in Chapter 13.

ABSORPTION COSTING VERSUS VARIABLE COSTING APPROACH TO INVENTORY VALUATION

L O 5

One theoretical issue in accounting that has generated considerable debate over the past 50 years is how to treat fixed overhead costs in the valuation of inventory. The debate centers around whether fixed overhead should be considered an *inventoriable product cost* and recorded initially as an asset or a *period cost* and recorded immediately as an operating expense. **Absorption costing** (also called **full costing**) treats fixed manufacturing overhead as a product cost, whereas **variable costing** (also called **direct costing**) treats it as a period cost. Therefore, fixed overhead cost is recorded initially as an asset (inventory) under absorption costing but as an operating expense under variable costing.

Suppose a company leases a plant for $25,000 per month, which is a fixed manufacturing overhead cost. Absorption costing assigns the $25,000 to the asset, inventory, and spreads it over the units produced in calculating the cost of each unit, whereas variable costing excludes this cost from the inventory cost calculation, recording it immediately as an expense. As Exhibit 12-8 illustrates, the only difference between absorption and variable costing is in the accounting for fixed manufacturing overhead. All other costs are treated the same under both methods.

Why does it matter whether fixed overhead is treated as a product cost or a period cost, since fixed product costs are eventually recorded as expenses under both variable and absorption costing? It matters because the recognition of fixed costs as an expense often does not occur during the same accounting period for absorption and variable costing. Also, there is the question of what constitutes an appropriate measure of product cost for purposes other than just preparing the income statement and balance sheet.

EXHIBIT 12-8: A COMPARISON OF ABSORPTION AND VARIABLE COSTING

Absorption Costing	Variable Costing
Product Costs	
Direct materials	Direct materials
Direct labor	Direct labor
Variable manufacturing overhead	Variable manufacturing overhead
Fixed manufacturing overhead	
Period Costs	
Variable selling and administrative	Variable selling and administrative
Fixed selling and administrative	Fixed selling and administrative
	Fixed manufacturing overhead

In pricing a product or evaluating its profitability, should a portion of fixed costs, or just variable costs, be considered in determining total unit cost?

These and other issues about the advantages and disadvantages of absorption and variable costing are considered on the following pages. The examples on the following pages illustrate the differences between these two methods with respect to inventory valuation and income determination. Keep in mind that *absorption costing is required for preparing financial statements for outside shareholders and lenders as well as for tax purposes but that variable costing is often used for internal reporting purposes.*

Inventory Valuations

To illustrate the difference in inventory valuations between absorption and variable costing, consider the following assumed cost data for the Morehart Company for a monthly volume of 4,000 units:

Direct materials	$7 per unit
Direct labor	$5 per unit
Variable manufacturing overhead	$4 per unit
Fixed manufacturing overhead	$8,000 per month

To determine the unit cost of inventory using absorption costing, average fixed overhead cost of $2 per unit is calculated by dividing the monthly fixed overhead of $8,000 by the monthly volume of 4,000 units. Even though fixed manufacturing overhead is not a variable cost, under absorption costing it is applied to inventory on a per unit basis, the same as variable costs. At a monthly volume of 4,000 units, Morehart's inventory costs per unit under variable and absorption costing are as shown below:

	Cost per Unit	
	Variable Costing	Absorption Costing
Direct materials	$ 7	$ 7
Direct labor	5	5
Variable manufacturing overhead	4	4
Fixed manufacturing overhead ($8,000 / 4,000 units)	-	2
Total unit cost	$16	$ 18

As expected, there is a $2 difference in total unit cost caused by including fixed overhead cost in the absorption costing valuation. The difference in the total inventory valuation on the balance sheet between absorption and variable costing will be $2 times the number of units in ending inventory. So if 1,000 units are on hand at the end of the month, they will be valued at $18,000 if absorption costing is used but only at $16,000 if variable costing is used. The $2,000 difference is equal to 1,000 units on hand times $2 per unit of fixed overhead cost included in the absorption valuation.

The $2 fixed cost per unit is dependent on the assumptions of $8,000 per month in total fixed overhead cost and 4,000 units of production. As illustrated later, if either total fixed overhead cost or the production volume is different, the fixed overhead per unit will be different.

Income Determination

Before discussing the income differences between variable and absorption costing, it is important to note that the income statement formats used for these methods are normally not the same. One of the primary benefits of *variable costing* is that it facilitates the breakdown of costs into variable and fixed costs on the income statement, making it possible to present the income statement in the *contribution format*. As illustrated in Chapter 2, in the **contribution income statement** format, variable costs are subtracted from revenues to get contribution margin, and fixed costs are subtracted from contribution margin to get net income.

When *absorption costing* is used, the income statement is usually formatted using the *functional format*, which classifies costs based on cost function such as manufacturing, selling, and administration. The **functional income statement** format subtracts manufacturing costs (represented by cost of goods sold) from revenues to get gross profit, and selling and administrative costs are subtracted from gross profit to get net income. The contribution and functional formats are summarized as follows:

Contribution Format			Functional Format		
Sales		$ xxx	Sales		$ xxx
Less variable expenses:			Cost of goods sold		(xxx)
Cost of goods sold	(xxx)		Gross profit		$ xxx
Selling	(xxx)		Operating expenses:		
Administrative	(xxx)		Selling	(xxx)	
Contribution margin		$ xxx	Administrative	(xxx)	
Less fixed expenses:			Net income		$ xxx
Manufacturing	(xxx)				
Selling	(xxx)				
Administrative	(xxx)				
Net income		$ xxx			

Notice that the contribution format provides information for determining the contribution margin ratio, which is calculated as total contribution margin divided by total sales. It also provides the total amount of fixed costs. These are the primary items of data needed to determine the break-even point and to conduct other cost-volume-profit analysis (see Chapter 2).

The functional format, on the other hand, reports the amount of gross profit, which is the amount by which products sold were marked up above their manufacturing costs to cover nonmanufacturing operating expenses and to provide a profit.

Not only is the income statement format usually different for absorption and variable costing methods, but also, as illustrated in the following examples for Morehart Company, the amount of net income reported on the income statement *may* not be the same because of the difference in the treatment of fixed manufacturing overhead. To compare variable and absorption costing for different levels of sales and production, assume the following additional information for the Morehart Company:

Selling price	$ 30 per unit
Variable selling and administrative expenses	$ 3 per unit
Fixed selling and administrative expenses	$10,000 per month

Sales Varies but Production Remains Constant

Assume production remains constant at 4,000 units per month for June, July, and August but that sales are 4,000, 2,500, and 5,500 units, respectively. For the three-month period, total production and total sales are both 12,000 units. Recall that the total unit cost to manufacture a unit is $18 using absorption costing and $16 using variable costing, the $2 difference being due to the difference in accounting for fixed overhead costs. Absorption and variable costing income statements for June, July, and August 19X6 are presented in Exhibit 12-9, and a summary of unit inventory changes is presented at the bottom of the exhibit. Note that the absorption costing statements are presented in a functional format and that the variable costing statements are presented in a contribution format.

In June, the first month of operation, when 4,000 units were both produced and sold, there were no units remaining in inventory, which means that all fixed manufacturing overhead cost was deducted as an expense during the current period under both methods. Under absorption costing, $8,000 (4,000 units × $2 per unit) of fixed overhead was deducted as part of cost of goods sold. Under variable costing, $8,000 was deducted as a period cost from contribution margin. No costs were assigned to ending inventory under either method since all units produced were sold.

In July, units produced (4,000) exceeded units sold (2,500) by 1,500 units. Because variable costing treats fixed manufacturing overhead as a period cost, the full $8,000 was deducted in July; however, note how absorption costing treated the fixed manufacturing overhead costs in July. At $2 per unit, absorption costing assigned $5,000 (2,500 units × $2) to cost of goods sold and $3,000 (1,500 units × $2) to ending inventory. Hence, because absorption costing deducted only $5,000 and variable costing deducted $8,000 of manufacturing overhead cost on the income statement in July, net income was $3,000 more under absorption costing than it was under variable costing. Further, since absorption costing assigned $2 more than variable costing to each unit produced as a product cost, ending inventory was $3,000 more (1,500 units × $2) under absorption costing than it was under variable costing.

EXHIBIT 12-9: ABSORPTION AND VARIABLE COSTING INCOME (PRODUCTION CONSTANT)

Morehart Company
Absorption Costing Income Statements
For the Months of June, July, and August 19X6

	(Sales Equal Production) June	(Production Exceeds Sales) July	(Sales Exceed Production) August
Unit sales	4,000	2,500	5,500
Sales (at $30 per unit)	$120,000	$ 75,000	$165,000
Cost of goods sold (at $18 per unit)	- 72,000	- 45,000	- 99,000
Gross profit	$ 48,000	$ 30,000	$ 66,000
Selling and administrative expenses:			
Variable (at $3 per unit)	$ 12,000	$ 7,500	$ 16,500
Fixed	10,000	10,000	10,000
Total	-22,000	-17,500	-26,500
Net income	$ 26,000	$ 12,500	$ 39,500

Morehart Company
Variable Costing Income Statements
For the Months of June, July, and August 19X6

	June	July	August
Unit sales	4,000	2,500	5,500
Sales (at $30 per unit)	$120,000	$ 75,000	$ 165,000
Variable expenses:			
Cost of goods sold (at $16 per unit)	$ 64,000	$ 40,000	$ 88,000
Selling and administrative (at $3 per unit)	12,000	7,500	16,500
Total	- 76,000	- 47,500	-104,500
Contribution margin	$ 44,000	$ 27,500	$ 60,500
Fixed expenses:			
Manufacturing overhead	$ 8,000	$ 8,000	$ 8,000
Selling and administrative	10,000	10,000	10,000
Total	-18,000	-18,000	-18,000
Net income	$ 26,000	$ 9,500	$ 42,500

Summary of Unit Inventory Changes

	June	July	August
Beginning inventory	—	—	1,500
Production	4,000	4,000	4,000
Total available	4,000	4,000	5,500
Sales	4,000	2,500	5,500
Ending inventory	—	1,500	—

In August, just the opposite of July's situation occurred: Sales of 5,500 units exceeded production of 4,000 units by 1,500 units. Where did the extra 1,500 units come from to make up the shortfall of production in August? They had to come out of beginning inventory left over from July. Once again, as in the two previous months, variable costing deducted $8,000 for fixed manufacturing overhead as a period cost, and absorption deducted $2 per unit for fixed manufacturing overhead as part of the product cost for units sold. But since 5,500 units were sold in August, absorption costing deducted $11,000 (5,500 units × $2) for fixed manufacturing overhead. Hence, because absorption costing deducted $11,000 and variable costing deducted $8,000 of fixed manufacturing overhead cost on the income statement in August, net income was $3,000 more under variable costing than it was under absorption costing. Or stated another way, since absorption costing deferred $3,000 more in inventory in July, when those units were sold in August, $3,000 more costs were deducted for units sold.

What can we conclude from this analysis? As long as units produced equal units sold, the two methods will deduct the same total costs on the income statement. However, net income is higher under absorption costing when production exceeds sales (i.e., in periods when inventories are increasing); and net income is higher under variable costing when sales exceed production (i.e., when inventories are decreasing). This is logical because when inventories increase, absorption costing defers some of the current period's fixed overhead costs in inventories as an asset on the balance sheet; but when inventories decrease, those costs are brought off the balance sheet into the income statement as an expense. Absorption costing assumes fixed overhead costs do not expire until the product is sold, whereas variable costing assumes they expire as incurred each period.

Sales Remains Constant but Production Varies

Assume that Morehart's unit variable and monthly fixed costs remain the same as above for the months of October, November, and December when 4,000 units per month were sold but 4,000, 5,000, and 3,200 per month, respectively, were produced. Unlike the previous illustration where production was constant and fixed manufacturing overhead cost was $2 per unit for absorption costing, this illustration has the following fixed manufacturing overhead costs per unit:

	October	November	December
Fixed manufacturing overhead	$8,000	$8,000	$8,000
Units produced	÷4,000	÷5,000	÷3,200
Fixed cost per unit	$ 2.00	$ 1.60	$ 2.50

As a result, the unit cost of inventory and, subsequently, the cost of goods sold, will vary each period, even if sales remain constant. Given that variable costs are $16 per unit, the total unit manufacturing costs for these three months under absorption costing are:

	October	November	December
Variable costs per unit	$16.00	$16.00	$16.00
Fixed costs per unit	2.00	1.60	2.50
Total manufacturing cost per unit	$18.00	$17.60	$18.50

Exhibit 12-10 (below and on next page) presents the income statements under absorption and variable costing for October, November, and December for Morehart. This exhibit illustrates again that when sales and production are equal (October), net income is the same for absorption and variable costing; when production exceeds sales (November), net income is greater under the absorption costing method; and when sales exceed production (December), net income is greater under the variable costing method. More significantly, this exhibit illustrates that even though unit sales are constant and manufacturing cost behavior is unchanged, net income can vary under the absorption method simply by changing the number of units produced.

EXHIBIT 12-10: ABSORPTION AND VARIABLE COSTING INCOME (SALES CONSTANT)

Morehart Company
Absorption Costing Income Statements
For the Months of October, November, and December 19X6

	(Production Equals Sales) October	(Sales Exceed Production) November	(Sales Exceed Production) December
Unit sales	4,000	4,000	4,000
Sales (at $30 per unit)	$120,000	$120,000	$120,000
Cost of goods sold:			
Beginning inventory	$ —	$ —	$ 17,600
Cost of goods manufactured	72,000*	88,000**	59,200***
Cost of goods available	$ 72,000	$88,000	$ 76,800
Less ending inventory	- —	- 17,600	- 3,700
Cost of goods sold	- 72,000	- 70,400	- 73,100
Gross profit	$ 48,000	$ 49,600	$ 46,900
Selling and administrative expenses:			
Variable (at $3 per unit)	$ 12,000	$ 12,000	$ 12,000
Fixed	10,000	10,000	10,000
Total	-22,000	-22,000	-22,000
Net income	$ 26,000	$ 27,600	$ 24,900

* 4,000 units produced at $18; **5,000 units produced at $17.60; ***3,200 units produced at $18.50.

EXHIBIT 12-10 (CONTINUED)

Morehart Company
Variable Costing Income Statements
For the Months of October, November, and December 19X6

	October	November	December
Unit sales	4,000	4,000	4,000
Sales (at $30 per unit)	$120,000	$120,000	$120,000
Variable expenses:			
Cost of goods sold (at $16 per unit)	$ 64,000	$ 64,000	$ 64,000
Selling and administrative (at $3 per unit)	12,000	12,000	12,000
Total	- 76,000	- 76,000	- 76,000
Contribution margin	$ 44,000	$ 44,000	$ 44,000
Fixed expenses:			
Manufacturing overhead	$ 8,000	$ 8,000	$ 8,000
Selling and administrative	10,000	10,000	10,000
Total	- 18,000	- 18,000	- 18,000
Net income	$ 26,000	$ 26,000	$ 26,000

Summary of Unit Inventory Changes

	October	November	December
Beginning inventory	—	—	1,000
Production	4,000	5,000	3,200
Total available	4,000	5,000	4,200
Sales	4,000	4,000	4,000
Ending inventory	—	1,000	200

Sales did not change from October to November, but net income increased by $1,600 merely by increasing the units produced. By producing more units and spreading the fixed overhead cost over more units, unit cost decreased from $18.00 to $17.60, thereby increasing net income by $1,600 (or 4,000 × $0.40 per unit). On the other hand, from November to December, the number of units produced decreased to 3,200 units; and the total unit cost increased from $17.60 to $18.50, or by $0.90 cents per unit. Under a first-in, first-out assumption, the 1,000 units in beginning inventory with a cost of $17.60 were sold first, followed by 3,000 of the units produced in December at a cost of $18.50. The other 200 produced in December remained in ending inventory. Hence, the decrease in net income from November to December was $2,700 (or 3,000 units × $0.90 per unit).

Summary and Reconciliation of Income Differences

To summarize, Exhibits 12-9 and 12-10 reveal several important relationships between absorption costing and variable costing net incomes and how net income responds to changes in sales and production under both methods:

- When production equals sales, absorption costing net income equals variable costing net income.
- When production exceeds sales, absorption costing net income is greater than variable costing net income.
- When sales exceed production, absorption costing net income is less than variable costing net income.
- Assuming sales prices and cost behavior remain unchanged, variable costing net income changes in response to changes in unit sales. Hence, if unit sales remain the same, net income stays the same; if unit sales increase, net income increases; and if unit sales decrease, net income decreases. *Variable costing net income does not change in response to a change in production level.*
- Assuming sales prices and cost behavior remain unchanged, absorption costing net income may change in response to a change in either unit sales or units produced. *If units produced remain constant, absorption costing net income*:
  - Increases as sales increase
  - Decreases as sales decrease
  - Remains unchanged if sales are unchanged

  If unit sales remain constant, absorption net income:
  - Increases as production increases
  - Decreases as production decreases
  - Remains constant if production is unchanged

  Of course, if both units produced and sold change, both factors may cause a change in absorption net income.

For each period, the income differences between absorption and direct costing can be explained by analyzing the change in inventoried fixed manufacturing overhead under absorption costing net income. In general:

$$\begin{array}{ccc} \text{Variable} & \text{Increase (or minus Decrease)} & \text{Absorption} \\ \text{costing} \quad + & \text{in inventoried fixed} \quad = & \text{costing} \\ \text{net income} & \text{manufacturing overhead} & \text{net income} \end{array}$$

This equation may be reversed to reconcile absorption costing net income to variable costing net income:

$$\begin{array}{ccc} \text{Absorption} & \text{Decrease (or minus Increase)} & \text{Variable} \\ \text{costing} \quad + & \text{in inventoried fixed} \quad = & \text{costing} \\ \text{net income} & \text{manufacturing overhead} & \text{net income} \end{array}$$

Exhibit 12-11 (page 666) presents a set of reconciliations for June, July, and August, which reconciles from variable income to absorption income, as well as a set for October, November, and December, which reconciles in the reverse order. Note in the following totals for the three-month period (June to August) that total production equals total sales and total absorption costing net income equals total variable costing net income.

Month	Unit Production	Unit Sales	Absorption Costing Income	Variable Costing Income
June	4,000	4,000	$26,000	$26,000
July	4,000	2,500	12,500	9,500
August	4,000	5,500	39,500	42,500
Total	12,000	12,000	$78,000	$78,000

For any given time period, regardless of length, if total units produced equal total units sold, net income will be the same for absorption costing and variable costing, all other things being equal. Under absorption costing, all fixed manufacturing overhead is expensed as a product cost through cost of goods sold *when inventory is sold*. Under variable costing, all fixed manufacturing overhead is reported as a period cost and expensed *in the period incurred*. Consequently, over the life of a product, the income differences within periods are offset since they are caused only by the timing of the release of fixed manufacturing overhead to the income statement.

An Evaluation of Variable Costing

Few accounting topics have generated as much controversy as variable costing. The central theoretical issue in this controversy is whether or not the incurrence of fixed manufacturing costs add value to products. Proponents of variable costing argue that the incurrence of these costs does not add value to a product. Fixed costs are incurred to provide the capacity to produce during a given period, and these costs expire with the passage of time, regardless of whether the related capacity was used. Variable manufacturing costs, on the other hand, are incurred only if production takes place. Consequently, these costs are properly assignable to the units produced.

Proponents of variable costing also argue that inventories have value only to the extent they avoid the necessity for incurring costs in the future. Having inventory available for sale does avoid the necessity of incurring some future variable costs, but the availability of finished goods inventory does not avoid the incurrence of future fixed manufacturing costs. They conclude that inventories should be valued at their variable manufacturing cost, and fixed manufacturing costs should be expensed as incurred.

When considering the accounting principle of matching, variable costing has an advantage over absorption costing because it matches revenues with the direct cost of producing the revenues. This results in net income varying only with sales, not with both sales and production, as is often found in absorption costing. In absorption costing, overproduction especially distorts net income during a period because the excess inventory is assigned fixed costs that would otherwise be assigned to the units produced and sold. Using absorption costing, a company may increase net operating income by simply producing more than it sells.

EXHIBIT 12-11: RECONCILIATION OF ABSORPTION AND VARIABLE COSTING NET INCOME

Reconciling from variable costing to absorption costing net income:

	June	July	August
Variable costing net income (Exhibit 12-9)	$26,000	$ 9,500	$42,500
Change in inventoried fixed costs:			
Fixed overhead in ending inventory	$ —	$ 3,000*	$ —
Less fixed overhead in beginning inventory	—	—	(3,000)#
Increase (decrease) in inventoried cost	0	3,000	(3,000)
Absorption costing net income (Exhibit 12-9)	$26,000	$12,500	$39,500

Reconciling from absorption costing to variable costing net income:

	October	November	December
Absorption costing net income (Exhibit 12-10)	$26,000	$27,600	$24,900
Change in inventoried fixed costs:			
Fixed overhead in beginning inventory	$ —	$ —	$ 1,600#
Less fixed overhead in ending inventory	—	1,600**	500##
(Increase) decrease in inventoried cost	0	(1,600)	1,100
Variable costing net income (Exhibit 12-10)	$26,000	$26,000	$26,000

  * 1,500 units × $2.00 of fixed cost per unit.
 ** 1,000 units × $1.60 of fixed cost per unit.
  # Ending of July is beginning of August, and ending of November is beginning of December.
200 units × $2.50 of fixed cost per unit.

Opponents of variable costing argue that fixed manufacturing costs are incurred for only one purpose—namely, to manufacture the product. Because they are incurred to manufacture the product, manufacturing costs should be assigned to the product. It is also argued that in the long run, all costs are variable. Consequently, by omitting fixed costs, variable costing understates long-run variable costs and misleads decision makers into underestimating true production costs.

On a pragmatic level, the central arguments for variable costing center around the fact that the use of variable costing facilitates the development of contribution income statements and cost-volume-profit analysis. If all costs are accumulated on an absorption costing basis, contribution income statements are difficult to develop, and cost-volume-profit analysis becomes very complicated unless production and sales are equal. Management Accounting Practice 12-4 shows how FMI Forms Manufacturers used a combination of absorption and variable costing to guide price bidding decisions.

Proponents of activity-based costing typically do not favor variable costing because ABC is based on the assumption that all costs are variable in the long run and that fixed costs should be assigned to products or services to represent long-run variable costs. Hence, inventory valuation using an ABC approach will tend to be closer to absorption costing values than to variable costing values. This does not mean that one who advocates ABC for inventory valuation purposes would not recognize the value of identifying variable and fixed costs for cost-volume-profit analysis or other short-term purposes.

As modern manufacturing techniques have led to major reductions in inventory levels in many companies, the significance of the absorption-versus-variable costing debate has declined. If a company has no inventories, all of its costs are deducted as expenses during the current period whether it uses absorption or variable costing, because all costs are deducted currently either as operating expenses or as cost of goods sold expense. Hence, from an income determination standpoint, it does not matter in such cases whether fixed costs are considered a product or period cost. Despite the emergence of inventory management techniques that substantially reduce inventory levels, few companies have been able to *completely* eliminate inventories. This topic is discussed in much greater depth in Chapter 13.

MANAGEMENT ACCOUNTING PRACTICE 12-4

FMI Forms Manufacturers Combines Absorption Costing and Variable Costing to Gain a Competitive Edge

FMI Forms Manufacturers, a medium-sized, machine-intensive printer of business forms, used a traditional costing system during the 1970s and 1980s designed to compute the direct costs (primarily paper cost) of each job and to apply overhead using a rate based on total direct costs. It became apparent that the total cost measurements produced by this system were not accurate because overhead was not driven by total direct costs but by factors related to the characteristics of the printing press used and the size of the forms printed. Hence, the first step in customizing its costing system was for FMI to determine the actual drivers of printing costs.

The critical use of "cost" information at a printing company such as FMI is for bidding jobs. FMI takes a two-pronged approach to bidding. It uses absorption costing for submitting initial bids to make sure that on an ongoing basis the company receives prices sufficient to cover full costs. If initial bids are turned down but allowed to be resubmitted, the company uses direct costing by subtracting all variable costs from the initial bid price to get the total contribution margin reflected in the bid price. This total contribution margin is divided by the number of estimated press-hours to get the contribution margin per press-hour, which is compared with a minimum acceptable contribution margin per press-hour. If the bid margin is above the acceptable minimum, the bid price is lowered; otherwise, it is not adjusted. According to FMI managers, with this new costing system—combining absorption costing, variable costing, and activity-based costing—"the company is profitable and has increased business in increasingly competitive markets."

Based on: Jacci L. Rodgers, S. Mark Comstock, and Karl Pritz, "Customize Your Costing System," *Management Accounting* (May 1993), pp. 134-135.

SUMMARY

Cost measurement involves assigning costs to cost objectives or reassigning them from one cost objective to another. The cost objective may be a product, department, activity, service, territory, or any other item of interest to management. For various reasons, it is not always possible or feasible to make a direct association between a cost objective and all of its costs. Although some costs can be directly identified with a particular cost objective, many other costs can be associated only indirectly with that cost objective. These indirect costs can be associated with a cost objective only by the process of reassignment, also called allocation.

If a cost objective has numerous indirect costs, it may not be feasible to allocate those costs individually. They are often placed into homogeneous groupings of related costs, called cost pools, which are then reassigned to cost objectives using an allocation basis that is common to all cost objectives. A good cost allocation basis has a logical cause-and-effect relationship with the costs in the pool. That is, the allocation basis has been determined to be the primary driver of the costs in the pool. An example of cost pools discussed in this chapter are costs for various service departments that are pooled together and assigned to users of the services based on the amount of services provided to each user. Because service departments often provide services to each other, it may also be necessary to recognize interdepartmental services in the allocation of service department costs.

Two approaches to inventory valuation were discussed: absorption costing and variable costing. The essential difference between absorption and variable costing is the inclusion—or exclusion—of fixed manufacturing overhead as a product cost. Under absorption costing, fixed manufacturing overhead is assigned to products and expensed as part of cost of goods sold when inventories are sold. Under variable costing, fixed manufacturing overhead is immediately expensed as a period cost.

Although absorption costing is required for external financial and income tax reporting, variable costing provides better information for use internally by management in evaluating the consequences of short-run decisions and in planning operations in the near-term. Variable costing is superior for short-run analysis primarily because it permits the development of contribution income statements, in which costs are classified by behavior (variable and fixed), to assist management in understanding cost-volume-profit relationships. Most ABC proponents consider all product costs to be variable in the long run; therefore, an ABC approach to inventory valuation would tend to be more consistent with absorption costing rather than with variable costing. From an income determination perspective, whether absorption or variable costing is used makes little difference for companies that have insignificant amounts of inventories.

SUGGESTED READINGS

Ajinkya, Bipan, Rowland Atiase, and Linda Smith Bamber. "Absorption versus Direct Costing: Income Reconciliation and Cost-Volume-Profit Analysis," *Issues in Accounting Education* (Fall 1986), pp. 268-281.

Fremgen, J.M. "The Direct Costing Controversy—An Identification of Issues," *The Accounting Review* (January 1964), pp. 43-51.

Fremgen, James M., and Shu S. Liao. *The Allocation of Corporate Indirect Costs* (Montvale, NJ: National Association of Accountants, 1981).

Johnson, Thomas H., and Dennis A. Loewe. "How Weyerhaeuser Manages Corporate Overhead Costs," *Management Accounting* (August 1987), pp. 20-26.

Martinson, Otto B. *Cost Accounting in the Service Industry—A Critical Assessment* (Montvale, NJ: Institute of Management Accountants, 1994).

Roth, Harold P., and A. Faye Borthick. "Getting Closer to Real Product Costs," *Management Accounting* (May 1989), pp. 28-33.

Schill, Michael. "Variable Costing: A Closer Look," *Management Accounting* (February 1987), pp. 36-39.

REVIEW PROBLEMS

12-1 Service Department Cost Allocation

Cotswald's Clothiers, Inc., is organized into four departments: Womens' Apparel, Mens' Apparel, Administrative Services, and Facilities Services. The former two departments are the primary producing departments, and the latter two departments exist to provide services to the producing departments. Top management has decided that, for internal reporting purposes, the cost of service department operations should be allocated to the producing departments.

Administrative Services costs are allocated on the basis of the number of employees, and Facilities Services costs are allocated based on the amount of square footage occupied. The service departments provide services to producing departments as well as to each other. Data pertaining to the cost allocations for February 19X7 are as follows:

Department	Direct Department Costs	Number of Employees	Square Footage Occupied
Womens' Apparel	$ 60,000	15	15,000
Mens' Apparel	50,000	9	7,500
Administrative Services	18,000	3	2,500
Facilities Services	12,000	2	1,000
Total	$140,000	29	26,000

Required:
(a) Determine the amount of service department costs to be allocated to the producing departments under the *direct method* and the *step method* of service department cost allocation.
(b) Discuss the *linear algebra method* of service department cost allocation, explaining circumstances when it should be considered over the direct and step methods.
(c) Should Cotswald's Clothiers, Inc., consider using the linear algebra method?

The solution to the review problem is found at the end of Chapter 12 assignment material. To maximize your learning, you should make a serious attempt to develop a written solution to the review problem before looking at the solution. If there are errors in your solution, you should then attempt to determine the causes of the errors.

12-2 Variable and Absorption Costing

Colorado Ski Company has just completed its first year of operations on December 31, 19X7. The president says she needs financial statements for both managerial review and external reporting purposes. The controller informs the president that two sets of statements will be needed: one based on absorption costing and the other based on variable costing. Although concerned about the cost of preparing two reports, the president agrees to let the controller try it.

The following data are from the first year of operations:

Direct labor	$200,000
Direct materials	250,000
Variable manufacturing overhead	100,000
Fixed manufacturing overhead	130,000
Variable selling expenses	75,000
Fixed administrative expenses	112,000

50,000 pairs of skis were manufactured, and 40,000 pairs sold at a price of $40.

Required:
(a) Compute the costs of the inventory at the end of the year using absorption costing and variable costing.
(b) Prepare income statements for 19X7 using both absorption and variable costing methods.
(c) Reconcile the difference in absorption costing and variable costing net incomes in requirement (b).
(d) Explain to the president why both sets of statements are needed.

The solution to the review problem is found at the end of Chapter 12 assignment material. To maximize your learning, you should make a serious attempt to develop a written solution to the review problem before looking at the solution. If there are errors in your solution, you should then attempt to determine the causes of the errors.

KEY TERMS

Absorption costing—an approach to costing products that treats both variable and fixed manufacturing costs as product costs.

Common cost—a cost incurred for the benefit of two or more cost objectives; an indirect cost.

Contribution income statement—an income statement format in which variable costs are subtracted from revenues to get contribution margin and fixed costs are subtracted from contribution margin to get net income.

Cost allocation base—a measure of a common volume of activity, such as direct labor hours or machine hours, that determines how much of a cost pool is assigned to each cost objective.

Cost objective—anything to which costs are assigned. Examples include departments, products, and services.

Cost pool—a collection of related costs, such as departmental manufacturing overhead, that is assigned to other cost objectives such as products.

Direct costing—see **variable costing**.

Direct department cost—a cost assigned directly to a department upon the cost's incurrence.

Direct method—a method of allocating service department costs to producing departments based only on the amount of services provided to the producing departments. It does not recognize any interdepartmental services.

Full costing—see **absorption costing**.

Functional income statement—an income statement format that subtracts manufacturing costs (represented by cost of goods sold) from revenues to get gross profit and subtracts selling and administrative costs from gross profit to get net income.

Indirect department cost—a cost reassigned or allocated to a department from another cost objective.

Interdepartmental services—services provided by one service department to other service departments.

Linear algebra method—a method of allocating service department costs using a series of linear algebraic equations, which are solved simultaneously, to allocate service department costs both interdepartmentally among service departments and to producing departments.

Service department—a department that provides support services to production and/or other support departments.

Step method—a method of allocating service department costs that gives partial recognition to interdepartmental services by using a methodology that allocates service department costs sequentially both to the remaining service departments and the producing departments.

Variable costing—an approach to costing products that treats variable manufacturing costs as product costs and fixed manufacturing costs as period costs.

REVIEW QUESTIONS

12-1

Distinguish between the following terms:

    (a) Direct product costs and indirect product costs
    (b) Direct department costs and indirect department costs
    (c) Product costs and period costs

12-2

Can any generalized distinctions be made about direct and indirect costs? Explain.

12-3

Explain the difference between cost assignment and cost allocation. What alternative term can be used to refer to cost allocation?

12-4

Can a specific cost item be both a direct cost and an indirect cost? Explain.

12-5

Why might cost allocations developed for financial reporting or tax purposes not be adequate for other purposes that require the accurate determination of individual product costs?

12-6

What is a cost objective? Give several examples of cost objectives that may be of interest to managers.

12-7

Why are cost pools used in allocating direct costs?

12-8

What is the primary advantage of allocating fixed and variable indirect costs separately?

12-9

To what extent are interdepartmental services recognized under the direct, step, and linear algebra methods of service department cost allocation?

12-10

Can period costs exist under the absorption method? If so, give some examples.

12-11

Explain the basic difference between absorption costing and variable costing.

12-12

What is the relationship between variable costing and the contribution income statement format?

12-13

Explain how the differences between variable costing and absorption costing net incomes are reconciled.

EXERCISES

12-1 Allocating Service Department Costs: Allocation Basis Alternatives

Clayton Glassworks has two producing departments, P1 and P2, and one service department, S1. Estimated direct overhead costs per month are as follows:

P1	$100,000
P2	200,000
S1	60,000

Other data:

	P1	P2
Number of employees	75	25
Production capacity (units)	50,000	30,000
Space occupied (sq. ft.)	2,500	7,500
Five-year average percent of S1's service output used	65%	35%

Required:

For each of the following allocation bases, determine the total estimated overhead cost for P1 and P2 after allocating S1 cost to the producing departments:

(a) Number of employees
(b) Production capacity in units
(c) Space occupied
(d) Five-year average percentage of S1 services used
(e) Estimated direct overhead costs (Round your answer to the nearest dollar.)

12-2 Indirect Cost Allocation: Direct Method

Springfield Manufacturing Company has two production departments: Melting and Molding. General Plant Management and Plant Security direct costs benefit both production departments. Springfield allocates General Plant Management costs on the basis of the number of production employees and Plant Security costs on the basis of space occupied by the production departments.

In November 19X5, the following costs were recorded:

Melting Department direct overhead	$125,000
Molding Department direct overhead	300,000
General Plant Management	90,000
Plant Security	25,000

Other pertinent data are provided below:

	Melting	Molding
Number of employees	20	40
Space occupied (sq. ft.)	10,000	40,000
Machine hours	10,000	2,000
Direct labor hours	4,000	20,000

Required:

(a) Prepare a schedule allocating General Plant Management costs and Plant Security costs to the Melting and Molding Departments.

(b) Determine the total departmental overhead costs for the Melting and Molding Departments.

(c) Assuming the Melting Department uses machine hours and the Molding Department uses direct labor hours to apply overhead to production, calculate the overhead rate for each production department.

12-3 Interdepartmental Services: Step Method

O'Brian's Department Stores allocates the costs of the Personnel and Payroll Departments to three retail sales departments: Housewares, Clothing, and Furniture. In addition to providing services to the operating departments, Personnel and Payroll provide services to each other. O'Brian's allocates Personnel Department costs on the basis of the number of employees and allocates Payroll Department costs on the basis of gross payroll. Cost and allocation information for June is as follows:

	Personnel	Payroll	Housewares	Clothing	Furniture
Direct department cost	$6,900	$3,200	$12,200	$20,000	$15,750
Number of employees	5	3	8	15	4
Gross payroll	$6,000	$3,300	$11,200	$17,400	$ 8,100

Required:

(a) Determine the percentage of total Personnel Department services that was provided to the Payroll Department.

(b) Determine the percentage of total Payroll Department services that was provided to the Personnel Department.

(c) Prepare a schedule showing Personnel Department and Payroll Department cost allocations to the operating departments, assuming O'Brian's uses the step method. (Round calculations to the nearest dollar.)

12-4 Interdepartmental Services: Direct Method

Portland Manufacturing Company has five operating departments, two of which are producing departments (P1 and P2) and three of which are service departments (S1, S2, and S3). All costs of the service departments are allocated to the producing departments. The table below shows the distribution of services from the service departments:

Services Provided from	Services Provided to				
	S1	S2	S3	P1	P2
S1	—	5%	25%	50%	20%
S2	10%	—	5%	45%	40%
S3	15%	5%	—	20%	60%

The direct operating costs of the service departments are as follows:

S1	$42,000
S2	80,000
S3	19,000

Required:

Using the direct method, prepare a schedule allocating the service department costs to the producing departments. (Round calculations to the nearest dollar.)

12-5 Interdepartmental Services: Step Method

Refer to the data in Exercise 12-4. Using the step method, prepare a schedule allocating the service department costs to the producing departments. (Round calculations to the nearest dollar.)

12-6 Absorption Costing and Variable Costing Inventory Valuation

Automotive Electric Company projects the following costs for 19X7:

	Per Unit
Direct materials	$6
Direct labor	8
Variable overhead	2
Fixed overhead ($40,000 for 20,000 units)	2

During May, 20,000 units were produced but only 10,000 were sold. During June, 20,000 units were produced and sold. During July, 20,000 units were produced and 24,000 units were sold. There was no inventory on May 1.

Required:

Compute the amount of ending inventory and cost of goods sold under variable costing and absorption costing for each month.

12-7 Absorption Costing and Variable Costing Income Statements

The Franklin Company sells its product at a unit price of $11.00. Unit manufacturing costs are: direct materials, $2.00; direct labor, $3.00; and variable manufacturing overhead, $1.50. Total fixed manufacturing costs are $30,000 per year. Selling and administrative expenses are $1.00 per unit variable and $10,000 per year fixed. Though 25,000 units were produced during 19X7, only 20,000 units were sold. There was no beginning inventory.

Required:

(a) Prepare an income statement using absorption costing.
(b) Prepare an income statement using variable costing.

12-8 Absorption Costing and Variable Costing Income Statements

The Uncontrolled Profit Corporation was disappointed to find that increased sales volume in 19X8 did not result in increased profits. Both variable unit and total fixed manufacturing costs for 19X7 and 19X8 remained constant at $10 and $1,000,000, respectively.

In 19X7, the company produced 100,000 units and sold 80,000 units at a price of $25 per unit. There was no inventory at the beginning of 19X7. In 19X8, the company made 70,000 units and sold 90,000 units at a price of $25 per unit. Selling and administrative expenses, all fixed, were $50,000 each year.

Required:

(a) Prepare income statements for 19X7 and 19X8 using the absorption costing method.
(b) Prepare income statements for 19X7 and 19X8 using the variable costing method.
(c) Explain why the profit was different each year using the two methods.

12-9 Absorption Costing and Variable Costing Comparisons: Production Equals Sales

Hammond Ketchup Company manufactures and sells 15,000 cases of ketchup each quarter. The following data are available for the third quarter of 19X9:

Sales price per case	$ 25
Direct materials per case	12
Direct labor per case	4
Variable manufacturing overhead per case	3
Total fixed manufacturing overhead	30,000
Fixed selling and administrative expenses	10,000

Required:

(a) Compute the cost per case under absorption costing and variable costing.

(b) Compute net income under both absorption costing and variable costing.

(c) Reconcile the income differences, if any. Explain.

12-10 Absorption Costing and Variable Costing Comparisons: Production Exceeds Sales

Daniel Derma Company produces hand lotion that it sells in bulk to distributors who, in turn, bottle the product under private labels. The sale price per five-gallon container is $10. The production information for July 19X9 is as follows:

Fixed selling and administrative expenses	$20,000
Fixed manufacturing overhead	66,000
Variable manufacturing overhead per container	2
Direct labor costs per hour	12
Direct material costs per container	1

The average direct labor per container is 15 minutes. During July, the company produced 30,000 containers of hand lotion but sold only 28,000 containers. There was no beginning inventory on July 1, 19X9.

Required:

(a) Compute the cost per container under both absorption and variable costing.

(b) Compute net income under both absorption and variable costing.

(c) Compute the ending inventories under both absorption and variable costing.

12-11 Absorption Costing and Variable Costing Comparisons: Sales Exceed Production

Goldberg Development sells commercial building lots. During 19X8, the company bought 1,000 acres of land for $5,000,000 and divided it into 200 lots of equal size. As the lots are sold, they are cleared at an average cost of $2,500. Storm drains and driveways are then installed at an average cost of $4,000 per lot. Selling costs are 10 percent of sales price. Administrative costs are $425,000 per year. The average selling price per lot was $80,000 during 19X8 when 50 lots were sold.

During 19X9, the company purchased and developed an identical 1,000 acres with all costs remaining constant. Sales totaled 300 lots in 19X9 at an average price of $80,000.

Required:

Compute net income under both absorption and variable costing for 19X8 and 19X9.

12-12 Conversion from Absorption Costing to Variable Costing Statements

The Greenville Company began operations on January 1, 19X6. The 19X6 income statement on an absorption costing basis is as follows:

Greenville Company
Absorption Costing Income Statement
For the Year Ending December 31, 19X6

Sales (15,000 units)		$450,000
Cost of goods sold:		
Beginning inventory	$ 0	
Cost of goods manufactured (20,000 units)	280,000	
Ending inventory (5,000 units)	- 70,000	-210,000
Gross profit		$240,000
Selling and administrative expenses		- 40,000
Net income		$200,000

All the selling and administrative expenses are fixed. Manufacturing costs include the following unit costs:

Direct materials	$ 4
Direct labor	5
Variable manufacturing overhead	2
Fixed manufacturing overhead	3
Total	$14

Required:
Prepare a variable costing income statement for 19X6.

12-13 Conversion from Variable Costing to Absorption Costing Statements
The variable costing income statement for Sahota Company is as follows:

Sahota Company
Variable Costing Income Statement
For the Year Ending June 30, 19X7

Sales (9,000 units at $50)		$450,000
Variable expenses:		
Cost of goods sold (9,000 units at $24)	$216,000	
Selling (10% of sales)	45,000	- 261,000
Contribution margin		$189,000
Fixed expenses:		
Manufacturing overhead	$100,000	
Administrative	45,000	- 145,000
Net income		$ 44,000

Selected data for 19X7 concerning the operations of the company are as follows:

Beginning inventory	0 units
Units produced	10,000 units
Manufacturing costs:	
Direct labor	$12 per unit
Direct materials	$ 9 per unit
Variable overhead	$ 3 per unit

Required:
Prepare an absorption costing income statement for 19X7.

12-14 Profit Planning with Absorption Costing and Variable Costing

The Profit Control Corporation wants to ensure that its profits do not decline in proportion to sales declines. To prevent profits from decreasing, Profit Control plans to increase production above normal capacity. For 19X5 and 19X6, the following budget information is available:

	19X5	19X6
Sales volume estimate	500,000 units	400,000 units
Normal production capacity	500,000 units	500,000 units
Planned production	500,000 units	700,000 units
Fixed manufacturing overhead	$1,000,000	$1,000,000
Fixed selling and administrative expenses	$100,000	$100,000
Total variable manufacturing costs	$10 per unit	$10 per unit
Sales	$20 per unit	$20 per unit

Required:
(a) Prepare pro forma income statements using absorption costing for 19X5 and 19X6. (Round computations to the nearest dollar.)
(b) Prepare pro forma income statements using variable costing for 19X5 and 19X6.
(c) Can the company actually control profits? Explain.

PROBLEMS

12-15 Predetermined Overhead Rates with Allocation of Budgeted Service Department Costs: Direct Method

The Albany Company applies manufacturing overhead in its two producing departments using a predetermined rate based on budgeted machine hours in the Stamping Department and based on budgeted labor hours in the Fabricating Department. The following data concerning next year's operations have been developed:

	Service Departments		Producing Departments	
	Human Resources	Maintenance and Repairs	Stamping	Fabricating
Budgeted overhead:				
Variable costs:				
Indirect materials	—	$16,000	$200,000	$ 80,000
Indirect labor	$60,000	50,000	140,000	200,000
Miscellaneous	—	—	28,000	30,000
Fixed costs:				
Miscellaneous	20,000	42,000	80,000	120,000
Other data:				
Direct labor hours (capacity)			20,000	30,000
Direct labor hours (budgeted)			14,000	20,000
Machine hours (capacity)			16,000	8,000
Machine hours (budgeted)			12,000	6,000
Number of employees (capacity)			20	30
Number of employees (budgeted)			12	18

Fixed Human Resources costs are allocated to the producing departments based on employee capacity, and variable costs are allocated based on the budgeted number of employees. Fixed Maintenance and Repairs costs are allocated based on machine hour capacity, and variable costs are allocated based on the budgeted number of machine hours.

Required:
(a) Prepare a schedule showing the direct allocation of budgeted service department costs to the producing departments.
(b) Determine the predetermined overhead rates for the producing departments.

12-16 Selecting Cost Allocation Bases and Direct Method Allocation

The Minot Company, a new company, has three producing departments, P1, P2, and P3, for which direct department costs are accumulated. In January, the following indirect costs of operation were incurred:

Plant manager's salary and office expense	$ 4,800
Plant security	1,200
Plant nurse's salary and office expense	1,500
Plant depreciation	2,000
Machine maintenance	2,400
Plant cafeteria cost subsidy	1,200
	$13,100

The following additional data have been collected for the three producing departments:

	P1	P2	P3
Number of employees	10	15	5
Space occupied (sq. ft.)	2,000	5,000	3,000
Direct labor hours	1,600	4,000	750
Machine hours	4,800	8,000	3,200
Number of nurse office visits	20	45	10

Required:
(a) Group the indirect cost items into cost pools based on the nature of the costs and their common basis for allocation. Identify the most appropriate allocation basis for each pool and determine the total January costs in the pool. (*Hint*: A cost pool may consist of one or more cost items.)
(b) Allocate the cost pools directly to the three producing departments using the allocation bases selected in requirement (a).

12-17 Evaluating Allocation Bases and Direct Method Allocation

The Cheyenne Company has two service departments, Maintenance and Cafeteria, that serve two producing departments, Mixing and Packaging. The following data have been collected for these departments for the current year:

	Cafeteria	Maintenance	Mixing	Packaging
Direct department costs	$176,000	$112,000	$465,000	$295,000
Number of employees			50	30
Number of meals served			9,000	7,000
Number of maintenance hours used			800	600
Number of maintenance orders			180	170

Required:

(a) Using the direct method, allocate the service department costs under the following independent assumptions:
   (1) Cafeteria costs are allocated based on the number of employees, and Maintenance costs are allocated based on the number of maintenance orders.
   (2) Cafeteria costs are allocated based on the number of meals served, and Maintenance costs are allocated based on the number of maintenance orders.
(b) Comment on the reasonableness of the bases used in the calculations in requirement (a). What considerations should determine which bases to use for allocating Cafeteria and Maintenance costs?

12-18 Reimbursement and Step Method

Community Clinic is a not-for-profit outpatient facility that provides medical services to both fee-paying and low-income government supported patients. Reimbursement from the government is based on total actual costs of services provided, including both direct costs of patient services and indirect operating costs. Patient services are provided through two producing departments, Medical Services and Ancillary Services (includes X-ray, therapy, etc.). In addition to the direct costs of these departments, the Clinic incurs indirect costs in two service departments, Administration and Facilities. Administration costs are allocated based on the number of full-time employees, and Facilities costs are allocated based on space occupied. Costs and related data for the current month are as follows:

	Administration	Facilities	Medical Services	Ancillary Services
Direct costs	$9,000	$2,000	$60,700	$24,800
Number of employees	5	4	12	8
Space occupied (sq. ft.)	1,500	—	8,000	2,000
Number of patient visits	—	—	4,000	1,500

Required:

(a) Using the step method, prepare a schedule allocating the common service department costs to the producing departments.
(b) Determine the amount to be reimbursed from the government for each low-income patient visit.

12-19 Step Service Department Cost Allocation: Pricing a New Product

Trimco Products Company is adding a new diet food concentrate, called Body Trim, to its line of exercise products. A plant is being built for manufacturing the new product. Management has decided to price the new product based on a 100 percent markup on total manufacturing costs. A direct cost budget for the new plant projects that direct department costs of $2,100,000 will be incurred in producing an expected normal output of 700,000 pounds of finished product. In addition, indirect costs for Human Resources and Computer Services will be shared by the Body Trim Division with the two exercise products divisions, Commercial Products and Retail Products. Budgeted annual data to be used in making the allocations are summarized below:

	Human Resources	Computer Services	Commercial Products	Retail Products	Body Trim
Number of employees	5	5	50	30	20
Computer time (hours)	500	—	1,500	1,250	750

Direct costs are budgeted at $90,000 for the Human Resources Department and $160,000 for the Computer Services Department.

Required:

(a) Using the step method, determine the total direct and indirect costs of Body Trim.
(b) Determine the selling price per pound of Body Trim. (Round calculations to the nearest cent.)

12-20 Allocation and Responsibility Accounting

The Austin Company uses a responsibility accounting system for evaluating its managers. Abbreviated performance reports for the company's three divisions for the month of March are presented below:

	Total	East	Central	West
Income before allocated costs	$165,000	$ 60,000	$ 75,000	$ 30,000
Less allocated costs:				
Computer Services	(66,000)	(22,000)	(22,000)	(22,000)
Personnel	(72,000)	(28,000)	(32,000)	(12,000)
Division income	$ 27,000	$ 10,000	$ 21,000	$ (4,000)

The manager of the West Division is very disturbed over his performance report and recent rumors that his division may be abolished because of its failure to report a profit in recent periods. He believes that the reported profit figures do not fairly present operating results because his division is being unfairly burdened with service department costs. He is particularly concerned over the amount of Computer Services costs charged to his division. He believes that it is inequitable for his division to be charged with one-third of the total cost when it is using only 20 percent of the services. He believes that the Personnel Department's use of the Computer Services Department should also be considered in the cost allocations.

Cost allocations were based on the following distributions of service provided:

		Services Provided to			
Services Provided from	Personnel	Computer Services	East	Central	West
Computer Services	40%	—	20%	20%	20%
Personnel	—	10%	35%	40%	15%

Required:

(a) What method is the company using to allocate Personnel and Computer Services costs?
(b) Recompute the cost allocations using the step method. (Round calculations to the nearest dollar.)
(c) Revise the performance reports to reflect the cost allocations computed in requirement (b).
(d) Comment on the West Division manager's complaint.

12-21 Allocating Service Department Costs: Direct and Step Methods; Departmental and Plant-Wide Overhead Rates

Brook Windshields, Inc., allocates Human Resources Department costs to the producing departments (Cutting and Welding) based on number of employees and allocates Facilities Department costs based on square footage occupied. Direct department costs, labor hours, and square footage data for the four departments for October 19X9 are as follows:

	Human Resources	Facilities	Cutting	Welding
Direct costs	$63,000	$90,000	$450,000	$600,000
Number of employees	50	50	200	250
Direct labor hours	—	—	8,000	10,000
Square footage occupied	3,000	3,000	30,000	15,000

Required:

(a) Prepare a schedule showing the percentage of services provided from each service department to each of the service and producing departments.
(b) Prepare a schedule showing the service department cost allocations using the direct method.
(c) Prepare a schedule showing the service department cost allocations using the step method. Allocate in the order of greatest interdepartmental services.
(d) Using the production department costs after step method allocation of service departments, calculate departmental overhead rates for Cutting and Welding, assuming both departments apply overhead to products based on direct labor hours.
(e) Calculate a plant-wide overhead rate for Brook Windshields, Inc., based on direct labor hours.
(f) Comment on using departmental overhead rates versus using a plant-wide overhead rate.

12-22 Service Department Cost Allocation: Direct and Step Methods

The Parker Manufacturing Company has two production departments (Fabrication and Assembly) and three service departments (General Factory Administration, Factory Maintenance, and Factory Cafeteria). The costs of the General Factory Administration Department, Factory Maintenance Department, and Factory Cafeteria are allocated to the production departments on the basis of direct labor hours, square footage occupied, and number of employees, respectively. A summary of costs and other data for each department prior to allocation of service department costs for the year ended June 30, 19X6, appear below:

	Fabrication	Assembly	General Factory Admin- istration	Factory Mainte- nance	Factory Cafeteria
Direct department overhead costs	$1,650,000	$1,850,000	$160,000	$203,200	$240,000
Direct labor hours	562,500	437,500	—	—	—
Number of employees	280	200	12	8	20
Square footage occupied	88,000	72,000	1,750	2,000	4,800

Required:

(a) Assuming that Parker elects to distribute service department costs directly to production departments without recognizing interdepartmental services, how much Factory Maintenance Department costs would be allocated to the Fabrication Department?

(b) Assuming the same method of allocation as in requirement (a), how much General Factory Administration Department costs would be allocated to the Assembly Department?

(c) Assuming that Parker elects to distribute service department costs to other service departments (starting with the service department with the greatest total costs) as well as to the production departments, how much Factory Cafeteria Department costs would be allocated to the Factory Maintenance Department?

(d) Assuming the same method of allocation as in requirement (c), how much Factory Maintenance Department costs would be allocated to the General Factory Administration Department?

(CPA Adapted)

12-23 Variable Costing Income Statement: FIFO

For the first three quarters of 19X7, Mustang Motor Company has had wide fluctuations in production and sales. Sales volume and the variable costs of production have increased with no increase in the selling price. Variable manufacturing costs per unit were as follows:

	Quarter		
	First	Second	Third
Direct materials	$1,500	$2,000	$2,500
Direct labor	2,000	2,000	3,000
Variable manufacturing overhead	500	1,000	2,000

The motors sell for $10,000 each. The fixed manufacturing costs are $250,000,000 each quarter. The variable selling and administrative expenses are $600 for each unit sold, and the fixed selling and administrative expenses are $80,000,000 a quarter. Beginning motor inventory at the start of the first quarter, 20,000 units, was recorded at $110,000,000, including $30,000,000 of fixed costs. The company uses the FIFO inventory method. Production and sales data are as follows:

Quarter	Produced	Sold
First	150,000	140,000
Second	160,000	150,000
Third	160,000	170,000

Required:
(a) Prepare income statements for each quarter using variable costing.
(b) Prepare income statements for each quarter using absorption costing.
(c) Reconcile the incomes for each quarter between the two methods.

12-24 Absorption Costing and Variable Costing Income Statements: FIFO
The operating data for the Silver Spoon Company are given below:

	19X7	19X8	19X9
Units manufactured	80,000	100,000	80,000
Units sold	70,000	90,000	100,000
Unit selling price	$ 10	$ 10	$ 10
Variable manufacturing costs per unit	$ 4	$ 4	$ 4
Fixed manufacturing costs	$200,000	$250,000	$300,000

There was no inventory on hand on January 1, 19X7. The company uses the FIFO method to maintain its inventories. Variable selling expenses are $1.20 per unit, and fixed selling and administrative expenses for each year are $60,000.

Required:
(a) Prepare income statements for each year using absorption costing.
(b) Prepare income statements for each year using variable costing.
(c) Reconcile the income differences for each year between the two methods.

12-25 Absorption Costing and Variable Costing Income Statements: All Fixed Costs
The Fixed Rock Company has only fixed costs. It built its building over a pile of rocks and simply sells them when customers visit the plant.

All employees of the plant are paid a fixed annual wage. There are no material costs and no variable overhead because the rocks came with the land and they do not need processing. They are washed in a creek that flows through the property. Costs are estimated as follows for 19X5 and 19X6:

Labor	$200,000
Depreciation	50,000
Insurance	20,000
Administration	40,000

Production capacity is 2,000 tons per year. Rocks sell for $200 per ton. Results for two years are as follows:

	19X5	19X6
Tons produced	1,600	2,000
Tons sold	1,500	2,100

Required:
Prepare income statements for each year under both absorption and variable costing. Which method is better? Why?

12-26 Absorption Costing and Variable Costing Comparisons

Never Quit Shoe Company is concerned with changing to the variable costing method of inventory valuation for making internal decisions. The absorption statements of income for January and February are shown below:

Never Quit Shoe Company
Absorption Costing Income Statements
For the Months of January and February 19X9

	January	February
Sales (8,000 units)	$160,000	$160,000
Cost of goods sold	- 99,200	-108,800
Gross profit	$ 60,800	$ 51,200
Selling and administrative expenses	- 30,000	- 30,000
Net income	$ 30,800	$ 21,200

Production data are as shown below:

Production units	10,000	6,000
Variable costs per unit	$ 10	$ 10
Fixed overhead costs	$24,000	$24,000

Selling and administrative expenses above include variable costs of $1 per unit sold.

Required:
(a) Compute the absorption cost per unit manufactured in January and February.
(b) Explain why the net income for January was higher than the net income for February when the same number of units was sold in each month.
(c) Prepare income statements for both months using variable costing.
(d) Reconcile the absorption costing and variable costing net income figures for each month. Start with variable costing net income.

12-27 Absorption Costing and Variable Costing Comparisons

The Sweet Company manufactures peach jam. Because of bad weather, the crop was small. The following data have been gathered for the summer quarter of 19X3:

Beginning inventory, cases	0
Cases produced	10,000
Cases sold	9,600
Sales price per case	$ 50
Direct materials per case	$ 7
Direct labor per case	$ 6
Variable manufacturing overhead per case	$ 3
Total fixed manufacturing overhead	$400,000
Variable selling and administrative expenses per case	$ 2
Fixed selling and administrative expenses	$ 48,000

Required:

(a) Prepare an income statement for the quarter using absorption costing.
(b) Prepare an income statement for the quarter using variable costing.
(c) What is the value of ending inventory under absorption costing?
(d) What is the value of ending inventory under variable costing?
(e) Explain the difference in ending inventory under absorption costing and variable costing.

12-28 Conversion from Absorption Costing to Variable Costing Statements

The income statement for Mug and Cup Company has been prepared on an absorption costing basis.

Mug and Cup Company
Absorption Costing Income Statement
For the Month Ending December 31, 19X9

Sales (5,000 units)		$25,000
Cost of goods sold:		
Inventory, beginning	$ 5,000	
Cost of goods manufactured	10,000	
Cost of products available for sale	$15,000	
Inventory, ending	- 2,500	12,500
Gross profit		$12,500
Selling and administrative expenses (all fixed)		- 3,000
Net income		$ 9,500

Variable unit costs have remained unchanged during the year. In 19X9, the monthly fixed manufacturing overhead was $2,000. During December, 4,000 units were manufactured.

Required:

(a) Recast the income statement for December to place it on a variable costing basis.
(b) Reconcile the two statements.

DISCUSSION QUESTIONS AND CASES

12-29 Whether or Not to Allocate: Selecting Bases for Allocation

Bonn Company recently reorganized its computer and data processing activities. The small installations located within the accounting departments at its plants and subsidiaries have been replaced with a centralized Data Processing Department at corporate headquarters responsible for the operations of a newly acquired large-scale computer system. The new department has been in operation for two years and has been regularly producing reliable and timely data for the past 12 months. Because the department has focused its activities on converting applications to the new system and producing reports for the plant and subsidiary managements, little attention has been devoted to the costs of the department. Now that the department's activities are operating relatively smoothly, company management has requested that the departmental manager recommend a cost accumulation system to facilitate cost control and the development of suitable rates to charge users for service. For the past two years, the departmental costs have been recorded in one account. The costs have been allocated to user departments on the basis of computer time used. The following schedule reports the costs and charging rate for 19X5.

(1) Salaries and benefits	$ 622,600
(2) Supplies	40,000
(3) Equipment maintenance contract	15,000
(4) Insurance	25,000
(5) Heat and air conditioning	36,000
(6) Electricity	50,000
(7) Equipment and furniture depreciation	285,400
(8) Building improvements depreciation	10,000
(9) Building occupancy and security	39,300
(10) Corporate administrative charges	52,700
Total costs	$1,176,000
Computer hours for user processing	2,750
Hourly rate ($1,176,000 / 2,750)	$ 428 (rounded)
Use of available computer hours:	
Testing and debugging programs	250
Setup of jobs	500
Processing jobs	2,750
Downtime for maintenance	750
Idle time	742
Total	4,992

The department manager recommends that department costs be accumulated by five activity centers within the department: Systems Analysis, Programming, Data Processing, Computer Operations (processing), and Administration. He then suggests that the costs of the Administration activity be allocated to the other four activity centers before a separate rate for charging users is developed for each of the first four activities. After reviewing the details of the accounts, the manager made the following observations regarding the charges to the several subsidiary accounts within the department:

1. Salaries and benefits—records the salary and benefit costs of all employees in the department.
2. Supplies—magnetic tape and disks costs, paper costs for printers, and a small amount for miscellaneous other costs.
3. Equipment maintenance contracts—records charges for maintenance contracts; all equipment is covered by maintenance contracts.
4. Insurance—records cost of insurance covering the equipment and furniture.
5. Heat and air conditioning—records a charge from the corporate Heating and Air Conditioning Department estimated to be the incremental costs to meet the special needs of the Data Processing Department.
6. Electricity—records the charge for electricity based on a separate meter within the department.
7. Equipment and furniture depreciation—records the depreciation for all owned equipment and furniture within the department.
8. Building improvements depreciation—records amortization of the depreciation of all building improvements required to provide proper environmental control and electrical service for the computer equipment.
9. Building occupancy and security—records the Data Processing Department's share of the depreciation, maintenance, heat, and security costs of the building; these costs are allocated on the basis of square feet occupied.
10. Corporate administrative charges—records the Data Processing Department's share of the corporate administrative costs; they are allocated on the basis of the number of employees.

Required:
(a) For each of the ten cost items, state whether or not it should be allocated to the five activity centers; and for each cost item that should be allocated, recommend the basis upon which it should be allocated. Justify your conclusion in each case.
(b) Assume that the costs of the Computer Operations (processing) activity will be charged to the user departments on the basis of computer hours. Using the analysis of computer utilization shown above, determine the total number of hours that should be employed to determine the charging rate for Computer Operations (processing). Justify your answer.

(CMA Adapted)

12-30 Cost Allocation and Performance Evaluation

The Village Branch of Citizens and Northern Bank is managed by Ron Short who has full responsibility for the bank's operations. The Village Branch is treated as a profit center within the company's responsibility accounting system. According to rumors throughout the company, if the Village Branch does not become more profitable, it is likely to be closed.

Ron is upset with the corporate accounting department because of the number of different indirect costs that are allocated to his branch each period. He believes that many of these costs provide no direct benefits to his branch and that they are not relevant to an evaluation of his performance or that of the Village Branch. An income statement for the Village Branch is presented below for February 19X4.

Branch revenues		$145,000
Direct branch costs		- 90,000
Branch margin		$ 55,000
Allocated costs:		
Computer Operations Department	$ 4,500	
Personnel Department	5,000	
Payroll Department	3,800	
Maintenance Department	6,000	
Accounting Department	5,200	
Legal and Audit Department	4,200	
Transportation Department	9,000	
Administrative Overhead	12,000	- 49,700
Branch net income		$ 5,300

An investigation of Mr. Short's complaint by the controller's office provided the following additional information:

- Computer operations costs are billed based on actual CPU and computer connect time used by the branch.
- Personnel and payroll costs are primarily fixed and are allocated to the various operating departments based on the number of employees in each division.
- Maintenance costs are charged to the operating departments based on the standard hours worked in each department, plus the actual cost of materials and supplies used.
- Accounting costs are allocated based on the number of transactions processed by the computer for each branch.
- Legal and audit costs are allocated based on total revenues of the operating departments. The Village Branch has been involved in only one lawsuit, which was about five years ago. Mr. Short gets a copy of the company audit report each year but seldom reads it.
- Transportation costs consist primarily of the costs of operating the company helicopter and the company airplane. The helicopter is used to deliver checks to the local clearing center and for local executive transportation, and the airplane is used primarily for executive travel out of town. Transportation costs are allocated to the operating departments based on revenues. Mr. Short has never flown in the corporate airplane.
- Administrative overhead consists of all other administrative costs, including home office salaries and office expenses. These costs are

allocated to the operating departments based on revenues. Mr. Short seldom ever sees anyone from the home office.

Required:

(a) Evaluate each of the cost allocations to determine whether it seems appropriate to allocate it to the operating divisions. Also, evaluate the basis upon which each cost is allocated to the operating departments.

(b) Prepare a revised income statement for Village Branch based on your evaluations in requirement (a).

(c) Do you agree with Mr. Short's complaint? How do the cost allocations affect the decision to continue or discontinue the Village Branch?

SOLUTION TO REVIEW PROBLEM 12-1

(a)
Direct method:

	Total	Womens'	Mens'
Administrative Services Department:			
Allocation base (number of employees)	24	15	9
Percent of total base	100%	62.5%	37.5%
Cost allocations	$18,000	$11,250	$6,750
Facilities Services Department:			
Allocation base (square footage occupied)	22,500	15,000	7,500
Percent of total base	100%	66.7%	33.3%
Cost allocations	$12,000	$ 8,000	$4,000

Cost allocation summary:

	Administrative	Facilities	Womens'	Mens'	Total
Departmental costs					
before allocations	$18,000	$12,000	$60,000	$50,000	$140,000
Cost allocations:					
Administrative	(18,000)	—	11,250	6,750	0
Facilities	—	(12,000)	8,000	4,000	0
Departmental costs					
after allocation	$ 0	$ 0	$79,250	$60,750	$140,000

Step method:
Allocation sequence:

	Administrative	Facilities
Allocation base	Number of employees	Square footage
Total base for other service *and* producing		
departments (a)	26	25,000
Total base for other service departments (b)	2	2,500
Percent of total services provided to other service		
departments (b) / (a)	7.7%	10.0%
Order of allocation	Second	First

Step allocations:

	Total	Administrative	Womens'	Mens'
Facilities Services Department:				
Allocation base				
(square footage occupied)	25,000	2,500	15,000	7,500
Percent of total base	100%	10%	60%	30%
Cost allocations	$12,000	$1,200	$ 7,200	$3,600
Administrative Services Department:				
Allocation base (number of				
employees)	24	—	15	9
Percent of total base	100%	—	62.5%	37.5%
Cost allocations	$19,200	—	$12,000	$7,200

Cost allocation summary:

	Facilities	Administrative	Womens'	Mens'	Total
Departmental costs					
before allocation	$12,000	$ 18,000	$60,000	$50,000	$140,000
Cost allocations:					
Facilities	(12,000)	1,200	7,200	3,600	0
Administrative	—	(19,200)	12,000	7,200	0
Departmental costs					
after allocations	$ 0	$ 0	$79,200	$60,800	$140,000

(b)

Another service department cost allocation method is the *linear algebra* method. This method simultaneously allocates service department costs both to other service departments and to the producing departments. It has an advantage over the *step* method in that it fully recognizes interdepartmental services.

(c)

If Cotswald's Clothiers wants the most precise allocation of service department costs to the producing departments, taking into account both direct services and indirect services, it will have to use the linear algebra method of service department allocation. As indicated in the "Allocation sequence" section of the Step Method in requirement (a), Facilities provides 10% of its services to Administrative, and Administrative provides 7.7% of its services to Facilities. The step method recognized the Facilities services provided to Administrative, but it did not recognize the Administrative services provided to Facilities.

In this case, the producing departments are using approximately the same proportions of services from each of the service departments (60% to 62.5% for the Womens' Department and 30% to 37.5% for the Mens' Department). Hence, using a more precise measure of cost allocation is not likely to produce significantly different results, especially since the interdepartmental services are so close (7.7% versus 10%). Just as the step method allocation results were quite close to the direct method results, the linear method results would likely be quite close to both the direct and step method results. Use of the linear algebra method is not recommended in this case. On the basis of simplicity and convenience, the direct method is probably the best method for Cotswald's to use.

SOLUTION TO REVIEW PROBLEM 12-2

(a)

	Cost per Unit	
	Absorption Costing	Variable Costing
Direct labor ($200,000 / 50,000)	$ 4.00	$ 4.00
Direct materials ($250,000 / 50,000)	5.00	5.00
Variable manufacturing overhead ($100,000 / 50,000)	2.00	2.00
Fixed manufacturing overhead ($130,000 / 50,000)	2.60	—
Total unit costs	$ 13.60	$ 11.00
Ending inventory units	10,000	10,000
Unit cost	× $13.60	× $11.00
Ending inventory value	$136,000	$110,000

(b)

Colorado Ski Company
Absorption Costing Income Statement
For the Year Ending December 31, 19X7

Sales (40,000 units × $40)		$1,600,000
Cost of goods sold (40,000 units × $13.60)		- 544,000
Gross profit		$1,056,000
Selling and administrative expenses:		
Selling expenses	$ 75,000	
Administrative expenses	112,000	- 187,000
Net income		$ 869,000

Colorado Ski Company
Variable Costing Income Statement
For the Year Ending December 31, 19X7

Sales (40,000 units × $40)		$ 1,600,000
Variable expenses:		
Cost of goods sold (40,000 units × $11.00)	$440,000	
Selling expenses	75,000	- 515,000
Contribution margin		$ 1,085,000
Fixed expenses:		
Manufacturing overhead	$130,000	
Administrative expenses	112,000	- 242,000
Net income		$ 843,000

(c)

Reconciliation of absorption and variable costing net income.

Absorption costing net income		$869,000
Change in inventoried fixed costs:		
Fixed overhead in beginning inventory units	$ —	
Less fixed overhead in ending inventory		
(10,000 units × $2.60)	- 26,000	- 26,000
Variable costing net income		$843,000
Variable costing net income		$843,000
Change in inventoried fixed costs:		
Fixed overhead in ending inventory units		
(10,000 units × $2.60)	$26,000	
Less fixed overhead in beginning inventory	- —	26,000
Absorption costing net income		$869,000

(d)

Generally accepted accounting principles require that absorption costing financial statements be used for external reporting. This includes all reports to creditors, stockholders, and governments. Absorption costing financial statements treat all manufacturing costs (fixed and variable) as product costs and assign them to the products produced, the premise being that all products should bear their share of all manufacturing costs. Although many companies use these statements for internal reporting, the analysis of operating results is quite limited because the various cost elements are not separated by fixed and variable behavior.

For variable costing financial statements, the analysis of cost behavior is required, which in itself provides an additional component in the overall analysis of the operating results. The fixed manufacturing costs are treated as period costs, not assigned to inventories. Therefore, variable costing provides a decision base for cost-volume-profit analysis, which includes a contribution margin (sales less variable costs) that permits an evaluation of costs that are directly related to the revenues.

ACTIVITY-BASED PRODUCT COSTING AND JUST-IN-TIME INVENTORY MANAGEMENT

In the previous three chapters, we introduced traditional product costing systems and discussed the assignment or allocation of indirect (manufacturing overhead) costs to products and services. In Chapters 10 and 11, job-order and process costing systems were introduced using the simplest manufacturing overhead allocation assumption: All indirect manufacturing costs were lumped together in one Manufacturing Overhead account and assigned to products using a single plant-wide overhead rate based on direct labor hours, machine hours, or some other single cost driver. In Chapter 11, we discussed the idea of product cross-subsidization that may result from using a single overhead rate and illustrated how multiple overhead rates may improve product costing. In Chapter 12, we illustrated how companies may benefit by using separate overhead rates for each production department and by establishing administrative, service, and other types of departments for accumulating certain indirect costs before assigning them to producing departments and, ultimately, to products.

*Throughout this text, we have emphasized the importance of identifying cost drivers; and in Chapter 4, we discussed the activity-based costing model, which assigns costs to cost objectives based on activities used by the cost objectives. ABC assigns overhead costs to products using a separate overhead rate for each activity cost pool. If the three approaches to manufacturing overhead cost allocation (plant-wide rate, departmental rates, and ABC rates) are presented on a continuum of complexity and precision, as in Exhibit 13-1, the plant-wide rate system is the simplest to apply and provides the least precise allocation of cost, and ABC is the most complex system and provides the most precise allocation of costs. **One purpose of this chapter is to discuss ABC in more detail as an approach to indirect cost assignment for product costing purposes and to illustrate how it can improve the accuracy of most product cost calculations.** We will also discuss the benefits of using ABC for costing nonmanufacturing processes such as marketing and distribution, selling, and customer service.*

EXHIBIT 13-1: MANUFACTURING OVERHEAD COST ALLOCATION SYSTEMS CONTINUUM

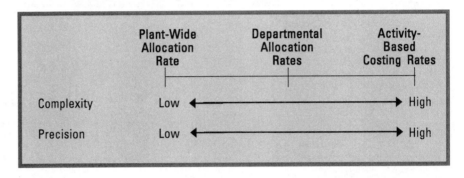

In addition to the task of determining the cost of products is the challenge of managing inventory levels. The nature of this challenge has changed in recent years with the development of a value chain approach to managing a business. No longer can managers consider only their companies' strategies, goals, and objectives in deciding the characteristics and quantities of inventory that should be acquired or produced and maintained. A value chain approach to inventory management requires them to also consider the strategies, goals, and objectives of their suppliers and customers as well if they hope to compete successfully in a global marketplace. Computer technology has affected how inventories are manufactured and handled (using robotics, fully computerized manufacturing and product handling systems, bar code identification systems, etc.), and it is also changing the way companies relate to other parties in the value chain. It has spawned worldwide use of new inventory management approaches and processes such as just-in-time (JIT) inventory management and electronic data interchange (EDI). Another purpose of this chapter is to discuss JIT and other techniques for managing inventories from a value chain perspective in today's high-technology environment and their implications for management accounting.

ACTIVITY-BASED PRODUCT COSTING

L O 1

The factory overhead cost pool has sometimes been referred to as a "blob" of common costs. The constant growth of costs classified as manufacturing overhead has forced accountants to search for increasingly detailed methods to analyze these costs. Increases in the use of expensive equipment, such as robotics, have dramatically increased overhead costs such as depreciation, maintenance, and utilities. When overhead costs were low in comparison with other costs, when factories produced few products in long production runs, and when there was little global competition, the use of a single plant-wide overhead rate may have been adequate. However, as overhead costs grew, manufacturing facilities began to produce a wider variety of products; and as competition intensified, the inadequacies of a single plant-wide overhead rate became evident. These conditions caused attention to shift to departmental overhead rates and the reassignment of service department costs.

As the trends toward product diversity, proportionately higher overhead costs, and global competition continue, management's need for accurate cost information becomes increasingly acute. To compete successfully, managers must be informed about the costs of their products or services so they can determine product profitability and make intelligent decisions regarding product mix, product design, sourcing (the internal or external acquisition of parts and services), and whether to continue or discontinue. Fortunately, advances in information technology and the declining costs of computerized information systems have facilitated the development and maintenance of increasingly detailed data bases. These and other factors, such as declining inventory levels that make product costing less significant for financial reporting, have led to the emergence of *activity-based costing* as an important product costing technique. See Management Accounting Practice 13-1 for a summary of how a New England soap company with 5,000 different products is using ABC to manage costs and profits.

As discussed in Chapter 4, activity-based costing involves determining the cost of activities and tracing the cost of activities to cost objectives on the basis of the cost objective's utilization of units of activity. To restate, ABC is based on the premise that activities drive costs and that costs should be assigned to cost objectives in proportion to the volume of activities they consume. Applied to product costing, ABC traces costs to products on the basis of the activities used to produce them.

The ABC Product Costing Model

As discussed in Chapter 4, ABC can be used to improve cost assignments in many different situations, including product costing, performance evaluation of responsibility center managers, and customer or business segment profitability assessment. ABC can also be used to determine the cost of various processes for efficiency assessment or for benchmarking purposes. Notwithstanding its large number of potential applications, ABC is most widely used to improve the costing of goods and services produced.

Recall that traditional costing considers the cost of a product to be its direct costs for materials and labor, plus some allocated portion of manufacturing overhead. On the other hand, activity-based costing is based on the notion that companies incur costs because of the activities they conduct in pursuit of their goals and objectives. For example, various activities take place to produce a particular product, such as setting up the machines to make the product, maintaining the machines, operating or monitoring the machines, physically moving raw materials and work-in-process, and so forth. Each of these activities has a cost; therefore, the total cost of producing a product using ABC is the sum of the direct materials and labor costs of that product, plus the cost of the various other activities conducted to produce that product.

Before proceeding further, take a few minutes to review the general ABC model illustrated in Exhibit 4-8 on page 194. Recall that two stages are involved in ABC: first, the assignment of resource costs, such as

MANAGEMENT ACCOUNTING PRACTICE 13-1

How a Private-Label Soap Manufacturer Cleaned Up Its Operations with ABC

The Original Bradford Soap Works, a New England-based manufacturer of 5,000 private-label soap products, reached its threshold in the mid-1980's when the following combination of factors brought the company to a crisis point: increased variety of products, increased volume of all product types, new customers with unique service requirements, and reaching full capacity of the current plant facilities. Within this setting, Bradford undertook to implement ABC.

Unlike many companies that experiment with ABC, Bradford did not linger on the fringes of this new technique. Instead, Bradford decided to integrate ABC fully into its financial and managerial reporting system. It developed an ABC data base of cost pools and cost drivers and recast the general ledger to match this data base so that the cost estimates being used to make managerial decisions would correspond to those reflected in the financial reports of operations.

The result was a management accounting system that tracked the job costs of products based on activities used to produce the products. Managers quickly started using the ABC costs for bidding new products, replacing the old system that tallied materials, labor, and an overhead charge with detailed estimates of activities and costs expected to manufacture the proposed products. Bradford's ABC system has provided the company the flexibility to organize data into useful information to "identify products and customers that provide an optimal mix of business to ensure long-term profitability." In addition, ABC "continues to help employees identify opportunities for improvement on the plant floor, reinforcing the total quality process." Finally, ABC is "helping management stabilize and control profitability, providing it with the funds it needs to grow its soap-making business."

Based on: Frances Gammell and C. J. McNair, "Jumping the Growth Threshold Through Activity-Based Cost Management," *Management Accounting* (September 1994), pp. 37-46.

---

indirect labor, depreciation, and utilities, to activity cost pools for the key activities identified; and, second, the assignment of those activity cost pools to cost objectives. Notice in Exhibit 4-8 that costs are assigned to activity cost pools from the various departmental accounts where incurred; hence, the costs in a particular activity pool may have been incurred in several different operating departments. It may be possible to directly assign certain resource costs to an activity cost pool; for instance, wages for the machine setup staff would be directly assignable to the setup activity cost pool. Other resource costs, such as payroll department costs, may have to be allocated to the various activity pools using a resource driver such as number of employees. Exhibit 13-2 presents a more detailed view of the ABC model for product costing purposes. This model is a modification of the general ABC model in Exhibit 4-8. Notice in Exhibit 13-2 that direct product costs, such as direct materials and direct labor, are directly assigned to products and are excluded from the activity cost pools.[1] Only indirect product costs (manufacturing overhead) are assigned to products via activity cost pools.

---

1 In highly automated companies, direct labor is often small; thus, it is not treated as direct cost. Instead, it is pooled with related activity costs and allocated to the products.

EXHIBIT 13-2: ABC TWO-STAGE PRODUCT COSTING MODEL

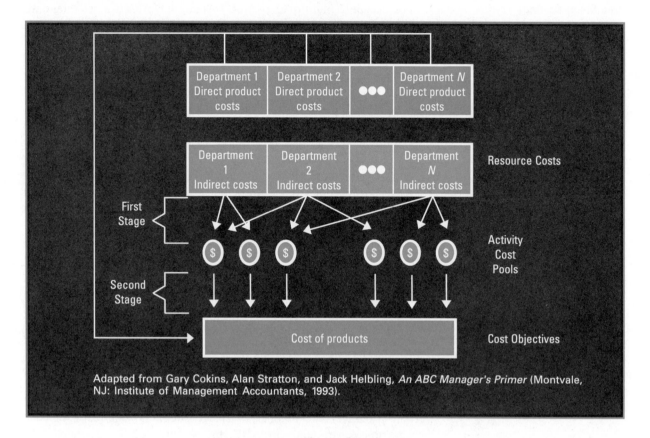

Adapted from Gary Cokins, Alan Stratton, and Jack Helbling, *An ABC Manager's Primer* (Montvale, NJ: Institute of Management Accountants, 1993).

Probably the most critical step in ABC is identifying cost drivers. The activity cost driver for a particular cost (or cost pool) is the characteristic selected for measuring the quantity of the activity for a particular period of time. For example, if an activity cost pool is established for machine setup activity, it is necessary to select some basis for measuring the quantity of machine setup activity associated with the costs in the pool. The quantity of setup activity could be measured by the number of different times machines are set up to produce a different product, the amount of time used in completing machine setups, the number of staff working on setups, or some other measure. It is important that the activity measure used has a logical, causal relationship to the costs in the pool and that the quantity of the activity is highly correlated with the amount of cost in the pool. Statistical methods, such as regression analysis, can be very useful in selecting activity cost drivers.

Once the total cost in the activity pool and the activity cost driver are determined, the cost per unit of activity is determined for the period by dividing the total cost by the total amount of activity. For example, if the total capacity and actual number of machine setups were 200 setups in July when $100,000 total costs were assigned to the setup activity pool, the cost per setup for the month was $500. If, during July, machines were set up 10 times to make product JX2, the total setup cost that would be assigned to product JX2 would be $5,000.

**Activity-Based and
Traditional Costing
Systems Compared**

Procedurally, ABC is not a new method for assigning costs to cost objectives. For decades, traditional costing systems have used a two-stage allocation model, similar to the ABC model, to assign costs to cost pools and, subsequently, to assign those cost pools to products using an allocation base. In many traditional systems, overhead is assigned to one or more cost pools, called Manufacturing Overhead accounts, and then assigned from these accounts to products using a general allocation base such as direct labor hours or machine hours. What is different about ABC is that it breaks the operations of the company down into processes, which are broken down into activities. ABC accumulates costs in cost pools for the major activities and then assigns the costs of these activities to products or to other cost objectives that benefit from these activities. *Conceptually*, ABC is different from traditional costing because it is a different way of viewing the operations of the company; *procedurally,* ABC uses a methodology that has been around for a long time.

The challenge in using ABC is specifying the model; that is, determining how many activity pools to establish for a given cost measurement purpose, which costs to assign to each activity pool, and the appropriate activity driver to use for each pool. Specifying the model also includes determining the resource cost drivers for assigning indirect resource costs to the various activity cost pools.

Four examples will help illustrate some of the differences between activity-based and traditional costing systems:

1. Using traditional cost allocation, maintenance department costs may be allocated to production departments on the basis of the number of repair orders or the number of service hours associated with each production department. In ABC, the resource costs associated with maintenance might be assigned to several different activity cost pools, all subsequently assigned to products.

2. In a traditional cost allocation system, all purchasing department costs may be allocated to production departments based on the dollar value of direct materials issued to each department. Using ABC, the purchasing function would be analyzed to determine the activities supported by its costs, such as processing and following up on purchase orders and processing receipt of ordered goods. If these activities are disproportionate across the various purchase orders processed, it may be necessary to establish a separate activity cost pool and allocation base for costs associated with (1) ordering and (2) receiving goods.

3. A portion of the plant manager's salary or security costs often are assigned to the producing departments by a traditional costing system using an arbitrary base such as number of employees or space occupied in the building. In ABC, these costs would not be assigned to production departments or to products unless they could be specifically associated with activities used by the production departments in making the products. If they were not assigned to products, they would be regarded as facility level costs.

4. In a traditional costing system, after all indirect costs of manufacturing are allocated to the producing departments through the various

administrative and service departments, the total indirect costs of the producing departments (allocated plus direct departmental costs) are usually allocated to products using a single cost driver such as direct labor hours or machine hours. Under ABC, many of these service department costs (such as purchasing) might be assigned directly to products using an appropriate activity cost driver; and any remaining indirect costs of the producing department costs would be allocated to products using not one, but multiple drivers, depending on the activities identified for the production process.

Several characteristics and conclusions of activity-based costing emerge from these examples:

1. *ABC uses a greater number of cost pools* than traditional cost allocation methods. Traditional costing tends to equate one department with one cost pool, but ABC often uses multiple cost pools within a single department. Or in some cases, ABC does not even use the established departmental structure for pooling costs if that structure does not coincide with key activities for which appropriate activity cost drivers can be determined.

2. Although traditional costing procedures as a general rule attempt to find causal bases for cost allocation, *ABC is even more insistent on the use of causal factors.* This is emphasized by the requirement that costs be assigned using their activity "cost drivers."

3. When a causal basis cannot be found for cost allocation, traditional costing procedures often resort to some arbitrary allocation basis judged to provide a "fair" allocation such as unit volume of output, labor hours, sales dollars, total direct costs, etc. By definition, *ABC assigns costs based on their activity cost drivers; and if they cannot be identified, ABC cannot be used to assign those costs.* In such cases, if full allocation of costs is required, such as for financial reporting purposes, a traditional, "arbitrary" costing approach would have to be used.

4. *Implementation of ABC requires an understanding of the production process, the activities that occur in the production process, and the cost drivers that generate the costs of those activities.* Hence, a team that includes accountants, engineers, production personnel, and information systems specialists is often required to implement an ABC system. At a minimum, the accountants designing the system must leave their air-conditioned offices, don hard hats, and seek assistance from operating personnel.

5. *Implementation and operation of ABC is more likely to involve the use of judgment* than is the operation of a traditional costing system. Many decisions pertaining to the establishment of activity cost pools, determining which costs to assign to each pool, and identifying cost drivers for allocating each pool are based on observation and interviews. Resorting to "most common practice" is not acceptable in ABC; each system must be tailored to the specific situation—and that requires judgment.

L O 2

THE PRODUCT COSTING CONTINUUM ILLUSTRATED

As stated earlier, product costing systems range from very simplistic ones where a single plant-wide overhead rate is used to very complex ones that use multiple activity cost overhead rates. The following scenario illustrates this continuum of cost allocation approaches for the Cyber Division of Neugenics, Inc.

The Cyber Division of Neugenics, Inc., specializes in the manufacture of two advanced technology components for the aerospace industry, referred to internally as T-1 and T-2. Recently, competition has become a problem for Cyber as new companies, including some in Europe and the Pacific Rim, have entered the market for these products, leading to falling sales for the Cyber Division. Speculating on the possible causes for the falling sales, Cyber's president expressed suspicion that some of its non-U.S. competitors were engaging in illegal dumping of products into the international market at prices below cost to try to eliminate their foreign competition. As a case in point, Cyber's president referred to a fax just received from a long-time customer who stated that it will no longer be able to purchase T-1 components at Cyber's current price of $550 per unit because of an offer from a Korean firm to provide the same component for $425 per unit—which is below Cyber's manufacturing cost of $455 per unit. In a staff meeting, the president suggested that maybe Cyber could no longer compete in the T-1 market and possibly should shift its emphasis to becoming the leader in the T-2 market where its selling price of $300 per unit provides substantial profit margins. The marketing manager for T-1 suggested that before making such a major change in corporate strategy, a study of revenue and cost data for both products should be conducted to see if possible cost-efficiencies could be made to help them become more competitive. A summary of Cyber's product costs for the most recent month is presented below. It is based on the current costing system, *which allocates manufacturing overhead using a single plant-wide rate based on direct labor hours*:

	Unit Costs	
	T-1	T-2
Direct materials	$125	$120
Direct labor	110	30
Manufacturing overhead*	220	60
Total unit cost	$455	$210

*Using a plant-wide manufacturing overhead rate of $20 per direct labor hour, based on $700,000 of plant-wide manufacturing overhead costs and 35,000 plant-wide direct labor hours.

In a meeting with the production manager, marketing manager, and controller, the president asked for a candid discussion about the company's manufacturing and cost control systems compared to those of Cyber's competitors. The manufacturing manager assured the president that Cyber was "state-of-the-art" in its production processes but raised some concerns about whether T-1 should have an overhead cost almost four times that of T-2. The controller responded that Cyber was using a plant-wide overhead allocation method, which it had used for many years, but followed up that some other firms in the industry were using different cost allocation methods, including a method called "activity-based costing."

(Product cost continuum observation: Note that by using a plant-wide rate, Cyber Division was at the end of the cost allocation continuum where the overhead rate is the easiest to calculate but provides the least precision in allocating overhead cost to products.)

Her curiosity piqued by the controller's comment about ABC, the president immediately contacted Cyber's public accounting firm (which also served as a consultant on accounting matters) to evaluate its product costing system. The consultant told the president that Cyber was operating a very antiquated costing system. However, before looking at ABC, Cyber should consider using departmental overhead rates, which could be developed without extensive consulting fees costs. The president agreed, and the consultant developed the following overhead cost data:

Direct departmental overhead costs:		
Composition Department	$215,000	
Assembly Department	140,000	$355,000
Common overhead costs:		
Production Support costs:		
Setup	$ 24,000	
Machining	75,000	
Engineering	96,000	195,000
Logistics costs:		
Receiving	$ 60,000	
Material handling	90,000	150,000
Total manufacturing overhead costs		$700,000

The consultant decided that the best way to allocate common costs to the producing departments was to use a direct allocation method with the following cost drivers:

Common Cost	Cost Driver
Production support	Machine hours
Logistics	Material moves

The allocation of common costs and the calculation of departmental overhead rates based on direct labor hours are presented below:

	Total	Composition	Assembly
Production Support costs:			
Cost driver (machine hours)	18,000	6,000	12,000
Percent of cost driver	100%	33 1/3%	66 2/3%
Cost allocation	$195,000	$65,000	$130,000

	Total	Composition	Assembly
Logistics costs:			
Cost driver (material moves)	225	135	90
Percent of cost driver	100%	60%	40%
Cost allocation	$150,000	$90,000	$ 60,000

Cost allocation summary:

	Common Costs		Production Departments		
	Production	Logistics	Composition	Assembly	Total
Costs before allocations	$195,000	$ 150,000	$215,000	$140,000	$700,000
Common cost allocations:					
Production (above)	(195,000)		65,000	130,000	
Logistics (above)		(150,000)	90,000	60,000	
Costs after allocations	$ 0	$ 0	$370,000	$330,000	$700,000

Production Department overhead rates:

	T-1	T-2
Total departmental overhead	$370,000	$330,000
Allocation base (direct labor hours)	÷ 25,000	÷ 10,000
Overhead cost per direct labor hour	$ 15*	$ 33

*Rounded

It was determined that each unit of product T-1 requires 9 direct labor hours in the Composition Department and 2 direct labor hours in the Assembly Department and that product T-2 requires 1 direct labor hour in Composition and 2 direct labor hours in Assembly. The unit cost summary based on the departmental overhead rates are as follows:

	T-1		T-2	
Direct materials cost (given earlier)		$125		$120
Direct labor cost (given earlier)		110		30
Factory overhead:				
T-1 - Composition (9 labor hours × $15)	$135			
Assembly (2 labor hours × $33)	66	201		
T-2 - Composition (1 labor hour × $15)			$15	
Assembly (2 labor hours × $33)			66	81
Total unit product costs		$436		$231

Allocating factory overhead costs based on departmental rates, rather than on a $20 per labor hour plant-wide rate, causes a shift in costs from T-1 to T-2 because T-2's overhead costs are incurred primarily in the Assembly Department, which has a $33 per labor hour overhead rate, whereas T-1's overhead costs are incurred primarily in the Composition Department, which has only a $15 per labor hour overhead rate.

(Product cost continuum observation: Note that as we move along the cost allocation system continuum for Cyber Division from a plant-wide rate to departmental rates, the calculations become more complex. However, the cost allocations are more precise measures of actual resources used to produce the respective products.)

The president agreed that using departmental rates is clearly an improvement over using a plant-wide rate in situations where departmental overhead costs are not the same and where various products use departmental activity in the producing departments in disproportionate amounts. Still, if $436 per unit for T-1 is an accurate cost, Cyber will not be able to compete with the competitive price of $425 per unit. Before making a final decision on the appropriate strategy, the president engaged an ABC consultant to look at Cyber's costs to see if ABC cost calculations were in line with costs based on departmental overhead rates.

The ABC consultant determined that the direct department overhead costs in the Composition Department are driven by machine hours, whereas direct department overhead costs in the Assembly Department are driven by units produced. It was also determined that each component of Production Support and Logistics costs represents a separate activity cost pool, and that these costs should be allocated to the products based on specific cost drivers. Accordingly, the consultant prepared the following overhead activity-based cost calculations:

Overhead Activity	Total Activity Cost	Activity Cost Driver	Quantity of Activity	Unit Activity Rates
Composition	$215,000	Machine hours	18,000	$ 11.94
Assembly	140,000	Units produced	5,000	28.00
Setup	24,000	Number of production runs	30	800.00
Machining	75,000	Machine hours	18,000	4.17
Engineering	96,000	Engineering hours	4,000	24.00
Receiving	60,000	Number of orders processed	140	428.57
Material handling	90,000	Number of material moves	225	400.00
	$700,000			

The amounts of activity attributed to producing 2,500 units each of products T-1 and T-2, and the factory overhead cost per unit based on ABC costs are as follows:

Activity (cost per unit of driver activity)	T-1 Quantity of Activity	T-1 Cost of Activity	T-2 Quantity of Activity	T-2 Cost of Activity
Composition ($11.94 per machine hour)	4,000	$ 47,760	14,000	$167,160
Assembly ($28 per unit produced)	2,500	70,000	2,500	70,000
Setup ($800 per production run)	10	8,000	20	16,000
Machining ($4.17 per machine hour)	12,000	50,040	6,000	25,020
Engineering ($24 per engineering hour)	1,600	38,400	2,400	57,600
Receiving ($428.57 per order processed)	40	17,143	100	42,857
Material handling ($400 per material move)	100	40,000	125	50,000
Total factory overhead product cost		$271,343**		$428,637**
Units produced		÷ 2,500		÷ 2,500
Factory overhead cost per unit of product		$ 109		$ 171
Direct materials cost per unit of product		125		120
Direct labor cost per unit of product		110		30
Total unit product cost using ABC		$ 344		$ 321

**Due to rounding, these do not total to $700,000.

(Product cost continuum observation: Note that ABC is considerably more complex for Cyber Division than are the previous two systems— plant-wide and departmental rate systems.   However, ABC provides the most accurate measurement of the costs of activities used in producing T-1 and T-2.)

After reviewing these costs provided by the ABC consultant, the president called the management team back into a meeting to discuss their strategy for competing with the Korean firm and to decide what actions to take regarding products T-1 and T-2.   They all agreed that ABC provided a more accurate measurement of overhead costs incurred in the production of the products than did the old system based on a plant-wide rate and the alternative system based on departmental rates.   In light of the ABC results, it now appears that T-2 is losing money and that the current price of $550 for T-1 makes Cyber particularly vulnerable to price competition from foreign firms.   The president announced that a price reduction for T-1 is in order—the only question is how much—and that the focus of cost control must now be shifted to T-2 if it is to survive.

Several limitations of the Cyber illustration should be mentioned. For the sake of simplicity, the example was limited to manufacturing cost considerations, but a complete analysis would also require consideration of nonmanufacturing costs, such as marketing, distribution, and customer service, before a final determination of product profitability could be made. Also, the costs illustrated represented only unit and batch level costs, but there would probably be product and facility level costs to consider in most situations.   Finally, the analysis was based on the assumption that actual capacity was the same as practical capacity.   Hence, there was no idle capacity involved.   These issues were all discussed in detail in the ABC discussion in Chapter 4.

The illustration of cost distortions (and, hence, profit distortions) for Cyber from using traditional costing systems, while hypothetical, is not uncommon.   Studies have reported that distortions of this type occur regularly in traditional systems where there is a significant variation in the volume and complexity of products and services produced.[2] Traditional costing systems tend to overcost high-volume, low-complexity products; and they tend to undercost low-volume, high-complexity products.   These studies indicate that the typical amount of overcosting is up to 200 percent for high-volume products with low complexity and that the typical undercosting is up to more than 1,000 percent for low-volume, highly complex products.   In companies with a large number of different products, traditional costing may show that most products are profitable. After changing to ABC, however, these companies may find that as few as the 10 to 15 percent most profitable products are producing 100 percent of the profits.   In these cases, the profits of the remaining profitable products are being offset by losses on the unprofitable products.   Adopting ABC often

---

2 Gary Cokins, Alan Stratton, and Jack Helbling, *An ABC Manager's Primer* (Montvale, NJ: Institute of Management Accountants, 1993).

leads to increased profits merely by changing the product mix to get rid of unprofitable products.

ABC IMPLEMENTATION ISSUES

L O 3

Most companies do not immediately abandon their traditional costing systems when they adopt ABC. Some maintain dual systems indefinitely—a traditional costing system for external reporting purposes and ABC for pricing and other internal decision-making purposes. Still others maintain dual systems only until they are satisfied that ABC is working well, and then they discontinue the traditional system and use ABC for both external reporting and internal decision making. As indicated in Chapter 4, a recent survey of costing systems in use indicated that 29 percent of companies surveyed are using ABC, instead of traditional costing systems, and that 56 percent are using ABC as an off-line analytical tool. Another survey conducted by the international accounting and consulting firm, Price Waterhouse, indicated that more than half of American manufacturing companies and one-third of service companies have at least experimented with ABC and that ABC is spreading quickly to companies based in Europe and the Pacific Rim. Commenting on this private survey and other issues about using ABC, Price Waterhouse partners Keegan and Eiler stated that "until management integrates activity-based costing into the company's formal system of reporting, ABC is in danger of remaining a sideshow exercise, championed by staff groups and consultants but of little real meaning to the day-to-day operations of the company."[3] Management Accounting Practice 13-2 describes how the international accounting firm of Ernst & Young goes about implementing an ABC system for its clients.

Proponents of ABC believe that managers must reassert their authority to control what are often dismissed as "common" or "fixed" costs. ABC attacks the shapeless mass of common costs, decomposing them into smaller, more homogeneous cost pools related to specific activities. ABC also takes a long-term view of fixed costs; and in the long run, all costs are variable—that is, fixed costs, such as depreciation, merely represent costs incurred for larger chunks of activity than those paid for on a per unit or per batch basis. And when one of these large chunks of activity is completed, another chunk will have to be purchased. Hence, managers must manage fixed costs and take action to bring them down when normal periodic activity levels decline. Certainly, there are difficult problems in determining how to treat fixed costs in either a traditional costing or ABC system, since fixed costs usually represent some amount of capacity of activity that may or may not ultimately be used. The full absorption inventory valuation approach requires an assumption about how much

---

3 Daniel P. Keegan and Robert G. Eiler, "Let's Reengineer Cost Accounting," *Management Accounting* (August 1994), pp. 26-31.

MANAGEMENT ACCOUNTING PRACTICE 13-2

Ernst & Young Consultant Reports on Implementing ABC Systems

A director of cost management consulting services for the international accounting firm of Ernst & Young reported on his experience in designing and implementing a "total cost management" (TCM) philosophy for client companies, both large and small. The TCM engagements involved several elements, including determining product costs that reflect true costs, process value analysis, cost reduction, improved performance measurements, responsibility accounting, and product line profitability.

The consultant identified four phases in implementing a TCM philosophy. Phase one begins with process value analysis, which includes identification of key processes and related activities along with cost behavior and activity/driver relationships. Phase two uses activity and cost analysis data from the processes identified in phase one to cost activities and to seek ways to reduce process costs. This phase also involves integrating activity cost and cost reduction information into the performance reporting system. Phase three produces a true picture of the internal value chain costs of providing products to the market using ABC. In the final phase, the consultants seek to fully integrate activity information into the reporting systems of both financial and managerial reporting purposes. They acknowledged that this phase was still on the horizon for TCM systems. Although this report was published in 1990, one of the major challenges of ABC that remains in 1996 is how to fully integrate ABC into the managerial and financial accounting and reporting systems.

Based on: Michael R. Ostrenga, "Activities: The Focal Point of Total Cost Management," *Management Accounting* (February 1990), pp. 42-49.

capacity will be used and over what period of time. This complex subject is addressed in much greater detail in advanced management accounting and cost accounting texts.

Possibly the greatest benefit of implementing an ABC system stems from the detailed analysis of the manufacturing process required to identify activity cost drivers. This analysis is likely to identify some activities that do not add value to the product, such as the unnecessary movement of materials or an inspection operation. Eliminating nonvalue-added activities will reduce final product costs and improve profitability. ABC analysis may also make design engineers aware of the probable costs of alternative product designs and manufacturing procedures, which may lead to redesigned products that are more competitively priced. In short, in addition to providing more accurate costs, ABC usually results in managers having an increased understanding of operational processes, improved product designs and processes, and better control of costs.

Once an ABC system has been developed for a production facility (including a detailed list of activities that occur in that facility, identification of activity cost drivers, and calculation of cost per unit of driver activity), the activity costs of a currently produced or proposed product can be readily determined. In ABC, manufacturing a product is viewed simply as the combination of activities selected to make it; therefore, the activity cost of a product or service is the sum of the costs of those activities. By viewing a product this way, management can evaluate the importance of each of the activities consumed in making a product. Possibly some activities can be eliminated, or a lower cost activity can be substituted for a more costly one without reducing the quality or performance of the product. For example, The Coca-Cola Company used ABC to determine that it was less costly—and, thus, more profitable—to deliver soft drink syrup to some fountain drink retailers such as fast-food restaurants in nonreturnable, disposable containers rather than in returnable stainless steel containers, which had been standard in the industry for many years.[4] When the final list of activities selected for making a product is determined, ABC data can be used to develop detailed standard costs for various operations conducted in making the product. These standards are the basis for calculating variances used for evaluating performance in a standard costing system (as discussed in Chapter 8).

Although an ABC system may seem complex, the system merely mirrors the complexity of an organization's design, manufacturing, and distribution systems. If a firm's products are diverse and its production and distribution procedures are complex, the ABC system will also be complex; however, if its products are homogeneous and its production environment is relatively simple, its ABC system should also be relatively simple. Even in highly complex manufacturing environments, ABC systems typically have no more than seven to ten cost pools per application. Many ABC experts in practice have observed that creating a large number of activity cost pools (more than about ten) for a given costing application normally does not improve cost accuracy significantly above that of a smaller number of cost pools. As with any information system design, the costs of developing and maintaining the system must not exceed its benefits; hence, although adding more activity cost pools may result in some small amount of increased accuracy, it may be so small as to not be cost-effective.

It is important to reiterate that ABC is not just a product costing system used to provide data for external financial reports. ABC's primary benefit from a product costing standpoint is that it provides more accurate cost data for internal decision-making purposes. Companies that sell virtually everything they produce obviously have little or no inventories. Consequently, they do not need a product costing system for external reporting purposes because all manufacturing costs are expensed as cost of goods sold each period. However, even these companies need a good costing system for internal management purposes, such as evaluating product profitability, tracking changes in costs over time, and benchmarking against their competitors. A 1993 survey discussed in Management Accounting Practice 13-3 reported that many companies still need a reliable product costing system for product pricing purposes.

---

4 From a presentation given by the Director of Activity-Based Costing for The Coca-Cola Company to the Executive MBA students at Goizueta Business School at Emory University.

Although ABC is normally adopted because of the internal benefits it provides, we believe that companies that have significant amounts of inventories should include accurate measures of inventories and cost of goods sold in their external reports. The accuracy of inventory costs affects the accuracy of reported net income; and for most companies—especially those publicly held—net income is the primary measure used by the owners to evaluate corporate performance and by the marketplace to value a company's shares of stock. This external use of inventory cost information is, arguably, no less important than the internal uses of inventory cost information.

In addition to using ABC for product costing purposes, other important uses for ABC have also been found. One of the most useful applications for ABC is in evaluating customer costs and distribution channel costs. Other applications include costing administrative functions such as pro-

---

MANAGEMENT ACCOUNTING PRACTICE 13-3

Product Pricing Approaches and ABC

A 1993 survey of 141 companies reported the extent that companies use cost-based pricing versus market-based pricing. It also reported on the use of ABC for product costing purposes. The survey, summarized below, included companies across U.S. industries, most of which were multiproduct organizations with an average of 75 products each:

	Number of Companies Using			
	Full-Cost Pricing	Variable-Cost Pricing	Market-Based Pricing	Total (%)
Fully or partially implemented ABC	26	6	6	38 (26.9%)
Plan to implement ABC	33	7	13	53 (37.6%)
Do not plan to implement ABC	39	4	7	50 (35.5%)
Total (%)	98 (70%)	17 (12%)	26 (18%)	141 (100%)

Two important observations about the above data are that 70 percent of all companies surveyed rely on a full-cost pricing method and that 64.5 percent (26.9 + 37.6) either already use or plan to use ABC product costing. Despite frequent criticisms (see discussion in Chapter 5), cost-based pricing is still very common in practice, according to this survey. As stated by the survey authors, "ABC systems provide more accurate product cost estimates that serve as a basis of determining full-cost price. The rapid implementation of ABC systems, therefore, tends to supply a support for the prevalent use of full-cost pricing practice." Whether cost-based or market-based pricing is the better approach to pricing, most should agree that ABC improves costs; and for those firms using cost-based pricing, it improves prices as well.

Based on: Eunsup Shim and Ephraim F. Sudit, "How Manufacturers Price Products," *Management Accounting* (February 1995), pp. 37-39.

cessing accounts receivable or accounts payable, costing the process of hiring and training employees, and costing such menial tasks as typing a letter or copying a document. Any process, function, or activity performed in an organization, whether it's related to production, marketing and sales, finance and accounting, human resource activities—even research and development—is a candidate for ABC analysis. In short, the total cost of any cost objective that has more than an insignificant amount of indirect costs can be more effectively measured using ABC.

Just as the Cyber Division of Neugenics, Inc., found that it was pursuing the wrong product strategy before obtaining ABC costs, strategic errors in other areas of an organization often are discovered by ABC. For example, one company's management was of the opinion that selling through distributors to small companies was its most profitable selling channel because selling prices through distributors were higher than those through direct selling alternatives. ABC showed that, in fact, direct sales at lower prices to large chains, such as Wal-Mart, were more profitable than sales at higher prices through distributors. In this case, ABC identified costs other than product costs and found that nonproduct costs of selling direct to large retailers were significantly lower than those made through distributors. As you would expect, as a result of ABC analysis, the company's marketing and sales strategy has shifted from selling through distributors to a large number of small to medium companies to selling directly to a small number of large companies.

JUST-IN-TIME INVENTORY MANAGEMENT

L O 4

Just-in-time (JIT) inventory management, a comprehensive inventory management philosophy, stresses policies, procedures, and attitudes by managers and other workers that result in the efficient production of high-quality goods while maintaining the minimum level of inventories. JIT is often described simply as an inventory model that maintains only the level of inventories required to meet current production and sales requirements. However, JIT is, in reality, much more than that. The key elements of the JIT philosophy include increased coordination throughout the value chain, reduced inventory, reduced production times, increased product quality, and increased employee involvement and empowerment. Approaches to reducing inventories of raw materials, work-in-process, and finished goods are considered below.

Reducing Raw Materials Inventories

The JIT approach to reducing raw materials includes: (1) developing long-term relationships with a limited number of vendors, (2) selecting vendors on the basis of service and material quality as well as price, (3) establishing procedures for production employees to order raw materials for current production needs directly from approved vendors, and (4) accepting vendor deliveries directly to the shop floor. Fully implemented, these steps would minimize or eliminate raw materials inventories. There would be sufficient raw materials on hand to meet only near-term needs, and the raw materials inventories would be located on the shop floor.

To achieve this reduction, it is apparent that vendors and buyers must work as a team and that production employees must be involved in decision making. The goal of the JIT approach to purchasing is not merely to shift raw materials carrying costs to vendors. A close and long-term working relationship between purchasers and vendors should be beneficial to both. Purchasers' scheduling information is provided to vendors so that vendors can also reduce inventories and minimize costs. Vendors are therefore able to manufacture small batches frequently, rather than to manufacture large batches infrequently. What's more, vendors are more confident of future sales. See Management Accounting Practice 13-4 for a discussion of how two computer companies' inventory strategies enable them to maintain small inventories of component parts.

Reducing Work-in-Process Inventories

Reducing **cycle time**, the total time required to complete a process, is the key to reducing work-in-process inventories. In a manufacturing organization, cycle time is composed of setup time, processing time, movement time, waiting time, and inspection time. Setup time is the time required to prepare equipment to produce a specific product. Processing time is the time spent working on units. Movement time is the time units spend

---

MANAGEMENT ACCOUNTING PRACTICE 13-4

Lower Inventories Are Key to Success at Dell Computer Corp. and Gateway 2000, Inc.

Dell and Gateway combined represent almost 50 percent of the direct-mail PC computer sales market. Unlike IBM, Apple, and other better established name brands that build PC computers for sale through dealers, Dell and Gateway build to order. Direct marketers build to customers' specifications after the orders are received. This makes their inventories much lower with 35 days of inventory on hand, compared to 110 days for Compaq Computer Corp.

These direct market sales companies maintain that they can respond to market changes much faster, too—up to three months faster than dealer-based companies to switch to new microprocessors or disk drives. For example, by the time Gateway had converted 50 percent of its computers to the Intel Pentium chip, IBM and Compaq had less than 10 percent of their models converted because of the need to sell 486 chips still in inventory. Because they were maintaining such a low inventory at any one time, Dell and Gateway also got past the problem of the Pentium chip flaws. They were among the first to announce they were shipping only the Intel replacement chip.

The ability to maintain lower inventories is inherent in some sales and marketing strategies such as direct marketing. However, firms using other strategies can realize some of the same benefits by using a JIT to minimize the need for inventories.

Based on: "The Computer Is in the Mail (Really)," *Business Week* (January 23, 1995), pp. 76-77.

moving between work or inspection stations. Waiting time is the time units spend in temporary storage waiting to be processed, moved, or inspected. Inspection time is the amount of time it takes units to be inspected. Of the five elements of cycle time, only processing time adds value to the product. Efforts to reduce cycle time are appropriate for both continuous and batch production.

Devising means of reducing setup times will directly reduce the cycle time for batch production, and, thus, reduce setup costs.[5] Setup times can also be reduced by shifting from batch to continuous production whenever practical. Rearranging the shop floor to eliminate unnecessary materials movements can help reduce movement time for continuous and batch production.

Many companies, especially in Japan, have created **quality circles**, which are groups of employees involved in the production of products and who have the authority, within certain parameters, to address and resolve quality problems as they occur without seeking managerial approval. Giving employees more authority and responsibility for quality, including the right to stop production whenever quality problems are noted, can reduce the need for separate inspection time.

In the case of batch production, waiting time can be reduced by better job scheduling. In the case of continuous production, waiting time can be reduced by moving from a materials push to a materials pull approach to production.

Under a traditional **materials push system**, employees work to reduce the pile of inventory building up at their workstations. Workers at each station remove materials from an in-process storage area, complete their operation, and place the output in another in-process storage area. Hence, they "push" the work to the next workstation. The emphasis is on production efficiency at each station. In a push system, one of the functions of work-in-process inventory is to help make workstations independent of each other. Inventories are large enough to allow for variations in processing speeds, disposal of defective units without interrupting production, and machine downtime.

Under a **materials pull system** (often called a **Kanban system**[6]), employees at each station work to replenish the inventory used by employees at subsequent stations. The building of excess inventories is strictly prohibited. When the number of units in inventory reaches a specified limit, work at the station stops until workers at a subsequent station "pull" a unit from the in-process storage area. Hence, the pull of inventory by a subsequent station authorizes production to continue. A pull, or Kanban, system's low inventory levels require a team effort. To avoid idle time, processing speeds must be balanced and equipment must be kept in good repair. Quality problems are identified immediately, and the low inventory levels require immediate correction of quality problems.

---

5 As discussed in the Appendix to this chapter, reducing setup costs reduces the economic lot size—that is, the size of inventory acquisition or production that is most economic.
6 Kanban, the Japanese term for "card," is a system created in Japan that originally used cards to indicate that a department needed additional components.

To make a pull system work, management must accept the notion that it is better to have employees idle than to have them building excess inventory. A pull system also requires careful planning by management, active participation in decision making by employees, and a shift from an emphasis on performance at each workstation to an emphasis on performance for the entire operation.

Reducing Finished Goods Inventory

Finished goods inventory can be reduced by reducing cycle time and by better predicting customers' demand for finished units. Lowering cycle times reduces the need for speculative inventories. If finished goods can be replenished faster, there is less need for large inventory levels to satisfy customer needs and to provide for unanticipated fluctuations in customer orders. Anticipating customers' demand for goods can be improved by adopting a value chain approach to inventory management, where the manufacturer is working as a partner with its customers to meet their inventory needs. This frequently involves having on-line computer access to customers' inventory levels on a real-time basis and being able to synchronize changes in production to changes in customers' inventory levels as they occur. Sharing this type of information, obviously, requires an enormous amount of mutual trust between a manufacturer and its customers, but it is becoming increasingly common among world-class organizations. An example of this type of vendor-customer relationship is the one between Procter & Gamble, one of the world's largest consumer products companies, and its largest customer, Wal-Mart. By having access to Wal-Mart's computer inventory system, Procter & Gamble is better able to determine and fill Wal-Mart's specific needs for products such as disposable diapers.

Other Aspects of JIT

While JIT focuses on procedures to reduce inventories, as a philosophy of management, it offers benefits that extend far beyond just cutting inventories. As indicated above, a critical element of the JIT "philosophy" is coordination with other organizations up and down the value chain. Also, it involves training and empowering employees to make decisions that are necessary to correct inventory production and quality problems when they occur. Giving workers a sense that they are important to the firm's success and that they are adding value to the firm is a key aspect of the philosophy. An example of a firm that has embraced JIT as a comprehensive philosophy of management is presented in Management Accounting Practice 13-5.

ACCOUNTING IN A JUST-IN-TIME ENVIRONMENT

L O 5

When organizations make significant changes in their operating procedures, they should reevaluate their accounting systems for any needed changes. Movement toward a JIT inventory philosophy requires changes in perfor-

---

MANAGEMENT ACCOUNTING PRACTICE 13-5

How Oregon Cutting Systems Used JIT to Become a World-Class Competitor

Oregon Cutting Systems (OCS), a $250-million company headquartered in Portland, manufactures steel products for cutting saws, timber harvesting equipment, and sporting equipment. OCS developed its own version of JIT called "zero inventory production system," or ZIPS, consisting of three primary components: (1) *just-in-time manufacturing*, which involved small lot production, setup reduction time, smoothing the production line, a pull system of inventory control, and cooperative supplier relationships; (2) *continual improvement*, which involved implementing statistical process control methods and waste avoidance; and (3) *people development and empowerment*, which involved continuing education, job security, and promoting employees' personal commitment to the company.

The adoption of ZIP also meant that accounting reports to managers had to be changed. Managers needed reports focused on strategic and operational measures (such as lead times, quality, inventory, actual product cost, and customer satisfaction), rather than on cost variances and other traditional financial measures. The new cost management system included a product line focus, identification of waste, a more simplified system, an operational versus financial focus, and both operational and strategic reporting.

OCS started implementing JIT in the early 1980s and within five years managed to reduce defects by 80 percent and to cut scrap and rework by 50 percent. Other results were equally dramatic. For example, at one Canadian plant, setup times were reduced from 6.5 hours to 1 minute and 40 seconds, space requirements were reduced by 40 percent, lead times were cut from 21 days to 3 days, and inventory was reduced by 50 percent. OCS met the challenges of worldwide competition by embracing JIT as a philosophy of management and by emphasizing quality, waste reduction, employee empowerment, and customer satisfaction. The result was a dramatic improvement in overall productivity.

Based on: Jack C. Bailes and Ilene K. Kleinsorge, "Cutting Waste with JIT," *Management Accounting* (May 1992), pp. 28-32.

---

mance evaluation procedures and offers opportunities for significant reductions in bookkeeping costs. These changes are considered below.

Performance Evaluation

JIT regards inventory as something to be eliminated. Hence, in a manufacturing organization, inventories are kept as small as possible; and under the JIT ideal, they do not exist. Raw materials are delivered by vendors in small batches directly to the shop floor. JIT also strives to minimize work-in-process inventory by minimizing the nonprocessing elements of cycle time and by having processing times as short as possible. Ideally, setup, waiting, movement, and inspection times are to be eliminated.

Dysfunctional Effects of Financial Performance Measures

There is a potential conflict between the goals of JIT and those of traditional financial performance measures applied at the department or cost center level. Although JIT emphasizes overall efficiency, many traditional financial performance measures emphasize local (departmental) cost savings and local (departmental) efficiency. Consider traditional performance measures for a purchasing agent and a departmental production supervisor:

- To achieve quantity discounts and favorable materials price variances, a purchasing agent may order excess inventory, thereby increasing subsequent storage, obsolescence, and handling costs.
- To obtain a low price, a purchasing agent may order from a supplier whose goods have not been certified as meeting quality specifications, thereby causing subsequent inspection, rework, spoilage costs, and, perhaps, dissatisfied customers further down the value chain.
- To avoid unfavorable labor efficiency and variable overhead efficiency variances, a departmental production supervisor may refuse to halt production to determine the cause of a quality problem, thereby increasing inspection, rework, and spoilage costs.[7]
- To obtain a favorable fixed overhead volume variance, a departmental production supervisor may produce in excess of current needs (preferably in long production runs), thereby causing subsequent increases in storage, obsolescence, and handling costs.[8]

Use of Nonfinancial Performance Measures

To avoid the problems associated with traditional financial performance measures that stress local efficiency and cost savings, nonfinancial performance measures should be emphasized for first-level control in a JIT environment. Financial performance measures are reserved for overall evaluation rather than for detailed or daily evaluation. In accordance with the goal of eliminating inventory and reducing cycle time to processing time, JIT performance measures emphasize inventory turnover, cycle time, and **cycle efficiency** (the ratio of value-added to nonvalue-added manufacturing activities).

When applied to a specific item of raw materials or finished goods, **inventory turnover** is computed as the annual demand in units divided by the average inventory in units:

$$\text{Inventory turnover} = \frac{\text{Annual demand in units}}{\text{Average inventory in units}}$$

Progress toward the goal of reducing inventory is measured by comparing successive inventory turnover ratios. The higher the inventory turnover, the better.

When stated in dollars, inventory turnover can be used as a measure of the overall success of the organization in reducing inventory:

$$\text{Inventory turnover} = \frac{\text{Cost of goods sold}}{\text{Average inventory (in dollars)}}$$

---

7 Labor and variable overhead efficiency variances are discussed in the body of Chapter 8.
8 The fixed overhead volume variance is discussed in Chapter 8, Appendix A.

This financial measure can be derived directly from a firm's financial statements.

Cycle time is a measure of the total time required to produce one unit of a product:

$$\frac{\text{Cycle}}{\text{time}} = \frac{\text{Setup}}{\text{time}} + \frac{\text{Process}}{\text{time}} + \frac{\text{Move}}{\text{time}} + \frac{\text{Wait}}{\text{time}} + \frac{\text{Inspection}}{\text{time}}$$

The lower the cycle time, the better. Under ideal circumstances, cycle time would consist of only processing time; and processing time would be as low as possible. Only processing time adds value to the product; hence, the time required for all other activities should be driven toward zero. If flexible manufacturing systems are used, jobs properly sequenced, and tools properly placed, setup time will be minimized. If the shop floor is optimally arranged, workers pass products directly from one workstation to the next. If production is optimally scheduled, inventory will not wait in temporary storage between workstations. If raw materials are of high quality and products are manufactured so that they always conform to specifications, there is no need for separate inspection activities.

Cycle efficiency is computed as the ratio of processing time to total cycle time:

$$\text{Cycle efficiency} = \frac{\text{Processing time}}{\text{Cycle time}}$$

The higher the cycle efficiency, the better. If all nonvalue-added activities are eliminated, this ratio equals 1.

Simplified Record Keeping

Just-in-time inventory allows significant reductions in the number of accounting transactions required for purchasing and production activities. This can result in cost savings for bookkeeping activities and shifting accounting resources from detailed bookkeeping to the development of more useful activity cost data.

Purchasing

In a traditional accounting system, every purchase results in the generation of several documents and two journal entries. Additional documents and journal entries record the issuance of raw materials to the factory. These items are discussed in detail in accounting information systems textbooks, but it is useful to consider them briefly here. The documents include:

- A *purchase requisition* completed by a computerized inventory control system or an inventory clerk who notes the need to place an order.
- A *purchase order* prepared in the purchasing department.
- A *receiving and inspection report* prepared by receiving room personnel.
- An *invoice* received from the vendor indicating the amount due.
- A *payment voucher* prepared by accounts payable authorizing the preparation of a check.
- A *check* prepared by the cashier.

After the goods and the vendor's invoice are received, a journal entry debiting Raw Materials or Merchandise Inventory and crediting Accounts Payable is made. The preparation of a check results in a journal entry debiting Accounts Payable and crediting Cash.

Tracking of inventory takes place as raw materials are issued to production. A *materials requisition* is used to document the transfer of inventory from the storeroom to the shop floor. This transaction is accompanied by a journal entry debiting Work-in-Process and crediting Raw Materials. In batch processing, appropriate notations are also made on *job-cost sheets*.

The above documents are required to ensure that purchases and issuances are authorized in accordance with company policy. Detailed documentation is especially important with high inventory levels and when purchases are made from a large number of vendors who compete on the basis of price.

JIT, on the other hand, attempts to minimize inventory levels and stresses long-term relationships with a limited number of vendors who have demonstrated their ability to provide quality raw materials on a timely basis and at a competitive price. Under a JIT inventory system, a company often has standing purchase orders for specified materials from specified vendors at specified prices. Production personnel are authorized to requisition materials directly from authorized vendors, who deliver limited quantities of materials as needed directly to the shop floor. Production personnel verify receipt of the raw materials. Periodically, each vendor sends an invoice for several shipments, which the company acknowledges and pays. The accompanying journal entries include a debit to Raw Materials-in-Process (discussed below) with an offsetting credit to Accounts Payable.

Electronic Data Interchange

Electronic data interchange (EDI), the electronic communication of data between organizations, is also affecting JIT inventory systems and accounting procedures. Using EDI, production personnel enter a materials requisition into a computer terminal and transmit the order by electronic mail to an authorized vendor. This procedure reduces the lead time required to order goods. When the vendor's EDI system is integrated in such a manner that data reentry is eliminated, order-processing costs and errors are reduced. Vendor invoices may also be sent using EDI. It is even possible to pay the invoice using EDI rather than by issuing a check.

Standing purchase orders and EDI reduce the number of documents and the amount of data entry involved in purchase transactions. In a traditional system, each purchase order might require a separate materials requisition, purchase order, receiving report, invoice, payment voucher, and check. Multiple copies are often required. The existence of all the documents and bookkeeping procedures associated with traditional accounting systems causes high order-processing costs. Standing orders with direct delivery to the shop floor and the electronic transmission of purchase orders, invoices, and payments significantly reduce order-processing costs.

The number of U.S. firms using EDI has increased at a rapid rate over the past five years. To illustrate the growth of this activity, Harbinger

Corporation began as an entrepreneurial effort in the late 1980s to offer EDI computer network services to client companies. Today, Harbinger has over 15,000 EDI corporate subscribers that use its network to exchange data with other companies, and the company is expanding into Europe and the Pacific Basin.[9]

Product Costing

Because JIT stresses low inventory levels and high inventory turnover, there is less need for inventory costing for external financial reporting. Ending inventories are nonexistent or so small that the costs assigned to them are insignificant in comparison with the costs assigned to goods sold.

Under these circumstances, when virtually all product costs are properly assignable to Cost of Goods Sold at the end of the period, it makes little sense to track product costs through inventory accounts. For financial reporting purposes, detailed product costing is not required when JIT inventory management is fully implemented. Instead, a simple costing procedure called backflush costing may be used.

Under **backflush costing**, costs are assigned based on outputs throughout the system after the process is completed. There are a variety of ways that backflush costing is applied in practice; but in one common form of backflush costing, Raw Materials and Work-in-Process are combined into a single account called Raw Materials-in-Process. The costs of purchases are immediately assigned to Raw Materials-in-Process rather than to Raw Materials. (Note how this parallels the direct delivery of raw materials to the shop floor.) At the end of the period, the raw materials costs associated with completed units are transferred to Finished Goods Inventory or Cost of Goods Sold. Conversion costs for direct labor and manufacturing overhead are accumulated in an account such as Conversion Costs. These costs are assigned to Finished Goods Inventory or Cost of Goods Sold at the end of the period, rather than to an in-process inventory account. The only end-of-period costs in Raw Materials-in-Process are those for unused or partially completed raw materials. Although backflush costing may result in an understatement of ending in-process inventory (to the extent that goods are partially completed), if inventories are very small, the understatement is acceptable.

To illustrate a backflush costing system such as the one described above, assume the following data for Marco, Inc., for October 19X7, its first period of operations:

Raw materials purchased (1,000 units × $10 per unit)	$10,000
(each unit of finished goods uses 1 unit of raw material)	
Direct labor (200 hours × $18 per hour)	3,600
Manufacturing overhead applied (at $8 per direct labor hour)	1,600
980 finished units were completed during the period, and 20 units of raw materials were on hand or in process at the end of the period.	
975 units finished during October were sold during the month.	

---

9 Based on an address by David Leach, Executive Vice President of Harbinger Corporation, in an executive education seminar at Goizueta Business School at Emory University.

The following journal entries record the flow of manufacturing costs in Marco, Inc.'s JIT system for the month of October 19X7:

JOURNAL ENTRIES			
	(1) Raw Materials-in-Process	10,000	
	Accounts Payable		10,000
	To record cost of raw materials purchases.		
	(2) Conversion Costs	3,600	
	Wages Payable		3,600
	To record wages for the period.		
	(3) Conversion Costs	1,600	
	Manufacturing Overhead		1,600
	To apply manufacturing overhead.		
	(4) Finished Goods Inventory	15,000	
	Raw Materials-in-Process		9,800
	Conversion Costs		5,200
	To transfer $9,800 (980 units × $10) of raw materials cost and all conversion costs for the month ($3,600 + $1,600) to Finished Goods Inventory. Unit cost of inventory is $15.31 ($15,000 / 980 units).		
	(5) Cost of Goods Sold	14,927	
	Finished Goods Inventory		14,927
	To record cost of goods sold for 975 units at $15.31 per unit.		

The balance in Raw Materials-In-Process at the end of October is $200, consisting of $10,000 for raw materials purchases less $9,800 transferred to Finished Goods Inventory. Finished Goods Inventory has a balance of $73 ($15,000 - $14,927) for the five completed units remaining in ending inventory. Because of the small amount of inventory on hand at the end of the period, no conversion costs are assigned to any units that may be in process.

Another way to apply backflush costing is to assign all raw materials purchases and conversion costs directly to Cost of Goods Sold. At the end of the period, an adjusting entry is used to assign (or backflush) costs to Raw Materials-in-Process and Finished Goods Inventory. At the start of the next period, a reversing entry assigns all costs to Cost of Goods Sold. The journal entries for this form of a JIT system for Marco, Inc., for October 19X7 are as follows:

JOURNAL ENTRIES			
	(1) Cost of Goods Sold	10,000	
	Accounts Payable		10,000
	To record cost of raw materials purchases.		
	(2) Cost of Goods Sold	3,600	
	Wages Payable		3,600
	To record wages for the period.		

(3) Cost of Goods Sold	1,600	
Manufacturing Overhead		1,600
To apply manufacturing overhead.		
(4) Raw Materials-in-Process	200	
Cost of Goods Sold		200
To flush $200 of raw materials		
cost out of Cost of Goods Sold		
for raw materials units not completed.		
(5) Finished Goods Inventory	77*	
Cost of Goods Sold		77
To flush $77 of cost out of Cost of		
Goods Sold for the production of		
five units in finished goods at the		
end of the month. Unit cost is		
$15.31, or ($10,000 + $3,600 +		
$1,600 - $200) / 980 units.		

*Rounded

There are other variations on these two approaches to the accounting procedures for JIT inventory systems. All emphasize a reduction in the number of accounting transactions and journal entries in an attempt to save bookkeeping costs. Given low JIT inventory levels, virtually all variations provide acceptable numbers for external reporting. If all end-of-period inventories are so low as to be negligible, the most extreme version of JIT would record all raw materials and conversion costs to Cost of Goods Sold as incurred, without any backflush entries at the end of the period. It is rare to find a company that manufactures goods without substantial amounts of ending inventories.

Management Still Needs Accurate Cost Data

Although JIT inventory management reduces the importance of product costing for external reporting, it does not reduce management's need for accurate product cost information for internal purposes. Indeed, the same competitive pressures that lead managers to adopt the JIT philosophy of inventory management also increase the need for detailed and accurate cost data. With simplified external reporting requirements, management has an opportunity to shift resources to the development of activity cost data.

SUMMARY

This chapter has focused attention on two of the most revolutionary managerial practices to be embraced worldwide by many managers over the past ten years—activity-based costing and just-in-time inventory management. ABC was introduced and discussed as an important strategic tool in Chapter 4; but in this chapter, it was addressed within the context of product costing, the application for which ABC is most often used.

ABC has distinct advantages over traditional costing alternatives because it focuses on production processes, the activities that make up those processes, and the costs of those activities. ABC has strategic superiority over traditional costing that relies on volume-driven, indirect cost allocations because it provides a more accurate measure of the economic cost of producing goods or services. ABC arms managers with useful information regarding product cost, which can be used to assess profitability and to make decisions about product mix and even customer mix. Possibly even more important is that ABC identifies costs for specific activities, giving managers relevant cost information useful for evaluating possible alternatives to existing production activities.

The just-in-time approach to inventory management was discussed not only as a methodology for reducing inventories, but also as a philosophy that embraces much more than procedures for limiting the scale of raw materials, work-in-process, and finished goods inventories. As a philosophy of management, JIT emphasizes managing from a value chain perspective and empowering employees to make decisions to ensure high-quality goods and services and to deal quickly with problems that develop at the production level. We discussed various nonfinancial performance measures that are helpful in a JIT environment and introduced backflush accounting methods for recording product costs when inventories are small or nonexistent.

Throughout this text, certain dominant conceptual themes have been developed: (1) costs are incurred in response to cost drivers—strategic, organizational, and activity; (2) the most effective approach to cost management has a value chain perspective—it embraces the total organization, its suppliers, and its customers; (3) different, but complementary, approaches and decision models are required for operational decision making and strategic decision making—it is necessary to understand the organizational context of decision making before selecting the tools and models to support the decision; and (4) organizational goals are achieved through the people in the organization—it is imperative that people be committed to those goals and be empowered to make decisions that enhance the achievement of those goals. Successful managers in world-class organizations of the future will understand and embrace these important concepts.

We began this text by quoting Peter Drucker, who posed the following questions that successful managers should be asking: "What information do I need to do my job? When do I need it? and From whom should I be getting it?" To help answer these questions, we have discussed many different concepts, models, and tools. Some of these tools (such as basic cost analysis techniques) have been around for a long time; but in recent years, they have begun to undergo change. Others are relatively new and will likely be modified in the future as they become better understood (such as just-in-time). Finally, there are those methods (such as value chain analysis and ABC) that are still in the experimental stages in many firms; but these methods will become more important decision aids as they are better understood. Having introduced you to a substantial body of management accounting concepts, methods, and tools to help you address the questions raised by Peter Drucker, it seems appropriate that we end with a recent and poignant Drucker insight about decision tools:

> What is important is not the tools. It is the concepts behind them. They convert what were always seen as discrete techniques to be used in isolation and for separate purposes into one integrated information system. That system then makes possible business diagnosis, business strategy, and business decisions.[10]

APPENDIX: ECONOMIC ORDER QUANTITY FOR PURCHASES

The operating budget (discussed in Chapter 7) specifies the number of units to be purchased or manufactured during a period of time. In merchandising organizations, for example, the number of units to be purchased is computed for each inventory item as the total expected sales, plus the desired ending inventory, less the expected beginning inventory. The operating budget does not specify the order quantity or the reorder point. The **order quantity** is the quantity of inventory ordered *at one time*, and the **reorder point** is the inventory level at which an order for additional units is placed. If 19X4 budgeted purchases of inventory item B-25 are 2,400 units, management might place one order for 2,400 units, three orders for 800 units, 80 orders for 30 units, or some other combination of number of orders and order size.

Assume that the demand for item B-25 is constant throughout the year and that new orders are timed to arrive just as the previous order is exhausted. In this case, an order quantity of 800 units might produce the variations in inventory level illustrated in Exhibit 13-3. The maximum inventory level is reached just as a new order is received. Subsequent to the receipt of an order, the inventory level falls at a constant rate per unit of time, and another order is received just as the inventory level falls to zero. With a maximum inventory of 800 units, a minimum inventory of 0 units, and a constant rate of decline per unit of time, the average inventory of item B-25 is 400 units ([800 + 0]/2).

INVENTORY COSTS

A variety of costs are associated with inventory, including the costs of the units purchased, of ordering inventory, of carrying inventory, and of insufficient inventory. Several costs in each of these categories are listed in Exhibit 13-4 (page 725). Management's objective is to determine the **economic order quantity (EOQ),** the order quantity that results in the minimum total annual inventory costs. Because only costs that vary with the order quantity are relevant to this decision, each of the cost categories in Exhibit 13-4 is examined to identify the relevant and the irrelevant costs.

---

10 Peter F. Drucker, "The Information Executives Truly Need," *Harvard Business Review* (January-February 1995), p. 62.

EXHIBIT 13-3: VARIATION IN INVENTORY LEVEL OVER TIME

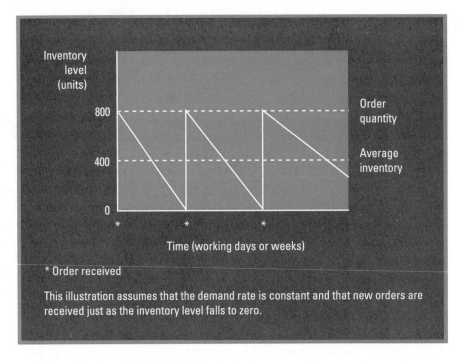

* Order received

This illustration assumes that the demand rate is constant and that new orders are received just as the inventory level falls to zero.

In the absence of quantity discounts, the total annual costs of the units purchased vary only with total units purchased, not with the order quantity or the number of orders. Consequently, the total annual costs of the units purchased are irrelevant to determining the order quantity and are excluded from order quantity models.

The total annual costs of ordering inventory are computed as follows:

$$\text{Total annual ordering costs} = \text{Cost of placing an order} \times \text{Number of orders per year}$$

Because the number of orders per year is computed as the annual demand divided by the order size, the total annual costs of ordering inventory vary with the order size. As the order size increases, the number of orders per year decreases, and the total annual ordering costs decrease. Conversely, as the order size decreases, the number of orders per year increases, and the total annual ordering costs increase. These relationships are shown in Exhibit 13-5 (page 726), which illustrates that the lowest total inventory costs occur where total annual ordering costs are equal to total annual carrying costs.

Assume that the cost of placing an order for item B-25 is $25. If the order quantity is 800 units, the total annual ordering costs are $75 ($25 × [2,400 / 800]). A decrease in the order size to 600 units would increase the total annual ordering costs to $100 ($25 × [2,400 / 600]).

As might be suspected, the costs of carrying inventory also vary with the order size. Increasing the order size increases the average inventory

EXHIBIT 13-4: INVENTORY COSTS FOR PURCHASED GOODS INTENDED FOR RESALE*

Costs of units purchased
Unit price
Transportation-in

Costs of ordering inventory
Processing the order
Receiving and inspecting the order
Processing payment for the order

Costs of carrying inventory
Insurance
Personal property taxes
Storage space costs
Deterioration and obsolescence
Handling costs
Opportunity cost of money
  invested in inventory

Costs of insufficient inventory
Lost contribution from missed sales
Lost customer goodwill
Cost of special orders
Cost of processing backorders

*In the case of manufactured goods, variable manufacturing costs are substituted for the unit price, and the cost of ordering inventory includes machine setup costs. If goods are to be processed further in a subsequent department, the costs of insufficient inventory include the costs of excessive idle time and the costs of expediting production once the goods are available.

and the total annual costs of carrying inventory. Conversely, decreasing the order size reduces the average inventory and the total annual carrying costs.

Note that the cost of carrying inventory includes an opportunity cost for the money invested in inventory. The interest rate on borrowed money is frequently used to estimate this opportunity cost. However, the rate of return management desires to earn on inventory investments is a better choice. The issues involved in determining this rate are discussed in corporate financial management textbooks.

Carrying costs are often expressed as a percentage of the unit purchase price. Assume the carrying costs for item B-25 are 25 percent of the unit purchase price. If the unit purchase price is $12 and the order size is 800 units, the cost of carrying 1 unit in inventory for 1 year is $3 ($12 × 0.25), and the total annual carrying costs are $1,200 ($3 × [800 / 2]).

Operations research textbooks sometimes contain sophisticated models that allow stockouts and backorders to occur. These models then include stockout costs in the determination of the economic order quantity. We shall assume that management does not intentionally allow stockouts to occur. Consequently, the costs of insufficient inventory are irrelevant to the determination of our economic order quantity.

In summary, only the costs of ordering and carrying inventory are relevant to determining the economic order quantity, and these costs vary inversely with each other. As the order size increases, total annual ordering costs decrease and total annual carrying costs increase. As the order size decreases, total annual ordering costs increase and total annual carry-

EXHIBIT 13-5: INVENTORY CARRYING COSTS, ORDERING COSTS, AND TOTAL COSTS

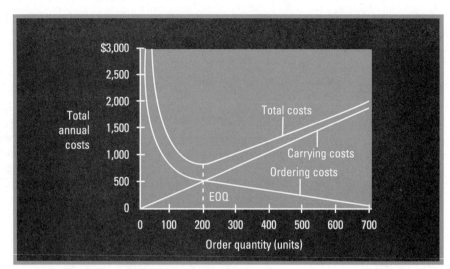

ing costs decrease.   The total relevant costs for determining the economic order quantity are computed as follows:

$$
\begin{array}{c}
\text{Total annual ordering} \\
\text{and carrying costs}
\end{array}
=
\left(
\begin{array}{c}
\text{Cost of placing} \\
\text{an order}
\end{array}
\times
\frac{\text{Annual demand}}{\text{Order quantity}}
\right)
+
\left(
\begin{array}{c}
\text{Unit carrying} \\
\text{costs per year}
\end{array}
\times
\frac{\text{Order quantity}}{2}
\right)
$$

DETERMINING THE ECONOMIC ORDER QUANTITY

The economic order quantity (EOQ) model, like many quantitative decision-making models, has several limiting assumptions.   The EOQ model assumptions are:

- The demand rate is known and uniform.
- There are no quantity discounts.
- Ordering costs are a known function of the number of orders.
- Carrying costs are a known function of average inventory.
- Stockouts are not deliberately allowed.

In using any quantitative decision-making model, the most important test usually is whether or not the model results are appropriate in the judgment of management.   Also, the failure to satisfy every assumption of a model does not necessarily render the model unusable; however, in such situations, managerial evaluation of the model results takes on greater importance.   Hence, when using the EOQ model in organizations where one or more of the above assumptions are not valid, management judgment is a critical factor in evaluating the EOQ model results.   As an alternative to setting order quantities entirely by managerial judgment, the EOQ model can be a valuable supplemental tool to management in determining the most economical order quantity.

The EOQ model is quite simple. The idea behind it is to determine the order quantity that minimizes total inventory costs, which is the point where annual inventory carrying costs and annual inventory ordering costs are equal. Hence, the economic order quantity equation is as follows:

$$\underline{\textbf{Annual Ordering Costs}} \quad = \quad \underline{\textbf{Annual Carrying Costs}}$$

$$\frac{\text{Cost of placing}}{\text{an order}} \times \frac{\text{Annual demand}}{\text{Order quantity}} = \frac{\text{Unit carrying}}{\text{costs per year}} \times \frac{\text{Order quantity}}{2}$$

$$\begin{array}{c}\text{Economic}\\\text{order}\\\text{quantity}\end{array} = \sqrt{\frac{2 \times \begin{array}{c}\text{Annual}\\\text{demand}\end{array} \times \begin{array}{c}\text{Cost of placing}\\\text{an order}\end{array}}{\begin{array}{c}\text{Unit carrying}\\\text{cost per year}\end{array}}}$$

For item B-25, the economic order quantity is determined to be 200 units:

$$\text{EOQ} = \sqrt{\frac{2 \times 2,400 \times \$25}{\$3}}$$

$$= \underline{\underline{200}} \text{ units}$$

Reorder Point

As stated earlier, the reorder point is the inventory level at which an order for additional units is placed. The reorder point must allow sufficient inventory to cover demand during the **lead time**, the time between the placement and the receipt of an order. Assuming demand takes place evenly throughout a year containing n work days, the equation for daily demand is:

$$\text{Daily demand} = \text{Annual demand} / n$$

If the lead time required to fill an order is known and certain, the reorder point that results in a new order arriving just as the previous order is exhausted is computed as:

$$\frac{\text{Reorder}}{\text{point}} = \frac{\text{Daily}}{\text{demand}} \times \frac{\text{Lead}}{\text{time}}$$

Assume the organization using item B-25 operates 240 days per year and that the lead time for this item is 5 days. Under these circumstances, the reorder point for B-25 is 50 units:

$$\text{Daily demand} = 2,400 \text{ units} / 240 \text{ days}$$
$$= 10 \text{ units per day}$$

$$\text{Reorder point} = 10 \text{ units per day} \times 5 \text{ days}$$
$$= \underline{\underline{50}} \text{ units}$$

Management places an order whenever the inventory level falls to 50 units.

SAFETY STOCKS

Safety stocks are extra units of inventory carried to prevent stockouts due to variations in the demand for units during the lead time. A **stockout,** which arises when there is a demand for a product that is not readily available, can occur because of delays in the receipt of an order or because of increases in the daily demand for an inventory item. If management desires to avoid stockouts and if daily demand and/or lead time are uncertain, safety stocks must be maintained.

Safety stocks can be computed as the difference between the maximum lead time demand and the reorder point without safety stocks. Safety stocks do not increase the economic order quantity; they do, however, increase the reorder point and total carrying costs. Assume the maximum daily demand for item B-25 is 12 units, and the maximum lead time is 8 days. Under these circumstances, the safety stock for this item would be set at 46 units.

Maximum demand per day	12 units
Maximum lead time	× 8 days
Maximum lead time demand	96 units
Reorder point without safety stocks	-50 units
Safety stock	46 units

Safety stocks can be viewed as a base inventory. If the safety stocks for item B-25 are never used, they will have an annual carrying cost of $138, computed as the $3 carrying costs per unit per year times 46 units of safety stock.

The economic order quantity for item B-25 will remain at 200 units, but the reorder point will increase to 96 units—the reorder point plus the safety stock. Possible patterns for item B-25's inventory level with safety stocks and variations in demand are illustrated in Exhibit 13-6. Note that the presence of the base inventory layer increases the maximum inventory to 246 units. Also, when some of the safety stock is used, the new order will not bring the total inventory level to 246 units, but to an amount equal to 246 less the amount of safety stock used.

ECONOMIC LOT SIZE FOR PRODUCTION

Production may take place in response to a specific customer order or to manufacture speculative inventories in anticipation of future sales. The manufacturing process may involve the continuous production of identical units or the production of batches of different products. As discussed in Chapter 10, job costing is appropriate for batch production, and process costing is appropriate for continuous production.

EXHIBIT 13-6: VARIATIONS IN INVENTORY LEVEL WITH SAFETY STOCK

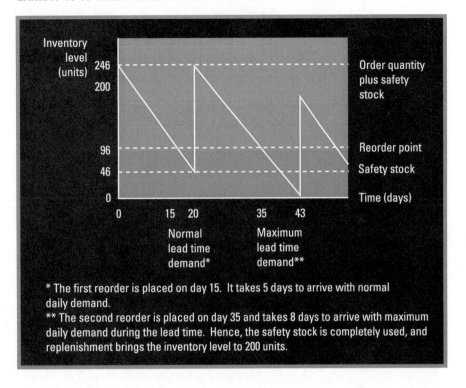

* The first reorder is placed on day 15. It takes 5 days to arrive with normal daily demand.
** The second reorder is placed on day 35 and takes 8 days to arrive with maximum daily demand during the lead time. Hence, the safety stock is completely used, and replenishment brings the inventory level to 200 units.

The economic order quantity model is applicable to the batch production of speculative inventory. In this case, variable unit manufacturing costs are substituted for the unit price, and the cost of ordering inventory includes machine setup and scheduling costs. With these modifications, the model is used to compute an **economic lot** (batch) **size (ELS)** that results in the minimum ordering and carrying costs.

Assume the annual use of subcomponent PK45 totals 2,500 units, spread evenly throughout the year. Variable manufacturing costs of subcomponent PK45 are $50 per unit; machine setup, scheduling, and other ordering costs total $125 per batch; and annual carrying costs are 20 percent of unit variable costs. In this case, the cost of carrying 1 unit in inventory for 1 year is $10 ($50 x 0.20), and the economic lot size is 250 units:

$$\text{Economic lot size} = \sqrt{\frac{2 \times 2{,}500 \times \$125}{10}}$$

$$= \underline{\underline{250 \text{ units}}}$$

The ELS size model should not be applied to situations in which continuous production is more appropriate than batch production. This would lead to excessive setup, scheduling, and other ordering costs as the production process is artificially segmented. When a job must pass through several operations in sequence, proper scheduling to minimize carrying costs normally calls for production in subsequent operations to begin before all units pass through preceding operations. When a job calls for the manufacture and subsequent assembly of several components, careful scheduling is required to avoid the buildup of excessive inventories between workstations. These and other issues, such as the proper timing of raw materials purchases and assembly of subcomponents for large jobs (materials requirement planning), are considered in operations management textbooks.

EOQ AND ELS WITH JIT

The economic order quantity model is intended to assist managers in making purchasing decisions. The economic lot size model is intended to assist managers in making decisions concerning the number of units in batches produced for speculative inventory. The JIT philosophy is applicable to all inventories and all production situations, batch and continuous. Hence, the JIT philosophy is more generalizable than are the EOQ and ELS models.

In recent years, the EOQ and ELS models have been criticized by proponents of just-in-time production. These proponents argue that management should try to minimize inventories rather than to optimize the batch size. The root of these criticisms appears to be a tendency of many managers to optimize production for the current cost structure. Often these managers attempt to manage by the numbers rather than becoming familiar enough with operations to try and change the numbers.

Meanwhile, managers in firms that do not rely solely on inventory quantity models have achieved significant reductions in inventories and cycle times while improving product quality. The by-product of their efforts has been a significant reduction in their organizations' cost structures. It appears that the blind application of quantitative models to a set of numbers is less profitable than becoming familiar with operations and engaging in actions that reduce cost structures.

Managers cannot shift the blame for bad decisions to a model. Managers, not models, make decisions. The economic lot size model is intended for batch production. It should not be used for situations in which continuous production is more appropriate. The model assumes the demand rate is known and uniform. If the demand rate is uncertain or variable, use of the model may result in excess inventory or inventory stockouts. Also, the model is intended to optimize for a given cost structure. If managers fail to make competitive reductions in ordering and setup costs (which will reduce the economic quantity), their firms will be less competitive, even if they properly use the model.

It is the authors' opinion that even better results can be obtained by adopting the JIT philosophy *and* using inventory models where appropriate. The results will be unsatisfactory if managers inappropriately apply EOQ or ELS models to situations in which the assumptions of these models are not valid, attempt to manage a business exclusively with the use of models, fail to develop a detailed understanding of the business, or fail to encourage employee involvement in improving operations. Managers of competitive firms must strive to reduce their firms' cost structures and to make appropriate use of quantitative models, such as EOQ, as decision aids.

SUGGESTED READINGS

Brimson, James A. *Activity Accounting—An Activity-Based Costing Approach* (New York: John H. Wiley & Sons, 1991).

Cokins, Gary, Alan Stratton, and Jack Helbling. *An ABC Manager's Primer* (Montvale, NJ: Institute of Management Accountants, 1992).

Keegan, Daniel P., and Robert G. Eiler. "Let's Reengineer Cost Accounting," *Management Accounting* (August 1994), pp. 26-31.

Ostranga, Michael R. "Activities: The Focal Point of Total Cost Management," *Management Accounting* (February 1990), pp. 42-49.

Romano, Patrick L. *Activity-Based Management in Action* (Montvale, NJ: Institute of Management Accountants, 1994).

REVIEW PROBLEM

Plant-Wide, Departmental, and Activity-Based Overhead Rates

Slack Corporation has the following predicted indirect costs and cost drivers for 19X6 for the following activity cost pools:

	Fabrication Department	Finishing Department	Cost Driver
Maintenance	$ 20,000	$10,000	Machine hours
Material handling	30,000	15,000	Material moves
Machine setup	70,000	5,000	Machine setups
Inspection	-	25,000	Inspection hours
	$120,000	$55,000	

The following activity predictions were also made for the year:

	Fabrication Department	Finishing Department
Machine hours	10,000	5,000
Material moves	3,000	1,500
Machine setups	700	50
Inspection hours	-	1,000

It is assumed that the cost per unit of activity for a given activity does not vary between departments.

Slack's president, Charles Slack, is trying to evaluate the company's product mix strategy regarding two of its five product models, ZX300 and SL500. The company has been using a plant-wide overhead rate based on machine hours, but Slack is considering switching to either departmental rates or activity-based costing rates. The production manager has provided the following data for the production of a batch of 100 units for each of these models:

	ZX300	SL500
Direct materials cost	$12,000	$18,000
Direct labor cost	$ 5,000	$ 4,000
Machine hours	500	700
Material moves	30	50
Machine setups	5	9
Inspection hours	30	60

Required:

(a) Determine the cost of one unit of ZX300 and SL500, assuming a plant-wide overhead rate is used based on total machine hours.
(b) Determine the cost of one unit of ZX300 and SL500, assuming departmental overhead rates are used. Overhead is assigned based on machine hours in the Fabrication Department and on inspection hours in the Finishing Department.
(c) Determine the cost of one unit of ZX300 and SL500, assuming activity-based costing overhead rates are used for maintenance, material handling, machine setup, and inspection activities.
(d) Comment on the results of the above cost calculations.

The solution to the review problem is found at the end of Chapter 13 assignment material. To maximize your learning, you should make a serious attempt to develop a written solution to the review problem before looking at the solution. If there are errors in your solution, you should then attempt to determine the causes of the errors.

KEY TERMS

Backflush costing—an inventory accounting system used in conjunction with JIT in which costs are assigned to inventories and cost of goods sold based on outputs throughout the system after the process is completed.

Cycle efficiency—the ratio of value-added to nonvalue-added manufacturing activities.

Cycle time—the total time required to complete a process. It is composed of setup time, processing time, movement time, waiting time, and inspection time.

Electronic data interchange (EDI)—the electronic communication of data between organizations.

Inventory turnover—the annual demand in units divided by the average inventory in units. It is also computed as cost of goods sold divided by the cost of average inventory.

Just-in-time (JIT) inventory management—a comprehensive inventory management philosophy that stresses policies, procedures, and attitudes by managers and other workers that result in the efficient production of high-quality goods while maintaining the minimum level of inventories.

Materials pull system (also called **Kanban system**)—an inventory production flow system in which employees at each station work to replenish the inventory used by employees at subsequent stations. The building of excess inventories is strictly prohibited. When the number of units in inventory reaches a specified limit, work at the station stops until workers at a subsequent station "pull" a unit from the in-process storage area.

Materials push system—an inventory production flow system in which employees work to reduce the pile of inventory building up at their workstations. Workers at each station remove materials from an in-process storage area, complete their operation, and place the output in another in-process storage area. Hence, they "push" the work to the next workstation.

Quality circles—groups of employees involved in the production of products and who have the authority, within certain parameters, to address and resolve quality problems as they occur without seeking managerial approval.

APPENDIX KEY TERMS

Economic lot size (ELS)—the size of an order or batch that results in the minimum ordering and carrying costs.

Economic order quantity (EOQ)—the order quantity that results in the minimum total annual inventory costs.

Lead time—the time between the placement and the receipt of an order.

Order quantity—the quantity of inventory ordered *at one time*.

Reorder point—the inventory level at which an order for additional units is placed.

Safety stocks—extra units of inventory carried to prevent stockouts due to variations in the demand for units during the lead time.

Stockout—a condition that arises when there is a demand for a product that is not readily available. It can occur because of delays in the receipt of an order or because of increases in the daily demand for an inventory item.

REVIEW QUESTIONS

13-1

Explain the product cost continuum.

13-2

What is the premise of activity-based costing for product costing purposes?

13-3

In what ways does ABC differ from traditional product cost assignment?

13-4

Explain why ABC often reveals existing product cost cross-subsidization problems.

13-5

How can ABC be used to improve cost analysis other than for product costing? Relate ABC benefits to value chain analysis.

13-6

Define activity cost pool, activity cost driver, and cost per unit of activity.

13-7

Name two possible activity cost drivers for each of the following activities: maintenance, materials movement, machine setup, inspection, materials purchases, and customer service.

13-8

Explain the concept of just-in-time inventory management.

13-9

What elements of the JIT approach contribute to reducing raw materials inventories?

13-10

Define and identify the elements of cycle time. Which of these elements adds value to the product?

13-11

Explain briefly how JIT benefits organizations that take a value chain approach to management.

13-12

Briefly describe backflush costing and its purpose.

13-13

Under what circumstances would it be appropriate to record all manufacturing costs initially in the Cost of Goods Sold account? Explain.

EXERCISES

13-1 Calculating Manufacturing Overhead Rates

Goldratt Company accumulated the following data for 19X4:

Milling Department manufacturing overhead	$320,000
Finishing Department manufacturing overhead	$100,000
Machine hours used:	
Milling Department	10,000 hours
Finishing Department	2,000 hours
Labor hours used:	
Milling Department	1,000 hours
Finishing Department	1,000 hours

Required:

(a) Calculate the manufacturing overhead rate using machine hours as the allocation base.

(b) Calculate the manufacturing overhead rate using direct labor hours as the allocation base.

(c) Calculate departmental overhead rates using machine hours in Milling and direct labor hours in Finishing as the allocation bases.

(d) Calculate departmental overhead rates using direct labor hours in Milling and machine hours in Finishing as the allocation bases.

13-2 Calculating ABC Overhead Rates

Refer to Exercise 13-1. Assume manufacturing overhead consisted of the following activities, activity cost drivers, and costs:

Setup (1,000 setup hours)	$100,000
Production scheduling (400 batches)	60,000
Production engineering (60 change orders)	120,000
Supervision (2,000 direct labor hours)	56,000
Machine operations (12,000 machine hours)	84,000
Total activity costs	$420,000

The following additional data were provided for Job 211X:

Direct materials costs	$6,500
Direct labor cost (5 Milling direct labor hours and 35 Finishing direct labor hours)	$ 800
Setup hours	5 hours
Production scheduling	1 batch
Machine hours used (25 Milling machine hours and 5 Finishing machine hours)	30 hours
Production engineering	3 change orders

Required:

(a) Calculate the cost per unit of activity driver for each activity cost category.

(b) Calculate the cost of Job 211X using ABC to assign overhead costs to Job 211X.

(c) Calculate the cost of Job 211X using the plant-wide overhead rate based on machine hours calculated in the previous exercise.

(d) Calculate the cost of Job 211X using the departmental overhead rates calculated in the previous exercise where the rate for Milling was based on machine hours and the rate for Finishing was based on direct labor hours.

13-3 ABC Product Costs

Olympic Company, a large, heavy equipment manufacturer, has determined the following activity cost pools and cost driver levels for the year:

Activity Cost Pool	Activity Cost	Activity Cost Driver
Machine setups	$400,000	8,000 setup hours
Material handling	120,000	2,000 tons of materials
Machine operation	250,000	5,000 machine hours

The following data are for the production of single batches of two products: J26Cams and Z43Shafts:

	J26Cams	Z43Shafts
Units produced	500	300
Machine hours used	3	6
Direct labor hours used	200	400
Direct labor cost	$ 5,000	$10,000
Direct materials cost	$25,000	$18,000
Tons of materials used	12.5	9
Setup hours used	4	7

Required:

Determine the batch and unit costs of J26Cams and Z43Shafts using ABC.

13-4 ABC Product Costs

Durite Company, a large paint manufacturer, has determined the following activity cost pools and cost driver levels for the year:

Activity Cost Pool	Activity Cost	Activity Cost Driver
Machine setups	$600,000	2,000 setups
Material handling	820,000	5,000 material moves
Electricity	250,000	25,000 machine hours

The following data are for the production of single batches of two products: Mirlite and Subdue:

	Mirlite	Subdue
Gallons produced	50,000	30,000
Direct labor hours used	400	250
Machine hours used	800	250
Direct labor cost	$ 10,000	$ 7,500
Direct materials cost	$350,000	$150,000
Setups required	15	12
Material moves	50	35

Required:
Determine the batch and per gallon costs of Mirlite and Subdue using ABC.

13-5 Activity Costs
Meriwether Company has determined its activity cost pools and cost drivers to be the following:

Cost pools:	
Setup costs	$ 30,000
Material handling costs	12,800
Machine operating costs	240,000
Packing costs	80,000
Total indirect manufacturing costs	$362,800

Cost drivers:	
Number of setups	200
Number of material moves	640
Number of machine hours	20,000
Number of packing orders	1,600

One product that Meriwether makes, metal casements, used the following activities during the period:

Number of setups	20
Number of material moves	88
Number of machine hours	1,900
Number of packing orders	150

Required:
(a) Calculate the cost per unit of activity for each activity cost pool.
(b) Calculate the manufacturing overhead cost per metal casement manufactured, assuming 500 units were produced.
(c) Comment on the adequacy of Meriwether's costing system.

13-6 JIT Product Costing with Backflush Costing Journal Entries
Speedo Cable manufactures drawn wire products in a JIT environment. Presented is cost information pertaining to September activities:

Purchase of raw materials on account	$200,000
Factory wages	80,000
Factory supervision salaries	15,000
Utilities bill for month	7,000
Factory supplies purchased	500
Depreciation	6,000

Raw materials costs associated with completed units amount to $180,000. Five percent of the units completed during the month are in the ending finished goods inventory.

Required:
(a) Prepare backflush costing journal entries for September, assuming Speedo uses a Raw Materials-in-Process account.

(b) Assuming September is a typical month, is it likely that the use of the company's shortcut accounting procedures will produce misleading financial statements? Explain.

13-7 JIT Product Costing

Presented is information pertaining to the standard or budgeted unit cost of a product manufactured in a JIT environment:

Direct materials	$15
Conversion	10
Total	$25

All materials are added at the start of the production process. All raw materials purchases and conversion costs are directly assigned to Cost of Goods Sold. At the end of the period, an adjusting entry is used to assign some costs to Raw Materials-in-Process and Finished Goods Inventory. The materials costs assigned to inventories are based on the standard or budgeted cost of materials multiplied by the number of units in inventory. The conversion costs assigned to inventories are based on the standard or budgeted cost of conversion multiplied by the percentage of completion of units in inventory. At the start of the next period, a reversing entry reassigns all costs to Cost of Goods Sold.

There were no beginning inventories on August 1, 19X7. During the month, the company incurred the following manufacturing related costs:

Purchase of raw materials on account	$300,000
Factory wages	125,000
Factory supervision salaries	30,000
Utilities bill for month	17,000
Factory supplies purchased	1,500
Depreciation	9,500

End-of-month inventories included raw materials-in-process of 600 units and finished goods of 400 units. One hundred units of raw materials were 0 percent converted, and the other 500 units averaged 60 percent converted.

Required:

(a) Following the company's accounting procedures, prepare summary August journal entries related to manufacturing activities. Also, prepare any appropriate September 1 reversing entry.
(b) Assuming August is a typical month, is it likely that the use of the company's shortcut accounting procedures will produce misleading financial statements? Explain.

13-8 Determining Order Quantity, Reorder Point, and Safety Stock (Appendix)

The annual demand for inventory item T-20 is 1,000 units, the cost of placing an order is $100, and the cost of carrying 1 unit in inventory for 1 year is $5.

Required:

(a) Use the economic order quantity formula to determine the optimal order size.

(b) Assuming a lead time of 10 days and a work year of 250 days, determine the reorder point.
(c) Assuming the maximum lead time is 15 days and the maximum daily demand is 6 units, determine the safety stock required to prevent stockouts.

13-9 Impact of Deviations from EOQ (Appendix)

Faced with a cash surplus, the Loveday Department Store increased the size of several inventory order quantities that had previously been determined using the EOQ model.

Required:
Use the words "increase," "decrease," or "no change" to indicate the impact of management's decision on each of the following:

(a) Average inventory
(b) Number of orders per year
(c) Total annual carrying costs
(d) Total annual ordering costs
(e) Total annual carrying and ordering costs
(f) Cost of goods sold

13-10 Cost Savings with Economic Order Quantity: Shelf Life (Appendix)

The Pleasant View Hospital places orders for a particular inventory item in lot sizes of 10 units. Additional information about this inventory item is as follows:

Annual demand	720 units
Ordering costs	$ 25 per order
Purchase price	$ 100 per unit

Annual inventory carrying costs are estimated to be 40 percent of the unit cost.

Required:
(a) Determine the economic order quantity.
(b) Determine the annual cost savings if Pleasant View changes from an order size of 10 units to the economic order quantity.
(c) The shelf life of this item is limited. Assuming that shelf life is based on the number of days it may be used after it is placed in inventory, determine the optimal lot size under each of the following circumstances. Assume a 360-day year.
(1) Shelf life of 20 days
(2) Shelf life of 10 days
(*Hint:* Determine how many days an order will last.)

13-11 Cost Savings with Economic Order Quantity: Quantity Discounts (Appendix)

The Mason Company currently purchases a particular item in sizes of 1,250 units. Mason's annual use of this item is 6,250 units. Ordering costs are $200 per order, and carrying costs are $10 per unit per year.

Required:

(a) Determine the economic order quantity.

(b) Determine the amount of the annual cost savings if Mason changes from an order size of 1,250 units to the economic order quantity.

(c) The supplier offers a discount of $2 per unit off the purchase price of orders in lots of 625 units or more. What action do you recommend? (*Hint:* Compare the annual cost savings from the discount to the increased total annual ordering and carrying costs required to qualify for the discount.)

PROBLEMS

13-12 Product Costing Continuum

The Maron Corporation, a small manufacturer of specialized medical care equipment, operates a plant that consists of two departments: Forging and Finishing. Each product requires processing in each of the departments. Expected indirect manufacturing costs for 19X8 are as follows:

Forging Department	$300,000
Finishing Department	200,000
Total manufacturing overhead	$500,000
Direct labor hours for the year	10,000

An activity-based cost analysis determined that manufacturing overhead was incurred to support the following activities:

Setups (500 setups)	$100,000
Engineering (5,000 engineering hours)	125,000
Material movement (6,000 movements)	75,000
Quality control inspections (1,000 inspections)	85,000
Machine operation (5,000 hours)	115,000
Total activity costs	$500,000

It was determined when the activity costs were being developed that similar activities that were performed in both departments, such as material movement, had similar costs in each department; hence, it was decided that separate departmental activity cost pools were not needed.

One of Maron's most successful products is a patented forceps that is produced in batches of 200. Each batch uses $3,000 of direct materials, all added in the Forging Department. Each batch uses 25 machine hours in the Forging Department. The manufacturing process is virtually totally automated in the Forging Department and completely dependent on direct labor in the Finishing Department. Direct labor costs, all incurred in the Finishing Department, are $1,000 per batch for 40 direct labor hours.

It was also determined that each batch of forceps requires 5 setups, 15 engineering hours, 50 material movements, and 25 inspections.

Required:

(a) Calculate the product cost per unit for forceps, assuming manufacturing overhead is assigned to products using a plant-wide overhead rate based on machine hours.

(b) Calculate the product cost per unit for forceps, assuming manufacturing overhead is assigned to products using departmental overhead rates based on machine hours for Forging and direct labor hours for Finishing.

(c) Calculate the product cost per unit for forceps, assuming manufacturing overhead is assigned to products using activity-based costing overhead rates.

(d) Comment on the reasons for the differences in the product costs calculated in requirements (a), (b), and (c).

13-13 Traditional and Activity-Based Costing Assignment

Mobar, Inc., produces three products in a single production department. For years, Mobar produced a single type of electric motor, the Standard A. Last year, Mobar added two new specialty products: Deluxe B and Special C. Although these new products have relatively low annual sales and are produced in relatively short production runs, Deluxe B and particularly Special C have proven to be so profitable that management is contemplating becoming a specialty producer of short-run products. The marketing manager observed that it made sense to move into areas where there is little foreign competition and where Mobar's ability to respond quickly to customer needs can be exploited.

The production supervisor is opposed to this action, arguing that the profits of Deluxe B and Special C are illusory. You have been called to perform a special study of the profitability of each product. You quickly obtain the following information:

| | Unit Data | |
Product	Selling Price	Direct Costs
Standard A	$35	$20
Deluxe B	50	30
Special C	65	40

After discussions with the production supervisor, you determine that Mobar uses highly automated equipment that has fast unit cycle times but relatively slow setup times. What's more, setups are expensive because they require the work of a supervisor and several highly trained production employees. Once set up, however, the machines operate with little attention. This information has led you to question Mobar's procedure of reassigning production costs on the basis of units produced.

Further discussions with production personnel and a statistical analysis of historical data revealed the following information pertaining to the actual production last year and the actual behavior of Mobar's manufacturing overhead costs:

Product	Total Units	Job/Batch Size (Units)	Setup Time per Job	Processing Time per Unit
Standard A	40,000	5,000	5 hours	0.10 hours
Deluxe B	10,000	500	10 hours	0.20 hours
Special C	5,000	100	5 hours	0.10 hours

Factory overhead costs:

Setup	$200 per hour
Operations	100 per hour

Required:

(a) Determine the gross profit per unit of each product when overhead is applied on the basis of (1) units produced and (2) processing time.

(b) On the basis of this analysis, what conclusions is management likely to reach about relative profitability?

(c) Determine the gross profit per unit when overhead is applied on the basis of the activities that drive overhead costs.

(d) Based on the analysis in requirement (c), what conclusions is management likely to reach about relative profitability?

13-14 Factory Overhead Allocation: One Cost Pool Versus Multiple Pools

For many years, the Underwood Motor Company has been using direct labor hours as the basis for allocating factory overhead to its two product lines: gasoline engines and diesel engines. As the company has moved toward a more automated assembly process, the company controller has suggested that direct labor hours are no longer an appropriate basis for reassigning costs to the products. Accordingly, she has engaged in a detailed study of factory overhead cost drivers with the factory engineers and is proposing a revision in the costing system that will better reflect activity-based costing. She is proposing that three cost pools and allocation bases be used: one pool for labor-related costs that will be assigned based on direct labor hours, another pool for machine maintenance and support based on machine hours, and another for space costs assigned on the basis of the number of hours the assembly line is set up to run the respective products. The following data have been collected for the most recent month of production activity:

Product	Direct Labor Hours	Machine Hours	Assembly Hours	Units Produced
Gasoline engines	20,000	2,000	320	1,000
Diesel engines	10,000	8,000	80	500
Totals	30,000	10,000	400	1,500

Factory overhead costs:

Indirect labor-related costs	$750,000
Indirect machine-related costs	300,000
Indirect space-related costs	150,000

Required:

(a) Under the old system of indirect cost allocation, how much factory overhead cost would be allocated to each gasoline and diesel engine produced during the month?

(b) Under the new system of indirect cost assignment, how much factory overhead cost would be allocated to each gasoline and diesel engine produced during the month?

(c) Assuming the new system is more accurate than the old system, which product has been cross-subsidizing the cost of the other and by how much?

(d) What are the consequences of product cost cross-subsidization?

13-15 ABC for Production and Pricing Decisions[11]

The budgeted manufacturing overhead costs of Beaver Window Company for 19X1 are listed below:

Type of Costs	Cost Pools
Electric power	$ 500,000
Work cells	3,000,000
Material handling	1,000,000
Quality control inspections	1,000,000
Product runs (machine setups)	500,000
Total budgeted overhead costs	$6,000,000

For the last five years, the Cost Accounting Department has been charging overhead production costs based on machine hours. The machine hour is the cost driver in determining the applied manufacturing overhead costs rate. The VP for production, Hal Jacobs, estimates the budgeted capacity for 19X1 to be 1,000,000 machine hours. The predetermined applied factory overhead cost rate will, therefore, be $6.00 per machine hour ($6,000,000 budgeted overhead costs divided by 1,000,000 budgeted machine hours).

Phil Stolzer, the president of Beaver Window Company, recently attended a one-day seminar on an ABC system that allocates overhead costs based on activity-based cost drivers. After attending the seminar, he believes that the ABC method results in more reliable cost data. This reliability will lead to better and more accurate pricing policies that will give the company an edge over its competitors. With this system, manufacturing overhead costs are correlated to various activity-costing bases rather than to one allocation base such as machine hours, direct labor hours, units of production, etc.

Stolzer plans to implement this application of overhead costs, based on ABC techniques that require the use of cost pools and cost drivers. Peter Brock, production manager, upon the president's request, has provided the following data regarding the expected total 19X1 activity of the activity-based cost drivers for those budgeted overhead costs listed above under the cost pool section:

11 The above case study, Beaver Window Company, was prepared by Professors Nabil Hassan, Herbert E. Brown, and Paula M. Saunders and was originally printed in the Fall 1990 *Management Accounting Campus Report*. It is reprinted with permission of the Institute of Management Accountants.

Type of Cost	Activity-Based Cost Drivers
Electric power	100,000 kilowatt-hours
Work cells	600,000 square feet
Material handling	200,000 materials moves
Quality control inspections	100,000 inspections
Product runs (setups)	50,000 product runs

Larry Ryan, the VP of marketing, received an offer to sell 5,000 windows to a local construction company that is currently building a high-rise office building adjacent to a shopping mall. Ryan asks Sue Pretora, head of the Cost Accounting Department, to prepare cost estimates for manufacturing the 5,000 windows. With this information, a comparison can be made between the present system of applying overhead cost on machine hours and the new ABC system based on various cost drivers. Pretora provided the following data concerning the production of 5,000 windows:

Direct materials cost	$100,000
Direct labor costs	$300,000
Machine hours	10,000
Direct labor hours	15,000
Electric power (kilowatt-hours)	1,000
Work cells (square feet)	8,000
Number of material handling moves	100
Number of quality control inspections	50
Number of product runs (setups)	25

Required:

(a) What are the manufacturing costs per window unit under the present cost accounting system that applies manufacturing overhead costs based on machine hours?

(b) What is the manufacturing cost per window unit if the activity-based costing system is implemented?

(c) If the above two cost accounting systems will result in different cost estimates, which cost accounting system is preferable as a pricing policy?

13-16 ABC and Conventional Costs Compared

The Digit Calculator Company manufactures two types of hand calculators: Custom Scientist and Consumer. The Custom Scientist is made to order in small batches. The Consumer is produced in large batches for distribution to discount stores. Presented is information pertaining to the manufacturing costs for February 19X6:

	Custom Scientist	Consumer
Units	5,000	25,000
Number of batches	50	10
Number of batch moves between workstations	250	20
Direct materials	$25,000	$75,000
Direct labor	8,400	19,000
Total prime costs	33,400	94,000

Manufacturing overhead:

Activity	Cost	Cost Driver
Materials acquisition and inspection	$20,000	Direct materials cost
Materials movement	10,800	Batch moves between workstations
Scheduling	24,000	Number of batches
Total cost	$54,800	

Required:

(a) Determine the total and unit costs of manufacturing the Custom Scientist and the Consumer during February 19X6, assuming all manufacturing overhead is assigned on the basis of direct labor dollars.

(b) Determine the total and unit costs of manufacturing the Custom Scientist and the Consumer during February 19X6, assuming manufacturing overhead is assigned using activity-based costing.

(c) Comment on the differences between the solutions to requirements (a) and (b). Which is more accurate? What errors might managers make if all manufacturing overhead costs are assigned on the basis of direct labor dollars.

13-17 Product Costing: ABC and Conventional Cost Allocation

Alpha Company manufactures two products: AA and BB. The overhead costs have been divided into four cost pools that use the following cost drivers:

Product	Number of Orders	Number of Setups	Number of Labor Transactions	Labor Hours
AA	30	10	25	1,000
BB	10	40	35	250
Cost per pool	$8,000	$6,500	$1,200	$10,000

Required:

(a) Allocate the overhead costs using activity-based costing to AA and BB.

(b) Using conventional costing, allocate the overhead costs based on direct labor hours to AA and BB.

(c) Presented are four arguments against using activity-based costing. Provide an appropriate response to each of these arguments.

(1) Conventional systems will do the job if we change to departmental overhead rates from a plant-wide overhead rate.

(2) A costing system should be kept simple so that it makes sense to managers and production employees.

(3) The market sets prices; so, we don't need accurate product cost information.

(4) Our current costing system produces financial statements that conform to generally accepted accounting principles.

13-18 JIT Performance Evaluation

To control operations, Justa Company makes extensive and exclusive use of financial performance reports for each department. Although all departments have been reporting favorable cost variances in most periods, management is perplexed by the firm's low overall return on investment. You have been asked to look into the matter.

Believing the Purchasing Department is typical of Justa's operations, you obtained the following information concerning the purchases of parts for a product Justa started producing in 19X1:

Year	Purchase Price Variance	Quantity Used (Units)	Average Inventory (Units)
19X1	$ 1,000 F	20,000	4,000
19X2	10,000 F	30,000	7,500
19X3	12,000 F	30,000	10,000
19X4	20,000 U	25,000	6,250
19X5	8,000 F	27,000	9,000
19X6	9,500 F	29,000	11,600

Required:

(a) Compute the inventory turnover for each year. Can any conclusions be drawn for a yearly comparison of the purchase price variance and the inventory turnover?

(b) Identify problems likely to be caused by evaluating purchasing only on the basis of the purchase price variance.

(c) Offer whatever recommendations you believe appropriate.

13-19 Materials Push and Materials Pull: Kanban

Media Storage, Inc., produces three models of hard disk drives for personal computers. Each model is produced on a separate assembly line. The production operation consists of several operations in separate work centers. Because of a high demand for Media's products, management is most interested in high production volume and operating efficiency. Each work center is evaluated on the basis of its operating efficiency. To avoid idle time caused by defective units, variations in machine times, and machine breakdowns, significant inventories are maintained between each workstation.

At a recent administrative committee meeting, the director of research announced that the firm's engineers have made a dramatic breakthrough in designing a low-cost read/write optical storage device. The president of Media Storage is very enthusiastic, and the vice president of marketing wishes to add an assembly line for optical storage devices as soon as possible. The equipment necessary to manufacture the new product can be purchased and installed in less than 60 days. Unfortunately, all available plant space is currently devoted to the production of hard disk drives, and expansion is not possible at the current plant location. It appears that adding the new product will require dropping a current product, relocating the entire operation, or manufacturing the optical storage devices at a separate location.

The vice president of marketing is opposed to dropping a current product. The vice president of finance is opposed to relocating the entire operation because of financing requirements and the associated financial risks. The vice president of production is opposed to splitting up production activities because of the loss of control and the added costs for various types of overhead.

Required:

Explain how switching to a materials pull (Kanban) system can help solve Media Storage's space problems while improving quality and cycle time. In your answer, be sure to describe how a materials pull system works and the changes required in management's attitude toward inventory and efficiency to make it work.

13-20 Inventory Costs, EOQ, JIT, and Systems Design

West Window and East Window were formed in 19X1 when the Glass brothers, who had jointly operated the Unity Glass Company, broke up their partnership. William Glass, the former general manager for business and finance of Unity Glass, became president of West Window; and Edwin Glass, the former chief engineer and production supervisor of Unity Glass, became president of East Window.

When they began operations in 19X1, West Window and East Window had similar products (aluminum storm windows and doors), similar cost structures, and similar facilities. However, William Glass made extensive use of optimizing models in an attempt to manage by the numbers, while Edwin Glass emphasized analyzing activities, breaking costs into small pieces for each activity, and then eliminating or cutting the cost of each activity. This difference in philosophy led to differences in each firm's approach to inventory management.

Presented is 19X1 and 19X5 information pertaining to the manufacture of aluminum storm windows for each company:

	19X1 and 19X5, West Window	19X1, East Window	19X5, East Window
Annual demand (each firm/units)	20,000	20,000	30,000
Costs:			
Production order, etc. (batch)	$ 60.00	$ 60.00	$ 21.25
Setup (batch)	100.00	100.00	40.00
Materials (unit)	20.00	20.00	20.00
Processing (unit)	40.00	40.00	40.00
Handling (unit)	8.00	8.00	2.00
Rework costs (average per unit)	3.00	3.00	0.00
Inspection (unit)	5.00	5.00	0.00
Carrying (unit/year)	10.00	10.00	30.00
Lot size (units)	800	100	50

West Window's production facilities and procedures are essentially unchanged over the period. William Glass is concerned about his firm's ability to compete against lower priced foreign and cross-town competitors in the mass market for aluminum storm windows. West Window has been forced to lower prices significantly during the past four years due to competitive pressure. William Glass is quoted as saying that, "At this point, profit margins are so fragile on aluminum storm windows that the sun may be setting on West Window's ability to compete in this market." He plans to change the firm's production and market strategy to produce specialty products for the government.

Edwin Glass, who says he saw the light of a new day dawning on East Window, implemented a just-in-time approach to inventory management in 19X2. The result has been a significant change in production procedures with an emphasis on reducing cycle time, lot size, and inventory levels. As a result, East Window has experienced significant reductions in production order and setup costs. The early identification of quality problems and constant work to prevent their recurrence have resulted in the virtual elimination of inspection and rework costs. The space previously devoted to inventory has been used to increase production facilities for a variety of products, thereby increasing the value of the remaining space and carrying costs.

Required:
(a) Determine the total annual and average unit costs associated with producing aluminum storm windows for each company in 19X1 and 19X5. Round answers to the nearest cent. (*Hint*: Ultimately all of the costs discussed in this problem are product costs.)
(b) Determine the economic lot size for both companies in 19X1 and 19X5.
(c) Comment on the approaches to inventory management followed by William and Edwin Glass. Might they have done better if they had not broken up the Unity Glass Company? Explain, using numbers to illustrate as appropriate.
(d) Can you recommend any additional changes in production procedures that might further enhance either company's competitive position?
(e) Describe an accounting system that seems most appropriate for the recommendation in requirement (d).

13-21 Plotting Variations in Inventory Levels with Safety Stocks (Appendix)

An inventory item with an average daily demand of 5 units and a maximum daily demand of 10 units has an economic order quantity of 100 units. In the absence of safety stocks, the item's reorder point is 25 units. Safety stocks are set at 75 units.

Required:
(a) Determine each of the following:
  (1) Reorder point with safety stocks
  (2) Maximum inventory level
  (3) Average lead time
  (4) Maximum lead time
(b) Graph the variations in inventory levels over a period of 60 days. Start at the beginning of day 1 (time 0) with maximum inventory. Assume that daily demand is normal during the first inventory cycle and that inventory is replenished at the end of the first cycle without the use of safety stocks. Assume that daily demand is normal during the second cycle until inventory is reordered. Assume maximum daily demand and lead time until the second order is received. Continue the

graph through the end of 60 days with normal daily demand and lead times.

13-22 Economic Order Quantity and Reorder Point: Missing Data (Appendix)

Supply the missing data in each case. Assume that all costs and quantities are optimal, according to the EOQ formula.

	Case 1	Case 2	Case 3	Case 4
Annual demand	250	?	200	?
Economic order quantity	?	?	?	200
Average inventory	?	50	?	?
Orders per year	?	30	5	?
Working days per year	250	?	?	?
Average daily demand	?	12	0.8	?
Lead time in days	10	?	5	8
Reorder point	?	60	?	80
Annual ordering costs	$?	$?	$?	$?
Annual carrying costs	?	1,500	?	?
Total	$?	$?	$?	$?
Cost of placing an order	$100	$?	$ 20	$ 80
Annual unit carrying costs	$ 20	$?	$?	$ 10

(*Hint*: For Cases 2 and 3, costs are equal at the EOQ; for Case 4, work backward from the EOQ.)

DISCUSSION QUESTIONS AND CASES

13-23 Detailed Application of ABC Product Costing[12]

CarryAll Company produces briefcases from leather, fabric, and synthetic materials in a single production department. The basic product is a standard briefcase that is made from leather, lined with fabric. CarryAll has a good reputation in the market because the standard briefcase is a high-quality item and has been well-produced for many years.

Last year, the company decided to expand its product line and produce specialty briefcases for special orders. These briefcases differ from the standard in that they vary in size, they contain both leather and synthetic materials, and they are imprinted with the buyer's logo, whereas the standard briefcase is simply imprinted with the CarryAll name in small letters. The decision to use some synthetic materials in the briefcase was made to hold down the materials cost. To reduce the labor costs per unit, most of the cutting and stitching on the specialty briefcases is done by automated

---

12 The above case study, CarryAll Company, was prepared by Professors Harold P. Roth and Imogine Posey and was originally printed in the *Management Accounting Campus Report*. It is reprinted with permission of the Institute of Management Accountants.

machines, which are used to a much lesser degree in the production of the standard briefcases. Because of these changes in the design and production of the specialty briefcases, CarryAll believed that they would cost less to produce than the standard briefcases. However, because they are specialty items, they were priced slightly higher—standards are priced at $30 and specialty briefcases at $32.

After reviewing last month's results of operations, CarryAll's president became concerned about the profitability of the two product lines because the standard briefcase showed a loss, while the specialty briefcase showed a greater profit margin than expected. The president is wondering whether the company should drop the standard briefcase and focus entirely on specialty items.   The cost data for last month's operations as reported to the president are as follows:

		Standard			**Specialty**
Units produced		10,000			2,500
Direct materials:					
Leather	1.0 sq. yd.	$15.00		0.5 sq. yd.	$ 7.50
Fabric	1.0 sq. yd.	5.00		1.0 sq. yd.	5.00
Synthetic					5.00
Total materials		$20.00			$17.50
Direct labor	(0.5 hr. × $12.00)	6.00	(0.25 hr. × $12.00)		3.00
Factory overhead	(0.5 hr. × $8.98)	4.49	(0.25 hr. × $8.98)		2.25
Cost per unit		$30.49			$22.75

Factory overhead is applied on the basis of direct labor hours. The rate of $8.98 per direct labor hour was calculated by dividing the total overhead, $50,500 for the month, by the direct labor hours of 5,625. As shown above, the cost of a standard briefcase is $0.49 higher than its $30 sales price, whereas the specialty briefcase has a cost of only $22.75, for a gross profit per unit of $9.25. The problem with these costs is that they do not accurately reflect the activities involved in manufacturing each product. Determining the costs using ABC should provide better product costing data to help gauge the actual profitability of each product line.

The factory overhead costs must be analyzed to determine the activities causing the costs. Assume that the following costs and cost drivers have been identified:

• Purchasing Department cost is $6,000. The major activity driving the Purchasing Department costs is the number of purchase orders processed.   During the month, Purchasing prepared the following number of purchase orders:

For leather	20
For fabric	30
For synthetic material	50

• Receiving and inspecting materials cost is $7,500. Receiving and inspecting costs are driven by the number of deliveries. During the month, the following deliveries were made:

Leather	30 deliveries
Fabric	40 deliveries
Synthetic material	80 deliveries

- Production line setup cost is $10,000. Setup activities involve changing the machines to produce the different types of briefcases. A setup for production of the standard briefcases requires 1 hour, while setup for the specialty briefcases requires 2 hours. Standard briefcases are produced in batches of 200, and specialty briefcases are produced in batches of 25. During the last month, there were 50 setups for the standard items and 100 setups for the specialty items.
- Inspecting finished goods cost is $8,000. All briefcases are inspected to ensure that quality standards are met. However, the final inspection of standard briefcases takes very little time because the employees identify and correct quality problems as they do the hand cutting and stitching. A survey of the personnel responsible for inspecting the final products showed that they spent 150 hours on standard briefcases and 250 hours on specialty briefcases during the month.
- Equipment-related costs are $6,000. Equipment-related costs include repairs, depreciation, and utilities. Management has determined that a logical basis for assigning these costs to products is machine hours. A standard briefcase requires 0.5 hour of machine time, and a specialty briefcase requires 2 hours. Thus, during the last month, 5,000 hours of machine time relate to the standard line and 5,000 hours relate to the specialty line.
- Plant-related costs are $13,000. Plant-related costs include property taxes, insurance, administration, and others. These costs are to be assigned to products using machine hours.

Required:

(a) Using activity-based costing concepts, what overhead costs should be assigned to the two products?
(b) What is the unit cost of the two products using activity-based costing concepts?
(c) Reevaluate the president's concern about the profitability of the two product lines.

13-24 Product Costing Using ABC and JIT: A Value Chain Approach

Wearwell Carpet Company is a small, residential carpet manufacturer started by Don Stegall, a longtime engineer and manager in the carpet industry. Stegall began Wearwell in the early 1990s after learning about ABC, JIT, total quality management, and several other manufacturing concepts being used successfully in Japan and other parts of the world. Although his was a small company, Stegall believed that with his many years of experience and by applying these advanced techniques, Wearwell could become a world-class competitor very quickly.

Stegall buys dyed carpet yarns for Wearwell from three different major yarn manufacturers with whom he has done business for many years. He chose these companies because of their reputation for producing high-quality products and their state-of-the art research and development departments. He has arranged for two carpet manufacturing companies to produce (tuft) all of his carpets on a contract basis. Both of these companies have their own brands, but the two carpet manufacturers also do contract work for other companies. For each manufacturer, Stegall had to agree to use the full output of one manufacturing production line at least one day each month. Each production line was dedicated to producing only one style of carpet, but each manufacturer had production lines capable of running each type of carpet that Wearwell sold.

Stegall signed a contract with a large transport company (CTC) that specializes in carpet-related shipping to pick up and deliver yarn from the yarn plants to the tufting mills and to deliver the finished product from the tufting mills to Wearwell's ten customers, which are carpet retailers in the ten largest residential building markets in the country. These retailers pay the shipping charges to get the carpets delivered to them. Wearwell maintains a small sales staff, which also doubles as a customer service staff, to deal with the retailers and occasionally even to deal with their customers on quality problems that arise.

Wearwell started out selling only one line of carpet, a medium-grade plush; but as new carpet styles were developed, it added two additional lines, a medium-grade berber carpet and a medium-grade textured carpet. Three colors are offered in each carpet style. By selling only medium grades with limited color choices, Stegall believed that he would reach a very large segment of the carpet market without having to deal with a large number of different products. As textured (trackless) carpets have become more popular, sales of plush have diminished substantially.

Required:
(a) Describe the value chain for Wearwell Carpet Company and identify the parties who comprise the value chain for Wearwell.
(b) Identify and discuss the cost categories that would be included in the cost of the product for financial reporting purposes.
(c) Identify and discuss the cost categories that would be included in the cost of the product for pricing and other managerial purposes.
(d) Discuss some of the challenges that Stegall will have trying to apply JIT to control the levels of inventory at Wearwell. Suggest changes that might be necessary to make JIT work.
(e) Does Wearwell seem to be an appropriate setting for implementing ABC? If so, what are likely to be the most important activities and related cost drivers?

13-25 JIT Performance Evaluation
The vice president of manufacturing is perplexed. When the new Southside Plant began operations three years ago, it appeared to live up to the expectations of top management. The plant was modern, well-lighted, and spacious. Cost variances were favorable, customers were highly satisfied with quality and service, and the plant reported large segment contributions to common costs and profits despite high start-up costs and early period depreciation.

Just three years later, the Southside Plant seems to be declining into crisis management. Although most cost variances, especially those dealing with cost center efficiency, remain favorable, the plant's segment contribution is declining, and customers are complaining about poor quality and slow delivery. Several customers have suggested that if the firm cannot correct its quality and delivery problems, they will take their business elsewhere. The shop floor is a mess with in-process inventory piled everywhere. Production employees complain of difficulty in locating jobs to be worked on, and scheduling personnel have recently requested a larger computer to help keep track of work-in-process.

The vice president said she does not even know where to begin to figure out how to solve the plant's problems. She commented, "What is really weird is that we all work so hard. Our facilities are the best in the business, and I know our employees are dedicated, well-trained, and hard-working. They do exactly what we ask, and we have never had any labor problems. It just seems like the harder we work, the worse our problems become."

Required:
Suggest the nature of the Southside Plant's problems and recommend how the vice president might begin to figure out how to solve the plant's problems.

SOLUTION TO REVIEW PROBLEM

(a)

$$\text{Plant-wide overhead rate} = \frac{\text{Total manufacturing overhead}}{\text{Total machine hours}}$$

$$= (\$120{,}000 + \$55{,}000) / (10{,}000 + 5{,}000)$$

$$= \$175{,}000 / 15{,}000$$

$$= \underline{\$11.67} \text{ per machine hour}$$

Product costs per unit:	ZX300	SL500
Direct materials	$12,000	$18,000
Direct labor	5,000	4,000
Manufacturing overhead:		
(500 machine hours × $11.67)	5,835	
(700 machine hours × $11.67)		8,169
Total cost per batch	$22,835	$30,169
Number of units per batch	÷ 100	÷ 100
Cost per unit	$228.35	$301.69

(b)

$$\text{Departmental overhead rates} = \frac{\text{Total departmental overhead}}{\text{Dept. allocation base}}$$

Fabrication:
$$= \$120{,}000 / 10{,}000 \text{ machine hours}$$
$$= \underline{\$12} \text{ per machine hour}$$

Finishing: = $55,000 / 1,000 inspection hours
                            = $55 per inspection hour

Product costs per unit:	ZX300	SL500
Direct materials	$12,000	$18,000
Direct labor	5,000	4,000
Manufacturing overhead:		
Fabrication Department:		
(500 machine hours × $12.00)	6,000	
(700 machine hours × $12.00)		8,400
Finishing Department:		
(30 inspection hours × $55.00)	1,650	
(60 inspection hours × $55.00)		3,300
Total cost per batch	$24,650	$33,700
Number of units per batch	÷ 100	÷ 100
Cost per unit	$246.50	$337.00

(c)

Activity overhead rates = Activity cost pool / Activity cost driver

Maintenance: = $30,000 / 15,000 machine hours
                    = $2 per machine hour

Material handling: = $45,000 / 4,500 material moves
                    = $10 per material move

Machine setup: = $75,000 / 750 setups
                    = $100 per machine setup

Inspection: = $25,000 / 1,000 inspection hours
                    = $25 per inspection hour

Product costs per unit:	ZX300	SL500
Direct materials	$12,000	$18,000
Direct labor	5,000	4,000
Manufacturing overhead:		
Maintenance activity:		
(500 machine hours × $2.00)	1,000	
(700 machine hours × $2.00)		1,400
Material handling activity:		
(30 material moves × $10)	300	
(50 material moves × $10)		500
Machine setup activity:		
(5 machine setups × $100)	500	
(9 machine setups × $100)		900
Inspection activity:		
(30 inspection hours × $25)	750	
(60 inspection hours × $25)		1,500
Total cost per batch	$19,550	$26,300
Number of units per batch	÷ 100	÷ 100
Cost per unit	$195.50	$263.00

(d)

The following is a summary of the product costs for ZX300 and SL500 assigning overhead costs based on a plant-wide rate, departmental rates, and activity-based costing rates:

	ZX300	SL500
Using a plant-wide rate	$228.35	$301.69
Using departmental rates	246.50	337.00
Using activity-based costing rates	195.50	263.00

When changing from a plant-wide rate to departmental rates, the cost of ZX300 increases by about $18, while the cost of SL500 increases by about $35. The plant-wide rate spreads the total overhead cost among products based on machine hours used, which does not recognize that it takes twice as much inspection time for SL500 than it takes for ZX300. Also, when changing to departmental rates, the total cost for both products increases because together they utilize 1,200 of 15,000 (or 8 percent) of the plant's total machine hours, but they use 90 of 1,000 (or 9 percent) of the plant's total inspection hours. By using departmental rates based on both machine and inspection hours, this causes more of the total overhead to be assigned to ZX300 and SL500 and less to be assigned to the other three products. Hence, using departmental rates reduces the amount of cross-subsidization of cost of ZX300 and SL500 by the other products.

When using activity-based costing rates, however, the costs of these two products drop dramatically because they use only a small portion (less than 2 percent) of the activities of setup (80 of 4,500) and material moves (14 of 750). Neither a plant-wide rate nor departmental rates recognize this fact, resulting in a large amount of cost cross-subsidization of other products by ZX300 and SL500 for these costs. Although this problem did not include cost analysis of the other three products, it clearly shows that they are less profitable than previously thought by management and that ZX300 and SL500 are much more profitable than previously thought.

GLOSSARY

A

Absorption cost: a method of inventory accounting that assigns all manufacturing costs, both variable and fixed, to inventory.

Absorption costing: an approach to costing products that treats both variable and fixed manufacturing costs as product costs.

Accounting rate of return: the average annual increase in net income that results from acceptance of a capital expenditure proposal divided by either the initial investment or the average investment in the project.

Activity: a unit of work.

Activity-based budget approach: budgets physical inputs and costs as a function of planned activity. Emphasis is on batches put into production and by the number of product lines. This approach traces costs to both volume-sensitive and nonvolume-sensitive driver costs.

Activity-based costing (ABC): a type of costing that is based on the cost of specific activities performed to fill customer needs. It determines the cost of activities and traces the cost of activities to cost objectives on the basis of the cost objective's utilization of units of activity.

Activity-based management (ABM): the identification and selection of activities that maximize the value of activities while minimizing the cost of activities from the viewpoint of the final customer.

Activity cost drivers: specific units of work (activities) performed to serve customer needs that consume costly resources.

Annuity: a series of equal cash flows received or paid over equal intervals of time.

Appraisal costs: quality costs incurred to identify nonconforming products or services before they are delivered to customers.

Automatic identification systems (AIS): the use of bar coding of products and production processes that allows inventory and production information to be entered into a computer without writing or keying.

B

Backflush costing: an inventory accounting system used in conjunction with JIT in which costs are assigned to inventories and cost of goods sold based on outputs throughout the system after the process is completed.

Balance sheet: a picture of the economic health of an organization at a point in time, showing the organization's assets and the claims on those assets.

Batch level activity: an activity performed for each batch of product produced.

Benchmarking: a systematic approach to identifying the best practices to help an organization take action to improve performance.

Bill of materials: a document that specifies the kinds and quantities of raw materials required to produce one unit of product.

Break-even point: the unit or dollar sales volume where total revenues equal total costs.

Budget committee: a committee responsible for supervising budget preparation. It serves as a review board for evaluating requests for discretionary cost items and new projects.

Budget office: the organizational unit responsible for the preparation, distribution, and processing of forms used in gathering budget data. It handles most of the work of actually formulating the budget schedules and reports.

Budgetary slack: sometimes referred to as "padding the budget," occurs when managers intentionally request more funds in the budget for their departments than needed to support the anticipated level of operations.

By-product: a product with insignificant value that is produced jointly with one or more other products.

C

Capacity costs: see committed fixed costs.

Capital budgeting: the identification of potentially desirable projects for capital expenditures, the subsequent evaluation of capital expenditure proposals, and the selection of proposals that meet certain criteria.

Capital expenditures: investments of significant financial resources in projects to develop or introduce new products or services, to expand current production or service capacity, or to change current production or service facilities.

Cash budget: summarizes all cash receipts and disbursements expected to occur during the budget period.

Centralization: when the top management controls the major functions of an organization (such as manufacturing, sales, accounting, computer operations, marketing, research and development, and management control).

Coefficient of determination (R_2): a measure of the percent of variation in the dependent variable that is explained by variations in the independent variable when the least-squares estimation equation is used.

Committed fixed costs (sometimes called **capacity costs**): costs required to maintain the current service or production capacity or to fill a previous legal commitment.

Common segment costs (also called **indirect segment costs**): costs related to more than one segment and not

757

directly traceable to a particular segment. These costs are referred to as common costs because they are incurred at one level for the benefit of two or more segments at a lower level.

Computer-aided design (CAD): a concept that involves the use of computers to design products.

Computer-aided manufacturing (CAM): a concept that involves the use of computers to control the operation of machines.

Computer-integrated manufacturing (CIM): the ultimate extension of the CAD, CAM, and FMS concepts to a completely automated and computer-controlled factory where production is automatic once a product is designed and the decision to produce is made.

Continuous budgeting: budgeting based on a moving time frame that extends over a fixed period. A budget system adds an identical time period to the budget at the end of each period of operations, thereby always maintaining a budget of exactly the same time length.

Continuous improvement: the constant evaluation of products, services, and processes, seeking ways to do better.

Continuous improvement (Kaizen) costing: costing method that establishes cost reduction targets for products or services an organization is currently providing to customers.

Contribution income statement: an income statement where costs are classified according to behavior as variable or fixed and the contribution margin that goes toward covering fixed costs and providing a profit is emphasized. Variable costs are subtracted from revenues to get contribution margin, and fixed costs are subtracted from contribution margin to get net income.

Contribution margin: the difference between total revenues and total variable costs that goes toward covering fixed costs and providing a profit.

Contribution margin ratio: the portion of each dollar of sales revenue contributed toward covering fixed costs and earning a profit.

Controlling: the process of ensuring that results agree with plans.

Conversion cost: the combined costs of direct labor and manufacturing overhead required to convert raw materials into finished goods.

Cost allocation base: a measure of a common volume of activity, such as direct labor hours or machine hours, that determines how much of a cost pool is assigned to each cost objective.

Cost behavior: how costs respond to changes in the number of units of an activity cost driver.

Cost center: a responsibility center whose manager is responsible for managing costs.

Cost driver: a factor that influences costs.

Cost driver analysis: the study of factors that influence costs.

Cost estimation: the determination of previous or current relationships between activity and cost.

Cost objective: anything to which costs are assigned. Examples include departments, products, and services.

Cost of capital: the average cost of obtaining the resources necessary to make investments.

Cost of production report: a document that summarizes total and unit cost data for each department for each period in a process costing system.

Cost pool: a collection of related costs, such as departmental factory overhead, that is assigned to other cost objectives, such as products.

Cost prediction: the forecasting of future costs.

Cost prediction error: the difference between a predicted future cost and the actual amount of the cost when, or if, it is incurred.

Cost reduction proposal: a proposed action or investment intended to reduce the cost of an activity that the organization is committed to keeping.

Cost tables: data bases that indicate the effect on costs of using different materials, production methods, and product designs.

Cost-volume-profit analysis: a technique used to examine the relationships among total volume, total costs, total revenues, and profits during a time period of interest.

Cost-volume-profit graph: an illustration of the relationships among activity volume, total revenues, total costs, and profits.

Cycle budgeting: is appropriate when the entire life of the cycle or project represents a more useful planning horizon than an artificial period of one year. Such cycles could be reduced to shorter planning periods by breaking the overall project into several components, such as construction phases.

Cycle efficiency: the ratio of value-added to nonvalue-added manufacturing activities.

Cycle time: the total time required to complete a process.

D

Decentralization: the delegation of decision-making authority to successively lower management levels in an organization. The lower in the organization the authority is delegated, the greater the decentralization.

Degree of operating leverage: a measure of operating leverage, computed as the contribution margin divided by income before taxes.

Denominator variance: see fixed overhead volume variance.

Depreciation tax shield: the reduction in taxes due to the deductibility of depreciation from taxable revenues.

Descriptive model: a model that merely specifies the relationships between a series of independent and dependent variables.

Design for manufacture: the explicit consideration of the costs of manufacturing and servicing a product while designing it.

Differential cost analysis: an approach to the analysis of relevant costs that focuses on the costs that differ under alternative actions.

Direct costing: see variable costing.

Direct department cost: a cost that can be traced directly to a department upon the cost's incurrence.

Direct labor: wages earned by production employees for the time they spend working on the conversion of raw materials into finished goods.

Direct materials: the costs of primary raw materials converted into finished goods.

Direct method: a method of allocating service department costs to the producing departments based only on the amount of services provided to the producing departments. It does not recognize any interdepartmental services.

Direct segment costs: costs that would not be incurred if the segment being evaluated were discontinued. They are specifically identifiable with a particular segment.

Discount rate: the minimum rate of return required for the project to be acceptable.

Discretionary cost center: a cost center that does not have clearly defined relationships between effort and accomplishment.

Discretionary fixed costs (sometimes called managed fixed costs): costs set at a fixed amount each period at the discretion of management.

Division margin: the amount each division contributes toward covering common corporate expenses and generating corporate profits. It is computed by subtracting all direct fixed expenses identifiable with each division from the contribution margin.

E

Economic lot size (ELS): the size of an order or batch that results in the minimum ordering and carrying costs.

Economic order quantity (EOQ): the order quantity that results in the minimum total annual inventory costs.

Economic value added: see residual income.

Electronic data interchange (EDI): the electronic communication of data between organizations.

Equivalent completed units: the number of completed units that is equal, in terms of production effort (cost), to a given number of partially completed units.

Ethics: the moral quality, fitness, or propriety of a course of action that may injure or benefit people.

External failure costs: quality costs incurred when nonconforming products or services are delivered to customers.

F

Facility level activity: an activity performed to maintain general manufacturing capabilities.

Feasible region: in linear programming models, includes all possible production volumes and mixes.

File: a collection of related records.

Financial accounting: a reporting system primarily concerned with providing financial information to persons outside the firm.

Financial reporting: the process of preparing financial statements (income statement, balance sheet, and statement of cash flows) for the firm in accordance with generally accepted accounting principles.

Finished goods inventories: the completed manufactured products held for sale to customers.

First-in first-out (FIFO) method: in process costing, a costing method that accounts for unit costs of beginning inventory units separately from those started during the current period. The first costs incurred each period are assumed to have been used to complete the incomplete units left over from the previous period.

Fixed costs: costs that are a constant amount for a time period. Their total amount does not respond to short-run changes in activity.

Fixed manufacturing overhead: all fixed costs associated with converting raw materials into finished goods.

Fixed overhead budget variance: the difference between budgeted and actual fixed overhead.

Fixed overhead volume variance: the difference between total budgeted fixed overhead and total standard fixed overhead assigned to production.

Fixed selling and administrative costs: all fixed costs other than those directly associated with converting raw materials into finished goods.

Flexible budgets: budgets that are adjusted to a particular level of production after the fact. These budgets, based on cost-volume or cost-activity relationships, are used to determine what costs should have been for an attained level of activity.

Flexible budget variance: computed for each cost as the difference between the actual cost and the flexible budget cost of producing a given quantity of product or service.

Flexible manufacturing systems (FMS): an extension of computer-aided manufacturing techniques through a series of manufacturing operations, including the automatic movement of units between operations and the automatic and rapid setup of machines to produce each product.

For-profit organization: an organization that has profit as a primary goal.

Full absorption cost: see absorption costing.

Full costing: see absorption costing.

Full costs: include all variable and fixed costs and costs at all activity levels.

Functional income statement: an income statement format that subtracts manufacturing costs (represented by cost of goods sold) from revenues to get gross profit and subtracts selling and administrative costs from gross profit to get net income.

Future value: the amount a current sum of money earning a stated rate of interest will accumulate to at the end of a future period.

G

General and administrative expense budget: indicates estimated expenses for the general administration of the organization, such as the accounting department, the computer center, and the president's office.

Goal: the purpose toward which an organization directs its activities.

H

High-low method of cost estimation: utilizes data from two time periods, a representative high activity period and a representative low activity period, to estimate fixed and variable costs.

Horizontally integrated organization: an organization that operates many entities in the same industry.

I

Imposed, or top-down, budget approach: top management decides on the goals and objectives for the whole organization and communicates them to lower management levels.

Income statement: a summary of economic events during a period of time, showing the revenues generated by operating activities, the expenses incurred in generating those revenues, and any gains or losses attributed to the period.

Incremental budget approach: budgets costs for a coming period as a dollar or percentage change from the amount budgeted for (or spent during) some previous period. It is often used where the relationships between inputs and outputs are weak or nonexistent, and particularly where fixed costs dominate.

Indirect department cost: a cost reassigned or allocated to a department from another cost objective.

Indirect segment costs: see common segment costs.

Input/output budget approach: budgets physical inputs and costs as a function of planned activity. This approach is often used for manufacturing and distribution activities where there are clearly defined relationships between effort and accomplishment.

Interdepartmental services: services provided by one service department to other service departments.

Internal failure costs: quality costs incurred when materials, components, products, or services are identified as defective before delivery to customers.

Internal rate of return (IRR) (often called the time-adjusted rate of return): the discount rate that equates the present value of a project's cash inflows with the present value of the project's cash outflows.

Inventory turnover: the annual demand in units divided by the average inventory in units. It is also computed as cost of goods sold divided by the cost of average inventory.

Investment center: a responsibility center whose manager is responsible for the relationship between the profits and the total assets invested in the center. In general, the management of an investment center is expected to earn a target profit per dollar invested.

Investment tax credit: a reduction in income taxes of a percent of the cost of a new asset in the year the new asset is placed in service.

J

Job production: see job-order production.

Job-cost sheet: a record used to accumulate the costs for specific jobs in a job-cost system.

Job-order production: a production environment where products are produced in single units or in batches of identical units.

Joint costs: all materials and conversion costs of joint products incurred prior to the split-off point.

Joint products: two or more products simultaneously produced from a common set of inputs by a single process.

Just-in-time (JIT) inventory management: a comprehensive inventory management philosophy that stresses policies, procedures, and attitudes by managers and other workers that result in the efficient production of high-quality goods while maintaining the minimum level of inventories.

K

Kaizen costing: see continuous improvement costing.

Kanban system: see materials pull system.

L

Labor efficiency variance: the difference between the standard cost of actual labor inputs and the flexible budget cost for labor.

Labor rate variance: the difference between the actual cost and the standard cost of actual labor inputs.

Lead time: the time between the placement and the receipt of an order.

Least-squares regression analysis: uses a mathematical technique to fit a cost estimating equation to the observed data in a manner that minimizes the sum of the vertical squared estimating errors between the estimated and actual costs at each observation.

Life-cycle costs: from the seller's perspective, all costs associated with a product or service ranging from those associated with initial conception through design, preproduction, production, and after-production support. From the buyer's perspective, they include all costs associated with a purchased product or service, including initial acquisition costs and subsequent costs of operation, maintenance, repair, and disposal.

Linear algebra method: a method of allocating service department costs using a series of linear algebraic equations, which are solved simultaneously, to allocate service department costs both interdepartmentally among service departments and to producing departments.

Linear programming: an optimizing model used to assist managers in making decisions under constrained conditions when linear relationships exist among all variables.

Long-range planning: a type of planning that emphasizes the selection of programs to move the organization toward its goals over the next several years.

M

Managed fixed costs: see **discretionary fixed costs**.

Management accounting: a discipline concerned with the use of financial and related information by managers and other persons inside specific organizations to make strategic, organizational, and operational decisions.

Manufacturing margin: the result when direct manufacturing costs (variable costs) are deducted from division sales.

Manufacturing organizations: organizations that process raw materials into finished products for sale to others.

Manufacturing overhead: all manufacturing costs other than direct materials and direct labor.

Margin of safety: the amount by which actual or planned sales exceed the break-even point.

Marginal cost: in economics, the varying increment in total costs with an additional unit of activity.

Marginal revenue: the varying increment in total revenue derived from the sale of an additional unit.

Materials price variance: the difference between the actual materials cost and the standard cost of actual materials inputs.

Materials pull system: an inventory production flow system in which employees at each station work to replenish the inventory used by employees at subsequent stations. The building of excess inventories is strictly prohibited. When the number of units in inventory reaches a specified limit, work at the station stops until workers at a subsequent station pull a unit from the in-process storage area.

Materials push system: an inventory production flow system in which employees work to reduce the pile of inventory building up at their workstations. Workers at each station remove materials from an in-process storage area, complete their operation, and place the output in another in-process storage area. Hence they push the work to the next workstation.

Materials quantity variance: the difference between the standard cost of actual materials inputs and the flexible budget cost for materials.

Materials requisition form: a record used to record the type and quantity of each raw material issued to the factory.

Merchandising organizations: organizations that buy and sell goods without performing manufacturing operations.

Minimum level budget approach: establishes a base amount for all budget items and requires explanation or justification for any budgeted amount above the minimum. An absolute minimum amount of expenditures is presumed necessary to support ongoing activities in the organization. It is very useful where many committed costs continue from period to period.

Mixed costs (sometimes called **semivariable costs**): costs that contain a fixed and a variable cost element.

Model: a simplified representation of some real-world phenomenon.

Mutually exclusive investments: the acceptance of one investment automatically causes the rejection of the other(s).

N

Net present value: the present value of a project's net cash inflows from operations and disinvestment less the amount of the initial investment.

Net sales volume variance: indicates the impact of a change in sales volume on the contribution margin, given the budgeted selling price and the standard variable costs. It is computed as the difference between the actual and the budgeted sales volume times the budgeted unit contribution margin.

Nonvalue-added activity: an activity that does not add value to a product or service from the viewpoint of the final customer.

Not-for-profit organization: an organization that does not have profit as a primary goal.

O

Objective function: in linear programming models, the goal to be minimized or maximized.

Operating activities: normal profit-related activities performed in conducting the daily affairs of an organization. These activities are the major concerns of management in preparing operating budgets.

Operating budget: a set of formal financial documents that details expected revenues and expenses, as well as all other expected operating and financing transactions, for a future period of time (usually one year). It is a plan of action.

Operating leverage: refers to the extent that an organization's costs are fixed.

Operations list: a document that specifies the manufacturing operations and related times required to produce one unit or batch of product.

Opportunity cost: the net cash inflow that could be obtained if the resources committed to one action were used in the most desirable other alternative.

Optimal solution: in linear programming models, the feasible solution than maximizes or minimizes the value of the objective function, depending on the decision maker's goal.

Optimizing model: a model that suggests a specific choice between decision alternatives.

Order filling costs: costs incurred to place finished goods in the hands of purchasers, for example, storing, packaging, and transportation.

Order getting costs: costs incurred to obtain a customer's order; for example, advertising, salespersons' salaries and commissions, travel, telephone, and entertainment costs.

Order quantity: the quantity of inventory ordered *at one time.*

Organization chart: a diagram illustrating the formal relationships existing between the elements of an organization.

Organizational cost drivers: cost consequences resulting from choices concerning the organization of activities and the involvement of persons inside and outside the organization in decision making.

Organizational structure: the arrangement of lines of responsibility within the organization.

Organizing: the process of making the organization into a well-ordered whole.

Outcomes assessment: see performance measurement.

Outlay costs: costs that require future expenditures of cash or other resources.

Outsourcing: the external acquisition of services or components.

P

Participation, or bottom-up, budget approach: uses the benefits of improved communication, coordination, and motivation. The participation budget requires managers at all levels—and in some cases even non-managers—to become involved in budget preparation.

Payback period: the time required to recover the initial investment in a project from operations.

Performance measurement (sometimes called **outcomes assessment**): the determination of the extent to which actual outcomes correspond to planned outcomes.

Period costs: expired nonproduct costs; they are recognized as expenses when incurred.

Physical model: a scaled-down version or replica of physical reality.

Physical quantity method: a joint cost allocation method that allocates joint costs to joint products based on the relative quantities of a common physical characteristic possessed by the joint products.

Planning: the formulation of a scheme or program for the accomplishment of a specific purpose or goal.

Practical capacity: the maximum possible activity, allowing for normal repairs and maintenance.

Predetermined manufacturing overhead rate: an overhead rate established at the start of each year by dividing the predicted overhead costs for the year by the predicted volume of activity in the overhead base for the year.

Present value: the current worth of a specified amount of money to be received at some future date at some interest rate.

Present value index: the present value of the project's subsequent cash flows divided by the initial investment.

Prevention costs: quality costs incurred to prevent nonconforming products from being produced or nonconforming services from being performed.

Price discrimination: illegally charging different purchasers different prices.

Price fixing: the organized setting of prices by competitors.

Price variance: the difference between actual and standard prices paid for resources and components times the quantity purchased.

Pro forma financial statements: hypothetical statements that reflect the "as if" effects of the budgeted activities on the actual financial position of the organization. They reflect what the results of operations will be if all the predictions in the budget are correct.

Process: a collection of related activities.

Process map (or **process flowchart**): a schematic overview of all the activities required to complete a process. Each major activity is represented by a rectangle on the map.

Process production: a manufacturing environment where a single product is produced on a continuous basis.

Process reengineering: the fundamental redesign of a process to serve internal or external customers.

Process-based management: an approach to the evaluation of activities emphasizing the importance of considering the entire process of which activities are a part.

Product costs: costs assigned to products as they are produced. These costs are carried in the accounts as an asset (inventory) until the product is sold, at which time they are recognized as an expense (cost of goods sold).

Product level activity: an activity performed to support the production of each different type of product.

Product margin: computed as product sales less direct product costs.

Production order: a document that assigns a unique identification number to a job and specifies the quantity to be produced in the job, the total raw materials requirements of the job, the manufacturing operations to be performed on the job, and perhaps even the time when each manufacturing operation should be performed.

Productivity: the relationship between outputs and inputs.

Profit center: a responsibility center whose manager is responsible for revenues, costs, and resulting profits. It may be an entire organization but is more frequently a segment of an organization, such as a product line, marketing territory, or store.

Profit-volume graph: an illustration of the relationship between volume and profits. It does not show revenues and costs.

Purchases budget: indicates the merchandise or materials that must be acquired to meet current needs and ending inventory requirements.

Q

Quality: conformance to customer expectations.

Quality circles: groups of employees involved in the production of products who have the authority, within certain parameters, to address and resolve quality problems as they occur, without seeking managerial approval.

Quality costs: costs incurred because poor quality of conformance does or may exist.

Quality of conformance: the degree of conformance between a product and its design specifications.

Quality of design: the degree of conformance between customer expectations for a product or service and the design specifications of the product or service.

Quantitative model: a set of mathematical relationships.

Quantity variance: the difference between the actual quantity and the standard quantity allowed for the production components times the standard cost.

R

Raw materials inventories: the physical ingredients and components that will be converted by machines and/or human labor into a finished product.

Record: a related set of alphabetic and/or numeric data items.

Relevant costs: future costs that differ between competing decision alternatives.

Relevant range: the range of activity within which a linear cost function is valid.

Reorder point: the inventory quantity level at which an order for additional units is placed.

Residual income: the excess of investment center income over the minimum rate of return set by top management. The minimum return is computed as a percentage of the investment center's asset base.

Responsibility accounting: the structuring of performance reports addressed to individual or group members of an organization in a manner that emphasizes the factors controllable by them. The focus is on specific units within the organization that are responsible for the accomplishment of specific activities or objectives.

Return on investment (ROI): a measure of the earnings per dollar of investment. The return on investment of an investment center is computed by dividing the income of the center by its asset base (usually total assets). It can also be computed as investment turnover times the return-on-sales ratio.

Revenue center: a responsibility center whose manager is responsible for the generation of sales revenues.

Revenues: inflows of resources from the sale of goods and services.

Robinson-Patman Act: prohibits price discrimination when purchasers compete with one another in the sale of their products or services to third parties.

S

Safety stocks: extra units of inventory carried to prevent stockouts due to variations in the demand for units during the lead time.

Sales budget: a forecast of unit sales volume and sales dollars. It may also contain a forecast of sales collections.

Sales mix: the relative portion of unit or dollar sales derived from each product or service.

Sales price variance: the impact on revenues of a change in selling price, given the actual sales volume. It is computed as the change in selling price times the actual sales volume.

Sales value allocation method: a joint cost allocation method that allocates costs to joint products based on the relative sales value of the joint products produced.

Sales volume variance: the impact on revenues of the change in sales volume, assuming there was no change in selling price. It is computed as the difference between the actual and the budgeted sales volume times the budgeted selling price.

Scatter diagram: a graph of past activity and cost data, with individual observations represented by dots.

Segment margin: the amount that a segment contributes toward the common (indirect) costs of the organization and toward profits. It is segment sales less direct segment costs.

Segment reports: income statements that show operating results for portions or segments of a business. Segment reporting is used primarily for internal purposes, although generally accepted accounting principles also require disclosure of segment information for some public corporations.

Selling expense budget: the costs and disbursements the organization plans to incur in connection with sales and distribution.

Semivariable costs: see mixed costs.

Sensitivity analysis: the study of the responsiveness of a model to changes in one or more of its independent variables.

Service costing: the process of assigning costs to services performed.

Service department: a department which provides support services to production and/or other support departments.

Service organizations: nonmanufacturing organizations that perform work for others, including banks, hospitals, and real estate agencies.

Sherman Antitrust Act: prohibits price fixing.

Short-range planning: the interpretation of goals and long-range plans into performance objectives for the coming year and the selection of specific actions to achieve these objectives.

Simplex method: a mathematical approach to solving linear programming models containing any number of variables.

Split-off point: the point in a joint product manufacturing process where joint products emerge as separate identifiable products.

Standard cost: a budget for one batch or unit of product. Standard costs indicate what it should cost to produce one batch or unit of product under efficient operating conditions.

Standard cost center: a cost center that has clearly defined relationships between effort and accomplishment.

Standard cost variance analysis: a system for examining the flexible budget variance, which is the difference between the actual cost and the flexible budget cost of producing a given quantity of product or service.

Statement of cash flows: a summary of resource inflows and outflows stated in terms of cash.

Statement of cost of goods manufactured: a report that summarizes the cost of goods completed and transferred into finished goods inventory during the period.

Static budget: a budget based on a prior prediction of expected sales and production.

Step costs: costs that are constant within a given range of activity but different between ranges of activity. Total step costs increase in a step-like fashion as activity increases.

Step method: a method of allocating service department costs that gives partial recognition to interdepartmental services by using a methodology that allocates service department costs sequentially both to the remaining service departments and to the producing departments.

Stockout: a condition that arises when there is a demand for a product that is not readily available. It can occur because of delays in the receipt of an order or because of increases in the daily demand for an inventory item.

Storyboard: a process map developed by employees who perform the component activities required to complete a process.

Strategic cost management: making decisions concerning specific cost drivers within the context of an organization's business strategy, its internal value chain, and its place in a larger value chain stretching from the development and use of resources to final consumers.

Strategic plan: a plan indicating the basic way people in the organization are to go about achieving the organization's long-range goals.

Strategic position analysis: an organization's basic way of competing to sell products or services.

Structural cost drivers: the result of fundamental choices about the size and scope of operations and technologies employed in delivering products or services to customers. These choices affect the types of activities and the costs of activities performed to satisfy customer needs.

Suboptimization: when managers or operating units, acting in their own best interest, make decisions that are not in the best interest of the organization as a whole.

Sunk costs: costs resulting from past decisions that cannot be changed.

T

Target costing: establishes allowable costs of a product or service by starting with the determination of what customers are willing to pay for a product or service Sand subtracting a desired profit on sales.

Territory margin: the result when all direct fixed expenses identifiable with each territory are subtracted from the contribution margin. It is the amount that each territory contributes toward covering common corporate expenses and generating corporate profits.

Theory of constraints: every process has a bottleneck (constraining resource) and production cannot take place faster than it can be processed through the bottleneck.

Time-adjusted rate of return: see *internal rate of return*.

Transfer price: the internal value assigned to a product or service that one division provides to another.

Transferred-in costs: the combined cost of materials, labor, and overhead transferred to a department as goods are received from the previous department.

U

Unit contribution margin: the difference between the selling price and the unit variable costs.

Unit level activity: an activity performed for each unit of product produced.

V

Value: the worth in usefulness or importance of a product or service to the customer.

Value-added activity: an activity that adds value to a product or service from the viewpoint of the customer.

Value chain: the set of value-producing activities stretching from basic raw materials to the final customer.

Value chain analysis: the study of value-producing activities, stretching from basic raw materials to the final consumer of a product or service.

Variable cost ratio: variable costs as a portion of sales revenue.

Variable costing: an approach to costing products that treats variable manufacturing costs as product costs and fixed manufacturing costs as period costs.

Variable costs: costs that are uniform for each incremental unit of activity. Their total amount increases proportionately as activity increases.

Variable manufacturing overhead: all variable, except direct labor and direct materials, costs associated with converting raw materials into finished goods.

Variable overhead efficiency variance: the difference between the standard variable overhead cost for the actual activity-based inputs and the flexible budget cost for variable overhead based on outputs.

Variable overhead spending variance: the difference between the actual variable overhead cost and the standard variable overhead cost for the actual activity-based inputs.

Variable selling and administrative costs: all variable costs other than those directly associated with converting raw materials into finished goods.

Vertically integrated organization: an organization that operates two or more units that might be regarded as independent links in a value chain.

W

Weighted average method: in process costing, a costing method that spreads the combined cost of beginning inventory and current manufacturing costs (for materials, labor, and overhead) over the units completed and in ending inventory on an average basis.

Work ticket: a document used to record the time a job spends in a specific manufacturing operation.

Work-in-process inventories: partially completed goods consisting of raw materials that are in process of being converted into a finished product.

CHECK FIGURES

Chapter 1

1-10 (a) Average unit cost at 100, $100.30
1-11 (a) 1. Total costs of 20,000 with current process, $45,000
1-12 (a) 1. Total costs of 500,000 with student help, $500

Chapter 2

2-1   Fixed costs, $40,000
2-2   (a) Fixed costs, $5,000
2-3   (a) Fixed costs, $2,900
2-4   (b) Fixed costs, $7,300
2-5   (a) Fixed costs, $7,750
2-7   (b) Fixed costs, $930
2-8   (a) Contribution margin, $90,000
2-9   (b) Margin of safety, $400,000
2-13 (b) Margin of safety, $475,000
2-14 (a) From other sources, $250,000
2-15 (a) 1. Capital-intensive unit break-even point, 210,000
2-16 (d) Operating leverage, 4
2-17 Case 1. Margin of safety, 200 units
2-18 Case 1. Margin of safety, $50,000
2-19 (c) 23,200 units
2-20 (b) 7,500 units
2-21 (a) 16,900 patient-days
2-22 (d) Sales volume, $880,000
2-23 (e) Total cost, $171.50
2-24 (a) Total costs, $117,125
2-31 (d) Predicted after-tax profit, $404,250

Chapter 3

3-5   (c) Net daily disadvantage, $525
3-6   (b) Net disadvantage, $630,000
3-7   (b) Advantage of buying, $5,500
3-8   Advantage of subscribing, $6,700
3-9   Disadvantage of further processing, $700
3-11 (c) Opportunity cost, $1,000
3-12 (b) Total commissions, $4,900
3-13 (b) Value of objective function at optimal solution, $680
3-14 (b) Value of objective function at optimal solution, $24,000
3-15 (e) Increase in monthly profit, $33,000
3-16 (b) Increase in monthly profit, $10
3-17 (b) Advantage of replacement, $30,000
3-18 (c) 2. Decrease in profits, $20,000
3-19 (d) Profit, $240
3-20 (b) Decrease in monthly profit, $8,200
3-21 (b) Decrease in monthly profit, $2,100
3-22 (a) 37,500 boxes
3-23 (c) Net income, $211,500
3-24 (c) Expected monthly profit, $3,700
3-25 (c) Expected monthly profit, $1,150
3-26 Coefficient of B1, $1.61
3-29 (b) Advantage of accepting, $37,500

Chapter 4

4-11 Introductory course cost per student, $54.375
4-12 Batch level salary, $20,000
4-13 Profitability of sales, $24,798
4-14 Total activity cost, $24,770
4-15 (a) Activity cost variance, $200 U
4-16 (a) Unit cost of specialty products, $32.75
4-17 (b) Total cost per task chair, $42.50
4-18 (c) 19X3 income, $45,640
4-19 (a) Cost of raw materials, $348,490; Average unit cost, $58.66
4-20 (b) Activity cost of routine visit, $10.21

Chapter 5

5-2   (c) 2. Markup for desired profit, 2.00
5-3   (b) 2. Markup for desired profit, 1.67
5-4   Price per cone, $0.80
5-5   (c) Required sales volume, 17,520 units
5-6   (b) Profit of 3 1/2-inch disks, $120,000
5-7   Target unit cost, $304.60
5-8   19X7 target cost of plastic case, $3.60
5-9   Labor productivity index, 1.43 units per hour
5-12 Internal failure costs, $86,000
5-13 Internal failure costs, $23,500
5-14 (e) Suggested selling price, $36
5-15 (c) Initial selling price with manufacturing cost markup, $313.20
5-16 External failure cost using toaster defect response rate, $424,000,000
5-17 (a) Internal failure costs, $330,000
5-19 (a) Cost of job 91-Z24, $4,751.05

Chapter 6

6-1   (f) Present value of deferred annuity, $3,570
6-2   (f) Present value of deferred annuity, $5,568
6-3   (b) Internal rate of return, 24 percent
6-4   (b) Internal rate of return, 18 percent

6-5   (b) Internal rate of return, 22 percent
6-6   (b) Internal rate of return, 24 percent
6-7   Payback period, 2.5 years
6-8   (b) Proposal C accounting rate of return on average investment, 0.20
6-9   (c) Minimum annual net cash flows, $44,610
6-10 (c) Required annual sales, 28,320 units
6-11 Required annual sales, 139,466 units
6-12 (a) Proposal X net present value, $9,112.50
6-13 (a) Plastic containers present value index, 1.6406
6-14 (a) Aluminum present value index, 1.3075
6-15 (a) Net present value of investment, $14,010
6-16 Present value of double-declining balance tax shield, $29,058
6-17 (b) 3. Present value index, 1.14
6-18 Net present value, $113,441
6-19 (a) Time-adjusted cost advantage of old processor, $1,650
6-20 (a) Time-adjusted cost advantage of new system, $27,880
6-21 Net present value of new equipment, $58,208
6-23 (a) Net present value of project, $31,083
6-24 (a) Net present value of compliance, $648,187
6-25 (b) Net present value, $495,296
6-26 (b) Net present value, $37,983
6-27 (a) Proposal A minimum annual net cash inflows, $40,555
6-28 (b) Net present value, $(85,680)
6-29 (b) Maximum payment, $768,625

Chapter 7

7-1   Total budget, $756,000
7-2   Total cleaning costs, $3,120
7-3   (a) Total sales for winter quarter, $4,455
     (b) Total sales for winter quarter, $3,410
7-4   Total sales for first quarter, $444,000
7-5   January purchase units, 144,000
7-6   (a) January production, 55,000
     (b) January purchases, $235,000,000
7-7   Cash balance, ending for February, $39,000
7-8   Cash available for July, $236,000
     Cash balance ending for December, $195,000
7-9   Total receipts for May, $49,030
     Total receipts for the three months, $192,365
7-10 Ending Accounts Receivable balance for June, $106,200
7-11 Total disbursements for April, $200,000
7-12 Net income, $154,385
7-13 Net income, $3,000
7-14 Net income, $960,750
7-15 (a) Net income, $135,616
     (b) Net income, $135,616
7-16 (a) Total cash receipts for July, $16,810
     (c) Cash balance, ending for July, $5,010
7-17 (a) Total cash collections, $42,720
     (b) Cost of purchases, $36,000

     (c) Total expenses, $13,950
     (d) Excess disbursements over receipts, $(2,563)
7-18 (a) Net income, $135,000
     (b) Total assets, $504,400
     (Schedule 1) Budgeted purchases for January, $144,000
     (Schedule 2) Cash balance, ending for January, $101,000; for March, $254,800
7-19 (a) Budgeted purchases for April, $31,000
     (b) Total cash receipts for May, $54,000
     (c) Total cash disbursements for April, $71,000
        Total cash disbursements for the quarter, $194,000
     (d) Cash balance, ending for April, $3,000
     (e) Net income for April, $(3,750); for the quarter, $3,650
     (f) Total assets, $123,500
7-20 (a) Unit buckle purchases, small, 360
     (b) Budgeted cost of materials, $2,241.60
7-21 Budgeted purchases for pecans for June, 49,200
7-22 (b) Budgeted purchases for April, 52,650
7-23 (a) Cash collections, $1,880,000
     (b) Budgeted production, 21,000
     (c) Purchases of frames, $352,000
     (e) Cash balance, ending, $284,000
     (f) Unit cost, $83
7-24 (a) Cash collections, first quarter, $429,000
     (b) Budgeted production, first quarter, 16,000
     (c) Plastic purchases, first quarter, $111,000
     (d) Disbursements, first quarter, $439,000
     (e) Cash balance, ending, first quarter, $160,000

Chapter 8

8-1   (b) Total flexible budget variance, $18,100 U
8-2   (c) Materials price variance, $176 U
     (d) Materials quantity variance, $1,200 F
8-3   (a) Materials price variance, $550 U
     (b) Materials price variance, $500 U
8-4   (c) Total flexible budget labor variance, $2,950 U
8-5   (a) Variable overhead spending variance, $500 U
8-6   (a) Fixed overhead budget variance, $400 U
8-9   (c) Net sales volume variance, $125 F
8-10 (a) Sales price variance, $110,000 F
     (b) 19X4 unit cost, $2.30
8-11 Direct materials flexible budget variance, $7,000 U
8-12 (a) Material A price variance, $207.50 U
        Material B quantity variance, $15 U
     (b) Total labor variance, $190 U
     (c) Variable overhead efficiency variance, $75 F
8-13 (a) Materials price variance, $700 F
        Labor efficiency variance, $2,400 U
        Variable overhead spending variance, $100 F
8-14 (a) Total standard costs per bag, $2.968
     (b) Materials quantity variance, $60 U
        Labor efficiency variance, $25.50 F

8-15 (a) Standard cost per unit, $19.20
    (c) Materials price variance, $183 F
    (g) Variable overhead spending variance, $230 F
8-16 (4) Effect on fixed overhead budget variance, $200 F
    (5) Effect on materials price variance, $60,000 F
8-17 (b) 2. Materials quantity variance, $675 F
    (b) 4. Labor efficiency variance, $900 U
    (b) 5. Variable overhead spending variance, $650 F
    (c) Total flexible budget variance, $1,475 U
8-18 (d) Fixed overhead volume variance, $10,000 F
8-19 Net sales volume variance, $700 F
8-20 (c) Sales price variance, $20,000 F
    (e) Administration Department variance, $1,500 U (or over budget)
8-21 (column 2) Total cost variances, $51,500 U
8-28 (b) Standard variable manufacturing costs per unit, $18
    Total Sales Department variances, $27,500 U
8-29 (2) Total flexible budget variance, $20,000 U
8-30 (b) Total standard variable costs, $28.35; Total flexible budget variance, $842 F
8-33 (a) 2. Total materials price variance, $133,000 U
    (a) 4. Labor efficiency variance, $30,000 F
    (a) 7. Net sales volume variance, $204,500 F

Chapter 9

9-4 Alaska territory margin, $10,600
9-5 Service 14 product margin, $55,000
9-6 Tax Consultants gross profit: (a) $240,000; (b) $234,000; (c) $225,000
9-7 Paper Division gross profit: (a) $560,000; (b) $600,000; (c) $520,000
9-9 Gross profit: (a) $3,720,000; (b) $2,232,000
9-11 Beta net income, $310,000
9-12 Proposed sales contribution margin, $45,000
9-14 (a) East ROI, 0.17; (b) East residual income, $15,000
9-15 (b) Residual income, $26,000
9-16 Division K sales, $2,500,000
    Division L investment turnover, 2.5
9-17 (a) Division 200 ROI on book value, 0.20
    (b) Division 200 residual income on book value, $4,800
9-18 (a) Southeast territory margin, $15,000
    (b) Southeast umbrella product margin, $20,000
9-19 (a) Cookware product margin, $(5,000)
    (b) Europe territory margin, $52,000
9-20 (a) Irmo territory margin, $712
    (b) Donut product margin, $260
9-21 (a) Accounting product margin, $(1,000)
    (b) Auditors market margin, $(12,800)
9-22 (a) Local territory margin, $310,000
    (c) Product A product margin, $185,000

9-23 Kiwi Division income, $20,000
9-24 (a) 19X5 net income, $240,000
9-25 (a) Current operation's ROI, 0.194
9-28 (b) Backing Division current net income, $540,000
9-31 (a) Division 11 19X1 ROI, 0.11
9-33 (a) Membership segment margin, $191,500

Chapter 10

10-2 (d) Cost of goods sold, $716,000
10-3 Net income, $54,000
10-4 Cost of goods manufactured, $384,000
10-5 Net income, $5,000
10-6 Underapplied overhead, $300
10-7 (d) Overapplied overhead, $30,000
10-8 (d) Credit Work-in-Process, $3,520
10-9 (c) Credit Cost of Goods Sold, $20,000
10-10 (b) Ending balance, $9,500
10-11 (b) Ending balance, $1,800
10-12 (b) Ending balance, $560
10-13 (d) Direct labor, $21,000
10-14 (e) Cost of completed contracts, $231,000
10-17 Net income, $45,000
10-18 Net income, $72,000
10-19 Case 1, purchases, $23,000
10-20 (a) Net income, $30,310
10-21 (a) Debit Finished Goods Inventory, $7,825
    (b) Debit Finished Goods Inventory, $8,000
10-22 (b) Work-in-Process ending balance, $27,600
10-23 (a) Credit Retained Earnings, $21,360; (b)3. Total assets, $527,150
10-24 (b) Ending balance, $16,100
10-25 (a) Credit Retained Earnings, $31,418; (b)3. Total assets, $657,034
10-26 (b) Required sales, 8,519 units
10-28 Unit profit of other products, $1
10-29 Lion Tamer gross loss, $27,820

Chapter 11

11-3 (c) Total costs, $49,440
11-4 (c) Total costs, $168,319.20
11-5 (b) Equivalent units of conversion, 225,000
11-6 (c) Equivalent units of conversion, 12,500
11-7 Cost per equivalent unit in process, $5.24
11-8 Cost per equivalent unit in process, $13.80
11-9 (b) Weedout, $2.83 per liter
11-10 (c) Product A allocation, $27,200
11-11 (a) Ending Work-in-Process, $33,550
11-12 (a) Ending Work-in-Process, $282,600
11-13 (d) Ending Work-in-Process, $88,200
11-14 Ending Work-in-Process: Machining, $89,290; Finishing, $94,571
11-15 (a) Ending Work-in-Process: Processing, $1,403,400; Bleaching, $1,356,024

11-16 (b) Allocation to Product X, $48,000

11-17 (d) Gross profit of Juice, $7,994.40

11-18 Last entry, credit Standard Cost Variances, $4,500

11-19 Last entry, credit Standard Cost Variances, $1,900

11-22 (b) Product A unit overhead costs, $198

11-23 (b) Product Alpha unit overhead costs, $43.80

11-24 (d) Total cost of job, $992

Chapter 12

12-1 (a) P2 total costs after allocation, $215,000
(b) P1 total costs after allocation, $137,500

12-2 (a) Plant Security costs allocated to Molding, $20,000
(c) Melting manufacturing overhead rate per machine hour, $16

12-3 (a) 10%
(c) Total Clothing Department costs after allocation, $25,387

12-4 Total P2 costs after allocation, $63,897

12-5 S2 is allocated last; Total P1 costs after allocation, $72,324

12-6 June absorption ending inventory, $180,000
June variable costing ending inventory, $160,000

12-7 (a) Absorption costing net income, $36,000
(b) Variable costing net income, $30,000

12-8 (a) Absorption costing net income for 19X7, $350,000
(b) Variable costing net income for 19X8, $300,000

12-9 (a) Absorption unit cost, $21; (b) Variable costing net income, $50,000

12-10 (a) Absorption costing unit cost, $8.20
(b) Variable costing net income, $26,000

12-11 Absorption costing net income for 19X8, $1,600
Variable costing net income for 19X9, $14,225

12-12 Net income, $185,000

12-13 Net income, $54,000

12-14 (a) Absorption costing net income for 19X5, $3,900,000
(b) Variable costing net income for 19X6, $2,900,000

12-15 (a) Total Fabricating Department costs after allocations, $514,000
(b) Stamping Department overhead rate per machine hour, $46

12-16 (a) Costs allocated based on space occupied, $3,200
(b) Total P1 costs after allocation, $3,760

12-17 (a) 1. Mixing Department costs for Cafeteria, $110,000
Mixing Department costs for Maintenance, $64,000

12-18 (a) Medical Department costs after allocation, $68,000
(b) Medical Department costs per patient, $17

12-19 (a) Total body trim after allocation, $2,152,000

12-20 (b) Total East Division costs after step allocation, $51,467
(c) Central Division income, $18,067

12-21 (a) Services provided from Facilities to Human Resources, 6.25%
(b) Total Welding Department costs after allocation, $665,000
(d) Cutting overhead rate per direct labor hour, $67.425

12-22 (a) $111,760

12-23 (a) First quarter variable costing net income, $426,000
(b) Second quarter absorption costing net income, $372,490

12-24 (a) Absorption costing net income for 19X7, $101
(b) Variable costing net income for 19X8, $122

12-25 Absorption costing net income for 19X5, $5,625
Variable costing net income for 19X6, $110,000

12-26 (a) Absorption cost per unit for February, $14
(c) Variable costing net income for February, $26,000

12-27 (a) Absorption costing net income, $(124,800)
(b) Variable costing net income, $(140,800)

12-28 (a) Variable costing net income, $10,000

12-30 (b) Branch net income, $26,000

Chapter 13

13-1 (c) Milling Department rate per machine hour, $32
(d) Finishing Department rate per machine hour, $50

13-2 (a) Production scheduling per batch, $150
(b) Total cost of Job 211X, $15,280
(d) Total cost of Job 211X, $11,600

13-3 Material handling costs per ton, $60; Unit cost of J26Cams, $62.20

13-4 Electricity cost per machine hour, $10; Cost of Subdue per gallon, $5.64

13-5 (b) Cost per casement, $70.12

13-6 (a) Debit: Cost of Goods Sold, $274,075

13-7 (a) Credit: Raw Materials-in-Process, $12,000

13-8 (b) Reorder point in units, 40

13-10 (b) Annual cost savings, $800

13-11 (b) Current annual ordering costs, $1,000

13-12 (a) Total unit cost of forceps, $32.50
(b) Total unit cost of forceps, $31.50
(c) Total unit cost of forceps, $43.50

13-13 (a) 1. Standard A unit gross profit, $1.40
(a) 2. Specialty C unit gross profit, $13.49
(c) Deluxe B unit gross profit, $(4.00)

13-14 (b) Manufacturing costs per unit for Diesel, $1,040

13-15 (a) Costs per unit, $92; (b) Costs per unit, $89.25

13-16 (a) Consumer cost per unit, $5.28; (b) Custom Scientist cost per unit, $13.68

13-17 (a) Product AA costs, $15,800; (b) Product BB costs, $5,140

13-18 (a) Purchase price variance for 19X4, $20,000 U

13-20 (a) Total 19X1 West Glass annual cost, $1,528,000
     (c) Total 19X5 East Glass annual cost, $1,897,500 (actual)

13-21 (a) 2. Maximum inventory level, 175 units

13-22 Case 1 average inventory, 25; Case 3 average inventory, 20

13-23 (a) Purchasing Department costs, Standard, $2,507; Total costs, Specialty, $30,560
     (b) Standard unit cost, $27.99